催化剂 CATALYST

(美)包弫(Jennifer Ball)⊙著

李 琪⊙译

苏州大学出版社
Soochow University Press

图书在版编目(CIP)数据

催化剂＝Catalyst：英汉对照/（美）包弨
(Jennifer Ball)著；李琪译. —苏州：苏州大学出
版社,2017.3(2017.11重印)
ISBN 978-7-5672-2044-7

Ⅰ.①催… Ⅱ.①包… ②李… Ⅲ.①英语－汉语－对照读物②长篇小说－美国－现代 Ⅳ.①H319.4：Ⅰ

中国版本图书馆 CIP 数据核字(2017)第 012197 号

Catalyst

催 化 剂

（美）包弨(Jennifer Ball) 著

李 琪 译

责任编辑 沈 琴

苏州大学出版社出版发行
（地址：苏州市十梓街1号 邮编：215006）
虎彩印艺股份有限公司印装
（地址：东莞市虎门镇北栅陈村工业区 邮编：523898）

开本 787 mm×960 mm 1/16 印张 35.25 字数 631 千
2017 年 3 月第 1 版 2017 年 11 月第 3 次印刷
ISBN 978-7-5672-2044-7 定价：58.00 元

苏州大学版图书若有印装错误,本社负责调换
苏州大学出版社营销部 电话:0512-65225020
苏州大学出版社网址 http://www.sudapress.com

目 录
Table of Contents

Chapter One Combustible	/ 2
第一章 易燃性	/ 3
Chapter Two Venting	/ 34
第二章 排放	/ 35
Chapter Three Catalyst	/ 58
第三章 催化剂	/ 59
Chapter Four Bench	/ 72
第四章 工作台	/ 73
Chapter Five Control	/ 94
第五章 对照	/ 95
Chapter Six Bonding	/ 112
第六章 联结	/ 113
Chapter Seven Reaction	/ 136
第七章 反应	/ 137
Chapter Eight Decomposition	/ 160
第八章 分解	/ 161
Chapter Nine Sabotage	/ 198
第九章 破坏	/ 199
Chapter Ten Rat Corner	/ 212
第十章 老鼠角落	/ 213

Chapter Eleven　Hottentot Venus	/ 268
第十一章　霍屯督·维纳斯	/ 269
Chapter Twelve　Chain Reaction	/ 288
第十二章　连锁反应	/ 289
Chapter Thirteen　Addiction	/ 318
第十三章　上瘾	/ 319
Chapter Fourteen　Chirality	/ 342
第十四章　手征性	/ 343
Chapter Fifteen　Rival	/ 368
第十五章　对手	/ 369
Chapter Sixteen　Karma	/ 390
第十六章　因果报应	/ 391
Chapter Seventeen　Piltdown Man	/ 416
第十七章　皮尔当人	/ 417
Chapter Eighteen　Mannitol	/ 442
第十八章　甘露醇	/ 443
Chapter Nineteen　Rate-limiting Reaction	/ 464
第十九章　控速反应	/ 465
Chapter Twenty　Moth to Flame	/ 478
第二十章　飞蛾扑火	/ 479
Chapter Twenty-One　Proof	/ 494
第二十一章　证据	/ 495
Chapter Twenty-Two　Adulterate	/ 526
第二十二章　掺假	/ 527
Chapter Twenty-Three　Unresolved: to Stay Together	/ 540
第二十三章　未溶解:保持一体性	/ 541

A singing telegram was a service initially provided by Western Union starting in 1933, but by the 1980s had been taken over by specialty companies that employed performers who dressed up in costumes and sang the message to the receiver, usually something like "Happy Birthday".

唱歌电报最初是由西部联盟电报公司于1933年开始提供的一项服务，但从20世纪80年代开始逐渐被专业公司取代。公司聘用艺术家们身着演出服装通过唱歌的形式将电报信息传达给收信人，通常是诸如"生日快乐"这样的祝福。

Chapter One Combustible

> Combustible: Capable of catching fire and burning ... easily excited.
>
> The Random House College Dictionary

A feeling of lethargy overtook her, the way she always felt just before she delivered a singing telegram. It wasn't that delivering a singing telegram was so hard or required much talent. In fact, it was amazingly easy: walk in, sing, make sixty dollars, how hard could that be? It was the humiliation of knowing that this was the result of a degree in theater, a rash decision she'd made in her youth that now haunted her daily. She was unequipped for anything else, except perhaps fraud. Deception was something she lived with daily. The pretense that you were loving every minute was essential to a telegram—not easy when your audience was a gaggle of pinheads who obviously didn't know how to have their own fun. When they laughed, you knew they didn't really know what was funny, so it wasn't much of a coup.

Shelby knew she would never get famous doing singing telegrams. One always heard stories about aspiring actresses delivering telegrams to big producers and then getting cast in a starring movie roles, but she believed this like she believed there were alligators living in Manhattan sewers. It had never occurred to her to hire a singing telegram herself because she hated enthusiastic, chipper people who moved too quickly in small spaces. Fortunately, though, clerical people loved them. It was the most excitement they would have in a month, the closest they would get to the entertainment profession. (Not very close, in other words.)

Okay, it was an easy way for office workers to have a party on company time. If she were a secretary, she'd probably be into it. No ... could she be that desperate? she wondered briefly, fumbling through her notebook for the next address while sideswiping people who were now entering the subway aggressively,

第一章 易燃性

> 易燃性：能够着火并燃烧的特性……易激动的。
> ——《兰登书屋大学辞典》

与往常一样，在发送唱歌电报之前，一股困倦感向她袭来。并不是因为这项工作需要多高的技术含量或者要求很高的天分；事实上，它简单得令人吃惊：走进屋里，亮起嗓子，60美金就到手了——这能有多难？真正的原因，是她深深意识到，现在的这每天缠绕自己的噩梦，是她年轻时鲁莽决定的后果——戏剧专业的文凭能带给她的，只有现在的这份工作，这不免使她感到有些丢脸。除此之外她无任何一技之长，除非欺骗也算是一种能力。她每天都与自我欺骗如影随形，因为在唱歌电报这一行，能够宣称"我热爱生命里的每一刻"是至关重要的——这项任务可不容易，尤其当你面对的观众是一群聒噪如鹅却很显然不知道如何制造属于自己的快乐的小市民的时候。他们哄堂大笑，可你知道他们并没有找到真正的笑点，所以这对谢尔碧来说也算不上什么成功。

谢尔碧一早就明白，现在的这份工作永远也不可能让自己声名鹊起，可是像下面这样的故事却总是口口相传：某个踌躇满志的女伶为名声显赫的制作人提供唱歌电报服务后，紧接着就一跃成为多部电影的女主角。但是要谢尔碧倾心这种"飞上枝头"的童话故事，就像让她相信曼哈顿的阴沟里面住着几只短吻鳄一样。她也从未想过要自己花钱雇人来提供这样的唱歌服务，因为她讨厌看那些狂热的、过度活泼的人在狭小的空间里左蹿右跳。幸好，文职人员对此情有独钟。也难怪，因为这也许是一个月当中最能激起他们兴奋的事情了，也是他们能与娱乐行业最接近的机会（换句话说，还是从来没有接近过）。

承认吧，这给办公室职员们在上班时间开派对找了个天衣无缝的借口。如果谢尔碧的职业是秘书的话，她对此的兴趣也许会更浓些。又或许不会……她真的会那么渴望喧闹吗？她短暂地思索了一下，接着边用手指笨拙地划过笔记本寻找下一个主顾的地址，边侧身躲过蜂拥进地铁车厢里的人群，

Chapter One Combustible

threatening to carry her backwards on one of the nine-to-five tides of humanity. The onslaught of New Yorkers as a physical wave was still an amazement to her, but she strode through it the way she stroke through the rest of her life—with one Wonder Woman foot forward. That wasn't working right now though, as a man in a large coat and a woman with a box converged, blocking her advance. Shelby hurled herself between the two, like a pea shot through a child's pincer grasp, toward the closing doors. Falling through, the bustle suddenly evaporated around her, except for one man tending to a schoolmarmish dog. The dog was nuzzling a large department store bag the man had set down in the middle of the subway platform. Like a honing device, Shelby made a direct hit, stepping on it and crushing something crackery inside.

"Oh, I'm so sorry..." she began, immediately hopping to her other foot, but the silver wing of her boot got caught inside the bag's handle and it started off with her as she took a quick step to catch herself. The owner snatched the bag back, pushing Shelby in the process, as a rush of students overtook the platform. "Hey!" Shelby yelled, turning around quickly, eager to vent, ready to give him the piece of her mind that was most turbulent. But the man and his dog had become enveloped in the ever-seething eddy of human activity that surged through Port Authority at rush hour.

Shelby winced, feeling for a moment embarrassed, and then headed for the stairs. People in New York were stupid. That was the explanation. It made everything make sense. The hassles with workmen, taxi drivers, her vocation even. Her husband Max always said, "Don't knock stupid people. Stupid people give you a job." He meant that someone lame enough to hire a telegram had to be mentally incapable of determining what a good time was. Possibly they'd never had a good time, for what else would possess you to invite actors to your work? She couldn't imagine. For some reason office people couldn't recognize high school theatrics. Big hand gestures and grimaces by former waiters who now called themselves "thespians". (The other deliverers were so full of it.) Granted, it paid better, telegrams. And the hours were flexible. She hated waiting tables and couldn't stand working the nine-to-five clerical shift. Daylight was so fleeting, who wanted to spend all of it indoors under florescent lights? For freedom you had to debase yourself more but for fewer hours.

Emerging from the underground, she blinked several times in the brittle daylight, momentarily happy that she was upstairs rather than deep in the earth watching the pastiche of gum go by. The underground caverns between Port Authority

极力避免被扯入那朝九晚五的人流之中。纽约客"人肉波浪"的猛烈冲击无论第几次经历都还是无法令人处之泰然,但是谢尔碧总是大跨步穿过这人群,一如她对待自己后半生的态度——总是像神奇女侠般一脚向前。可这一招现在却不管用了,因为一个穿长外套的男人与怀抱纸盒的女子肩头并到了一起,挡住了谢尔碧的去路。于是她像是孩子用弹弓射出的豌豆粒一般,冲破那两人的阻碍,从正在关闭的门间蹿出。周围一切的嘈杂声都瞬间蒸发了,只剩下眼前的一个男人,牵着一只打扮得像个女学究似的狗,那只狗正"咻咻"地用鼻子摩擦主人随手放在站台中间的大号百货公司购物袋。谢尔碧跃出车厢时像安装了自动引导装置一般,一脚踩上了那只购物袋,并听到了里面脆脆的碎裂声。

"噢,真是抱歉……"她立刻跳到另一只脚上做支撑,正准备迅速向前跨一步找回平衡时,却发现自己靴子上的银色流苏勾住了购物袋的提手,并把它向前拖了一小段距离。那男人见势便劈手将袋子夺回,同时将谢尔碧一把推开,在这期间一群学生迅速占领了整个站台。"嘿!"谢尔碧吼道,她急急地转过身去,迫切地想要让那男人尝尝自己怒火的厉害,以此来发泄自己的不满。但由于是交通黄金时间,他和他的狗已经淹没在了从港务局站涌出的沸腾人流中。

谢尔碧的脸抽搐了一下,有那么一秒钟她感到非常窘迫,随后她就径直走向了楼梯。纽约客们脑筋都有问题——这是唯一的解释了。这样一来一切都解释得通了:与工人的摩擦,与计程车司机的冲突,甚至在自己这一行里遇到的各种搅扰。她的老公麦克斯总是这样说:"别招惹这些脑筋短路的人了,没有他们你就没有工作了。"他的意思是,差劲到要雇佣别人来做唱歌电报的人,他们的心智肯定连什么叫快乐都无法判断。也许他们从来就没有真正开心过,不然是什么使他们迷了心窍,竟然请演员到他们上班的地方去?谢尔碧实在想不出其他的理由。不知什么原因,办公室职员总是无法领会具有戏剧效果的包袱,比如现在称自己为演员的人,在过去做服务生的时候就会做出的夸张的手势,扭曲的鬼脸,这些就属此类(许多深谙此道的人都成了我的同行)。当然了,可以确定的是,这行的报酬十分可观,工作时间也非常灵活。她讨厌在餐馆里点单端菜,也无法忍受职员朝九晚五循环往复的生活。白日稍纵即逝,谁愿意头顶荧光灯的冷光,整天闷在室内呢?为了自由,你牺牲的程度得更深一些,但持续的时间却可以短一些。

从地铁出来,终于重见天日,谢尔碧迎着薄薄易碎的阳光眨了几下眼睛,一股短暂的愉悦感立刻涌上了心头:脱离了地底,就不用再提防着黏在地面上

Chapter One Combustible

and Grand Central were the catacombs of New York, the fallout shelter of the fallen. Bodies strewn in corners like some economic centrifuge had flung them there. She felt so terrible seeing the carnage of poverty, watching the unwatchable, but carefully, not wanting them to see her pity or to draw attention to herself in case they might follow her home. The men, clothed in ragged cast-offs, faces darkened as if by the smoky remains of their lives, soiled sweat jackets with holes in the shoulder, or at the wrist, a mere nod to the inclimate weather, with shoes that disengaged from their soles and limbs that were missing; and the women, if you could tell the difference, with no teeth, ski caps pulled over their steel gray hair, talking about Jesus or sex or throwing empty bottles of Colt 45 at the subway tracks. Some days she walked up the stairs with tears in her eyes. Some days she didn't even see them. That too could make her cry, when she realized how much they'd become part of the landscape.

The weather was cold—she had her big tweed coat and gloves on—and it had rained earlier that day, but now the sky was a vivid of blue which made the concrete so much more insulting: the heavens taunting her with exhibitionism. She could feel her excitability rising. She laughed at the irony because it honestly made her feel like singing, being in New York, the aliveness of it, the weather—but not musical show tunes, not "New York, New York"—how many times had she heard tourists humming that? People were so average. No, you'd wanna sing "People Who Died" by Jim Carroll, someone who really knew the city.

"Herbie pushed Tony from the boys' club roof
Tony thought that his rage was just some goof
But Herbie sure gave Tony some, some bitchin' proof.
And Herbie said, 'Tony, can you fly?'
But Tony couldn't fly.
Tony died."

Their band did that song. On the chorus she and Max would shout the lyrics, harmonizing in a dry punk way:

"Those are people who died, died. Those are people who died, died.
Those are people who died, died. Those are people who died, died.
They were all my friends, and they died."

It was truth and it was brutal, but it made for great music.

的拼贴画似的口香糖走路了。联通港务局与中央火车站之间的地下洞穴，是纽约市的茔窟，是堕落在最底层人们的防空洞。角落里横七竖八地躺着一些人，就像是被廉价的离心机甩到四处的。谢尔碧偷偷瞥过这被贫穷席卷的战场，感到心疼，但却小心翼翼地不让他们感觉到自己的同情，更不想引起他们的注意，因为他们很有可能会跟踪自己回家。在烟雾缭绕的生活残渣里，那里的男人们脸颊都被熏黑了，他们穿着已经破烂成锯齿状的捡来的衣服，污渍斑斑的运动夹克在肩膀或手腕处磨出了好几个破洞，遇到天气恶劣便毫无抵御之力；有的人没有了鞋底，有的人残缺了四肢。那里的女人们——如果你还能将她们与男人区分的话，她们用滑雪帽将钢铁般冷灰色的头发向后撸过去，干瘪着牙齿都掉光了的嘴巴在一起谈论着上帝、性，或者是将 Colt 45 [译者注：一种饮料] 的空瓶子扔向地铁的轨道里。有的时候，谢尔碧在走出地铁口时会发现泪水盈满了自己的眼眶。但有些日子里，她经过时看不到他们，也会想要掉眼泪，她意识到这些人已经成为这里景致的一部分。

天气很冷——谢尔碧裹紧了呢大衣并戴上了手套。那天早些时候下了雨，但现在的天空已经恢复成生动的蓝色，使得周围混凝土大楼的矗立更像是一种侮辱：天空展尽了风头，极尽嘲讽之能事。谢尔碧可以感觉到自己兴致逐渐高涨，因为这个讽刺的场景使她想要放声歌唱，身在纽约，感受着它的生机，它的天气——但不是那种音乐剧的调子，不是那句"New York, New York"——她已经多少次听见游客们兀自哼哼着这个曲子了？他们都太过中庸了。你真正想唱的应该是吉姆·卡罗尔的"People Who Died"（《逝去者》），他才是真正了解这个城市的人。

  赫比将托尼推下屋顶，在男生俱乐部
  托尼以为他的愤怒，只是一时失误
  赫比却毫不，毫不留情
  赫比说，"托尼，你会飞吗？"
  托尼不会飞
  于是他就这样死去

谢尔碧所在的乐队曾演唱过这首歌，在和声部分她和麦克斯会用嘶哑的朋克风格将歌词吼出来：

  那些人已经死去，死去。那些人已经死去，死去。
  那些人已经死去，死去。那些人已经死去，死去。
  他们曾是我的朋友，现在他们已经死去。

它残忍地吟唱着事实，造就了伟大的音乐。

Chapter One Combustible

Shelby quickly stretched her arms as she walked, the buffeting crowd thinning briefly if only to make room for the buildings that suddenly came close, even by New York standards, invading one's personal body space and pushing the pedestrians off the sidewalk. Everyone walked in the street here, these older apartments being nearer to the curb, remnants of a previous New York, as if it had been a more intimate city then. But no longer. Every day blocks of crumbling granite were replaced by glinty polymers, shiny, indulgent materials that gave you a clear view of yourself and blocked out the rest of the world. "Gentrification," they called it, like naming it made it okay. Perfect example: Hunan Balcony. Shelby looked up as she passed underneath its sign. Great food but ugly, like a Denny's hoisted to the second floor. It was built when architects were influenced by the Jetsons. Chrome and Naugahyde. Hardly Chinese at all. It looked fast food. Her first month in New York, Shelby had thought Hunan was a franchise. Growing up in white suburbia, who knew?

She paused for a moment, stretching her left leg. Her pantyhose was pulling on the inside of her thigh. Always. The biggest hassle of telegrams was the clothes. Well, them and the monkey. Shelby jerked her hand between her legs, reaching underneath her coat in a quick attempt to free up some room. She glanced around quickly to see if anyone noticed, but it was a shifting wall of people. Sometimes New York reminded her of driving in L. A. because you were armored by your own anonymity. No one wanted to know you. (Thank God.) So you whizzed by with minimum interaction.

Someone bumped into her and she held tight to her large gym bag. It was easier to walk through New York with a shield, something to sling around. But it slowed her down. At night she would go without it, somewhere out with Max. They would slip through the crowd like snakes. Max's rule was that you had to get out of the house before you got high. Otherwise, he figured, you'd never leave. He'd always wave his hand at her, flicking it in his impatience. "Out of the house. Come on. Let's go." He knew she had to leave the apartment three times before they could truly be called gone.

Three hundred fifty-four Grosvenor. Stumbling into consciousness, she realized she'd just passed it. She felt like she was pulling into an offramp, disengaging herself from the caravan of people marching by. The Roland School of Chiropractic. Max had given her a bunch of shit. "They're gonna wanna align your back."

谢尔碧这样走着的时候迅速地伸展了一下胳膊,突然之间急匆匆向前的人群自动地收缩成了细长的队伍,仿佛是在给两旁向人群逼近的大楼让路。路人纷纷被挤到人行道的下面,即使是按照纽约市的标准,现在每个人也都毫无私人空间可言了。每个人都曾在这条街上走过,这些老公寓楼是旧纽约城的残余景象,它们离马路沿要近很多,好像在试图证明它过去曾是一个比现在要亲密得多的城市。但好景不长在。每一天,渐趋脱落的花岗岩都会被闪闪发光的聚合物建筑材料取代,它们有些任性——清楚地呈现着你的镜像,却将外面的世界隔绝;它们闪耀着阳光,却使你迷失其中。"低端住宅高档化",他们这样称呼它,就好像只要给它命名,一切就都搞定了似的。最能体现这一点的就是纽约市的湖南阳台餐馆了,谢尔碧路过的时候抬头看了看它的招牌:食物很不错,只是建筑太丑了,就像是丹尼斯餐馆建在了二楼。在它建造的时期,建筑家们都深受杰森家族的影响——铬合金和瑙加海德革材质,因此毫无中国风可言,看起来就像一家快餐店。她来到纽约的第一个月里,一直以为湖南是一个连锁店的名称。从小在郊区的白人社区里长大,谁会知道湖南是什么呢?

　　她稍稍停顿了一会儿,舒展了一下左腿,大腿内侧立刻就感觉到了连裤袜的拉扯。总是这样。做唱歌电报这一行最麻烦的就是服装问题了——好吧,服装,还有那只猴子。谢尔碧迅速将手伸到大衣底下两腿之间,试图给大腿释放一些空间。她赶快瞥向四周,看是否有人注意到她的动作,但周围只是快速移动的人墙而已。有时候纽约这样的场景使她想起驾车行驶在洛杉矶的感觉,因为从内到外你都是一个无名之辈,没有人想要了解你(感谢上帝)。所以你开着车呼啸而过,与任何人都没有交集。

　　有个人猛地撞上了谢尔碧,她立刻警觉地攥紧了自己的大运动包。随身携带着这样一个盾牌,穿行在纽约街道上会更有安全感一些,因为它还可以作为自我防御的武器。但这也会减慢她走路的速度,所以晚上和麦克斯一起出门的时候她就不会带着大包了,他们会像蛇一样在人群间滑过。麦克斯的规矩就是,在喝高了之前必须得出门,不然的话,他觉得,你就出不了门了。他总是向她招手,轻轻的摆动里透露出不耐烦的神气:"快出来吧!得了,我们走吧!"他知道,谢尔碧还要再进出公寓三四次他们才能真正出得了门。

　　格罗夫纳街354号。突然回过神来的时候,她才意识到自己刚刚已经错过了那里。她渐渐与沙漠商队般向前行军的人群分离,那感觉就像将车开进了出口坡道上。到了——罗兰指压疗法学校。麦克斯曾经狠狠地嘲笑过她:"他们

Chapter One Combustible

She had grinned at him. "Nah, they're gonna wanna cure me of bedwetting."

Opening the swinging glass door, she stared at the floor, a sense of dread coming over her. Her hatred for singing telegrams went beyond rational. She was philosophically opposed to them, but the amount she made more than overcame her principles. And, in a strange way, telegrams made her appreciate the rest of her life because in the rest of her life she wasn't doing them.

She felt her body temperature drop as the moment came closer. Her pulse slowed. She knew that what she felt wasn't calm, actually, but overload. Synapses firing to a numbing degree. Her thoughts flew too fast for her to think them, piling on each other like used laundry. It was preservation, a way to hide her feelings from herself. And it worked until her fears surfaced, bubbling violently in her hot little mind. Maybe it was her period. Of course that was the easy out, the excuse many women use for unmanageable lives. If she'd been living a happy, fulfilling life, she could shrug off a little crankiness, a little bloating, but now it pervaded her demeanor like an example of all that was wrong with the world.

Punching the elevator for the third floor, Shelby jumped up and down a few times, trying to get herself in the mood. The doors parted and she took a deep breath, tightening her stomach muscles for added stamina. Sense memory work— now she felt like Wonder Woman. Oh, yeah.

"Four forty-five for Keller. Monkey Business," she said to a young woman reading *Vogue* whose several body piercings suggested that her name might be "Velvet" or "China". Without looking up, the girl buzzed the door open and Shelby went through. The waiting room was a small area with shiny metallic-flecked seats, upholstery straight from the back of a Ford Fairlane. Shelby took off her long coat and folded it into a neat square, setting it down carefully. Then she grabbed a protruding leg and shook her monkey out of the gym bag, dropping it unceremoniously on the floor. The toy monkey was a handy vehicle for relieving tension. She felt the need to use the bathroom, but instead she forced herself to sing "People who died" in her head. An image of the band the last time they played gave her a moment of fortitude. They'd set up in the basement of the chemistry building, a yeasty-smelling cavern that echoed like a dormitory bathroom. She remembered their rendition of "Suzy Q", how she'd found a swivel chair in the back of the place, and did the whole song scooting around on the floor,

会想要把你的背好好直一直的。"谢尔碧则冲他咧嘴一笑："才不会,他们会想先治好我的尿床的。"

　　穿过旋转门后,她紧紧地盯着地板看了一会儿,一阵恐惧感向她袭来。她对于唱歌电报的憎恶已经超出理性范围了,虽然内心深处她是持反对态度的,可这行给她所带来的可观收入战胜了她的原则。再者,虽然有些奇怪,但这份工作使她对后来的生活更加珍惜,因为在那些日子里她终于可以不用再做这件事情了。

　　随着那一刻越来越近,她觉得自己的体温有些下降,脉搏也渐渐变缓。谢尔碧知道,这种感觉事实上不是镇静,而是超负荷的表现。突触灼烧到了使人麻木的程度,脑海中千万种思绪迅猛地划过,甚至都还来不及经过思考,就已经如同待洗的脏衣服一样堆叠在一起了。这是一种自我保护的方法,使她感觉不到自己真实的情绪。但等到谢尔碧的恐惧浮出水面,开始在她发热的脑海中剧烈沸腾时,这个方法就失效了。也许这一切只是因为她正处于月经期。当然了,这是最简单的解释方法——当生活脱离了掌控,许多女人首先找的就是这个借口。假如谢尔碧过着幸福而令人满意的生活,她也许会对别人的一点暴躁或自负的表现不予理会,可是现在,她的一言一行都像是在说,这世界一定是出毛病了。

　　谢尔碧一拳砸在电梯的三楼键上,然后纵跳了几下,努力让自己进入状态。电梯门慢慢打开的时候,她深吸一口气,收紧了腹部的肌肉,使自己精神更抖擞一些。启动所有的感官记忆——现在她感觉自己就是神奇女侠。噢,太棒了。

　　"四点四十五分送给凯勒的唱歌电报,猴子事务所。"谢尔碧对一个正在阅读《时尚》杂志的年轻女子说道。她身上的文身让人觉得她的名字也许叫 Velvet 或者 China［译者注：当时很多的电台 DJ 会起类似的名字,比如 September, California 等,这是当时嬉皮士的潮流］。她连头都没有抬一下,门在她摁下按钮的瞬间"嘶嘶"地打开了,谢尔碧径直走了进去。休息室很小,金属座椅反射着光芒,但有些掉漆斑驳,坐垫就像是从福特汽车的座位上扯下来的。谢尔碧脱下长外套,叠成齐整的方形,仔细地放好。随后她抓住玩具猴露出来的一条腿,将它从运动包里扯出来,粗暴地丢到地上。它可是用来缓解紧张气氛的好帮手,随叫随到。虽然她现在很想去洗手间,但却强迫自己在脑海里唱起了"People Who Died"的旋律。回想起自己乐队上一次演出的场景,谢尔碧瞬间又充满了面对一切的勇气。那次他们把地点定在了化学大楼的地下室,所有乐器都准备就绪,空气里弥漫着发酵的味道,洞穴般的构造使回声效果像宿舍卫生间里的一样。谢尔碧还记得他们演唱"Suzy Q"这首歌的情景,她在地下室的后面找到了一把转椅,整首歌下来她都坐在转椅上滑过来滑过去,有时双脚向墙面一蹬,

Chapter One Combustible

launching herself off the wall and into the audience. They'd loved it. Moments like that made her life liveable.

Sighing, she started through her prop check. Truth rope. Tying a large knot in the black silken cord, she tried to think of a particularly rude but acceptable question she could ask the guy in the event that everyone was comatose. *Can you get it up?* Nah, maybe that was too aggressive. *Handcuffs?* When she asked this question she didn't wait for a response. A friend of hers had handcuffed one of the San Diego Chargers out on the field during half-time. That was fame in the telegram biz. She wasn't sure, but she thought they might have dated for a while afterward. The client/performer relationship wasn't quite as sacred here as in other lines of work.

Chained to the bag's strap, Shelby's handcuffs caught her eye and she deliberated. They were actually a prop for a different character she did, Policewoman Betty, a frumpy officer that Shelby loved to do, first scaring the telegramee with a phony citation, and then stripping down to hot pants and bustier while swinging her handcuffs. But Gary never sold any of those because it was Shelby's idea and he was jealous. So sometimes she used the handcuffs as Wonder Woman if she thought she wouldn't have enough material. She went out and bought the goddamn things, might as well get some use out of them. Anyway, it was a good bit to handcuff the guy to you. That was when you got the best tips. Once she handcuffed the telegramee to *her* ankle. The place had gone crazy. What a party. Sometimes she'd hang around. That was really why Gary kept her on. She delivered lousy telegrams, but she could schmooze good. People loved Wonder Woman if she was really smart-mouthed and could tell wild stories, like about her friend Delilah who used to chain herself to a B. Dalton's with pictures from Playboy plastered all over her body. And Delilah always claimed that this was nothing to her friend who got arrested for purposefully throwing up on two Santa Cruz policemen. Shelby had a thousand weird stories, all true.

Sometimes at the parties they would even tell her to invite her husband. These were the wild, after-hours telegrams, usually in someone's penthouse. And she would call Max, laughing, already drinking. Occasionally he would come. She treasured these telegrams, the few and far between, the hoped for but also the most painful: seeing how the other half lived. Wealth can't help but dazzle. It luminates, drawing you in. You can't avoid comparing your life to theirs as your poverty is flashed in your face. And then the light goes out, and you're left in the dark with your trifles.

就将自己推向了观众人群中。大家都对这表演倾心不已。谢尔碧觉得,那些瞬间才赋予自己的人生价值。

想到这她叹了口气,开始检查自己的道具情况。真心话绳索。她一边在那条黑色绸带上打一个大大的结,一边试图想出一个可以在这个大家都恹恹欲睡的活动中问的问题,既显得刁钻又不至于无法接受。"你能勃起吗?"还是算了吧,也许这问题太有攻击性了。"你想让我用上手铐吗?"问这个问题其实并没有期待什么答案。她有个朋友曾经在球赛中场休息的时候将圣地亚哥电光队的一个队员给铐了起来,并带到了球场上。这件事在电报界名噪一时。谢尔碧不是很确定,但是在那之后他们俩似乎约会过一段时间。在这一行里,客户与业务员之间的关系并没有其他职业中那么神圣不可侵犯。

谢尔碧的目光落到挂在背包带上的手铐上,她思忖了片刻。这手铐其实是谢尔碧喜欢扮演的另一个角色的道具——衣着邋遢土气的女警贝蒂:她会先用一张假的法院传票来吓唬观众,然后边挥舞着手铐,边将身上的衣服扯到只剩热裤与紧身胸衣。但是加里却从来不向外推销这套表演,因为这是谢尔碧的创意,这使他感到嫉妒。所以当谢尔碧觉得神奇女侠的表演里包袱不够用的时候,她就会把手铐的元素加入进去。她既然都专门买了这该死的道具——也就不妨让它发挥点作用吧。不管怎样,当着大家的面把一个男人铐起来都是一个很好的套路,这时候拿到的小费也往往最可观。曾有一次,谢尔碧把自己的脚踝与活动男主角的铐在了一起,当时全场都沸腾了。那样的派对真是让人难忘!有的时候她就会留在那里玩个尽兴——这也是加里之所以还一直雇佣她的原因。虽然她的唱歌电报做得不是很精致,但她却擅长和顾客们聊成一片。大家喜欢神奇女侠,因为谢尔碧巧舌如簧,脑袋里储存着无数疯狂的故事。比如说那个关于她的朋友黛利拉浑身贴满《花花公子》杂志中的插图,并将自己拴在 B. Dalton 连锁书店前门上的故事;而黛利拉则坚持说和她的朋友一比,自己只能算是小巫见大巫——她的朋友因为故意在两个圣克鲁斯的警员身上呕吐而被逮捕了。谢尔碧脑子里有成百上千个这种怪异的故事,并且全部都是真事。

有时在电报表演结束后,通常在某个人的顶楼公寓房间里,还会有后续的疯狂派对,他们甚至会让谢尔碧把麦克斯也叫来。已经喝了不少的她就会大笑着打电话给麦克斯,而麦克斯偶尔也会来。这些回忆被谢尔碧视若珍宝,这些少之又少的希望与痛苦并存着的回忆:看着不同于自己的另一部分人如何生活。钱财使生活变得光怪陆离,它装点着你的生活,同时也将你吸进生活的漩涡。当贫穷无情地鞭打在你的双颊时,你就会不由自主地会将自己和其他人比较。当灯光渐灭,你被黑暗吞没,还是要转头面对生活的琐碎。

Chapter One Combustible

Pulling out a mirror, she checked her lipstick, scratching at a crease above her lip that the lipstick was wont to crawl up. Her hair looked bouncy. It felt good against her face. Tickly hair. That's what an old boyfriend had called it. It reminded her of static, crackling, the light glimmering in your eye. Max called her a burr head because her hair would get really frizzy in the rain. She hated it. Not always, maybe every third day. The mugginess made it too wild. Somedays she would lash it back with a piece of phone cord. People always asked her where she bought that, thinking the phone cord too cool. People were imbeciles.

The door opened and a sandy-haired woman with really big front teeth came out smiling broadly. "Shelby Mitchell? Hi. I'm Molly. I'm so excited. We all chipped in." She shook Shelby's hand, holding it too long. Chipping in usually meant no tip.

"Oh, what a nice gesture. I'll be sure to mention his promotion, as you requested." Shelby, done with civilities, sensed the woman wanting to prolong her stay. People were goofy about deliverers. They tended to gravitate toward you. Wanted to touch you. It was something Shelby had never really been able to figure out. Handing the woman her gym bag, Shelby used it as an opportunity to nudge her toward the door. "Let's do this now, I have a five-fifteen in Midtown. Can you watch this for me?" she asked, mixing lie with request to make smoother the transition. "What's this guy look like?" she asked, picking up her monkey by the leg, letting him swing head downward. They began walking down a corridor with Shelby moving faster than Molly, trying to anticipate the direction they were going.

"Dennis? Well, he's medium height, medium weight. He has brown hair," she drawled, halting their progress. Shelby bounced on her feet. "Well—oh, I know, he's wearing a red bowtie." She touched her palms together on the word "know", somehow reminding Shelby of a praying mantis.

"That'll be my clue." Shelby nodded tersely, charging off in the direction they'd been headed but changing when the woman belatedly squeaked, "Oh, we're going this way," and turned through some double doors. "You're an idiot," Shelby thought loudly, hoping that the woman had at least been blessed with telepathy. Walking behind the pant-suited posterior, Shelby imitated her, trying to get the mincing down, trying to get the teeth. She laughed silently at her attempts, dry lips sticking to her upper gum, getting some small token of satisfaction from the spoof but feeling desperate all the same.

谢尔碧掏出一面镜子来检查自己的唇膏,她用指甲刮了一下唇膏容易溢出的上唇纹。她的卷发看起来蓬松有弹性,贴着自己的脸颊感觉很舒服。有个前男友叫她"刺毛头",这使她联想到因为静电而炸起的头发,连续的爆裂声,还有阳光下反射的如同眼眸里闪烁的光芒。如果淋了雨,她的头发就会变得卷卷的,麦克斯会叫她"刺梨头"。谢尔碧讨厌自己的头发,但并不总是,大概每隔三天吧。闷热潮湿的头发使她看起来像个野人,有时候她就直接用一段电话线将头发束在脑后。总是有人觉得她的发带很酷,问她是在哪买的。有时候人们就像傻瓜似的。

突然门被推开,一位浅黄色头发的女职员满脸堆笑地走了进来,露出了巨大的门牙。"你就是谢尔碧·米歇尔吧?你好!我叫莫莉。你来了我真是太高兴了!我们大家一起凑的钱请你来表演呢。"她和谢尔碧握了手,但长时间没有松开。大家凑份子的话,通常意味着小费是不会有人给的了。

"噢,你们真是太贴心了!我一定会照你要求的那样顺带提及他升官的事情的。"谢尔碧做完表面的寒暄之后,感觉到这个女人想让自己待得久一些。人们在面对唱歌电报表演者的时候行为都显得有些怪异,他们好像被你给吸引过来,想和你有更亲密的接触。关于这一点谢尔碧始终都没有想明白为什么。谢尔碧把自己的运动包递到那女职员手里,并借机轻轻地将她推搡向门口的方向。"我们现在就开始吧!我五点十五在市中心那边还有预约。你能帮我看一下包吗?"谢尔碧这样说道,撒了个谎之后又提了个要求,这样能够过渡得自然一些。接着她提起玩具猴的一只脚,让它头向下悠荡起来,"男主角长得什么样子啊?"这时候她们已经一前一后地走在过道里了,谢尔碧步伐更快地走在前面,猜测着她们应该走的方向。

"你说丹尼斯啊,他嘛,身高中等,体重中等,头发是棕色的。"她故意慢条斯理地说,好减缓她们行进的速度。谢尔碧双脚并拢向前跳了一下。"噢,对,我知道了!他现在打着一个红色的领结。"她在说"知道"这个词的时候击了一下手掌,不知怎么的使谢尔碧想起了螳螂。

"这就是我找他的线索了。"谢尔碧简单地点了下头,继续向同一个方向快步前进。但那个女人却突然迟钝地发出一声短促的尖叫:"哦!我们该向这边走!"并顺势拐进了一个双开门里。谢尔碧只能随她改变方向,心里有个声音怒吼着"你这个白痴",暗暗希望着自己的怒意可以通过心灵感应传给她。看着前面包裹在职业套装里的肥臀一扭一扭,谢尔碧忍不住开始模仿起来,试图抓住那造作姿态和可笑门牙的精髓。她不发出声音地狂笑着,干燥的嘴唇紧紧地贴着上牙龈。虽然这个小恶作剧让谢尔碧产生了些许快感,但她内心还是渗透着极度的绝望。

Chapter One   Combustible

They were walking along a corridor now. Yellow walls. Narrow but clean. The woman opened another door and whispered, "Wait here", like she was in a some spy movie. With the turn of a plump heel, the woman disappeared. Looking around the room, Shelby tried not to smile when she saw the chart on the wall. "Do you understand the damaging effects of subluxations?" it read. There was a large drawing of a body in profile and at the bottom was the word "dis-ease". She could hear Max's voice in her head asking where the bed-wetting coordinate was. Which bone did you have to crack for that? Max could be so scathing about chiropractors. Quackery in general made him go off. For him, the stresses of graduate school were taken out by yelling about the world's ignorance. Tirades, his friends called them. Chiropractors and New Age medicine got to him the most. Max often called it the Green Party mentality because their friend Eberhard had said that it started in Germany: women who henna their hair and let their chickens roam free. Not that there was anything wrong with those two things per se, but they often accompanied a belief that shunned science or anything that was built on logic. As if logic were contrary to goodness. It was this trend toward wanting everything "natural", like nature couldn't kill you. Shelby shook her head. Take natural childbirth. What an oversold concept. You think a guy would go through that without drugs? Hell, no. What good is living in the age of pain-killers if you don't take them? Or as Shelby always joked, "I have drugs in my regular life. Why would I give them up for childbirth?"

She laughed out loud, remembering a magazine a friend had mailed her, *Earth Mother*. The average reader seemed to be an unwed, poor Canadian, Australian, or Southern woman who had more than three children, hated doctors, didn't vaccinate her kids, breastfed children who could walk to the store and buy their own milk, with Baby #n on its way in June somehow conceived in a family bed with a boyfriend who was unemployed. The magazine's appeal ran a weaving trail between humor and pathos. When Shelby joked about the magazine to friends, she wasn't sure if she was making fun or giving homage. Many readers were women trying to take control of their lives, something she could understand.

Shelby had read Max a letter about a new mother who admitted to pumping one time when she had run out of milk and was in the middle of making coffee cake. After she'd shared the cake with friends, she told them the truth,

现在她们已经来到了另一个走廊,有些窄但是很干净,两侧的墙面是黄色的。那女人打开一扇门后,小声说道"在这等着",那神态就好像是在演出间谍电影似的。踩着圆圆粗粗的鞋跟,她转了个弯,就不见了身影。谢尔碧开始打量四周的环境,墙上的一张画报让她忍俊不禁,上面写着:"你知道半脱位的破坏性后果吗?"旁边配着人体侧面解剖图,底部则写着"疾病"两个字。这时候她脑海里响起了麦克斯讽刺的声音:"控制尿床的协调中枢在哪里?""要治好尿床得整治哪根骨头?"麦克斯对脊椎按摩师一直都颇有微词,因为任何一种招摇撞骗却没有实际效果的庸医行为都让他气不打一处来。对他而言,释放研究生生活巨大压力的方法就是大声地谴责这个世界上的无知与愚昧,因此他的朋友们都叫他"长篇演说家"。最能引燃他的两个话题就是脊椎按摩师和新时代药业了。麦克斯将其统称为"绿党思维",因为他们有个朋友艾伯哈德曾经说过,这个理念最先起源于德国:那里的女人们会用指甲花染料来给自己的头发染色,而她们养鸡的方法则是任由它们四处漫游。并不是说这两件事本身有什么不妥的地方,只是它们的观念往往具有逃避科学或是逻辑思维的倾向。他们就好像认定了逻辑推理一定无法带来好的结果一样,在事事都崇尚"自然"的大潮中,却忘记了"自然"也是可以置你于死地的。谢尔碧摇了摇头,就比如说自然分娩这个概念吧,实在已经被过分吹嘘了。你觉得如果是一个男人要经历这样的过程,他会选择不用麻醉药吗?鬼才信呢!在这样一个止痛药唾手可得的时代,你选择不用的话岂不是浪费了吗?或者就像谢尔碧经常开的玩笑那样,"反正我平时都会嗑药的,为什么我要为了生孩子而放弃这一习惯呢?"

谢尔碧想起了一位朋友曾邮寄给她的杂志《地球母亲》,她忍不住笑出声来。一般来说,这份杂志的读者很有可能是来自加拿大、澳大利亚或是南方地区的贫困未婚女人,她们生育了不止三四个孩子,痛恨医生,从来没有给孩子注射过疫苗,而当孩子们长到了已经可以自己去商店买牛奶的年龄,她们还是采用母乳喂养,即将在6月份出生的第N个孩子是不知怎么与游手好闲的男友在家里的床上造出来的。这份杂志吸引人的地方就在于,它用幽默的方式引起了读者们的共鸣。当谢尔碧拿这份杂志和朋友与开玩笑的时候,她也不确定自己到底是在嘲笑还是心怀敬意。读者中的相当一部分都是在努力尝试掌控自己生活的女性,这一点谢尔碧非常能够感同身受。

有一次谢尔碧给麦克斯读过一封信,信中一位刚生产完的妈妈承认说,自己在做咖啡蛋糕的时候牛奶用光了,于是就挤了自己的奶。她在和朋友们分享了蛋糕之后才告诉她们事实,从那以后那些朋友就再也没有和她说过话。

and the friends never spoke to her again. Max and Shelby had laughed about that one, imagining the woman breaking the news, wondering how the woman could mistake her friends so grievously. "Hell, there are people who'd pay extra for that," Max had hooted, perceiving a business venture. "Mother's Milk bakery," he had called it. "Okay, it would be a small clientele, but they'd be dedicated."

After reading the letter to Eberhard and Hadley on the way back from rehearsal, Shelby and Max had replayed their conversation from the night before, their routine building, a captive audience making them funnier. Max had yelled, "You'd have to have a stable of lactating women." Shelby had added dryly, "You could market it under La Leche Loaf." This was how they entertained at parties, honing their comedy in taxis.

Eberhard had laughed out loud. "Why not just have places where people can suckle?"

"Mother's Milk Bakery and Boudoir," Max had said, his face lighting up.

Shelby had noticed that even Hadley couldn't help but smile. "I wonder if you would be breaking laws?" he had asked coolly.

"In New York?" Shelby had pushed Hadley's shoulder, defying his stoicism. He always acted as if laughing was a pastime with which he was inexperienced.

A door opened with a thump. Shelby shook her head to stop daydreaming. "Come on!" the woman whispered loudly, ushering Shelby into some kind of office, perhaps the school's administration. Shelby settled the monkey's fuzzy bottom in the crook of her arm like it was Charley McCarthy, a puppet with some dignity. She walked quickly, her silver boots clicking on the floor. For some reason that made her feel important. Her legs, covered only in hose, felt a little chilly, but she knew she'd forget about that in seconds. Over her hose she was wearing an outfit that reminded her a little of Esther Williams. Blue dance trunks, like the bottom of a swimming suit, then a bodice that snapped in the back and fanned out the front, silver breastplates over red spandex. She looked okay. Fuckable. God, why did she think things like that? She shook her head, trying to erase the thought from her mind. She saw herself reflected ghostly in a whiteboard and smiled, amazed at her idiocy. She was no different from the crazy New Yorkers. A nutcase. She was itchy, seething, ready for something. But something would have to wait. She sucked in her stomach once more, cleared her mind, and went for it.

谢尔碧和麦克斯一边大笑一边想象着她说出真相那一刻的场景,想着她怎么可以这么不了解自己的朋友。麦克斯大声辩驳道:"见鬼,愿意为此多付钱的大有人在呢!"他似乎从中嗅到了"商机"。"就取名叫'母乳烘焙'!客户群确实会比较小,但是品牌忠诚度是可以保障的。"

在乐队彩排结束回家的路上,念完信里的内容给艾伯哈德和哈德利听以后,谢尔碧和麦克斯又把他们前一天晚上的对话给重演了一遍,这是他们一贯的做法,因为有了全神贯注倾听的观众,他们的讲述往往会更有趣一些。麦克斯叫道:"这样一来你必须得找到一群处于稳定哺乳期的女人!"谢尔碧则干干地补充了一句:"你可以用西班牙语'La Leche loaf(鲜奶面包)'的名字来做市场推广。"不论是在派对里给大家逗乐儿的时候,还是在出租车里斟酌喜剧包袱的时候,他们都是这样你一言我一语。

艾伯哈德发出响亮的笑声:"为什么不索性开一家店让人们可以直接吮吸乳汁呢?"

麦克斯的脸上泛起了亮光,他接口道:"母乳烘焙坊和闺房直销。"

谢尔碧注意到,甚至哈德利也忍不住咧开了嘴角。可他还是用平静的语调问道:"我在想你这样做会不会是违法的?"

"在纽约这样一个城市?"谢尔碧顺势推搡了一下他的肩膀,对他的禁欲主义嗤之以鼻。他的一言一行都好像在表明,放声大笑是一种他极其不熟练的娱乐方式。

门"砰"的一声被打开了,谢尔碧甩了甩头从白日幻想中恢复过来。"快进来吧!"先前那个女职员用悄悄话的语气大声叫道,接着她将谢尔碧领进一个类似办公室的房间里面,也许是学校的教务处。谢尔碧把道具猴毛茸茸的屁股放在自己的臂弯处,摆出查理·麦肯锡的姿态,这样一来他就是一只有些尊严的玩偶了。她快步地向前走着,银色的靴子敲击着地板发出"咔嗒咔嗒"的声音,不知为何她觉得这很重要。只穿了丝袜的双腿,略微感觉到些寒意,但她知道,过不了几秒钟她就会忘记这回事儿了。她觉得自己穿在丝袜外面的装束有点像埃斯特·威廉姆斯。下身穿蓝色的舞蹈短裤,有点像泳衣的下半截儿,上身着红色的紧身衣,胸前是扇面打开状的设计,搭扣在背后系紧,银色的胸带连接前后。她觉得自己看起来还不错,凑合能让男人产生"性趣"。天哪,为什么自己总是从这个角度想事情呢!她又甩了甩头,试图把这些想法全部赶出自己的脑袋。看见白板上映出的自己幽灵般的影像,她笑了,惊讶地发现自己的白痴程度和那些疯狂的纽约客们没什么两样。她心里总是痒痒的,身体内有一股热血沸腾,随时准备着做些什么,一触即发。但现在这个档口什么事儿都得放一边了,谢尔碧再一次地吸气收腹,理了理思绪,正式开始了工作。

"Dennis Trantin? I have a telegram for Dennis Trantin!" She caught sight of a bowtie. A skinny man with a saggy face. It occurred to Shelby that perhaps the body had grown too tall for the face, and the drag of gravity was a little much for the jowls. "Dennis Trantin? I am from Monkey Business Singing Telegrams, and this here is Chuckles." She smacked the monkey on the head with the heel of her hand. "Say hello Chuckles." She quickly bent forward and hit him hard on the floor. "Chuckles?" She hit him a couple more times. A few people moved back.

"May I use your desk?" she asked politely. The young woman's eyebrows raised a notch, but she nodded and quickly stepped aside.

Shelby couldn't take her eyes off the woman's fingernails—blood red and an inch long. "Nice nails," Shelby lied, smiling. They looked like Volkswagen fenders, lined up in a row, lacquered and shining, somehow malevolent.

Shelby raised the monkey high over her head and brought it crashing down, giving the leg of the metal desk a good wallop.

"Ee-ee-ee-ee-ee-ee," it began to scream, grinning ludicrously and clapping its cymbals. Looking up, she smiled chipperly at the stunned and silent audience. "Sorry. Bit I gotta do."

Shelby launched into a suggestive version of "Let me entertain you" while walking up to Mr. Trantin with the chattering monkey. She sang a few bars and then asked, "Can you hold him for me? He doesn't bite, but he might pee." For a chemistry professor she had actually done that—had actually put a small balloon in the monkey's pants filled with perfume, holding the opening with her finger until the last moment. It was a great thing to do to guys. It really messed them up to smell like violets.

After giving Mr. Trantin the monkey, which he took with a sheepish smile like his old heart was going to give out, she put her arm around his shoulder and steered him to the front of the room where there was a little more space.

"Molly!" he said weakly but with an obvious thrill, tilting his head shyly at the woman with big teeth. It was a cry like "How could you, you crazy thing?" The way people say, "Oh, you shouldn't have," all titillated at the prospect of excitement.

Glancing at Molly, Shelby watched her teeth increase in wattage.

"丹尼斯·特兰汀在吗？我这有一封唱歌电报要发送给他。"谢尔碧瞥到了一个打领结的男人。他高高瘦瘦，脸上的肉有些下垂。谢尔碧心想也许是因为他长得太高了，地吸引力超出了他颚骨能够承受的范围的缘故。"你是丹尼斯·特兰汀吗？我是猴子唱歌电报事务所的电报员，我手里这位是'咯咯笑'。"她一掌拍在猴子的脑袋上，"咯咯笑，快问好！"见没反应，她随即迅速地弯下腰去并把它重重地砸在地上，"咯咯笑，你怎么了？"她又打了好几下。有些人向后退了几步。

"我能用一下你的桌子吗？"她礼貌地转向一个年轻的女职员。女职员皱了一下眉头，但她还是点了点头并且迅速地站到旁边去。

谢尔碧目不转睛地盯着她的手指甲——鲜血般的红色，有一英寸长。"你的美甲真好看！"谢尔碧笑着撒了个谎。它们的形状像是大众汽车的挡泥板，排成了一排，油漆一般闪着莫名的恶毒的光芒。

谢尔碧将玩具猴高高举过头顶，随后猛地甩手将其砸在金属办公桌的一条桌腿上。

猴子终于开始尖叫："咿咿咿咿咿咿——"咧开嘴笑的样子滑稽至极，还不停地敲打着手里的铙钹。谢尔碧抬起头，看向一旁惊讶得说不出话来的观众们，爽朗地笑了。"抱歉，我一定得这样做才能奏效。"

谢尔碧一边拿着那只仍然叨叨不休的猴子向特兰汀走去，一边开始试探性地演唱"Let Me Entertain You"。唱了几句之后，她开口道："你能帮我拿一会儿吗？它不会咬人的，但是也许会尿尿。"她曾经这样捉弄过一个化学教授——她在猴子的裤子里藏了一只装满香水的小气球，并且一直用手捏住开口处，直到交接的一刻才松开。这一招对男人们使用屡试不爽，面对自己身上散发的紫罗兰香气，他们往往会惊慌得手忙脚乱。

特兰汀带着羞怯的微笑接过那只猴子，就好像他那颗上了年纪的心都要融化一样。房间的前面空间略大一些，于是谢尔碧把胳膊搭在他的肩膀上，引导着他向前走去。

"莫莉！"他有些害羞地将头转向那个长着巨大门牙的女人，低低地叫了一声，语调里带着明显的兴奋。潜台词就是："你怎么能这样做呢！你这小疯子！"人们在说"哦，你完全不必这样做"的时候，总是兴奋地期待着即将到来的惊喜。

谢尔碧扫了一眼莫莉的脸，看到她的牙齿像通上电的灯泡一样亮起了一排。

"Now someone was nutty enough to send you a telegram," Shelby started in a chummy voice, clutching him to her. "And I happen to have no better job than to spend my days wandering the city in this outfit. The bums love it. You know, you just don't look at the world the same after being dressed as Wonder Woman." She gave a frank smile. "Well, of course you know. You used to have this job. Here, just wear the tiara for old time's sake. It'll go good with your promotion." She quickly stuck the tiara on his head while the room guffawed. What was it about men in women's clothing? Never failed to get a laugh. That and people falling. Those were the underpinnings of comedy.

"Wonder Woman, let me see you break my arm," someone yelled from the back. Shelby flinched, already into her patter, not ready for a bar scene. It was different at bars. A lot rougher. Alcohol brought out the testosterone.

She looked toward the voice. "Wha'd I say? The bums love it. Okay, Mr. Trantin. I have here a truth rope. Step right up, anyone who would like to ask Mr. Trantin a question." Shelby made Mr. Trantin hold one end of the truth rope while she walked slowly around him, running her hand through his hair, messing it up, knocking the tiara sideways. Tying a bow in front of him, she said, "Don't fight it Mr. Trantin. You won't be able to stop. The truth will spring from your lips ... or wherever." Her eyes traveled his body, the implication obvious. She paused, waiting for someone to ask him a question. There was about twenty people in the room now. Clerical people, clusters of jeans, business suits, a hodge-podge of onlookers. And nobody was saying nothing. Great. She hated these low-energy telegrams. It was better when the people were only interested in laughing at their own witticisms. Then Shelby purely had to act like Ed McMahon. She was such a prostitute. But sometimes, when the place was hip, she'd have a religious experience. She was hired by some animators once; they wanted her to do a telegram while the animation was rolling, so that the cartoons went on her body. She didn't do her usual schtick. Instead, because the animation had a blues score, she danced and sang, harmonizing with the music. They loved it. They were stoned. They got her stoned. Those were the ones she lived for.

A loud voice yelled, bringing Shelby back to earth. "When was his shirt last washed?"

"Mr. Trantin?" She sniffed the air. "Hmm."

"好啦，有人傻到要送你一份唱歌电报，"谢尔碧一把抓住他的胳膊，亲昵地说道，"而恰好我能找到的最好的工作就是穿着这身衣服每天在城市里瞎逛。流浪汉们可是我的忠实粉丝呢。你知道吗，打扮成神奇女侠之后看待这个世界的眼光都不一样了。"她露出了一个大大的微笑。"对了，你当然知道了，曾经你也干过这一行呢。来吧，看在过去那段时光的份上，把这个凤冠给戴上。正好你升职，戴着多合适呀。"说话间谢尔碧就把凤冠套在了特兰汀的头上，房间里立刻爆发出一阵哄笑。究竟让男人穿戴成女人的样子有什么魔力呢？每次这样都能博得人们一笑。除此以外还有人们摔倒的情形，这些都是喜剧中的经典桥段。

"神奇女侠，让我看看你能不能把我的胳膊给掰折了！"有人在房间的后面嚷道。已经进入自说自话单口模式的谢尔碧并没有预料到会出现这样的情况，她有些发怵。通常这样的叫嚣会发生在酒吧，在那里表演要困难多了，因为酒精会激起过剩的雄性激素。

她循着那个声音的方向望去。"我说什么来着？流浪汉最爱加入我的表演了。好的，特兰汀先生，现在我这里有一根真心话绳索，请你向前一步走。现场有人想问特兰汀先生任何问题吗？"谢尔碧让特兰汀握住绳索的一头，自己则带着另一头慢慢地绕着他走，她把手指插进特兰汀的头发里，把它搅得乱蓬蓬的，头顶的凤冠也被弄歪到了一边。谢尔碧开始在他的胸前打一个蝴蝶结。"别做无谓的挣扎，特兰汀先生。真话将会源源不断地从你嘴里冒出来，你无法停止这一切……"谢尔碧的目光在他的身体上游离，做着明显的挑逗。她停顿了一下，等别人问特兰汀问题。现在房间里大概有二十多个人，一群办公室职员们不是身着正装，就是蹬着工装裤，聚集成一堆等着看热闹，可却没有人说一句话。棒极了。谢尔碧特别讨厌遇到这种活跃不起来的场面，哪怕是大家只被自己说的俏皮话逗笑，也比现在的情形好多了。那种时候谢尔碧只需像爱德华·麦克马洪一样行事就好了——像妓女一样任人摆弄。但是有时候，如果遇到一群真正懂她的人，她就会表演到精彩忘形。有一次她的雇主是一群动画制作人，他们希望谢尔碧在动画片放映的同时进行表演，这样一来动画的影像就会在她的身上游离。她发现动画的配乐中有蓝调成分，于是放弃了一贯的表演内容，一边舞动，一边给配乐唱和声部分。他们超级喜爱这个表演，看得如痴如醉，而谢尔碧也沉醉在大家的瞩目当中。谢尔碧努力地生活就是为了这样的时刻。

"他的衬衫最近一次洗是什么时候？"一声大吼将谢尔碧拉回了现实当中。

"特兰汀先生，"她嗅了嗅周围的空气，"唔……"

"I washed it last night," he said taken aback.

"Well, would you look at this." Shelby asked. "There's a knot in the rope." She turned Dennis Trantin around to show the audience the obvious snarl, a large pink ribbed condom hanging from it. This was Gary's idea. Telegrams gave her little respect for the masses.

Shelby nudged Mr. Trantin. "Looks like you're too busy to be doing laundry." Some people laughed, and Shelby whipped the rope away from him, going at warp speed. No one had really said that there was a time limit on these things. She knew some girls did twenty minutes, and that Gary had once said "at least ten to fifteen," when she had eight telegrams in one day. The less time she spent, the higher her hourly rate went. That kind of power made her heady. She thought maybe she could get this in at just under nine. Of course she didn't want them calling up and complaining, but if you gave them a rousing nine minutes, they were usually happy.

Making a big production of untying the knot in the rope and tucking the condom inside Mr. Trantin's shirt, she listened to the sudden rise of hoots and catcalls. Shelby pulled the untangled rope around herself and Mr. Trantin, tying them both together. Several people giggled. She could see him turn red. This was why people enjoyed telegrams. It was play sex, safely stimulating. She truly was a prostitute.

"Okay, we have time for just one more question." Several people called out questions now, loosened up by the revelry. Someone asked how many company pens he'd taken home. Someone else asked how many company pens he had in his pant's pocket right now. This made several people laugh.

Shelby shook her head imperceptibly. Pity them, she reminded herself. It was condescending and that's why she thought it. She needed an inferior ruler with which to measure her own life. Happiness was a relative thing. In a moment she would be happy. You only had to experience something terrible then wait. It would eventually go away and that would make you glad. Pain made her philosophical. She wondered if it was self-inflicted for that very reason. She knew torture made her sing from her gut. Could she afford to quit singing telegrams if the horror made her a better singer? Tough call. She was drifting now. Going through the motions. Making Mr. Trantin do the hula with her. Gary didn't know all the stupid stuff she did on her telegrams, he just cared that she did them and that people didn't complain.

"我昨天晚上还洗了呢。"他显然吓坏了。

"好吧,那你们来看看这个,"谢尔碧叫道,"绳子上有个结。"谢尔碧把他转了个圈,以便观众都能看到那个明显的绳结,上面还挂着一个用粉色丝带扣起来的大号避孕套。这是加利的主意。做这一行,容不得谢尔碧给予观众更多一些的尊重。

谢尔碧轻轻推搡了一下特兰汀,"看来你是太忙了没时间洗衣服呀。"有一部分人笑了起来,接着谢尔碧以极快的速度抽走了绳子。从没有人规定过唱歌电报的时间限制,就谢尔碧所知,有些女演员会做大概 20 分钟,而有一次谢尔碧一天要做八个电报,加利则告诉她"每个都至少要有 10 到 15 分钟"。每份电报持续的时间越短,她时薪就越高。能够这样控制自己的时薪使她感到很兴奋。她在想也许眼前的这个九分钟就可以搞定。当然咯,她不希望收到顾客的电话投诉,但是如果你可以使这九分钟高潮迭起的话,通常情况下他们还是会心满意足的。

谢尔碧花了一些功夫解开绳索上的结,然后又将避孕套塞进了特兰汀先生的衬衫里,尽情享受着房间里突然爆发出的尖叫声和笑骂声。谢尔碧又重新用那根绳索把自己和特兰汀先生绑在了一起,观众里有几个人"吃吃"地笑出了声,她看见特兰汀的脸红了。这就是人们喜欢唱歌电报的原因:它就是在安全范围内进行性感挑逗。她真是有些淫荡。

"好的,现在我们剩下的时间只够一个问题了。"先前的欢腾让大家都放开了,有好几个人都大声喊出了问题。有人问他带了多少支公司的签字笔回家。还有人问现在他裤子口袋里有几支公司里的笔。好几个人都被这个问题给逗笑了。

谢尔碧难以察觉地摇了摇头。她提醒自己,应该对他们给予同情。虽然这样想带有高人一等的意味,但这正是她需要的。如果要来衡量谢尔碧自己的人生的话,她需要一把等级低一些的标尺。幸福是一个相对的概念,转瞬间就可能出现在她的生命中。你只需要经历一些痛苦的事情,然后耐心等待。烦心事最终会走开,而你会因之高兴。苦痛让她变成了一个哲学家。她有时候会想,是不是因此她才产生了自我打击的倾向,因为她知道内心的折磨能够使自己的演唱更加发自心底。如果真的只有恐惧可以使她唱得更好的话,她会因此而放弃这一行吗?很难说。谢尔碧现在带着特兰汀先生一点一点地移动,跳起了哗啦圈舞。加利完全不知道谢尔碧在做唱歌电报时做的这些傻事,他只在乎谢尔碧做完整个流程,并且没有顾客抱怨就好了。谢尔碧现在心里想着,要不了一会儿她

She was thinking about how in a few moments she could go home and get stoned. Hell, she might even have a roach on her. Where had she put last night's joint? In her—?

"Wonder Woman, when are you free?" The disembodied voice from moments earlier walked its face up front, an urgent face, on the edge of surly. He had shaggy blond hair and was kind of scrawny, not that tall but thin and hunched. An uglier Squiggy.

"He's had a little to drink," Dennis, the telegramee, whispered in Shelby's ear, turning only his head. "He's really not like this … He's Mr. Roland's son."

Oh, that explains it, Shelby thought. His dad's rich, he thinks he's God's gift to women. Every heckler had a story.

Molly had been motioning to the son for a while now, smiling hugely and maternally. Shelby watched, confused as to what was going on, then realized that there was silence and everyone was staring at her, waiting for the next bit. Forced from her rote patter, Shelby forgot what had she been doing. She stuttered, "And now … " then looked at Mr. Trantin and realized they were still tied together. Oh, she was going to ask him about his promotion and then have him take his telegram out of her boot.

"I said when are you free?" The guy leaned in toward her, his rasta hair brushing her arm and giving her the creeps. He grinned at her, obviously thinking he was too cool. Like he was saying, "Give it up, I get all the babes."

"Does this work for you?" Shelby asked dryly, quickly freeing herself and Mr. Trantin from the truth rope. Her only thought was to get out of there. Spotting trouble was almost a sixth sense of hers. Or perhaps her whole life—rock bands and singing telegrams—lent itself to abetting trouble and so, invariably, she was never wrong. Guys like this were usually just about ready to throw up, and you wanted to make sure it didn't happen on you.

Molly whispered, "Ethan?" and smiled painfully.

Trying to finish the telegram as quickly and smoothly as possible, Shelby tucked the rope in her boot, pulled out the scroll that said Happy Birthday on it, and put her arm around Mr. Trantin. "Dennis—" she said while batting her eyes at him. "May I call you Dennis?"

"You can call me Dennis," the heckler said, sidling up to her, rubbing his

就可以回家了,然后在大麻的作用下欲仙欲死。见鬼,现在她身上可能有支烟卷。昨天晚上那支被她放哪了?难道放在……

"神奇女侠,你什么时候有空啊?"几分钟之前出现过的那个匿名声音这回带着自己的身体走向前来,那一张急于求成的脸,近乎不怀好意。他有一头乱蓬蓬的金发,个子不是很高但是瘦瘦的,背微驼。比斯珪奇还丑。[译者注:斯珪奇是美剧《快乐的日子》续集中的一个人物。]

"他喝了点儿酒,"今天的主角丹尼斯,转过头在谢尔碧的耳边小声说道,"平时不是这样的……他是罗兰德先生的儿子。"

哦,原来如此,谢尔碧心想道。老爸有钱,所以他觉得自己在所有女人眼里都是个香饽饽。每一个问问题最凶的人,背后都是有故事的。

莫莉已经带着大大的充满母性的笑容向这个富家子弟暗送秋波好一会儿了。谢尔碧看着四周,正困惑着到底发生了什么,突然意识到一个说话的人都没有,大家都盯着她,等着她下一步的表演。已经滚瓜烂熟的套路被打断,谢尔碧突然忘记自己刚才进行到了哪一步。她结结巴巴地说:"那么现在……"然后她看向特兰汀先生,瞬间意识到他们还被绑在一起。哦,对了,她刚才是想要问起特兰汀先生升职的事情,然后让他从自己的靴子里取出祝贺电报的。

"我在问,'你什么时候有空'!"那个家伙身体向谢尔碧倾过来,密密麻麻的辫发摩擦在她的肩膀上,谢尔碧冒起了鸡皮疙瘩。他咧着嘴笑了起来,很显然觉得自己很酷。那模样就好像在说:"投降吧,我看上的女人没有得不到的。"

"你觉得这样合适吗?"她冷淡地问道,并且迅速地将缠绕在自己和特兰汀先生身上的真心话绳索解开。她现在唯一的想法就是尽快离开这个地方。预见麻烦几乎是她的第六感。或者说她全部的生活——摇滚乐队和唱歌电报——都是在试图煽动起一些麻烦,所以在这一点上,她从来都没有错过。像这样的家伙通常随时都有可能会吐出来,你想确定的一点是,不会吐在你身上。

莫莉小声叫道:"伊桑?"并费力地挤出了一个微笑。

谢尔碧想要迅速自然地结束这一切,于是把绳索塞进靴子,并拿出了上面写着"生日快乐"的卷轴,接着将胳膊搭在特兰汀先生的身上。"丹尼斯——"谢尔碧盯着特兰汀说道,"我可以叫你丹尼斯吗?"

那个插话者又接嘴道:"你可以叫我丹尼斯。"他顺势贴近了谢尔碧,用自己

shoulder against her free one and starting to put his hand around her waist. She felt herself tense. That was it. She didn't want the fucker touching her and she was gonna have to seriously break character, get ugly, and make it clear to him. It pissed her off when people did this. It wasn't often, but it did happen: The guy who stuck his tongue in her ear once at a bar mitzvah, the woman who followed her into a bathroom stall at a dyker bar. That one still cracked her up, but at the time it was unnerving. It pissed her off that people would not respect her privacy when she was just trying to make a living.

"Listen, buddy," Shelby said, turning sharply, and shoving him away from her. It crept her out to have strangers touch her. And after a day of strangers touching her on the subway, in the street, she'd had enough. It wasn't that they meant to touch her, at least not always, it was just the common physicality of life in New York City. She hadn't even known she was going to shove him. It was an involuntary response, an equal and opposite reaction. In a daze she watched him move away from her, off-balanced, spinning to the floor and ending up face downward, a heap of ratted hair and skinny blue-jeaned legs. There was a stunned pause, some people shaking their heads, some laughing, some looking at the others for a clue as to what to do. Shelby watched incredulously, thinking how much it had reminded her of Mousetrap. The ball knocking the shoe tipping the bucket. And the strangest thing was, this guy suddenly looked familiar to her. She racked her brain, trying to figure out who he looked like.

Molly immediately went over to Ethan—Shelby realized that she actually knew the guy's name now, reinforced because people were murmuring it. She certainly had no interest in even knowing that much about him. She *hadn't* meant to push him that hard. She hadn't pushed him that hard. Walking toward him, she asked worriedly, "Is he okay?" as he lay unmoving by the watercooler. She could hear the room get noisy. Her cheeks burned.

Shelby stood next to Molly nervously. Molly had knelt next to Ethan and was feeling his forehead and talking softly. Shelby noticed a finger moving on his hand, tapping the floor. She watched it puzzled, not sure what it meant. A tremor? A muscle out of whack? No one else noticed. Then she heard the background Muzak, faint but audible. She hadn't noticed it before. Staring at the finger for a moment, she slowly digested the fact that the rhythm and the finger moved together. Jesus.

的肩膀摩擦着谢尔碧空着的一只胳膊,借机用另一只手环住了她的腰部——她立刻就感觉到自己浑身绷紧了。到达底线了!她不想让这个混蛋碰自己,她这回是真的打算撕破脸,跟他挑明了。每次有人这样做谢尔碧就气不打一处来,虽然不是很经常,但确实发生过:在一个犹太男孩的成人仪式上有个男人曾经把舌头伸进了谢尔碧的耳朵里面;还有一次在女同性恋酒吧有个女人尾随着谢尔碧一直走进了洗手间的隔间里。现在每次回想起第二件事谢尔碧都会想笑,但当时却是紧张害怕得要命。每当她为生活拼命努力,而自己的私人空间却得不到人们的尊重时,谢尔碧就烦透了。

"听着,伙计!"谢尔碧提高了音调说道,同时一把将他推开。陌生人一碰她她就会浑身起鸡皮疙瘩,再加上一天下来在地铁、街道上不停地被人碰撞,这对谢尔碧来说已经够受的了。其实他们也并不是有意地要去碰自己,至少不是每个人都是有意的,因为这就是纽约市生活的常态。谢尔碧在做这个动作之前都没有意识到自己会去推他,这只是一个站在他对面的人会做出的合理的下意识反应。眼神迷蒙中她看见那家伙从自己身上飞离,失去平衡后打着转儿地向地板跌去,最终脸与地来了个亲密接触,只能看到那一堆蓬松的头发和包在牛仔裤里的两条竹竿似的腿。所有人都惊呆在原地,有的人在摇头,有的人大笑不止,还有的人盯着别人看,揣摩着现在该怎么做。谢尔碧不可置信地看着他们,眼前的场景使她想起了电影《捕鼠器》里的情节:球撞飞了鞋,鞋打翻了桶……最奇怪的是,眼前这个家伙突然看起来很眼熟。她绞尽脑汁地思索着,他到底像谁。

莫莉立刻向伊桑走去——谢尔碧突然意识到自己已经记住了那家伙的名字,因为大家一直在小声嘟囔,强化了她的记忆,但她连知道他的名字都嫌多余。她没想推那么重,其实也没有用多大力气。那家伙却一动不动地躺在饮水机的旁边,谢尔碧走过去,担心地问道:"他还好吗?"房间里喊喊喳喳的声音渐渐大起来了,谢尔碧的脸颊烧得滚烫。

她紧张地站在莫莉的身旁,莫莉则单膝着地蹲在伊桑的旁边,一边摸着他的前额,一边轻声地说着话。谢尔碧突然发现,伊桑有一根手指不停地击打着地板。她很困惑,不知道这意味着什么。难道是抽搐吗?还是肌肉遭到猛烈碰撞后的反应?其他人都没有注意到这一点。然后她听到了隐约传来但仍可辨析的背景音乐声,之前一直都没有注意到。她又盯着那根手指看了一会儿,慢慢地思忖着:那根手指一直在跟着音乐的节拍敲打地面。天哪,他这是在拖延时间。

He was keeping time. Shelby looked around. Nobody seemed to realize. She stood up, ready to kick the little jerk. There was nothing wrong with him. He was playacting. Like she needed more of that. "What an asshole," she said under her breath, moving back toward the front of the room.

Ethan's eyes popped open as she started away and he reached out a hand to grab her ankle, missing it. He jumped up laughing.

"I'm sorry, I have to leave," Shelby said, turning to Mr. Trantin and handing him the Monkey Business Singing Telegram card, like these people were going to order another telegram. She picked up her monkey, knowing that she was now over her ten minute absolute cut-off time. "My bag?" she said, looking at Molly.

"Ah, don't go ... "

Shelby turned toward Ethan with the attitude of "don't fuck with me, buster", but then realized her mistake. He would only perceive it as challenge.

Putting his face up to hers, he asked, "How about a dance?" and grabbed her left hand, smashing the monkey to her chest. "Look," he shouted, "I'm dancing with Wonder Woman." Shelby leaned back, cocked her right hand hard, and before she knew it, it was ricocheting, bounding back with her best jujitsu punch, the monkey along for the ride. She'd taken classes years ago, never knowing that her body would respond with such precision. Upon impact, the monkey flew from her hand and, landing head down, started screaming with laughter. The one time in its life when it had come through.

Stunned, she looked at her hand, then at Ethan. He hadn't fallen, but a big bruise was coming into view on his cheek. He backed up and yelled, "You hit me!" There was a mixture of shock and something else on his face, perhaps a doggyish sense of misunderstanding. "I'm gonna sue." Shelby looked at him blankly, wondering why he wasn't on the ground. She'd hit him with all her might. She'd connected. It was a strange feeling, believing yourself to be a fairly strong person, able to open stuck jars, lifting band equipment, and then discovering it was all an illusion. But, she reasoned, maybe it was him. After all, inebriated pledges often live after falling off frat balconies. Perhaps only later would he truly feel it. If there were a God.

Someone official came in the room which was bulging with people now and more coming in. He had on a badge, but he wasn't with the police department.

谢尔碧环顾了一下四周,没有人发现这个蹊跷的行为。谢尔碧站直了身子,准备好一脚踢飞这个小混蛋。他明明什么事都没有,却一直在演戏。就好像谢尔碧在工作生活中还没有看够戏似的。"这该死的。"她低声咒骂了一句,随后向房间前面走回去。

她一转身伊桑的眼睛就突然睁开了,并且伸出一只手试图抓住她的脚踝,不过失手了。他一跃而起,开始大笑起来。

谢尔碧转向特兰汀先生,说道:"我很抱歉,但是我得走了。"虽然明知这些人不会再花钱雇她做唱歌电报了,她还是递过了一张猴子唱歌电报事务所的名片。她捡起了地上的猴子,断定现在已经超过了自己十分钟内解决的时间标准。于是她看向莫莉,"我的包呢?"

"啊,别走呀……"

带着一脸"你这小子,别惹老娘"的表情,谢尔碧转过身去看着伊桑。但她瞬时就意识到这是一个错误:他只会把这看成是一种挑战。

他猛地把脸凑到谢尔碧的脸面前,问道:"跳支舞怎么样?"不等回答,他就一把抓起谢尔碧的左手,猴子顺势砸在了她的胸部。"快看哪!"他叫道,"我在和神奇女侠跳舞呢!"谢尔碧向后一侧身,举起自己紧握的右拳,当她意识到的时候,这个拳头已经结束了漂亮的柔道一击,带着反冲力向回收了,那只猴子则搭着顺风车飞了出去。几年前谢尔碧上过柔道训练班,但她不知道自己身体的应激反应竟然这么精准。不可避免的,那只猴子从她手里飞出去后,大头着地,接着就开始大笑并发出刺耳的尖叫,这是到现在为止唯一的一次成功案例。

愣在原地的谢尔碧看了看自己的手,又看向了伊桑。他并没有跌倒,但是一个大大的瘀青开始慢慢显现在他的脸颊上。他向后倒退了几步,大吼道:"你竟然敢打我!"他脸上的表情十分复杂,除了震惊之外还有些别的东西,就像是小狗在做错了事情之后却不明所以的困惑样子。"我要告你。"谢尔碧毫无表情地望着他,奇怪为什么他没有倒在地板上。她那一击可是用尽了全身的力气,就像所有的筋脉都被打通连接在一起。这种感觉很奇怪,你本以为自己是一个很强壮的人,可以拧开卡住的盖子,也能够搬动乐队的设备,最后却发现这一切都是幻象。但是,谢尔碧又回头推理了一下,觉得也许是那个家伙的原因。毕竟,宣誓入会的人在喝醉后经常会从兄弟会阳台上摔下来,之后也没什么大碍。也许过一段时间他就会感觉到真正的痛苦了。如果上帝真的存在的话。

有个警官模样的人走了进来,本来就略嫌拥挤的房间又陆续增加着来客。他胸前佩戴着一个徽章,但他并不是警察。麦克斯叫他们"临时条子",在加州

Chapter One Combustible

Rent-a-pigs, Max called them. You saw a lot of them in California. On the freeway you'd think they were the police and then realize that you'd thrown the joint out the window for nothing. Shelby didn't want to get stuck having to explain what happened and really lower her hourly wage, so she grabbed her monkey, snatched her bag out of Molly's hands, and ran to the elevator.

She didn't know where her aggression came from, and it scared her. She couldn't remember ever hitting anyone before. Not hard like that. She tended to be punchy as a joke, slugging padded shoulders or poking panted legs, a safe way of feeling close that couldn't be taken for sexual. Maybe it really was her period. Maybe it was New York. Maybe it was disgust that guys thought they could just touch you whenever they wanted and they relied on the fact that you, as a woman, couldn't do anything about it, especially if there wasn't a strong man around to intervene, specifically a man who would claim you. It just pissed her off. And being Wonder Woman had gone to her head.

Out on the street, she started laughing, unable to believe what had just happened. She looked back at the building. Three guys were standing in the window. "Good job!" one of them yelled. She grinned at him a little embarrassedly. He hoisted a champagne glass to her, and the guy standing next to him threw an air punch and nodded. Well, it seems to have gotten all the guys excited, she joked to herself, flattered and sarcastic at the same time. She stuck the monkey into her open gym bag, its lecherous face peering up at her, then started running down the sidewalk in costume, wanting to get lost in the crowd, if that were possible dressed as a superhero. She heard people yelling at her, strangers. She didn't care. She only wanted to be home. Stoned. She had a sudden desire for rude sex, and laughed that that would be the case, that sticking up for herself had been an aphrodisiac. Max had never fucked her in her Wonder Woman costume. Kind of amazing considering that they'd tried almost everything else. That's really why she bought the handcuffs. It was only afterward that she'd come up with Policewoman Betty, so they could write the handcuffs off on their taxes. She liked wild sex, but sometimes, even with all the accessories, she just couldn't seem to relax. Deep down she knew there was a reason that she played at kink. And it left her wanting. Like the rest of her life.

随处可见。在高速公路上看到他们的时候,人们会误认为是警察,可后来就意识到,就算你把吃剩的大麻烟卷扔出车窗外也不会发生什么事情的。谢尔碧实在是不想被困在这里解释事情的始末,因为这会使她的时薪大打折扣,于是她一把抓起猴子,从莫莉手里抢过自己的包,向电梯跑去。

　　谢尔碧完全不知道自己刚才那么强烈的攻击性是从哪冒出来的,着实把她自己都给吓了一跳。在她的记忆里,自己从来没有打过人,至少没有打得那么重过。她的本意是开玩笑般的打两下,一拳打在垫肩处或是踢一下他的腿,这些都是可以拉近距离但不会引起暧昧误解的方法。或许真的是由于谢尔碧正处于生理期的缘故,或许是因为身在纽约,又或许是因为这样的事实让谢尔碧感到恶心:男人们觉得自己想什么时候随便摸你都可以,因为他们笃信,作为一个女人,你对此毫无办法,尤其是当你身边没有一个强壮的男人,具体来说,也就是一个宣称拥有你的男人,来干预这一切的时候。一想起这个她就火冒三丈,而且神奇女侠的角色已经融入她的性格里面了。

　　终于走到了大街上,谢尔碧开始放声大笑起来,觉得刚才发生的一切都有些不可置信。她回头看向那座大楼,有三个男人站在窗口的位置。"干得好!"其中一个冲谢尔碧喊道。她有些窘迫地咧嘴笑了一下。他又对谢尔碧举起了香槟酒杯,而旁边的另一个男人则向空气中挥了一拳并向谢尔碧点了点头。好吧,我的行为好像使那些男人们都感到挺痛快的。谢尔碧和自己开起了玩笑,既觉得荣幸,又感到有些讽刺。她将猴子一把塞进了敞开的运动包里,那只猴子则脸上带着挑逗的表情一直瞪着谢尔碧。谢尔碧顺着人行道向前跑去,想要消失在人群中——可是穿着这一身超人的衣服想做到这一点好像有些不现实。她听到有人冲她大吼,是些陌生人。但是她不在乎。她只想回家。抽上几口大麻。她突然产生想要野蛮做爱的冲动,然后大笑着意识到,原来为自己挺身而出这件事对她来说是一剂催情药。但她从来都没有穿着神奇女侠的衣服与麦克斯做过爱,这倒是有些令人惊讶,因为他们几乎把所有其他的方式都试过了。这也是谢尔碧最初买手铐的真实原因,只是到后来她才想出了"女警贝蒂"的这个电报角色,这样他们在填自己的税单时就可以不填手铐这一项了。谢尔碧喜欢疯狂的性爱,但有时候,即使用上了各种道具,她似乎也总是放松不下来。内心深处她知道,自己之所以这么喜欢带有性虐色彩的性爱一定存在着什么原因。这也让她总是想要更多。一辈子都是如此。

Chapter Two Venting

Venting: *verbs.* open, ope [poetic], open up; lay open, throw open; fly open, spring open, swing open, tap, broach; cut open, cut, cleave, split, slit, crack, chink, fissure, crevasse, incise; rift, rive ...

Roget's International Thesaurus

Max thumbed through the Merck Manual, a thick brown book listing nearly every disorder known to mankind. "A dictionary for hypochondriacs," Max called it knowingly. His was well-worn. Today he had the beginnings of a sore throat, and he was checking to see if it was something he could die painfully from. Not finding "sore throat" in the index, Max riffled the pages, learning a little bit about giantism ("excessive secretion of GH caused by an acidophilic adenoma of the pituitary"), precocious puberty ("an activation of the hypothalamic-pituitary axis with a consequent enlargement and maturation of the gonads") and other relatively obscure conditions, when suddenly he let go a loud fart. Shelby wasn't home which disappointed him because he liked farting loudly and wished that someone else had been there to hear it. He knew this was on the edge of crude, but there it was all the same. As a consolation, he looked it up. "Like it's really gonna be there."

Page 792. Just like that. He felt perhaps he knew just a little more about the authors. Turning to it, he began reading all about "The Irritable Bowel Syndrome". ("Star Trek" wouldn't be on for another fifteen minutes.) First, he read through the possible causes (stress was a big one, with women more affected than men by 3 to 1), through the symptoms and signs, and then focused on the one case cited where gas passage reached uncanny proportions.

One careful study noted a patient with daily flatus frequency as high as 141, including 70 passages in one 4-h period. This symptom, which can cause great psychosocial distress, has been unofficially and humorously described according to its

第二章 排放

> 排放：动词，打开，启[诗歌]，完全打开，开着，推开，弹开，甩开，轻敲，钻开，切开，切割，裂开，劈开，撕裂开，破裂，成裂缝，分裂开，崩溃，割裂开，断裂开，撕开……
>
> ——《罗格特国际成语词典》

麦克斯将《默克诊疗手册》从头到尾给翻阅了一遍，这本大部头有着棕色的封面，里面罗列了几乎所有人类已知的障碍性疾病。"这本字典对有疑心病的人很实用。"麦克斯机智地说道。他的这本书早已磨损得不成样子了。今天他有些咽喉痛的症状，这会儿他正检索着自己是不是患上了什么折磨人的不治之症呢。最终他也没有在索引里找到"咽喉痛"这个症状，于是就哗啦啦翻了好几页，开始了解一些关于巨大畸形症（由嗜酸性垂体腺瘤引起的生长激素的过度分泌引起）、性早熟（对下丘脑—垂体轴的激活及其引起的性腺肿大与化脓症状）以及其他一些定义相对模糊的病症。突然间，他放了一个特别响亮的屁。谢尔碧这时候却并不在家，他感到很失望，因为他喜欢在放响屁的时候有人在场听到。他明知道这样近乎粗俗，但还是克制不住会产生这样的想法。为了给自己找些安慰，他又去那本书里搜寻这个症状。"就好像书里真的会有似的。"

792 页，还真的就找到了。他感觉自己对作者的了解又更近了一步。翻到那页之后，他就开始从头阅读关于"肠易激综合征"的种种描述（反正《星际旅行》还有 15 分钟才开始放呢）。先从各种可能的诱因开始读起（压力是重要罪魁之一，女性的患病率比男性要高出两倍），然后是症状和体征，最后再集中阅读文中引用的那个排气量达到不可思议程度的个人病例。

曾有实验记载，有位患者每天"放气"频率高达 141 次，其中在某连续的四小时内达到 70 次之多。这种症状可能带来严重的心理焦虑，根据其一些显著的特征，人们对它进行了非官方的颇具幽默色彩的分类：1."悄无声息型"（常见

salient characteristics: (1) the "slider" (crowded elevator type) which is released slowly and noiselessly, sometimes with devastating effect; (2) the open sphincter, or "pooh" type, which is said to be of higher temperature and more aromatic; and (3) the "staccato" or "drum-beat" type, pleasantly passed in privacy.

While questions of air pollution and degradation of air quality have been raised, no adequate studies have been performed. However, no hazard is likely to those working near open flames and youngsters have even been known to make a game of expelling gas over a match-flame. Rarely, this usually distressing symptom has been turned to advantage, as with a Frenchman referred to as "Le Petomane," who became affluent as an effluent performer on the Moulin Rouge stage.

Max smiled, tilting for a moment. It stunned and pleased him that the writers of the Merck Manual had a sense of humor.

He was wasting time. But he was a postdoc. He could do that. In the old days, not so long ago, he would have left the lab, come home, eaten a quick dinner, usually a pound of Tatertots and some macaroni and cheese, then gone back to the lab. In graduate school, you have to work your ass off. Five years of slavery. But it had its positive sides. You slaved for a purpose. It was perhaps a little bit of boot-camp mentality, but there was more to it than that. You were doing something at such an intense level, learning things that other people didn't know. By your second year, you were the expert on your particular molecule. There was the joke they always made in the lab that you had the world's supply of whatever compound you were working on—pretty heady stuff. Okay, it was esoteric, but that added to the ego fulfillment. You knew you were smart, that someday people would call you doctor (though when they found out you were a mere Ph. D. they would be less impressed).

Life had been simple in graduate school. You went to the lab. You came home. There were no decisions required. What would you do tonight? It was obvious. You worked for your research director, a man who resembled God more than God. He could make or break your career.

But now Max had his own money. A grant from the American Cancer Society. His way wasn't being paid out of Dr. Scotia's money, so Scotia had a little less power over him than his research advisor at Irvine had, not that he'd want to piss Scotia off or anything. But Max could come and go as he pleased now. No one checked up on him. It certainly made being married easier. Or at least it should have. It used to.

于拥挤的电梯中）；通常徐缓且无声，有时具有"杀伤性"后果；2."毫无顾忌型"（又称"一冲而出"型）：据传温度更高，气味更刺鼻；3."断断续续型"或"鼓点儿型"：不引人注意地完成整个过程。

　　随着空气污染与空气质量下降问题的日益突出，人们对"放气"这一现象进行的研究还远远不够。但其实，最危险的情况是，让患者在有明火的环境中工作，以及年轻人发明的对着火柴的火苗放屁的游戏。令人惊奇的是，这个通常情况下会使人苦不堪言的症状，竟然被转变成了一种特长，法国的"放屁表演家"拉·派多曼就因为在红磨坊的舞台上表演放屁而身价百万。

　　麦克斯笑了，顺势翘起了半边屁股。虽然作者在《默克诊疗手册》中体现出的幽默感使他有些吃惊，但他对此感到很满意。

　　麦克斯现在做的事情就是在浪费时间，但他已经是个博士后了，这样做没什么不可以的。然而就在不久之前的那些日子里，他每天离开了实验室之后就会直接回家，吃一顿简单的晚饭，通常是一磅左右的炸黄金土豆球，还有一些意大利通心粉配上芝士，随后又一头扎进实验室里去。待在研究生院里，你就必须没日没夜地做事，就像服五年的奴役一样。但这种生活还是有积极一面的——你是为了达到最终的目标而在做奴隶。有点像身处新兵训练营里的心态，但又不止于此：因为你如此高强度地投入一件事情，是在学习别人所不知道的东西。到第二年的时候，在你研究的那个特定小分子的领域，你就已经是专家了。在实验室里，他们经常说这样一句玩笑话，"无论你在试图合成什么样的化合物，整个世界的资源都在你手边"——这不免会使人有些飘飘然。好吧，这个笑话仅限于圈内人，但这一点更使他们为此而骄傲。他们清楚地知道，自己智力不凡，总有一天人们会称呼自己为博士的（但如果别人发现你只是一个哲学博士，印象就会打些折扣了）。

　　在研究院的日子是简单的：去实验室，然后回家。不需要你做任何决策。你今晚做什么呢？答案显而易见——你得给研究室主任干活儿。这个人比上帝还像上帝，因为你职业生涯的成败全在他一念之间。

　　可现在麦克斯拥有自己的基金来源了——美国癌症协会的研究拨款。他所做的研究现在并不是由斯考蒂亚博士来出资了，所以斯考蒂亚对麦克斯的掌控权比麦克斯在加州大学欧文分校时的导师还要少——虽说如此，麦克斯并没有过成心激怒斯考蒂亚或是其他的想法。重要的是现在麦克斯可以来去自由，没有人会查他的岗。这样一来结婚就容易多了，至少理论上是这样的——从过来

He frowned. Lately something had been going on between them, something he couldn't put his finger on. Shelby was a little bit manic depressive. He'd known that before they got married. But he used to be able to calm her down. To win her over to the side of happiness. These days, though, his efforts seemed less effective. He didn't mind the effort. He loved her. But he was beginning to be at a loss as to what to do.

She'd had a troubled childhood. Her father had discovered, or at least revealed, that he was gay when she was in junior high. He'd left her mom. It had been ugly. She said she used to think him so liberated, getting *Playboys* for him, *Playgirls* for her. Little had she known, the *Playgirls* were for him, and the *Playboys* just a cover. Had she lived in New York it might have been more obvious. That's what she said now. She wouldn't have been so naive. But she grew up in a small Californian town where such things were rare, and once out, discussed to death. She didn't blame her father. How could he continue to pretend? But she missed their family. Going home. She'd wanted the quintessential childhood, and Max had learned not to remind her that it didn't exist.

Max could afford to be supportive. Overall, he'd had a happy childhood. The only disconcerting thing about his family had happened when he was in college, when his father had had a very fast onset of Alzheimer's. Fortunately he'd died shortly after that, fortunate because it was painful to watch him deteriorate. He would do completely incomprehensible things. One Christmas break Max came home and found that his dad had completely disassembled Max's Yamaha motorcycle. Every nut had been unscrewed from every bolt, every gasket, every pinion dislodged. It lay spread over the floor of the garage like a diagram from a do-it-yourself magazine. Max stood in the doorway, completely shocked. His mother had found him there, and held him while he just kept shaking his head. He didn't want to say anything to make her feel worse. He couldn't help being bummed about the motorcycle. There was no way to put it together again. But it was hard to wrap words around what he felt about his dad. There was no way to put him together again either.

Everyone had some tragedy in their lives. But it was how you let it affect you that made it a curse or a strength. Max knew that overall he'd been lucky. His parents were the kind that anyone would have liked to have had. It made missing his dad harder, but that was okay. When Shelby was down, he would try to explain this philosophy to

人的经验上看理应如此。想到这里麦克斯蹙了蹙眉：最近他和谢尔碧之间发生了一些事情，让他感到无从下手。谢尔碧这些日子里有些狂躁抑郁的倾向，虽然这点在他们结婚前麦克斯就知道了，但是过去在他的安抚下，是可以成功地将她领到幸福的一边的。可现在，他的努力似乎收效甚微。因为爱她，麦克斯并不介意自己的付出，但他却逐渐开始感到茫然，不知道自己还可以做些什么。

谢尔碧的童年并不平坦。在她还在上初中的时候，她的父亲发现，或者说是承认了自己的同性恋取向。随后他就离开了母亲，整个过程少不了争执吵闹。父亲过去会买《花花公子》来看，顺便也会给谢尔碧买上相应的男色杂志，那时谢尔碧误以为父亲的思想足够开放才会这样做。她当时完全没有想过，其实那些男色杂志是为他自己买的，而《花花公子》不过是个幌子。如果她生活在纽约这样的城市的话，也许会更轻易地看出蹊跷来。但这是后话了，否则她也不会还像现在这样头脑简单。谢尔碧从小在加利福尼亚的一个小镇长大，在那里，这样的事情极其少见，一旦公之于众，就会无休止地被拿来作谈资。她并不怪自己的父亲：他如何能继续伪装下去呢？但她还是很怀念那个他们共同组建的家，还有回家的日子。她心心念念着一段完美的童年生活，而麦克斯也习惯了不去提醒她，这样的童年根本不存在。

麦克斯对谢尔碧如此支持包容，是因为总体来说他的童年生活还是充满了幸福感的。他的家庭里发生的唯一令人措手不及的事情，就是在他上大学期间，麦克斯的父亲突然患上了阿尔兹海默症（老年痴呆症）。幸运的是，不久之后他父亲就去世了——说幸运是因为麦克斯实在不忍心看着他一点点地恶化，有时候他会做一些常人完全无法理解的事情。有一年圣诞节，麦克斯回到家里，发现自己的雅马哈摩托被父亲拆得零零散散：每一个螺钉都被拧开了，螺帽、垫片、小齿轮，无一幸免。这些小零件散落在车库的地面上，就像是某个教你如何组装杂志的教程插图。麦克斯站在车库门口，沉浸在震惊当中。之后母亲在那里找到了他，挽起他的胳膊，而他却一直摇着头。麦克斯不想再说任何会让母亲更伤心的话，但是却无法抑制地为自己的摩托车而感到难过——要想把它再重新组装回去是门都没有了。麦克斯很难找到合适的词来形容当时他对父亲处境的感受——要想把他重新组装回去，亦是痴人说梦。

每个人的生命中都有过悲剧。但它究竟是会成为诅咒还是动力则取决于你让它通过什么方式影响你的生活。麦克斯深知，总的来说自己是个幸运的人。他的父母是所有孩子心目中理想的类型，而这让思念过世的父亲成为一件更加痛苦的事情，但是麦克斯还能挺过去。谢尔碧情绪低落的时候，麦克斯就会将

Chapter Two Venting

her, and though she could grasp it rationally, emotionally she couldn't hold onto it. She hadn't liked her childhood that much. She had a lot of anger. Because of it, she suffered twice, once as a child, and again as an adult. But how to change? It was something they talked about a lot. Once you find all the roots of your behavior, then what do you do? Max didn't know how to help her. He only knew that he loved her.

The front door opened with the weighty sound of wood wearied from overuse. Shelby clomped in. She walked straight to their bedroom and dropped her gymbag on the waterbed. The bed rolled with undulations. Slow semi-circles that rustled the covers. She paused for a second, staring at the room, having forgotten that she'd seen it earlier in the day and nothing had changed; it still looked like a disaster area. The floor was completely coated with a grayish powder except for where large bootprints showed the grain of the hardwood underneath. A dirty pair of overalls lay in a pile near the bathroom door with an empty cigarette pack crumpled companionably by it. Shelby gritted her teeth, her anger returning to her in an amazing swoop, as if a switch had been flipped and the current was running. The apartment felt as private as Grand Central Station. She was afraid to look in the bathroom. Unsuspecting, she had gone in there at lunch. Someone had made a huge hole in the wall and a smaller one in the floor. She couldn't believe that New York was a place where people could just come in and demolish your apartment, and that they would be paid to do it.

Shelby sat heavily on the edge of the waterbed. She pulled off her Wonder Woman costume, and tried to think of something to look forward to. Sometimes there were parties looming ahead. That could perk her up. Sometimes the band excited her, and sometimes it didn't. She usually found herself dreading performing and then loving every minute of it. Even when the place was empty. She'd stand in front of the speakers and lean against the wall of sound, feeling the music pour over her body, listening to her voice weave through the melody, find its place in the harmonies, fitting alongside a wavelength like its best friend.

"Shel! You got to listen to this!" she heard Max yell from the living room. It drove her crazy when he did that. She hated it when he talked to her from another room because their apartment had such high ceilings, the sound echoed throughout the place. She would yell, "I can't hear you," and he would yell, "What?" in a way that both amazed her and made her wonder if this really was how comedy was born.

自己的这套人生哲学解释给她听,尽管理智上谢尔碧可以听进去,但总是无法产生情感上的共鸣。她对自己的童年感情淡薄——从那时起她就有很多的怒火。就因为如此,谢尔碧必须要经受两次煎熬——还是孩童的时候,以及成年之后的现在。但是要如何改变呢?他们俩经常讨论这个话题——找到了行为的根源之后,该怎么做呢?麦克斯不知道该如何帮助她,他只知道,自己爱她。

门被打开的时候发出了一阵年久失修的"吱嘎"声,谢尔碧步履沉重地走了进来。她径直走向卧室,随手将运动包扔在了水床上。水床随之而波动起来,圆弧形的水波徐徐摩擦着表面,发出沙沙的声音。停顿了一秒之后,谢尔碧开始环顾整个房间,忘记了今天早些时候就已经看过了一遍,而现在还是什么变化都没有:仍然像是一个灾难现场。地板上全部蒙上了一层灰色的粉末,只有个别被踩过的地方,才露出了木地板的纹路,呈现出巨大的靴子形状。一条脏兮兮的工装裤团成一团堆在浴室的门口,旁边还躺着一个皱巴巴的香烟盒。谢尔碧磨了磨牙齿,突然之间整个人又充满了无名的怒火,就好像有个开关被打开了,电流全速通遍全身。这间公寓就跟中央火车站一样,毫无隐私可言。她都有些害怕向浴室里望去了——午饭时间她进去过一次,震惊地发现墙上被人打了一个巨大的洞,地板上还有一个小洞。谢尔碧怎么都无法相信,在纽约这样的城市,竟然有人可以随意进出你的公寓肆意破坏,而且这些人还能够为此而拿到报酬。

谢尔碧一屁股坐在水床的边缘,一边脱下神奇女侠的服装,一边认真地想着最近有什么值得期待的事情。有时,临近的派对会为她注入活力;而乐队的演出对她的振奋作用却时有时无。通常情况下,在表演开始之前,她总是感到担心惧怕,而后却又觉得其中的每一分钟都是享受。即使是观众寥寥无几的时候,她也会站在麦克风的前面,依靠着一面无形的声墙,感受着洒满全身的音乐,听着自己的声音在旋律中徜徉,找到和声中合适的位置,与声线的波长水乳交融。

"谢尔!你得听听这个!"她听见麦克斯从客厅里传来的喊声。每次他这样做,都让谢尔碧感到抓狂:这间公寓的天花板特别高,因此当两个人在不同的房间里大声地对话时,声音就会不停地在空气中回响,让谢尔碧尤其讨厌。她总是会回喊道:"我听不见你说什么!"然后麦克斯又会喊:"什么?"这样的对话使她自己都感到吃惊,同时也有些好奇,或许这就是喜剧真正的起源?

"I'm too tired to listen." She knew she should tell him she slugged a guy, but something perverse in her wanted him to ask how her day had been, wanting proof that he cared. She hung her coat in the hall closet, then went back into the bedroom and started to take off her boots, kicking aside the work clothes. "Where were you? I left a note in your lab." Her voice was irritable. She heard the tone of it and winced. She didn't mean to take it out on Max. Although, now that she felt mad at him, she did wonder if it would have occurred to him to start cleaning up this mess.

"I had to go downtown and get my guitar repaired. I just got home a second ago."

"Oh, shit, I completely forgot." She walked to the glass-paneled door that separated the living room from the entry hall, and leaned in. Her face softened into an apology. "I don't mean to sound crabby. I missed you. I just wanted to see you," she said, sliding into pseudo-baby talk by her last sentence. Then she couldn't help herself. "I slugged a guy today," she said lightly, and went back into the bedroom, accidentally sitting on the toy monkey. She yanked it out from under her and hurled it to the floor where it slid under the bookcase.

"What?"

She didn't bother to answer, instead pulling off her hose. Why was it that happiness always seemed so short-lived, like there was no way to stock up on it? You might think you were happy only to have something break or go wrong or make you slug someone and suddenly that wrong became a metaphor for your life. Okay, she hadn't been that happy, but just to be done with a day of telegrams, knowing there was a bong waiting for her, elevated her to at least an acceptance of life's banality. But now she had to clean up the filth left her by pinhead maintenance men (she just knew they were men) if she hoped to go to bed later without tracking plaster dust into bed.

"I'm gonna have to find another line of work. I just wish I knew how to do something else. That goddamn monkey never works."

"So don't take the fucking monkey. How will he know?"

"Oh, he'll know," Shelby said glumly. "Somebody'll complain. They'll say they paid to see the monkey." The monkey was supposed to bare its teeth in some pretense of a grin, chatter, and clap its cymbals together when you lightly cuffed him on the head, but it never worked. During telegrams she would now hit the monkey

"我太累了，不想听。"她知道，自己应该将今天对那个家伙动手的事情告诉麦克斯，但心里有那么一股倔强的情绪，希望麦克斯会主动问起她今天过得怎么样，至少证明他还关心自己。她把外套挂进门厅的衣橱里，然后回到卧室，开始脱靴子，并把演出服踢到一边。"你今天早些时候去哪了？我留了一张便条在你的实验室。"她的声音满是抱怨的口气。觉察到这一点后她感到自己有些过分了，毕竟她并不想把怒气发泄在麦克斯身上。尽管如此，既然她现在已经有些生麦克斯的气了，她在想这会不会促使他产生将这一团糟的房间打扫一下的念头。

"我去了市中心修吉他，这会儿刚到家不久。"

"哦，天哪，我完全把这回事儿给忘了。"谢尔碧走向隔开客厅与走廊的玻璃门，将身体探向前去，并做出歉意的表情。"我不是故意恶声恶气的。我很想你，很想见你。"最后一句话几乎到了奶声奶气的程度。这时候她再也忍不住了，轻声说道："今天我动手打了一个男的。"然后转身回了卧室，不小心坐在了玩具猴的上面。她一把将它从屁股下面拉出来，扔到地板上，它顺势滑到了书架的下面。

"什么？"

谢尔碧懒得回答，开始伸手脱丝袜。为什么幸福总是那么短暂，好像没有任何方法能够将它储存起来呢？有时候你觉得自己很幸福，但是下一秒生活就出了差错，被迫要动手打人，而这些差错，变成了你生活的真正的隐喻。虽然原本也没有多么开心，但在结束了一天的工作之后，有一杆大麻可以使自己的情绪振奋起来，她就能够继续忍受生活的索然无味了。但是眼下，她却必须先把那些没脑子的维修工（不用猜都知道是男人）留下的一地狼藉给打扫干净，否则她就得一路踩着石灰上床睡觉了。

"我得换一行工作干干了，真希望我还会点别的什么。那只破猴子一到关键时候就掉链子。"

"那就别带那只该死的猴子了，你老板又不会知道。"

"他会知道的，"谢尔碧闷闷不乐地说，"有人会投诉的，他们会说，他们花钱就是为了看那只猴子的。"只要你在那只猴子的头上轻轻地拍一下，它就应该龇起牙，露出虚假的笑容，并开始"唧唧"地叫个不停，同时敲打手里的铙钹，但它总是出毛病。所以谢尔碧在表演的时候，会将它砸在任何离自己最近的东西

on anything in the vicinity, not just desks, but lamps, watercoolers, once even a bald man's head—gotta big laugh. It was a cheap plastic monkey, made in Taiwan, not really built to take the abuse. Shelby didn't care. She'd told Gary she needed a new monkey and he said that none of the other girls needed new monkeys and they'd worked there longer than her. Chuckles had served him well and he expected that Chuckles would continue to do so. (All the monkeys had their names written diagonally on their T-shirts. Gary always called them by name. Gary wasn't gifted mentally.)

"If you require a new partner, it'll have to come out of your wages," Gary had said.

"As long as I can shove Chuckles up your ass," she fantasized her response as she walked out onto the crowded street, Chuckles under one arm.

Yesterday Chuckles wouldn't move a muscle, not through four separate telegrams. She thought he'd expired for good, but as soon as she got on the subway, Chuckles started clapping and hissing. Finally she just had to sit on him. Fortunately a young man with a fuzzy upper lip walked in from the car in front of them. As soon as he opened the heavy door at the end of the train, music blared from his earphones. At least it gave the subway occupants someone else to stare at. The music was so incredibly loud, she imagined that while everyone else was suffering the piercing din, he was really hearing a deep and complete silence.

Shelby foggily heard Max ask her a question, and she repeated herself, "He'll definitely find out. He makes it his business to nose around." Looking in the mirror that hung on the back of the bedroom door, she rubbed a pimple on her neck, wanting to probe it but knowing if she did it would get much uglier. "He'll probably find out I slugged someone." She gave it a tentative poke to see if it was worth picking. "The son of the client." She realized that she was talking to her reflection in the mirror, watching her expressions, noticing how her nose wrinkled snottily then seductively, mugging for the mirror. This somehow depressed her. As compensation for her mood, she went after the pimple.

"You hit someone?" Max asked loudly.

"He wouldn't leave me alone." Having drawn blood, which she now dabbed with a Kleenex, Shelby put on her sweats and socks, then picked up her costume and walked past Max into the living room, her index finger holding a piece of Kleenex to her neck.

上面，不仅仅是桌子，还有台灯、冷水器，有一次甚至砸在了一个光头男人的脑袋上——引起了一阵哄堂大笑。这是一只廉价的塑料猴子，产地是台湾，最初的生产目的应该不是用来承受这样的虐待的。但是谢尔碧才不在乎呢。她曾经向加利说过自己需要一只新的猴子，加利却说其他的姑娘们在这一行做得比她要久得多，却从没提过要新猴子。"咯咯笑"当年跟着他的时候表现得很好，因此希望它也能继续满足谢尔碧的需求。（所有的猴子都有自己的名字，并且成对角线方向地写在它们的 T 恤上。加利一直以来都是直接用名字称呼它们，由此可见他的心智没有很高。）

"你要是想要一个新搭档，得从你的薪水里面扣掉。"加利这样说过。

"除非让我用'咯咯笑'抽你的肥屁股！"谢尔碧一只胳膊夹着猴子，脑海里想象着自己对加利的回复，一边走上了人潮拥挤的街道。

昨天的四场电报表演里，"咯咯笑"连动都没有动一下。谢尔碧以为它总算是"寿终正寝"了，但是等到她一上地铁，"咯咯笑"就开始又是敲铙钹又是"嘶嘶"叫，最后她只能一屁股坐在了上面。还好这时候有一个年轻人从他们前面的一节车厢走了过来，他的上唇长有密密的茸毛。当车尾沉重的门被打开的时候，刺耳的音乐声从他的耳机中迸发出来。至少这样一来，地铁上的人们就有了其他可以盯着看的目标。音乐声大得不可置信，以至于谢尔碧觉得是不是当周围所有人都在饱受这噪音折磨的时候，那个男生的耳边其实只有一片深深的寂静。

模模糊糊中谢尔碧听到麦克斯问了自己一个问题，于是她又重复说道："他一定会发现的。他把每天四处打探当成正事来做。"接着她向挂在卧室门后的镜子里望去，搓了搓脖子上的一个青春痘，想把它给挤掉，但她知道这只会让它变得更红肿。"他很有可能会发现我动手打人了。"谢尔碧试探性地拨了拨，看看是否值得一挤。"该死的。"她意识到自己正在和镜子里的影像说话，她看着自己的表情：鼻子有些烦躁地皱着，一副挑逗的鬼脸。不知怎么，这使她变得愈加沮丧起来。为了弥补自己的心情，她就对那个青春痘下手了。

"你打人了？"麦克斯大声问道。

"他一直烦我。"谢尔碧抽出一张纸巾，擦了擦挤出来的血，然后穿上了毛衣和短袜。她一边用食指将一小片纸巾捂在脖子上，一边捡起地上的演出服向客厅走去，经过了麦克斯的身边。

Chapter Two Venting

Max stood up, following Shelby, and put his arm around her. "You should quit."

"I know."

Max kissed her forehead gently.

"I shoulda just left, but he pissed me off. He looked like Squiggy from *Happy Days*."

"*That's* why you hit him," Max joked. Shelby smiled and kissed him back, then went to hang up her costume in the crowded walk-in closet, knowing that she wouldn't quit. Sometimes she thought about going back to school. Becoming something. But what? She sighed and thought instead about marijuana. It was a more immediate solution.

She hastened her mission, whipping open the closet door at the far end of the living room. Its location only made sense if you had spent any period of time in New York. "We forgot the bedroom closet, but, not to worry, we'll just put it in the living room," she imagined the contractors explaining. Not having a closet in the bedroom made dressing awkward at times, especially when they had guests. These were the quirky inconveniences of apartments in New York: that your vision or possessions didn't match the original designers'. Their living room, for example, was built to resemble a ballroom. "The cave" Max called it. The ceiling loomed fifteen feet away. It was dark living in a cave. Changing the lights on the top of the ceiling required a device that made Shelby's neck ache, a long pole with a wire cage at the end in the shape of a light bulb. Needless to say, out of five bulbs, generally only two were actually lit. And the light filled the room hesitantly, becoming faded and tired by the time it reached the floor.

An enormous stone could be seen through all five of the floor-to-ceiling windows, the bedrock of Manhattan, too big to move, so they built around it. It was one frame of nature, a brief respite from the constancy of buildings. During the day, that is. At night it took on more sinister fantasies: a hideout for thieves, a stepping stone to their apartment. Their first week, Shelby had bought rolls of wallpaper on sale and hung them, one roll per window, unable to stand the thought of burglars looking in. Max thought it a deterrent if the burglars could see they owned nothing, but he didn't stop her.

麦克斯站起来，紧一步跟上了谢尔碧，并用双手环住了她。"你应该放弃这一行。"

"我知道。"

麦克斯轻轻地吻了一下她的额头。

"我本应该一走了之的，但是他实在是把我给气坏了。他长得就像《幸福生活》里面的斯奎奇。"

"难怪你要打他了。"麦克斯开玩笑道。谢尔碧笑了，回吻了麦克斯，转身走向衣帽间，将衣服挂了进去，她心里十分清楚，自己是离不开这一行的。有时候她想过要回学校去，并能最终学有所成。但是学什么呢？她叹了口气，转而想到了大麻——这个解决方法更迅速一些。

她加快了自己的速度，用力地打开在客厅最尽头的衣橱。只有曾经或多或少在纽约待过一阵子，才会对这样的房间格局感到习以为常。"我们忘了安装卧室衣橱了，不过别担心，把它放在客厅就行了。"谢尔碧想象着承包商这样解释道。卧室里没有衣橱有时会让穿衣服变得很尴尬，特别是有客人在的时候。居住在纽约的公寓里就会遭遇各种离奇的不便：你的想法或者所拥有的物品都与原设计者的意图不相符。比如说，他们的客厅本来是想设计成舞厅的样子，但是现在却被麦克斯称为"山洞"，因为它的天花板有15英尺高。住在这个"山洞"里面总是感觉很晦暗；每次更换天花板上的灯，谢尔碧都要使用一种尾端固定有灯泡形状绝缘笼的杆子，这样做使她的脖子僵酸无比。不消说，一般五个电灯泡里，只有两个是能点亮的。灯光闪了几下，极不情愿地洒满房间，等到它到达地板上的时候，早已经变得昏黄暗淡了。

五个落地窗都从天花板延伸到地板，透过每一扇向外看，你都可以看见一块巨大的岩石——这是曼哈顿的基岩，因为太过巨大而无法移动，人们就围绕着它来建造楼房。它是自然残存的一角，使人在满目的高楼林立中得到短暂的喘息。但这只是在白天，一到晚上它所带来的联想就要恐怖多了：盗贼们的藏身之所，以及他们进入公寓的垫脚石。住进这里的第一周，谢尔碧就买了好多卷降价的墙纸挂在每个窗户上。她一想到小偷们可以从外面看到自己的家，就无法忍受。麦克斯则觉得，如果小偷能够看见他们家"家徒四壁"，也就不会再光顾了，可是他并没有阻挠谢尔碧这样做。

Chapter Two Venting

Shelby thought about this as she went to the kitchen. Max never tried to deter her. She liked that about him. She smiled, knowing that he would consider it effort wasted. He knew her too well. She touched his hair fondly as she passed him, then turned the quick right to the kitchen. The apartment was laid out like a cross. From the entryway, it was nine steps to the living room, four to the kitchen and the same to the bedroom. The kitchen door had been removed, most likely because a previous tenant had suffered claustrophobia after using the oven, an act that would have reduced the available floor-space by half. The refrigerator door could only be opened to a forty-five degree angle, making the right crisper drawer useless. A person could trap a small child in the corner of the kitchen with the refrigerator door open, no doubt why small children weren't allowed in the building.

Having suddenly lost her desire for pot, Shelby instead poured herself a glass of wine, chugged half of it, then set it on the counter, and got the broom and dustpan from the entry hall closet.

"So why were you at the lab?" Max asked. She could tell he was placating her, and she felt guilty. Sometimes she was really mean to him, and he was so nice to her.

"You weren't home when I called, so after my telegram I went there to write. I have to turn in a story for my class." Shelby's voice continued out of the bedroom while she swept the plaster dust into a little pile and then coaxed it into the dustpan. "You know, that weird Indian woman—"

"Rahda?" Max asked.

"—I guess that's her name, anyway, she came in and called someone and then proceeded to bawl for what seemed like a half-an-hour. I couldn't get anything done. So I just listened to her weep in Indian."

"Jeeze." Max turned the sound up, "Star Trek" having just come on. "I think you mean Hindi."

"Hindi ... Indian ... " Shelby started to say, but then paused. "You know, I never noticed how similar those words are. Like 'gypsy' and 'Egyptian'." She bit her lip, then realized she was staring at the overalls and wondered what she should do with them. Gingerly picking them up, she carried them out the front door and put them on the large brass ashtray that sat three feet from their door, spotless and gleaming. The doorman, sitting in his red high-backed chair, glanced over at her. She

谢尔碧在走向厨房的时候意识到了：麦克斯从来都不试图阻挠她做任何事情，这一点她很喜欢。她会心地笑了，因为麦克斯深知试图劝她也是无用功——他实在是太了解自己了。经过麦克斯身边的时候她温柔地揉了揉他的头发，然后右转进了厨房。这间公寓的构造就像是一个迷宫：从入口进来，走向客厅需要九步，而通往卧室和厨房则各需要四步。厨房的门被拆掉了，很有可能是因为之前的房客在用完烤箱之后患上了幽闭恐惧症，因为打开烤箱门之后可供人移动的地板空间又减小了一半。冰箱的门只能打开45度角，使得它右边的保鲜储藏格完全变成了摆设。打开的冰箱门与厨房角落形成的空间足以让一个小孩子藏身了，难怪这栋楼不许小孩子进入呢。

突然间，谢尔碧对大麻的兴趣就消弭殆尽了，于是她转过身去给自己倒了一杯红酒。她咕嘟喝掉了一半，将杯子放回台面，便去走廊壁橱里取了扫帚和簸箕来。

"对了，你今天为什么会去实验室？"麦克斯问道。谢尔碧能够感觉到，麦克斯是在试图调节她的心情，这更让她产生了愧疚感。有的时候她对麦克斯真的很刻薄，而他却总是一如既往地对自己好。

"我给你打电话的时候你不在家，所以做完一份唱歌电报之后我就去你那里写东西了，有一份作业要交。"谢尔碧的声音继续从卧室里传来，她此时正将满地的白石灰扫成一小堆，然后慢慢地拨进簸箕里面。"你知道吗？那个奇怪的印度女人……"

"拉达吗？"麦克斯问。

"应该是叫这个名字吧。不管怎么样，当时她走了进来，拨通了一个电话，接着便对着那头鬼吼鬼叫，持续了大概有半个小时。我什么都做不成，只好一直听她用印第安语(Indian)哭诉。"

"天哪，"麦克斯把电视的音量调大了一些，《星际旅行》刚刚开始播放，"我想你说的是印度语(Hindi)吧……"

"印度语……印第安语……"谢尔碧开始嘟囔道，然后停顿了一下。"你知道吗，我从来没有注意到这两个词有这么相似。比如说'gypsy(吉普赛人)'和'Egyptian'(埃及人)。"她突然咬到了自己的嘴唇，然后意识到自己正盯着那条脏兮兮的工装裤看，并思忖着该怎么处理它。她小心地将其拎起，拿到了门外，门前三英尺左右的地方放了一个巨大的黄铜烟灰缸[译者注：纽约的烟灰缸ashtray非常大，直径约有半米]，擦得一尘不染还微微泛着光，于是谢尔碧就把裤子放在了上面。门卫坐在红色的高背椅上，向这边瞟过来。谢尔碧冲他露了一个甜甜的笑容，不知道他会不会因为这件事而找自己麻烦。但就在这时候，几对衣

smiled sweetly, wondering if he was going to hassle her about leaving the overalls there, but just then some well-dressed couple came to the door with their scuttling floor-mop of a dog and he jumped up to open the door.

"… that arranged marriage thing?" Max was asking.

Shelby closed the door behind her and answered tersely, "That'd be enough to make anyone depressed." She knew Max so well that she could continue their conversation without even knowing what had been said. "I wonder who would marry her."

"Someone who likes midgets."

Shelby laughed. "You're so mean." She went back to the kitchen to get her wine glass. "I think her family must have a ton of money. That's the inducement. Big dowry. She's always wearing new clothes."

"I think half of them are Paige's."

"Paige loans her her clothes? They're not even the same size. Anywhere." Paige was famous for being the most buxom chemist in the building.

"Not according to Paige."

"What? Rahda steals them?"

Max shrugged.

Shelby sat down on the arm of the big chair in which Max was splayed, digesting this bit of information. Max's legs were straightforward in a "V" in front of him, the chair perfect viewing distance from the TV. Max handled the remote like a phaser, laying one program to rest while bringing forth another with the expert click of a button. Shelby nonchalantly tried to reach her hand behind him and grab the control, but he knew this game and moved it ever-so-slightly out of her reach.

"How come you always get to be king?"

"Because I'm a man," Max said gruffly, taunting her. Shelby slid from the arm of the chair to his lap and stretched out her arms and feet, obstructing his view. "Hey, cut it out. Star Trek's on." When she didn't move, he said in his most exasperated voice, "Okay, here, you can have it for two minutes," and handed her the remote. She flipped around, stopping at a Spanish-speaking station where she tried to understand even one word until Max started sighing loudly. Knowing that his desire to watch television outshone hers, she gave him back the remote and stood up.

着光鲜的夫妇牵着他们的狗来到了门前,那些狗长着拖布条一样的长毛,前前后后地嗅着,门卫赶忙从椅子里跳起去开门。

"……那个包办婚姻的事情?"麦克斯在问她什么话。

谢尔碧转身并随手关上了门,简洁地答道:"谁遇到这种事都不会好过的。"她已经对麦克斯如此了解,即使没听到他说的前半句话也可以将对话继续下去。

"我想知道跟她结婚的人会是什么样的。"

"喜欢侏儒的人呗。"

谢尔碧被逗乐了:"你真是太坏了。"她又走向厨房去拿红酒杯。"我觉得她的家庭肯定超级富有,这就是诱饵——一大笔嫁妆。因为她总是在穿新衣服。"

"我想那些衣服里面有一半都是佩琪的。"

"佩琪把衣服借给她穿?她们的身材根本都不一样,没有一点相似的地方。"佩琪被公认为是那座大楼里身材最丰满和健美的女化学家。

"佩琪可不是这样说的。"

"什么?拉达偷了她的衣服?"

他耸了耸肩。

麦克斯四仰八叉地陷在椅子里,谢尔碧则顺势坐在了椅子的一边扶手上,开始消化刚听到的这点信息。椅子与电视之间留出了最佳观看距离,麦克斯的腿伸得笔直,摆出"V"字的形状。遥控器在麦克斯手里,就像是物理实验中的相位器,调出一个节目,另一个就进入休眠状态,连按下按钮的姿势都像个专家。谢尔碧假装漫不经心地从他背后伸手去拿遥控器,但麦克斯早就看透了这个把戏,轻易地就将手移到了她够不着的地方。

"为什么总是你说了算?"

"因为我是男人。"麦克斯粗着嗓子说道,充满了调侃的口吻。谢尔碧从椅子扶手上滑坐到麦克斯的膝盖上,尽力伸展开四肢,遮挡住麦克斯的视线。"喂,快停下。《星际旅行》要开始了。"看到谢尔碧完全没有移动的迹象,他终于用充满恼怒的语气说道:"好吧,拿去,你只能用两分钟。"然后把遥控器递到了她的手里。谢尔碧飞快地转换着频道,最终停在了一个讲西班牙语的电视台,试图听懂里面的只言片语,哪怕一个单词也好,直到她听到麦克斯开始大声地叹气。她还回了遥控器并站起身去,因为她知道自己看电视的欲望远没有麦克斯那么强烈。

Chapter Two Venting

"Someone was yelling at her," Shelby said, going into the kitchen for more wine.

"Yelling at who?" Max asked distractedly.

"Who are we talking about?" Shelby yelled from the kitchen. Max drove her crazy sometimes.

"Rahda?"

"Is she doing badly in chemistry?"

"No way. She's a molecular machine." Max laughed. "I've never seen someone get so much done."

"Big social life, I guess," Shelby said, putting the wine back in the refrigerator.

"Hell, Scotia announced at group meeting the other day that lawyers were coming to draw up patents on her work. She's going to get a third of the profits. That's unheard of."

"Why she's getting it then?" Shelby walked back into the living room with a glass of wine.

"Because it's that big."

Shelby knit her brow, confused. "She doesn't seem that smart. Are you jealous?"

"Trust me, it'll only help my career. Scotia could get a Nobel prize for this. I would have worked with a Nobel-prize winner."

"Wow." Shelby sat down on the sofa and cracked her neck. She looked at Max. "Doesn't it seem odd to you then that she was crying?"

"No," he said with a jaded laugh. "She is weird. The other day when she was drawing a chemical structure on the Macintosh, she thought the mouse was moving on its own."

"I don't get it."

"Like she was getting messages from God or something." Max rolled his eyes. "I have to admit, she's so odd, sometimes it makes me wonder."

"About what?"

"How did she get so lucky as to discover something this big and she's only a second year graduate student?"

"You think she got it from God?"

Max farted his answer.

"有人对她大吼大叫的。"谢尔碧走向厨房去再添一些红酒。

"对谁呀?"麦克斯心不在焉地问道。

"我们刚才一直在谈论谁呀?"谢尔碧怒吼的声音从厨房里传来。麦克斯有时候会让她抓狂。

"拉达吗?"

"她最近做实验是不是成果很差?"

"怎么可能,她就是一台分子机器。"麦克斯笑道,"我从来都没有见过有人完成了这么多任务的。"

"那我想,应该是社交生活太丰富了吧……"谢尔碧将酒瓶放回了冰箱里。

"真是见鬼!斯考蒂亚那天在组会上宣布不久就会有律师来给她的工作成果申请专利了,她能够得到三分之一的利润,这是前所未闻的事情。"

"那为什么她能得到这些呢?"手握酒杯,谢尔碧又回到了客厅。

"因为她的发现很重要。"

谢尔碧禁不住皱了眉头,感到十分困惑。"她看起来没有那么聪明啊,你嫉妒她吗?"

"相信我,这只会对我的职业生涯有帮助的。斯考蒂亚会因此而拿到一项诺贝尔奖,而我则会成为与诺贝尔奖获奖者一起工作的人。"

"哇哦。"谢尔碧坐在沙发上转动着脖子,发出"咔咔"的声音。她向麦克斯看去,"那她今天下午还在痛哭,你难道不感到奇怪吗?"

"一点也不。"他露出了疲倦的笑容,"她这个人很怪异。有一次当她在苹果电脑上绘制一个化学结构的时候,她觉得鼠标是在自己移动。"

"我没听懂。"

"就是说她觉得自己正在接收来自上帝或者其他神力的指示。"麦克斯翻了个白眼,"我不得不承认,她这个人真是太奇怪了,有时候我都感到纳闷。"

"纳闷什么?"

"纳闷为什么她才只是个研二的学生而已,就能这么幸运地有如此大的发现?"

"你认为她是有上帝的帮助吗?"

麦克斯放了个屁,作为回答。

Chapter Two Venting

"That's revolting," Shelby said, trying not to laugh. Sometimes she felt like a hypocrite. Though she laughed and found Max genuinely funny, she also felt put off by his brusque, blue collar way of behaving. He had no pretensions to class. Sometimes she found herself embarrassed to introduce him to her friends, and knew that she, ultimately, was the one lacking in grace, or at least charity. But she couldn't help it. She aspired to a better life, and that meant loftier humor.

"You should be over here," Max suggested. "Hey, listen to what I found in the Merck Manual." Sensing an opportunity, he quickly opened the book, and read, " Among those who are flatulent, the quantity and frequency of gas passage can reach astounding proportions—"

"You looked up farting?" Shelby asked slowly, rubbing her forehead with her hands.

"Let me read this to you. You won't believe it—"

"Max," Shelby interrupted him, "hard as this may be to believe, I don't want to hear about farting right now." She knew she was being mean again. But when life felt so serious, she just couldn't be amused by bodily functions, even if they came under the auspices of so revered a reference as the Merck Manual. Another time, she'd probably be interested, but now, she hadn't the patience.

Max looked slightly hurt. He leaned forward and put the Merck Manual on the coffee table. "What's for dinner?" he asked. "What about Chinese food?"

"Oh yeah," Shelby said huskily. She loved fried dumplings better than sex. Food was her one consolation. "Since it's your night to cook, I think you should at least call them." Shelby lay back on the sofa.

"What's their number?"

"Look it up." He was so helpless sometimes.

Max went to find the phone book in the kitchen. Shelby continued talking to him from the living room, trying somewhat to make amends.

"You know, I never cease to wonder about people coming here from other countries. It's so crazy; here she is, obviously smart, getting a Ph.D., soon to be a wealthy woman but still succumbing to something as archaic as a pre-arranged marriage. It just doesn't make sense to me."

Off the coffee table, Shelby picked up a book she was reading about Chinese footbinding. It had some of the most revolting pictures. She read it like Max watched

"你真是太恶心了。"谢尔碧尽量忍住笑说道。有时候她觉得自己很虚伪：尽管她会被逗笑，并且由衷地觉得麦克斯是一个有趣的人，她还是会对麦克斯这种工人阶级式的唐突粗鲁的行为方式感到迟疑和反感；麦克斯从来不主张划分社会阶层。谢尔碧在把麦克斯介绍给自己的朋友时，甚至偶尔会感到难为情，但其实她知道，真正缺少风度，或者说没有宽容品性的，是她自己。即使如此，她还是情不自禁，因为她渴望更好的生活，而这意味着你的幽默方式也得更高雅一些。

"快到我这儿来，"麦克斯建议道，"听听我在《默克诊疗手册》里的发现。"他迅速地翻开书，并读出声来："患有肠胃气胀的病人，他们每天的排气总量及频率可达到惊人的比例……"

"你竟然去查放屁了？"谢尔碧拖长了声调问道，并用手背揉了揉前额。

"让我读给你听吧，你会感到不可置信的——"

"麦克斯，"谢尔碧打断了他，"也许真的就像你说的那样不可置信，但我现在没心情听关于放屁的事情。"她知道，自己又开始刻薄了。但是当生活给她的感觉是如此严肃的时候，她怎么也没办法被这关于身体机能的事情逗笑，即使有《默克诊疗手册》这样的权威引证也不行。如果换个时机，她很有可能会感兴趣，但此时此刻，她没有这样的耐心。

麦克斯看上去有些受伤。他倾身把书放在了咖啡桌上。"晚饭吃什么？"他问道，"中国菜怎么样？"

"噢，那再好不过了，"谢尔碧不假思索地说道。她对煎饺的热爱比性爱还更胜一筹。食物是他唯一的慰藉。"既然今晚轮到你负责晚饭，我觉得至少应该由你来打电话叫外卖。"谢尔碧向沙发后面仰去。

"号码是多少来着？"

"自己去查一下。"他有时候真的很没用。

麦克斯去厨房里找电话簿了，谢尔碧待在客厅里继续跟他说着话，试图做出一些补偿。

"你知道吗，我一直都对从不同国家来到纽约的人充满好奇。真是太疯狂了，就像拉达，很明显是一个聪明女人，拥有博士头衔，不久就会成为富婆，但却还是要向封建婚姻这样古板的事情低头。对我来说这简直就不可理喻。"

谢尔碧说着从茶几下面取出一本自己正在读的书，是关于中国女人裹脚现象的，里面的插图让谢尔碧尤为反感。她阅读这本书的心态和麦克斯看那些令

those horrific true-to-life TV mystery shows where at least once per show they show a woman bound and gagged. She couldn't watch those, but the footbinding book was grossly compelling. Shelby just couldn't understand how a culture could purposely cripple half its population, and for a thousand years. The book referred to the men at that time as Lovers of the Lotus. For many of them it was an aesthetic. For many of them it was the smell of rotting feet. They wrote poems praising the Golden Lotus, the perfect three-inch foot. Some men, driven by passion, would even drink the foot-binding water. It was a country gone mad. And to Shelby, it didn't seem that far from an arranged marriage.

For a moment she envied Rahda, marriage and all. A scary thought, but Rahda could do what she wanted, she just didn't know it. What a waste. To have the intellect, and the fortune, but be so bound by culture that it does you no good.

Max was saying something in the kitchen, but she couldn't hear him. "Are you going to call for Chinese food?" Shelby's stomach was growling.

Max leaned around the corner. "I can't find the phone book."

"Why is it that I know where everything is in this apartment?"

"Because you're perfect. Are you going to tell me where the phone book is, or are we going to starve?"

Shelby made an exhausted face. "It's not under the sink?"

"No."

Shelby exhaled, puzzled. "Oh! I put it in the bathroom."

There was silence.

Max cleared his throat. "What's it doing in the bathroom?"

"There's a big hole there that the workman made today, but I guess you haven't seen it. They were looking for a leak. In New York, they look for leaks with pickaxes. I don't know. I wasn't here. All I know is that when I came home at lunch the water in the bathroom was turned off, no one was around, and there were things climbing out—"

"Things?" Max looked confused as he started for the bathroom.

"I sprayed a big can of something poisonous down there and then covered it with the phone book. I was gonna use your thesis, but I thought you might want that."

Max came back without the phone book. "Maybe I'll just call information."

人毛骨悚然的真人悬疑剧的心态一样，只是她无法忍受电视里至少每隔一集就会出现的女性被捆绑起来并堵住嘴巴的场景，而这本关于裹足的书却对她有着巨大的吸引力。她怎么也想不明白，为什么会有文化将其几乎一半的人口故意致残，并持续了千年之久。书中提到，那时的男人们被称为是"爱莲之人"。他们中的一些认为这是一种审美行为，还有一些人则是迷恋那腐坏的双脚散发出来的气味。他们曾写诗赞美"金莲"——完美的三寸之足。甚至有些人会在强烈欲望的驱使下，饮用裹足时使用的水。这是一个已经疯狂了的国家。而在谢尔碧看来，这与包办婚姻的性质也相差无几了。

有那么一个瞬间，谢尔碧嫉妒过拉达，包含婚姻在内的一切。这个想法似乎有些可怕，但其实拉达完全可以做自己想做的事情，只是她没有意识到这一点。多么浪费啊。拥有了如此的智力和财富，却被文化束缚得太紧，而没有好的结局。

厨房里的麦克斯好像在说什么，可她听不清。"你准备好要打电话叫中餐外卖了没？"她的肚子已经在低低地吼叫着了。

这时麦克斯向后倚在了拐角处，"我找不到电话簿。"

"为什么我就知道公寓里每一件东西摆放的地方？"

"因为你太完美了。你是准备告诉我电话簿在哪呢还是准备一起挨饿？"

谢尔碧露出了一脸的疲惫。"不在洗碗池的下面吗？"

"不在。"

她吐了口气，有些迷惑。"噢！我把它放在洗手间了。"

房子里有一阵子静默。

麦克斯清了清喉咙，"它待在洗手间干吗呢？"

"今天有工人进来把洗手间弄出了一个大洞，但我想你应该还没看到吧。他们是为了找管道上一个漏水的地方。在纽约这样的地方，他们都是用锄头来找漏洞的。我并没有在场，不知道发生了什么，只知道我中午回来吃饭时发现洗手间里的水被切断了，屋子里没有其他人，有东西从大洞里往外爬——"

"东西？"麦克斯正向洗手间走去，脸上充满了困惑。

"我对着那里喷了整整一大罐有毒喷雾，然后用电话簿把洞口给盖了起来。本来是想用你的论文的，但我觉得你也许还需要它。"

麦克斯回来了，手里没拿电话簿。"我还是打电话到信息台询问吧。"

Chapter Three Catalyst

> Catalyst: that which causes activity between two or more persons without itself being affected.
>
> The Random House College Dictionary

That afternoon, when she'd first seen the bathroom, she'd scowled and actually closed her eyes, thinking, somehow, that she was in the wrong apartment. She took a sharp inhale. Then she started screaming. "Those goddamn motherfuckers." She was so pissed, so angry that maintenance crews could tear your apartment apart, make a disaster area of your home, and yet end up with such little result. Manhattan was bursting. Mains were breaking everywhere. The plumbing was going. The buildings were crumbling. Basically the whole place should be razed, but instead, they repaired it a leak at a time.

She had jumped hard on the bedroom floor, trying to get some release, scattering plaster dust with her feet. A light coating of drywall covered the wood floor, muffling the usual clump of her high heels. Shelby had felt like she wanted to hit someone, anyone, but instead hurled her gym bag to the wall of the bedroom. She'd tried breathing slowly, hating the feeling of being enraged, so controlled by others as to provoke out-of-controlledness in herself. This place was like the movie *Brazil*. Next thing you'd know, the workmen would be living with you. Hell, their clothes were already here, she almost snorted, noticing that by the bathroom door there was a wad of white canvas with a cigarette pack sticking out the front pocket. They'd smoked in here too. Shelby sniffed the air, not sure if she could detect smoke, but wincing her nose all the same. She realized there was no point in trying to clean up now. It might be years before she and Max would live alone again.

A movement in the bathroom caught her eye. She could see activity by the open cleft, the slightly damp floor resembling an urban swamp, the proverbial watering hole, drawing the wildlife. Shelby went and got the Raid, spraying a whole can

第三章　催化剂

催化剂：能够引起两种或者多种物质之间反应，本身性质没有变化的物质。

——《兰登书屋大学辞典》

那天下午，当谢尔碧第一眼看到洗手间里的情景时，不由得蹙起了眉头，她甚至闭上双眼，开始怀疑自己是不是进错了公寓。深深地吸了一口气之后，她开始放声尖叫："这帮该死的狗娘养的！"最让谢尔碧怒火中烧的是，这些维修工可以拆掉你的公寓，把你的家搞得像个灾难现场，最终却不用负一点儿责任。当时曼哈顿已经是"遍地开花"了，主要的输水管道都发生了爆裂，四处的修复工作都在进行当中；许多楼房也都开始摇摇欲坠。总体来说这整片区域都应该拆毁重建，但相反的，他们却一次只修一个水管洞。

谢尔碧重重地在卧室地板上跳了几下，想借此来发泄一些愤懑，双脚落地时却震起了阵阵石灰粉。木地板上附着了一层薄薄的墙面涂料，使得谢尔碧高跟鞋的"咔嗒"声也比平时低沉好多。谢尔碧那一刻很想揍人，揍谁都行，但她却只能用力地把运动包向墙面砸去。她讨厌这种被激怒，情绪被他人所掌控，最后逐渐失控的感觉，于是她开始试着放缓呼吸节奏。现在整个屋子就像是电影《巴西》里面的场景；说不定第二天，那些工人们就搬进来住了。天哪，他们的衣服已经留在这里了——她一眼瞥到洗手间门口裹成团的帆布工作服，上衣的口袋里还露出了一盒烟，谢尔碧几乎是愤慨地"哼"了一声。他们还在这儿抽烟了。她在空气中嗅了嗅，并不确定真的闻到了烟味，但还是蹙起了鼻子。她意识到，现在打扫的话等于白搭，因为要想和麦克斯再次单独相处可能是很久以后的事了。

这时谢尔碧注意到，洗手间里似乎有什么在移动。她能够看见那个洞口有东西在动——微微潮湿的地面模拟了城市里的湿沼环境，而这个"泉眼"则招徕了四处的"野生动物"。谢尔碧去取了雷达杀虫剂，看都没有看一眼就将整整一

down the hole without one glance toward the opening, not wanting to know that nothing was dying, not wanting to see it if they were. Elevating her eyes, she tried the sink taps, which didn't work, closed the door, and then immediately went to find the super even though she knew it would make her late for her next telegram.

She rode in the building's elevator, an ancient machine with a metal pantograph cage that you had to pull across before the outer doors would close. Shelby loved old elevators, but she was so deficit in her happiness, one small credit didn't do much good. When she got to the top floor she found the little stairwell to the roof that the doorman had told her to take. The stairs were wooden and unpainted, curving around quickly as they ascended, hastening her pace. There was a door at the top. The gray daylight suddenly illuminating the staircase as she swung it open. A fierce wind took hold of the door, throwing it into a wire clothesline and then rebounding, making Shelby shield her face with her arms. She stepped over the raised wooden threshold, grasping the doorknob to steady herself. She'd never been on the top of a building in New York before. It was only nine stories, but Shelby had a desire to see the view, to be tall, to feel removed from the chaos below. Widening the door, she realized that the clothesline was in the door's trajectory, so she slipped out the half-opened door, and found herself in a maze of wet sheets, all luffing in the wind. A light rain grazed her face, stinging slightly. She felt as if she were on a ship sailing through the city, blasts of wind panting and gasping around her. An island moving upstream.

Turning to check that the door wouldn't lock on her, Shelby was startled by the slap of a wet sheet that suddenly clung to the door affectionately, magnetized by wind and water. It embraced the gray door with folds and curves of yellowing fabric, swaddling material, Christo in miniature. The gusts of wind made it hard to close the door, and Shelby imagined the sheet holding tight, not wanting to let go of its lover.

Why would they dry sheets outside on a day like today? she wondered. Nothing in New York made sense to her.

She made her way between the aisles of undulating sheets, trying to avoid contact, so cold and clammy was one that touched her hand. She came to a railing, some distance from the edge, not close enough for a great view, but she could see the dark green of Central Park between tall buildings and church spires. She watched the flow of humanity moving down Broadway, units and clumps, bitlike about its business, census digits interweaving.

瓶都喷进了洞里,不管它们是生是死,她都不想看见。她就这样向上翻着白眼,又试了试水池上方的龙头——毫无反应;于是她关上洗手间的门立即动身去找管理员,即使她知道,这样一来肯定无法按时赶上下一场唱歌电报了。

她进了这栋大楼的电梯——有着金属导电笼的古老机器,里面的人必须先得把笼子的门给拉上,外面的电梯门才能关闭。谢尔碧对这种老式电梯情有独钟,但是这一点小小的开心事根本无法弥补她巨大的幸福赤字。当她到达顶楼的时候,看见了门卫说的那架通往天台的楼梯井——木制的旋转楼梯,并没有涂漆,越向上幅度越大,谢尔碧的脚步也随之加快了。楼梯顶端有一扇门,被谢尔碧推开的时候它摇晃了几下,灰蒙蒙的日光突然之间就洒到了台阶上。一股强风攫住了那扇门,猛地摔向后方的晾衣绳,然后又反弹了回来,谢尔碧下意识地用手臂挡住了脸。她跨过突起的木头门槛,紧紧抓住门把手来保持平稳。在此之前,她从来都没有登上过纽约任何一座建筑的楼顶。虽然这里只有九层高,但此刻谢尔碧只想要恣意享受这里的风景,想要永远身处高处,想要与下面的纷纷扰扰隔离开。她准备把门向外再推开些,但随即意识到晾衣绳挡住了门向后运动的趋势,索性便从半开的门里一跃而出。此时她发现自己置身于一个由湿答答的床单构成的迷宫之中,每一条床单都在风中飒飒飞舞着。一滴雨点擦过她的脸颊,微微有些痛。谢尔碧觉得自己仿佛身处一艘正在穿越这个城市的船上,一阵又一阵的狂风在她耳边喘息贲张。又好像一个岛屿在逆流而上。

谢尔碧转过身去,想确定一下门不会自动锁上,却被突然甩过来的湿床单给吓了一跳,它像献媚似的紧紧地贴在了门上,仿佛风和水给它注入了磁力一般。那是一种用于做婴儿襁褓的布料,而现在它那泛黄的身体紧紧地裹挟住了铅灰色的大门,缱绻出了无数的折痕,就像是迷你版的克里斯托的作品[译者注:克里斯托因用床单罩住整个建筑物或其他景观的行为艺术而闻名]。一阵阵的强风加大了关门的难度,谢尔碧觉得那条床单是在牢牢抓住自己的情人,舍不得放手。

为什么会有人在今天这样的天气晒床单呢?她想不通。纽约发生的一切都让她想不通。

波浪起伏的床单形成了一道走廊,谢尔碧艰难地在其中穿行着,努力避开那冰冷湿黏的接触。她终于走到了栏杆处,但离楼的边缘还有一些距离。虽然在这里还看不到最好的风景,但是高楼大厦与教堂尖顶之间的中央公园,已经将那一片深深的绿色呈现在她的眼前。她就那样看着人潮向百老汇的方向涌动,三五成群,打着各自的小算盘,在人口普查中互不相干的人生在这里交织。

The air was brisk and the wind blustered as though it wanted to push her off the building. She held tightly to the rail and closed her eyes, feeling a sudden passion, as if she'd just been crowned queen or been given an Academy award. Emotion churned up in her. A tingle ran along her extremities and culminated at her lips, causing her to shout in laughter. She swore loudly, trying to make up new combinations of curses, hoping someone would look up. But no one did, the wind taking her profanities and delivering them to the birds. It was in her nature to confront authority, the status quo, even in silly ways like swearing at the top of her voice. She didn't care that if Max were up here, that's the first thing he'd do. The obvious, anti-establishment reaction. It felt good.

She laughed and opened her eyes, a flash of white drawing her attention. She was reminded of the painter's overalls downstairs and realized that she had to go. But the white flapped at her, taunting her. At first she thought it was a flag of some sort, partly hidden by a chimney. Rounding the corner, she saw that it was a sheet which had flown away from its place on the clothesline. Caught on something near the corner edge of the building, it flailed over the crevasse, trying to escape its mooring. Leaning on the cold pipe railing, Shelby was tempted to go beyond the confines of safety to free it, just to see it sail in the air. She started to crawl between the horizontal pipes, but then told herself not to be an idiot. Instead, she looked for a rock to throw at the sheet in hopes of dislodging it. Beneath her feet was only gravel and tar paper, but near one of the clotheslines she found a wire hanger. Untwisting it, she lengthened the hanger, hurting her fingers slightly. The unbent hanger reminded her of roasting marshmallows as a child. "Golden brown," an old friend of her parents had jokingly admonished her, her fascination more for setting them on fire than eating them.

Shelby took the hanger and approached the sheet, avoiding the shallow pools of water that had formed on the roof. Damn, she thought, leaning over the railing and waving the hanger at the sheet as if that would bring them closer together. Trying not to think about what she was doing, Shelby squeezed through the crosspieces of the pipe-metal railing and held tightly to the lower rung with her right hand as she leaned toward the sheet, poking with her left. Still a foot away from the corner she hoped to loosen, she pursed her lips. Very carefully, Shelby let go of the railing and crouched down on all fours, moving slowly toward the linen, realizing that she'd lost her mind.

天台上空气凛冽,身边不停咆哮的风像是要把谢尔碧给推下楼去。她握紧扶手,闭上了双眼,胸中突然涌起一种澎湃的情感,仿佛自己刚被加冕为女王或者是荣获了一项奥斯卡金像奖似的。强烈的感情在她体内激荡,有种微小的刺痛感奔突遍她的四肢,最终在双唇处聚集并不可抑制地在她响亮的笑声中爆发。她大声地咒骂着,试图想出新的骂人话来,并希望会有人向上看过来。但是没有人这样做,风带走了她所有的亵渎话语并传给了鸟儿听。直面强权和现状是她天性的一部分,即使是用声嘶力竭地咒骂这样的愚蠢方法来执行。就算麦克斯现在在楼顶,谢尔碧也不会在乎,况且这也是他在第一时间会做的事情——最容易的,反对体制的方式。这种感觉真好。

谢尔碧大笑着睁开了眼睛,眼前闪过的白色吸引了她的注意力。这使她想起了楼下油漆工们留下的工装裤,她意识到自己得赶快走了。但是那抹白色一直在她眼前上下翻飞,好像在逗弄她一样。一开始谢尔碧以为可能是面旗子,被烟囱给遮住了一部分。她绕出那个角落,发现那其实是一条从晾衣绳上飞走的床单,被大楼边角的什么东西给勾住了,此时正奋力地拍打着墙上的裂缝,试图逃脱束缚。谢尔碧倚在冰冷的空心栏杆上,突然很想越过这道安全护栏去解放那条床单,只是为了能够看它在空中自由飞翔的样子。她立刻就开始从两根横栏之间向外翻去,但下一秒又告诫自己不要做这种傻事。于是作为折中,她开始寻找石头向床单砸去,希望这样可以起作用。她脚下只有碎石子和沥青纸,但是在一条晾衣绳的旁边谢尔碧找到了一个金属衣架。她用力将它扳直,弄得手指头都有些痛。扳直后的铁丝使谢尔碧想起了自己小时候烤棉花糖的情景。"要烤成金灿灿的棕色才好",父母的一位老朋友当时还开玩笑般的劝告她,但是谢尔碧更感兴趣的是把棉花糖放在火上烤的过程而不是吃掉它们。

谢尔碧持着衣架向床单靠近,极力避开屋顶上沉积的潜水坑。该死的,她咒骂道,却仍然继续倚靠在栏杆上挥舞着衣架,就好像这真能让自己离得更近一点似的。她努力不去想自己现在到底在做什么,俯身穿过栏杆,右手紧紧抓住低一些的那根扶手,身体向外倾斜,左手拿着衣架不停地捅着床单。可是离她想要够到的角落还是有一尺之遥,她不满地地撅起了嘴巴。接着她小心翼翼地松开抓着栏杆的手,四肢着地伏在屋顶上,缓慢地向那块亚麻布移动。她意识到,自己

She jabbed the hanger at the closest corner of the sheet, trying to see what was holding it. Sliding the end of the hanger under the material, Shelby started to lift the sheet above a possessive nail. It moved slightly, then got caught in a different place. Just as Shelby tried dislodging it again, this time getting more of the hanger underneath, the wind abruptly gusted down along the corner of the building, scaring the hell out of Shelby, and in an instant the sheet was free, sailing over the tops of buildings like a magic carpet, almost getting caught on a taller building two buildings down, but a change of wind shifted its direction and it billowed onward, a phantom of the city.

"Be free, be free," Shelby yelled, feeling light-hearted and silly. The sight of the white linen borne by the wind made her extraordinarily happy. It lifted and surged, pirouetting in the air: choreography for bed sheet and city. The fabric gave presence to the breeze, molding itself to the unseeable force. Shelby watched the sheet until it disappeared in the distance, a milk-white butterfly flitting between concrete flowers, perennials in the garden of New York. Now only an indelible fleck of remembered whiteness, the sheet pulsed in Shelby's brain, a glowing after-image. Shelby realize she was holding her breath. She let it out slowly, almost hiccuping, reliving the moment. She'd made art. It was like an orgasm of a very subtle concatenation. Paroxysms of the mind.

She felt the way she often felt after a particularly good rendition of a song, when her soul took over and sang the song for her. Eberhard would grin at her, Max would nod, his approval always understated but present, and Hadley would stare at her for a moment and then look at his drums. He was so weird. Maybe later he would say gruffly, "That was okay." It was about the highest praise you could get from him. He made her feel nervous because he intimidated her with his ability. And for that reason, she found herself wanting his approval. He could write songs that impressed her with their emotion, and yet he seemed so controlled, always proper, always somewhat distant. She didn't know why, but she wanted to get under his skin, pierce his superiority. But of course, she majored in theater. She wanted to affect everyone.

The wind started blowing more viciously, and Shelby quickly crawled back to the railing, truly fearful of the height now that her quest was over. Grabbing the railing firmly and ducking through, she looked back to where she had been,

已经疯了。她用衣架挑起离自己最近的床单一角,想看看它到底是被什么给勾住的。顺着布料继续滑下去,床单便一点一点地被揭起来,一颗顽固的钉子露了出来。可是刚移动了一点点,钉子就又刮住了床单的另一个角。谢尔碧准备再试一次,这次把衣架伸得更远一些。这时,一阵狂风突然从楼顶的一角席卷而来,把谢尔碧吓得七魂掉了三魂半。也就是在那瞬间,床单获得了自由,像魔毯一般漂浮过林立的建筑群顶端,差点又被两楼之外的另一幢更高的大厦给勾住,但突然改变的风向使它向上翻腾了一下,如同城市的幽灵。

"自由吧,自由吧,"谢尔碧喊道。虽然觉得自己有些蠢,但是心情却无比轻松。看到那白色的亚麻布在风中鼓动翻飞,她感到格外得幸福。它时而突然上升,时而如波浪起伏,又像芭蕾舞者一样踮起脚尖在空中旋转:为床单和城市而舞。它使风的形状得以显现,无形的力量得以彰显。谢尔碧一直看着它消失在远方,像一只乳白色的蝴蝶,轻快地掠过钢筋水泥的花朵——纽约花园里四季不败的植株。那条床单的影像仍然在谢尔碧脑海中跳动,成为记忆中一道不可磨灭的白色荧光。谢尔碧这才意识到自己一直在屏住呼吸,于是她缓慢地向外吐气,脑海回放着刚才的画面,差点打了个嗝。她的这种行为是艺术,就像一系列微小的连锁反应所引起的性高潮。一次大脑的爆发。

在每次演唱到情深处的时候,谢尔碧的灵魂就会取代自己放开歌喉,而现在谢尔碧的心情就像是结束了这样的一场表演。然后艾伯哈德会咧开嘴向她笑,麦克斯则点点头——他的赞扬总是很低调,但从不缺席。而哈德利却总是盯着她看好一会儿,然后低下头去看自己的鼓。他总是这么奇怪,或许过些时候他会粗声粗气地说:"还不错。"这几乎是你能从他那得到的最高褒奖了。他在音乐方面的天赋让谢尔碧有一种威胁感,也会激发出她的紧张情绪。也正因为如此,谢尔碧发现自己特别希望得到他的认同。哈德利写的歌充满了丰沛的感情,总让谢尔碧为之动容,但是他本人看上去却始终那么自我克制,行为规矩,给人一种距离感。不知道为什么,谢尔碧想要潜入到他的皮肤底下,刺穿他那不可一世的高傲。不过这并不奇怪,她学的是戏剧,理所当然地想要影响所有人。

风势越来越大了,谢尔碧赶紧往回爬,现在任务已经完成了,对高度的恐惧开始从心底涌上来。终于牢牢抓住了扶手并俯身穿回天台,她向自己刚才待的

a hanger's length from the edge, and chastised herself. But then she grinned. "Fuck you all," she yelled at the city, laughing. This was the best she'd felt in weeks.

Suddenly Shelby remembered that she had a telegram in less than an hour, and she still hadn't found the super. She brushed the gravel from her coat where she'd knelt on it and then walked around the whipping laundry to the other side of the roof, tripping once on a loose bit of tar paper and catching her balance by grabbing the railing. This made her start laughing all over again. What a simp she was. Clumsy and giggling. She realized that nothing had changed except her mood.

The roof was flat except for three structures: the door Shelby had come from, which stood like a sentry, angling sharply down to the gravel-spattered tar paper, the chimney, and on the opposite end of the building, a square cottage with a pitched roof that sat primly, almost as if the Wicked Witch had dropped it there. Shelby went to the house and knocked on the weathered front door. Flecks of green paint stuck to her knuckles. A bent old woman with a kerchief about her head opened the door and looked at Shelby with a scowl. The aroma of tomato sauce and garlic percolated out of the house, mixing with the scent of rain. Shelby could feel an ache in her stomach and remembered that she hadn't eaten lunch yet.

"I need to see the super," Shelby said politely.

"Not here." The woman made as if to close the door. In the gray light, the woman's face reminded Shelby of a road map, an excess of meandering lines forming a network of wrinkles, all headed toward old age.

"It's important. Do you know where he is?" Shelby asked quickly.

"Downstairs." With every word, the opening between door and jamb grew narrower.

"I just came from downstairs." Shelby was close to pleading.

The woman scowled even more, her bottom lip protruding grotesquely. "Try laundry," she said, shutting the door firmly.

Shelby sighed and shook her head. Every time she dealt with New Yorkers it made her pissed. No one was ever forthcoming with information. How hard was it to be civil? Shelby retraced her steps, realizing that her moment of privacy had been rejuvenating. But how to hold onto it? In this city, one's lack of solitude was wearing. The fact that, as Max put it, the only place to be alone was in the bathroom.

地方看去——离大楼边缘只有一个衣架的距离。她骂了自己一句。但突然咧嘴笑了。"去你们的吧!"她对着城市大喊,大声地笑着。这是几周以来她觉得最开心的时刻了。

猛然间,谢尔碧想起来离下一个电报表演只剩不到一个小时了,但是到现在自己还没有找到楼层管理员呢。她掸了掸刚才跪在地上时外套上粘的沙砾,然后穿过风中"飒飒"作响的湿床单向天台的另一边走去,一不小心被翘起的沥青纸绊了个趔趄,慌乱中抓住栏杆才找回了平衡。她又忍不住开始放声大笑起来——她觉得自己像个傻瓜,笨手笨脚,总是咯咯傻笑。她意识到,除了自己的心情以外,什么都没有改变。

整个屋顶的结构都是平的,除了三处地方以外:谢尔碧来时穿过的大门,它就像个岗哨似的杵在满是沙砾的沥青地面上;烟囱;还有对面的方形小屋,它顶着倾斜的屋顶拘谨地坐在那里,就像是被邪恶的女巫放置在那里的。谢尔碧走上前去,敲了敲被风雨侵蚀的前门,绿色的油漆块登时粘在了她的指节上。开门的是一个驼背老妇人,头上裹一块方巾,她皱着眉头看着谢尔碧。番茄酱与大蒜的味道从屋里飘散出来,与雨的气味混合到一起。谢尔碧感到肚子有些痛,这才想起自己还没有吃午饭。

"我在找管理员,"谢尔碧礼貌地说道。

"不在这。"那老妇顺势就要把门关上了。在灰蒙的灯光下,谢尔碧觉得她的脸看起来像一张地图,蜿蜒的线条构成了一张皱纹的网络,每一条都通向衰老。

"我有很重要的事,你知道他在哪吗?"谢尔碧快速地问着。

"楼下。"她每说一个字,门和墙壁之间的缝隙就变得更窄一些。

"我刚从楼下上来。"谢尔碧几乎是恳求的语气了。

那妇人眉头皱得更深了,她的下嘴唇以一种搞笑的方式向外突出着。"去洗衣房看看。"门彻底地关上了。

谢尔碧摇着头叹了口气,每次她和纽约客打交道总是搞得一肚子气。他们从没有人能够提供一点有用的信息,做个有教养的人能有多难?谢尔碧循着来时的路线返回,感到自己的私人空间正一点点地恢复,但是要怎么把它给持续下去呢?在这座城市里,你永远无法独处,这点令人感到疲倦。就像麦克斯说的,唯一可以让你一个人待着的地方就是洗手间。

Taking the elevator to the basement, she turned right and immediately found the skinny, bow-legged super folding towels. She went for a straight-forward attack.

"What the fucking hell have you done to our bathroom!"

He looked up in surprise, taken off-guard, and cautiously lifted a towel, a reluctant toreador fending off a menacing bull.

"It was an emergency," the super said, shuffling his feet and not even pretending that he didn't know what she was talking about. "There was a leak."

"There's been a leak there for almost a year! That's why large pieces of plaster continually fall off the wall whenever someone above us takes a shower." Shelby took a step toward him and he backed up, running into his laundry basket and toppling a stack of towels.

"Different leak," the super mumbled under his breath and began to fold towels again and lay them in the basket.

"Six months ago they took a pickax to our tile and made an ugly little rat hole near the floor. They would have made a bigger hole, but my husband pointed out that if you could see water leaking on our ceiling, didn't it stand to reason that the leak must be higher?"

"Not the same leak," the super mumbled again.

"So the workmen went to the other side of our wall and completely demolished it. You know how long that took?" Shelby's voice was getting louder and louder, irritated by his defenseless nature.

"They work as fast as they can," he said seriously but with an air of exhaustion. He looked down at his folded towels as if to find an answer there.

"Three months! It took them three goddamn months to fix a leak that they would have been fixing in our apartment if we hadn't said something. How long is it going to take them to fix the leak this time?"

He breathed heavily at her.

"There is plaster dust all over our bedroom. Dirty clothes lying around our floor!"

"Ma'am, I'm sorry you're so upset—"

"Upset!" Shelby was on the verge of hysteria. Her voice broke, squeaking an octave higher than normal. "I'm more than upset! My goddamn bathroom is falling down to the basement." She looked up and was stunned that she wasn't exaggerating.

乘电梯到了地下室，谢尔碧右转之后一眼就看到了那个瘦不拉几、长着罗圈腿的管理员，他正在叠毛巾。谢尔碧直接就展开了攻势。

"你他妈的对我们的浴室做了什么！"

他吃惊地抬起头来，随后又放松了警惕，小心翼翼地提起了另一条毛巾，就像一个满心不情愿的斗牛士正试图避开气势汹汹的牛。

"是紧急情况，"他开口道，交叉的双脚换了个方向，他甚至都不打算伪装不知情，"有个地方漏水。"

"漏水都漏了一年了！每次楼上有人洗澡，我们的墙上就会有大片的石灰掉下来。"谢尔碧向他逼近了一步，他跟着向后退了一步，碰到了衣物篮，里面一沓叠好的毛巾随之坍塌了。

"是另一个地方漏水，"管理员小声嘟囔道，然后又开始折叠毛巾并重新放回篮子里。

"六个月之前他们带着锄头进来，在地板旁边的瓷砖上留下了一个丑得要命的老鼠洞。本来他们还要把洞凿得更大，但是我老公跟他们说，如果是天花板在漏水的话，水管洞不是应该在更高的地方吗？"

"这次是另一个洞。"管理员又嘟囔了一句。

"然后他们就走到另一面墙前，把那面墙完全给拆了。你知道那花了多久吗？"谢尔碧的音量越来越高了，管理员丝毫不准备为自己辩护的态度激怒了她。

"他们已经能多快就多快了。"他严肃地说道，但是透出一股疲倦的神气。然后低头向叠好的毛巾看去，好像能在那找到答案似的。

"三个月！修个水管洞他们花了整整三个月！如果我们没有说什么的话，他们本来就要在我们的房子里动工了。这次他们又要修多久？"

他对谢尔碧喘着粗气。

"我们的卧室里现在满地都是石灰粉，地板上到处是乱扔的脏工作服！"

"女士，很抱歉让你这么不高兴——"

"不高兴！"谢尔碧几乎到了歇斯底里的边缘，因为激动而破了音，音调跟着高了八度，听起来像是短促而尖利的叫声。"我不只是不高兴！我那该死的浴室都快塌到地下室来了。"她抬头看去，惊讶地发现自己并没有夸张。"看那儿！"

"There!" she yelled, pointing to the huge water stains in the far right of the basement. "I want it fixed *now*! And I want a rent credit for as long as I have to use the lobby bathroom!"

"Can't give rent credits. Have to go to the housing office," he said firmly, waving his hands at her. He kept shaking his head and muttering under his breath.

"This place just sucks!" Shelby yelled, starting to cry. The housing office would waste an entire day.

"They'll be back tomorrow," the super mumbled, obviously embarrassed by her tears.

"What? They can't work afternoons?" Shelby asked sarcastically, trying to dab her eyes furtively with her coat sleeve.

"Wrong width of pipe." He started moving the laundry basket toward the elevator.

"No wonder there's so many murders in this fucking city," Shelby said loudly. "Nobody can take a goddamn bath!"

她吼道,向地下室最右边的一个巨大的水渍指去。"你现在就得修好它,还得减免我的月租,直到我不需要再用大堂里的洗手间为止!"

"我没法给你减免,你得去房产办公室。"他坚定地说道,同时对谢尔碧摆了摆手。然后一直摇着头,低声嘀咕着什么。

"这个地方简直糟透了!"谢尔碧叫道,然后开始放声大哭。去房产办公室会浪费掉整整一天的时间。

"那些工人明天会再回来的。"管理员含糊地说了一句,显然被谢尔碧的眼泪搞得有些窘迫。

"什么?他们不能今天下午就开始工作?"谢尔碧讽刺地问道,偷偷地用袖子擦了擦自己的眼睛。

"他们带来的水管口径不对。"他开始把衣物篮向电梯的方向移动。

"怪不得在这鬼城市里有这么多杀人犯,"谢尔碧大声说道,"因为大家连个该死的澡都洗不上!"

Chapter Four Bench

> Bench: ... the seat where judges sit in court ... the place where justice is administered ... a long worktable.
> Webster's New Collegiate Dictionary

The chemistry lab was dark at eleven in the morning, the air piercingly cold. Outside it was a blustery day. Leaves everywhere. Rain pelting the unsheltered. A bluish light crept tentatively in the window, illuminating a rack of glassware on Rahda's bench. The glassware answered back with minor glints of light, parallel tapers lighting up the fraction collector, a battalion of glass tubes that stood at the ready. The minute flickerings were quickly absorbed by the dark room, sucked into the shadow's subtle vortex.

Rahda was sitting at her desk near the window, her head bent over her paper. Where her straight hair met the desk, it folded smoothly, like an embanked roadway. A freeway to her brain. She felt her thoughts run out her hair, leaving an abandoned infrastructure. The form, but none of the content. She circled on that thought, repeating it, riding the same words as before. It was so easy to veg. Veg wasn't the word she thought, but it was the word she meant.

She was drawing a molecule. Many molecules. With diligence, Rahda connected one perfectly drawn benzene ring to another. Flawless hexagons covered her page, looking like so much chicken wire. Someone had explained to her that synthesizing chicken wire was an old chemist joke because molecules often have six-membered rings. She had nodded politely, wondering at American humor.

Rahda scratched her nose, leaving a smudge of black on the tip, then continued adding to the molecule until it extended past the edge of the paper and she was forced to draw on her desk, which she did without pause, defining the lines with a metal ruler, a gift from her father, and determining the angles with a plastic protractor. There were templates for drawing molecules, but she preferred to do it this way. The

第四章　工作台

（法官席位，工作台）：……法庭上法官坐的位置……正义得以贯彻伸张的地方……长长的工作台。

——《新韦伯斯特学院字典》

上午十一点的时候化学实验室里还是一片漆黑，空气冷得刺骨。室外风很大，树叶在各个角落打着卷儿，清泠的雨无情地打在无家可归的人身上。拉达工作台前的窗口犹犹疑疑地划过一道略略发蓝的光线，照亮了桌上的一排玻璃器皿。玻璃反射着些许微光，分馏收集器的双芯也被点燃了——那一整套玻璃管构成的装置已经准备好，随时待命。那微茫的闪光瞬间就被黑暗的房间给吸收了，被吸进阴影中稀薄的漩涡里。

拉达坐在靠窗的桌前，整个头几乎都要埋进稿纸里。她的直发落在桌上，形成了自然的蜷曲，就像沿着海岸线的高速路，通向她的大脑。她觉得自己的思想都从头发上流泻了出来，只剩下一个空空的脑壳儿。只剩形式，但没有内容。这个想法在她脑海里挥之不去，不断地重复着，每次都漂浮着同样的词语。要想虚度时间非常容易。"虚度"并不是她想用的词，但她想表达的就是这个意思。

拉达正在画分子结构，很多的分子结构，然后再努力将一个个精确绘制的苯环相互连接起来。她的笔记本上画满了毫无瑕疵的六边形，看上去就像是围成鸡圈的六边形铁丝网。有人曾经跟她说，过去的化学家会拿"合成鸡圈网"来开玩笑，因为许多分子都具有六个原子支撑的环状结构。她当时礼貌地点了点头，内心却对美国式的幽默感到奇怪。

拉达搔了搔鼻子，在鼻尖上留下了一点黑色的墨迹，然后又开始继续延长分子链。直到延伸到了笔记本的边缘，不得不继续在桌子上画下去的时候，她也毫不犹豫地这样做了。她用来测绘线条的金属尺子是父亲给她的礼物，还有一把用来量角度的塑料分度器。其实绘制分子有现成的模板，但是她更喜欢这种方

templates seemed like cheating.

As the molecules began to resemble honeycomb, Rahda thought about bees. There had been a beehive near her home in Jodhpur. She remembered that a little neighbor boy had been stung to death. Shortly after, the beehive had been destroyed. Moving back to her open notebook, she drew one tentative bee and then another and another, scribbling frantically until her molecule had become unrecognizable. Soon her page was covered with ink. She realized, belatedly, that she shouldn't be doing this. Someone might want to see it. But she couldn't seem to stop. The pen moved on its own accord and she watched, powerless. She could just say it leaked. Or maybe that she'd made a mistake and crossed everything out. But you were never supposed to destroy anything in a scientific notebook. That would be a problem. A scientific notebook was perfect bound, with all the pages consecutively numbered, and you were supposed to sign and date each page to verify authenticity. A dated notebook page was admissible evidence in a court of law. Of course, for the patent, they would only require copies of her notebook pages, but someone might notice one was missing. Perhaps not if they were bad xeroxes. Who would strain to read an illegible page number?

Rahda chewed her lip as she continued to draw and contemplate the problem. The page had become black and creepy. It reminded her of a dream she'd had as a child, a nightmare really, of a scanner that she'd seen years ago in her father's lab, a circular instrument with a beam of light that swept the diameter, leaving a trail of fluorescent green blips and dots. In her dream, there was one scanner, and another, and another, until her whole dream was filled with scanners, swinging away at the empty space in a neurotic frenzy. They were uncontrollable, devouring each other with every sweep, leaving ragged, half-eaten remnants, brutalized pieces of neon light. She could even smell the slaughter in her dream. The scent would be in her nostrils when she awoke.

It was the dreams that forced her into chemistry. A way to control the nightmares was to harness their power. Knowledge gave her strength. She became her father's assistant, learning what he knew despite his belief that it was wasted on her. But he liked a companion, someone who would listen without comment. He hadn't a son, so she filled the emptiness. He never expected her to be a chemist, thinking her interest a childish pastime, but she insisted, knowing it was one step

法,用模板的话看上去像是作弊。

那些分子群开始越来越像蜂巢了,拉达不由得想起了蜜蜂。在印度久德浦,她家的房子附近有一个蜂窝。她还记得邻居有一个小男孩曾经被蜜蜂给蜇死了。不久之后,那个蜂窝就被捣毁了。她回过神来,在摊开的笔记本上试着画了一只蜜蜂,然后又画了一只,再一只。她疯狂地画着,直到她的分子链变得完全不可辨认为止。不一会儿笔记本的页面上就满满的都是墨水了,她后知后觉地意识到,自己不应该这样做,因为也许有人会想要看那条分子链。但是她根本就停不下来,手里的钢笔按照自己的意愿不停移动着,拉达只能无力地看着。她可以说自己的钢笔漏水了,或者说自己画错了于是就把所有内容都给涂掉了。但是在一本实验记录本里,你永远都不应该毁掉任何东西,否则就会引起问题。因为一本完美的实验记录本需要在每一页都标上连续的页码,并且签上自己的姓名和日期,以确保其原创性。在法庭上,这样的一本记录本是可以用来作为证据使用的。当然了,如果要申请专利的话,他们只会要求上交记录本的复印件,但也许会有人发现少了一页。如果复印机质量不好的话可能就不会发现了,再者说,谁会费尽心力地去辨认那模糊的页码呢?

拉达边继续画下去,边思忖着这个问题,下意识地咬着自己的嘴唇。已经变得乌黑诡异的纸面使她想起了一个小时候做过的梦,说起来其实是个噩梦。她梦到了几年前在父亲实验室看过的光电子扫描仪,那是一个环形仪器,光电波发射器沿着直径方向发射光线,留下一串发绿色荧光的光点轨迹。在她的梦里,先是出现了一台扫描仪,然后又出现了一台,一台一台直到最后整个梦里都是,每一台都像失去控制般疯狂地在空洞的空间里荡来荡去。它们用每一次的撞击和扫射互相摧毁,最后只剩下锯齿状的半半拉拉的残骸,霓虹灯管被残忍地撞成了碎片。在梦里她甚至都可以闻得到厮杀的血腥味,在她醒了之后那气味还残留在她的鼻孔里。

正是那个梦促使她进了化学这一行,要想控制住她的梦魇就只能通过学会驾驭化学的力量。知识使她充满了力量。她先是成了父亲的助手,学习他所知道的各种化学知识。虽然她父亲一直认为女孩子学习化学是一种浪费,可是他喜欢有人陪伴着自己,一个能够倾听而不会多加评论的人。他没有儿子,所以拉达填补了这个空缺。他从来都没有期待拉达会成为一名化学家,并且认为她的兴趣只是一种幼稚的消遣方式,但是拉达却一直坚持了下来,因为她深知这能

closer to freedom. Since she had no immediate prospects of marriage at the time, he agreed. What else was he to do with her? She knew she wasn't good-looking. But she also knew that in some ways, that had been her savior. Until last year. That's when her luck ran out. A marriage had been arranged. And she couldn't go against her family. It was unthinkable.

Rahda shifted her weight and her chair groaned suddenly, wood swelling against wood and chaffed about it. The noise made Rahda quit drawing and listen. Hearing nothing, she switched from drawing bees and started drawing chicken wire again. Underneath the notebook, her desk was completely covered with spectra and reports from other graduate students. A sixteen-ounce cup of cold coffee, half full, was perched on the edge of the desk. The powdered cream had collected on the top, mimicking a fungus.

Rahda lifted her head and listened. A door had opened somewhere deep in the building. She slammed her notebook shut and listened some more. She waited, willing herself to decipher who it was, what they were doing. Her mind quickly ran through several possible scenarios, imagining individual chemists in their labs. Paige? It didn't sound like her. Paige walked heavier than that. Max? He was never in this early. Hadley? He could be getting a result. She'd have to do something.

Glancing at the clock, Rahda stood up and pushed the chair back from the desk. It complained as it went, and she felt perturbed by the sound, a harmonic that resonated unpleasantly with her bones. She realized she was trembling, and she clenched her hands to stop. Her nervousness had ramped up after the last group meeting. Scotia had added Hadley to her project because so much needed to be done, now that patents were being filed. The pressure was on.

In the beginning, Scotia had only given her two mildly difficult reactions. He had stopped by the lab her second day to wish her well and see if she needed anything. This was last year, and Rahda had felt as uncomfortable with American men then as she did now. They looked you in the eye. They asked you questions. Rahda had spoken to him softly, not lifting her head at first. Casually, as he was about to leave, he handed her drawings of two molecules, her graduate project, and explained that he had this idea about adding a catalyst to the first molecule that would change it into the second, creating a mixture very close to a steroid, a goal worth pursuing.

够使自己向自由更进一步。况且当时看来,拉达并没有近期结婚的可能,父亲就同意了。不然让他拿拉达怎么办呢?拉达知道自己并不好看,但她意识到某种意义上,正是这一点拯救了自己的命运。直到去年,她的运气用光了。家里给她安排了一桩婚事,而她无法违背家人的意愿。她简直都不敢细想。

拉达移动了一下重心,椅子突然发出了"吱嘎"的呻吟声,木头与木头摩擦发出嘲笑般的声音。拉达停下笔凝神听了一下,什么动静都没有,她又继续回头转而开始画六边形了。在记录本的下面,满满的都是其他研究生的光谱图和实验报告,桌角放着一杯十六盎司的冷咖啡,半满。粉末状的奶油聚集在咖啡的表面,像是菌丝。

楼里某处的门被打开了,拉达又抬起头来听。她合上了记录本静静地等着那个声音再次出现,想听个仔细。她在心里猜想着到底是谁,他们在做什么。她在脑海中迅速将可能的场景过了一遍——熟识的化学家们在自己的实验室里的样子。佩琪吗?听起来不像,她的脚步声要更重一些。麦克斯吗?他从来不会这么早的。难道是哈德利?也许是他来取实验的结果。她得做些什么了。

拉达瞟了一眼钟,随即站起身,将椅子推了进去。它又发出了不满的声音,那谐波与拉达的骨头产生了令人不舒服的共振,搞得她心神不宁。她突然发现自己正在发抖,于是抓住了自己的手试图停下来。自从上一次组会之后,她的紧张就开始泛滥了——斯考蒂亚把哈德利加到了她的组里,因为申请了专利以后,工作任务实在太重了,压力也日渐增加。

最开始的时候,斯考蒂亚只分配给拉达两个中等难度的实验,并在第二天就顺便来了拉达的实验室,祝她一切顺利并且看看她有什么需要的。这已经是去年的事情了,那时候拉达跟现在一样——对与美国男人接触感到不舒服,因为他们会直视你的眼睛,还会问你问题。拉达最初和他说话的时候是轻声轻语的,也不会抬头。他快要离开的时候,突然递给拉达一张画了两个分子的结构图——那是拉达的研究生课题,然后跟她说自己有这样一个想法,可以在第一个分子上加上一个催化剂使之转化成第二个分子,并且合成一种与类固醇很相似的化合物,他说这是一个值得研究的方向。

Chapter Four Bench

"It's the steps," he explained the next time he dropped by, checking on her progress. He gestured with his hands that of course she understood, but he elucidated anyway. "You take a ten-step reaction and reduce it down to four. Six less steps. There's a lot of money to be saved in six steps." Scotia leaned back on Rahda's bench, crossing his arms confidently, a man used to being right. He was a bright guy; being right was a natural consequence. "With six fewer steps, the reaction might be a hundredth the cost. People would be very interested." Scotia smiled kindly at Rahda. She could look at him, but not in his eyes. She found herself mostly staring in his right nostril. Then, when she forced herself to look elsewhere, ended up staring at his mouth, moving up and down, the motion as hypnotic as television.

"And if the process works for other molecules, the money could be astronomical." He looked at Rahda, both serious and excited, placing his hands back against the waist-high bench as though he needed grounding. "Of course, you would share in whatever remunerations ... but I'm being very premature. I just like to be straight-forward. I don't believe in graduate students as slave labor. I want their opinions, I want their candor. Feel free to tell me anything. And just to let you know, my wife Birdie and I will be having a Christmas party. I'll let you know when exactly; we do it every year. People carpool. It's not far. You'll have a good time." He nodded, waiting for a response.

"I would like that." She looked at his chin, wondering if she should say more. She was having trouble making the catalyst. She opened her mouth to say something, but her hands started shaking and she put them behind her, pressed against the bench, pushing her body backward to hold them still. She was afraid to tell him she was having difficulties. That a matchmaker had found her a husband. That she couldn't concentrate.

He smiled kindly again. "Let me know if you have any problems. New York can be overwhelming, but it's a great city. You're all moved in, right?" Rahda nodded. "Well, good. Be sure to meet the other chemists. I believe Bineet comes from a region very near yours. Maybe you have friends in common. And Paige is another woman in the group."

"I live with her," Rahda whispered.

"She—what? What did you say?"

他第二次来造访检查拉达进度的时候说道:"是步骤问题。"说着用手比画了一下。当然了,这些拉达都懂,但他还是开始进一步解释起来:"如果你把一个十步的反应减少到四步,就可以节省六步,在这六步间就可以省很多钱。"斯考蒂亚向后倚在拉达的工作台上,自信地将双手交叉在胸前,男人习惯性地认为自己总是正确的。他是个聪明的家伙,所以自然而然就觉得自己一定不会错。"减少了六个反应步骤,实验的总成本兴许就只有原来的百分之一。人们会很感兴趣的。"他和善地对拉达笑着。她可以看着他,但是不能直视眼睛。拉达发现自己大多数时候都是盯着他右边的鼻孔看的,然后当她强迫自己看向别处的时候,目光便会落在斯考蒂亚的嘴巴上,那两片嘴唇上下翻飞时就像电视机一样催人入眠。

"如果这个过程对其他分子也适用的话,可以省下的钱就是个天文数字了。"他既认真又兴奋地看着拉达,双手向后撑在齐腰高的工作台上,就好像他需要靠什么来支撑住自己的身体似的。"当然咯,不论酬劳如何都会有你一份的……但我这些都还是提前预期。我这个人喜欢直来直往,我不觉得研究生是免费苦力,我需要他们的观点和坦白直率。有什么话就直接对我说。顺便提一句,我和我的妻子准备举办一个圣诞晚会,这是我们每年的传统,具体时间会再告诉你的。大家一起拼车出行,你会玩得很开心的。"他点了点头,等待拉达的回复。

"我很愿意去。"她看着他的下巴,寻思着自己要不要再多说两句。她当时在合成催化剂上遇到了困难,于是张了张嘴想要再说些什么,但她的双手却突然开始发抖,于是她立刻把手藏到身后,撑在工作台上,身体向后倚着来抑制手的抖动。她不敢开口说,说自己遇到了麻烦,说媒人给她找到了一个丈夫,说自己无法集中注意力。

斯考蒂亚再次露出温和的笑容,"有什么问题的话就告诉我,纽约有时候会让人喘不过气来,但它是一个很棒的城市。你们都搬到市里来住了,对吧?"拉达点了点头。"这就好,记得和其他化学家打个照面。我记得贝内特的家离你的家乡很近,也许你们还有共同的朋友呢。还有佩琪,是我们组里的另一个女性组员。"

"我现在和她住在一起,"拉达小声道。

"她——什么?你说什么?"

"I share her apartment. Also with Dermot from Chesterton's group."

"Oh," Scotia nodded, looking satisfied. "I didn't realize that's who you had moved in with. Well, good. That should work well for you. I think you'll really like each other. Well. Okay. I'll drop by next week." He gave Rahda a short smile and walked out. She sat there, blowing air into her closed mouth and then letting her lips deflate with a puff, sounding like a turbine, a continuous machine of moving flesh.

Rahda had a break through and was two steps away from making the catalyst when Scotia came by one morning a week later, whistling "Darktown Strutter's Ball". In the lab Scotia's graduate students used his whistling as a guide to behavior, a jaunty tune a good time to ask questions, something in a minor key a time to lay low. But no matter the tune, the whistle was everyone's cue to look busy.

She almost jumped when she heard the sound. He was too early. She wasn't done yet. Why hadn't he waited till the afternoon? She would have been finished and could tell him that she'd made the catalyst. She wanted to have something completed, something she could say definitively. Almost was such a despicable word, it hinted at uncertainty, weak-kneed and pathetic. You either had nothing or you had something. You didn't almost have it.

He didn't ask her right away, making small talk, giving her the date of the party, asking her if Paige had taken her shopping yet. He laughed, saying that Paige was known in the group as being addicted to Bloomingdales. He leaned against her bench. "So, how's it going?"

"I'm taking an NMR of it right now," Rahda heard herself say. It wasn't a big lie. Certainly it implied that she'd made the catalyst, but also that she didn't really know if it was exactly right. It was the final step. She was done, now she was just verifying.

He had given her a wide-eyed look of anticipation, obviously pleased with her work. She allowed herself to smile back, happy that she'd given him the answer he'd wanted. Scotia had talked with her for a moment about what she should do next, then excused himself, saying he was late for a meeting. He would come back when he had more time.

It was only after Scotia walked out her door that she remembered she was still two steps away. But only two steps. It was almost made. She wouldn't leave the lab until she made it. There. It was settled. So she stayed in for lunch. Around six

"我和她合租一个公寓,还有切斯特通组的德莫特。"

"哦。"斯考蒂亚点点头,看上去很满意。"我完全不知道这件事。既然这样,那好吧,这应该对你有好处。我觉得你们一定会喜欢对方的。就这样吧,我下个星期还会来看你的。"他给了拉达一个短暂的微笑便走了出去。拉达坐在那儿,深吸一口气,发丝都被吸进了嘴巴里,然后又嘴唇颤动着将发丝噗了出来,听起来就像是涡轮的声音,一个持续运转的人肉机器。

一周以后,拉达已经有了突破性的进展,只差两步就可以合成那个特定的催化剂了。这时候斯考蒂亚又来了,嘴里吹着《达客镇舞会》的调子。在实验室里,斯考蒂亚带领的研究生们把他的口哨当作晴雨表,如果曲调欢快就代表是个问问题的好时机,若是比较沉闷,那么还是低调行事的好。但不管是什么调子,只要听到那个口哨声,每个人都会立刻意识到,要让自己看起来很忙。

拉达听到那声音的时候差点跳了起来:他来得太早了,实验还没有完成呢,为什么他不等到下午再来呢?那个时候就已经大功告成了,自己也可以告诉他催化剂已经合成好了。她想要先完成一些东西,自己可以百分之百确定的东西。"差不多"是一个让人看不起的词,它暗示着不确定性,缺乏支撑,显得很可悲。要么一无所获,要么有一定的成果,你不可能"差不多"得到了想要的结果。

他并没有直接就问拉达这个问题,而是先拉了拉家常,告诉她聚会的具体时间,并且问起佩琪有没有带她去购物。在说到佩琪是组里出了名的布卢明戴尔品牌(Bloomingdale)的忠实粉丝的时候,他大笑了起来,装作不在意地向拉达的工作台靠了靠,"那么,做得怎么样了?"

"我现在正在做核磁共振。"拉达听到自己这样说。这并不算是一个谎言,当然了,这么说意味着自己已经合成了这种催化剂,但是这也表明自己还并不确定它的精确性。这已经是最后一步了,前面都完成了,现在只是进行核实。

斯考蒂亚的眼睛瞪得老大,闪烁着期许的光芒,显然对拉达的成果感到十分满意。拉达也迟疑地露出了笑容,能给出他想要的答案,自己也很开心。斯考蒂亚接着和她谈了一会儿她接下去应该怎么做,然后说自己开会快要迟到,就离开了。他说有时间还会再来的。

直到斯考蒂亚走出门口拉达才回过神来,自己离最后成果还差两步呢。但是只剩两步了,基本都完成了。不成功合成催化剂她是不会离开实验室的,嗯,就这样决定了。所以她连午饭都在实验室里草草解决了,到了大概晚上六点的

o'clock she thought about leaving and going to the American Way for a hamburger but decided to wait. She was having trouble with the last step. The reaction was supposed to turn white and it was still colorless. She must have done something wrong. She tried the whole thing again with some material that she'd saved, running a second batch through chemical hoops. At eleven o'clock, after making numerous runs to the candy machine, she decided to go home and think. She would feel better with sleep.

But after a tortured night of dreams, she didn't feel up to the task of solving the problem. The thought of telling Scotia that the reaction hadn't worked, that she had lied, made sweat pool on her forehead, water abandoning a sinking ship, her bangs adhering to her brow. She wanted him to think she'd done it right. His authority scared her. He was nicer than most research directors, but he could be scathing if he thought you were incompetent. She'd seen this on her interview trip, briefly, when he'd been talking to a student who was no longer here. She felt herself start to tremble. What would she say when he came by again? She had no idea.

But the gods were in her favor. When she got to the lab, she saw Hadley walking down the hall. Hadley was one of the few chemists who had stopped by to say hi when she'd first gotten there. He had loaned her his Modern Synthetic Methods. When she saw him, she ducked her head shyly, a subtle hello that could easily be ignored. But he stopped and asked her how things were going. He told her that Scotia was gone for a week, giving a talk in France. At first it didn't register. She looked at him oddly, replaying the movement of his lips. Scotia was gone. She almost smiled. She didn't have to make the catalyst immediately. She'd think about it and do something else. No need to get in a panic. Instead, she'd run the reaction without the catalyst. It was one of the controls he had wanted her to test. She shrugged to herself, knowing her science was a little out of order. Usually you ran the controls last. But at least she could accomplish something.

As much as chemists tried to deny it, chemistry was not unlike cooking, the kind of cooking an experienced chef might do, trying different combinations of ingredients for the best result. You had a hypothesis; you tested it. For example, does anise make the cake taste better? You would then make the cake with anise. That would be the experiment. Then you would make the cake without anise. That would be the control.

时候，她本想去美式快餐吃个汉堡，但最终还是决定留下来等结果。她在最后一步上还有些问题：反应最后的产物应该是白色的，可现在却还是无色透明，肯定是自己哪里做错了。于是她用剩下的反应原料又从头做了一遍，做了第二组实验，她感觉自己像是马戏团的动物一样，一遍又一遍地钻着圈。十一点，在跑了无数次的糖果贩卖机之后，她终于决定回家再想想，睡一觉可能就会感觉好一些。

但是经过了一夜梦魇不停的折磨之后，她对解决这个问题仍然没有头绪。一想到要告诉斯考蒂亚反应没有成功，自己撒了谎，她的前额就冒出了一层汗珠，刘海紧紧地贴在眉毛上，就像一艘即将沉没的船，船体也渐渐开始渗水。她只是希望让斯考蒂亚觉得自己做得还不错，但他的权威把她给吓坏了。虽然他比其他大多数的研究所主任都要和蔼可亲，可一旦他觉得你的能力不够，就会变得非常严厉。她是在自己的面试之旅中见识到这一点的，当时斯考蒂亚正在跟一个后来离开了这里的学生讲话。想到这里她的身体又开始不由自主地战栗。他下次再来的时候自己要说什么？拉达一点主意也没有。

但上帝还是偏爱她的。当天她到达实验室的时候，她看到哈德利正往大厅走去。哈德利是少数几个在拉达刚来的时候来实验室打过招呼的化学家之一，还曾经把自己的《现代合成方法》那本书借给拉达。看到哈德利的时候，她有些羞涩地低了低头，问好的声音轻得几乎可以忽略。但是他却停下来问起拉达的近况，并且告诉她斯考蒂亚去法国演讲了，要待一个星期。一开始他的话完全没有进到拉达的脑子里，她奇怪地看着他，然后把他嘴唇的动作又回放了一遍：斯考蒂亚走了。她差点笑了出来：不用立刻就把催化剂给做出来了。自己可以一边想一边做点别的事情，没必要陷入恐慌。事实上，她可以不加催化剂做一下对比实验——这是斯考蒂亚想让自己测验催化剂性能的变量实验之一。她耸了耸肩，知道自己的研究顺序有点乱——通常这一步是放在最后的。但这样一来最起码自己还可以完成一些东西。

虽然化学家们都很想要否认这一点，但化学与下厨其实没什么不同，只是你需要像经验丰富的大厨那样，为了得出最好的结果尝试使用不同组合的原材料。先有一个假设，然后再进行验证。比如说，茴香能不能使蛋糕的味道变得更好？接下来你就会在做蛋糕的时候加上茴香，这就是实验。然后你还会做一个不加茴香的蛋糕，这就是控制变量的对比实验。

In Rahda's particular project, the experiment had four components: the starting molecule, which was a compound that could be bought from a supplier, metal, chlorine, and the catalyst, which was the molecule she'd been unable to make. So the control she ran was a three-step synthesis, everything but the catalyst, three discrete chemical transformations that created a yellow crystalline substance. It only took her two days to make. It looked right, glomming onto her glass; she shook it free and watched it sparkle in the light of her Bunsen burner. But when she picked up the printout of the NMR data, she sucked in her breath violently, hurting her lungs. One tight inhale that chilled her heart. It wasn't right. She didn't get the control result, which should have been simply the separate materials swirling around together, not forming anything. *Instead, she got the product*, the thing that Scotia wanted from the *experiment*. She'd got the product without a catalyst. How was that possible?

She stared at the sheet of paper pinched tightly between her fingers, digesting. It had made what he said, but all by itself. She didn't need the catalyst. She repeated that. She didn't need the catalyst. Proceeding slowly, she worked out that if it didn't need the catalyst, then she didn't need to make the catalyst. She'd already made what Scotia wanted. With relief she realized that she could be done with this project and could go work on another molecule he had suggested in passing, one that had been partly her idea. That was the one she was really interested in. What did the catalyst matter anyway? She had the product, that's what counted.

She tapped her fingers together, thinking down all the roads of thought. She could find a catalyst that didn't do anything, and no one needed to know it wasn't necessary. Maybe this time she'd extend the truth a little, but it wouldn't be much because she wasn't lying about having the product. You couldn't lie about that. Going over to her open notebook, she looked at the description of how she made the control. There was enough space for another line. Just this once she would say she added the catalyst, just until he knew she was good. On the next project she wouldn't have to lie.

When Scotia got back from France, he had come by to see her the next day wearing an actual beret. She'd noticed that he liked dressing ostentatiously, sweaters with little bobbles, ties from the MoMA collection. She had stood before him, her notebook in her hands, twisting it nervously. She looked up and blurted, "I have

在拉达的项目中,实验有四个组成部分:起始分子——是可以从原料商那里买来的化合物;金属,氯,还有就是催化剂——也就是她一直没能成功研制出来的物质。所以她要做的对比实验就是由三个步骤组成的合成过程,在不添加催化剂的条件下,经历了三次独立物质转化过程后,会产生一种黄色的具有水晶结构的物质。拉达只花了两天时间就完成了:看上去没什么问题,紧紧依附在玻璃管上;她试着摇匀,看着它在本生灯的灯光下熠熠生辉。但当她拿起打印好的核磁共振数据时,她猛地倒吸了一口气,隐约地感觉到肺有些痛。这一下急促的呼吸让她的心都有些发凉:不对!她得到的并不是对比实验的结果,否则她看到的应该是只有各种反应物分散地在玻璃管里打转儿才对,而不会形成任何物质。相反,她直接得到了产物——斯考蒂亚一直想从实验中得到的东西。她没用催化剂就得到产物了,这怎么可能呢?

她盯着紧紧夹在手指之间的那张纸,慢慢消化着这个内容。做出了斯考蒂亚所说的东西,但却是在什么也没加的情况下。催化剂并不是必要的。她又重复了一遍:不需要催化剂。她一点一点地咀嚼着,没加催化剂就做出了斯考蒂亚想要的产物,那么自己也就不用再合成催化剂了。她顿时感到如释重负,这样一来这个项目就可以告一段落,而自己也可以如愿以偿地投入另一种分子的研究工作中——在那当中有一部分是拉达自己的见解,而斯考蒂亚也曾经暗示会审核通过这个项目。那才是她真正感兴趣的领域呢。反正催化剂有什么重要的呢?她手里已经有产品了,这才算数。

她轻轻地打起了响指,顺着所有的思路想下去:可以找一种对实验没有任何影响的催化剂,至于这一点别人就没必要知道了。也许这样是有一点夸大事实的成分,但是也不算过分,因为得出了产品这一点她并没有撒谎,这也没法撒谎。拉达走到摊开的记录本前,浏览着自己做对比试验的记录,发现空白处足够再加上一行字的。就这一次,她会说自己加了催化剂,直到斯考蒂亚意识到她足够优秀就行了。下一个项目上她就用不着再撒谎了。

斯考蒂亚来实验室看拉达是他从法国回来的第二天,头上戴着一顶如假包换的贝雷帽。她注意到,斯考蒂亚平时就喜欢穿得惹人眼球:两侧垂着小球的毛衣,配上摩玛精品各种款式的领带。拉达站在他面前,紧张地翻着手中的笔记本。她猛然抬起头,脱口而出:"我得到产品了。"虽然猜测到他可能会很兴奋,

the product." She had thought he might be excited, but she wasn't prepared for his abrupt fervor. He had fired off several ideas immediately, almost talking to himself, and Rahda had watched, breathing carefully, in a kind of stupor at what she had unleashed. She kept waiting for him to ask to see her notebook. He never did. He believed her. She told him that she'd done the reaction and it had worked. She realized that she was actually telling *two* lies, not just the one she'd planned. She hadn't made the catalyst, *and* she hadn't run the reaction with the catalyst. Maybe lies come in pairs she thought, each a half-lie. Well, not a lie as much as a Mobius strip of veracity—she convinced herself—a switching of two truths in an enclosed system. But this was it. Everything else would be the systemless truth.

Except that she forgot about Scotia. She didn't consider the outpouring of research that her words would put into motion. Her little rotation of the facts had started a tornado of experiments. Electrifying immediately, he had the face of confidence, of knowledge, pleased with how well he understood chemistry, how well in fact he understood it more than others. He had asked her some questions, what the compounds had looked like at various points, then he nodded and pulled out his power-user ball-point pen, inviting her over to her bench. We could try this, he'd said generously, the "we" including her in the decisions, making her feel important. He was drawing structures all over scraps of paper and handing them to her, then saying, "Oh, wait, that's too hydrophobic," or something similar, and taking some of them back while giving her more, his mind obviously working out the puzzles of interaction, modeling molecules in his brain. She had fifteen drawings by the time he had left. Fifteen new possibilities of improving her yield, of simplifying her synthesis, of even better ways to synthesize the product which would make it more desirable to potential investors.

Ten minutes later, still holding the pages of molecules, Rahda had sunk down dully in her chair. What could she do? She searched her brain, trying not to let terror take over. Then an idea jolted her. She would have to make the catalyst. She had no choice. She would camp out in the lab.

Rahda went home and got a sleeping bag and some books, planning to make a food run once a day. She stayed up till four o'clock on many nights, trying every method she could think of, but nothing worked. Pretending to run Scotia's reactions during the day and trying to make the catalyst at night, Rahda hid her fear from the

但她还是对那阵突然爆发的热情感到措手不及——斯考蒂亚立刻就谈起好几个后续的计划,几乎演变成了自言自语,拉达就在一旁看着,小心翼翼地呼吸着,还处在对自己说的那句话的恍惚状态之中。她一直静静地等着斯考蒂亚要求看自己的记录本,但他从始至终一字未提——他相信她。因为她已经说了,自己完成了实验并且奏效了。刹那间,她意识到自己撒了两个谎,而并不是当初计划的一个。她没有研制出催化剂,也没有把催化剂加到反应中去。也许谎言总是成双吧,她暗暗想道:互相拼合成一个。任何谎言都没法像莫比乌斯带一样完美精确——她开始自我安慰——在一个封闭的系统内将两个真相翻转相扣。这就是一切,其他所有真相都是系统以外的。

除了一点——她把斯考蒂亚的做事方式给忘了。自己说的话所带来的势如洪水般的后续试验,让拉达始料不及。一个对事实的小小扭曲,使得一连串的实验像龙卷风一样接踵而至。听到这个消息之后的振奋之情,让斯考蒂亚的脸上立刻充满了自信与博学的神色,他满意于自己对化学的了如指掌,以及比其他人都更在行的优势。拉达被问到了几个问题,诸如那个化合物在各个阶段的形色等,斯考蒂亚点了点头,拿出了自己的高级商务圆珠笔,请拉达到工作台边上来。"我们可以这样试试。"他大方地用了"我们"这个词,将拉达也包含在决策权之内,这使她感觉到了自己的重要性。斯考蒂亚在碎纸片上画起各种结构图,然后递给拉达,"噢,等等,那张的结构有点太疏水了,"或是其他一些类似的话,然后拿回一些,但同时又递过更多张图纸。很显然他正在自己的大脑里试图解决物质间相互反应的谜题,并且在脑海中建立起了分子模型。等到他离开的时候,拉达的手里握着整整十五张构图,十五种全新的关于拉达的实验的可能性,有的可以提高产率,有的可以简化反应步骤,甚至还包含了更好的合成产品的方法,使其对潜在投资人更具吸引力。

十分钟后,拉达没精打采地陷在椅子里,手里仍然握着那一沓图纸。她能怎么办呢?她搜刮过自己的每一寸大脑皮层试图寻找解决方案,尽量不让自己的意识被恐惧攻占。一个突然的想法使她打了个寒战:这样一来她就必须要把催化剂给做出来了,别无选择,看来要在实验室里打地铺了。

拉达回到家里取了一个睡袋、一些书,并打算每天回来取一次食物。许多个夜晚,她都熬夜到凌晨四点,每一种她能想出来的方法都尝试过了,但无一奏效。白天假装进行着斯考蒂亚要求的实验,晚上就努力研究催化剂的合成,拉达将睡袋扔进满是蟑螂断腿的橱柜里藏起来,同样被藏起来的还有她内心深深的恐惧。

Chapter Four Bench

others like she hid her sleeping bag which was thrust down in an empty cabinet filled with roach husks. She would occasionally go home to rumple her bed, leave dishes around to look like she'd been there. She said very little to the others, only answering questions if she couldn't avoid it. She finally moved back home when she herself couldn't avoid the truth. The catalyst wasn't to be made. It was over a year since her initial results and she spent most of her time doing cover-up work. But now that Scotia had assigned Bineet and recently Hadley to her project, they were continually coming to her for samples. Hadley wanted product, Bineet the catalyst. Giving Hadley what he wanted was easy. Anytime she needed more product, she would run the control. But Bineet wouldn't leave her alone. She told him, pointedly, that he would have to make the catalyst himself. He told her he hadn't been able to do so and could he please just use some of hers. She had apologized tersely and said that hers was all designated for other reactions. He was a caste below her and she used it to her advantage. She suspected that Bineet was on the verge of knowing, except that so far no one suspected, because to lie was unthinkable. Scientists don't lie. They believed her research. So when the others got unfavorable results, Scotia blamed it on bad yields or lousy technique or other assorted logical excuses. Theories that could keep her safe for a while. The question was, how long?

Rahda rubbed her face, smearing more pen on her cheek, tired of thinking about her situation. Time to act. Her shoes made a scuffling noise as she walked to her bench. She picked up four test tubes from a small rack, each with a different-colored cap on it: red, blue, yellow, and green. Inside each test tube was an identical solvent, a light yellow liquid the color of saffron. If not for the colored tops, it would have been impossible to tell them apart. The test tubes were small enough to slip inside her right lab coat pocket, which she did. Cocking her head slightly, like her brain had shifted, Rahda paused, then walked to the door of her lab and opened it. Her normal shuffling gait took her out of her lab and to the NMR room. The NMR, an acronym for Nuclear Magnetic Resonance, was a huge silver hulking bubble of a machine, a chemists' magnet that causes known atoms to resonate in a particular direction, like a compass pointing to polar north, or a tuning fork spontaneously humming. Setting the NMR for known frequencies is a way for chemists to be sure that what they *think* they have is what they *actually* have.

她偶尔会回趟家,把被褥弄得凌乱一些,再四处放些脏盘子,营造出一副她在家住过的样子。平时她很少和别人提起实验的事,只有实在避免不了的时候才会回答几个问题。最终,她搬回了家里,因为她再也无法逃避事实了:催化剂根本就做不出来。此时离最初做出产品已经超过一年了,这段时间里她大部分的精力都投入在"伪装"工作上。但是如今斯考蒂亚把贝内特分到了她的项目上,最近又加进了哈德利,他们俩不停地追着自己要样本:哈德利需要产品,而贝内特要催化剂。前者很容易应付——任何时候需要更多的产品,只要做对比试验就行了。但是贝内特却阴魂不散地揪着自己不放,于是她只能跟他强调,他得自己把催化剂给做出来。贝内特解释说自己还没能成功做出来,并且央求着拉达借一些样本。拉达简短地说了句抱歉,并解释说她的样本都已经被分配到指定的实验上了。贝内特的印度种姓要比拉达的等级低,因此拉达就利用了这一点。不过她仍然怀疑贝内特已经接近真相的边缘了,只是到目前为止,没有人起疑,因为在这上面撒谎简直是不可想象的。科学家是不会撒谎的,他们都相信拉达的实验,所以当其他人得到的结果不尽如人意时,斯考蒂亚会将其怪罪在收益不好,设备不精或者是总结为其他一系列合理原因的综合后果。这些借口可以让她暂时处于安全地带,但问题是,能撑多久呢?

拉达厌倦了总是为现状烦恼,她挠了挠脸,留下了更多的墨汁。是时候行动了。她向工作台走去,鞋子在地板上发出拖沓的声音。接着她从小木架上取了四个有不同颜色盖子的试管:红色、蓝色、黄色,还有绿色。每个试管里的试剂都是一样的,一种淡黄色的液体,有点偏近藏红花的颜色。如果不是盖子的颜色不同,要想区分它们几乎是不可能的。试管小到可以滑进她的实验服口袋里,于是她就顺手放进了右边的口袋。就好像大脑的重心转移了一般,拉达微微地仰起头,向实验室门口走去,停顿了一下,然后打开了门。出了自己的实验室,她拖着一贯的步子向核磁共振(NMR)室走去,核磁共振是核能磁性共振的缩写(Nuclear Magnetic Resonance),那是一个巨大而笨重的透明罩仪器,闪烁着银色的光泽。它的作用就是化学家的磁铁,可以让已知的原子向着特定的方向共振,就像是总是直指北极的罗盘,或是自发嗡鸣的音叉。将共振仪调到特定的频率,化学家就可以确定他们手里的物质是否就是他们以为自己获得了的东西。这是

It is proof, in the way that ancient chemists used to burn the compounds for their color, or taste them for their acidity, a less reliable but more theatrical way to determine exactly what one has in hand.

Rahda opened the door to the NMR room and walked in, carefully shutting it behind her. A clipboard hanging on the back of the door swung with a slowing beat. Rahda's name was written in the 11:15 to 11:30 time slot in such precise penmanship that she felt compelled to study the handwriting admiringly. A smile crept to her lips. She liked the swish of her name in ink. Then it occurred to her that not much longer would it be her name. With an effort, she forced herself to turn from the door. She walked over to the NMR terminal where she sat down and started entering a nonexistent job. She typed and deleted and typed and deleted the same two numbers for thirteen minutes, practicing her speed, toggling between the keys in time to the humming in her mind, finally sending the command to run the analysis at 11:28. Her fingers left damp spots on the keyboard.

Suddenly the door opened and Hadley ducked his head inside.

"Oh, sorry," he said, startled by her presence, the clipboard making an irritating tapping sound as it swung back and forth. Having glanced at the sign-up sheet earlier, he'd thought that the slot before him had been empty. His plan was to get his job going and then take an early lunch. He wasn't hungry as much as he needed some air. The lab felt so airless to him on these damp and muggy days, the several radiators creating a sauna-like environment in the lab.

"That is no problem," Rahda said politely. "I am nearly done here. Give me just five more minutes." She paused and started to turn back to the keyboard. "Unless you would like for me to put it in the probe for you." She looked at him questioningly.

"Well, sure, if you don't mind."

"It is no problem. Really. I will be done very soon."

"Okay." Hadley handed her a red-capped test tube filled with a familiar light yellow liquid, and backed out the door. Rahda transferred the test tube to her left hand. She waited a moment after Hadley closed the door, the ball of her left foot grazing the earth, poised for quick movement. She listened. She heard the large door at the end of the hallway close with its characteristic skronking of metal. Walking back to the terminal and quickly canceling her job, Rahda fished in her right lab coat

一种证据，就像古代的化学家们通过煅烧化合物来观察颜色变化，或者亲自品尝来确定其酸性，那些方法可靠性更低一些，但却包含着更多的戏剧性。

拉达走进共振室，小心地关上身后的门，门后挂着的签到板随之左右摇晃起来，然后渐渐趋于平缓。在 11:15 到 11:30 的时间段后面写着拉达的名字，那隽秀的字体使她深深感到练习书法的必要。一丝微笑爬上了她的嘴角：她喜欢用墨水写自己的名字时发出的"沙沙"声。可她却突然想到，要不了多久自己的名字就永远不会再出现在这里了。她强迫自己离开那扇门，走向共振终端机。坐定之后，她开始进行那项并不存在的工作——同样的两个数字被输入又删除，再输入，再删除，拉达这样持续了 13 分钟，手指在两个按键之间切换着，频率与大脑中的"嗡嗡"声一致。终于在 11:28 分的时候她发送了运行分析的指令——她的手指在键盘上留下了湿湿的痕迹。

突然门开了，哈德利的脑袋探了进来。

"噢，抱歉。"他说道，显然被拉达的存在吓了一跳，门后的签到板不知疲倦地左右晃着，发出恼人的"啪啪"声。哈德利之前瞥了一眼签到表，本以为他前面的时间段是空的，便打算着让自己的实验运行着，然后早早地去吃午饭。其实比起饥饿，他更需要一些新鲜的空气——在这种潮湿闷热的天气里，实验室里的空气都变得稀薄了，屋里的几个散热器则营造出了一种桑拿房的环境。

"没关系的，"拉达礼貌地答道，"我快做完了，再给我五分钟就好。"她顿了一下，又转过头去面对着键盘。"除非你愿意让我一会儿帮你把它放进探针里去。"她带着询问的眼神看着哈德利。

"如果你不介意的话，那当然好了。"

"没问题，我很快就好了。"

"好的。"哈德利将一个红色盖子的装满黄色液体的试管递给拉达，然后转身出了房间。拉达将试管换到左手上，左脚的前脚掌内侧蹬在地上，做好要迅速移动的准备，耐心地等待着哈德利关上门。她倾身听着，直到走廊的尽头传来大门关上时的特殊金属碰撞声。她走到终端机前面，迅速取消了自己的实验，并把

pocket for her own red-capped tube. She held her pocket open and spied Hadley's test tube's twin. Momentarily holding the two samples before her, she smiled. Identical in appearance, they were not so in substance. One would give the right result, and one wouldn't. She quickly dropped Hadley's tube into her left lab coat pocket. The one in her right hand she put into the NMR probe, the repository of tubes to be evaluated. Rahda started the new job in an instant. It was the right thing to do. She knew Hadley was working on scaling up the product, making it in large batches, and she couldn't afford for him to get the wrong result.

With relatively little emotion, she took Hadley's red-capped test tube back to her office and poured the contents down the drain. She ran the water faucet for half-an-hour while she drew more bees and chicken wire.

手伸进右口袋里搜寻她自己的红色盖子试管。用手撑开口袋,她瞥了一眼哈德利试管的"双胞胎",将它们并排放在眼前,拉达笑了——外观一样,本质却不一样;一个能得出正确的结果,另一个却不行。转眼之间她已经把哈德利的试管塞回了自己的口袋里,自己的那支则放进了检测器里,与其他的试管一同进行评估。拉达毫不犹豫地按下开始键——这是她应该做的事情。她知道哈德利当时正在测量产品的数值范围,以便进行大量生产,所以她不能让哈德利得出错误的结果。

内心几乎没有什么情感波动,拉达带着哈德利的试管回到了自己的办公室,然后倒进了水池里,让水龙头一直流了半个小时,自己则在一旁继续画起了蜜蜂和六边形铁丝网。

Chapter Five Control

> Control: to test or verify (a scientific experiment) by a parallel experiment or other standard of comparison.
>
> *The Random House College Dictionary*

No matter what Max did, he could not get the cockroach to walk across the cord of the venetian blinds. He had looped the cord into a simple trap on the corner of his desk, clearing away a space among the various papers and empty Pepsi cans. He'd even dripped a small lake of Pepsi in the loop, thinking it the perfect bait. What didn't like Pepsi? As Max watched the cockroach, he wondered if this is what chemists did right before they cracked up. He laughed, thinking of people he'd personally known who'd wigged, all scientists. There were perhaps a higher proportion of nutcases in science than in the rest of society. Other people were too boring to lose their minds. Max remembered his labmate at Irvine, the one who quit chemistry to become an alcoholic somewhere in Idaho. Then there was the guy who just walked out of the lab one day, went home and watched TV for nine months. Max would come over to visit his friend Bruce, and Harv would be there, eating refried beans straight from the can and lying on the Barcalounger. Eventually Harv became a lawyer. "Because that's what nutcases do," Max joked to himself.

Leaning back and putting his feet up, Max surveyed his mental health. He knew quick movements weren't his style, like suddenly quitting school, or losing his mind and becoming a lawyer. Instead, he bugged out this way, a semi-deviant line of behavior. Luring roaches. Yelling at parties. Letting out little bits of steam was much more his mode, much healthier, though perhaps it drove other people crazy. But better them than him.

He watched the cockroach as it whirled its wiry antennae about. It appeared to know something was up, and was trying for better reception. The roach's sci-fi body was a brittle khaki with specular glints that resembled burnished metal. It was this

第五章　对照

> 对照：在科学实验中通过平行试验或者其他标准的对比实验进行检测或者核查。
>
> ——《兰登书屋大学词典》

无论麦克斯怎么做，都无法让那只蟑螂爬过威尼斯风格的百叶窗拉绳。他在满桌子的稿纸和空可乐罐中清理出了一角，并将拉绳结成了一个简单的陷阱。他甚至还在绳圈的中间倒了一小滩的百事可乐，构成了一个完美的诱饵。谁不喜欢百事可乐呢？麦克斯一边盯着那只蟑螂，一边心想着这是不是就是化学家精神崩溃之前会做的事情。他大笑了起来，试着回忆那些自己认识的已经发狂了的人，全部都是科学家。也许科学界的疯子比例要比社会其他领域的疯子比例的总和还要高，其他人都太无聊了，根本不可能进入癫狂状态。麦克斯还记得自己在欧文分校的实验室伙伴，他放弃了化学这一行最终沦为了酒鬼，游荡在爱达荷州一带。还有一个家伙，突然有一天就离开了实验室，回到家里连续看了九个月的电视。麦克斯偶尔会去拜访他的朋友布鲁斯，哈弗也会在那儿，他们就躺在苏丹式按摩椅上，直接从罐头里舀炸豆泥吃。最终哈弗成了一名律师。"因为这就是疯子会做的事情。"麦克斯对自己开玩笑道。

他身体向后仰去，并将双脚搭在了桌面上，他开始检查自己的心理健康状况。麦克斯知道，雷厉风行不是自己的作风，比如说突然辍学，或是大脑抽风去改行做律师；相反的，他用自己的方法来逃逸——略微有些奇怪的行为，比如诱捕蟑螂，在派对上大吼大叫等。让情绪一点一点地宣泄出来才更符合他的模式，也更加健康，尽管也许他的行为会把其他人给逼疯。但是总比自己疯癫要好。

那只蟑螂不停地旋转着自己尖细的触须，麦克斯就这样盯着它看。它好像知道有什么事情要发生了，一直试图获取更多的信息。它那带有科幻色彩的躯壳是卡其色的，给人易碎的感觉，闪着镜面一般的光芒，如同擦得锃亮的金属表

mechanical visage of cockroaches that bothered Max the most. They didn't seem biological. No wonder they'd survived for so long. This one certainly had. It was a good two inches, and the height of an eraser. Max's distaste for roaches was overcome by his desire to control something. He fancied a pet.

The cockroach suddenly ran out of sight. Bummer. Max sighed, then went down the hall to get his mail, collecting it from his square cubbyhole in the department office and immediately throwing away an alumni newsletter and some junk mail. As he started back down the hall, he remembered seeing these four-inch long Madagascar cockroaches in one of the labs at Irvine. The roaches produced a pheromone that was being studied, an attractant, a call to the species that could be harnessed, perhaps used in insect repellent: "Here baby, come get these drugs." The act of stimulating cockroaches was the kind of thing you discussed in a bar, shit-faced and abusive. Or at least that's where Max heard about it. Some biology students were boasting that when they fed the roaches dog food you could actually hear crunching sounds. Going to check it out the next day, Max watched grimly as a phalanx of cockroaches devoured a whole bowl of dry dog chow. He thought he was going to throw-up. His head hadn't felt too good to begin with. He'd left quickly, thanking God he'd gone into organic chemistry.

Having now remembered the incident, he couldn't get the sound of crunching out of his head and it began to make him faintly ill. He tried to think of something else, but it was either that or his chemistry, and both made him squeamish. He couldn't get shit to work. He had no decent ideas about what to do next, and this seemed as good a time as any to loaf around. Better, really. He pulled aside the curtain and looked out the steamy window, the rain and forced-air heating meeting side by side on the glass, drizzling rivulets and beaded sweat facing off. It was after six and the sky had gotten very dark outside. There'd been a hurricane that day, a baby one. The winds blew like mad but found little to destroy in Manhattan. The city was a fortress. Max had wanted to order Chinese food just to watch the guy bicycle in the storm, but no one else would go in with him. Laughing, Paige told him that he was the meanest person she'd ever met.

"Whaddya talkin' about mean? I'd tip him!"

"You're worse than Dermot."

"No way. He'd have *done* it." Dermot worked for Chesterton on the sixth floor.

面。就是它这样机械感浓重的外表让麦克斯百思不得其解——它们看起来不符合生物规律。怪不得它们存活了这么久,尤其是眼前这个——足足有两英寸,大概跟橡皮一样高度。麦克斯想要控制某样东西的欲望超过了他对蟑螂的厌恶之情——他想要一个宠物。

突然间那只蟑螂就跑出了他的视线之外,太糟糕了。麦克斯叹了口气,然后走向大厅去取邮件。走进部门办公室,他从自己专属的信件小橱中取出所有来函,随手就扔掉了一封校友实时通讯,还有其他一些垃圾邮件。正当他开始往回走的时候,他突然想起,曾经在欧文分校的实验室里看到过的那些四英寸长的马达加斯加大蟑螂。这种蟑螂会分泌一种叫作费洛蒙的引诱剂,是当时的研究项目之一,它向其他可以加以利用的蟑螂物种发出信号:"这儿,宝贝儿,来喝碗迷魂汤。"这一点也许能够用来制作驱虫剂。这种关于如何挑逗蟑螂的讨论往往发生在酒吧里,喝得醉醺醺的,骂骂咧咧地讨论着;至少麦克斯是在这样的情景下听到的。有些生物专业的学生自豪地说起,当他们给蟑螂喂食狗粮的时候,真的可以听到"嘎吱嘎吱"的咀嚼声。听到的第二天麦克斯就准备一试真假,当他严谨地观察完一大群蟑螂将整碗的狗粮风卷残云之后,他感觉到自己几乎要吐出来了。实验最开始的时候他就感到头部有些不适。随后他就迅速地离开了那里,暗暗庆幸自己选择的是有机化学这个研究方向。

现在又再回忆起那次实验,麦克斯满脑子都是"嘎吱嘎吱"的声音,挥之不去,这让他又开始有些不舒服了。他试图想些别的事情,但除了这个之外就是他的化学研究,而两者都让他反胃。什么都做不成。对于接下来要做什么麦克斯毫无头绪,所以现在,就像往常一样,是个闲逛的好时机。甚至,是个更好的时机。他将窗帘拉到一边,透过雾气氤氲的窗户向外看去,雨水和室内蒸腾的热气在玻璃的两侧相遇,毛毛雨联结成了微流,随后便像是断了线的汗珠。已经六点多了,外面夜色也愈加浓重。当天有一场飓风,规模不大,大风如同发狂一般席卷而来,却发现曼哈顿的一切都坚不可摧——这座城市就像是坚固的堡垒。麦克斯本来想打电话叫中国菜,只是为了看送外卖的人在暴风雨里骑车的样子,但是没有其他人愿意加入他。佩琪一边大笑着一边对麦克斯说他是自己认识的人里面最刻薄的一个。

"你怎么会觉得我刻薄呢?我会给他小费的!"

"你比德莫特还坏。"

"不可能,要是他的话早就已经打电话了。"德莫特在六楼的彻斯特通公司

Chapter Five Control

Dermot, Paige, and Rahda shared an apartment. Dermot called Rahda the Couch Samosa because recently all she would do when she got home from the lab was watch television. Granted, she was often at the lab, but that was the only other thing he ever saw her do, eating her meals while transfixed by the TV. Paige thought the name stupid, but the more she groaned, the more Dermot said it. Max secretly thought that Dermot and Paige were on the edge of a romance because they fought constantly, like brother and sister, but when he asked them separately, they both vehemently denied it. The other day Dermot threw a half-gallon of ice cream out their kitchen window just so Paige wouldn't eat the whole thing. Paige was exceptionally buxom and good-looking, especially for a chemist, but tended toward the zaftig end of the spectrum. Dermot was constantly watching out for Paige, and it drove Paige crazy.

Recently, Paige's new boyfriend had spent the night, a wrestler with biceps that seemed cancerous, as if the muscle couldn't stop proliferating. In the morning the boyfriend's left tennis shoe was missing. He and Paige searched the apartment. No luck. Angrily, the boyfriend pounded his massive fist on Dermot's door. When Dermot opened it, the boyfriend thrust his right shoe into Dermot's sleep-swollen face.

"Hey, buddy, have you seen my other shoe?"

"I duh know. What's it look like?" Dermot joked. He was so practiced at being a smart aleck that he could even do it in the haze of just waking.

"You *must* have a death wish," Max had said later, shaking his head. Dermot had used the story as a pretense for showing Paige's room to Max and Shelby, proving to them that small livestock could be hidden in there and no one would know. (A mouse had been crushed to death when Paige dropped a pile of books on a mound of clothes. A week later, the stench was so bad, Dermot wouldn't let her out until she found what was stinking up the apartment.)

Laughing at the thought, Max thumbed through a copy of *Chemical and Engineering News*, a trade magazine that would get tossed as soon as he read it, and then glanced at his hood, the glass-fronted area where most of the serious chemistry is done. Argon, nitrogen, and propane were accessible through silver spigots on the left side. Hot plate stirrers, ring stands, clamps, and glass tubing all filled the hood in ordered confusion. Above the hood a yellow bumper sticker read, "Back off man, I'm a scientist." Down below, two flasks, one with white powder, the other with

工作，他和佩琪、拉达合租一间公寓。德莫特把拉达叫作"印度沙发饺子"［译者注：英语中把整天赖在沙发上看电视的人叫作"沙发土豆"，此处为衍生笑话］，因为她从实验室回家以后，所做的唯一一件事情就是看电视。不消说，拉达大部分时间都在实验室里待着，但这是德莫特在家里唯一看到她做的事情———一边吃饭，一边牢牢地钉在电视机的前面。佩琪觉得这个名字太蠢了，但是她越是抱怨，德莫特说的次数就越多。麦克斯私下里一直以为德莫特和佩琪就快要成为一对了，因为他们经常会像兄妹那样斗嘴。但当他分别问他们的时候，他们却双双强烈否认。有一天德莫特把半加仑的冰淇淋从厨房窗户给扔了出去，这样佩琪就不会把它整个都给吃掉了。佩琪身材丰满，姿色可人，尤其是对一个化学家来说更为难得，但是却越来越发福了。德莫特总是时刻注意着佩琪，都快把她给搞疯了。

最近，佩琪的新男朋友在她家过了夜，他是一个摔跤手，长着像肿瘤似的二头肌，就好像他的肌肉无法停止增殖一样。早上的时候，佩琪男友左脚的那只网球鞋不见了，佩琪和他一起找遍了整个公寓，还是一无所获。带着怒气，她的男友用硕大的拳头砸响了德莫特的门，门打开的瞬间，右脚的那只网球鞋就被提到了德莫特那睡得有些浮肿的脸前面。

"喂，伙计，你看到我另一只鞋了没？"

"我不知道，它长什么样子？"德莫特用玩笑的口气说道。他对装傻充愣已经熟练到了即使在刚睡醒的朦胧状态下也能进行的程度了。

"你肯定是活够了。"事后麦克斯摇着头对他说道。后来德莫特用这个故事做借口，带麦克斯和谢尔碧参观了佩琪的卧室，试图证明这个房间里可以藏得下一只小型的牲口而没有人会知道。（曾经有一次，当佩琪把一大摞书扔在一堆衣服上的时候，压死了一只老鼠。一周之后，因为实在恶臭难忍，德莫特直到佩琪找出臭味的源头才让她离开公寓。）

想到这里麦克斯笑了，同时快速地翻阅着手里的《化学与工程新闻》杂志的副本，这是一本读完就会随手扔掉的商业性杂志。随后他瞟了一眼正前方是玻璃屏的通风橱，大多数重要的实验都是在那里完成的。分别打开左手边的银质龙头就可以获得氩、氮、丙烷这些物质。通风橱里面摆满了磁力搅拌器、铁环架、铁夹、玻璃试管等，虽然是按照一定的规律摆放的，但还是令人眼花缭乱。它的上方贴了一张黄色的汽车保险杠贴纸，写着"让开点，伙计，我是个科学家"。在最下面放着两个长颈烧瓶，一个装着白色的粉末，另一个装着黄色的，瓶底都垫

yellow, sat on cork rings. Max noticed that his magnetic stirrer was still on, spinning a small teflon-coated stir bar around in an orangish solution. Turning the stirrer off, he took the solution, poured it into another small flask and labeled it in his scrawly, illegible handwriting. That's enough work for today, he decided.

Max started to sit back in his chair and put his legs on the desk when he noticed that the cockroach had come back. Two legs rested just inside the trap. All Max had to do was pull the plastic tassel and he'd have the thing. The question was, did he really want him? After so much engineering, it seemed a waste of energy not to try. And he felt the need to have accomplished something today. Grimacing, Max carefully leaned over and slowly moved his left hand into position. He grasped the tassel between his thumb and forefinger. His other hand held the line taut that ran up to the curtain rod. Just as he began to slowly tighten the loop, a pile of journals landed with a whack on his desk, making him jerk the cord too hard. The cockroach escaped and ran along the edge of the desk, disappearing behind some papers.

Max yanked his head around, slightly embarrassed at his pastime. "Hadley, goddamn you." He felt irritated at Hadley, even though they were best friends. There was a constant competition between them, uncomplicated by reason. Deep down, Max knew that his irritation stemmed from the fact that Hadley excelled at the same things Max excelled at, and Max was used to being the best. And yet, Max liked the company. He liked having someone who understood complexities in the way he understood them. Hadley was both a comrade and a rival, and Max's ambivalence sometimes made him feel faintly confused, which most likely was the true source of the irritation. Max was a person who liked clear-cut cause-and-effect: tough problems, simple solutions. The only area in which Max had the better of Hadley was when it came to women. Hadley just didn't exude the kind of confidence necessary to attract women the way Max did. In all the years they'd known each other, back at UCLA, and then long-distance during graduate school, Max at Irvine, Hadley at MIT, Max had only known Hadley to have had one girlfriend. It wasn't that Max was a ladies' man or anything, but he certainly thrived on the company of women. Shelby always joked that it had been hard to get him between girlfriends.

Hadley raised one eyebrow at Max. "You were trying to catch a cockroach?"

"*Maybe*," Max said defiantly, removing his glasses and rubbing the length of his nose. It was his way to relax when he wasn't near a shower.

着软木圈。麦克斯注意到他的磁力搅拌器还是开着的,一个裹着聚四氟乙烯的小小搅拌子正在一种近橘黄色的溶液中旋转着。停下搅拌器,麦克斯取出了溶剂,将其倒进另一个小烧瓶中,并用自己潦草的、几乎不可辨认的笔迹给它写上了标签。今天做这么多工作就够了,他做出了决定。

麦克斯重新坐回椅子上,双腿翘到桌上,这时候他注意到那只蟑螂又回来了。它正好有两条腿停在了陷阱里面,麦克斯唯一需要做的事情就是拉一下窗帘的塑料流苏,就能够擒获这个家伙了。问题是,他真的想要这只蟑螂吗?已经在陷阱设计上花了这么多工夫,如果不试一下似乎浪费了付出的精力。况且,他觉得自己今天至少需要完成些什么。麦克斯对自己做了个鬼脸,小心翼翼地倚身过去并慢慢让左手就位。他用拇指和食指捏住了流苏,另一只手紧紧抓住绕在窗帘杆上的绳子。正当他开始渐渐拉紧那个圈的时候,一大沓学术期刊重重地落在桌面上,吓得麦克斯用力拽了一下绳子。那只蟑螂立刻沿着桌子的边缘逃走了,消失在一摞纸的后面。

麦克斯猛地转过头去,略微为自己打发时间的方式感到窘迫。"哈德利,去你的。"他被哈德利的行为给激怒了,尽管他们是最好的朋友。他们俩之间一直都有竞争存在,而理由其实并不复杂。内心深处麦克斯知道,自己的怒气来源于哈德利在他擅长的领域也毫不逊色的事实,而麦克斯一直以来都习惯了第一的宝座。不过,麦克斯也喜欢有这样一个同伴——一个可以用同样的方法来理解复杂事情的人。哈德利既是战友,又是对手,而这种矛盾心理有时候让麦克斯感到困惑,这也是引发他怒气的真正原因。麦克斯喜欢清晰明了的"原因——结果"模式:艰涩的问题,简单的解决方案。麦克斯胜过哈德利的唯一一点就是在女人这方面,哈德利就是无法像麦克斯那样表现出吸引女人所必需的自信。他们相识的这么多年里:在加州洛杉矶大学共度的时光,然后是研究生时期远距离的友谊——当时麦克斯在欧文分校,而哈德利在麻省理工学院,麦克斯只知道他有过一个女朋友。也不是说麦克斯是个万人迷,但是女人的陪伴不可否认地使他更加焕发光彩。谢尔碧总是开玩笑说,麦克斯几乎没有单身的时候。

哈德利对着麦克斯挑起了一边眉毛,"你刚才在抓蟑螂?"

"也许吧。"麦克斯挑衅地说道,顺手取下眼镜并挠了挠鼻梁。不能立刻冲澡的时候,他就用这种方法来放松。

Chapter Five Control

"You need to get out more," Hadley said, shaking his head. He leaned against the bench cluttered with an assortment of beakers and funnels, accidentally elbowing a flask.

"Tell me about it." Max sighed and wiped the Pepsi up with his shirt-sleeve. It was a dark shirt and Shelby would never know. She hated it when he ruined perfectly good clothes by wearing them in the lab. He figured, what's a few stains? Of course, there were always stories about people spilling chemicals on their clothes and the clothes disintegrating. Chemist legends. Although he did remember an undergraduate at Irvine breaking a bottle of sulfuric acid. A male labmate told the woman that she had to take her clothes off now, but some kindly soul rushed her to the women's where there was a shower. She was sent home in a lab coat, but her frayed, disintegrating clothes (including her bra) somehow ended up pinned to a department bulletin board with the note "See what *you* missed?" Chemistry was one of the last male bastions.

"You stuck?" Hadley picked up a cork ring off of Max's bench and started twirling it around his finger. Hadley was always doing something, clicking his pen in and out, tapping his foot. It could drive Max crazy.

"Nah, it's just what to do with this damn quinazoline. I can't get the protecting group off." Max was trying to make a derivative of Rahda's final product, a slightly different steroid component that could work for alternate inflammations.

"You tried vapping it ... " Hadley said this as a statement because it was the obvious thing to try.

Max answered leisurely. "Yeah, I put it on the rotovap, I tried treating it with sulfuric acid, maybe I'll try vapping it again with a different reagent. I just got the slows today." Max leaned back in his chair and rested his head in his hands. He crossed his feet on top of his desk, trying not to crumple the papers that lay there.

"Did you talk to Rahda? Maybe she has some ideas."

"She hasn't been around all day. I left her a note." All Max could think about right now was food.

"She was here this morning. When did you get in?" Hadley glanced sideways at Max, a faint smile on his lips.

"I don't remember," Max stonewalled. "It was dark." Max reached down, opened his lower desk drawer, and retrieved a magazine.

"你该多出门走走了。"哈德利摇了摇头说道。近处的工作台上面摆满了烧杯和漏斗等各式各样的器皿,哈德利倚过去的时候不小心手肘碰到了一只细颈瓶。

"还用你告诉我。"麦克斯叹了口气,用衬衫袖子擦掉了桌子上的一小摊百事可乐。那件衬衫是深色的,所以谢尔碧不会发现。她最讨厌麦克斯穿着一件毫无瑕疵的好衣服去实验室,回家的时候却已经毁了。麦克斯却觉得,沾一些污点有什么关系呢?当然了,总会有化学试剂被撒到衣服上导致后者分解的事情发生,化学家的传奇故事。麦克斯记得在欧文分校时,曾有一个本科女生打翻过一瓶子的硫酸。同实验室的一个男生告诉她,她得立刻脱掉自己的衣服,但有个"好心人"却催促她进带淋浴的女洗手间里冲洗一下。最后她被用实验服裹着送回了家里,但她那被腐蚀得破烂不堪的衣服(包括文胸)不知怎么被钉在了部门的公告栏上,旁边贴着一张字条:"看看你错过了什么?"化学已经是仅存的为数不多的男性领域之一了。

"你卡在这一步了吗?"哈德利从麦克斯的工作台上拿过一个软木圈,并开始用手指玩转起来。哈德利总是闲不下来,不是将圆珠笔按进按出,就是用脚打拍子。这有时候让麦克斯感到抓狂。

"也不是,只是不知道该拿这该死的井苯丙阿尔法嘧啶怎么办。我想不出办法把保护基团给去掉。"麦克斯当时正在尝试做出拉达的最终产物的衍生物,一种略有不同的能够用于治疗间歇性炎症的类固醇物质。

"你试过将它汽化了……"哈德利用的是陈述的语气,因为这种方法很容易想到。

麦克斯悠闲地答道:"是啊,我把它放进过旋转蒸发仪里,试图用硫酸来与它反应,也许我应该再用一种不同的试剂来汽化试试。我今天状态不太好。"他说着将双手搭在头上,向椅子后面靠去。双脚又翘到了桌子上,但尽量不将那里的一摞纸碰倒。

"你和拉达聊过了吗?没准儿她有什么想法呢。"

"她一整天都不见人影,我给她留了一张字条。"现在麦克斯脑子里唯一的想法就是吃的。

"她今天早上还在呢,你什么时候来的?"哈德利斜眼瞟了一下麦克斯,嘴唇上泛起了一丝笑意。

"不记得了,"麦克斯小心翼翼地回避着,"当时天还没亮。"说着弯下腰去从下面的抽屉里取出一本杂志。

Chapter Five Control

"Well, at least I did something today. I took an NMR. But it doesn't make much sense ... " Hadley paused and looked down at his jeans. He rubbed at a white spot on his pant leg with the edge of the cork ring. Little bits of cork trickled to the floor. Max waited impatiently. Hadley could just lapse into silence in the midst of a sentence. It was like that sleep disorder where a person falls unconscious in the middle of a word. Hadley seemed to forget that he had been talking. Finally Max leaned forward on his chair and the front two legs hit the floor with a thump.

"You gonna tell me or do I gotta guess?" Max felt grumpy that his own research wasn't going so well.

"When I ran a control, the reaction still took place." Hadley paused. "*There wasn't any catalyst.*" Hadley, normally reserved and unemotional, had occasional moments of theatricality. "I don't get it." Hadley sighed. "It shouldn't have worked."

"Why are you running controls? I thought you were scaling up."

"Well I was, but when I took an elemental analysis of the product after I ran the NMR, there was no trace of the catalyst, which I thought was odd. The product and the catalyst should have both been there. So I talked to Scotia, and he said try running scaled up controls and see what happens."

"Hmm. Maybe it doesn't need the catalyst?" Max volunteered, knowing that this was pretty far-fetched, but he couldn't think of anything else because he was hungry and Shelby was late. Max put the magazine in his lap, quickly flipping past the naked women to a page he wanted to show Hadley. Wanting to shock Hadley just a little, he slowed his pace as he neared the center of the magazine.

Oblivious to Max's game, Hadley looked out the window, puzzled. "Well, that's a possibility I guess, but it doesn't agree with any of the other data. The only thing I can figure is that somehow there must be trace amounts of catalyst, enough to make it work, but not enough to show up in the elementals. How is that possible? Where would it come from?"

"A dirty flask?"

Hadley gave him a look of disdain.

"Sorry, I'm just trying to help." Max laughed. Hadley's fanatical cleanliness was a joke in the lab. His bench was a model of organization. Every test tube was racked in perfect alignment. The glassware was ranked by shape and size. It was a vision of

"好吧，至少我今天还做了一些事情，我做了一个核磁共振测试，但是结果好像解释不通……"哈德利停顿了一下，然后低下头去看着自己的牛仔裤。接着他用软木塞的边缘擦刮着裤腿上的一个白色斑点，少许的碎木屑悠悠地飘落到地板上。麦克斯耐心地等待着。哈德利会在话说到一半的时候就突然地陷入沉默，就好像患了睡眠紊乱症的人，正说话的时候就进入了无意识状态。看上去哈德利好像忘记了自己刚才正在说话。麦克斯终于从椅背上倾身起来，两条腿落地的时候伴随着重重砸在地板上的声音。

"你是准备告诉我还是让我自己猜呢？"因为自己的研究进展不是非常顺利，麦克斯的脾气有些暴躁。

"当我进行对照实验的时候，反应仍然是可以进行的。"哈德利顿了一下，"没有加任何的催化剂。"通常情况下哈德利是镇定自如，从不外露感情的，但偶尔会出现像现在这样夸张的表现。"我不明白，"他叹了口气，"本来不应该进行的。"

"你为什么会想起来做对照实验？我还以为你的任务是按比例增加催化剂的用量。"

"对的，本来是这样的，但当我做完核磁共振测试之后对产品进行元素分析时，没有发现催化剂的痕迹，我当时觉得很奇怪。本来产物和催化剂都应该被检测到的。于是我就告诉了斯考蒂亚，他让我试着做不同量级的对照实验，看会发生什么。"

"嗯……也许本来就不需要催化剂？"麦克斯猜测道，虽然知道这种揣测实在是太离谱了，但他想不出其他任何原因了。他现在很饿，再加上谢尔碧又迟到了。麦克斯把杂志放在自己的膝盖上，迅速翻过有裸女的那一页，并找寻着他想给哈德利看的那一页。他想要出其不意，于是在快翻到杂志中间的时候故意放慢了速度。

哈德利完全没有注意到麦克斯的"阴谋"，带着一脸的迷茫看向窗外。"好吧，我想这也是其中一种可能性，但这个猜测与其他任何的数据都不符合。我现在能给出的唯一解释就是，当中肯定还存在一定量的催化剂，足够推动实验进行，但是却达不到元素分析所要求的含量。怎么会这样呢？它到底是从哪来的呢？"

"来自没洗干净的烧瓶？"

哈德利不屑地看了他一眼。

"对不起，我只是想帮忙而已。"麦克斯大笑了起来。哈德利的洁癖在实验室里经常被拿来开玩笑，他的工作台就是一个井井有条的模板。所有的试管都整齐地排成一列，玻璃器皿都按照形状和大小来分类，放眼看去一片和谐井然。

harmony and order. Max often asked Hadley if he ever got anything done or if he just arranged things.

"Did the glassware come straight from the dishwashers?" Max asked, concentrating on Hadley's problem now that he had found the page he was looking for. Hadley shrugged and glanced at the magazine as Max folded back the cover.

"What the hell are you reading?" Hadley asked calmly.

"Oh, Shelby sent this to the lab as a joke." Max pointed to an illustration on the page. "Look at this."

With obvious resignation, Hadley read dryly, "The John Holmes Dick Enlarger."

"Look at the picture!" Max said excitedly.

"It looks like a hand pump."

"It's only twelve dollars! The ones from Aldrich are fifty!"

Hadley narrowed his eyes at Max. "You're gonna buy a dick enlarger to pump your reactions?"

"Just think, I can write in my footnotes, All filtrations were done with the John Holmes Dick Enlarger.'"

Hadley shook his head, laughing despite himself. "Why did Shelby send you that?"

Max held his hands out as if to say, "Go figure." Then he said, "She also sent me a sheep suit."

Hadley waited.

"The two of us have been practicing that song by Sam the Sham and the Pharaohs, you know, 'Little Red Riding Hood'. Shelby's teaching me to sing. She likes the line where he says he's gonna put his sheep suit on."

There was a pause. Then Hadley said, "So did you put it on?"

"Of course not. What are you, nuts?"

"Yeah, *I'm* nuts." Hadley started tossing the cork ring into the air and catching it.

"Shh!" Max said, listening for a moment. "I thought I heard whistling." Then he stuck out his hand and caught the cork ring as it came down. "You wore away one of my initials," Max complained, looking at the edge of the abraded ring. "MC" had been sloppily scrawled in black permanent marker on the edge of the cork

麦克斯经常问哈德利，他是否真的能做出成果，还是所有的时间都花在了整理上面。

"那些玻璃器皿是不是从清洗机里直接取出来的？"麦克斯找到了那一页，于是开始专注在哈德利的问题上。哈德利耸了耸肩，瞥了一眼麦克斯合上的封面。

"你到底在看什么鬼东西？"哈德利语调平静地问道。

"噢，是谢尔碧为了搞笑把这本杂志送到实验室来的。"麦克斯指着页面上的插图，"快看这个。"

哈德利无奈地顺从了，开始干巴巴地读起来："约翰·福尔摩斯牌阳具放大器。"

"看图片！"麦克斯的语气里充满了兴奋。

"看起来像个手动打气筒。"

"只要12美元！阿德里奇牌的要50美元呢！"

哈德利眯起了眼睛瞅着麦克斯，"你准备买一个阳具放大器来辅助你的实验？"

"你想一下，我可以在脚注里这样写：'所有的过滤都由约翰·福尔摩斯牌阳具放大器完成。'"

哈德利摇了摇头，忍不住大笑起来。"谢尔碧为什么要送这个过来？"

麦克斯双手一摊，好像在说："谁知道呢。"他接着说道："她还给我寄来一身绵羊服装。"

哈德利等待着。

"我们两个一直在排练'骗子山姆和法老们'组合的那首歌，你知道的，就是那首《小红帽》。谢尔碧最近正在教我唱，她最喜欢那句要穿上羊皮的歌词。"

又是一阵停顿。然后，哈德利问道："所以呢，你穿上了吗？"

"当然没有了。你是傻子吗？"

"对呀，我就是傻子。"哈德利开始把软木圈扔到空中去，然后再接住。

"嘘！"麦克斯说道，然后侧耳静静听了一小会儿。"我还以为我听到口哨声了。"然后他伸出手去接住了正在往下掉的软木圈。"你把我名字缩写的其中一个字母都给磨掉了。"他看着那个边缘磨损了的木圈，抱怨道。那个木圈的边缘上用粗粗的黑色记号笔潦草地写着"MC"两个字母，但是现在字母"M"的一条腿

Chapter Five Control

ring, but now one leg of the "M" was almost missing.

"You are so possessive." Hadley shook his head. "Why don't you just pee on everything?" Hadley laughed at his own joke.

"If I thought that would keep my cork rings from disappearing, I would," Max said, taking a black marker out of his desk and fixing the "M".

Walking to the door of the lab, Hadley tapped his fingers on the doorjamb briefly. He looked back at Max. "Let me know if you can think of any reasonable explanations."

"If the dishwashers rinse with New York water, who knows what could be on those flasks, probably body parts and whatever else, metals maybe, residue alcohols. They would be minor amounts of course ..." Max trailed off, thinking that the explanation wasn't really good enough. The catalyst wasn't a complex molecule, but it didn't seem likely to be found in the water. In New York, however, who knew? He remembered a report of trace amounts of benzene in the Manhattan water supply.

"I just don't know." Hadley paused and scratched at his perfectly clipped mustache. Shelby had once joked that he must take it off at night so that it wouldn't get mussed. "Maybe I'll do an analysis of the tap water. See what's in there." Hadley started out the door.

"By the way," Max put his cork ring down. "Were we going to rehearse tomorrow?"

Hadley turned around. "I thought that was the plan."

"I didn't know if you were going to go down to Scotia's talk."

"Damn, I forgot that was tomorrow night." Hadley pursed his lips while he thought for a second. "Were you?"

"Nah. He'll probably tell us everything he's gonna say at group meeting. I'd rather play. I *need* to play." Max grinned at Hadley, baring his teeth ape-like, as if the stress was making him crazy.

Hadley just shook his head. The sound of clicking of high heels could suddenly be heard coming down the hallway. Hadley turned his head slightly.

"It's about time!" Max said loudly. "I'm weakened by malnourishment."

Shelby turned the corner, her lips in the expression of mock disgust.

"It's true," Hadley said. "I found him roping a cockroach for dinner."

"Sometimes those are the only dates Max can get," Shelby said dryly.

几乎都看不见了。

"你的占有欲真是太强了,"哈德利摇了摇头,"你怎么不在所有东西上尿尿做记号呢?"哈德利因为自己的笑话而哈哈大笑起来。

"如果我知道这样做可以让我的软木塞不再凭空消失的话,我早就做了。"麦克斯说着从抽屉里取出一只黑色记号笔,开始修补那个"M"。

哈德利向门口走去,手指在门框上短促地敲了几下,又回头望向麦克斯,"你要是想出任何合理的解释,就告诉我一声。"

"如果清洗机用的是纽约市的水,谁知道烧瓶上会留下什么呢。很有可能是部分尸体残余和其他一些乱七八糟的东西,也许是金属、酒精残留。当然了它们的比重都是很小的……"麦克斯声音慢慢小了下去,因为他开始觉得这个理由站不住脚。这个实验所需的催化剂并不是一种很复杂的分子,但也不像是能在水里找到的物质。可在纽约这样一个城市,谁知道呢? 他还记得自己看过一篇文章,里面报道了在曼哈顿的饮用水源里发现微量苯的事情。

"我就是搞不明白。"哈德利顿了一下,挠了挠他那修剪得近乎完美的胡子。有一次,谢尔碧开玩笑说他到了晚上得把胡子给摘下来才不会弄乱。"也许我应该给自来水做一下分析实验,看看里面都有什么。"哈德利开始向门外走去。

"对了,"麦克斯放下了手里的软木圈,"乐队明天要排练吗?"

哈德利转过身来,"我以为早就定好了的呢。"

"我并不知道你要不要去听斯考蒂亚的演讲。"

"该死,我忘了演讲是在明天晚上了,"哈德利噘了噘嘴,想了几秒钟,"你要去吗?"

"我才不去呢,他无非就是把要在组会上说的话先说一遍。我宁愿排练。我需要去排练。"麦克斯咧开嘴笑了。他的牙齿龇得像猿猴一样,似乎是被压力给逼疯了。

哈德利只是摇了摇头。突然间有高跟鞋"咔嗒咔嗒"的声音从走廊上传来,他微微地转过头去。

"是时候了!"麦克斯大声说道,"我都因为营养不良而虚弱不堪了。"

谢尔碧出现在转角处,嘴唇上显现出伪装出来的厌恶之情。

"是真的,"哈德利说,"我刚才撞见他抓蟑螂来做晚餐。"

"有时候麦克斯也就只能和小强约会了。"谢尔碧干巴巴地回复道。

Chapter Five Control

"Ba-dum-*ba*," Max said, imitating a rim shot on his desk. "And here you are," he said, gesturing to Shelby as if presenting her. Shelby just shook her head and then gave Max two sideways pecks on the lips, first twisting her lips to the left and kissing the right side of his mouth, and then reversing it. Originally he had liked to kiss her that way because then he didn't get her lipstick on his mouth. Now it had become ritual. Shelby told him that they kissed the way jive people shook hands.

"What took you so long?" Max asked, standing up and stretching his legs.

"I've never seen such a drunken office party. One man lifted me in the air and yelled, 'I caught me a Wonder Woman!' over and over again. I had to pinch him hard on his arm several times before he put me down."

"Oh those super powers," Hadley said.

Shelby ignored him. "Anyway, they gave me an extra large tip."

"Well let's go spend it," Max said, putting his arm around her. "Pizza?" Max looked inquiringly at Hadley.

"I should probably run a couple more reactions," Hadley started to hedge.

"Oh, come on! Go with us," Shelby said, almost exasperated. "You just want to be begged. Here, you can bring your magazine with you," she said, throwing it at him.

"I think I'll stay here," Hadley said, looking at the ground.

"Suit yourself," Shelby said flippantly.

"啪——咚——啪",麦克斯在桌上模仿着架子鼓鼓边敲击的节奏。"你终于来了。"他双臂迎向谢尔碧,就好像在介绍她出场一样。谢尔碧只是摇摇头,并在麦克斯嘴唇两边轻轻啄了两下,先是向左面撅起嘴亲了他的右嘴角,然后换一个方向。最开始的时候麦克斯喜欢这样,因为如此一来他就不会满嘴都是谢尔碧的口红了。现在这已经变成了他们之间的一种例行公事。谢尔碧对他说,这种亲吻就像嬉皮士们用拳头问好的方式一样。

"你怎么这么久才来?"麦克斯站起身来,舒展了一下双腿。

"我从来没有见过喝得这么烂醉的办公室派对。有个男的把我举到半空中,还一遍又一遍地大叫着'我给自己抓了个神奇女侠!'直到我用力地掐了几下他的胳膊他才把我给放下来。"

"噢,有些人可是有超能力的。"哈德利评价道。

谢尔碧没有搭理他。"无论如何,他们最后给了我一笔特别多的小费。"

"那么,让我们现在去把它给花了吧。"麦克斯说着用双臂环住了谢尔碧。"比萨?"他用询问的眼神看向哈德利。

"我最好再多做几个实验。"哈德利开始闪烁其词。

"噢,来吧,和我们一起去吧。"谢尔碧的口气几乎有些恼怒了,"你就喜欢别人求你。来,你可以把你的杂志给带上。"她顺手就给扔了过去。

"我觉得我还是留下来吧。"哈德利盯着地面说道。

"随你便。"谢尔碧满不在乎地回道。

Chapter Six Bonding

> Bonding: The bond is not a physical "thing" such as a rod or spring; rather, it represents an attraction between species.
>
> Study Guide to Chem One

Hadley was adjusting his drums in the far corner of Max and Shelby's enormous living room. Because of the vastness of space, a rarity in New York, it seemed like the furniture was camping out by the TV, huddled close for warmth. In fact, Max often joked that when the TV was on, the room felt a lot hotter. He used this as a reason for never turning off the television. Even when he wasn't watching it—when all the lights were out and he was going to bed—he would turn the sound down but leave the picture, bathing the room in flickering images that danced along the furniture, reflecting a postmodern flame. During Christmas Max discovered a station that featured a twenty-four-hour telecast of a crackling fire. Even if you had no fireplace in your apartment—and who did in New York?—you could still enjoy a warm moment of Christmas cheer there tuned in to the Yule log. Max used this as proof of his theory: everyone found a lit TV to be more homey.

Hadley didn't share Max's love of television. He hated trying to carry on a conversation while the TV was on. Against his will his eyes would gravitate toward the set, the animation of the screen more enticing than real life. It was moth-like behavior, being seduced by the sparkle of light and the promise of entertainment. Television permeated an environment like the stale smell of cigarette smoke, constantly reminding one of the addicted.

As Hadley unzipped his black drum bags and took out his tom-toms, he thought about Max's latest addiction: Channel J. Max said that Bineet had told him about Channel J, which surprised Hadley. Bineet seemed too refined to watch sex videos. "It comes with regular Manhattan cable!" Max would yell at parties, waving his hands in that flat, cartoon-character way he had. "Fourteen dollars a month and it's

第六章　联结

> 联结：并不是指物理上的"实体"如木棒或弹簧等，而是代表着物种之间的吸引力。
>
> ——《化学学习指南一》

在麦克斯和谢尔碧宽敞无比的起居室里，哈德利远远地在一个角落里调节着自己的架子鼓。这么宽敞的空间在纽约很少见，它使所有的家具看上去就像在电视机的周围开展野营，互相依偎在一起取暖。麦克斯经常开玩笑说，当电视机打开的时候，整个房间里面都感觉暖和一些了，他把这个作为永远不关电视的借口。即使不看——当所有灯都熄灭了，而自己也要上床睡觉的时候——他也要把音量调小，让屏幕仍然亮着。闪烁的画面在家具上摇曳起舞，反射着后现代风格的光芒，整个房间都沐浴其中。圣诞节的时候，麦克斯发现了一个电视节目，24小时不间断播放篝火噼啪作响的场景。这样一来，即使你的公寓里没有壁炉——在纽约能有几个人拥有呢？——你还是可以在大块木柴燃烧的声响中享受圣诞节的温暖瞬间。麦克斯以此来证明自己的理论：每个人都觉得亮着的电视更有家的感觉。

哈德利并不像麦克斯那样对电视情有独钟，他讨厌在电视开着的时候聊天那种费力的感觉。但他的眼睛却会违背他的意愿，视线总是被电视机给牵引过去——屏幕上的多姿多彩要比现实生活诱人多了。这种行为就像是飞蛾扑火，都是受到光亮的火花和潜在的快乐所诱惑。电视就像香烟烟雾的陈腐气味，渗透进周围环境中，不停提醒着人们"瘾君子"的存在。

哈德利拉开黑色鼓包的拉链，取出自己的长鼓来，他的脑海里想着麦克斯最近的新癖好：J频道。麦克斯说是贝内特把频道J介绍给自己的，这使哈德利有些吃惊。贝内特看上去非常有涵养，不像是会看成人视频的人。"普通的曼哈顿有线网就能收到！"有时麦克斯会在派对上这样大叫，并且用他那特有的卡通人物风格的方式在一个平面内挥舞自己的双手。"一个月14美元，而且和儿童

Chapter Six Bonding

on the same channel as Nickelodeon!" This had amazed Hadley as well. Perhaps children were just that much more sophisticated in New York.

Al Goldstein, the publisher of *Screw* magazine, had a show on Channel J called "Midnight Blue". Legally they could show anything on "Midnight Blue" except the heterosexual point of insertion. This juncture would be covered up by a blue dot, expanding as the camera zoomed in. Because the law was made before homosexuality was in the public conscience, for a short time gay sex could be shown in its entirety, with nothing disturbing the view. New York is so strange, Hadley thought, shaking his head and tightening the pivot on a jointed cymbal stand.

Hadley assembled his tom-toms, screwing them to the metal support that rose above the bass drum. He had taken them downtown to get new drumheads. He wanted to see if it was worth the forty-eight dollars they charged him. He took a drumstick and started tapping the right tom, turning one of the pitch keys. Lately he'd had to really crank the key to get the pitch high enough. It reminded him of high school. Nothing would tighten on his school's drum set because over the years the threads had all been stripped. So many average drummers had passed their time there, wearing out the drums by their inexperience. He'd grown up in the Midwest and moved with his family to California in his senior year of high school. California had opened his eyes for sure. But nothing had prepared him for New York. It shocked him. And yet he loved it here. It made him feel erudite rather than just nerdy. He could sit in Washington Square for hours, entertained by the locals, the fire-eaters and unicyclists, the marimba players, the androgyny, the psychedelic profusion of clothing and hairstyles and tattoos. Things were just more interesting here, and once you'd been exposed, how could you go back to mediocrity?

Of course, that didn't mean that he wanted to watch Channel J all the time like Max and Shelby did. They were even talking about recording it and mailing it to friends! Performance art they said. Proof that New York was crazy. And it was. There was the old woman, sixty at least, who demonstrated how to give head on a variety of dildos. There was the S & M club, Hellfire, where a guy who looked like Mister Rogers was dragged around by his balls by a woman he called "Mistress Supreme". And then there was Al Goldstein himself who would drive around in a limo, find a guy who had just let his dog defecate on the sidewalk, and then point a rifle at the guy, forcing him to eat the shit. Of course, as Max said, a lot of this was

点歌机是在同一个频道!"这一点也让哈德利感到不可置信。但也许纽约的孩子们就是比一般孩子更成熟世故一些吧。

阿尔·古德斯坦,《性交》杂志的出版商,他在J频道上有一个叫《午夜之蓝》的节目。从法律角度来说,除了男女交媾时的关键部位不能够出现在荧屏上以外,他们想播放什么都行。禁播镜头会打上蓝色的马赛克,当视角渐近时,色块也会随之变大。在制定有关法律的时候,同性恋还没有出现在公众视野里,因此有那么一小段时间内,同性的性交过程可以毫无遮挡地完整播放出来。哈德利拧紧铙钹支架上的旋钮,摇着头心想道,纽约这个地方真是太怪异了。

哈德利拼装起了长鼓,并用螺丝将其拧紧在大鼓的金属支架上。先前他到市中心给长鼓换上了新的鼓皮,现在想看看到底值不值那四十八美金。取过一只鼓槌,他一边在右鼓上轻轻敲打着,一边调整着音调旋钮。最近,他非得使劲儿扭转调音器才能使音调足够高。这使他想起了高中的时光,学校里的那套架子鼓没有一个部位能够调紧,因为日复一日的磨损已经使许多线都崩脱了。有那么多平庸的鼓手曾在那里消磨过时间,他们的经验匮乏也加重了鼓的磨损程度。哈德利在美国中西部长大,高二的时候随着家人搬到了加州。毫无疑问,加州使那时候的他大开了眼界,但即使是那里的一切也并没有让他对纽约做好必要的心理准备。纽约常常让他感到震惊无比,但他还是爱上了这座城市。在这儿他觉得自己是一个满腹学问的人,而不仅仅是一个书呆子。他可以在华盛顿广场坐上好几个小时,当地人的表演从来不会让他感到无聊:吞火球的人,骑独轮车的人,双性人,以及穿着各式服装、发型迥异、有着个性文身的人,他们共同营造了一种魔幻的氛围。总之,这里的一切都更加有趣,而一旦你有了这种体验,你要如何再回到平淡无奇的生活中去呢?

当然咯,这也不意味着他像麦克斯和谢尔碧一样,总是一直想看J频道的节目。他们甚至还打算把它给录下来然后邮寄给其他朋友看!他们说,这是表演艺术。这足以证明纽约疯了,彻底疯了。有一期节目中,一个至少60岁的老妇人用各式各样的人造阴茎示范如何口交。另一次是在一个名叫炼狱之火的S&M(施虐者与受虐者)酒吧里,一个长得很像密斯特·罗杰的家伙被一个他称作"霸道情人"的女人扯着睾丸到处跑。再有就是阿尔·古德斯汀本人开着房车四处转,当他发现有个人让自己的狗在人行道上大便时,他就用来复枪指向那个人,强迫他把狗屎给吃掉。当然了,就像麦克斯说的,当中有很多都是演出来

Chapter Six Bonding

staged. Like that made it acceptable.

Now that he'd thought about it, Hadley couldn't get that one advertisement out of his head, the one Max loved to imitate. "Hi. I'm Steve. I'm six-four and well-hung. I cater to men, women, and couples." The guy would announce this while standing there in his underwear in front of a blue backdrop. It disturbed Hadley, but the commercial had a catchy rhythm to it. Hadley found himself tapping it out. Disturbed, Hadley bent down to adjust the bass drum pedal slightly and then pressed the pedal several times, checking the fit of the beater against the drum. The soft, fuzzy, mallet beat a low booming noise out of the bass drum. It was pleasantly loud, a sound you could depend on. The stability of the band.

Hadley thought about the last time they'd played. It was at a grad student hangout across the street from the campus. Some guy had come up to him in the bathroom and said, "Hey. You guys don't suck." It made him laugh now as it had then. He remembered telling the rest of the band afterwards, when they were all sitting around Max and Shelby's living room. Shelby had said, "That's better than this guy saying to me, 'It's nice to see a chick in the band.'" They now referred to her as "the chick" because it both bugged and flattered her. Hadley realized that the band filled out his life. It was something he was good at without effort. The only cool thing he'd ever done. He laughed again because it was so true, and continued beating the bass drum.

The living room ceiling was so high that the sound spread, like an exterior heartbeat pulsing throughout the room. Hadley absent-mindedly glanced at the television while listening to the beat. A dog was chasing a tiny wagon train. Then two little kids were eating cereal. Hadley jerked his head away, irritated that he'd succumbed for even a minute. He was suddenly reminded of chickens, the brainless way you could hypnotize them. All you had to do was draw a line in front of their eyes, you could even use your finger, and they would freeze, mesmerized by trying to watch your finger with opposing eyes. It would also work if you laid them on their backs, handy if you were planning dinner. A friend who was in 4-H had shown him this back when he lived in North Dakota. The guy said if you hypnotize turkeys and then leave them like that, they would die. Turkeys were that stupid. Hadley wondered what would happen if you put a turkey in front of a television.

"Ow." Shelby walked into the living room looking cross. "Every fucking thing

的。好像这样一来这一切就能够被接受了一样。

想到这里,有一个广告在哈德利的脑子里总是挥之不去,麦克斯总爱模仿的那个:"你好!我是史蒂夫。身高六尺四,那活儿大如牛。男人女人通吃,单身已婚皆宜。"那个家伙站在蓝色的背景前面,浑身只穿了一条内裤,大声地说出这些台词。哈德利被搅得心神不宁,但是这个广告的韵律朗朗上口,他甚至发现自己在不自觉地跟着打节拍。他觉得自己的思绪受到了扰乱,于是就弯下腰去轻轻调了调大鼓的踏板,并向下压了几下,测试击打的力度是否合适。又软又毛茸茸的鼓槌敲击出一声低低的轰鸣,震耳却令人愉悦,这是一种使人依赖的声音,维持着整个乐队的稳定性。

哈德利想起了他们上一次演出时候的情景,那是在校园对面一个研究生们经常聚会的地方。在洗手间里,有个家伙走到他面前说:"嘿,你们的表演没有很烂!"现在回想起来,哈德利还是像当时一样哈哈大笑起来。他记得后来把这件事情告诉了大伙儿,当时大家都坐在谢尔碧和麦克斯家的客厅里。谢尔碧说:"这比那个家伙走到我面前跟我说'能在乐队里看到个小妞真不错'要好多了。"他们现在都叫谢尔碧"小妞",因为这对她既是一种挑逗又是一种恭维。哈德利意识到,乐队使他的生活更加完整了,这件事他不用付出很多努力,就可以做得很好,也是他做过的唯一一件最酷的事情。真是太对了。他又开始大笑起来,继续打起了鼓。

客厅的天花板非常高,以至于那声音像漏出来的心跳声一般回荡在屋子里。哈德利一边听着节拍,一边漫不经心地瞥几眼电视。电视上一条狗正追着玩具小火车跑,两个小孩子在一旁吃着燕麦片。他立刻就将头转向了一边——即使是只向电视屈服了一分钟也使他感到生气。他突然想起,鸡会被一种非常愚蠢的方法给催眠。你需要做的就是在它的眼前画一条线;你甚至可以用手指头来画,它都会定在原地,因为它会试图用自己的斗眼同时看你的手指头,然后就会被迷惑住了。如果你将它背朝地放着的话也会产生同样的效果,你要是正准备做晚饭的话这样就很方便。过去哈德利住在北达科他州的时候,一个在 4 - H [译者注:帮助孩子圈养动物或了解其他农场活动的学校或组织]里的朋友曾经给哈德利展示过。那个朋友说如果你把火鸡催眠了之后,就那样放着然后自己离开的话,它们就会死掉。火鸡竟然笨到了这样一种程度。哈德利想知道,要是把火鸡放在电视机前会发生什么。

"哎呀!"谢尔碧走进了客厅,一脸的怒气。"每一件该死的事都不顺心。"她

shocks me." She reached out to turn on her keyboard and was shocked again, the air charged with electricity. She started playing the chords to "Dead Flowers", confusing the verse with the chorus and starting over again. Suddenly the keyboard stopped working. There was nothing but the soft click of the keys as they touched the padded insides. Mystified, she squinted and flicked the power switch off and on.

"Could you plug this in somewhere else?" Hadley held the nine-volt adapter out to her. It had been connected to the wall socket near his drums and every time he turned to adjust his cymbals his arm hit the cord.

"Sure." She walked over to his drum set and he handed her the heavy plug. She looked at him quizzically. "Are you in a pissy mood?"

"Why do you always ask me that?"

"Because it always seems like you are," she said, bugging her eyes out at him.

Hadley bent down to fish around in his drum bag for his cow bell. Finding it, he looked back at Shelby. "I don't understand."

"'Could you plug this in somewhere else?'" Shelby said, snotty, like a little kid imitating a grown-up.

Hadley tried to look apologetic. "It was in my way."

Shelby plugged the connector into a different wall socket and started to play again.

Hadley was practicing a drum fill. The sound penetrated the room explosively, thick and fulfilling, like a roomful of people crumpling newspaper and eating Saltines. Suddenly Hadley stopped playing, the drop in sound unnerving, like the freefall of an elevator. He asked, "Where's Max?"

"Oh, out foraging for dinner. You know, one of those hunter/gatherer things."

Not knowing how to respond, Hadley hit his cowbell a few times, then played a ska rhythm, fitting the cowbell in on an offbeat. He searched in his mind for something to say that would soften his earlier bluntness. He didn't think of himself as abrupt; he just didn't like to waste energy. Manners were fine with people you didn't know, but among friends they seemed excessive and time-consuming. Of course that left more time for conversation, but he was at a loss as to what he should say. He wondered if continuing to play seemed really rude. He didn't mean it that way, it was just something he knew how to do. He was a better drummer than he was conversationalist. Feeling more tense, he finally he asked, somewhat lamely, "So,

伸手打开电子琴开关,又被电了一下,因为空气中有微弱的电量。接着她就弹起了《死亡之花》的和弦,但是却把独奏与和声部分的旋律搞混了,于是又从头开始。但是键盘突然就失灵了,只剩下琴键按下去摩擦内垫时轻柔的声音。谢尔碧摸不着头脑,也斜着眼睛,不停地开关着电源按钮。

"你不能把它插到其他地方吗?"哈德利把那个 9 伏的转换器递给她。它一直都插在墙上的插孔里,而哈德利的鼓就在旁边,所以他每次转身调整铙钹时胳膊都会碰到接线。

"好的。"谢尔碧走到鼓架旁,接过那个沉沉的插座,有些揶揄地看着他。"你是不是心情不爽?"

"你为什么总是问我这个问题?"

"因为你看上去总是这样的。"她对着他翻了个白眼。

哈德利弯下腰去在鼓包里摸索了一圈,找到了想要的牛铃,又转过身去看着谢尔碧,"我不明白。"

"'你不能把它插到其他地方吗?'"谢尔碧拿腔拿调地说道,就像是小孩子在模仿大人的样子。

哈德利努力做出抱歉的表情,"它碍着我的事了。"

谢尔碧把连接器插到另一面墙上的插孔里,又重新开始了演奏。

哈德利正在练习鼓花。那爆炸式的声音穿透了整个房间,厚重地填满每个角落,就像是满屋子的人在折报纸和吃咸饼干。突然间,他就停下了,声音的骤降搅得人心神不宁,感觉就像是电梯在做自由落体运动。"麦克斯在哪?"

"哦,他出去张罗晚饭了。你知道的,就是打猎采摘那一档子事。"

哈德利一时不知道怎么回答,便敲了几下牛铃,然后演奏了一个 ska 旋律[译者注:20 世纪 50 年代起源于牙买加的一种音乐风格],在弱拍的地方敲击牛铃。他搜肠刮肚地想说些什么,来缓和自己之前太过直接而引起的尴尬气氛。其实他并不觉得自己的行为很唐突,只是不想浪费精力而已。对你不熟识的人礼貌也许有必要,但在朋友之间就显得有些多余而浪费时间了。当然了,这样一来就省下更多的时间来聊天,但现在他却满心茫然不知该说什么了。他有些困惑,不知道如果自己继续演奏的话会不会显得很没有礼貌。这并不是他的本意,但这是他唯一知道该怎么做的事情。与和人聊天相比,他更擅长做个好鼓手。随着房间里的紧张感逐渐增加,他最终开口了,问得有些蹩脚:"那么,今天你做

Chapter Six Bonding

did you deliver any telegrams today?"

"Five. From ten until four-thirty. I had to go all the way to Queens. And I only get five dollars more for travel time. But they had the cutest little baby there at this one office. The mom was breastfeeding it—"

"She was breastfeeding while you were doing a telegram?" Hadley's eyes opened wide and his voice cracked. "In an office."

"Well, she was discrete. I didn't notice her until afterward." Shelby paused, then looked intently at Hadley. "Why? What's wrong with that?"

"It just seems a little odd, that's all." He bent down to his bass drum.

"You'll probably banish your wife to the bathroom." Shelby sat on her piano stool, planting herself, looking ready for battle.

Hadley rolled his eyes. "I should be talking to you about pissy moods."

"I'm just tired of everyone thinking that there's something obscene about breastfeeding."

"Now who says that?" Hadley asked indignantly.

"Oh, Max, and these friends that came over. They didn't even think that a woman should do it in the living room if there were guests. It's like, why should I be sent to the bedroom simply because I had a child?"

"It's your house. You can do what you want." He didn't understand her sometimes, even though they'd known each other for years, though often at a distance. Pen pals more than intimates. Shelby was large in her letters, but larger in life. She overwhelmed Hadley, who philosophically exhausted easily, preferring music, or reading, or hiking in the woods. Talk, like manners, was also a timewaster. And yet, he felt something when he talked to Shelby, a kind of energy. She was an inflamer, an event. She got people worked up. And partly because she wanted to know what you thought. She would draw you out, gathering your stories together like strands of twine, then helping you retell them to others, knotting them together in a web of cause and effect.

Perplexed by Shelby's mood, Hadley incautiously asked, "Does Max control you that much?"

"No," she said petulantly. "I just want everyone to have my opinions."

Hadley laughed and she smiled sheepishly at him. "This wasn't even what I wanted to say. I wanted to tell you about the baby. See, I was watching it, and at

唱歌电报了吗?"

"做了五个。从早上十点到下午四点半。最远的一个我还得大老远地跑到皇后大街,却只得到五美元的路费补贴。但是在那间办公室里有一个超级可爱的小宝宝,他妈妈当时正在给他喂奶——"

"她在你做唱歌电报的时候给孩子喂奶?"哈德利的眼睛瞪得老大,声音都变了,"在办公室里?"

"但是她做得很低调,我直到后来才注意到她。"谢尔碧顿了一下,目不转睛地盯着哈德利。"怎么了? 这有什么问题吗?"

"只是有点奇怪,就这样。"他向着大鼓俯身下去。

"换作是你的话,你八成会把老婆打发到卧室里去。"谢尔碧一屁股坐在钢琴凳上,调稳坐姿,一幅准备"战斗"的架势。

哈德利向上翻了翻眼皮,"现在是我应该跟你聊'心情不爽'这个话题了吧。"

"我只是厌倦了每个人都觉得喂奶是一件很见不得人的事情。"

"谁说过那样的话了?"哈德利愤愤地问道。

"哦,麦克斯,还有上门来的这些朋友都这样觉得。他们甚至认为如果有客人的话,女人不应该在客厅里面喂奶。我就不明白,为什么因为我有个孩子我就得被打发到卧室里去?"

"这是你家,你想做什么就做什么。"他们已经相识很多年了——尽管是有距离的相处,有时候哈德利还是搞不懂她。与其说是亲密挚交,他们作为笔友的关系则更为融洽。谢尔碧在写作方面很擅长,在生活方面更强势,让哈德利喘不过气来。哈德利一卷入哲学范畴的思辨就很容易疲倦,因此他更偏爱音乐,或是阅读,或是在森林里漫步。他觉得,聊天和礼节一样,都是一种时间的浪费。但是,当他和谢尔碧说话的时候,能够感觉到一些不一样的东西,一种能量。她能点燃气氛,引起事端,使人激动起来。一部分原因是,她想要知道你在想什么,她会先引导你讲出自己的故事,将它们像麻线团一样卷到一起,然后帮助你重新复述给别人听,以便将其织成一张由因果关系构成的网。

哈德利对谢尔碧的心情变化感到有些不知所措,随口问道:"麦克斯管你这么多吗?"

"不,"她任性地答道,"我只是想让所有人都知道我的观点。"

哈德利大笑了起来,谢尔碧也不好意思地对着他笑了。"这根本不是我想说的事,我本来是想告诉你关于那个宝宝的事情的。当我盯着他看时,他叼着乳

one point, it'd lost the nipple but its mouth kept sucking and it was making these little cooing sounds, like 'mm' 'mma', and suddenly I realized that's where the word 'mama' comes from, from babies making the sound of nursing. I'll bet every language has an 'm' word for mother."

"I guess that makes sense," Hadley said hesitantly. It seemed obvious now that she said it, but it had never occurred to him before.

"And then I realized that's where all these other words come from: *mammal*, *mammary* ... " Shelby stopped, unable to think of any others.

"Hmm." Hadley's voice was muffled by the bass drum as he bent down once more to adjust the pillow.

A moment of silence went by, then Shelby started playing the chords to "Dead Flowers" again.

Sitting back up and beating the bass drum loudly, making up for his inattention, Hadley said, "You know, there are mammals that don't have breasts—or teats rather." He looked down at his drums, fumbling with his sticks.

Shelby stopped playing. Looking suspicious at his sudden offer of conversation. "How is that possible?"

"They're monotremes. The platypus for example. They lay eggs, but they nurse their young."

"With what!" She asked scoffingly, then walked over and sat on the back of the sofa.

Hadley looked up at her. "Lactating patches."

Shelby glanced sideways at him and they broke out laughing. It was a freeing moment, cracking the ice, letting them fall beyond their glacial mannerisms and standoffish behavior.

"You're making this up!" Goofy with laughter, Shelby fell backwards onto the sofa cushions, her legs over the back of the sofa, her head hanging toward the floor. Hadley knew that Max constantly warned her that one of these days she was going to hit her head on the coffee table, so he noticed that now she did it when Max wasn't there.

"I'm not," Hadley said earnestly. He stood up and stretched his legs, then walked across the room to where the floor-to-ceiling windows looked toward the spire of bedrock outside, in the near-dark, a building of no one home. The window

头的嘴突然松掉了,但是他的嘴巴还是继续保持吸奶的状态,结果就发出这种低低的声音,就像'么么''嗯妈',那个瞬间我意识到这就是"妈妈"这个词的来源——婴儿吃奶的时候发出的声音。我打赌所有语言中的妈妈这个词都包含'm'的音。"

"我想或许有点道理。"哈德利有些犹豫地说。现在看来,经过谢尔碧这么一说,他觉得联系非常明显,可是之前他从来都没有这么想过。

"接着我又想到,这也是其他词,比如 mammal(哺乳动物),mammary(乳腺的)的来源……"

"唔……"哈德利又弯下腰去调整大鼓的轴架,他的声音被鼓声给遮盖住了。

有那么一会儿,谁都没有说话,然后谢尔碧又接着开始演奏"死亡之花"的旋律了。

哈德利也坐下开始敲起了鼓,为了弥补先前没有搭话的不重视,他说道:"你知道吗,有些哺乳动物是没有乳房的,或者说没有乳头。"接着他低下头看向自己的鼓,不经意地摆弄着手里的鼓槌。

谢尔碧停下演奏,怀疑地看着突然主动挑起对话的哈德利。"这怎么可能呢?"

"它们被统称为单孔类动物,比如说,鸭嘴兽。它们通过产卵来繁衍后代,但是会给幼仔进行哺乳。"

"用什么喂呢?"谢尔碧带着嘲讽的语气说道,接着走过去坐在沙发背上。

哈德利抬起头看着她,"乳袋。"

谢尔碧斜眼瞥了他一下,两人便爆发出一阵大笑声。那一瞬间,所有冰冷的态度和僵持都不复存在了,束缚被打破,隔阂也消失了。

"你肯定在瞎编!"谢尔碧吃吃地笑着,身体向后倒在沙发的坐垫上,两条腿翘在沙发背上,脑袋垂下来,向着门口的方向。哈德利知道,麦克斯经常警告她,这样下去总有一天头会撞到茶几上的,所以他注意到现在谢尔碧都是趁麦克斯不在的时候才会这样做。

"我没有。"哈德利认真地说,紧接着他站了起来,舒展了一下双腿,然后穿过房间向落地窗走去。他看着窗外巨石的尖顶部位,在渐临的夜色中,它就像一栋无人归家的大楼。窗户上的阴影使外面的景色变得有些朦胧,那石块看起来

Chapter Six Bonding

shades confused the view, creating the effect of a giant bar graph, the dark outside rising and falling. Turning, Hadley's knee grazed the wall-length window seat, and he sat down. "I just read an article about it in *Science*. It was about the echidna, a spiny anteater related to the platypus."

Shelby looked at Hadley upside down. "You look like Clutch Cargo this way. Say something else." Hadley remained silent. Shelby inched her body forward until her head almost touched the floor. "What did you call them? Mono—what?"

"Monotremes. One hole."

"Ohhhh ..." Shelby drew out, and then wrinkled her brow. "I've seen that word recently."

Hadley laughed. "I know where. Someone renamed Scotia's secretary's computer 'Monotreme' because it only has one disk drive. I wish I'd thought of that. I don't think she knows how to rename it."

Shelby laughed. Hadley played with one of the little curtain pulls tied to the wallpaper shades, a miniature clay armchair that Shelby had made last year. He accidentally pulled too hard and the window shade shot up at sixty miles an hour. "Sorry," he said.

"It's okay, you just need to climb up and get it."

Hadley looked at her pointedly. The bottom of the shade was now a good ten feet away. "Isn't that giving you a head-ache?" He watched her slide closer to the floor.

"Not as much as if I were standing on my head," she answered nonsensically.

Hadley looked puzzled for a moment, then turned to the window.

"Have you ever had sushi?"

"Yeah, it's okay." Hadley was used to her non-sequiturs. They were a part of Shelby. In a way he liked them because you never had to worry about awkward silences. She always filled them up. "I prefer cooked fish."

"See, that's so weird because all my life I never liked cooked fish, and then, after having sushi, I discovered how fish was meant to be eaten. Fish at fish temperature."

"What?"

"You know, fish are cold-blooded, you should eat them cold. Cows are warm-blooded, you eat them warm."

就像一个巨大的柱状图,而四周昏暗的夜色起伏不定。哈德利转了个身,膝盖擦过与墙同宽的窗台,坐了下去。"我最近刚在《科学》杂志里读到一篇相关的文章,是关于针鼹的,它是一种和鸭嘴兽有关系的多刺食蚁兽。"

谢尔碧从颠倒的视角看着哈德利,"倒着看,你很像柯腊池·卡勾。说点儿别的吧。"哈德利保持着沉默。谢尔碧一点一点地将自己的身体向前移,直到她的头几乎碰到了地面为止。"它们被称作什么来着?单——什么?"

"单孔动物,一个孔。"

"噢⋯⋯"谢尔碧拖长着声音,皱了皱眉头,"我最近在哪见过这个词。"

哈德利大笑了一声,"我知道在哪:有人给斯考蒂亚秘书的电脑重新起了个名字——'单孔动物',因为它只有一个硬盘驱动器。我怎么就没想到呢。我敢肯定她自己是想不出这个名字的。"

谢尔碧扑哧一声笑了。哈德利摆弄着系在窗帘百叶上的拉手,那是一个谢尔碧去年做的迷你陶瓷椅子。他不小心拉得重了一些,百叶纸便以每小时六英里的速度向上弹去。"对不起。"他说。

"没关系,只要你爬上去把它给拉下来就可以了。"

哈德利讽刺地看着她——现在那窗帘纸足有十英尺高。他看着谢尔碧又向地板滑了一点,问道:"你那样不会头痛吗?"

"没有我站在自己的头上的时候痛。"她胡言乱语道。

一瞬间他的表情显得很困惑,随即又转向了窗户。

"你吃过寿司吗?"

"吃过,还可以。"他已经习惯了谢尔碧的逻辑混乱了,这就是她这个人的一部分。他甚至还有点喜欢这点,因为这样一来你就用不着担心会陷入尴尬的沉默了——谢尔碧会把它们都填满的。"但我更喜欢吃煮熟了的鱼。"

"你看,这真是奇怪,因为我从来都不喜欢吃煮熟了的鱼,然后在试过寿司之后,我终于知道了吃鱼的真正方法——在鱼的正常体温下吃掉它们。"

"你说什么?"

"你知道的,鱼是冷血动物,你就应该冷着吃,牛的血是热的,所以牛肉就得煮熟了吃。"

Hadley just stared at her.

"What's wrong?" She tilted her head, accidentally hitting the floor.

"I've never heard anyone put it that way."

"Maybe you hang out with really stupid people."

"I'd be careful if I were you." Hadley smiled at her, raising his eyebrows.

She was speechless for a moment. There was some satisfaction in that. He'd rarely seen Shelby without something to say.

She asked abruptly, "So, did you discover anything today?"

He knew this was a standard question she always asked Max. She constantly complained that they were doing all that research, they should be discovering *something*.

Hadley thought. "Let's see. I discovered that you don't answer a ringing pay phone." He laughed.

"Why?"

"You know that pay phone down on the corner there?" He pointed in the general direction.

"The one across the street?"

"Right. I answered it and the guy asked if Tom was there. I said, 'This is a pay phone' and he said, 'I know. Could you just look down the block and see if Tom is anywhere around?' So I walked down to—"

"No way!" Shelby yelled, laughing and almost sliding off the sofa. "You actually looked for the guy?"

Hadley said nothing.

"Sorry, sorry." Shelby paused. "Jesus, you're so touchy," she said, still laughing. "You knew that Tom didn't really exist, right?"

"Okay, I'm gullible. What do you want from me? So I came back and told him that there wasn't anyone around and then he asked if *I* was interested in coming up for a drink." Hadley's voice cracked just slightly.

Shelby gave a deep throaty laugh. "So did you?"

"I gave him your guys' number," Hadley said.

"Yeah, right."

Hadley stood up, stretched, and walked back toward his drums. "Oh, by the way." He was working at sounding offhand. "I heard you hit somebody." A smile twisted the corners of his lips.

哈德利就那样盯着她看。

"有什么问题吗?"谢尔碧撇过头去,不小心碰到了地板。

"我从来没听别人这样说过。"

"也许是因为你总是和笨蛋在一起玩儿。"

"如果我是你的话,我就会小心一点。"哈德利挑起了眉毛,对谢尔碧笑着。有那么一会儿谢尔碧都没有说话,他感到很满意,因为她无话可说的情况实在是少见。

她突然问道:"那么,你今天有什么发现吗?"

哈德利知道,这是一个她经常用来刁难麦克斯的标准问题。她总是抱怨说,你们每天都在做各种各样的实验,总该发现点什么。

哈德利搜索了一下脑海,"让我想想看,我发现了你不接公用电话亭打来的电话。"他放声大笑起来。

"为什么这么说?"

"你知道那边角落里的电话亭吗?"他指了个大概的方向。

"街对面的那个?"

"对,就是那个。我接了电话,那个家伙问我汤姆在不在,我说,'这是个公用电话',他回答说知道,并问我能不能帮他看一下汤姆在不在这个街区附近,于是我就走到——"

"天哪!"谢尔碧尖叫了起来,笑得几乎从沙发上滑下来。"你真的去找那个汤姆了?"

哈德利一声不吭。

"对不起,对不起,"谢尔碧停顿了一下,"天哪,你真是敏感。"说的时候她还是没有止住笑声,"你知道汤姆其实并不存在的,对吧?"

"好的吧,我就是容易受骗,你还想让我怎么样呢?之后我又回去告诉他附近没有这个人,接着他就问我有没有兴趣一起喝一杯。"哈德利的声音变得有些沙哑。

谢尔碧喉咙里发出一声低沉的笑声,"那么你去了吗?"

"我把你的号码给他了。"他说道。

"哦,对。"

哈德利站了起来,舒展了一下四肢,向他的鼓走去。"哦,对了,"他装出漫不经心的语气,"听说你今天打人了。"一抹笑意爬上他的嘴角。

Chapter Six Bonding

Hitting her knee on the coffee table and cursing, Shelby extricated herself from the sofa. "Did Max tell you?" She was indignant and embarrassed.

"No. My new roommate."

Shelby furrowed her brow. "How would he know?"

"He's the guy you hit." Hadley laughed for real now. He wasn't sure why. It was just funny. He could see someone like Shelby hitting someone like Ethan.

"You're living with *that* guy?" Shelby's face clouded, her eyelids batting.

"He's a chemist. He works for Chesterton."

"He's a chemist?"

"I've known Ethan for a year. He's not my closest friend or anything—"

"He's a complete asshole! What are you talking about?" She stared at him, open-mouthed.

"Well, I really only know his chemistry. He moved in a couple of months ago but I hardly ever see him." Hadley leaned against the wall and tapped his fingers against it. "I think he does drugs."

"Well, who doesn't?" Shelby looked at him like he was lame.

"I mean, serious drugs."

"How do you know?"

"There are unmarked vials in the refrigerator."

"Maybe he's taking his work home with him."

"That's what I mean."

"Oh ..." Shelby drew out. "Did you tell him you know me?"

"He knows who you are. He's seen the band."

Shelby frowned. "You mean ..."

"He saw you do that telegram for Closky."

Shelby scowled even deeper. "God. What? Is he following me?"

"He's too busy for that. He's got a girlfriend and he's starting to write up his thesis. He's never home."

"Yeah, because he's out stalking!"

Hadley shook his head at Shelby.

"Did he tell you why I hit him?"

"He said something that was mostly unintelligible. I think he said he was goofin' you."

谢尔碧从沙发上缩了回来,膝盖不小心碰到了茶几,她嘴里咒骂了几句。"麦克斯告诉你的吗?"她带着些怒气,觉得很丢人。

"不,是我的新室友。"

谢尔碧的眉头皱得更深了,"他怎么会知道的?"

"因为他就是你打的那个家伙。"哈德利现在才爆发出了真正的笑声。他也不知道为什么,只是觉得这件事情很搞笑。他非常能够理解像谢尔碧这样的人为什么会打伊桑这种人。

"你和那个家伙住在一起?"谢尔碧的脸顿时阴沉下来,不断地眨着眼。

"他是个化学家,在切斯特通公司工作。"

"他是个化学家?"

"我已经认识他一年了,他并不是我非常亲近的朋友或是什么的——"

"他是个彻头彻尾的混蛋,你到底是怎么搞的?"谢尔碧目瞪口呆地盯着他看。

"好吧,我只知道他在化学方面的作为。他是几周前搬进来的,我几乎没怎么见过他。"哈德利倚在墙上用手指敲打着墙面,"我觉得他嗑药。"

"这年头谁不嗑药呢?"谢尔碧像是嫌弃他差劲似的看着他。

"我说的是真正的毒品。"

"你怎么知道的?"

"冰箱里放着很多没有标记的小药瓶。"

"也许是他把没做完的工作带回家去了。"

"我也是这么想的。"

"哦……"谢尔碧拖长了声音,"那你告诉他你认识我了吗?"

"他知道你是谁,他看过我们乐队的表演。"

谢尔碧蹙起了眉头,"你是说……"

"他看过你给克劳斯基做的唱歌电报。"

谢尔碧脸上的怒气更重了,"天哪,什么,他一直在跟踪我吗?"

"他可没时间那么做,他有个女朋友,而且刚刚开始着手写论文了,几乎从来都不回家。"

"当然了,因为他一直在跟踪骚扰别人。"

哈德利对谢尔碧摇了摇头。

"他告诉你我为什么打他了吗?"

"他说的大部分话我都没听懂,但我想他的意思应该是说他逗了你一下。"

Chapter Six Bonding

Shelby snorted. "He makes it sound so innocent."

The doorbell rang and Shelby went to answer it, still stunned that Hadley knew Ethan, *lived* with him in fact. Eberhard sauntered in, the perpetual grin on his face. He was carrying his bass with him and a six-pack.

"So. How many songs haf you learned?" he asked jovially.

"We were waiting for you," Hadley retorted.

"Where iss Max?" Eberhard asked, looking around and then propping his bass against the wall and setting the beer down next to it.

"He just went to get some pizza. He should be back any minute," Shelby said walking over to Eberhard.

"Beer?" Eberhard offered. He leaned down and pulled out a bottle for Shelby. She motioned for another and he handed it to her in one of his massive, bass-playing hands. He was a big guy, a bear-like man with dark brown hair that he wore in a pony tail, knowing that one day, when he went back to Germany and became a professor, he would have to cut it off. Postgraduate school in the U.S. offered him a moment of personal freedom, and so he took it.

"You want one?" Shelby asked Hadley almost hesitantly, knowing that the intimacy of their conversation was over.

"Sure." Hadley shrugged, taking one from her.

"Ah, beer! But first I must use the basroom." Eberhard started to open the bedroom door.

"Oh, you have to go outside in the lobby. Our bathroom is all torn up," Shelby said, shaking her head and grimacing.

"Unt why is your basroom torn? May I look?"

Shelby nodded, wanting him to look, wanting to impress them both with the horror of their apartment. She followed Eberhard as he walked through the bedroom and opened the door to the bathroom. There was silence and then he started laughing and shaking his head.

"I'm glad you find it funny," Shelby said, starting to laugh herself. "Because it pisses me the fuck off!"

"I want to see," Hadley said, coming through the bedroom door. On the bathroom wall facing them, a gaping hole ran floor-to-ceiling exposing several layers

谢尔碧嗤了一下鼻子,"把自己说得那么无辜。"

门铃响了,谢尔碧便走过去应门,仍然对哈德利认识那个家伙——事实上,是和他住在一起这件事而感到吃惊。艾伯哈德悠闲地走进来,拿着他的贝斯和半打瓶装啤酒,像往常一样嬉皮笑脸的。

"那么,你们已经学了几首歌了?"他带着愉快的语调问道。

"我们在等你呢。"哈德利辩解道。

"麦克斯去哪了?"艾伯哈德边问,边向四周看了看,顺手把贝斯和啤酒放在了墙角。

"他刚出去买比萨了,这会儿就该回来了。"谢尔碧向艾伯哈德走去。

"要啤酒吗?"他弯下腰去取出一瓶啤酒递给谢尔碧,谢尔碧示意他再来一瓶,于是他便用那只巨大的弹贝斯的手递了过来。艾伯哈德是个大个子,虎背熊腰的,一头棕发扎成了马尾辫,他知道等有一天自己回到德国,成为教授的时候,就必须得把它给剪掉了。美国的研究生院给他提供了短暂的个性自由,他也欣然抓住了这个机会。

"你来一瓶吗?"谢尔碧几乎是有些犹豫地问哈德利,因为她知道他们的对话已经尴尬收场了。

"当然了。"哈德利耸了耸肩,从她手里拿过一瓶。

"哈,啤酒,但我得先用一下洗手间。"艾伯哈德说着打开了卧室的门。

"你得去外面大厅里,我们的洗手间被拆掉了。"谢尔碧说道,一边摇头,一边扮了个鬼脸。

"为什么被拆了?我能看看吗?"

谢尔碧点了点头,她希望让他看到,希望让他们俩见识一下这座公寓的糟糕程度。她跟在艾伯哈德的后面,穿过卧室,打开了浴室的门。房间里先是一阵寂静,随后爆发出一阵大笑,艾伯哈德还不停地摇着头。

"我很高兴这能逗你一笑,"谢尔碧说道,并且也开始笑了起来,"因为我都快被气疯了!"

"我也想看,"哈德利说着也穿过卧室的门走过来。洗手间里正对着他们的那面墙上,有一个巨大的洞,几乎同时触及地板和天花板,里面露出了好几层

Chapter Six Bonding

of decaying greenish copper pipes. Plaster hung in clumps off the edge of the opening, barely connected to the papery surface of the drywall. A stain of wet discoloration started at the top corner of the bathroom, turned left for a ways, and then followed the cleft downward, warping the edges of the drywall and ending in a half-an-inch of dirty water on the floor next to the tub. Plaster muck, grout, and clods of drywall lay all over the sodden floor, along with a pipe wrench, a massive crow bar, and some crushed cigarette butts.

"It smells like a cave. Why is the phone book in here?" Hadley asked. He and Eberhard peered from the bedroom, looking in amazement at a bathroom which only a few days ago had been completely intact.

"Look. This hole was made by somebody's hand," Shelby said knowingly, squeezing between them and gingerly tiptoeing into the bathroom, ready to prove her detective ability.

"You can't punch in a floor," Hadley said with exasperation.

"This one you could." The floor rumbled at Shelby's weight and she could feel its softness, a kind of giving at every step like she was walking on a very thick pudding.

Eberhard warned, "Be careful."

Hadley gave him a look. "Shelby's never careful."

She didn't acknowledge this comment, other than a small twist of a smile as she bent down and picked up the soggy phone book. Hadley and Eberhard leaned forward into the bathroom in order to have a better look at the pit of blackness that the phone book had covered. Hair line cracks emanated from the hole.

"I poured some Raid down there. The roaches were abandoning the basement," Shelby said, lowering the phone book back over the hole. It was gross, but she had an audience. She wanted to seem butch. A tough New Yorker. Sexy and aggressive. Shifting her grip, the sodden New York phone book buckled in Shelby's hands and she lost it. It dropped solidly to the floor and instantly disappeared through the hole, taking part of the floor with it. Shelby could feel herself starting to sink as her left foot slid toward the opening. She had the sudden vision of an ant lion lying in wait in his casbah under the sandy ant pit. Briefly she wondered if she was smoking too much pot these days. "Shit!" she yelled and stepped backward with her right, catching it on the crowbar and losing her balance. The hole in the floor was widening further along fault

已经腐蚀成绿色的铜水管。洞的开口处,大块的石灰悬吊在空中,与薄如纸般的墙壁似连非连。从浴室屋顶的一个角落开始,墙面因为泡了水而开始褪色,接着水流被向左引去,顺着裂缝向下渗漏,使得干涂料糊的墙角都变了形;最后在浴缸旁边形成了一个半英寸深的脏水泊。浸透了水的地板上到处都是石灰残渣,水泥浆,以及墙上掉下来的土块,还有水管扳手、撬棍和一些被踩扁了的烟头。

"这里闻起来就像是个山洞。为什么电话簿会在这里?"哈德利问道。此刻他正和艾伯哈德站在卧室里,用惊讶的目光打量着这个几天前还是完完整整的浴室。

"你们来看,这个洞是有人用手弄出来的。"谢尔碧在行地说道,然后从他们两人中间挤过去,小心翼翼地踮起脚尖走进了浴室里,准备展示一下她的侦查能力。

"没人能把地板给打穿。"哈德利有些恼怒地说。

"这个地板就可以。"地板在谢尔碧的体重压迫下发出"咕噜噜"的声音,她每走一步就可以感觉到一个柔软的反弹力,就好像走在一大块很厚的布丁上一样。

艾伯哈德提醒道:"小心点儿。"

哈德利瞥了他一眼,"她从来不知道小心是什么。"

谢尔碧对这个评价不予置评,只在刚开始弯腰去捡那本湿软的电话簿时露出了一点笑容。哈德利和艾伯哈德这会儿都又向前倾了一些,希望更清楚地看到电话簿覆盖着的那个漆黑的小洞。毛细血管般的裂痕从小洞周围蔓延开去。

"我对着里面喷了些雷达杀虫剂,因为那些蟑螂都开始从地下室里往上爬了。"谢尔碧说着又慢慢把电话簿放回去盖住它。她觉得很恶心,可是还好她有观众在。她想让自己看起来男性化一点,一个强悍的纽约人,性感而好斗。换手拿的时候,那本湿透了的纽约黄页突然从她手里滑了下去,结结实实地砸在了地板上,眨眼的工夫就消失在了洞里,还带走了一部分的地板。谢尔碧的左脚开始滑向洞口,她感觉到自己正在下沉。她突然有一种幻觉,觉得在这个蚂蚁沙丘的下面有一只蚁狮在他那九曲回环的迷宫里等着自己。又有那么一闪念,她在想最近自己是不是大麻吸多了。"该死!"她大叫了一声,右腿向后退了一步,却正好踩在撬棍上,身体失去了平衡。随着即将到来的微震,地面开始产生断层裂

Chapter Six Bonding

lines of a tremor-to-be. Shelby started to tilt. She instinctively flung herself backward, arching her body in a kind of pole vault fashion. This caught Eberhard and Hadley unawares as she fell toward them. Eberhard reached for Shelby's flailing left arm and missed it, while Hadley, having taken one step in to help her, was on the receiving end of the fling. She fell on him before he was prepared, knocking him back into the bedroom, where they skidded across the bedroom floor.

While they fell, they heard the bathroom floor slowly folding downward, collapsing with a minimum of dust and noise. Eberhard turned to watch it go, a time-lapse sequence of a neighborhood black hole, reverse detonation, as the surface implodes and speeds toward a mass. The toilet, moored by the back wall, stayed in place, but the flooring around it disappeared, leaving the glowing white fixture suspended in space. It was a toilet of the future, when gravity was of no concern and astronauts could fly by and grab hold, lowering themselves, hand over hand, to the seat. The tub, firmly affixed to three walls, didn't move a muscle.

"Jesus fucking Christ!" Shelby was yelling, trying to stand up but not able to because every time she turned to the left she felt something tugging at her belt loop. She thought that Hadley was still holding onto her. "Lemme go," she said loudly, somewhat embarrassed. She was sweating; her heart pounding. Hadley finally jerked his arm forward, pulling out the end of his watchband where it was catching on Shelby's belt.

Eberhard started laughing at the two of them. Part of Shelby's problem in getting up was that her jeans were too tight. She had limited mobility. Eventually Eberhard gave her an arm, saying, "I have never seen such excitement."

A little frightened and embarrassed, Shelby turned to help Hadley, but then started laughing uncontrollably at the sight of him lying on the floor. He looked so vulnerable. He made her so nervous that laughing was the easiest thing to do.

They heard the front door open. Max walked in, bringing the odor of pizza with him. He paused at the bedroom door, looking at them suspiciously. Eberhard and Shelby started laughing all over again.

"Why are you on the floor?" he asked Hadley, looking down for a straight answer.

Eberhard and Shelby laughed louder. Hadley just stood up and brushed off his pants.

"Because your wife's an idiot."

缝,而那个洞也沿着断层越裂越大。谢尔碧开始向一边倾斜,但她下意识地向后倒去,将身体弯成了撑竿跳的姿势。谢尔碧向他们倒去的时候艾伯哈德和哈德利都有些措手不及,艾伯哈德伸手去抓谢尔碧四处乱挥的手,但是没抓到;而哈德利当时已经向里跨了一步准备帮谢尔碧,正好站在了谢尔碧倒下的方向。他还没准备好,谢尔碧就一下子将他撞倒在卧室里,两个人在地板上滑行了一段距离。

他们跌倒的同时,听到浴室地板一层一层缓慢向下塌陷的声音,它正以最小量的灰尘和噪音坍塌着。艾伯哈德转过身去观看这个场景,就像站在一个有时间延迟效应的黑洞旁边。当整个地面加速向内崩塌成一片废墟,这场景就像是一个逆向的爆炸过程。马桶由于固定在后墙上,还是牢牢地待在原地,但四周的地面都已经塌陷了,只留着那泛着白光的固定设施悬在半空中。这就是未来的马桶,当重力不再是问题,宇航员可以飞到附近然后抓住把手来让自己降下来,两只手交换地移到座位上。浴缸因为牢牢地钉在三面墙上,也纹丝未动。

"真见鬼!"谢尔碧大叫着,试图站起来却没能成功。因为每次她向左转的时候都感觉到有什么钩在了她的皮带搭扣上。她还以为是哈德利仍然抓着她没有放手,"放开我!"她大声说道,或多或少有些尴尬:她开始流汗,心跳也加速起来。哈德利终于把另一只胳膊抽到前面去,解开了钩住谢尔碧皮带的手表。

艾伯哈德开始嘲笑起他们两个来。谢尔碧起不来的部分原因是她的牛仔裤太紧了,移动很艰难,最终还是艾伯哈德把手伸给了她,"我从来没见过这么刺激的场面。"

谢尔碧惊魂未定之余还感到有些丢脸,于是转过身去帮哈德利。但她刚看到哈德利躺在地板上那一脸无辜的样子就控制不住地大笑起来;哈德利让她感到紧张,以至于对她来说最容易的事就是放声大笑了。

他们听到了前门打开的声音,麦克斯走了进来,周身萦绕着比萨的香味。他在卧室门口停了下来,一脸怀疑地打量着他们。艾伯哈德和谢尔碧又一次笑得前仰后合。

"你为什么躺在地板上?"他问哈德利,期待着一个直截了当的答案。

艾伯哈德和谢尔碧的笑声更响亮了,哈德利只是站起身来,用手拂了拂裤子。

"因为你老婆是个傻瓜!"

Chapter Seven Reaction

The meeting of two personalities is like the contact of two chemical substances: if there is any reaction, both are transformed.

Carl Jung

The entrance hall of the chemistry building was a mausoleum of cold yellow limestone, big blocks of calcite that almost looked like marble. It made Shelby feel chilly, as if she'd walked into the Middle Ages. Max had told her that marble was simply calcium carbonate that had fused during some volcanic process.

"You mean like Tums?" she had asked him.

"Exactly."

"You mean if we take Tums and melt them, we could make marble?" The thought made her smile.

"Just think of that," he had smiled back, "our own little marble factory." She had meant to try it but forgot. The idea of home chemistry appealed to her. She wanted sparks and explosions. She wanted the excitement that would accompany them. Dermot had given a bachelor party and hired a stripper who lit herself on fire. Shelby never forgave him for not inviting her. After she groused about it excessively, Max promised to bring home some potassium when it snowed. He said it would be like firecrackers when you threw it on the snow. Living with a chemist had its percs.

Shelby turned left and went through some wooden doors. They had massive iron bars holding the wooden ties together. It reminded her of the movie *Lion in Winter*. She always wondered what they did in those days if they just wanted to sit down and relax. Instead of furniture they had big furs spread everywhere. You had a rug or a robe depending on how cold it was. Still, there was something to be said for simplicity. Looking down an empty stone corridor, Shelby tried to imagine she was in a cavern, the looming rock walls shiny and wet. She fantasized she would turn the corner and see a monk. It was a game she liked to play. How far could she let her

第七章 反应

> 两个人格的相遇就像是两种物质之间的接触:如果有化学反应发生,两者就都被改变了。
>
> ——卡尔·荣格

化学楼的大厅是由黄色的石灰石建造而成的冰冷陵墓,原石就是大块的方解石,质形与大理石十分相似。谢尔碧觉得冷飕飕的,就好像走进了中世纪中的场景。麦克斯告诉过她,大理石就是在火山喷发过程中熔融过的碳酸钙。

"你是说就像咀嚼钙片一样?"她问道。

"没错。"

"你的意思是,如果我们把钙片融化掉,就可以制成大理石咯。"谢尔碧想到这一点就不由自主地笑了。

"这样一想的话,"麦克斯也回笑了一下,"我们就能够拥有自己的迷你大理石工厂了。"谢尔碧本打算尝试一下,但后来便忘记了。她一直都对家庭实验室的想法倍感兴趣,因为她想要火花和爆炸,想要可以陪伴他们的新鲜刺激的感觉。德莫特曾经举办过一个单身汉告别派对,并且雇了一个脱衣舞娘,她在表演的时候在自己的身上点燃了火焰。谢尔碧却没有被邀请,她一直对这件事耿耿于怀。在她就这件事抱怨了无数次之后,麦克斯答应她等下雪的时候带一些钾回来。他说如果你把钾扔在雪上的话,就会产生鞭炮一样的效果。和一个化学家生活在一起还是有很多福利的。

左转之后,谢尔碧穿过了几扇木头门,枕木的后面安放着粗大的铁棍加以固定,这让她想起电影《冬狮》里的场景。她总是好奇,过去那些年代,如果他们想要坐下来休息的话会怎么做。他们没有家具,却用巨大的兽皮铺在地面上;至于是铺小地毯还是穿兽皮袍则取决于寒冷的程度。不过,简单朴素的信条还是得到了推崇。谢尔碧向下面空荡荡的石头走廊看去,努力想象自己正身处于一个阴森的洞穴里,岩石墙壁反射着湿答答的光亮。也许转过下一个拐角她会碰到一个和尚。这是一个她很喜欢玩的游戏:她的想象力到底能飞多远?她能够描

imagination go? Could she picture him? Could she hear him? Shelby liked hallucinations. Or the moment before. She wanted to hear voices.

Listening intently, Shelby slowed her walk, loathe to see a chemist. It was monk or nothing. She loved the silence but wanted to hear it filled. She strained for echoes. The hollow crunch that her boots made on the stone floor pleased her and made her crave the swishing of robes, the murmuring of prayers. She stopped and sang one note. Claiming the air. Barely loud enough to hear. There was an echo. She listened to it die away. She sang two notes quickly, trying to make a harmony, the sonority of the cloister making her voice sound deep and melodious as she let the volume rise. She sang something Gregorian chant-like. Fourths and fifths made her happy. She couldn't explain it. Perhaps they resonated with the bony structures of her body, the cavities, the alcoves. Her skin tingled. There was something alive in her. Something that she felt but couldn't put into words. But it made her feel like singing. Something was making her happy and she hadn't a clue. She laughed at herself, singing a bad note because she wasn't paying attention, trying instead to put her finger on what made her want to laugh for no reason. It wouldn't come to her. Maybe she was just happy. It cracked her up.

Shelby took another left which lead to the heavily balustraded stairs, and began to climb the four sets of twisting stone steps to Max's lab. The building had no elevator. She was tempted to slide down the banister when she got to the top, but recognized that—clumsy as she was—probably not a good idea. So instead, she leaned way over the railing, like she was in some Civil War epic looking to see who was returning home from the war. These enactments humored her. She enjoyed being nuts.

When Shelby got to the top, she glanced at the sign that was posted on one of the swinging doors. It warned pacemaker wearers of the presence of a magnetic field. On the other door a radiation emblem was painted with a warning below. The type forced her to read the words against her will. There were too many signs in New York; they fought for the eye. Warnings about buildings crumbling on you and fines if you honk too loud. Shelby wondered if perhaps the car horns were sonicating the buildings. Maybe if they explained it, people would be more understanding. But instead, most warnings were posted and terse. Hell, there was even one in their bathroom. A little stand-up fluorescent sign that sat on the toilet and read "Caution",

画出那个和尚的具体长相吗？能否听到他的声音？谢尔碧喜欢这样的幻想，或者说是幻想产生的前一秒。她想要听到声音。

　　谢尔碧放慢了脚步，专注地听着，不愿意眼前出现一个化学家。要么是和尚，要么就最好什么都没有。她喜爱这种寂静，但是又想听到它被填充起来。接着她又竖起耳朵，收集着回声。自己的靴子踩在石地板上发出的"咔哒"声使她感到满意，也让她更加想要听到道袍摩擦的"窸窸窣窣"声和做祷文的咕哝声。她停了下来，唱了一个音节，试图宣称对空气的拥有权，声音小得几乎听不见。但还是有回声产生，谢尔碧听着它渐弱直至消失。接着她又迅速地唱了两个音节，试图营造出和声的效果。当她慢慢提高音量的时候，走廊的浑厚感使她的声音变得更加深沉悦耳起来。她哼唱了几句类似格列高利圣歌的旋律，音符 fa，so 使她感到开心。关于这一点她也不知道怎么解释，也许是这两个音符与她身体的骨骼结构——遍布全身的孔腔，以及凹处产生了共鸣。她感觉到了皮肤上的微微刺痛感：她的身体中有一些活跃的因子，可以感觉得到，却无法言说。这些因子让她产生唱歌的冲动，并开心起来，连她自己都不知道为什么。谢尔碧自顾地大笑起来，因为她只顾着思索自己会无缘无故大笑的原因，反而一不留神唱跑调了。但答案却始终不肯出现，也许她就只是开心而已，就那么没由来地想要捧腹大笑。

　　谢尔碧又向左转了个弯，安装了厚重扶手的楼梯出现在眼前，于是她便开始了由四段弯弯曲曲的台阶组成的征程，向麦克斯的实验室走去。这座楼里没有电梯，所以每次谢尔碧爬到顶端以后都有一种顺着扶手滑下来的冲动，但她意识到对于她这么笨手笨脚的人来说，这应该不是什么好主意。于是作为弥补，她会将身体伸出栏杆外，就好像身处某个讲述内战的史诗情节当中，遥望着远方归来的良人。这种表演总是让谢尔碧忍俊不禁。

　　谢尔碧到达顶端之后，瞟了一眼贴在其中一扇旋转门上的标语，内容是提醒佩戴心脏起搏器的人这里存在着磁场。在另一扇门上贴有一张辐射的标识，下面写有"警告"两个字。尽管她很不情愿，但是那种打印字体还是迫使她读了下去。在纽约有太多的标识，它们争相吸引人们的眼球。提醒你注意可能在你头顶坍塌的楼房，警告你鸣笛声过大就会收到罚单。有的时候谢尔碧会想，也许汽车鸣笛中的声波也在无形中摧毁着楼房建筑。如果有关部门这样解释的话，没准人们就能更加理解他们的工作。但相反的，他们只会张贴出冰冷简短的标语。真是见鬼，连她自己的浴室里都贴着一张荧光标识：小心。它就那样显眼地

taunting them. Their bathroom was a hazard area too.

She'd forgotten about it for a moment, but now the frustration of the day before looped in her mind, the events cycling as she felt her anger mount. How did people stay happy? She couldn't seem to do it. Forgetting her laughter of a moment ago, she mentally walked through the chaos in their apartment, enumerating all the things that pissed her off. She imagined possible confrontations with the housing office, what she would say. In the end she always saw herself yelling, forcing the entire office to listen to a description of what she had seen when she walked into her bathroom. The demolition. The wildlife. And then, in a stupor from my anger (she would say), she nearly went through a hole in the bathroom floor, a hole that looked as if someone had punched it with their fist. She would assure them that the punching probably happened when the plumbers took the wall out and realized the leak was above them.

Shelby knew she was flamboyant. The way she figured it, everyone had eccentricities, only hers were louder. It was a way to deal. To live largely despite diverse obstacles. She used to live by the motto: if you have to be depressed, you might as well be beautiful (eye-lining and speed dating when she was despondent). But now she preferred to be outrageous. Demanding what she needed out of life. It had its advantages as one got older.

Swinging the doors open to the lab floor, she looked down the hall, hoping someone was there. Seeing no movement of any kind, she walked down the hallway, occasionally glancing left and right into open labs, curious about the people who worked there. The barbaric feeling of the ground floor had dispersed by floor four, replaced by a 1950s office ambiance, wood molding over the doorway, pale green walls the color of mint ice cream. The place seemed sterile, laden with cabinets of glass tubing and the occasional refrigerator. There was an audible hum of machinery, making the quiet more ominous. Sometimes being completely alone in New York was worse than being around people. There was an unexpected eerie quality at the surprise of their sudden absence. Shelby fingered her mail-order mace in her bag, a gut-reaction to the solitude.

She was relieved to see Bineet standing in front of his hood as she passed his door. She stopped by and nodded, exchanging small talk. She liked him but didn't know him very well. She knew a lot of stuff about him from Max, but she couldn't let on

贴在马桶上方,嘲笑着谢尔碧和麦克斯。他们的浴室也属于危险地带。

她本来都已经把那件事给暂时忘记了,但现在,昨天那种极度沮丧的情绪又开始盘踞在她的脑海里。整个事件不断地重复回放,她的怒气也不断地上涌。人要怎么样才能保持开心呢?反正她是做不到。刚才的开怀大笑已经抛诸脑后,谢尔碧想象着自己正走在公寓的一片狼藉中,一一细数着惹恼她的每件事情。她还设想着与物业人员见面时的各种场景,以及自己会说些什么。不管哪个场景,她都预见到自己的歇斯底里,她要让整个物业的人都来听她描述自己走进浴室时所看到的景象。拆除的惨象、满地的虫蚁,以及自己是怎样在恍惚的愤怒中(她决定这样说)差点掉进了浴室地面那个洞里的。那个洞看起来就像是有人用拳头砸出来的;她敢保证,这肯定是那些水管工在把墙面拆除并发现漏洞是在天花板上之前干的。

谢尔碧知道,自己做事喜欢夸张化。但她觉得,每个人都有自己怪异的行为方式,只不过她的有点大声而已。这是一种处理事情的方法。不论遇到各种各样的阻碍,都要勇敢地为自己而活。过去她有一条生活格言:如果你一定要感到沮丧的话,你不妨也打扮得漂亮一些(当她低落的时候她会给自己画眼线,然后再去速配约会)。但现在她更倾向于肆无忌惮地把自己的情绪都发泄出来,要求获得自己生活需要的东西。当一个人渐渐老去的时候,会发现这一点非常有用。

谢尔碧推开通向实验室区域的门,向走廊望去,希望有人在,可是却没有看到任何移动的迹象。于是她走了进去,抱着对在这里工作的人的好奇心,不时地向左右两边开着的实验室张望着。到达四层以后底层大厅的阴森感就消失无踪了,取而代之的是一种20世纪50年代的办公室装潢风格:木地板从门前延伸开去,墙壁涂成了浅绿色,就像薄荷冰淇淋的颜色。这个地方看起来有些荒凉,四处都是装满玻璃管的橱柜,冰箱偶尔可见。仪器的嗡鸣声隐约可以听见,使得这寂静中渗透进了一丝不祥的感觉。在纽约,有时候完全一个人待着的感觉比身处人群中还要糟糕。这种因为人群的突然消失而产生的惊奇,带来了一种意想不到的怪异恐怖的氛围。独处的时候,谢尔碧本能地拨弄着包里那瓶邮购的防狼喷雾。

路过贝内特的实验室门口时,谢尔碧看到他正站在仪器保护罩的前面,顿时松了一口气。她停下脚步,微微点了点头,随意聊了几句天。谢尔碧挺喜欢他的,但不是非常了解他。她从麦克斯那里听说了很多关于他的事,却不能表现

that she knew. Like his arranged marriage and his fascination with anything sexual. He was good-looking; he could get women if he wanted, but Max had told her that Bineet was a virgin. He was saving himself for marriage. This was incomprehensible to Shelby.

She walked by Hadley's lab. Unbidden, the idea that he still might be a virgin occurred to her. Was that possible? In this day and age? Leaning in Hadley's doorway, just in case he was hidden by the wall, she said loudly, "Boo," but there was no response. She noticed his leather jacket on the back of his chair and wondered if that meant he was coming back. She felt more like talking than writing and Max was at a guitar lesson. She left a note on Max's desk anyway, then continued down the hall and turned right again, this time at the research adviser's door. The secretary's desk nearly blocked the passage to the inner office, a room jokingly referred to as "The Knitting Room." Shelby liked the man for that alone. Apparently, he didn't try to hide it; Max said you'd go into his office to ask him a question, and he'd sit there from a moment, knitting needles clicking. He'd ask a few of his own, untangle some yarn, and pause briefly, halting progress on his sweater or afghan. Then, as you stood there dumb-founded, he'd give you this elegant solution to your problem. One Christmas Dr. Scotia made stockings for all his graduate students. Shelby smiled, remembering that Max was worried that someday he might get a sweater and have to wear it. Max hated sweaters.

Amused by the thought, Shelby rounded the desk and sat down, pushing on the computer switch. Even though she wasn't a chemistry student, or even attending the university, she felt very comfortable using the facilities. It was what she loved most about academia: resources for the elite and their friends. She was taking a writing class on Tuesday nights. Some woman had asked the teacher whether it was better to write in the morning or the afternoon or the evening. That was the problem with extension classes.

Shelby put her hands on the keyboard to type, but she couldn't think of anything she wanted to say. She cracked her neck and then combed her hair with her fingers for a while, her mind making lists of things she needed to remember, like beer, which they were nearly out of. Shelby looked at the clock. It was already 7:20. She could see a sliver of darkness through the subset of door and window in a lab across the hall. She'd already wasted ten minutes. It was so easy to drift and do

出自己知道的样子,比如他的包办婚姻,还有他对任何与性有关的事物的迷恋。贝内特五官英俊,如果愿意的话可以得到很多女人的青睐,但是麦克斯告诉她,他还是个处男之身。他是为了婚姻而这样做的,这对谢尔碧来说实在无法理解。

接着她路过了哈德利的实验室,毫无预兆地,她脑子里闪过哈德利也许也还是处男的想法。有可能吗?在今天这个时代,以他的年纪?她倚在门框上,为了试探他是否被墙挡在了后面,谢尔碧大声叫了句"嗨",结果没有人回应。谢尔碧注意到,他的皮夹克挂在椅子的后背上,便寻思着他是不是正在回来的路上。比起一个人待着写东西,她现在更想跟人聊天,而麦克斯又在上吉他课。即便这样,她还是在麦克斯的桌子上留了一张纸条,然后继续沿着走廊走下去。又向右转了个弯之后,这次出现在眼前的是导师办公室。秘书的桌子几乎挡住了通往里间办公室的通道,那里被打趣地称作是"织毛衣的房间"。仅仅这一点就让谢尔碧对斯考蒂亚博士产生了好感。很显然,他本来也没准备隐藏;麦克斯说,当有人走进他的办公室请教他问题时,他会先静坐一会儿,手里的毛衣针却一刻不停地发出"咔嗒咔嗒"的声音。接着他会反问你几个问题,理一理毛线团,停顿个几秒钟,整个对话因为他手里的毛衣或者阿富汗针织毯而停滞下来。正当你不知所措地站在原地时,他会就你的问题给出一个简洁明了的解决方案。有一年圣诞节,斯考蒂亚给自己带的所有研究生都织了一双圣诞袜。谢尔碧笑了,她想起麦克斯一度担心自己某天会收到一件毛衣,那样就不得不穿了。麦克斯讨厌毛衣。

谢尔碧被这个想法给逗乐了,她绕过桌子坐了下来,按下了电脑开关。尽管她不是化学专业的,甚至都不上这所大学,但在使用这里的设备时她一点儿也不拿自己当外人。这是学术界最让她满意的一点:资源的开放针对所有精英,以及他们的朋友。她当时正在上一个星期二晚上的写作课程,有个女同学竟然问老师写作是在早上进行比较好,还是在下午或是晚上。这就是扩招课程的弊端。

谢尔碧把双手放到键盘上准备打字,却想不出任何想说的话。她转了转脖子,又用手指捋了一会儿头发,同时在脑海里罗列着需要记住的东西,比如说啤酒,家里的快喝完了。接着她瞟了一眼钟,已经 7:20 了。透过走廊对面实验室的门缝和窗缝,她可以看到长条状的夜色。她已经浪费了十分钟了。漫无目的

nothing. Writing felt so much like day-dreaming to her that it was hard to free-associate on the one hand and actually type on the other. She missed her old typewriter, the one she'd had during college. It had palsy. The whole thing shook like her mother's washing machine with a full load. She constantly had to resettle the carriage or it would have ended up on the floor. But it gave her something to do, forced her to pay attention to it, a jealous medium. It died the day a bookcase fell off the wall at the university's cooperative housing and crushed it. The Co-op, as it was called, was more than one step up from slum housing but not as many as ten.

Actually, that was what Max always said. She'd stolen it from him. She stole a lot of her humor from others, but it seemed more like homage. People forgot their bon mots; she catalogued them. Everyone has at least one good story. The problem is, they usually think they have more. Her job was to sift through. Some people keep their troubled stories inside, letting them walk along on their day, a constant presence. It shows in their manner. Their hands. Their rhythm. She freed them, letting the stories loose on the world.

They met at the Co-op—Hadley, Max, and Shelby—legendary for being the low-rent district of Westwood, California. One hundred and ten dollars a month for room and board—the place invited destruction. Looking at it, it was hard to imagine that it could be significant: the structure a wall of concrete, like a freeway upended. Someone had tried to grow ferns in the front, but years of uric acid had tainted the soil and now the ground was covered only by crushed cigarette butts and some hardy weeds.

At the time they had no idea that they would be re-living their college days for years to come; that college had been a time in their lives when freedom was as simple as breaking everything in the vicinity. Life was uncomplicated. Time was now. As a lark, they even made a date to see each other when they would all be fifty-five, thinking they would be at opposite ends of the world, not knowing two would marry, two would postdoc, their three lives thus intertwined. At a bar in Westwood they drunkenly penned the date on the back of their driver's licenses, never imagining that they would ever actually be fifty-five. The pressure of scholastic competition egged them on to feats of sexual prowess and minor acts of depravity, and they thought it would always be this way.

地瞎转悠实在是太轻松容易了。写作对她来说就像是做白日梦，要一边天马行空一边把它们打出来真是太难了。她想念自己大学时用的旧打字机，它就像患了抽搐性中风一样，加足马力的时候它抖动起来就像谢尔碧母亲的洗衣机。她经常要把滑架重新归位，否则最后就会摔到地上去了。但是这样一来谢尔碧就有事情可做了，她不得不把注意力集中在它身上，真是一台爱刷存在感的机器。它最终"死于非命"：有一天合作公寓里的书架突然从墙上掉了下来，把它给压扁了。合作公寓比贫民窟的条件要好上不止一点，但是没有超过十点。

事实上，这是麦克斯总会说的一句话，谢尔碧偷来用的。她的很多幽默段子都是借用别人的，但其实更有一种致敬的意味。人们往往会忘记自己说过的连珠妙语，而谢尔碧就给它们分门别类。每个人至少都有一个好故事可以讲。问题是，人们通常会认为自己有不止一个。谢尔碧的任务就是对它们进行筛选。有些人倾向于把不堪的故事埋在心底，让它们在自己每一天的生活中大摇大摆地存在着。但是这会体现在他们的行为上，他们的双手上，他们的节奏上。谢尔碧使他们得到解脱，让他们的故事在天地间不受束缚地驰骋。

合作公寓的传奇名声是因为它在加利福尼亚西区的廉租房地位，当初哈德利、麦克斯和谢尔碧就在这里初次相遇。每月110美元，包含食宿——这地方真是在自取灭亡。向这座楼房望去，很难想象它能有什么重要作用：整栋大楼由水泥墙面构成，就像是立起的高速公路。有人曾经试着在楼前种一些蕨类植物，但是长年累月的尿酸侵蚀已经把土壤给污染了，如今，那里只有遍地踩扁的烟头和少许生命力顽强的杂草。

当时他们想都没有想过，未来的几年自己还要再体验一遍大学生活；那所大学代表了他们生命中一段自由的时光，那时的自由，就像随手打碎身边的东西一样唾手可得。生活是那么的简单。时间就是当下。他们甚至玩闹着约定，等到他们都到了55岁的时候再相见，想着那时候应该各自分散在了世界的不同角落，却不知道他们中有两个彼此牵了对方的手，还出了两个博士后，而且他们三个的生活也因此而紧紧地缠绕在了一起。在西区的一家酒吧，他们醉醺醺地把这个约会的日期写在各自驾照的背面，却从来没有想过自己真的会有到五十五岁的那一天。学业的竞争压力鼓动他们在性生活方面表现得英勇无畏，也有过轻微的堕落，他们还以为，生活永远都会是这个样子。

Shelby felt the freedom of no parents. She liked to try out other beds. It was both innocent and sexual, going only so far as bra and underwear, but fooling around extensively. Her excuse was her room. It was the size of a large dog kennel. And she shared it with two disparate coeds, Bets, a psychology major who thought she looked like a turtle, and Olga, one ton of girlhood from Sweden. Olga rested heavily on the bed above Shelby. Everyone thought Shelby was crazy to let Olga sleep there, a good two-hundred and fifty pounds suspended over her by the frame of one slightly swaying Co-op bunk bed. ("Look at your goddamn typewriter!" Max would yell. He lived on the fifth floor.) Still, she let Olga snore loudly in Swedish above her. "If it happens, it'll be over so fast ... " Sometimes Shelby thought this might be the best solution. Especially if it meant that she no longer had to listen to Olga throw her weight around. Shelby was just concerned that she and Olga would end up in the same heaven. Or worse, some waiting room where they both had to lose weight before they could get in. (Like many coeds, Shelby's personality verged on anorexic.) What do you do if you're too fat for heaven and too good for hell?

Olga was the source of much Co-op lore. For example, at the Co-op everyone had to put in four hours of work a week. Some brilliant mind had given Olga the job of calling out people's names when their omelets were ready during Sunday brunch. (Brunch sounds like such an elegant repast for a place like the Co-op, but it really was an excuse for them to serve only two meals on Sundays.) The main problem with this arrangement was that Olga's accent was so very Swedish that no one could recognize their own name. "They all sound like 'Bean'," Max would joke during brunch, and everyone around would imitate Olga: "One ex for Bean. Two exxs easyover for Bean. Bean, Beean, and Bean please to come get your exxs." Max and the guys he hung around with would laugh till they choked.

And plates of eggs would end up in a line along the counter, congealing, the whites becoming so hard that an hour later degenerates would be throwing them at the ceiling where they would stick for a period of time and then fall on the unsuspecting. People would begin yelling for their breakfast and Olga would yell right back, saying that she'd been calling them all morning. Olga liked to heave her temper around too. She was majoring in theater and this gave her a chance to try out all her emotions.

谢尔碧感觉到了没有父母管教的自由。她喜欢尝试不同的床。这种行为既天真无辜,又充满了性的意味;虽然到目前为止她最大的尺度就是只穿着内衣和内裤,但是却到处留情。她的借口就是自己的宿舍。那里充其量就算是一个大一点的狗窝,而且她还必须与另外两个与自己迥然不同的女生分享:贝蒂,心理学专业,觉得自己长得像一只海龟,还有欧佳,来自瑞典的"胖妞"。欧佳沉重的身躯躺在谢尔碧的上铺——所有人都觉得谢尔碧是疯了才会同意让欧佳睡她上铺:足足两百五十磅的重量,仅仅借助一个微微有些晃动的公寓上下床床架支撑,悬浮在谢尔碧的上方。("看看你那该死的打字机的下场!"麦克斯曾经对她吼道。他住在五楼。)可是谢尔碧还是同意了,让欧佳在她的头顶上带着瑞典腔调大声地打着呼噜。"如果真的发生意外的话,也会非常快……"有的时候谢尔碧觉得这也许是最好的解决办法,尤其是一想到这就意味着她可以不用再忍受欧佳骄横跋扈的样子了。她只是有些担心自己最后会和欧佳进入一样的天堂。或者情况更糟糕,她们两个都被困在某个等候室里,等到瘦了才能进天堂。(与许多男女混合学校的女生一样,谢尔碧的性格也接近于神经性厌食症的患者。)如果太胖了进不了天堂,但是对于地狱来说又太善良了,你要怎么办呢?

欧佳是合作公寓的传说来源之一。比如说,在合作公寓里每个人都得一周义务工作四个小时,某个机灵鬼给欧佳安排了这样一份工作:在周日早午餐供应的时间段,每一份食物做好以后,她都得大声地叫出点单者的名字。(早午餐听起来像是合作公寓这种地方的一顿丰盛的餐宴,但其实就是他们为了星期天只提供两顿饭找的借口。)这个安排的主要问题就是,欧佳的瑞典口音非常浓重,以至于没有人能够辨别出自己的名字来。"听起来全部都像'豆子'。"麦克斯会在吃早午餐的时候开这样的玩笑,然后周围的人都开始模仿欧佳:"一份鸡蛋是豆子的。两个微焦的鸡蛋给豆子。豆——子,豆子请来取走你的鸡蛋。"麦克斯和几个玩得好的男生会一直大笑到呛到为止。

许多碟的鸡蛋就会在餐台上排成一条长队,慢慢开始凝结,蛋白变得僵硬,一个小时以后那帮无赖就开始将它们向天花板上扔去。鸡蛋会在那里粘一段时间,然后掉在毫无防备的人头上。当人们叫嚣着要求自己的早餐时,欧佳就立刻大声吼回去,说自己整个早上都在叫他们来取。欧佳也喜欢四处发脾气。她的专业是戏剧,这让她有机会可以把自己所有的情绪都尝试一遍。

Eventually the kitchen monitor, a grumpy thin guy, ordered Olga to start delivering the eggs. She did it in her usual laconic way, dropping plates of cooked eggs heavily in front of the people, whether or not they had ordered them. There was a shuffling of breakfasts before people realized Olga's method. In the characteristic Co-op way, insults started flying, but Olga seemed to pay no attention. She worked so hard at paying no attention that she also didn't notice that one of the milk-machine nozzles had a slow leak. Milk dribbled out, making an atoll on the floor of the dining commons, linoleum-locked islands of cream, on the verge of melding into a pool of whiteness. Their combined slipperiness was her undoing. Almost as if in slow motion, Olga stepped into the splashings of milk, lost her footing, tilted—her huge girth quivering in descent—and hit the wet floor with a whoosh. Milk spoogied everywhere. The momentum shot her between the legs of the table that supported the monstrous toaster.

The toaster was a Co-op fixture. It had a constantly moving belt of metal racks that shuttled the toast four-across past heated coils, a minute-and-a-half ride, till the individual racks finally tilted near the bottom and the warm toast slid down a silver bank to the condiment table, a war zone of greasy knives, empty gallon containers of peanut butter, jelly, and margarine, and the charred remains of carbonized toast (sometimes the racks didn't tilt well enough and the toast made more than one trip). The toaster was the watering hole of the Co-op, where late at night the drugged and drunken would accumulate to eat peanut butter and do toast experiments. The place where Co-op legends were born. Everyone remembered exactly what they were doing the instant Olga's supine form came to a rest beneath the toast table, the crumbs and residual crusts trickling down on her, like snow blanketing a hillside.

Shelby felt sorry for Olga except for when she was around her. Olga was not a nice person, but Shelby still felt guilty when people teased Olga, as if she had participated in a stoning. Sometimes when Max would be yelling, "Be-ean, Be-e-e-ean," Shelby would leave, thinking that the spoof was old now. Of course then Shelby would go upstairs and find that Olga had brought home fifty bottles of Liquid Paper, all of it sitting on the floor of their dorm room. Liquid Paper had been recently outlawed and at Olga's part-time secretarial job she'd been instructed to toss them. Fifty bottles of Liquid Paper—what a coup.

最后，厨房班长——一个脾气暴躁的瘦家伙，命令欧佳开始把鸡蛋端给别人。与往常一样，她采用了简单粗暴的方法：不论是不是他们点的，她都一律把盛着煎好鸡蛋的碟子重重地扔在别人面前。在人们意识到欧佳的做事方式之前，有过一阵忙乱的早餐交换。按照典型的合作公寓风格，人们的谩骂声已经飘荡在了空气中了，但是欧佳看上去却一点都不在意。她非常努力地不理会周围的一切，以至于她也忽略了牛奶机的喷嘴里面有一个正开始慢慢渗漏。牛奶成小股地流下来，在餐厅的地面上形成了一个环状珊瑚岛：被油毡毯包围的奶油岛屿，几乎快要融合成了乳白色的一摊。就是这湿滑的地面成了欧佳覆灭的祸根。以一种近乎慢放的速度，欧佳一脚踩了上去，牛奶飞溅，她失去了平衡，身体向一边倾斜过去——坠落的过程中她那粗壮的腰部不停地抖动着——带着一阵风声撞向地面。那一刻，牛奶"哗啦"一声溅得四处都是。随之产生的动量将她向放着巨大吐司机的桌底推去。

这个吐司机是合作公寓的固定财产。上面的传送带持续不停地运转着，金属托盘带着面包片经过用来加热的电线圈，一共四次，全程一分半钟，直到某一个托盘最终倾斜，热乎乎的吐司就会顺着一个银色的通道滑到调料桌上——那里是一个挥舞着油腻餐刀的战场，到处是曾经装满花生酱、果酱和人造黄油的空瓶子，还有被烤煳了的面包残渣（有时候托盘倾斜得不够好，吐司就会多停留很久）。这个吐司机所在的地方就是合作公寓的酒吧，到了半夜里，嗑了药和醉酒的人就会聚集到这里吃花生酱，并且拿吐司来做实验。合作公寓的传说都是在这里诞生的。欧佳仰面朝天摔倒在桌子下面的时候，每个人都清楚地记得自己当时在做什么，面包碎屑和剩余的残渣纷纷扬扬地飘洒在她身上，就像白雪渐渐覆盖小山坡时候的情景。

除了和她在一起的时候，谢尔碧还是十分同情欧佳的。虽然欧佳的性格不是特别好，但当别人嘲笑她时，谢尔碧还是会产生内疚感，就好像自己也参与其中了一样。有时，当麦克斯大喊大叫"豆子——，豆——子"的时候，谢尔碧就会转身离开，她觉得捉弄人这种事情已经过时了。但当她走上楼以后，不出意料的，看见宿舍地板上摆满了欧佳带回来的五十瓶修正液。最近修正液的使用刚被规定为违法行为，而欧佳做的兼职秘书工作收到的最新一项任务就是把它们都给扔掉。五十瓶修正液——多么大的便宜啊！

Chapter Seven Reaction

After Olga fell in the dining commons, she took her grievances to MemCom, the judicial system of the Co-op. She didn't want to work on the kitchen crew anymore. It turned out that this was no problem. No one wanted her. Incompetence had gotten Olga out of a job. Shelby knew there was a moral there, but it wasn't one you'd find in Aesop's fables.

She remembered that night. She'd gotten to MemCom late because she'd had to oversee a towing. She was head of parking, a hellish position because there weren't enough spaces. There was at least a towing a week. People with no cars would sit along the retaining wall outside, cheering and smoking as the truck nabbed another victim. Shelby had hurried into the lounge and slid into her seat just as Myron, the head of MemCom, went on to the next line of business: a new guy who'd been fined by the kitchen monitor for disrupting the dining commons. The kitchen seemed to be a hotbed of problems.

Glancing at the accused, Shelby remembered thinking he looked too boring to be a troublemaker. Apparently, on the pretense of being highly allergic, the accused had asked permission to go into the kitchen in order to read the "Fishfingers" ingredients, the entree being served that night. After reading them, he had torn the label off, thinking he was only going to show his roommate. (He volunteered this as evidence that the act had not been premeditated.) Returning to the dining commons and seeing the long line of people waiting for dinner, something had come over him. Instead of taking the list to his room, he stuck it on the slanted plexiglas cover that protected the food, the "spit shield" as people called it. He hadn't intended this as a symbolic stand, but he was irritated that he had paid for room and board and nothing was edible except for the tubs of peanut butter put out nightly for the stonies. Once he'd posted the label, everyone stopped eating the Fishfingers, as if the list of ingredients could possibly have made more of an impression than their appearance.

Shelby had yelled in indignation, "Why are you fining him ten dollars? Someone should give this man a medal."

Unfortunately, no one on MemCom had a sense of humor. A hubbub started as the result of Shelby's comment. "Can we have quiet in here or we will have to throw you out." Myron hit his gavel on the flimsy folding table in front of him. It was later discovered that Myron hadn't attended school for two years and was not even eligible to live in the Co-op, much less preside over MemCom.

欧佳在餐厅里摔倒以后,心怀不满,便向合作公寓的仲裁部门反映,要求不在厨房里工作了。这完全不是问题,因为本来也没有人想要她。能力的欠缺使欧佳丢了工作。谢尔碧知道,这件事是有寓意的,但是与伊索寓言里的故事揭露的不一样。

她还记得那天晚上,因为要监督拖车流程,很晚她才赶到仲裁部门。谢尔碧是停车处的头头,这个职位十分令人伤脑筋,因为停车位总是不够。每周至少会有一辆车被拖走。无车一族会在防水墙上面坐成一排,抽着烟,欢呼着看卡车拖走又一个"受害者"。谢尔碧匆匆走进休息室,一屁股坐在自己的位置上,这时仲裁处的主席麦伦正转向下一个待处理的问题:一个新来的家伙因为扰乱就餐秩序被厨房班长罚款了。看起来,厨房真是问题滋长的温床。

谢尔碧瞥了一眼被指控的人,她记得自己当时觉得他长得很无聊,不像是会惹麻烦的人。很显然,尽管表面上看上去是个很容易过敏的家伙,但他却要求进到厨房里去,看一下当天晚上的主菜"炸鱼条"的配料表。在看完之后,他将那个标签撕了下来,心想着给室友看一下。(他主动供述了这件事,因为他想证明自己后来的行为并不是预谋好的。)回到餐厅之后,他看着排着长队等晚餐的人们,突然脑子里闪过一个念头。那张配料表他并没有带回宿舍,而是贴在了用来保护食物的倾斜的有机玻璃上,那个隔层被大家叫作"防痰玻璃"。他本意并不是想做什么出格的行为,只是觉得生气,自己付了食宿的钱而他们提供的食物——除了深夜供给瘾君子们的花生酱之外,却都不可食用。他刚把标签贴上去,所有人就都放下了正在吃的"炸鱼条",就好像那张配料表给大家留下的印象比实物还要深刻一样。

谢尔碧愤愤不平地叫嚷道:"你们凭什么罚他十美元?应该有人给他颁发一个奖章才对!"

不幸的是,仲裁处里没有一个人有幽默感。谢尔碧的话引起了一阵骚动。"请肃静,否则你将被强行驱逐。"麦伦用小木槌砸了一下他面前不太结实的折叠桌。后来人们才发现,麦伦已经两年没有去学校上课了,根本就没有资格住在合作公寓,更别谈主持仲裁处了。

"You can't throw us out, this is the lounge," someone said. The sergeant-at-arms started walking toward the voice and it shut-up.

As he ruffled through some pages, Myron said, "If we turn to our Co-op handbook, it says on page thirty-four that the kitchen staff does not have to tolerate roughhousing, yelling, causing a disturbance—"

"He was posting ingredients!" Shelby interrupted.

"He was causing a disturbance," the kitchen monitor volunteered, still in his long white smock as if to prove his dedication to the kitchen. "People started throwing Fishfingers at the toaster."

"Why?" Myron looked confused.

The kitchen monitor shrugged.

"Because they suck and you know it!" someone yelled.

"Yeah! Let's see you eat one."

"Shut-up!" Myron yelled, striking the table so hard that it knocked over a soda, flinging sticky syrup around.

"Fine him! Fine him!" people began to yell and the meeting was disbanded for ten minutes while the radical element was ousted from the lounge.

Eventually the fine was reduced to five dollars. It made Shelby angry that civil liberties didn't extend to the Co-op. It also perturbed her that the new guy so easily paid it, forking over five dollars after the vote. She expected someone like that to have more persistence. Big ideas, small deeds, she thought sarcastically. Seeing him a few days later in the dining commons, Shelby said, a little snidely, "Well, if it isn't the Fishfingers guy."

He looked at her slowly and said, "I'm hoping that will die quickly." He put a piece of bread in the toaster. "As I recall, you were the one who wanted to give me a medal."

"I was drunk." Shelby grinned at him. It was rare to find people who liked their conversations aggressive.

They had come in on the tail end of brunch and all the kitchen staff had gone. Only a few students remained inside on such a nice day, huddled over books and papers, setting up camp early for midterms. Shelby noticed that the Fishfingers' guy—what was his name? she couldn't remember—would occasionally tap his fingers on the toast table, playing small but complete fills, odd cadences.

"你没权赶我们出去,这里是休息室。"有人说道。一旁的卫士开始向那个声音的方向走去,他立刻就闭嘴了。

麦伦快速地翻了几下,接着说道:"我们把合作公寓手册翻到三十四页,上面写着,厨房工作人员没有必要忍受打架斗殴,鬼吼鬼叫以及其他造成干扰的行为——"

"他只是贴了一张配料表!"谢尔碧打断道。

"他造成了干扰,"厨房班长主动说道,他还穿着那件长长的白色罩衣,仿佛要证明自己对厨房的奉献精神一样,"大家都开始把炸鱼条扔到吐司机上去了。"

"为什么?"麦伦看上去有些困惑。

厨房班长耸了耸肩膀。

"你自己清楚,因为那些炸鱼条难吃得要命。"

"就是!你自己怎么不吃。"

"闭嘴!"麦伦大叫了一声,重重地在桌子上捶了一拳,甚至都把苏打水给震翻了,黏糊糊的饮料四处飞溅着。

"罚款!罚款!"人们开始指着麦伦叫道,接着会议被迫中止了十分钟,期间所有激进分子都被驱逐出了休息室。

最终"炸鱼条罚款"被减少到了五美元。谢尔碧感到气愤的是,文明与自由竟然没有普及到合作公寓里来。那个新来的家伙如此轻易地就交了罚款,投票之后立刻就心甘情愿地掏出了钱。她本来还期待,这样的一个人会具备一些韧性呢。想得大,做得却少,谢尔碧不无讽刺地想道。几天之后谢尔碧在食堂里见到了他,便带着挖苦的口气说:"哟,这不是炸鱼条先生嘛。"

他慢慢转过来看着谢尔碧,"我希望这件事快点过去,"接着他往吐司机里放了一片面包,"如果我没记错的话,你就是那个说应该给我颁发奖章的人。"

"我当时喝醉了。"谢尔碧对着他咧嘴一笑。很少有人会喜欢这样咄咄逼人的对话。

这时候已经是早午餐的收尾阶段,所有的厨房工作人员都已经离开了。在这样一个好天气里,只有少数学生选择待在室内,蜷缩在成堆的书本后面,早早地为期中考试复习扎营。谢尔碧注意到,那个家伙——什么名字来着?她当时完全记不住他的名字——时不时地用手指在桌子上敲打,演奏着简短但完整的鼓花,节奏很新奇。

"You're a drummer." Shelby's toast hit the deck and she grabbed it, lathering it with a swipe from the bucket of margarine that sat on the toast table.

He nodded.

"What's your name?"

"Hadley."

"Shelby," she said, gesturing self-consciously to herself.

"Mind if I join you?"

Shelby shrugged. They both walked to a table near the back wall where a window looked out toward the campus and below to the Beta fraternity house. The swimming pool behind the house still showed signs of being dyed pink. The water had a rosy hue to it and streaks of red could be seen on the cement that surrounded the pool. The frat had accused the Co-op and promptly lit a fire on one of the Co-op floors. It was a small fire and was eventually extinguished, but no one bothered to leave the building, everyone being fairly unemotional about fire alarms because they went off at least twice a week. And as Max liked to say, "What's to burn? This place is fucking concrete."

"Where do you drum?"

"I don't." He sighed. "I was in a band in San Louis Obispo, but I transferred here."

"What was the name?"

"Boomslang. You wouldn't have heard of us."

"So what are they doing now?"

"Playing." He sighed. "They found another drummer."

"Were you guys any good?"

"We were okay." Hadley paused. "We opened for the Beach Boys a couple of months ago."

"And you quit!"

"I want to get my education," Hadley said dryly.

"Jesus, though. I mean, what's so great about UCLA?"

"There's a better chemistry program here—"

"Chemistry! I already know too damn many chemists."

"Is that possible?" Hadley smiled at her.

"你是个鼓手。"谢尔碧的面包跳出了底层,被她一把抓住了,然后她从装着人造黄油的小桶里挖了一块涂抹起来,顺势坐到了放吐司机的桌子上。

他点了点头。

"你叫什么名字?"

"哈德利。"

"我叫谢尔碧。"她做了个指代自己的姿势。

"介不介意我和你一起?"

谢尔碧耸了耸肩。他们一起走向靠近后墙的一张桌子,透过那里的窗户可以看到外面的校园,还有贝塔大学生联谊会会堂。会堂后面的游泳池仍然残留着曾被染成粉色的痕迹。池水带着玫瑰色的色调,池子四周的水泥边缘上缕缕红色若隐若现。联谊会的人认为合作公寓的人是罪魁祸首,并且当即在公寓的楼梯上点了火。火势很小,最终也被扑灭了,但当时大家都懒得离开那栋楼,因为每个人都已经对火警习以为常了:一周至少两次。况且,就像麦克斯所说的,"能烧坏什么呢? 这地方全是钢筋混凝土。"

"你在哪个乐队打鼓?"

"没有,"他叹了口气,"我以前在圣路易斯奥比斯波的时候在一个乐队里,但是现在我转学到这里来了。"

"那个乐队叫什么名字?"

"炼狱蝰蛇。你不可能听说过我们的。"

"那他们现在在做什么?"

"还在演出,"他又叹了口气,"他们另找了一个鼓手。"

"你们的演奏水平高吗?"

"还算过得去。"哈德利顿了一下,"几个月之前我们给'沙滩男孩儿'组合做了开场秀。"

"但是你现在却退出了乐队!"

"我只是想完成我的学业。"哈德里干巴巴地说。

"天哪,可还是……我的意思是,UCLA 这所学校有什么好的?"

"这里有一个更好的化学项目——"

"又是化学! 我已经认识太多的化学家了。"

"真的吗?"哈德利看着她笑了。

Chapter Seven   Reaction

"Wait till you meet Max." She rolled her eyes. "He's a friend of mine who lives here too. Although, you might like him. He's always talking about starting a band. I don't know how good he is. He plays guitar. I don't think he'd be up to opening for the Beach Boys though."

"That sounds more impressive than it actually was." He looked at her wryly. "Another band canceled. We mostly played dive bars where you'd have to protect yourself from flying bottles. Our lead singer got hit in the face with a mug once, split his lip. That's the one good thing about playing near the back."

"Except that the women can't see you as well."

Hadley looked at her levelly. "I don't play to get women."

"What do you do then? Cause disturbances? Rile the kitchen staff?"

Shelby watched in amazement as Hadley's face actually flushed red. It was very touching for some reason.

"My best friend Delilah went to San Luis. Know her? That's what she called it." Shelby tried to rescue the conversation, knowing that hers was a purposefully stupid question. Still she liked finding she knew the same people as others. You feel like you have more in common with people than you really do. It was a way to take a pulse, to get a sampling, see if you concurred over a reference object. One saved a lot of energy that way.

Hadley shook his head.

"She was famous for dismantling a bathroom at my high school. Every day she would go in and unscrew one screw. Late in the semester a girl went in there and the whole front of the stalls fell forward onto the sinks."

"You're making this up."

"No, I'm not. I swear." Shelby was laughing like she was lying.

"What was her major?"

"Veterinary."

He paused. "What's your major?"

"Theater. But it's not something I'm proud of. Though I did see something really great the other night. Performance art." Shelby grinned at him.

"What's that?"

"Well, this was where two women drenched the stage in stage blood and dropped large fish down their shorts."

"等着你见过麦克斯你就知道了。"谢尔碧翻了个白眼。"他是我的一个朋友,也住在合作公寓。你也许会喜欢他的,他是一个吉他手,总是在说想组建一个乐队,但我不知道他技术到底怎么样。但我不觉得他能胜任给'沙滩男孩儿'做开场表演的任务。"

"那次演出实际上没有它听起来那么光鲜。"他苦笑着看了看谢尔碧。"另一个乐队取消了演出,我们大部分是在'非主流酒吧'里演奏,在那儿你必须得躲开飞过来的酒瓶子来保护自己。有一次我们乐队主唱的脸被杯子给砸中了,嘴唇划出了一道口子。这就是在靠后的位置演奏的好处之一。"

"只是在后面的话,女观众也看不见你了。"

哈德利平静地看着她,"我演奏不是为了泡妞的。"

"那你为了什么呢?造成干扰吗?还是为了惹恼厨房工作人员?"谢尔碧吃惊地发现,哈德利的脸居然红了。"我最好的朋友黛利拉去了圣路易斯上大学,你认识她吗?"谢尔碧试图挽救这场对话,但她知道自己问了个非常白痴的问题。可是,她就是喜欢发现自己和别人有共同的交友圈时的感觉。这时你会觉得实际上自己与其他人有很多的共同点。这是一种把脉和采样的方法,看看自己与分析对象是否一拍即合。这样一来可以省很多精力。

哈德利摇了摇头。

"在高中的时候,她因为把学校的洗手间给拆了而名噪一时。每天她都会走进洗手间卸掉一颗螺丝钉,就这样快到学期结束时,有一个女生进去了之后,所有隔间的门都倒塌下来,砸在了洗手池上。"

"你在编故事吧。"

"不,我没有,我发誓。"谢尔碧大笑着,就好像自己是在撒谎似的。

"她的专业是什么?"

"兽医学。"

他停顿了一会儿,"你呢?"

"戏剧。但我并没办法以此为傲。尽管如此,前几天晚上我确实看到了一场非常精彩的表演——行为艺术。"谢尔碧笑嘻嘻地看向他。

"那是什么?"

"这个嘛,就是现场有两个女人用人造血洒满了整个舞台,然后又将硕大的鱼顺着自己的短裤往下扔。"

Chapter Seven Reaction

Hadley looked at her blankly. "Is everyone around here so intense?"

"I don't think so because everyone thinks I'm from New York."

He laughed.

"Anyway, think about it. Blood and fish ... ?" She paused as he looked at her blankly. "What two things do they have in common? Women and ... ?" She gestured, as if that would help the connection.

"Fish?" He looked startled.

"You can't be that naive." She said wonderingly, and his face turned color.

"You sure blush a lot." She smiled at him and he looked at his hands, tapping them on the table. "I like that in a man."

He looked at her with the barest twitch of a smile. "Women and?" He gestured for her to continue.

"Jesus! Women and Jesus. See, they also had a cross onstage covered with Kotex. Because blood and fish are symbolic of Christ and they also pertain to women. And this is the cleverest part. They talked about if immaculate conception had really occurred, Christ would have had to have been a woman because women don't carry Y chromosomes. Blood and fish were clues from the ancients."

"Amazing." Hadley caught Shelby's eyes, and for a heartbeat of time, he smiled at her, until she broke his gaze and looked at her food. She could tell that he was interested in her. A fleeting urge to touch him, his hand or maybe his shoulder, came over her, but she knew she had a tendency to fall in love with whoever liked her, a kind of romantic responsibility, so she squelched the idea. And wouldn't think of it again for another five years. But by then it would be a sin.

哈德利一脸困惑地盯着她,"这里所有人都这么激进吗?"

"我不这么觉得,因为这里的每个人都觉得我才是从纽约来的。"

他被逗笑了。

"重要的是,你想想,血和鱼……"看着他不解的表情谢尔碧停顿了几秒,"它们有哪两个共同点?女人,还有……"她做了个手势,好像这样就能帮哈德利建立联系似的。

"鱼?"他一副受到惊吓的样子。

"你不可能这么单纯的,"谢尔碧惊讶地说,然后哈德利的脸瞬间又变了颜色。

"你真是容易脸红。"谢尔碧对他笑了,他立即把目光投向自己的双手,在桌子上不停地敲打着。"我喜欢会脸红的男人。"

哈德利看着她,脸上挂着明显是扯出来的笑意,"女人,还有……"他示意谢尔碧继续。

"上帝!女人还有上帝。你看,那些表演者还在舞台上放了一个用高洁丝卫生棉盖住的十字架。因为血和鱼都是基督的象征,同时它们又都与女人相关[译者注:鱼是基督教的符号象征之一,详见维基百科词条"ichthys";在英语中女人与鱼相似的腥味经常被拿来开玩笑]。这就是整场演出最聪明的地方。他们说,如果圣灵感孕真的发生过的话,上帝本应该是女性的,因为女性是不携带Y染色体的[译者注:圣母受圣灵感孕生耶稣,未曾与约瑟同房]。血和鱼就是古人给我们留下的线索。"

"真是不可思议。"哈德利迎上谢尔碧的目光,对她笑了,持续了一拍心跳的时间,直到谢尔碧低头看向自己的食物,打断了他的凝视。她能够感觉到,哈德利对自己有兴趣。她产生了一阵短暂的冲动,想要去触碰哈德利,他的手,或者是肩膀。但是她非常了解自己,只要别人喜欢她,她就会轻易坠入爱河,因为她觉得这是一种浪漫的责任。这样一想,谢尔碧立刻就压制了自己的想法。在那之后的五年里,她也强迫自己不去想它。但是到那时,这种想法就已经成为一种过错了。

Chapter Eight   **Decomposition**

> Decomposition: Geology. Chemical breakdown of rock minerals with the resultant disintegration of the rocks themselves.
> *The Tormont Webster's Illustrated Encyclopedic Dictionary*

Hadley's new roommate was starting to drive him nuts. He hated to think that Shelby had been right about Ethan. It's always the little things that get you, the accumulation of insignificances that tilt you over the brink. Trifles mount until you're forced to face that you've just let things go too far, like when you're suddenly nose to nose with a bloody syringe on the kitchen counter. Nearly dropping his cereal bowl on it, Hadley choked back a yell, accidentally kicking an open cabinet door in his sudden panic. This was the final provocation. Waking up in the morning was hard enough without having to face the horrors of New York in your own apartment.

So subtle had been Ethan's decline into the underworld that it took something like a bloody syringe to make Hadley realize how much Ethan had degenerated. There'd been other signs, but none quite as flagrant as the brilliant red of a recently used needle, blood strung between needle tip and countertop like the plumb line of a web. It made Hadley's stomach turn. The need to inject one's high. The dependence. The impact of flowing bodily fluids. That was how much you needed it. To have to spill your blood.

Hadley was used to the smaller side effects of Ethan. The personality changes. The refrigerator of mystery, filled with experiments of one type or another. In the fog of his usual mornings, Hadley would find that he had a stoppered bottle in his hand when he had only meant to grab the milk. Among other things, Ethan regularly kept methadone in the refrigerator just in case he couldn't score any heroin. He'd gotten the methadone from a rehab center, quitting the program the same day he'd joined. Ethan wasn't interested in being rehabilitated.

第八章　分解

> 分解：地质学术语。岩石中矿物质的化学分解以及伴随而来的岩石自身的分解。
>
> ——《托蒙特韦伯斯特图解百科词典》

哈德利快被自己的新室友给搞抓狂了，但他却不想承认谢尔碧对伊桑的看法是对的。最后让你发怒的总是小事情，一些不起眼的事不断地堆积，让你忍无可忍。琐事叠加到最后你不得不承认，你的放任换来的是一步步的得寸进尺，比如说你竟然沦落到与厨房桌子上的一个该死的注射器大眼瞪小眼。哈德利差点把装麦片的碗放到上面，他强忍住怒吼，突然的惊慌却使他不小心一脚踢上了敞开的储藏柜的柜门。这件事成了最后的导火索。光是早起就已经够受的了，更别提还要在自己的公寓里直面纽约市的种种怪异事件了。

直到看见带血的注射器，哈德利才意识到伊桑的堕落程度，他平时的表现该有多细微啊。其实也有其他的征兆，只是没有一个像刚使用完不久的鲜红的针头那样明目张胆：血丝就像织网时的铅垂线一般贯穿针筒首尾。看到这样的场景，哈德利的胃里开始翻腾起来。一个人竟然需要注射才能让自己兴奋起来，随之产生的依赖性，体液流动的影响。你对它的渴望如此之强烈，即使是自己的鲜血也在所不惜。

以前，对于伊桑带来的较小些的副作用，哈德利已经习惯了，但一个人的个性是会改变的。冰箱变成了一个不可预知的地方，摆满了各种实验品。一个普通的早晨，哈德利迷迷糊糊地伸手想拿牛奶，却发现手里握着一个带塞子的瓶子[译者注：实验室里的试剂瓶]。还有就是，以防自己搞不到海洛因，伊桑通常会把美沙酮储藏在冰箱里[译者注：美沙酮是海洛因等阿片类毒品的替代性药物]。他是从一个戒毒中心领到的美沙酮，在加入项目的那一天他就立刻退出了——他对恢复正常生活一点兴趣也没有。

Chapter Eight   Decomposition

He wasn't the ideal roomer, but there were worse. That was the deal when you lived in New York. As long as your roommate paid his share of the rent and didn't trash the place, you considered yourself lucky. But that was the problem. Just this month, Ethan's rent check had bounced, even after Hadley had loaned him half of it. Hadley didn't ask him what he did with the money. It's pretty obvious what an addict would do with ready cash. Until now, Ethan had always been reliable, although he did have checkbooks lying all over the place and pretty much wrote checks out of any one of them. Generally Ethan's dad came through with the money, but Hadley remembered that lately his dad had been threatening to disown him.

He dreaded having to give Ethan an ultimatum—as if his opinion were going to matter to a heroin addict. But it was easier than moving. Running through possible scenarios of reasoned discussion, Hadley started to make a sack lunch when Ethan startled him by showing up, waving a wad of money. Ethan grandly paid Hadley back, flaunting the fifties as he snapped them into Hadley's hand. Then he fluttered a cashier's check to the housing office around under Hadley's nose. "Chesterton loaned me three thousand dollars," he finally said in response to Hadley's insistent questioning. Ethan sat down at the kitchen table, taking a swig off his natural protein drink of carrot juice and malt.

"Why would Chesterton loan you all that money?" Hadley squinted and opening the kitchen window. The protein drink had a smell that irritated Hadley's nose.

Ethan had a mustache of carrot juice which he licked off with his tongue, missing the left side. "I told him my grant money was late and I owed three months in rent."

"And he believed you?"

"I'm his best chemist."

Hadley couldn't argue with that. Ethan was a really smart guy. It made Hadley kind of depressed. He liked Ethan. He had a likable quality. The charming loser. You got so pissed off at him but you couldn't not like him. But lately Ethan was more distant, a Stepford chemist with a hidden secret. Who knew what sums he owed people? Obligations he had? Hadley didn't think Ethan would steal. The question was, would he synthesize? Would he make drugs for others? He was hanging around people he never would have spoken to in the past—bony, emaciated creatures who wouldn't

第八章 分解

伊桑并不是一个理想的室友人选,但是比他更差的大有人在。住在纽约,你就得接受这个现实。只要你的室友按时交了自己的那份房租,并且没有把整个房子搞得像个垃圾堆,你就应该觉得自己幸运了。但是问题又出现了:就在这个月,伊桑的房租支票被退回了,即使是在哈德利借了一半的房租钱给他之后。哈德利没有问他钱花到哪里去了,因为一个瘾君子会把手里的现金用来做什么实在是太明显了。尽管他会把支票簿扔得到处都是,用的时候随便捡一张来写,但在这件事情之前,总的来说伊桑还是一个可以信任的人。大多数时候伊桑的爸爸会带着钱来看他,但是哈德利回忆起来最近他好像一直威胁说要与伊桑断绝关系。

哈德利害怕有一天自己得给伊桑下最后的通牒——就好像他的看法对一个吸毒者会产生什么影响似的——但这对他来说比自己搬走要容易一些。哈德利在脑海里把所有与伊桑对质的可能场景都过了一遍,然后开始做便当,这时候伊桑突然出现了,手里挥舞着一沓钱,哈德利被吓了一跳。伊桑炫耀似的扬着手里一叠面值为五十美元的钞票,姿势夸张地"啪"一声甩到哈德利手里。然后他又在哈德利眼皮底下挥了挥给住宅办公室的银行本票。"切斯特通给我贷了三千美元,"在哈德利的一再追问下,他终于说道。伊桑在厨房里的桌子前坐下,喝了一大口他特制的纯自然高蛋白饮料——胡萝卜汁与麦芽威士忌的混合物。

"为什么你老板会借钱给你?"哈德利撇斜着眼看了看他,打开了厨房的窗户。那种蛋白饮料的味道让哈德利的鼻子无比不舒服。

伊桑的嘴边沾上了胡萝卜汁,他用舌头舔了舔,却把左边给忘了。"我告诉他我的实验经费发放迟了,而我的房租已经欠了三个月了。"

"他就这样相信你了?"

"我是他旗下最好的化学家。"

这一点哈德利无话可说。伊桑确实是一个很聪明的家伙。这让哈德利感到有点低落。他喜欢伊桑这个人——他身上有一种让人产生好感的品质。他是个有魅力的失败者。虽然他会让你火冒三丈,你却没办法不喜欢他。但是最近,伊桑变得更有距离感了,像是个怀有秘密的斯戴普福德化学家[译者注:*Stepford Wives*(《斯戴普福德主妇》)是一部美国电影,片中人物大多毫无个性,心怀鬼胎]。谁知道他一共欠别人多少钱呢?还有多少应该负的责任?哈德利倒不认为伊桑会去偷,但问题是,他会不会为其他人合成药品呢?当时和他混在一起的那帮人,放在过去伊桑是绝不可能和他们说上一句话的——他们都骨瘦如柴,

look you in the eye. They reminded Hadley of walking skeletons, only coming around at night, staying until dawn, slipping away without their shadows, without any vestige of daylight. When drugs become the reason to exist, all else is unimportant. Friends are just people who can help you score.

Hadley grew up around dead people. His father was the town mortician. It wasn't something that got you a lot of friends. He was used to hanging out by himself, used to jokes about the family car. He'd learned to avoid confrontation, preferring books to people. He'd retreated into music. Death was not something he feared. But it was Ethan's semblance of death, this pre-death that bothered him. Death without the benefits.

Hadley watched as Ethan drank his carrot juice, remembering that not long ago—or at least last year, which didn't seem that long ago—they had run into each other at the glass blower's, both of them needing specialized flasks. They had talked to this old man with the unplaceable accent for an hour, down in the basement of the chemistry building, a dark and fiery throw-back to blacksmiths and brickyards and dangerous crafts, watching him fire the glass until it was a blistering orb, bright cyan at the surface, shimmering, the Northern Lights in miniature.

Hadley watched the glass transform from a molten lump to an Ehrlemeyer flask while Ethan talked the old man into making him a water pipe. He didn't call it that of course, but drew a picture of what he wanted, and told the glass blower he'd pay him on the side. Setting down his iron rod, the man stroked his gray stubbled jowls, looking pointedly at Ethan. He shrugged, nodding in acquiescence, never saying a word; it was obvious that he knew what Ethan wanted. Hadley had thought this exchange funny at the time, not realizing that Ethan would be one of those people for whom drugs was an obsession; it filled a vacancy in his personality.

Two days ago detectives from the New York police department had come to the chemistry labs to ask Ethan questions about a murder that had happened at The Lunar Room, a local bar Ethan frequented. There had been a point in Hadley's life when something like this would have stunned him, the fact that the NYPD was investigating a drug-related murder at the university chemistry labs, not to mention questioning his roommate. So much was implied. And yet, he'd actually forgotten about it until now. It was just another day in New York City. You would think a story like that would make the papers. But no. It was small news. A place like

从来不看别人的眼睛。他们让哈德利想起行走骷髅来，只在午夜出现，一直待到黎明，悄无声息地溜走，没留下一丝阴影，不带走一片日光。当毒品成为存在的理由，其他所有事都不再重要了。朋友也沦为你获取毒品的工具。

哈德利从小就在死人周围长大。他的父亲在家乡的小镇里做殡葬。这一点导致哈德利交不到什么朋友，他习惯了形影单只，习惯了别人拿他们家的车来开玩笑。他学会避免与他人正面接触，比起人来，他更喜欢看书；他还会退到音乐这个避风港里。对于死亡，他并不感到惧怕。但是笼罩着伊桑的死亡外壳，以及生命终结的前兆，使他不安。死亡的所有好处都无法获得；虽然还活着，却如同行尸走肉。

哈德利看着伊桑喝他的胡萝卜汁，想起不久之前——还是至少有一年以前，那也不是很久——他们在吹玻璃的师傅那里第一次见面，当时他们都需要制作特殊的细颈烧瓶。就在化学楼的地下室里，他们和那个吹玻璃的老头儿聊了一个小时的天，却搞不清他的口音到底是哪个国家的。他们看着他用火烧制玻璃，直至它成为一个不断冒气泡的球状，表面呈现青色，闪烁着光芒，像极了微型的北极光。那个老头黝黑的皮肤和暴躁的脾气使人想起过去的铁匠和搬砖工，还有其他从事危险行当的工人。

玻璃从融化的块状物渐渐成形为锥形瓶，哈德利一直在一旁观看着。与此同时伊桑正试图说服老人给他做一个水烟管，当然他并没有直接说，而是把自己想要的东西给画了出来，并且告诉老人，他会直接付现金。老人将铁棒放下，轻轻摸了摸下巴上的胡茬，目光尖锐地看着伊桑。伊桑耸了耸肩，默许地点了点头，一个字都没有说；很显然那老头知道伊桑想要什么。哈德利当时还觉得这种交流很有趣，却没有意识到伊桑日后会成为瘾君子；毒品填充了他人格中的一部分空缺。

两天前，纽约警察署的警探们来到化学实验室里询问伊桑一些问题，因为伊桑经常光顾的当地酒吧"月桂屋"里发生了一起谋杀案。在哈德利人生的某个阶段，总会发生像这样的事，使他震惊无比：纽约警署竟然来到大学实验室里调查跟毒品有关的谋杀案，更不要说还审讯了自己的室友。很多事都已经很明显了，但在此之前他竟然都把这件事情给忘了。但这只不过是纽约市普普通通的又一天而已。别以为像这样的故事就可以登上报纸了，没门。这只是则小消息。

Chapter Eight Decomposition

Manhattan had too much on its mind.

Hadley looked at Ethan sitting there, swishing carrot juice around in his mouth as if he were the healthiest person in the world. Sometimes he would be wild, strung out on something, coke or meth. Hadley had only seen him this way twice, but it was a wonder more people than just Shelby hadn't slugged him. He'd yell at policemen as they drove by him. Insane stuff. Other times he'd be nearly comatose, glued to the TV set like it was his only friend.

Hadley would try to pull Ethan back with science. Talk about his chemistry. Science was what they had in common. Intellectual banter that had no emotional attachment. Sometimes Hadley, after establishing this mode, would slowly bring the conversation around, trying to inch in, appealing to Ethan's rational side. Reminding him of how he used to be. Reminding him how bad it had gotten. Sitting down at the table with Ethan, Hadley now tried to work the murder.

"So your friend Eli was killed—the one who wears all his shirts inside out?" The weird way Eli wore his shirts seemed too personal a memory, as if someone that quirky couldn't just *die*.

Ethan nodded and took another drink of carrot juice. He was a vegetarian. He also made a lot of sun tea. Hadley glanced at the big jar of sepia-colored water that sat along the windowsill of the kitchen. Several bags of herb tea hung down inside, held in place by the screwtop lid. For Ethan there was no irony.

"He was a good friend of yours."

Ethan just shrugged.

Sometimes Hadley felt as if there were an atmospheric condition between Ethan and himself that made Hadley's words incomprehensible, a cloud or an unusual vapor state that dopplered his meaning. He wanted to shake Ethan out of his haze and say, "Get the hell back here!" But there was nothing Hadley could say that would make any difference. He knew this absolutely, but something in him still refused to accept it. He wasn't sure why.

Ethan interrupted his thoughts. "You haven't seen my keys anywhere have you? I've misplaced them."

"Again?" Hadley couldn't help himself.

"A simple yes or no. That's all I'm looking for."

"But the door was locked when I came home—"

像曼哈顿这样的地方每天要过滤的事儿太多了。

哈德利看着伊桑坐在那里，将胡萝卜汁在嘴里"唰唰"地漱来漱去，仿佛他是世界上最健康的人似的。有的时候他却会变得毫无节制，不停嘴地吃东西，不是可乐，就是冰毒。他像这样的情形哈德利只看见过两次，但是除了谢尔碧之外竟然没有更多的人动手揍过伊桑，这真是个奇迹。他会在警车开过身边的时候冲着警察大喊大叫——简直是疯了。其余的时候他都近于迷糊状态，死死地扎根在电视机前面，就好像那是他唯一的朋友一样。

哈德利曾试过用科学把伊桑给拉回正轨。他会和伊桑聊化学——他们的共同点也就是科学研究了。但只是学术上的打趣开玩笑，而没有感情的连接。有时在建立了这个模式之后，哈德利会循序渐进地将对话打开，试图进一步靠近伊桑神智清晰的那一面。提醒他自己过去是什么样子的；提醒他现在的状况变得多么糟糕。此时此刻哈德利与伊桑同坐在一张桌子上，哈德利想要试图了解更多关于那件谋杀案的事情。

"听说你的朋友艾莱被谋害了——就是那个总是把T恤反着穿的朋友？"这段关于艾莱怪异穿衣习惯的记忆带有鲜明的个人色彩，仿佛如此古怪的一个人不应该就这么死掉。

伊桑微微点了点头，又喝了一口胡萝卜汁。他是个素食主义者。他还会经常泡太阳茶。哈德利瞥了一眼厨房窗台上盛着棕褐色液体的大罐子，几包草本茶的茶包固定在盖子上悬挂在罐子里。对伊桑来说，这没有什么可讽刺的地方。

"他可是你的好朋友之一。"

伊桑只是耸了下肩。

有的时候哈德利觉得他和伊桑之间存在一种气场，像是云层或者蒸气态，使得哈德利的话变得无法被理解。他想要将伊桑从迷蒙的状态中摇醒，对他说："你给我回来！"但事实上哈德利不管说什么都不会产生效果的。这一点他心知肚明，但他内心有一股力量仍然拒绝承认。他也不确定为什么。

伊桑打断了他的思绪，"你有没有看见我的钥匙？我不知道把它们给放哪儿去了。"

"又找不到了？"哈德利不由自主地反问道。

"我就要你一个简单的回答，有还是没有。"

"但我回家来的时候门是锁着的——"

"I've been using the fire escape."

Realizing this meant that Ethan had been leaving the living room window open, Hadley said sarcastically, "Why don't you just put a sign out that says 'please rob me'?"

"Okay, okay, I only did it today. You got a spare?"

"As soon as I finish here with my lunch, I'll go make you one." Hadley knew that he should make Ethan get his own key made, but if he could do that, they wouldn't be having this conversation.

Hadley opened the refrigerator for some mayonnaise and luncheon meat, and got the bread out of the cupboard. As Hadley spread the mayonnaise slowly and painterly, coating the bread's surface with a thin veneer, the preciseness of his spreading exerted a calming influence; he paused and tried to use his most persuasive tone.

"Ethan, I hate to sound like your dad or something, but you've gotta get some help. I mean, I'd be worried if my best friends were getting murdered." He paused, waiting for Ethan to say something. Hadley realized that the whole situation confused him. Ethan was one of the smartest people he knew and, as a rule, smart people didn't make stupid mistakes. What did they call this in psychology? Something like unresolved dissonance, where the three things didn't add up: Ethan was smart. Ethan was a drug addict. But being a drug addict was stupid. It was A equals B and B equals C, but C doesn't equal A. Logically, one of the conditions must be wrong. But life wasn't very mathematical. That was the problem. In life, all those things could be true and that's what was making Hadley crazy. He liked things to make sense. That's why he did research. Chemistry was complex, but it worked out. You had some amount of control. Hadley looked back at Ethan, unable to lecture him. "Why was he murdered?"

"Sold somebody some bad shit. He needed the money."

"When's the funeral?" Hadley watched Ethan's face, looking for any flicker of emotion. The funeral of someone your own age was sobering. Hadley paused as he opened the refrigerator for some lettuce, feeling the weight of his own sad memories.

"No funeral. His body disappeared—"

"How could his body just disappear?" Hadley interrupted. His head was pounding.

"Come on. This is New York. Someone thought he had drugs *in* him."

第八章 分解

"我一直用的是紧急出口。"

这意味着伊桑一直以来都是不关卧室窗户的，哈德利意识到这一点以后，挖苦地说："你还不如在外面挂个标语，上面写着'请打劫我'呢！"

"放松，放松，我就只有今天这样做了。你有备用钥匙吗？"

"我一做完手头的午饭，就去给你配一把。"哈德利知道，他应该让伊桑自己去配，但是如果伊桑能做到这件事的话，这段对话也就不会发生了。

哈德利打开冰箱，取出蛋黄酱和午餐肉，又从橱子里拿了面包。哈德利一边慢慢像画家般地涂抹着蛋黄酱，给面包的表面镀上一层薄薄的装饰，精准到位的动作产生了一种安抚人心的效果；他停顿了一会儿，酝酿出自己最具说服力的语调来。

"伊桑，我也不想用你老爸的口吻跟你说话，但你必须得寻求一些帮助了。我是说，如果我最好的朋友被谋杀了的话，我会非常担心的。"他停了下来，等伊桑说些什么。哈德利意识到，现在整个事态都让自己困惑不已。伊桑是他所认识的最聪明的人之一，而理所应当的，聪明人不会犯愚蠢的错误。当三个条件之间的等价关系不成立时，在心理学上被称作什么来着？好像是未知不协调症状之类的：伊桑很聪明；伊桑是个瘾君子；但是染上毒瘾是非常愚蠢的。现在的情况是，A 等于 B，B 等于 C，但 C 不等于 A。从逻辑上来说，其中一个条件必然是错误的。但生活本身并不能用数学逻辑来计算。这就是问题所在。在生活中，以上所有陈述都有可能是真的，这就是为什么哈德利快被搞疯了的原因。他喜欢让所有事情都有据可循，所以他才会选择做研究。化学虽然复杂，但在一定数量控制实验的协助下，它最终会产生效果。哈德利回过头去看着伊桑，一时间不知道该怎么给他讲道理。"他为什么被杀了？"

"卖了一些不太好的货色给别人。他需要钱。"

"葬礼是什么时候？"哈德利打量着伊桑的脸，寻找哪怕是一丝的感情流露的迹象。同龄人的葬礼能够让人肃然清醒。哈德利打开冰箱拿生菜的时候顿了顿，体味着自己悲伤的回忆。

"没有葬礼。他的尸体不见了——"

"他的尸体怎么可能就这么消失了呢？"哈德利打断道，他的头有点突突作痛。

"得了吧，这里可是纽约。有人觉得他体内有毒品。"

Chapter Eight Decomposition

"What do you mean '*in* him'?"

"Up his butt." Ethan finished his juice and stood up. He was five-ten but seemed taller because his flesh clung tightly to his bone. His skin had the translucence of a grub or something that lives in perpetual darkness. Ethan always wore long sleeve shirts, even in the summer. He never wore shorts. His clothes were of a serious nature, gray, concealing, like urban camouflage; Ethan could blend into concrete and steel like a reptile of the city.

Walking to the kitchen door, Ethan said cynically, "Without a body, not much point in having a funeral."

Hadley watched him leave, feeling less amenable to Ethan and more angry. He didn't buy Ethan's callousness. He knew that Eli was his best friend. Why couldn't he admit it? It seemed so terrible not to have a funeral. People need funerals. Without them, you never get to lay your dead to rest. His father would go on about this, his salesman spiel, but it was true. Funerals gave you the right to grieve. They were freeing. It was the proximity of funerals that had pulled Hadley toward music. He began his career as the funeral home organist. Music had the power to soothe, to infuse the body with emotion so that eventually you could just let it all go. Otherwise you end up like Ethan. Angry instead of sad. Never able to lose the pain, only dulling it with drugs. In Hadley's experience, sadness could be tolerated and would become more distant. Anger bred its own.

Hadley was still holding the refrigerator door open; he'd forgotten what he was looking for. He glanced back at his sandwich for a clue. Oh, lettuce, he remembered and opened the crisper drawer, almost afraid of what he'd find in there. Tearing off a few leaves, he started to let the door close again when he noticed something out of place, more odd than the unmarked bottles. Snatching the door open, Hadley replayed his previous moments, bending back down and looking on the shelf. Jesus. There were Ethan's keys behind the milk. He'd only seen them because he had to bend down to reach into the crisper and the refrigerator light had glinted on them.

"Now how the hell..." he thought, knowing the question would go unanswered because Ethan never remembered anything. Hadley was sure that much of Ethan's life was lived by remote control. He was like the three faces of Eve without two of the faces. Those spots were just filled with white noise.

"体内是什么意思?"

"屁股以上。"伊桑一口喝完了果汁站了起来。他身高五尺十寸,但是看上去更高,因为他身上的肉紧紧地依附在骨头上。他的皮肤有着幼虫或是长久生活在黑暗之中的生物般的透明感。即使是在夏天,伊桑也总是穿长袖T恤,从来不穿短裤。他的着装体现了一种严肃的天性,灰色的,具有隐藏的性质,就像是城市里的伪装;伊桑可以像变色龙一样将自己转变为与城市一体的钢筋和水泥。

伊桑向厨房的门走去时,口无遮拦地说道:"没有尸体,办葬礼也没多大意义。"

哈德利看着他就这样离开,内心对伊桑的责任感少了一些,愤怒多了几分。他不吃伊桑冷酷无情的那一套,他知道艾莱是他最好的朋友。为什么他就不能承认呢?不举办葬礼看上去实在是太说不过去了。人们需要葬礼,否则的话,逝去的人就无法得以安息。虽然哈德利的父亲会一直用这套说辞来招揽生意,殡葬行当的其他销售员也会对此夸夸其谈,但这却是千真万确的。葬礼给人们提供了悲伤的权力;他们是在寻求释放。正是对葬礼的接近拉近了哈德利与音乐的距离。他最初的音乐生涯是从殡仪馆的风琴演奏开始的。音乐具有抚慰的能力,它向人体内注入一种感情,最终你就可以让一切都随风而逝。不然的话,你就会落得像伊桑一样的下场——感到生气而不是悲伤。永远都无法让痛苦彻底离开,只能用毒品来钝化它。从哈德利自己的经验来看,悲伤是可以忍受的,然后就会渐行渐远;愤怒则会不断衍生。

哈德利的手仍然搭在打开的冰箱门上,他已经忘记了本来是要找什么的。他转过头去瞥了一眼三明治,想找找线索。噢,生菜,他想起来了,于是打开了保鲜层,他几乎都有些害怕,不知道自己会在里面找到什么。当哈德利取了几片叶子,放手让门慢慢关上的时候,他突然注意到了某样东西,比没有标记的试剂瓶还要格格不入。他猛地抓开门,脑海里回放着刚才的画面,重又弯下腰去扫视了一遍架子。见鬼,牛奶的后面不就是伊桑的钥匙嘛。要不是哈德利躬身去保鲜层时,冰箱的灯正好反射到钥匙上的话,他是不会发现的。

"这到底是怎么……"他寻思着,但他知道答案显然易见,因为伊桑从来就不记得任何事情。哈德利十分确定伊桑大部分的生活都是由遥控器来控制的。他就像是三面夏娃,只是缺少了两面,空白处被白噪声给填满了[译者注:《三面夏娃》是关于多重人格的美国影片;白噪声的物理定义为随机起伏噪声的统称]。

Chapter Eight Decomposition

It was nine in the morning. Hadley shook his head as he listened to Ethan's choking snores—everyone of them starting with silence of breath and then making up for it by a deep inhale that caused Ethan to nearly gag in his sleep. Ethan had obviously been up all night. A recurrent suspicion of why he put up with Ethan surfaced in his brain, but he didn't want to deal with it now. He just wanted to do chemistry, so he took his sack lunch and went to the lab. He was going to figure out why the control worked when it shouldn't have. His plan was to run an analysis of the tap water. It was a relief for him to do chemistry. In a way he understood why Ethan continued to go to the lab. Working with your hands was therapeutic. Solving difficult problems forced you to concentrate so completely on them that the rest of the world just passed by. Night turned to day, day to night without your having to think about it. To plan anything else, to fill your time with dates or parties or relationships was unnecessary. You could, of course, but you didn't have to. Chemistry could become your lover, your bridge to posterity. If you made your mark, you could live on, whether or not your genes ever replicated.

Hadley knew this was desperate, so he started a new reaction to keep himself from thinking about it. But it didn't help. He thought about how much he'd like to have kids. He thought he'd be a good dad. Then he chided himself. His life wasn't over. Anyway, New York was no place to raise a child. He remembered visiting a friend from high school. He and his family lived on a farm in Iowa. They'd had a horse. His youngest—what was she? two years old?—carried around this black negligée the whole time he was there, her security object. She called it a "neigh". The mom had shrugged apologetically. "She found it in the back of my drawer." Then she'd laughed. "I hadn't seen it for years." Something about that moment, how cute the little girl was, sucking her thumb and dragging this nightie around the farm, and how down-to-earth his friend's wife had been, stuck in his mind, representing what life could be like. Perhaps he'd been too single-minded, intent on his career. But he certainly couldn't see himself as a farmer. He shook his head, knowing he was being stupid, knowing that changing jobs would not find him a family, and he forced himself to get to work, pouring a concentration of dye into a flask of water just as Max sauntered in. Max staked out an area on Hadley's bench. "You know, Dermot's having a party tonight."

第八章 分解

现在是早晨九点。哈德利听着伊桑那令人窒息的呼噜声,摇了摇头——每一声打呼的开始,都先是安静的呼吸,然后突然深深地吸气来弥补,他几乎在睡梦中就被呛住了。很显然,他是彻夜未归,凌晨才回来。对于自己为什么要忍让伊桑的疑问不停地出现在他的脑海里,但他现在不想考虑这个问题。他只想研究化学,于是他就拿起午餐便当出发去实验室了。他要去搞明白为什么对照实验本来不应该产生产品,结果却奏效了。他的计划是对实验用的自来水进行分析实验。对他来说,做化学实验是一种减压释放。在某种程度上,他能够理解为什么伊桑会一直频繁地去实验室。使用双手工作对健康有益:在解决难题的时候,你被迫完全集中注意力在上面,以至于剩下的世界就只会从你身旁倏忽经过。日复一日,夜复一夜,你完全都不用去费神评估这件事。任何其他计划——用约会、派对或是恋爱关系来填满自己的时间都完全没有必要。当然你也可以做这些,但不是非得做。化学可以成为你的爱人,你与后世之间的桥梁。如果你给这个世界留下了印记,不论你的基因是否得到了复制,你都可以永存。

哈德利感觉到了这个想法的绝望性,于是就开始了一项新的反应来分散自己的注意力,但是没起效果。他在想,自己其实非常想要孩子,而且自己会成为一个好父亲。接着他又把自己给责备了一顿——他的生活还没有结束呢。再说了,纽约也不是一个抚养孩子的好地方。他还记得去拜访一个高中同学时的情景:他们一家人一起住在爱荷华州的一个农场里,他们拥有一匹马。他最小的女儿——几岁来着?两岁?——在哈德利拜访期间一直拿着一件女式的晨袍跑来跑去,那是她的安全符。她把它称为"咳儿"。女主人抱歉地耸了耸肩,"她在我的抽屉里面翻出了这个,我都已经好几年没见到了。"随后她就大声笑了起来。那一瞬间,某种东西——那个小女孩儿吮手指和拖着睡袍满农场地跑时有多么的可爱,还有朋友的妻子是多么的朴素真实,深深烙印在了哈德利的脑海里,提醒他生活原来是可以这样的。也许他有些太死脑筋了,执意追求自己的事业。但他也十分确定自己无法成为一个称职的农夫。他甩了甩头,意识到自己又在犯傻了,明知道换工作也不会帮助他组建起一个家庭的。他强迫自己投入工作中,将一定浓度的染液倒入有水的烧瓶中。这时候,麦克斯悠闲地走了进来,盯着哈德利工作台上的一块区域,"你知道吗?今晚德莫特要办派对。"

Chapter Eight Decomposition

Hadley looked at Max for a long moment, then half-shrugged, half-winced, a certain brand of arrogance and humility to match Max's own. "I'm not much in the party mood."

"Neither is Shelby. But I convinced her to go." Max waved his hand in fast-forward, a beckoning motion that almost went too fast for the eye. "Come onnnn. Free alcohol."

"What's wrong with Shelby?" Hadley turned back around and attended to his reaction.

"I think she wants to take a shower."

"It's not fixed yet?" Hadley asked, swirling the flask. The mixture inside was turning from clear to a light orange.

"No. So Shelby went to the housing office yesterday because she can cry better than I can—"

Hadley paused swirling. "I'm glad to see her theater major is worth something," he said dryly. Thinking of her crying in the housing office confused him. He rarely cried. Growing up above a mortuary had taught him how to deal with grief. He saw it everyday. Most people had no control over it. It was common for them to take out their emotions on his father. One widow had even punched his dad, just hauled off and hit him in the eye because he'd ordered the wrong color flowers. For the funeral his father had had to wear the same makeup as the corpse, his purple eye more disfiguring than her husband's death.

Hadley realized that he'd never seen Shelby cry, couldn't even imagine her sad. She was always so sarcastic. She always thought he was unhappy, which was funny to him because he didn't think of himself as anything—particularly happy, particularly sad.

Max glanced at the flask in Hadley's hand. "What the hell is that?"

"Qualitative assay," Hadley said simply, looking at the now dark orange solution. "Impurities," he nodded, tapping the flask. He'd guessed that the water would only turn slightly golden, but the result already made him feel somewhat better. The orange color started sinking toward the bottom. Hadley quickly filtered the precipitate and weighed it. "Two percent. You think that's enough to make the reaction happen?" Hadley looked concerned. It didn't seem like enough.

"Depends what it is."

哈德利盯着麦克斯看了好一会儿,半耸肩半皱眉地说:"我现在没什么心情去派对。"他下意识所展现出来的傲慢和谦逊并存的表情仿佛是在模仿麦克斯。

"谢尔碧也这么说,但我最后还是说服了她。"麦克斯极其快速地向前挥了挥手,示意哈德利,"来吧,免费酒水。"

"谢尔碧是怎么了?她怎么会不想去?"哈德利转过身去,照看着他的实验。

"我觉得她应该是想洗澡。"

"你们的浴室还没有修好?"哈德利问道,一边摇晃着手里的烧瓶,里面的混合物已经开始从透明变为浅橘色了。

"还没有。谢尔碧昨天去了物业办公室,因为她哭能比我哭得更有效果……"

哈德利停下手里的活儿,干巴巴地说道:"我很高兴看到她的戏剧专业也派上了点用场。"一想到谢尔碧在物业那里大哭的情形,哈德利感到有些困惑。他很少哭。从小生活在太平间的楼上教会了他如何处理悲伤的情绪。他每天都会看到这样的情景,而大部分的人对悲伤都毫无掌控力可言。有的人会将情绪发泄在哈德利的父亲身上,这并不少见。有一个寡妇甚至揍了他父亲一拳,就那样手臂向后一缩猛地打在了他的眼睛上,仅仅是因为他订错了花的颜色。哈德利的父亲不得不顶着一张尸体一样的脸度过了整个葬礼,他那紫了的眼睛比那个女人老公的死相还要丑。

哈德利这才意识到自己从来没有看到谢尔碧哭过,甚至连她难过的样子都无法想象。她总是充满讽刺挖苦的意味,总是觉得哈德利不开心,这一点对哈德利来说很有趣,因为他对自己什么看法都没有——没有特别开心,也不难过。

麦克斯瞥了一眼哈德利手里的烧瓶,"那个鬼东西到底是什么?"

"定性检验,"哈德利简洁地回答,目光一直没有移开那已经变成深橘色的溶液,"有杂质。"他点了点头,轻敲着烧瓶。他本来猜测溶液只会变成浅金色,但现在的结果已经让他感觉好一点了。橘色开始向瓶底沉淀了,哈德利迅速地过滤出沉淀物并将其称重。"2%。你觉得这杂质的比例足够推动对照实验进行吗?"哈德利看上去有些担心,这个量似乎不够。

"取决于杂质是什么。"

Hadley nodded, thinking. He played with his fingers for a moment. "What if it's not the water?"

"You mean, what if you don't need the catalyst?" Max looked at him archly. "Isn't that what I asked the other day?"

"It didn't seem as plausible then." Hadley stared at Max. Both of them knew that this would be big news. Max shrugged. They both considered how the chemicals might come together, which would give up electrons, how the new configuration might look.

"If the pyridine ring hooked up on its own, it might not need the catalyst." Hadley looked at Max, wondering if he'd thought of this already.

"Rerun it without the catalyst. It's the only way you'll know. Just rinse everything with solvent."

Hadley wrote some figures down in his open notebook. While he was writing, he said calmly, "Ethan told me Chesterton loaned him three thousand dollars." Hearing Max's outrush of air, Hadley sparked up. Max liked to think he knew everything.

"Why?"

Ignoring Max's question, Hadley, added, "And Ethan was questioned about a drug murder. Did you know that the police were here looking for him two days ago?"

"Here?" Max's voice was loud. Hadley shushed him. "At the lab?" he whispered.

Hadley nodded, then added lightly, "Must've been before you came in."

Max ignored the dig. He picked up a clamp off of Hadley's bench and began spinning the gripper around with his index finger. When it got to one extreme he spun it back in the other direction. Max looked up at Hadley. "Maybe you should think about moving."

"*Where?*" Hadley asked irritably. He was tired of Max harping on this. Hell, lots of people slept on the floor of other friends' apartments, waiting months for one of their own.

Hadley placed the flask back on his bench and made a couple of notations in his notebook. Grabbing a graduated cylinder, Hadley poured some solvent into the cylinder, swirled it well, and then did the same with a clean flask, preparing to repeat

哈德利点头表示同意，又陷入了思考。同时玩着自己的手指头，"万一不是自来水的问题呢？"

"你的意思是，万一其实不需要催化剂？"麦克斯狡黠地看着他，"我上次不就问过这个问题吗？"

"当时看起来并不怎么合理，"哈德利瞪着麦克斯。他们俩都知道这会成为大新闻。麦克斯耸了下肩。他们都考虑了一下化学试剂可能结合的方式，以及失去电子后新结构的产生情况。

"如果吡啶环自动连接上了的话，也许就不需要催化剂了。"哈德利看向麦克斯，好奇他是不是已经想到了这一点。

"不加催化剂再做一遍实验。这是找出真相的唯一方法。记住用清洁溶剂把所有器皿都洗一下。"

哈德利在摊开的实验记录本上记下几个数字，同时他声音平静地说道："伊桑告诉我切斯特通借给他三千美元。"听到麦克斯大口呼气的声音，哈德利的眼里闪起了光。麦克斯喜欢自以为对所有事都了如指掌。

"为什么？"

哈德利忽视了麦克斯的问题，补充道："伊桑还因为一件与毒品有关的谋杀案被问询了。你知道两天前警察来这儿找过他吗？"

"这里？"麦克斯的声音大了起来。哈德利示意他小声点儿。"来实验室里？"他又低声问。

哈德利点了点头，轻描淡写地说道："肯定是在你每天来实验室的时间点之前咯。"

麦克斯忽视了他的讽刺。他从哈德利的工作台上取下一个铁夹，开始用食指转了起来。当转到头的时候，再反方向转回来。麦克斯抬起头看着哈德利，"或许你应该考虑搬家了。"

"能搬到哪呢？"哈德利烦躁地说。麦克斯总是喋喋不休地谈论这个问题，导致他都有些厌烦了。再说了，有那么多人都还住在朋友公寓的地板上，为了分配给自己的公寓等上好几个月呢。

哈德利把烧瓶放回工作台上，在本子上做了几个标记。然后他抓起一个标有刻度的筒形容器，倒了一些溶剂进去，将其摇匀，接着又用洁净的烧瓶做了同

the reaction. If he got the product again, he'd have to go to Scotia and say that something's wrong. He wouldn't want to say that he thought the mechanism was wrong, because that would be a little too confrontational, but he'd make it clear that things were not adding up.

Max pulled him back to their conversation. "I'd be worried about one of these guys breaking into the apartment and mistaking you for Ethan."

"Tell me about it," Hadley said glumly, thinking about Ethan leaving the window open. He weighed some white powder out on a balance, carefully piling it on a square of waxed paper. "I just hate the thought of trying to find a new place to live," Hadley groaned.

"Why would Chesterton loan him three thou?" Max looked perplexed. "Doesn't he know Ethan's a drug addict?"

"Apparently not. Ethan told him that his grant hadn't shown up and he was three months late with his rent."

"*And Chesterton believed him?*" Max laughed out loud.

Hadley laughed without meaning to. He looked at Max, shaking his head. "That's what I said."

"How can Chesterton be that out-to-lunch?" Max put the clamp down and ran his fingers through his hair.

Hadley was writing down the weight of the powder in his notebook and didn't respond to Max's comment right away. He folded the waxed paper in half, carried it over to the flask, and slowly poured it into the solvent, watching it dissipate into the liquid. When he was done, he turned to Max and said thoughtfully, "Ethan doesn't look like a drug addict. Well," he amended, "he didn't used to. I think his change in appearance has been so gradual that someone like Chesterton wouldn't notice."

Hadley turned on the hot plate with a magnetic stirrer hidden inside and set an oil bath on top. Inside this he suspended his flask, tightening the ringstand. Then he walked over to his desk and added one more line to his notebook. He abruptly started out the door but turned quickly to add, "He's started to write up. Maybe Chesterton isn't planning on letting him go yet."

They both had been schooled on the concept of graduate students as slave labor. Getting a Ph.D. was not unlike a lengthy puberty rite. If you got a lot of work done, a research director wasn't keen on letting you go. Indeed, sometimes

样的操作,准备将实验再重复一次。如果这次又得到最终产物的话,他就必须得亲自去告诉斯考蒂亚,实验出现问题了。他当然不想直接对他说自己觉得实验机理是错误的,因为那样有点太正面冲突了,但他一定会说清楚中间有环节出问题了。

麦克斯又将他拉回了对话中来,"我只是担心那些人会冲进你们的公寓把你错当成伊桑。"

"这我也知道。"哈德利忧郁地说着,回想起了伊桑让窗户敞开着的事情。他正用天平称量一些白色粉末,在一张方形的蜡纸上不断小心翼翼地添加着。"我只是一想到要费力地重新找个住处就心烦。"哈德利抱怨道。

"为什么切斯特通会借三千美元给他?"麦克斯一脸的不解,"他难道不知道伊桑吸毒吗?"

"很显然不知道。伊桑对他说他的研究资金还没有到位,而他自己已经欠了三个月的房租了。"

"切斯特通竟然相信他了?"麦克斯禁不住大声笑了起来。

哈德利也不由自主地笑出了声。他看着麦克斯,摇着脑袋,"我也是这么说的。"

"切斯特通怎么会这么好骗啊?"麦克斯放下手里的夹子,用手梳了梳头发。

哈德利正把粉末的重量记录到笔记本上,没有立即回复麦克斯的评论。他将蜡纸对折,移到烧瓶处,缓慢地倒进溶剂中,看着粉末渐渐溶解消失。做完之后,他转向麦克斯,略一沉思,说道:"伊桑看上去并不像个瘾君子。好吧。"他改正道:"他以前并不像。我觉得因为他外表上的变化不是非常明显,所以像切斯特通这样的人并不会注意到。"

哈德利打开内置磁力搅拌子的热盘,并在热盘上方放了一个油浴装置。随后将烧瓶放入其中,调紧铁夹。紧接着他走到自己的桌前,在笔记本上又写下一行字。突然,他向门口走去,但又迅速地转过头来补充道:"他已经开始对实验认真起来了。没准切斯特通还没有打算让他离开。"

他们都早已熟知研究生就是免费劳动力的事实了。拿到博士学位的过程就像青春期一样漫长。如果你能够完成很多任务的话,你的导师是不太想让你离开的。事实就是如此,有时导师甚至会做到过分的程度,比如有一个学生在读了

Chapter Eight Decomposition

research directors went too far, as in one case where a student who had worked for ten years on his Ph. D. was finally told by his director that he just wasn't up to snuff. Shortly after, the student killed the director with a ball-peen hammer. Just whacked him on the head. Many graduate students had the newspaper clipping of the incident pasted above their hoods. A kind of homage to an anti-hero.

Hadley walked next door to the instrument room where the lab refrigerator hunched in the corner snuggling up to the lab computer. The room was a claustrophobic's nightmare. Books cantilevered in at you, large equipment blocked your path. Hadley opened the refrigerator and reached behind some larger bottles for his small vial of clear liquid. It was labeled in Hadley's precise hand which contrasted harshly with the scribbled note taped to the outside that screamed, "DO NOT STORE YOUR LUNCH IN HERE!!!" A skull and crossbones had been added below in red. Someone else had added, in green, what looked like puke and worms. There was no telling what other additions might be made during a late night in the lab. It amused Hadley, but he could never see himself participating. It was like writing on a bathroom wall. If that was fun, you should be worried.

Returning to his lab, he picked up a clean syringe off a rack on his bench. "Oh yeah," Hadley said meaningfully, "And this reminds me—" he gestured toward Max with the empty syringe, "—I found one of these on the kitchen counter this morning."

"*Used?*" asked Max.

Hadley nodded.

"Does Chesterton know about the police?"

"Apparently not."

"Jesus."

"I had to tell you."

"But that's my point. Why doesn't anybody tell Chesterton? Why doesn't he make it his job to find out? I don't think he wants to know. He'd be too human. It's guys like Chesterton that make me want to avoid academics."

"I don't think you have to be like that," Hadley said. Max always said this and Hadley didn't want to believe it. He wanted to go into academics. It seemed so much less commercial. If you could make a name for yourself, you could have autonomy.

十年的博士之后,导师最终却告诉他他就是不够毕业标准。不久之后,那个学生用一把半球形的铁锤把导师给杀了,在头上给了重重的一击。许多研究生都把报纸上的报道剪下来贴在实验室的通风橱上。这是一种对反面英雄的致敬。

哈德利走到隔壁的仪器室,角落里的实验用冰箱蜷缩电脑旁边。这个房间对于幽闭恐惧症患者来说简直就是噩梦——书架悬在空中,过道则被大型设备挡住了。哈德利打开冰箱,伸手去够大瓶子后面的小瓶无色试剂。上面的标签是哈德利的清晰字迹,与冰箱外面潦草刺耳的标语形成了鲜明的对比:"不要把你的午饭放在里面!!!"下面贴了一张红色的骷髅图。有人在下面用绿笔画上了像是呕吐物和毛毛虫样的东西。谁也猜不准下一次有人在实验室熬夜之后冰箱里又会多出什么来。哈德利觉得这种涂鸦接力很好笑,但他自己是永远不会加入其中的。这好比是在浴室的墙上乱涂乱画,如果这样做能够给你带来乐趣,才真的应该要担心了。

回到自己的实验室以后,他从工作台的支架上取下一支干净的注射器。"噢,对了,"哈德利意味深长地说,"这倒提醒我了——"他手里拿着注射器示意麦克斯,"——我今天早上在厨房的台子上发现了一支这个。"

"使用过的?"麦克斯问。

哈德利点了点头。

"切斯特通知道警察来找他的事吗?"

"很显然不知道。"

"上帝啊。"

"这件事我必须得告诉你。"

"没错儿。可为什么没有人告诉切斯特通呢?为什么他不觉得了解这一切是他的职责呢?我不认为他想知道这些事,那样的话他就显得太人性了。就是切斯特通这样的人才让我有远离学术的冲动。"

"我不这么觉得。"哈德利说。麦克斯总是这样说,哈德利不想相信他。哈德利自己是想进入学术界的,因为它看上去商业气息没那么浓。假如你可以建立名声的话,你就有了自主权。

Chapter Eight Decomposition

Sticking the needle into the flask, Hadley slowly injected the contents of the syringe into the warming solution and watched as the fluid spun into the mixture, creating a trickle of distortion, like gasoline vapor, deceptively warping a thin strand of matter. He enjoyed pure science, not needing the glitz of industry always beating the path to patents. He just wanted to discover stuff. "I don't think Scotia's like that," Hadley added.

"Chesterton's a lot younger than Scotia and doesn't have his reputation yet," Max countered. "Maybe someday Chesterton will be real, after he gets the divorce." Chesterton's wife was spectacularly peculiar, wanting all the graduate students to make a video in Grecian garb for the holiday Chemistry party. She had a reputation of getting saucy with the graduate students when Chesterton would have dinner parties. "Chesterton only has time to read the literature and lasso his wife. He probably forgot what Ethan used to be like."

Hadley looked up at Max and grunted, laughing. "He *doesn't* lasso his wife. God, the thought of that is almost overwhelming."

"Almost?" Max grinned at Hadley. "I'm thinking that's the answer. That's why he isn't clued in to Ethan. The guy's simply too busy."

"And he's not the only one." Hadley shot Max a look.

"You think Scotia's bonin' her?"

"NO!" Hadley's voice dripped with distaste. "He's not the only one who's too busy. Lately Scotia's never around either. This project needs some guidance." Hadley shook his head as he poured the contents of his flask into an NMR tube, then walked out the door of the lab. He remembered that he'd signed up for an afternoon slot, and he was almost out of time. He nearly ran into Rahda in the hallway and apologized without stopping. It would take about ten minutes to take the NMR, and he didn't want someone coming in and moving his tube because he was over his allotted time. After he mounted the sample, Hadley quickly wrote, "Acquisition in progress" on a piece of scrap paper, leaving it on the NMR keyboard. As he turned to leave, he saw Rahda standing there, waiting for him by the open door. Great, now what did she want? Hadley didn't feel like talking reactions which was the only thing Rahda was ever interested in. Hadley continued down the hall and Rahda followed him, nearly side by side, but never quite catching up.

哈德利将注射器伸入烧瓶中，缓慢地把内容物注射到加热了的溶液中去，看着它像纺丝一般旋转形成混合物，呈现出一种像汽油蒸汽般的细流状的扭曲态；让人误以为是一缕细丝状的物体正在被弯曲变形。他享受纯粹的科学，不需要工业的浮华气不时提醒他向专利看齐。他只是想要有所发现而已。"我不觉得斯考蒂亚是那样的人。"哈德利补充了一句。

"切斯特通要比斯考蒂亚年轻很多，还没有建立起名声。"麦克斯反驳道，"也许在他离婚之后有一天切斯特通就会变得更贴近生活了。"切斯特通的老婆特别古怪，有一次她想让所有的研究生都穿上古希腊式的服装给化学大楼举办的节日派对拍一个视频。她名声不太好，因为她会在切斯特通举办晚餐派对的时候和研究生打情骂俏。"切斯特通的时间只够用来阅读文献和管好他的老婆。很有可能他已经忘记了伊桑原本的样子。"

哈德利抬起头看向麦克斯，哼哼了一声，大笑起来。"他从来不管老婆。天哪，只是想一想这件事就几乎能够让他窒息了。"

"只是几乎？"麦克斯龇牙对哈德利笑了。"我猜这就是答案了，他对伊桑的改变没有丝毫察觉的原因，就是这个家伙真的是太忙了。"

"并且他还不是唯一的一个。"哈德利迅速地看了麦克斯一眼。

"你认为斯考蒂亚也和他老婆有一腿？"

"不是！"哈德利的声音中充满了反感。"他不是唯一一个忙得不可开交的人。最近斯考蒂亚也很少出现，而我们的项目需要一些指导。"哈德利说着摇了摇头，将烧瓶里的内容物倒进了一个核磁共振试管里，然后走出了实验室。他突然想起自己只申请了下午一个时间段的使用，而现在快到截止时间了。在走廊里奔跑的时候差点儿撞上了拉达，他急忙道歉，却也没有停下脚步。完成核磁共振实验大概需要十分钟，他不希望仅仅因为自己分配到的时间用完了就有人进去移走他的试管。提取出样本之后，哈德利快速地在一张纸头上写下"中间产物"的字样，并随手留在了核磁共振仪的键盘上。正当他转身准备离开的时候，他看见拉达站在打开的门旁边，在等他。这回好了，她想怎么样？哈德利当时没有心情聊反应的事情，而拉达唯一感兴趣的东西也就只有实验了。哈德利继续沿着走廊向前，拉达跟着他，几乎肩并肩了，但始终没有并排。

Chapter Eight Decomposition

"Nice sweater," Hadley said for lack of anything better, hoping that if he said something she would get to the point and leave him alone. He wished he could just be rude and ignore her, but he was a sucker for the socially inept. It was a condition he knew too well.

"Thank you."

"Did you need something?"

"Oh, I was on my way to dinner when I remembered that I was going to leave Bineet my mass spec and NMR data. I thought perhaps you might want me to give him a copy of yours as well. Or you could," she finished belatedly.

He said quickly, "Well, I'm running mine again. I got the final product when I was only running a control."

"Oh, you're running a control?" Rahda asked, stopping suddenly. "I thought those had already be run several times."

"Well, the elemental analysis of the final scaled up product didn't show any traces of catalyst, and I thought this was odd, so I figured I'd run another control." Hadley stopped at the door of his lab.

Rahda looked at the floor and then back at Hadley. "That is not odd. There is such a small amount needed, it most likely would not show up. I regret to think of you wasting your time. I already discovered this and mentioned it at the last group meeting. You do not remember?"

"Unfortunately I don't, but I came in late."

"Well, I hope to spare you the work. I was going to put a probe in now. Dr. Scotia was hoping I would call him with the results very shortly. Might I remove yours since we no longer need the data?"

"It's almost done," Hadley said somewhat tersely, a little irritated at the implication that her research was more important than his. "I can come get you as soon as it's through."

"That is fine. I was also wondering if you had that article about folate inhibitors? I would like to read it."

"I'm still reading it." He'd told her this before. "I'll bring it to work when I'm through." He knew he sounded kind of rude and amended it with, "Is next week okay?"

"你的毛衣挺不错的。"哈德利找不到什么更好的话来说了,暗自希望如果自己主动开口了,她就能开门见山,然后不再来烦自己。哈德利也希望自己能够表现得粗鲁一点,无视她的存在,但他在"社交低能儿"面前总是无法脱身。现在这个情况他再熟悉不过了。

"谢谢。"

"你找我有事吗?"

"噢,我正准备去吃晚饭,但我突然想起来我得把自己的实验质谱图和核磁数据交给贝内特,我想也许你想让我把你的实验结果也拷贝一份带过去。或者你一起带过去——"末了她又迟疑地补了一句。

哈德利快速答道:"是这样,我现在正重新做一遍分配给我的实验。因为我在做对照实验的时候竟然得到了最终产品。"

"噢,你在做对照实验?"拉达问道,突然地停顿了一下,她又接着说:"我还以为对照实验已经做过好几次了。"

"在将最终产品按比例增加进行元素分析的时候没有发现任何催化剂的痕迹,我觉得这很奇怪,于是我就想再做一次看看。"哈德利在自己实验室的门口停下了脚步。

拉达先盯着地板看了一会儿,转而又看向哈德利。"这并不奇怪。需要用的催化剂量很小,很有可能在元素分析中无法显现出来。我也不想这样说,但是你是在浪费时间。我早已经发现了这一点并且在上次组会上提过,你不记得了吗?"

"很不幸,我不记得了。我当时进去得迟。"

"好吧,我希望能帮你不做无用功。我现在打算放一支探针进去,斯考蒂亚博士期望我尽快打电话告诉他最终的结果。既然我们不需要对照实验的数据了,我能把你的东西拿出来吗?"

"快结束了,"哈德利简洁地说。拉达言语之间暗示着自己的实验要比哈德利的更加重要,这让哈德利有些恼怒。"一做完我就告诉你。"

"这样也行。我在想你有没有那篇关于叶酸抑制剂的文献?我想借来读一读。"

"我也正在读。"他之前已经告诉过她了。"等我读完了就带过来。"他知道自己的口气听起来有些粗鲁,于是又补救了一下,"下周可以吗?"

Chapter Eight Decomposition

"That is fine. I had better go. I need to run downstairs to see if my new column came in before receiving closes," Rahda said, starting to leave. Then she turned back around. "Oh, yes. Workmen were to come today to fix my argon line. I have not been able to run any reactions for a week. If you see them, could you send them into my lab?"

"I'm going to be leaving here in a minute myself," Hadley said, starting to move into his lab.

"Well, if you see them ... " Rahda pressed.

"Sure," Hadley said quickly. Rahda nodded good bye and left. Hadley wondered what that was all about. The exchange felt ... he wanted to say rehearsed, but that didn't make any sense.

Eberhard was sitting in Hadley's chair and talking to Max, when Hadley came back. Max promptly shut up. He looked at Hadley, smiling innocently. Hadley glanced at them both and then said, "Okay, what is it?"

Eberhard shrugged, and Max gave Hadley his "Why are you looking at me?" look.

"You want me to go back outside so you can finish your conversation?"

"Oh, no, no, no," Max said. "After all, this is your lab."

Hadley said sarcastically, "Well, don't let that stop you."

Max sighed. "Oh, all right. Eberhard was just saying you're an idealist."

"I'm an idealist!" Hadley said, looking at Eberhard.

Eberhard laughed. "I think Max imagines much conversation?" Eberhard always ended his sentences with an upward inflection, making it sound like he was asking a question. Hadley suddenly realized that Max was putting words in Eberhard's mouth. Hadley raised his eyebrows at Max. He didn't feel like a lecture.

"I know you, Hadley," Max said. "As fucked up as Ethan is—and Jesus Christ, he is—I know you think that he can be salvaged. You think you're responsible for the happiness of the world—"

"No, I don't," Hadley said, exasperated.

"Yes you do," Max insisted. "Ethan depresses you so much because he's so damn smart."

Hadley just shook his head and turned toward his bench, replacing the bottle of sulfuric acid and racking an unused test tube. He knew that Max and Eberhard could

"没问题。我得走了,取件处关门之前我要下楼去看看我订的层析柱有没有到。"说话间,拉达已经在往外走了。然后她转过身来,"噢,对了,今天会有工人来修理我的氩气线路。我已经一个星期没有做任何实验了,如果你看到他们的话,能让他们来我的实验室吗?"

"我也马上就要离开了。"哈德利向自己的实验室走去。

"我是说,如果你看见他们的话……"拉达强调道。

"好的。"哈德利给了一个简短的回答。拉达点头再见之后离开了。哈德利犯起了嘀咕,刚才到底发生了什么事情。他和拉达的对话感觉像是……他想说"像是排练好的",但却讲不通。

哈德利回到实验室的时候,艾伯哈德正坐在椅子上和麦克斯聊天。麦克斯立刻就不说话了,他抬起头看着哈德利,露出无辜天真的笑容。哈德利先后瞥了他们一眼,"好了,你们在说什么?"

艾伯哈德只是耸了下肩膀,而麦克斯则用一种"你看着我干什么?"的表情应对哈德利。

"你们是想让我到外面去,好让你们结束未完成的对话吗?"

"噢,不不不,"麦克斯说,"毕竟,这是你的实验室。"

哈德利讽刺地回击,"别,可千万别让这件事阻拦了你。"

麦克斯叹了口气,"好吧,艾伯哈德刚才只是在说,你是一个理想主义者。"

"我,是一个理想主义者?!"哈德利不可置信地看着艾伯哈德。

艾伯哈德突然放声大笑起来。"我想,麦克斯是自己幻想了这段对话?"艾伯哈德说的每一句话总是以上扬的语调收尾,听起来就好像他在问问题。这时,哈德利意识到麦克斯是在借艾伯哈德的嘴说话,于是他不屑地扬起了眉头,因为他不想听人说教。

"我了解你,哈德利,"麦克斯开腔了,"不管伊桑堕落到了何种地步——见鬼,他真的已经无可救药了——我知道,你仍然觉得他可以被拯救。你觉得自己对整个世界的幸福都有责任——"

"不,我不这么觉得。"哈德利有些恼怒。

"你就是这么认为的,"麦克斯坚持道,"伊桑之所以让你变得这么沮丧,是因为他的头脑实在是太他妈好了。"

哈德利只是摇着头转向工作台,给硫酸溶液换了个瓶子,又把未使用过的试管放回支架上。他知道,麦克斯和艾伯哈德都无法理解为什么自己还要和伊桑

not understand why he continued to share an apartment with Ethan. But they hadn't looked around lately. The last thing he wanted to do was end up in a worse situation, and in New York that was easy.

"Well?" Max said.

Hadley sighed and turned around. He knew Max was just being practical. Where was the logic? he would ask. Living with Ethan, Hadley was forced to watch his downfall. He had witnessed tragedies before. It wasn't pleasant. But he couldn't turn away from it either. He said haltingly, "There's a real person in there that's dying. I think he's dying." Max made a face like Hadley was getting melodramatic which Hadley ignored.

"He tells me these stories … He told me that all the addicts wait in line outside a storefront for their fix. When the police drive by, everyone disperses. But when the police are gone, everyone gets right back into line in exactly the same place." Hadley paused. "He said it impresses him how civilized addicts can be."

No one said anything. The hum of the lab got louder. Hadley tossed some used glassware away into the recyclable garbage, where it shattered car-crash-like in the silence.

Max scuffed his feet. "Just don't blame yourself if he doesn't get better."

Hadley stared at the ground as he walked back toward the NMR room, wondering why he felt so shitty today. It wasn't a word he often used, even to himself. He just felt so complicatedly troubled. Ethan was not his problem. Why *did* he feel responsible? He ultimately knew why, and that's what aggravated him the most. Ethan reminded him of his brother. It had dawned on him this morning after listening to Ethan snore. But knowing this didn't seem to help. Self-knowledge doesn't always equal immediate action. It may only make you painfully aware. He couldn't seem to divorce himself from Ethan's problems. There was something about Ethan that made Hadley miss his brother. A kind of wild abandon that was appealing, that made you want to see what would happen next. They both shared a knack for making decisions that would lead to their eventual downfall, but a downfall witnessed in glorious specificity, a more personal version of Jim Morrison. Even as a child, Hadley's brother had this inverse genius. He used to build nine-story card houses in his parents' travel trailer, paper castles quickly erected at the

合租公寓，但那是因为他们没有关注周围的近况。哈德利最不想看见发生的事情就是改变之后的处境比原来还差，而在纽约这样的概率很大。

"怎么样？"麦克斯又追问道。

哈德利无奈地叹了口气又转向他们。他知道麦克斯只是在从实际角度为他考虑。但是他想问，逻辑又在哪呢？和伊桑住在一起，哈德利被迫目睹了他堕落的过程。过去他也看过很多悲剧，这绝不是一种享受。但是他却也没有办法允许自己逃避。"现在有一个活生生的人在走向死亡，我觉得他正在走向死亡。"哈德利一字一顿地说道。麦克斯做了一个嫌哈德利太夸张的表情，被哈德利给无视了。

"他给我讲了一些事情……他告诉我，所有的瘾君子们都在店面门口排队买毒品，当警车经过的时候，大家就火速散开。但当警察们离开之后，每个人又重新回到原本站的位置继续排队。"说到这里哈德利顿了几秒，"他说瘾君子们的文明有礼给他留下了很深的印象。"

没有人说话。机器的嗡鸣声被衬托得更响了。哈德利将一些废弃的玻璃器皿扔进循环垃圾箱里，在一片寂静中玻璃破碎的声音就像是一场车祸。

麦克斯拖沓着脚步准备离开，"如果他没有好转的话，不要责怪你自己。"

在走回核磁共振室的路上，哈德利一直盯着地面看，思忖着为什么今天自己感觉这么糟糕。这个词，即使是对他自己也不常用。他只是觉得，自己陷入了错综复杂的麻烦之中。伊桑并不是困扰他的症结。为什么自己会觉得有责任呢？其实从根本上来说他知道为什么，也正因如此才导致他的恼怒升级。伊桑使他想起了自己的弟弟。他是在今天早晨听到伊桑打呼噜之后才突然意识到这一点的。但似乎知道了，也没有多大的帮助。自我认知不总是等同于即时行动，有时候它只会使你痛苦地洞悉一切却无能为力。哈德利似乎没有办法从伊桑的问题中抽身出来，伊桑身上有一种东西让哈德利开始想念自己的弟弟。这是一种疯狂的放纵，无比的诱人，让你想要知道下面会发生什么。他们俩有一个共同的习惯，他们做出的决定会导致自己最终的堕落，但是人们可以通过种种光辉的细节见证这个堕落的过程，是更贴近生活版本的吉姆莫里森[译者注：著名美国摇滚歌手，诗人]。即便在还是个孩子的时候，哈德利的弟弟就具备了这种反常的天赋。他过去常在父母开的旅游房车上搭九层的纸牌楼，当他们一家人在暑假里穿越整个国家的时候，偶尔停下来休息的间隙，"纸牌城堡"就会迅速拔地而起。

occasional rest stops as their family crossed the country on summer vacation. It didn't bother Colin that he was wasting his time, that a travel trailer is possibly the worst place to build card houses. Just opening a closet could topple an hour's worth of effort. Colin's hubris was his knack for short-term accomplishments. He simply didn't care. It drove Hadley crazy. Even in those days, Hadley thought that every moment of a person's life should count for something, should weigh in as meaningful. But for his brother, everything was an equal burden. Wasting time was a way to avoid meaning.

Hadley's feet stopped, so intent was he in thinking about his brother. Missing his brother. He could almost see him, slouching in a chair, laughing. Colin always found the world funny, but it wasn't a happy humor. Hadley sighed, then he shook his head and continued on. He didn't see the blue-suited workman looming in the middle of the hallway until he almost ran into him.

"Hey, I can't find no one else around and we got a problem."

Hadley looked up, still in a fog. He wasn't normally addressed by people he didn't know. He preferred it that way. Hadley looked at the man quizzically. The last thing he wanted to do was to talk to some maintenance man with a problem.

"Ya know da big silver thing down there?"

Hadley had no idea what he was talking about.

"Ya know, in that room. The big tank or something."

Hadley did a doubletake. "The NMR?"

"Yeah, whatever, well, Louey, he got his wrench stuck."

"On the NMR!" Hadley started down the hall quickly. This was the last thing he needed. He'd been working all day to get this one bit of data, and now... He felt such a wave of disappointment, such an incredible let down as the one final thing that he cared about was sabotaged by idiots, that he cast about in his mind for anything to cheer him up. It was an effort, but he'd been remembering something funny on the way to the lab. Something that bobbed on the edge of his mind. A thought that had occurred to him more than once but he hadn't really paid attention. Oh, yeah. The sight of Shelby falling in with the bathroom floor. The memory had many components: Humor, fear, relief, replayed in his mind from every angle. The complete predictability of it. That was perhaps the funniest part. Shelby was the clumsiest person he knew. He remembered how she constantly hit her head when she

柯林一点儿也不介意自己是不是在浪费时间，也不介意旅游房车大概是建纸牌屋最差的环境这个事实。就只是随便打开一扇衣橱的门，就有可能让一个小时的心血瞬间坍塌。每次取得小小的短期成就，柯林就变得傲慢自大起来。简言之，他对什么都不那么在乎。这让哈德利几乎快要疯了。即使是小时候，哈德利就已经觉得人生的每一个瞬间都应该是有意义的，都对以后的人生有着决定性的作用。但对于他的弟弟来说，所有事情都是同样的负担，浪费时间是一种用来逃避意义的方法。

哈德利专心地想着弟弟的事情，想念着他，以至于他都不自觉地停下了脚步。他几乎看见了弟弟懒洋洋地躺在椅子上笑的样子。柯林总是觉得这个世界好笑，但那并不是一种快乐的幽默感。哈德利叹了口气，摇了摇头继续向前走去。他一点儿也没有注意到走廊中间隐约靠近的着绿色工作服的工人，直到几乎撞上他们。

"你好，我在附近没看见其他人，但我们现在出现了一个问题。"

哈德利抬起头来，仍然一脸的迷茫。通常他不认识的人是不会和他说话的。他也更习惯这样。他诧异地盯着那个男人。他最不想做的事就是应付某个有问题要问的维修人员。

"侬知道这块儿那个银色的大机器么？"

哈德利对他在说什么完全没有头绪。

"侬晓得的，在那个房间里。一个大罐子还是什么的。"

哈德利先是一怔，恍然大悟："那个核磁共振分析仪？"

"对，管它叫什么名儿。是这样，洛伊，他的扳手给夹在那里了。"

"在分析仪里？"哈德利开始快步地向走廊尽头走去。这是他最不想发生的事。一整天他都在为了获得这一点数据而忙碌，现在却……这是他在意的最后一件事情，却被几个白痴给毁掉了。一阵难以形容的失望感向他袭来。他努力地回想任何可以让自己心情好起来的事情。但在走向实验室的路上，他的脑海里却开始浮现出一件好笑的事情，一直在大脑的边缘时隐时现。其实它已经在哈德利的思绪中出现不止一次了，但他没有认真注意过。噢，对的。就是谢尔碧和浴室的地板一同跌下去的情景。这段回忆具有很多要素：幽默、恐惧、如释重负，它们变幻着角度在哈德利的脑海里重复播放。这件事结果的可预测性，也许是最好笑的部分。谢尔碧是他认识人里面最笨手笨脚的一个。他还记得她是如何

climbed into cabs. She claimed it was because her eyes were much lower in her head than most people's and therefore the clearance was much higher. He thought of Shelby sometimes when he needed a laugh. Her mind surprised him; what you would think were non sequiturs would suddenly relate fifteen minutes later. And you would realize that she'd made these connections long ago and was leading you through her maze of thought, knowing that at the end that you would realize she'd planned it all out.

Hadley noticed that his thoughts of Shelby had become more frequent. It had a feeling of being not completely harmless. But he couldn't think about the ramifications right now because the imposing workman was following him, chatting away unendingly.

"Yeah, we been pullin' and pullin' but that wrench is stuck. It ain't budgin' for nuttin'."

"You can't pull it off the NMR." Hadley shook his head with annoyance.

"Louey's pretty strong."

"It's a magnet. You'll never pull it off. And it would cost fifty thousand dollars if you did!"

"Huh," said the big workman thoughtfully. "Maybe we should tell Louey to stop pullin'."

Hadley opened the door and saw the NMR, shimmering like a misplaced object from outer space, the size of beer vat from a mini-brewery. Louey had a stained red rag looped through the end of the wrench. One of his feet was planted on the NMR and the other on the ground, both sporting big work boots that looked capable of stomping small rodents. Sweat was pouring off his face as he strained to move the wrench. He looked up in exasperation as Hadley and the other workman entered the room.

"Louey, relax. That thing ain't comin' off there. This here's—" the heavy-set workman patted the NMR, "—a big magnet. That guy—" he jerked his thumb at Hadley "—says no way."

"It'll come outta this week's pay," complained Louey, not pulling anymore, but also not changing his position.

Hadley looked at Louey and shook his head. He couldn't believe it. He just couldn't believe it. This would mean that the NMR would be out of commission for

在每次钻进出租车的时候碰到自己的头的。她宣称那是因为自己的眼睛在头上的位置要比大多数人低很多，因此额头的面积要大得多。有时候，哈德利在需要轻松一笑的时候会想起谢尔碧。她的思维方式使哈德利吃惊；在她那里，看上去完全没有因果关系的事情十五分钟之后就会突然联系到了一起。然后你就会意识到，其实她在很久之前就已经建立了那些关联，刚才她只不过是在引导你走过她的思维迷宫，并且知道你最终会意识到其实一切都是她计划好的。

哈德利注意到近来他想起谢尔碧的次数更加频繁了。这样做似乎不是完全无害，但他现在却无暇思考后果了，因为那个工人一直紧紧地跟在他后面，没完没了地和他聊着天。

"我们一直不停地在拔呀拔，但那扳手就是卡在那里，动都不动。"

"你不可能把它从分析仪上拔下来。"哈德利恼怒地摇了摇头。

"洛伊很强壮的。"

"分析仪上是磁铁。你拔不下来的。再说如果你拔下来的话，你得赔偿五万美金！"

"啊，也许我们应该告诉洛伊不要再拔了。"

哈德利打开门，看到了分析仪，像搁错地方的外太空物品一样闪烁蒸腾着，有微酿啤酒作坊里的啤酒桶大小。洛伊在扳手的尾部用带污渍的红布条扣了一个环儿。他一只脚固定在分析仪上，另一只蹬在地上，脚上穿的工作靴足以踩死一只老鼠。他用力地想要移动扳手，汗如雨下。哈德利和另一个工人走进房间的时候，他气急败坏地抬起头来。

"洛伊，别用力了。那个玩意儿不会下来的。这儿，这个是——"那个身材矮小粗胖的工人拍了拍分析仪，"——一块儿大磁铁。那个家伙——"他跷着大拇指指向哈德利，"说没门儿。"

"扳手的钱会从这周的薪水里面扣的。"洛伊抱怨道，同时停下了拔的动作，换了个姿势。

哈德利看了一眼洛伊，摇了摇头。他不想相信。简直就不能相信。这意味着一整周分析仪都不能用了。这还是在走运的情况下。"你要是把它拔下来

a week. If he was lucky. "If you pull it off, you'll quench the magnet." Hadley said this calmly, purposefully using a word he thought the guy didn't know.

"Yeah, fifty thousand big ones."

Somehow the two of them reminded Hadley of Tweedledum and Tweedledee, dressed alike in green work clothes, portly, and stupid. The situation was laughable, except for the fact that Hadley really wanted to know if the reaction produced a product the second time without a catalyst. If it did, the patent would have to change. A lot of things might happen. It would also mean that Rahda never ran all the controls. That wouldn't look very good. He didn't want to get Rahda in trouble, but if he had the product, he'd have to let Scotia know. Scotia would do the rest on his own. Hadley frowned in despair. He wouldn't know now for a week. Here he was on the verge of a discovery but everything seemed to be conspiring against him.

"I want my wrench." Louey pouted for a moment.

"Relax. We bill the university. Wrenches ain't cheap you know." The big guy leaned against the wall like he was ready for a heart-to-heart.

"They're gonna have to shut down the magnet anyway." Hadley moved toward the door, too irritated to think. "Someone will have to come out and shim it and those guys are expensive." Hadley opened the door and then turned. "There's a sign on the door that says 'electromagnetic field'." He underlined the words. "Didn't that make you wonder?"

"Bub, it says 'electromagnetic-hocus-pocus' all over this damn place." The large workman waved his hands like a wizard. "Don't mean nothin' to me. If they don't want wrenches in there, they should say so. Or just hang one of them crossed signs with a wrench in it. It ain't my fault. Besides, it was Louey's wrench." The workman let out a belch of finality. "Damn brie."

Hadley felt a wave of dizziness pass over him and he rubbed his temples, walking back into the room.

"Hey, maybe it'll still work. You can see, it's not a very big wrench."

Ignoring him, Hadley reached in to get his sample out of the NMR probe. He'd have to label it and put it in the refrigerator for next week when the NMR was working again. Feeling an overwhelming desire to sit down, he turned to leave. The workmen followed him. Unseen by them, Hadley rolled his eyes as he walked up the

的话,磁铁就会被去磁了。"哈德利平静地说,故意用了一个觉得他们听不懂的词。

"知道,五万美金的大磁铁。"

不知道为什么,他们俩使哈德利想起了《爱丽丝梦游仙境》里的胖子兄弟,穿着相似的绿色工作服,都略微发福,都很傻。现在的情景很荒唐可笑,只是哈德利笑不出来,他非常想知道第二次不加催化剂的反应到底有没有产生最终产品。如果产生了,专利就必须要改变了。很多事情都有可能发生。那就意味着拉达从来就没把所有对照实验都做一遍。这样看上去就不妙了。他不想给拉达制造麻烦,但是若是他真的得到了产品的话,他必须得让斯考蒂亚知道。斯考蒂亚自己会处理剩下的事情。哈德利绝望地皱了皱眉头。现在好了,他一周之内都不可能知道结果了。明明他已经接近发现的边缘了,可所有事情都像是合起伙来跟他对着干。

"我得拿回我的扳手。"洛伊噘了一会儿嘴。

"放心。我们会把账单寄给这个大学的。扳手可不便宜,你知道的。"那个大个子的家伙斜倚在墙上,好像准备好要来一场掏心掏肺的谈话似的。

"反正他们会把机器给关掉的。"哈德利向门的方向走去,他实在是太恼怒了,无法思考。"得有人来给它垫片,而那会很贵。"哈德利打开门,然后转过身来。"门上有个声明说这里是电磁场区域,"他重读了那几个字,"难道你们没有注意吗?"

"兄弟,这个破地方到处都贴着电磁场之类的鬼话。"那个大块头的工人像个巫师似的挥舞着双手。"那些标语对我来说什么意思都没有。要是他们不想让人带扳手进来,他们就应该直接那么说。要不就贴一个扳手被划掉的图片在门上。这可不是我的错。再说了,那是洛伊的扳手。"他最终决断似的打了个嗝。"该死的布里奶酪。"

哈德利感到一阵晕眩传遍全身。他搓揉了两边的太阳穴,接着走回了分析仪实验室里。

"嘿,没准还能用呢。你看看,那个扳手也不是很大。"

哈德利无视了他,探头从分析仪探针里取出自己的样品。现在他得给它贴上标签,放进冰箱里保存到下周核磁共振仪修好了为止。这时他感到一阵强烈的想要坐下休息的欲望,于是转身向门外走去。那两个工人就一直跟着他。在走廊里,哈德利知道他们看不见自己的表情,便翻了个大大的白眼。他试图回忆

Chapter Eight Decomposition

corridor. He tried to think of something that would bring the day back to zero, reverse the polarity and swing his mood into equilibrium. He needed to talk to someone, make jokes about stuff, remember the relative importance of things. He thought of Shelby hanging upside down on the sofa. She was nuts. But that's the kind of weird shit—there, he was swearing again—that made her happy. She reminded him a little of his brother too, only not so out of control. But the glitter factor was there. The thing that drew you in.

"Hey, can we weigh ourselves on this?"

Hadley turned around, confused that the workmen would be so gauche as to get a wrench stuck on the NMR, and then ask permission to use a scale to weigh themselves.

"I don't care," Hadley said, wondering if they'd wagered on which one weighed more. He started back towards his lab. Then, realizing that he might be asked questions about this encounter, he turned back and watched Louey step gingerly on the foot-square pan. Normally the scale sat on a bench, but there was some construction going on in one of the labs, so a lot of stuff had been set in the hallway. The scale was a heavy-duty model, used for weighing kilo flasks. Even together those guys couldn't hurt it.

Hadley interrupted their weigh-in. "Excuse me, can I ask what you guys were looking for in the first place?"

"We came to fix a faulty gasline. Someone said it was in here."

Hadley looked perplexed.

"Guess we got the wrong room," Louey said with a grin.

Hadley suddenly realized that these were the guys Rahda had mentioned. The whole deal with the NMR had flustered him. "I know where you're supposed to be. In Rahda's lab. It's her argon line. You want me to show you where it is?" At least he could benefit chemistry in some way today.

Louey's partner shrugged himself into a smile. "Won't do us no good. Don't gotta wrench." He raised his hands wide open. The New York form of karma.

一些事情,可以使这一天重新归零,让时间调转,而自己的心情也能够随之恢复平衡。他需要和人聊聊天,随便开些玩笑,区分出事情重要性的相对大小。谢尔碧头朝下躺在沙发上的样子在他脑海里浮现出来。她真是个白痴。但就是这种奇奇怪怪的屁东西——看,他又说脏话了——会让谢尔碧开心满足。哈德利觉得她也有点像自己的弟弟,只是还没有到那么失控的程度。但是闪光点是一样的,那是一种让你不自觉被吸引过去的东西。

"喂,我可以用这个称体重吗?"

哈德利转过身去,有点不解:笨手笨脚的连扳手都能卡到分析仪上的人,竟然会在称体重之前寻求许可。

"无所谓。"哈德利心里想着他们会不会打赌谁体重更重。他向着自己实验室的方向走去,但突然意识到有人可能会问起这件事情,于是又转回头去。洛伊正小心翼翼地站到英尺见方的秤盘上去。通常情况下,这个秤是应该放在工作台上的,但最近有一个实验室正在装修,所以很多东西都被堆在了过道里。这个秤是用来称量公斤烧瓶的,属于重载型秤,即使他们两个都站上去都不会把它给压坏的。

哈德利打断了他们的称量过程。"打扰一下,我能问一下你们一开始来这儿是做什么的吗?"

"我们是来修出了毛病的气体线路的。有人告诉我们在那个房间里。"

哈德利有些困惑不解。

"我猜可能是我们找错房间了吧。"洛伊咧着嘴笑道。

哈德利猛然想起,他们就是拉达先前提到的修理工。核磁共振仪那一档子事儿已经把他给搞晕了。"我知道你们应该去哪儿,去拉达的实验室,她的氩气线出问题了。要我告诉你怎么过去吗?"至少今天他还可以用这种方法对化学做一点小贡献。

洛伊的搭档笑着耸了耸肩。"告诉我们也没用,没有扳手。"说着摊开了空空的双手。这就是纽约风格的宿命因缘。

Chapter Nine Sabotage

> To throw a spanner in the works: To deliberately sabotage a plan or enterprise or spoil a scheme by creating difficulties, obstructions, etc. to promote failure, as some machinery can be wrecked by literally throwing a spanner or a piece of metal into moving parts.
>
> *Brewer's Dictionary of Phrase & Fable*

Rahda heard the clank as the wrench hit the outside shell of the NMR. If she'd grown up in America she would have said, "Yes!" under her breath and clenched her fist downward in a show of sitcom-inspired happiness. Instead, she was much more subtle, much more deeply moved. She just clenched her teeth and exhaled through her nose, the breath long and smooth, like a smoker enjoying a good cigar. Things were going her way.

Rahda had only pretended to leave after talking to Hadley. She'd waited instead in the tiny supply room near the stairway until the echo of Hadley's footsteps diminished into the grumbling sounds of the building. The chemistry lab had a constant drone of sonicators, stirrers, and especially noisy hoods that pulled a loud vacuum, a hollow sucking sound, inhaling all the vile fumes necessitated by the chemistry. The sound reminded Rahda of her childhood, walking through her father's labs at the university, waiting quietly at his side while he spoke to a student. She'd grown up with these sounds and the constant noise had become a part of her life. A hum that was constantly with her, an anxiety that she could actually hear in her ears.

The realization that she had substituted the wrong compound in the NMR stunned Rahda in a dull way. She hadn't dreamed that Hadley would still be running controls. She couldn't mess up like that again. She wondered if he'd mentioned it to Scotia. Was Scotia suspicious? He didn't act it. Scotia was always so solicitous on Rahda's behalf. Always honoring her. In any case, she'd explained to Hadley why

第九章　破坏

　　To throw a spanner in the works(从中捣乱)：通过制造麻烦、阻碍等打乱原有步骤,以导致失败为目的,蓄意破坏某项计划、事业或活动;因为如果向正在运行的部位投掷扳手或其他金属,某些机器会被毁坏。

——《布鲁尔短语寓言词典》

　　拉达听到"哐啷"一声,是扳手砸到分析仪外壳上面时发出的。如果她从小在美国长大的话,很有可能会像美剧里面那样,攥紧拳头,低声欣喜地说一句:"太棒了!"而事实上,她的表现更细微一些,更多的是内心深处的翻腾。她仅仅是咬紧了牙关,用鼻子长长地呼着气,气息平稳圆润得像是吸烟的人在享受一支上好的雪茄。一切都在向她希望的方向发展。

　　拉达在和哈德利说完话之后,只是假装离开了。其实她一直躲在楼梯旁边狭小的储藏室里,听着哈德利的脚步声渐渐消失在大厅沉闷的回声中。这里有着长年不断的嗡嗡声,超音波处理器,搅拌器,尤其是通风橱里的洗尘装置发出的巨大噪音,那是一种空洞的吸附声,将化学实验产生的无法避免的有害气体通通吸走。这些声音让拉达想起了自己小时候,她会跟在父亲的后面穿行在大学实验室之间,父亲和学生讲话时自己则安静地在一旁等待。这些声音伴随着她长大,已经成为她生活的一部分。与她形影不离的嗡鸣声,是她能够真真切切听到的焦虑。

　　自从意识到自己在分析仪里替换了错误的化合物之后,拉达一整天都惶惶不已。她做梦也没有想到哈德利竟然还在做对照实验。不能再搞砸了。她有些好奇,哈德利有没有把实验结果告诉斯考蒂亚?斯考蒂亚起疑了吗?不过他倒是没有表现出来。毕竟他一直以来都站在拉达这边,对她表示关心,总是肯定她的成果。不管怎样,她已经跟哈德利解释过为什么催化剂没有和最终产物同时

the catalyst wouldn't show up with the final product and verified that Scotia was aware of this, so perhaps Hadley would move onto other things and forget about this one anomaly. She thought for a moment about Hadley. Would he forget? Not likely. He was running another control right now. If it confirmed the first result, he'd go to Scotia for sure. Rahda thought hard about how to fix the damage. What mixture of chemicals should she concoct in order to produce the right result?

She contemplated going to her lab right now, grabbing some baking soda, and simply adding it to his control. Sodium bicarbonate was base and normally prevented any reaction from occurring. It was a reaction-stopper, an uncatalyst. If she added it, the control wouldn't do any chemistry—or at least it shouldn't. Rahda wasn't completely sure. But it only had one proton and would never show up on the NMR spectra, so if the baking soda worked, that would be the perfect solution. No one would suspect.

She had stood in the supply room, thinking about what she should do next while she shuffled boxes of KimWipes and disposable gloves. If anyone walked in, she would look as if she were simply picking up some stuff. She wasn't really hiding out, but sometimes she could overhear bits of information as people walked down the hall, what they were working on, what they were running next. It was from in here that she heard the sound of the workmen clomping up the stairs, their voices breaking into the stillness of the low mechanical rumble. Instinctively she knew this was a stroke of luck, but how to harness it? Glancing carefully out of the supply room, she saw them looking into labs, unhurried, discussing the Giants. One of the guys was waving a wrench around to make his point. These must be the guys to fix her argon line. A plan came to her. Sometimes she thought she was brilliant. She walked out of the supply room, holding a couple pairs of white latex gloves. Turning at the sound of her movement, the workmen asked her if she knew where the faulty gasline was. Closing her eyes and tilting her head sideways, she appeared to be thinking. Through the slits of her eyes she watched them look at one another and then grin. These scientists were all wacko, you could tell they were thinking. They played right into her hands.

She pointed to the NMR room and, as they opened the door, she left quickly, ducking outside the swinging doors to the stairs, knowing they would never read the signs. One can do well in New York if one is a student of human

出现，并且跟他确认斯考蒂亚已经知晓这件事了，那么也许哈德利会继续做其他的事情，而淡忘这一反常现象。他会吗？不太可能。他现在又在做对照实验了。假如这次实验确认了第一次的结果，他一定会去跟斯考蒂亚汇报的。拉达绞尽脑汁地想着该如何弥补自己犯的过错。要配制什么样的试剂才能产生正确的结果呢？

深思之后，她打算回到自己的实验室去取一些发酵苏打，加到哈德利的实验中去。碳酸氢钠呈碱性，通常会阻碍所有反应的进行。它是反应终结者，反催化剂。如果加进去的话，对照实验就不会发生任何化学反应了——至少不应该。拉达也不能完全肯定。但是它只有一个质子，永远也不会在核磁共振图谱上显现出来，因此如果这招奏效了的话，问题就被完美地解决了。没有人会怀疑的。

拉达站在储藏室里，一边想着下一步该怎么做，一边挪动着盛放金佰利牌无尘擦拭纸和一次性手套的纸箱。万一这时候有人进来的话，她就可以装作自己正在找东西的样子。其实她并不是在躲藏，但有时候她在这里能够零星听到别人走进大厅时正在谈论的话，他们正在做什么课题，下一步要怎么做之类的。就在这时她听到了修理工人们在楼梯上沉重的脚步声，他们的说话声打破了单调低沉的机器嗡鸣声。本能般地，拉达感觉到这是一次机会，但是怎么把握呢？她小心翼翼地从储藏室向外瞥去，看见他们正不慌不忙地一间一间实验室地查看，一边还谈论着巨人队的比赛，其中一个正挥舞着手里的扳手在强调自己的观点。他们肯定是来给自己修氩气线的。一个计划在她脑海中形成了。有时候她自己都佩服自己的聪明才智。她走出了储藏室，手里拿着几副白色的乳胶手套。工人们听到了她的脚步声，转过身来，询问她是否知道故障的线路在哪里。拉达闭上了眼睛，把头歪向一边，做出思考的样子。透过眼角的缝隙她看到那两个工人互望了一眼后无声地咧嘴笑了。她知道他们在想什么——这些科学家都古怪的不得了。而他们现在完全在拉达的掌控之中。

她指向了核磁共振室，当他们把门打开以后，拉达迅速地离开了。她知道他们是不会去读门上贴着的警告的，于是便抽身跨进了通向楼梯的旋转门中。如果你是一个人类心理学专业的学生的话，在纽约一定可以混得很好。听到自己

nature. Hearing the success of her quick-witted scheme, the clonking sound as wrench cleaved to magnetic, she almost ran down the four flights of stairs, buoyed by her luck. She couldn't have timed this better, and the joke was, her argon line really didn't work. She hadn't faked that part, but it too would give her more time. For what? Another plan.

Walking down the wide stone steps, she felt happy that it was the weekend. She didn't intend to go back to the lab once. Usually she worked seven days a week; it was the only way to cover her tracks. But now, with the NMR not working, she could take a break. And for at least two days she wouldn't have to fend off Bineet who never ceased to ask her questions, hovering over her desk when she was trying to think. If she could only think of a way to fudge his results. But she couldn't do it because he was trying to recreate her catalyst, a compound she'd never made.

She didn't really care that Bineet was constantly in trouble with Scotia, unable to make the catalyst for his own set of experiments. He thought he was better than her, though he was of the working-class Vaisya caste. She suspected it was because he was marrying a Kshatriya woman; his intelligence and—what some thought—good looks elevated his status so that he could marry above himself. Rahda's husband-to-be was a caste below her, even though he too was in graduate school. A matchmaker had found him, and, as he was also in the U.S., the match seemed perfect to everyone except Rahda.

It had once been a convention in India that girls were to be married before the onset of menstruation. Though legally this had changed long before Rahda was born (the age being raised to a ripe fourteen) society had been slow to comply. Young marriages were still quite common—puberty a symbol of spinsterhood for some. But it was this extension of a woman's childhood that had led to the chance of higher education. Something had to be done with the single women. In Rahda's case, education became a means to excuse her unmarried state; it had been said to friends and relatives that she was doing so well in science that marriage was unthinkable right now. No one really believed it, but it was a way to save face.

Upon receiving her B. S., Rahda still had no immediate prospects, so her father, grudgingly, decided to let her continue with her schooling, even allowing her to live

急中生智的计划成功的声音——扳手被吸到磁铁上的"哐啷"声,拉达几乎是跑着下的楼梯,她为自己的幸运而感到振奋。时机被她掌握得恰到好处,而讽刺的是,她的氩气线确实坏了。这个部分不是她伪造的,但这也让她有了更多的时间。用来做什么?想出另外一个计划。

从宽阔的石台阶上走下来,拉达为现在正是周末而感到开心。她不打算立刻回实验室。通常情况下,她一周工作七天;这是唯一能够隐瞒她的实验进度的办法。但现在,核磁分析仪不工作了,她也可以休息一下了。至少整整两天,她都可以不用再应付贝内特连珠炮一样的问题了,他总是在拉达试图思考的时候在她桌边阴魂不散。要是她能想出一个办法把贝内特的实验数据篡改掉就好了。但是她无计可施,因为她得再现催化剂——一个她从来都没有做出来的催化剂。

贝内特没法为自己的那套实验做出催化剂来,斯考蒂亚一直在找他麻烦,但是拉达不在乎。尽管贝内特只属于工人阶级的瓦斯牙种姓,但他觉得自己比拉达等级要更高。她怀疑是因为贝内特娶了一个沙翠雅种姓的女人;他的聪明才智以及——有些人觉得——英俊外表使他的地位提升了,可以迎娶比自己种姓地位高的女人。拉达未婚夫的种姓比自己要低,尽管他也是一个研究生。这个人是媒婆牵的线,正好也在美国,因此这场婚姻在所有人眼里都完美无缺的,除了拉达。

在印度,女孩儿在月经出现之前就结婚曾经是一种习俗。虽然早在拉达出生之前法律就规定废除了这一惯例(法定结婚年龄被提升到了较成熟的十四岁),但是社会适应这条法规的速度还非常缓慢。未成年婚姻仍然非常常见——对一些人来说青春期时就已经算是老处女了。但正是这一女性童年时期的延长使得她们接受高等教育的概率大大提高了。有些事情只有单身女性才能够做。就拉达的例子来说,教育就成为她未婚状态最好的借口;她的朋友和亲戚得到的解释是,她在化学方面正大有作为,现在结婚对于她来说是难以想象的。其实没有人相信,但是这是一种可以保全面子的方法。

拿到学士学位之后,拉达仍然没有什么立即结婚的可能性,于是她的父亲十分不情愿地决定让她继续学业,甚至同意让她住在美国这样一个男人不怎么在

in the United States where men didn't mind as much an educated wife. Rahda was relieved. People couldn't be so bossy thousands of miles away. Friends close to the family constantly offered their advice that Rahda's "co-education", that is, education with men, would result in a marriage of love, something they felt should be avoided at all costs. Or even worse, Rahda, they felt, would certainly want someone smarter than her, and the bridegroom's family could use this to exact an excessive dowry. Rahda's father gestured to the heavens as if to say it was out of his hands. Karma was his usual way of ending an argument. But her mother had found a matchmaker. The marriage had been hurriedly agreed upon, Rahda's father secretly worrying that graduate work might make Rahda too smart for the average husband.

Rahda shook her head and squeezed her eyes closed. The thought of her upcoming wedding gave her a headache. She had met her husband-to-be last week at a mutual friend's house for dinner. He was older than her and had too many moles. He was also fat. He seemed to laugh when things weren't funny and this made Rahda suspicious of his intellect. Rahda had left early, feigning illness. She knew it was an insult to her husband-to-be, but she didn't care. She would be spending all her days with him soon, why add one more night? When her mother found out that she had met him, she was very angry. Rahda had called to complain about his moles. Her mother chastised Rahda, pointing out that this was the very reason that one should not meet one's husband until the wedding day. Rahda said nothing, glad that she had not wasted her own money to call her family, using instead the departmental telephone. She would not call again. She would take things into her own hands.

She stopped suddenly in the middle of the sidewalk and breathed loudly out of her mouth, letting the air whoosh past her lips, pursing them inadvertently, a plan forming. As she stood there, breathing, a "Hi, Rahda" caught her attention, causing her to flinch. She started to smile, but when she saw it was Max's wife, she looked the other way and continued to move quickly down Broadway. She had nothing to say to her. She knew that Max and his wife hung out with Dermot and Paige, a fast kind of crowd she had no interest in. It was probably a joke for Max's wife to say hi, a taunt to see if she would respond. Everyone wanted to suck you in, to get you to trust them so that they could laugh at you, make you into a fool. She

乎妻子是否受过教育的国家。拉达如释重负。远隔千里,再爱发号施令的人也没法施展。和她的家庭走得近的朋友不断进言,说拉达的"副教育",也就是关于男人的教育,会导致一场有爱情存在的婚姻,而他们觉得这件事是无论如何都要避免的。情况甚至可能更糟,他们认为,拉达一定会想要找一个比她聪明的丈夫,而新郎的家庭则会以此为借口索要巨额的嫁妆。拉达的父亲向上天做了一个手势,好像在说这已经不是他能控制的了。"因缘际会皆有注定"是他常用的结束争论的方法。但是她的母亲找到了一个媒人,于是这场婚事就这样草率地被定了下来。拉达的父亲私下里有些担心研究生的生活把拉达锻炼得太过机敏,而不会满足于这样一个平庸的丈夫。

拉达甩了甩头,紧紧地闭上了双眼。一想到自己即将到来的婚礼,她就头痛。上个星期在一个共同朋友的家里吃晚饭时,她已经见过自己未来的丈夫了。比她年长,脸上长了很多的痣,而且身材臃肿。不好笑的时候他也总是大笑,这让拉达有些怀疑他的智商。那晚拉达假装身体不舒服提前离开了。她知道,这对她的未婚夫来说是一种侮辱,但她不在乎。过不久她就要和他一起过一辈子了,何必再加上这一晚呢?当拉达的母亲发现他们已经见过面之后,非常生气。拉达还打了个电话回家抱怨他脸上的痣,却被训斥了一顿,她的母亲还说这就是为什么结婚之前不应该和丈夫见面的原因。拉达没有吱声,很庆幸她没有浪费自己的钱来打电话回家,而是用了实验室的电话。她不会再打电话回去了,从现在起她要为自己做决定。

她突然停在了路中间,大口地喘着气,让空气"呼呼"地掠过自己的嘴唇,接着她下意识地撅起了嘴,一个计划渐渐在她的脑海中成形。正当她站在那里调整呼吸时,一声"你好,拉达"让她回过神来。她向后踉跄了一步,开始微笑起来,但当她看见来人是麦克斯的老婆时,便看向其他地方,继续沿着百老汇大街快步走开了。她没什么可对她说的。她知道麦克斯和他的老婆会经常和德莫特还有佩琪一起消磨时间,但在她眼里,这群人放荡无度,对她毫无吸引力。麦克斯的老婆之所以会问候自己八成是为了开玩笑,看自己是否会回应。每个人都想把你吸过去,等你完全信任他们了,他们就可以肆意地嘲笑你,让你看上去像

had thought Hadley her friend, but even he was turning on her. Checking up on her. They underestimated her. Her family did too. They thought they could still control her. But she had a plan. It was bold, but if she could prove to her intended that she was pregnant, perhaps the marriage would be called off. She didn't want to really get pregnant, of course, but with the right chemicals, anything could be manufactured.

As she walked home she thought about going into a store and stealing something, a reward for cleverness, but the practical side of her talked herself out of it. Instead, she went into some stores and played at shoplifting, carrying something around each shop and then putting it down right before she walked out the door. She wanted to fool them. To have the security guards search her and realize she had nothing on her. To make them look stupid. She almost walked out with a purse at Woolworth's, taunted by their indifference. She carried her backpack in front of her, a handbag sandwiched between it and her chest, but she let the handbag drop at the last minute, not prepared for the torrent of activity that might ensue. Instead she went home, wanting something else, a change of clothes maybe, to assuage her desire for excitement.

At home, Rahda rummaged through her dresser quickly but carefully. Even though she was feeling more frantic as the minutes went by, she forced herself into placidity, meticulously putting each article of clothing back after she had disturbed its position. She paused in her search and re-examined the situation. She couldn't find the pink mohair sweater. She remembered placing it in her dresser. Someone had obviously taken it. She sat on her bed, trying to think where it could be, but there was a low-frequency hum in her head that made thinking painful. The hum reminded her of the lab, as if she'd taken the whirrings of science home with her, the suction of the hoods, the rattling of the vacuum pumps. The doctor had told her to stop drinking coffee, but that was ridiculous. How could coffee make you hear things? Her stomach rumbled angrily, but she refused to pay attention. She had calculated that if she gave up breakfast and lunch and only ate dinner she could lose ten pounds by her wedding. Then she remembered that she wasn't getting married.

Rahda gritted her teeth in determination and went into Paige's room. Not an inch of floor space could be seen. Walking across several T-shirts and a Rolling Stones magazine, Rahda made her way past Paige's bed to the closet. Paige had a

个傻瓜。她原以为哈德利是自己的朋友，但竟然连他都翻脸不认人了。竟然在检测她的实验。他们都低估了她。她的家里人也是。他们以为她还会继续受控制。但她已经为自己想好计划了。虽然有些大胆，但是如果她可以向未婚夫证明自己怀孕了，也许这场婚礼就会被取消了。当然，她并不想真的怀孕，只要用对化学品，任何事情都可以伪造。

走在回家的路上，拉达突发奇想地想要去商店里偷东西，作为对自己聪明才智的嘉奖，但是理智阻止了她。最终她决定走进店里，假装自己在行窃，在每家店里她都藏了一些东西在自己身上，然后在走出去的前一秒放下来。她想要捉弄别人。保安会来搜查自己，结果却发现她身上什么都没有。这让他们看上去很傻。在一家伍尔沃思店里，店员的漠不关心让她觉得受到了冷落，拉达差点就带着一个钱包走出了大门。她把自己的背包背在前面，将一个小手提包夹在背包和身体之间，但是最后一秒的时候她还是让手提包掉回了地上。对偷窃可能带来的一系列后果，她还没有准备好。她继续往家走，想做些别的，也许应该换身衣服，来缓解一下自己想要寻求刺激的欲望。

回到家里之后，拉达快速又仔细的在衣橱里翻找了起来。时间一点一点地过去，她却越来越焦躁，为了强迫自己镇静下来，她每弄乱一件衣服，都会一丝不苟地叠好再放回去。她突然停下了手里的活儿，审视着现在的情况。她找不到那件粉色的马海毛毛衣了，记忆当中明明放在了这里的。很显然有人把它给拿走了。她坐在床上，努力想着它可能会在哪里，但是她脑海中的低频嗡鸣声使得思考也变得痛苦不堪。这又让她想起了实验室，就好像她把那恼人的声音带回家了一样——保护罩抽气的声音和真空泵空洞的轰鸣。医生告诫拉达远离咖啡，但拉达觉得这个要求太无理取闹了。咖啡怎么可能使一个人产生幻听呢？她的肚子开始愤怒地咕噜起来，但她却故意置之不理。拉达计算过了，假如自己可以省掉早餐和午饭，只吃晚饭的话，到婚礼那天她就可以瘦下十磅来。这时她又记起来，自己并不打算结婚。

拉达咬了咬牙，下定了决心，然后转身走进了佩琪的房间。地板上没有一寸面积是裸露着的。拉达艰难地跨过摊在地上的几件 T 恤和《滚石》杂志，绕过佩琪的床，走到衣橱前面。佩琪的床是皇后尺码的，在床垫和衣橱的中间只留下了

queen-size bed and there was a mere hips' width between mattress and closet. Consequently, the closet doors remained perpetually opened. Because of this, there was no need to clear the area, so clothes tumbled out over the closet threshold, covering the entire floor. Rahda had to stand on a pile of clothes just to look into the closet. She felt something hard under her foot and bent down, fishing for whatever was jabbing her heel. She pulled out a vibrator and immediately flung it aside in a panic, not knowing exactly what it was, but recognizing it as something forbidden. She could choose not to think about something, to put it out of her mind—and in an instant, it was gone. As she began to search through Paige's clothes, her mind had already moved on to what she should do next.

Thumbing through hangers, Rahda accidentally knocked an unbuttoned blouse to the floor. She left it there knowing that Paige wouldn't know the difference. She wished Dr. Scotia could see what a disorderly person Paige was. Even though Rahda basked in the knowledge that she was Scotia's star student, he didn't joke with her the way he joked with Paige. There was a fatherliness to him that he exhibited to Paige, and Rahda was jealous of their special relationship. Even though Scotia was always very deferential to Rahda, she preferred the familiarity that he had with Paige and the other students. Why did they deserve such treatment? She imagined herself in charge of a large research group and Paige, poor and destitute, groveling for a job. First she'd make Paige get on her knees. Then she'd slap her across the face. Acting out her fantasy, she knocked more of Paige's clothes to the floor. That's for stealing my sweater, she'd say. And Paige would cry and beg, but it would be too late. Rahda smiled calmly at the thought.

Pushing aside the section of clothes she'd already looked through, Rahda pulled the next hanger toward her and was about to shove it left when she felt a particular softness, uncharacteristic of a regular cotton shirt. There it was! Hidden underneath. What a little sneak. Stronger words came to mind, but she silenced them. Rahda shook her head, amazed that Paige would think her so stupid as to not find the sweater. She pulled them both off the hanger, letting the checkered cotton shirt fall to the floor. The soft pink sweater, its color the shimmering incarnadine of a seashell's underside, seemed the pinnacle of femininity. It bequeathed upon the wearer a dainty bearing and sensitive manner. Rahda felt different the moment she pulled it on and buttoned up the front. It was a little tight through the shoulders;

一个臀部的宽度。结果就是,衣橱的门总是敞开的,也就没有必要整理它,所以衣服滚落出来,散了一地。拉达要站在一堆衣服上才能看见衣橱的里面。她感觉到脚下有个硬硬的东西,于是弯下腰去,看看到底是什么硌住了她的鞋跟。她从T恤下面抽出一个震动按摩器,随即就慌张地把它扔到一边去,虽然不能确切地知道,但直觉告诉她那是个禁品。拉达有控制自己不去想某些事情的能力,只要她决定从脑海中删除掉——转眼之间,那个思绪就不见了。她继续搜索着佩琪的衣橱,脑子里早已开始谋划下一步该怎么做了。

她用拇指翻动着衣架,一不小心把一件没有扣扣子的衬衫碰落到了地板上。拉达没有去管它,她知道佩琪不会注意到有什么不同的。她希望斯考蒂亚也能看到眼前的场景,他就会知道佩琪有多么的没条理。尽管拉达深知自己才是斯考蒂亚的明星学生,并以此为豪,但是他从来没用和佩琪开玩笑的语气和自己说过话。他对佩琪的态度里包含了一种父亲般的慈爱,而这种特殊的关系让拉达心生妒意。斯考蒂亚对拉达,总是彬彬有礼的,但她却更想要佩琪和其他学生得到的那种亲密感。凭什么她们能够得到这样的待遇?她想象着自己将来主管一个很大的研究团队,一贫如洗的佩琪卑躬屈膝地向自己恳求一份工作时的样子。首先她要让佩琪给自己下跪,然后掴她一巴掌。拉达不自觉地做出了想象中的动作,一下打掉了更多的衣服。这一下是为了被你偷走的毛衣的,她会愤愤地对她说。然后佩琪就会大哭着求自己原谅,但是那时候已经太迟了。拉达想到这里平静地笑了。

拉达把已经搜查过的一排衣服推到旁边,把另一拨衣架移到自己面前,正准备再把它们推向左边,这时她摸到了一种特别柔软的料子,通常的棉质衬衫是不会有的。就在这儿!藏在衬衫的下面。真是太无耻了。拉达的脑海里闪过更脏的话,但是被她遏止住了。她摇了摇头,感到有些惊讶——佩琪竟然认为自己会傻到找不到这件毛衣。她一把将它从衣架上扯下来,任由一摞叠好的衬衫跌落到地板上。那件质地柔软的粉色毛衣,闪烁着海贝壳内侧般的肉粉色,使女性气质显露无遗。穿上它的人顿时就会被赋予一种娇小可爱的姿态和善解人意的气质。拉达将毛衣套在自己身上,系上前面的纽扣,瞬间就感觉到了它的变化。以

Chapter Nine Sabotage

however, Paige had stretched out the front of it. Rahda felt her irritation increase as she looked down at the sweater's bagginess. She started tucking it into her skirt, but the label at the back of her neck bothered her. Taking the sweater off, she went into the bathroom and found a pair of nail scissors. Carelessly she cut off the label and it fell to the floor along with a few puffs of clipped mohair.

After putting the sweater back on and checking herself proudly in the bathroom mirror, Rahda went back to her bedroom to collect some things. Her head felt so fuzzy. She was thinking of moving. The downstairs neighbor had made fun of her furniture. She heard him talking to Dermot and say something about a Volkswagen missing a seat cover. She was hidden behind the door, but her plaid sofa had been in view. That wasn't the only reason she wanted to move, but it was the last straw. She was thinking about going down and talking to him.

Lately everyone seemed so rude to her. Earlier today, just before she'd sat down at the lunch table to eat, she cleared off all the old newspapers and cans of soda that the rest of the group had left. She didn't want to eat amidst all the debris. She wanted a clean table. Next thing she knew Max was calling her "den mother" and giving her a hard time for throwing away his Pepsi. How was she to know? He made some remark about her making sweeps of the lab, and also about having to write his name on everything so it wouldn't disappear, and then he stormed off. He was completely out-of-line. They had no respect for her, even though she, and only she, was the one bringing serious money into the chemistry department.

Rahda's neck tensed up as she thought of this, and she reached around to massage it. The armpit of the sweater strained, breaking the threads slightly. She heard footsteps outside the door. Rahda threw a jacket on and zipped up the front. Then she hurriedly grabbed her black backpack from off the bed. She opened the front door just as Dermot and Paige paused in front of it, Paige looking for her key. Dermot said, "Hi, Rahda," but she ignored him. They all moved around one another like magnets distanced by a polarized field, bouncing sideways, never getting closer than a certain radius.

"See you later," Dermot yelled.

She hunched down inside her jacket, and she went to eat her solitary dinner.

前毛衣的肩膀处是有点紧的，但是现在被佩琪给撑大了。当她低下头看见松松垮垮的下摆时，更加怒火中烧。拉达开始把毛衣掖进短裙里去，但是衣领后面的标签让她感到很不舒服。于是她又脱了下来，去浴室找了一把指甲剪，草草地把标签给剪掉。标签掉在地上，几缕马海毛在空气中悠悠地飘荡着。

毛衣又重新穿到了拉达身上，她在浴室的镜子里骄傲地打量了一回自己，随后回到自己的卧室收拾些行李。她感到脑袋有些晕晕乎乎的。一直以来她都在考虑搬家的事情。楼下的邻居曾经嘲笑过她的家具风格，她听见他对德莫特说什么福斯汽车少了一个椅套的事情。拉达当时躲在门后面，但是她的格子沙发就摆在眼前。这不是她想要搬家的唯一理由，但却是最后一根稻草。她思忖着走之前要下楼去和他谈一下这件事。

最近，似乎每个人都跟她过不去。今天早些时候，坐下来吃午饭之前，她把组里其他人留在桌上的所有旧报纸和汽水罐给清理干净了。因为她不想坐在一片废墟里吃饭。而不消多久，麦克斯就已经在背后叫她"女学监"了，仅仅是因为拉达把他的百事可乐给扔掉了，他就开始找她麻烦。她怎么能够确定呢？因为哈德利对拉达清扫实验室的行为颇有微词，还抱怨说他得在所有东西上都写上自己的名字，它们才不会凭空消失，并因此大发了一通脾气。他真是太过分了。他们一点都不尊重自己，尽管她，并且只有她，才是给化学部门带来盈利的人。

想到这里，拉达的脖子变得酸胀起来，于是她伸出胳膊按摩了几下。毛衣的腋窝处受到了拉伸，线头有微微的绷裂。听到门外传来一阵脚步声，拉达迅速套上一件夹克衫，拉紧了拉链，匆忙从床上抓起自己的黑色背包。打开公寓门的时候德莫特和佩琪正站在门口，佩琪在找钥匙。德莫特立即说道："你好，拉达。"但是拉达没理他。三个人就像是互相排斥的磁铁一样移动交换了位置，始终各自侧着身子以保持一定的距离。

"待会儿见。"德莫特大声说道。

拉达蜷缩进夹克衫里，一个人出门去吃一顿孤独的晚饭。

Chapter Ten   Rat Corner

> Rat Corner at the end of the block
> Rat Corner—it's on their mailbox
> Rat Corner, they're there everyday
> Rat Corner—
> USA!
> *Olé.*
>
> Hadley Gresham

"Why would the bottom fall out?" Shelby asked Max half-heartedly. Sometimes he talked and talked, not realizing that she was far away, high up in the top of her head, looking down on the world. Her balcony of thought. These were the times when she had millions of hours to plan, but only in lots of five minutes at a time.

They were standing in front of Dermot and Paige's front door, waiting for someone to answer their ring. Shelby was considering going back home and crawling into bed. She wasn't sure she was up to a party.

"The Coke bottle would get so hot that it would just fall off," Max said, startling her with an answer. She had to think back to remember her question. He had been telling her how he and his friends used to make exploding balloons in junior high by filling a Coke bottle with Drano and water, throwing in pieces of aluminum foil, and then capping the bottle with a balloon. The balloon would fill up with hydrogen ("the by-product of the reaction," Max liked to say), then they would tie the balloon off, light the string, and let it float away. Max grinned as he told Shelby, remembering the neighbors yelling after several blew up over their swimming pool, the pieces of ripped elastic floating on the water's surface like leaves from a motley tree.

"How did you know how to do this?" Shelby asked wonderingly, momentarily interested, thinking that her childhood had covered so many different things—piano, for instance, and tap dance—but nothing so spectacular as explosives.

第十章　老鼠角落

> 老鼠角落，在街区的尽头
> 老鼠角落——写在信箱的上面
> 老鼠角落，每天都在上演
> 美利坚！
> 万岁。
>
> ——哈德利·格雷斯汉

"为什么瓶底会掉下来？"谢尔碧心不在焉地问麦克斯。有时候他会滔滔不绝地讲话，却没有注意到谢尔碧已经走神了，她任由思绪游走在脑海的顶端，向下俯视着这个世界。那里是谢尔碧思想的阳台。这种时候，谢尔碧需要给无数的时间做出规划，但却只能用许多个分散的五分钟来完成。

他们俩正站在德莫特和佩琪的公寓门口，等人来开门。谢尔碧正寻思着要不要回家去，一头钻进被窝里。她也不确定自己现在是否有心情去参加派对。

"可乐瓶被加热到一定程度，瓶底就掉下来了。"麦克斯的回答把谢尔碧惊回到现实中来。她得努力回想才能记起自己刚才问的问题。麦克斯在给她讲初中时和朋友一起制作气球炸弹的事情：在一个可乐瓶里装满水和极效凝胶，扔进几片铝箔，然后用气球将瓶口套紧。不一会儿气球里面就会充满氢气（"化学反应的副产物"，麦克斯喜欢这样说），接着他们取下气球，扎紧，点燃细绳末端，然后将其放飞。麦克斯一边咧嘴笑着一边讲给谢尔碧听，他记得当时的邻居还抱怨来着，因为有几个气球在他们的游泳池上方爆炸了，碎片漂浮在水面上，就像树上掉下的五彩树叶。

"你怎么知道制造气球炸弹的方法的？"谢尔碧暂时被吸引住了，好奇地问。她以为自己的童年已经囊括了足够多东西了——比如说钢琴，还有踢踏舞——但是还从没有过像爆炸物这么引人注目的东西。

"I don't know. I think Jimmy Mahoney's brother told us. Maybe he learned it in the army."

Shelby rang the doorbell again. "Why would the balloon explode?" she asked, suddenly curious.

Max smirked. "Hydrogen is very flammable."

"Oh …" Shelby said, realizing that she knew this. Of course, the hydrogen bomb. The Hindenberg. She always felt slow around Max. Explosives had been the topic of the evening. Max had been watching a documentary on Alfred Nobel, the inventor of dynamite, when she came home from a day of telegrams. On the screen were faded pictures of Nobel's younger brother. A solemn English voice was explaining that one of Nobel's brothers had died in an factory explosion.

"They said that people who couldn't read the warnings were using nitroglycerin as axle grease!" Max had said, shaking his head and laughing, laughter apparently being a reasonable response to incredibly bad luck.

Shelby had nothing to say to this, so instead she sat on the sagging couch and took off her right shoe, a low-heeled blue pump marred by scuffs and gouges and life lines of wrinkles across the toe, enough for any palm reader to decipher the myriad journeys of the foot. She slipped off her white cotton sock, the fold-down kind that little girls wear. Her last telegram had been for a kid's birthday party. She'd come as Alice. Looking at her feet, Shelby noticed that several of her toenails had grown very long and were starting to push her shoe into the shape of her foot, as well as cut into the adjacent toes. Absentmindedly she started ripping the white, tearable end of her toenails off and placing them in the palm of her left hand.

She said pensively, "You know, I just remembered this time in L. A. when the man upstairs from me was having a heart attack. And his girlfriend told me that he was taking nitroglycerin for his heart. I knew that was dynamite. And while I was giving him artificial respiration I kept thinking that any minute I might blow up, but—"

Max laughed. "Why'd you keep doing it if you thought you were gonna blow up?"

"I couldn't just let him die."

"He lived?" Max had never heard this story.

Shelby scrunched her face apologetically, comical yet pensive.

"我也记不清了,好像是吉姆·马哈尼的哥哥教我们的。也许他是在军队里面学到的。"

谢尔碧又摁了摁门铃,"为什么气球会爆炸呢?"她有点抑制不住自己的好奇心。

麦克斯得意地笑了,"氢气是易燃气体。"

"噢……"谢尔碧突然意识到自己是知道这一点的。当然会爆炸咯,氢弹利用的就是这个原理。这也是兴登堡号飞艇失事的原因。在麦克斯身边的时候,她觉得自己总是慢半拍。炸弹理所当然地成为当晚聊天的话题。最近,谢尔碧每天做完唱歌电报回来之后,都会看见麦克斯在看一部关于炸药的发明者阿尔弗雷德·诺贝尔的纪录片。她还记得屏幕上展示过一张诺贝尔的弟弟的褪色照片,一个庄严肃穆的声音用英语在一旁解说着,诺贝尔的兄弟之一在一次工厂爆炸中丧生了。

"有人说看不懂警告标语的人会用硝化甘油来做车轴的润滑剂!"麦克斯一边不停地摇着头,一边大笑起来,很显然是在嘲笑那个人的糟糕运气。

谢尔碧对此没什么好评价的,于是就一屁股坐进软趴趴的沙发里,脱下了右脚的鞋子,一只蓝色的低跟鞋,上面布满磨损刮擦的痕迹,还有大脚趾的纹路,多到任何看相先生只需一眼就可以估测出那只脚跋涉过的无数旅程。她又脱下了白色的棉袜,是小女生会穿的那种卷边式样的。上一个唱歌电报是在一个小孩子的生日派对上,她装扮成了爱丽丝出场。谢尔碧看着自己的双脚,注意到有几个脚指甲长得太长了,已经把鞋子撑出了脚的形状,并且会扎到旁边的脚趾头。她开始漫不经心地撕扯脚指甲的白色边缘,然后放在左手的手掌里。

谢尔碧沉思了一会儿说道:"你知道吗,我想起了在洛杉矶时发生的一件事,住我楼上的那个男人心脏病突发,他的女朋友告诉我当时他正在服用硝酸甘油救心丸[译者注:含在舌下服用]。我知道那是炸药的成分,所以在我给他做人工呼吸的时候,我一直在想,我可能随时都会爆炸,可是——"

麦克斯放声大笑了起来,"既然你以为自己会爆炸,那你为什么还要那样做呢?"

"我也不能眼睁睁看着他死呀。"

"所以他活过来了?"麦克斯之前从来没有听过这个故事。

谢尔碧的脸抱歉地皱成一团,有些滑稽,但又很沉重。

Max laughed louder.

"It wasn't my fault," Shelby said bashfully, smiling despite herself. "The paramedics got his heart started but he never came back. His girlfriend said he had a wife and kids in Pennsylvania and he was wanted by the police." She paused. "So— why wouldn't he blow up?"

"It's not concentrated enough. Nitro needs a critical concentration to catalyze its own decomposition. That's how it detonates."

"Nitro?" Shelby gave him a look. He knew jargon made her ill.

Max shrugged.

The commercial that they had been talking through was over, and now Max turned the sound back up. The sedate voice from the TV announced that the scientist who had discovered nitroglycerin was a man named Ascanio Sobrero. He had put a drop of it on his tongue and found that it made him very sick.

"I can't believe that chemists used to taste their compounds," Shelby said over the TV, dropping another curved nail into her hand. They lay there like an assortment of crescent moons, prehistoric and brittle.

"Hell, the Curies used to carry uranium around in their pockets. Nobody had a clue," Max said. He yawned widely and rubbed up his nose a couple of times. He stuck his right thumb inside, scratching the interior.

"I wonder if you guys do anything dangerous now," Shelby said, thinking of how Max always had vestigial odors of cocaine when he came home. It was a joke with them. She knew it wasn't cocaine, but it was one of the few medicinal smells she recognized and so she always teased him about it. Now it occurred to her that if these odors so easily clung to him, obviously molecules of his various compounds would as well. She remembered Franco, a friend of theirs, always saying how if you were smelling shit, you were tasting it. While Franco was going to UCLA he was also training to be a pilot and was always picking up phrases like "You wanna kiss your daddy 'fore I go shake the piss out of him?" and "I would suck the dick of the dog that pissed on the tree in front of her house". Shelby remembered Hadley once asking Franco if this was a special class he took, or if these just came with the regular flying lessons.

Max broke into her thoughts. "The only dangerous thing we do is live in New York."

麦克斯笑得更大声了。

"那不是我的错。"谢尔碧有些羞愧，不情愿地扯了扯嘴角。"急救人员恢复了他的心跳，可是最终没有救活他。他的女朋友说他在宾夕法尼亚有一个老婆和几个孩子，并且正在被警方通缉。"她停顿了一下，"那么，他为什么没有爆炸呢？"

"浓度不够大。硝甘达到特定的浓度才能触发自身的分解反应，这才是引爆点。"

"硝甘？"谢尔碧冲他翻了个白眼。麦克斯知道，谢尔碧不喜欢听化学术语。

麦克斯只能耸耸肩。

他们用聊天来打发的广告时间过去了，麦克斯重新把音量调大。电视里一个从容淡定的声音介绍着发现了硝化甘油的人——一个名叫安斯坎尼欧·索布雷娄的科学家。他曾经在自己的舌尖上滴了一滴硝化甘油，后来因此而病得很严重。

"我简直就不敢相信，过去的化学家们会品尝自己合成的化合物。"谢尔碧评价着电视里的内容，说着又向手掌里扔了一缕弯曲的指甲。它们躺在掌中，就像史前各种形状的新月，敏感而又脆弱。

"还有更惊人的呢，居里一家还经常把镭放在口袋里带来带去呢，当时也没有人知道那意味着什么。"麦克斯说着打了个大大的哈欠，用手指来回揉了几次鼻子。他紧接着又把右手拇指伸进了鼻孔，挠了挠里面。

"我有些好奇，你们现在还会做什么危险的事吗？"谢尔碧回想起来，麦克斯回家的时候身上总会残留一股可卡因的气味。这只是一句玩笑话，因为她知道那不是可卡因的味道，这是她能辨别气味的为数不多的药物之一，所以她总是拿这个来取笑麦克斯。这时她突然意识到，如果那些气味这么容易就附着在他身上，很明显他合成的各种化合物的小分子也会这样。她还记得他们的一个朋友——弗兰克欧，总是说这样一句话，如果你闻到了大便的气味，你也就正在品尝它。当时弗兰克欧正在加州大学洛杉矶分校上学，同时还在接受飞行员训练课程，于是他总是零零星星地学会一些句子，像是"在我把你老爹打得屁滚尿流之前，你不想去亲他一下吗？"还有"要是我看到在她家门前树根上撒尿的那只狗，我会上去亲它的老二的"。哈德利曾经问过他，这种语言到底是一门特殊的课程，还是夹杂在平常的飞行课里面的？

麦克斯打断了她的思绪，"我们现在会做的唯一的危险的事情就是住在纽约市。"

Shelby laughed. Even when she was mad at him, he could make her laugh. Why was she mad at him? She felt begrudging, but she couldn't remember why. That made her feel stupid, but she was sure there had been a good reason. Maybe it was because he was so good at everything. That made her feel stupid, too. He used big words that he could then explain to her. She liked learning things, but it felt one-sided. What could she offer him? The band was the only place they were equals. They were all equals in the band. That's why she enjoyed it so much. It was refreshingly democratic. She was as much involved with the sound of the band as any one of them. It made her feel like a feminist. One on one with the boys. They were exciting. They weren't genetically programmed to have more interesting conversation, but ultimately they did. Women let it be conditioned out of them. They were too nice. They didn't dig. They didn't associate with dirt. And men knew that's where all the risky conversation was. That's where rock'n'roll was. Dirty. Sweary. Foul-mouthed and guttural. Rock was an emotional wrenching that compelled beyond all comprehension.

Shelby knew she attracted men with her performance. They would come up and talk to her, a kind of radiance emanating toward her; sometimes she would mention being married, sometimes she wouldn't. Guilt would tug at her omission. Sometimes she wished she were lesbian. Or at least a swing in that direction, something to lessen the effect of her need of men. She needed Max. She didn't feel complete unless she was with him. That felt very unfeminist. But in her need, she also felt competition. In the rock band they were equals, but in life Max held fifty-one percent. He knew he was going somewhere. Shelby was jealous of his future, that something lay out there for him, that school would soon be over and then they would pay him well. Shelby wondered why she hadn't paid attention in chemistry. If someone could have only told her, if someone could have said, "This is where the big bucks will be." Max had the self-confidence of someone you would pay well. She knew he considered his chemistry impeccable. Certainly compared to his English labmate Kyle. Max said that chemists from England would often do things like not wear gloves or leave traces of compound on the balance. Kyle would dribble a trail of white powder wherever he'd been, and, Max would yell later, waving a beer in his hand, "Who knows what the hell it is? An acid, a carcinogen ... Okay, it's not completely his fault. In England a Ph. D. program is three years and you're out, whether you're

谢尔碧被逗笑了——麦克斯总是能做到这一点,即使是在谢尔碧生他气的时候。为什么她会生气?因为嫉妒,可是她也记不起来是为了什么。这让谢尔碧觉得自己有些蠢,但是她确信自己一定有足够的理由。也许是因为麦克斯对一切事情都那么擅长,让她感觉到了自己的愚蠢。他会用一些高级的词汇,然后再解释给她听。谢尔碧喜欢学习新东西,可是她觉得这种方式不平衡。那么她可以给麦克斯提供什么呢?只有在乐队里他们才是平等的,所以她才能够那么尽情地享受。那里的平等氛围让人精神振奋,她对乐队总体效果的贡献与其他任何一个成员一样不可或缺。这样的感觉使谢尔碧觉得自己像女权主义者。一对一地和男人单挑。男人们总是能够令人兴奋起来,虽然基因编码并没有注定他们具有让谈话更加有趣的能力,可最终他们却能够做到这一点。而女人就任由社会驯服,渐渐失去了这种能力。女人会过度地友好,不喜欢讽刺挖苦,不涉及下流粗俗。而男人则知道,只有在这些方面冒险才有可能促成成功的对话,才能够点燃激情。带点色情,掺杂些脏话,伴随着咽喉音。摇滚是一种感情上的挣脱,能够极大限度地激发一个人。

谢尔碧知道,男人会被她的表演所吸引。他们会走上前来和她搭讪,就像光线一般纷纷向她辐射过来;有时她会提到自己已婚的事实,有时则不会。愧疚感会提醒她不去做刻意的隐瞒。她甚至曾经暗自希望自己是个同性恋,或者至少摇摆不定一些,这样就可以减少她对男人的需要了。她需要麦克斯,只有和他在一起的时候谢尔碧才觉得自己是完整的。这种感觉有悖于女权主义。但是她的需求之中,还有竞争。在摇滚乐队里,他们是平等的,可是在生活中麦克斯却占了51%。他明确地知道自己人生的方向。谢尔碧嫉妒他的未来,计划好的一切——大学即将结束,而他将有一份很高的薪水。谢尔碧后悔着自己当初为什么没有多留心一下化学。要是当初有人告诉她就好了,跟她说一声:"这就是能挣大钱的领域。"麦克斯具有应该得到高薪的人的那种自信。她知道,麦克斯觉得自己的化学研究是无可匹敌的,要是跟他同实验室的英国人凯尔比起来,更是不在话下。麦克斯曾说过,来自英国的化学家会经常做一些不靠谱的事情,比如不戴手套,或是在将化合物散落在天平的托盘上。凯尔无论走到哪里,身后都会留下一条白色粉末的痕迹,过了不久麦克斯就会挥舞着手里的啤酒冲他大喊:"鬼知道这他妈到底是什么?是酸还是致癌物……好吧,这也不完全是他的错。在英国读博士项目三年一满你就可以出师,管你准没准备好呢。"这是麦克斯经

ready or not." This was one of the tirades Max went on: the illogic of graduate school as handled in certain countries. He was both funny and right. He had a persuasive argument. That's what drove her crazy. He always had the persuasive argument.

"Were we thinking about going—" Max started to say, startling Shelby out of her reverie; she had been staring across at the rock that starred in their window.

She looked toward him, interrupting him. "Don't pick your nose. Jesus Christ. That's disgusting!" Max's habits made her feel like she was living with a caveman. Someone had once said that you can tell you're married when you go into the bathroom while your spouse is taking a crap—come to think of it, that was probably Franco too. Shelby hated the thought of marriage being equated to something as base as that. It meant you were comfortable, but was that kind of familiarity a good thing?

Looking a little bit embarrassed at having been discovered, Max quickly wiped his finger on the underside of his chair. "Well, you're picking your toes!" he said defensively.

"No, I'm not!" she said with irritation, amazed that he would try to associate the two. "I'm tearing off my nails. I haven't seen the clipper for days. It used to be in the bathroom cabinet—"

Max interrupted in measured tones, "I haven't touched it."

Shelby shook her head. "This doesn't even compare."

They sat in huffy silence for a while, the only noise the educated voice of the television. Shelby went into the kitchen to throw her clippings away, liking the scrabbling sound they made as they filtered through the trash. She opened the refrigerator as if commanded to do so, but nothing looked good enough to entice her to eat it.

"We should go," she sighed, not sure if she was up to a party, still staring into the refrigerator just in case something started to look more appetizing. A block of cheddar cheese seemed the most inviting, but she didn't feel like going to the effort of taking it out of its baggy and cutting a piece off just to find that it wasn't really what she wanted. She craved something better than cheese. Something better than food even. "Why does everyone say that chemists only have girls then?" she asked, closing the refrigerator and walking back into the living room. The implication was that the male sperm wasn't hardy enough to survive after being exposed to chemical substances.

常发表激烈演说的话题之一：某些国家实施的研究生项目有悖于逻辑常理。他总能做到又有趣又正确，想出有说服力的理由来。这就是让谢尔碧不能接受的地方——他的观点总是那么令人信服。

"我们还打不打算去——"麦克斯开口道，将谢尔碧从遐想中惊醒过来；她一直在盯着窗外的那块大岩石出神。

谢尔碧转过头去，打断了他的话。"别挖鼻孔了，上帝啊！太恶心了！"麦克斯的习惯让她觉得自己是和一个原始野人生活在一起的。有人曾说过，如果你的另一半在大便的时候你也会走进洗手间里去，那么就可以断定你已经结婚了——仔细想一想，这句话很有可能也是弗兰克欧说的。谢尔碧不喜欢这种观念——把婚姻等同于那么龌龊琐碎的事。那样的行为意味着你们在一起的时候很舒服自然，可是那么亲近真的是一件好事吗？

被发现之后麦克斯看上去有些窘迫，迅速地在椅子下面擦了擦手指。"怎么了，你还在抠脚呢！"他不甘心地争辩道。

"我才没有！"谢尔碧有些恼怒，他竟然试图把这两件事联系起来。"我在撕指甲。我已经好几天找不到指甲剪了，本来是放在洗手间的小柜子里的——"

麦克斯用慢条斯理的语调打断了她，"我可没有碰过。"

谢尔碧不满地摇了摇头，"这两件事根本不能相提并论。"

他们就那样在僵持的寂静中坐了一会儿，唯一的声音就是电视机里传来的富有涵养的嗓音。谢尔碧走进厨房去扔指甲，它们穿过垃圾时的刮擦声使她愉悦。她鬼使神差地打开冰箱门，但却找不到任何可能诱惑她去吃的食物。

"我们该出发了。"她叹了口气，并不确定自己有心情去参加派对，眼睛仍然盯着冰箱，以防有什么能突然引起她的食欲。最具引诱力的是一块切德干酪，但是谢尔碧害怕在自己费事地把它从袋子里拿出来切下一小片之后，却发现那不是自己想要的。她想要比乳酪更好的东西，甚至是比食物更好的东西。"为什么人们都说化学家只能生出女儿来？"谢尔碧问道，随后关上冰箱走回起居室去。这个问题暗示的就是男性精子无法在暴露于化学物质中之后继续存活。

Chapter Ten Rat Corner

Shelby threw this out as a peace offering, an awkward attempt to start their conversation back up. She still only had one shoe on and it made her feel lopsided. For some odd reason that pleased her, that simply the novelty of walking crooked was enough of a difference to be interesting.

"I think that's kind of a chemist joke. *C & E News* mentioned it the other day even, but admitted that no one's ever done a study." Max leaned back in his chair. "You ready to go?"

"I'll bet they're afraid to find out," Shelby said, looking pensively at the bedroom door and wondering if she felt like changing her clothes. Walking with one bare foot had made her clothes feel too formal. She was still wearing a baby blue dress and a white pinafore, her Alice costume, which she'd intended on wearing to Dermot's, but now she felt like being low-key. It took more personality to be overdressed; people expected you to be the life of the party. Maybe she'd wear jeans.

She left Max watching the television, knowing that TV required no energy from him, there was no need for participation, and that's why he liked it. The sound was so loud, she could hear the narrator explaining that Nobel had established the Nobel prize in his will for the encouragement of persons who work for humanity. Nobel had remorse about all the people who had been killed and was very upset when a newspaper obituary for his older brother had mistakenly thought Alfred had died, describing him as the "merchant of death". She heard Max flick off the TV, and say, obviously for her benefit, "Death Merchant, Vendor o' Death, Dead Salesmen, Door-to-Door Death, Death du Jour ... Ennh. They're just too heavy metal."

Walking out of the bedroom, Shelby said, "You forming a new band?"

"Just trying out some names."

"I kind of feel sorry for him." She grabbed a jacket out of the hall closet and opened the front door. Max followed her.

"Yeah, people will always hold the inventor responsible. But cause and effect is much more complex than that. I think about that with things like anticancer compounds. Basically you're trying to kill the cancer just before you kill the human who's probably going to die anyway, but you want to make sure it's not from your drug."

"Yeah, but responsibility and decency are two different things. If you made something that did kill someone, wouldn't you want to do something about it?"

谢尔碧提出这个问题作为和解,重新开始他们的对话,虽然有些笨拙。她脚上仍然只穿着一只鞋,因此感到自己有些向一侧倾斜。由于某种奇怪的原因,这种感觉让谢尔碧很满意,仅仅是与众不同地一瘸一拐地走路,就足够新鲜,足够有趣了。

"我认为这是一个跟化学家开的玩笑。甚至《化学与工程新闻》还刊登过一次,不过同时也承认没有人做过相关实验。"麦克斯向后嵌进椅子里,"你准备好出发了吗?"

"我打赌他们不敢找出真相。"谢尔碧看着卧室的门,沉思了一会儿,纠结着要不要换个衣服。一直光着一只脚走路,使得她现在穿的衣服显得太正式了。她还穿着扮演爱丽丝的服装,宝蓝色的裙子外面系着一条白色的围裙。她本来是打算穿着这身去德莫特的派对的,但现在她却想低调一些。盛装出席是需要勇气的,因为人们会期待你给派对带来活力。也许她应该穿牛仔裤。

她把麦克斯丢在那里看电视,知道这不需要他消耗任何精力,也就是因为不需要任何参与,麦克斯才会喜欢看电视。电视的音量大得谢尔碧在卧室都能听见,旁白解释着诺贝尔设立诺奖的原因是为了鼓励人们为人道主义而奋斗。诺贝尔对那些因炸药而死的人心怀愧疚,再加上诺贝尔的弟弟去世时,当时的一份报纸误以为是诺贝尔,在讣告中将其称为"死亡商人",这也使他十分不快。谢尔碧听到麦克斯把电视给关掉了,很显然是为了讨好她,"死亡商人,死亡小贩,死亡推销员,死神上门,死亡的颜色… 唔。就是重金属感太强了。"

谢尔碧从卧室里走出来,"你要成立新乐队吗?"

"只是在想一些名字。"

"其实我有些同情他。"她从走廊衣橱里抓了一件夹克,打开了前门。麦克斯跟在她的后面出了门。

"是啊,人们总是把一切都算在发明者头上,但其实因果关系要比那复杂得多。就比如说抗癌化合物的例子,总的来说你要做的就是在杀死人类健康细胞之前一点把癌细胞给杀死。虽然患者无论如何还是会死,但你想要确保他不是死于你的药物。"

"确实如此,可是责任感和个人操守是完全不同的概念。如果你合成出来的药物真的害死了人,你难道不想做些什么吗?"谢尔碧招手示意正从椅子里起

Chapter Ten Rat Corner

Shelby waved down the doorman as he started to rise out of his chair. She didn't care that it was his job, it still made her feel part of a class system. Especially since it seemed that most of the doormen in New York were black.

Max whispered, "It's exciting to alter the course of history every time we walk through the lobby."

Shelby ignored him and walked faster. He skipped to catch up. "Anticancer drugs are very toxic. That's why they work. If they work too well, you might kill the patient before the cancer does. When patients die because of the drugs, people want a scapegoat."

"And shouldn't that be the company who stands to make a profit? I think that's why Nobel felt so guilty, because he did make a profit." Shelby felt irritated, the effect of walking outside into the cold, the real cold unfamiliar to a Californian.

They walked across the street in silence, the quiet better company than each other. She knew that Max thought that she saw a very simple side of the issue, the emotional side. That she didn't consider the fact that advances in science are risks and a person has to weigh the risks to the possible benefits. They'd been through this before. An ugly argument that never went away.

Jumping onto the sidewalk, Max said, "Guilt is an interesting motivator," and laughed, changing to a lighter subject. "I gave Jimmy Mahoney my erector set after he almost lost his finger." Max looked at Shelby. "It was kind of my fault."

Shelby looked at him sullenly. She didn't feel like figuring out what he was talking about.

"I knew it would get hot, but I didn't actually think that the bottom of the Coke bottle would blow off with such force," Max said, trying for levity as he opened the front door of the building. It was supposed to be locked so that people could buzz you in, but it never was.

Dermot's building was across the street from theirs and closer to Riverside Park, a nicer park than Morningside, but every park had its liabilities. The building was old and dark, with threads the length of the hall missing from the carpet, as if someone had rolled them up to make a nappy, slate-colored sweater. The building's foyer had checkerboard linoleum and seemed larger than it was because the walls were covered with those once-trendy mirror tiles that had veins of black and gray running through them as if someone on the other side's cigarette smoke had been trapped within the glass.

身的看门人不必麻烦了。她不在乎这是不是他的分内之事,起立问好这种事情在她眼里是在课堂里才会发生的事情。尤其是鉴于纽约几乎所有的看门人都是黑人的情况。

麦克斯小声嘀咕道:"我们每次经过大厅都会改变历史的习惯,真是激动人心。"

谢尔碧无视了他的话,又加快了脚步。于是麦克斯跳过这个话题,接着上一段对话说了起来。"抗癌药物毒性是很高的,所以它们才会起作用。假如它们疗效过强的话,也许癌细胞还没被杀死患者就已经被药给毒死了。当有人是被药物夺走了生命的时候,人们就需要找到一个替罪羊。"

"难道不应该是借此来挣钱的公司吗?我觉得这也是诺贝尔那么内疚的原因,因为他曾经从中获利。"突然走到冷风中,谢尔碧感到有些心烦,这种寒冷对加州人来说很少见。

他们穿过街道,一路默默无言,安静给予了他们比对方更好的陪伴。谢尔碧知道,麦克斯认为她只看到了问题最肤浅的一面,感性的那一面;她没有考虑到会推动科学前进的正是风险以及权衡风险与收益的那个人。这个论点揭露了丑恶的现实,他们以前就讨论过,但是永远也得不出结论。

麦克斯跳到人行道上,"内疚感是一种很有意思的驱动因素,"然后就大笑了起来,旋即换了一个轻松一点的话题。"吉米·马哈尼差一点就失去了一根手指头,我就把自己的建筑拼装玩具套装给了他。"麦克斯看着谢尔碧说道:"因为那件事大体来说是我的失误。"

谢尔碧一脸阴郁地回看着他,一点儿也不想去猜他在讲什么。

"我知道瓶子会变得很热,可我也没有预料到可乐瓶的瓶底爆炸会有那么大的威力。"麦克斯说话的空当试探地推了推大楼的前门,这扇门本来应该是锁起来的,只有里面的住户按下按钮,你才能进去,但它却一直都是开着的。

德莫特住的公寓楼和他们的只有一街之隔,离河畔公园更近一些。虽然总体来说河畔公园要比晨边公园更宜人,可是每个公园都有自己的角色要扮演。这栋公寓楼老旧阴暗,大厅的地毯抽丝严重,就好像有人曾经把它给卷起来做成一件毛茸茸的石灰色毛衣似的。门厅里铺的是棋盘图案的油地毡,因为墙上新贴了曾经风靡一时的镜面瓦片,所以整体看上去比实际空间要大,黑色和灰色的纹路流淌于玻璃间,仿佛对面的抽烟人的烟雾被困在了玻璃里面。

Chapter Ten Rat Corner

Shelby checked her lipstick in one of the tiles, scraping away an errant streak with her fingernail where it violated the line of her lip. The two-person elevator yawned slowly open. They entered and felt the carriage of the elevator rise fitfully, the movement shaking them to the center of the sloping floor like a saggy bed that succeeds in having its occupants touching by morning.

"You should have seen it; his finger was cut through to the bone," Max said, taunting her with more of the story, apparently wanting her to ask questions.

"Because of the carbonation?" Shelby asked, wrinkling her forehead fretfully. She didn't feel like talking anymore. That was okay, though, Max was willing to do it for both of them. Her mind drifted as they walked down the hall to Dermot's. Max always told her that she was too emotional, and she thought him too unfeeling. Their conversations would reach a dead-end of frustration where neither felt like negotiating. This made her feel sad. How did you stay married and not wear on each other, not grind each other down? Shelby cleared her throat in preparation for announcing that she didn't feel well. She just wanted to go home, get stoned, and go to bed. But then Dermot answered the door.

"Hey, check this out," Dermot said, grinning. He always acted like you were in the middle of a long conversation with him even if you hadn't seen him for a week. A Renaissance man, left brain and right brain, Dermot had a B.A. in Sculpture and a Ph.D. in Chemistry. Recently, when Shelby was at the New York Public Library, she'd been looking through a book of famous playwrights. She was amazed to discover that Dermot looked just like Molière, curls and all. She had suggested it to him as a Halloween costume. But he preferred to go as a woman.

Dermot was wild. His favorite thing to do when drunk was to take a running dive into the ever-present piles of plastic garbage bags that line the streets of New York. They'd all be walking home from dinner—chemists mostly—and suddenly Dermot would be off and running, lifting his body like a pole vaulter, then landing on his back in the midst of all the garbage. They would laugh because it was funny and then they would try to scare him out of ever doing it again. "What if there were syringes in there?" someone would say. "Or knives?" "He has a death wish," they would joke, wondering if it were really true. Paige had given up trying to convince him. She just insisted he take a shower afterward.

第十章 老鼠角落

谢尔碧对着一块镜面检查了一下嘴巴,用指甲擦去了越过唇线的口红。电梯门慢慢吞吞地开了,他们走了进去,立即感觉到这个限载两人的电梯开始断断续续地上升。地板是向中间倾斜的,他们不知不觉地被晃悠得越来越近,就像睡在松软床铺的两人一早醒来发现正彼此亲密接触一样。

"你要是能亲眼看见就好了,他的手指骨头都露出来了。"麦克斯添油加醋地对谢尔碧形容道,很显然他想让她追问下去。

"就因为碳酸饱和作用的威力?"谢尔碧烦躁地皱起眉头,不情愿地问道。她实在不想再说话了,不过也没什么大碍,反正麦克斯愿意自己把他们两个人的话都给说了。走在通向德莫特公寓的走廊上,她的思绪早已就不知道飘到哪里去了。麦克斯给她的评价是,太过感情用事,而且把他想象得太过冷酷无情。有时他们的对话会困在死胡同里,两人都沮丧到不想和谈的地步。这一点让谢尔碧感到难过:要如何才能维系婚姻,但又不会越过对方的忍耐限度而导致互相折磨呢? 谢尔碧清了清嗓子,准备声明自己觉得不舒服。她只想回家,来一口大麻,然后倒头就睡。但就在这时候德莫特打开了门。

"嘿,快来看。"德莫特得意地笑着。他总是表现得仿佛你和他聊了很久一样,尽管事实上你已经一个星期没有见过他了。他是一个文艺复兴型的男人,左脑和右脑兼顾,他有一个雕塑艺术的硕士学位和一个化学的博士学位。前几天,谢尔碧在纽约公共图书馆看一本关于著名剧作家的书时,惊讶地发现德莫特和莫里哀长得一模一样,不论是卷发还是其他特征。她建议德莫特万圣节的时候装扮成莫里哀,但是他更想伪装成一个女人。

德莫特是一个疯狂的人。他喝醉了以后最喜欢做的事情,就是助跑之后一头扎进纽约市街头司空见惯的塑料袋垃圾堆里。他们一群人吃完晚饭之后会一起走回家——大部分是化学家——冷不丁地,德莫特就会脱离队伍,开始助跑起来,然后像个撑竿跳运动员那样让身体一跃而起,最后背朝下降落在一大堆垃圾中。大家便会被这个滑稽的场景给逗得前仰后合,接着他们就会开始恐吓德莫特,让他下次不敢再这样做。"万一里面有针筒怎么办?"有人会说,"或者是刀子呢?"大家还会开玩笑说,"他真是不想活了",同时也好奇到底是不是真的如此。佩琪已经放弃说服他的可能性了,她只是坚持让德莫特做完这件事之后一定要洗澡。

Chapter Ten Rat Corner

"Read this," Dermot ordered Shelby and Max, stopping halfway down the hall. Taped to the wall outside the bathroom was a creased, typewritten letter.

Shelby read it out loud, as fast as she possibly could. "'I am fucking tired of having your filthy bath water drip down from the ceiling onto my gun collection. If it doesn't stop IMMEDIATELY or sooner, I will be up there to do something about it. This is not an idle threat. FIX THE PROBLEM!!!! The neighbor in 4B.' So?" She looked at him defiantly. Dermot liked you to grovel for his stories.

"Dermot, this is nuts!" Max said, looking at him in amazement. "Did you call the police?"

Dermot brightened. "It's being handled."

"What do you mean 'it's being handled'?" Max asked mockingly.

"He doesn't come up with a rifle anymore—"

"You're not serious," Shelby interjected, turning back toward him. She really didn't know if she should believe him. Dermot's stories always sounded made-up. Even if the facts were true, Dermot's way of telling the story could pervert what Shelby considered the "real" truth of the situation. To him, being funny was paramount. He had a profound interest in standup comedy and had even considered quitting chemistry and becoming a comic ... for about a day. His adviser told him to go do it, thinking perhaps that he would get it out of his system and not need to use the chemistry group meetings as a forum for trying out new material. Dermot finally went to a comedy club that had an open mike night. After he performed, the MC told him, "I'm sure you'll do well at whatever it is you end up doing."

Dermot pushed the door to the bathroom open. "See along the bottom there, how black it is? Our shower drips down to his apartment. I told him that I'd already talked to the housing office. But that didn't seem to make an impression. He said, 'Next time, I won't just bring my gun!' Two days later this letter shows up under the door. I posted it here so that anyone taking a shower would be conservative with the water." Dermot grinned. He reveled in conflict.

"I don't doubt that your bathroom is falling apart." Shelby said dryly, and leaned against the wall.

"Shelby nearly fell through ours."

"You should move." Shelby shook her head. Dermot's cavalier attitude confused her. He acted like a neighbor brandishing a gun was an everyday occurrence.

"读一下。"德莫特在门厅的中间停了下来,给谢尔碧和麦克斯下了一道命令。洗手间外的墙上贴着一张皱巴巴的打印出来的信。

谢尔碧用她最快的语速大声地读了出来:"我他妈的受够了!你们的脏洗澡水从天花板滴下来,流到我收集的枪上面了!如果这件事不能立刻,或者尽快被解决的话,我会亲自上楼去采取措施的。这可不是随便说说的威胁,给我立刻解决!!!住在4B的邻居。""所以呢?"谢尔碧挑衅地反问道。德莫特就是喜欢别人求着他讲出整个故事的始末。

"德莫特,这件事太疯狂了!"麦克斯无比讶异地看着他。"你打电话报警了吗?"

德莫特的脸亮了起来。"正在解决当中。"

"你说'正在解决当中'是什么意思?"麦克斯嘲弄道。

"他不会再拿着来复枪冲上楼来了——"

"你肯定是在吹牛。"谢尔碧忍不住插了嘴,表示不相信。她真的没法确定该不该相信德莫特,因为他所有的故事听上去都像是编造出来的。即使事情是真的,德莫特的叙述方式也会歪曲掉谢尔碧认为的"真正的"事实。对德莫特来说,别人觉得他有趣才是最要紧的事。他对单口喜剧有着浓厚的兴趣,甚至考虑过要不要放弃化学转行做喜剧演员……持续了大概一天。他的学业顾问鼓励他这样做,心想着也许这样就可以让他得到彻底的打击,他也就不会再把组会发言当成他试验新段子的舞台了。德莫特最后终于加入了一个喜剧俱乐部,参加了他们的"公开表演之夜"。在他的表演结束后,主持人对他说:"我很确定,你以后无论做什么都会比这个做得好的。"

德莫特推开了洗手间的门。"沿着拐角看,看到有多黑了吗?我们的洗澡水会沿着地板滴进他的房间里去。我告诉他我已经跟物业办公室的人谈过了,但是他似乎不为所动。他说,'下一次,我就不只是带枪上来了!'两天之后,这封信就出现在了我的门缝里,我就把它张贴在这里,这样大家在洗澡的时候就都会少用一点水了。"德莫特得意地笑了,冲突让他乐在其中。

"我一点儿都不怀疑你的公寓就快要散架了。"谢尔碧斜倚在墙上,干巴巴地说道。

"谢尔碧差点儿就掉进了我们房间的浴室里。"

"你应该搬家了。"谢尔碧摇了摇头。德莫特满不在乎的态度让她困惑,就好像邻居拿着一把枪气势汹汹地冲你挥舞是再平常不过的事一样。虽然知道德

Chapter Ten Rat Corner

She knew he liked to milk things. But how could you make more of a guy with a gun standing at your door?

"You should go to the police," Max said.

Dermot leaned against the wall and folded his arms. "He's not a bad guy. He says it's ruining his Indian rugs."

"Oh, well in that case ... " Shelby said sarcastically, and walked away, badly wanting a glass of wine.

There was a knock at the door.

"Everybody duck," yelled Max.

Dermot opened it, and Eberhard and his wife Estrid walked in. As they entered, Hadley rounded the corner from the elevator.

"Guns?" Max asked.

"Were we supposed to bring some?" Eberhard asked. Nothing Max said ever surprised him. "I haf my Swiss Army knife—for my beer!"

"Guns?" Estrid asked, her eyes wide open.

"It's just Max," Hadley said to her as they all walked into the narrow hallway and he closed the front door. "He never makes any sense."

"Don't say I didn't warn you," Max said pointedly to Hadley.

Shelby didn't know why, but Max was irritating her. She expected Dermot to act like that, but Max? He was so competitive that he always had to sink to the lowest common denominator.

The doorbell rang again. It was Paige. She was carrying two big grocery bags.

"Thanks, I couldn't reach my keys," she said to Hadley, giggling apologetically after he opened the door and took one of the bags from her, following her to the kitchen. The doorbell rang again. Paige yelled from the kitchen, "Dermot, just prop it open."

"Don't do it," Max yelled from the living room, taking an opened beer from Eberhard.

"It is very warm," Eberhard said, taking off his jacket and sitting back on the sofa. "Could I open a window?" Eberhard put equal weight on all of his syllables, making English more like German lieder.

"Just don't take a shower," Max said. Shelby sensed that Max was trying too hard because she was annoyed with him, and this only annoyed her more.

莫特喜欢讲故事,但是都已经有个家伙持枪站在你的门口了,还能怎么美化事实呢?

"你应该报警。"麦克斯建议道。

德莫特倚在墙上,双手交叉在胸前。"他不是个坏人,他说滴下来的脏水把他的印度地毯给毁了。"

"哦,这样一来就可以理解了……"谢尔碧不无讽刺地补充了一句,一边走向厨房,她现在急需一杯酒。

这时一阵敲门声传来。

"大家快躲起来。"麦克斯大喊了一声。

德莫特去开了门,艾伯哈德和他的老婆爱丝翠走了进来。就在这个时候,哈德利也从电梯旁的拐角处走了过来。

"带枪了吗?"麦克斯问道。

"我们应该带些枪来吗?"艾伯哈德反问。无论麦克斯说什么,他都不会感到惊讶的。"我随身带着瑞士军刀呢——用来开啤酒!"

"枪?"爱丝翠瞪大了眼睛。

"只是麦克斯在瞎扯而已,"哈德利在大家都从狭窄的门厅通过之后,顺手关上了门,"他总是说些疯话。"

"可别怪我没警告过你。"麦克斯的语气中充满挖苦。

谢尔碧也不知道为什么,麦克斯现在的言行让她感到生气。德莫特这样哗众取宠还在预料之中,但是麦克斯也这样?他的竞争欲实在是太强了,所以要一直堕落到最低的分母当中去。

门铃又响了。是佩琪,拎着两个大大的购物袋站在门口。

哈德利打开门之后接过了其中一个袋子,跟着她一起进了厨房。"谢谢,我刚才没有手拿钥匙。"佩琪抱歉地吃吃笑着。门铃再次响起,佩琪的叫声从厨房传来,"德莫特,就把门一直打开吧。"

"千万不要!"麦克斯从艾伯哈德手里接过一瓶打开的啤酒,大喊道。

"这里太热了,"艾伯哈德说着脱掉了夹克衫,退后一步坐在了沙发上,"我能把窗户打开吗?"艾伯哈德说话总是每个音节都用一样的重音,使他说英语的口音听起来更像是德国经典歌曲的唱腔。

"只要你不洗澡就行。"麦克斯揶揄道。谢尔碧感觉到麦克斯更加努力地想要表现,因为他知道自己在生他的气,可是他这样做只会火上浇油。

Chapter Ten Rat Corner

"Someone else's bathroom is falling apart?" Hadley asked innocently, walking into the living room.

"Dermot's neighbor is psycho and Dermot's getting all the mileage out of it he can," Shelby said bluntly, sitting on the edge of a sofa, ready to spring, to take off. She was already sorry she came. She was tired of talking about the things Dermot wouldn't deal with. Anything that couldn't be fixed Shelby didn't see a purpose in continuing to discuss unless there was some benefit in it, a kind of emotional stock exchange. She saw people telling her their problems as a trade that had four possible modes of transaction: She either 1) got to tell them a solution, 2) got to tell them her problems, 3) got to laugh at their problems (which meant that their problems had to be funny) or else, 4) they paid her as they would any good therapist. She looked at Hadley and saw that confusion was ruffling his face.

"Read this," Shelby said, standing up and walking down the hallway, hoping that once he read it and showed his amazement, they could then talk about something else. She tried to analyze why talking about the neighbor made her so angry. She wasn't sure, and it hurt to think that hard, but she thought it was because it was a serious problem that no one was taking seriously and that seemed somehow irresponsible. Shelby went into the kitchen to refill her glass. She was drinking fast. As she poured, the calming influence of watching the pale yellow liquid fill the wine glass forced Shelby to admit to herself that she was just really moody right now and she had to be careful not to weigh other people down with her testiness. She prided herself in being a real person, never phony or fake, but that meant she didn't hide her frustrations. She realized that this was really an excuse for giving other people her baggage and it didn't correspond to her idea of emotional fair exchange. But being nice was hard work when you felt so unhappy.

Standing at the kitchen door and toying with the idea of joining the party, Shelby watched Paige walk to the coffee table, hugging two bowls of chips. Paige was wearing a black fuzzy sweater and her breasts swelled before her like the prows of attendant ships. Max had admitted to Shelby that occasionally he had dreams about Paige. Shelby was irritated that Max had told her. She hadn't asked and didn't want to know. Paige played the cute game. She knew the right combination of silly little me and cutting-edge woman chemist. Sometimes Paige even played cute around Shelby, acting the part of a confused girl. Shelby wanted to say, "You forget,

"还有其他人的浴室也快塌了吗?"哈德利一脸天真地走进客厅。

"德莫特的邻居是个疯子,而他正充分地利用这一点,让自己有好故事可以说。"谢尔碧坐在沙发的扶手上,不留不情面地总结道。她准备好要闪人了,随时随地,事实上,她已经后悔自己来了这里。大家都苦口婆心地提建议,而德莫特却决心不采取任何措施,这让她非常不满。任何不能被解决的事情,谢尔碧都觉得没有继续讨论的必要,除非能够从中获得一些好处,一种类似于感情证券的交易。她把人们找她倾诉问题看成是一种交易,通常有四种可能的模式:她要么(1)给他们提供一个解决方案;(2)转而向他们倾诉自己的问题;(3)有机会可以嘲笑他们的问题;或者是(4)他们会付给她任何一个优秀的心理治疗师能得到的报酬。她看了一眼哈德利,疑惑占据了他的整个表情。

"读一下这个吧。"谢尔碧站起身来向门厅走去,希望哈德利读完那封信,表达过他的惊讶之后,大家就可以换一个话题了。她试着分析了一下,为什么聊关于这个邻居的话题会让自己这么生气,她也不是十分确定,不过那么投入地思考让她头疼。大概是因为没有人拿这么严肃的问题当回事儿,这在她看来有些不负责任。谢尔碧手里的酒杯很快就空了,于是她走进厨房去再给自己添一些。倒酒的时候,谢尔碧看着那浅黄色的液体缓慢地将高脚杯填满,感到了一种抚慰作用,她不得不承认自己现在的情绪有些阴晴不定,一定要很小心才能不让自己的暴躁破坏别人的心情。她一向以自己的真性情为傲,从不作假或是伪装,但这也意味着,她从来都不隐藏沮丧失落的情绪。她现在意识到这其实是一个把自己的负面情绪转移到他人身上的借口,而这违背了她所倡导的公平情感交易。但话说回来,要想在自己非常不开心的时候对每个人都态度友善实在是太难了。

谢尔碧站在厨房的门口踌躇着要不要回去加入大家的派对时,她看到佩琪怀里抱着两大碗薯片向咖啡桌走去。佩琪穿着一件毛茸茸的黑色毛衣,她的双乳晃动得像波浪中的救生艇。麦克斯曾经向谢尔碧坦白过,他有时候会梦到佩琪。谢尔碧从来没有开口问过,也不想知道,可是麦克斯却主动告诉她,这让她很恼怒。佩琪懂得如何运用装可爱那一套,她知道如何将"傻傻的小女人"和"尖端女化学家"的形象给完美地结合起来。有时候佩琪甚至会在谢尔碧的面前故作可爱,装作是个困惑的小女生。谢尔碧很想对她说:"你别忘了,我知道

I know that game. I've played it myself."

Shelby told Max that she'd seen Paige in a bra when they were shopping together. "It was industrial-strength," she'd said, intentionally catty and feeling mean, but not stopping. "At least four hook-and-eyes." Shelby rarely wore a bra and associated the wide bands of Paige's with one her grandmother had worn, some crazy size like double E's. It had been so long since Shelby had worn a bra, she happily couldn't remember her size. Seeing Paige in a bra, roped in, strapped up, had seemed so restrictive, hearkening back to bustles and crinolines, corsets that made you faint. Feet that made you bound.

In the kitchen window Shelby looked at herself, lifting her breasts so she could see them in the wobbly panes. She had average breasts and she liked them. They were best when they were naked. Full at the base but not jutting out so far as to need more support. When she was younger and fatter, her breasts got so big during her period that she was forced to wear a bra, and she hated it. It was hot and sweaty, the straps pulled against her shoulders. Big breasts were really a hassle. They were the male model that women subscribed to, but in reality they only made life more cumbersome. One Halloween Shelby had dressed as Adrienne Barbeau in Swamp Thing (an artist's conception—she'd never actually seen Swamp Thing). On Max's suggestion she'd blown up balloons and fitted them in her dress. At the Halloween party some woman dressed as a witch made a tacky comment about her "breasts". Shelby said to her in amazement, "But they're just balloons!" The woman admitted, "You know, I like you much better for saying that." Max told that story for a while: What had society come to when women were threatened by balloons? Shelby had considered writing a book called Big-Titted Like Me about a woman who had breast implants and then viewed the change in the way society treated her, but lost interest before the first chapter. It seemed too ardently feminist and she didn't need more reasons to be angry at life.

Shelby opened the kitchen window and looked across at the apartment building next door. She could see herself in a far window. She could see the party going on in the windows next to that one. She watched Paige still hugging one bowl of chips, eating from it and carelessly littering her chest with crumbs. Watching Paige laugh, seeing Max's mouth move but not able to understand the words, Shelby felt like she wanted to be in there and have fun too. To laugh so easily. But she just couldn't

你玩的是什么把戏,我也是从那里过来的。"

　　谢尔碧告诉麦克斯,她曾经在和佩琪一起购物的时候看过她只穿内衣时候的样子。"真是坚挺无比,"谢尔碧故意恶毒地说道,她也感到了自己的刻薄,可是仍然没有停下来,"至少要四个扣子的那种。"谢尔碧自己很少穿胸罩,但是她看到佩琪的宽带文胸就联想起了她祖母穿过那种,大得离谱的双 E 罩杯。上一次穿胸罩已经是很久以前的事了,谢尔碧早已忘记了自己的罩杯,不过她丝毫不觉得有什么损失。内衣紧绷在佩琪身上的情景,在谢尔碧眼里是那么的束缚,使人想起过去的裙撑和紧身胸衣,能勒到让人晕倒。还有将女人禁锢在家的裹足习俗。

　　谢尔碧看着厨房窗户里的自己,抬起自己的双乳,在晃动的玻璃镜像中打量着它们。大小适中,她很满意。它们裸露着的时候才是最好的状态。饱满圆润,并没有过分突出到需要额外支撑的地步。在她更年轻一些也更丰满一些的时候,每次月经期间她的胸部就会变得特别大,她不得不穿上胸罩,她讨厌那种感觉。又热又容易出汗黏腻,而且胸带紧紧地绷在两个肩膀上。大胸真的很麻烦。它们只不过是男人所向往的标准,而女人也如此认同了,但现实生活中它们只会成为累赘。有一次万圣节谢尔碧装扮成了《沼泽怪物》里的奥德丽·芭比欧(建立在自己的艺术理解上——她从没真正看过《沼泽怪物》)。在麦克斯的建议下,她吹了两个气球从裙子里面塞了进去。在派对上,一个扮成巫婆的女人阴阳怪气地评价了她的"胸部"。谢尔碧吃惊地回答她:"但它们只是气球而已啊!"那个女人承认道:"你知道吗,听你这样说完之后我还是挺喜欢你的。"麦克斯把这个故事作为谈资讲了好一阵子:气球竟然也被女人视为威胁,这个社会已经变成什么样子了啊?谢尔碧考虑过要写一本书,名字就叫《像我这样的大胸女》,讲述一个女人在隆胸之后如何看待这个社会对她态度的改变,但是第一章还没写完她就失去了兴趣。这个题材看上去就充满了女权主义的色彩,但她不需要更多的理由来增加自己对生活的暴躁情绪了。

　　谢尔碧打开了窗户,向街对面的公寓楼看去。在一面远远的窗玻璃里,她可以看见自己的倒影。而在那扇窗户旁边的房间里,也有一个派对正在进行。她又回过头来,佩琪仍然怀里抱着一大碗薯片,另一只手不停地往嘴里送,毫不在意地任由碎屑掉在她的胸前。佩琪开怀大笑着,麦克斯的嘴巴快速运动着,可是他的话在谢尔碧听来却模糊不清,她突然也想加入她们,尽情地开心,轻松地大笑。可是不知怎么的,她就是没办法振作起精神,没办法抬起腿来。她试着想象

seem to pull herself up enough to get a leg over. Shelby tried to imagine herself in the living room, then she imagined herself at home. Ultimately, which would make her happier? She sighed and didn't move.

"Sorry, all the living room windows are painted shut." Paige made a face of dismissal as she sat down on an easy chair that had been covered with a large piece of orange chenille. With her right hand, Paige slowly placed her bowl on the coffee table while her left hand worked the chips, shuttling them back and forth to her mouth.

"Yeah, and the concept of a thermostat hasn't reached the East Coast yet," Max said loudly. The lack of thermostats in New York was a particular theme with him. He couldn't believe that the heat for all the apartments was regulated several blocks away, somewhere in the bowels of the university. They all lived in university housing because it was subsidized and, therefore, about one third the cost. No one could turn the heat down—except possibly some janitor who must have once lived in the tropics. Every apartment building was always overheated. The best you could do was to simply open the windows and let the cold air flow in. That is, if you could open the windows.

"Too bad some idiot painted your windows," Max said, laughing and taking a handful of chips himself. Watching Paige eat always made him hungry. He figured it was because you could see how much she loved food, and her enthusiasm was hard to resist.

"But we have a solution!" Dermot yelled from the kitchen. "Oranges!" He came out with a big bag of oranges and set them on the coffee table which was starting to overflow with beer bottles and food.

Estrid took an orange from the bag and started to peel it.

"Don't eat them! We're gonna play baseball!" Dermot said excitedly.

Estrid stopped peeling and looked confused.

"Don't listen to him," Max said.

Eberhard laughed, "Not to listen is good advice." Estrid continued to peel the orange.

Paige paused long enough in her eating to look suspiciously at the oranges on the coffee table. She glanced at Dermot and brushed off her sweater.

了一下自己在客厅里的状态,还有在家里的情景。到底,哪一个才让她更开心呢?她叹了口气,还是待在原地没有动。

"不好意思哦,客厅里所有的窗户都在以前的一次粉刷里被涂料给封住了。"佩琪做了一个驳回要求的表情,顺势坐在了简易椅子上,上面盖着一条橘黄色的针织垫。她用右手慢慢地把碗送到咖啡桌上,左手仍然一刻不停地在碗和嘴边来回。

"就是啊,温度自动调节器这个概念还没有普及东海岸这边呢。"麦克斯大声评论道。麦克斯对纽约没有温度自动调节器这件事一直耿耿于怀。他简直就不能相信,所有公寓楼的供热竟然都是在几个街区之外的地方调控的,在大学建筑群的最深处。他们都住在有补贴的学校公寓里,因此省下了三分之二的钱。但是却没有人能够把暖气给关掉——除了某个很可能曾经在热带住过的看门人以外。每一栋宿舍楼都被过度加热了,最好的办法就是打开窗户让冷空气吹进来。前提是,你得能打开窗户。

"竟然有个弱智家伙给窗户涂上了油漆,这真是太糟糕了。"麦克斯手里抓着满满的一把薯片,放声大笑起来。看着佩琪吃东西,总是会让他也感到饥肠辘辘起来。他猜想这也许是因为你能看到佩琪到底有多爱吃东西,而她的热情总是很难抵制。

"但是我们还是有解决办法的!"德莫特的喊声从厨房传来。"橘子!"他手里拎着一大袋橘子走了出来,放在已经摆满啤酒瓶和食物的咖啡桌上。

爱丝翠从塑料袋里拿了一个橘子开始剥皮。

"别吃呀!我们是要用它们玩棒球的!"德莫特一脸兴奋地说道。

爱丝翠停下手上的动作,困惑地看着他。

"别听他的。"麦克斯嫌弃地说。

艾伯哈德也笑了,"不听德莫特的话是一个好建议。"于是爱丝翠又重新开始剥手里的橘子。

佩琪一声不吭地吃着薯片,用怀疑的眼光打量着桌上的橘子,又瞟了一眼德莫特,然后掸了掸胸前的碎屑。

"Paige's looking forward to this, I can tell," Max said, noticing her expression.

"All I'm saying is I'm not cleaning it up, whatever it is."

"Hell, we already know that. We've seen your room!" Max gestured expansively with his beer.

"Who's seen my room?" Paige asked pointedly, directing the question to Dermot who was across the living room looking for something. "Did Dermot show you my bedroom!" She was both laughing and annoyed.

"We were looking for a tennis shoe," Max covered, realizing that he'd fucked up.

"Where's that black felt pen?" Dermot asked quickly, searching in a basket hanging on the wall.

"I keep it messy to hide my valuables."

Max asked teasingly. "Is Dermot stealing your underwear?"

"No, Rahda is!"

"Rahda steals your underwear?" Max asked.

"And my sweaters, and my hair comb, and my hot water warmer." Anything food-related had a great effect on Paige. "I'm telling you, she's psycho."

"I found it," Dermot yelled, holding up the felt pen. He walked to the end of the narrow living room where two large windows looked out toward the street. There was a foot-wide band of wall between the windows, and it was here that Dermot drew an irregular polygon and wrote the word "Home" in it in big letters.

The doorbell rang just then. Dermot grabbed a couple oranges and went to answer it. He yelled back over his shoulder, "The only rule is that if you throw an orange, you have to throw it as hard as you can. No aiming!"

Max tossed Paige an orange. "Here. Vent."

"I can't throw." Paige threw it immediately and it didn't make the wall. She sat down on the sofa and ate more chips.

"Here's the line." Max pointed to the edge of the sofa. Home plate was about thirty feet away. Between the sofa and home plate were just bare boards, the blond pine shiny and expansive. Max could only view the floor as yet another example of the insensitivity of New Yorkers. They went on and on about hardwood floors, but they were so cold and barren during the winter. They looked great in magazines, but who really wanted to live on one?

第十章 老鼠角落

"我能看出来,佩琪已经等不及了。"麦克斯注意到了她的表情。

"我只是想事先申明,不管最后变成什么样子,我是不会打扫的。"

"放心,我们早就知道这一点了,见识过你的房间了!"麦克斯一手拿着啤酒,夸张地展开了双臂。

"谁见过我的房间了?"佩琪立刻警觉地问道,矛头指向在客厅另一边找东西的德莫特。"是不是德莫特把你们带去我的房间了!"她既觉得生气又感到好笑。

"我们当时是在找一只网球鞋。"麦克斯赶忙圆场,他意识到自己说漏嘴了。

"那只黑色毡头笔去哪了?"德莫特一边在墙上的篮子里翻找,一边急促地问道。

"我让房间杂乱是为了把贵重物品给藏起来。"

麦克斯揶揄地问:"德莫特偷你的内衣了吗?"

"他没有,是拉达!"

"拉达偷你的内衣了?"麦克斯问。

"还有我的毛衣、梳子,还有我的热水加热器。"任何跟食物有关的事情佩琪的反应都会很大。"相信我,她就是心理变态。"

"我找到啦。"德莫特突然一只手高举着毡头笔大声吼道,接着他走到狭长客厅的尽头。那里有两扇临街的巨大窗户,窗户中间隔着大概一英尺宽的墙面。德莫特就在那面墙上画了一个不规则的多边形,然后在里面用大写字母写下"HOME"(本垒)。这个时候门铃又响了起来。德莫特抓过几个橘子,走过去开门,又转过头来大声说:"唯一的规则就是扔橘子的时候一定要使出你最大的力气。不许瞄准!"

麦克斯扔了一个橘子给佩琪。"接着,发泄一下吧。"

"我不会扔。"佩琪一接到就扔了出去,连墙都没有碰到。她坐回沙发上继续吃她的薯片。

"这就是起始线。"麦克斯指着沙发的边缘说道。本垒离这里大概有三十英尺远,在沙发和那面墙之间只有光滑的木地板,金黄色的松木质地又阔又亮。在麦克斯看来,这地板只是纽约人感官麻木的另一证明。所有人都对硬木地板赞不绝口,可是冬天的时候它们就变得冰冷不近人情。在杂志里硬木地板看上去确实不错,可是谁愿意天天在上面生活呢?

"Okay I'll throw. This is for the idiot that got the wrench stuck to the NMR!" Max yelled. He screwed up one eye and threw the orange with all his might. It hit the glass part of the window with a resounding whack, shaking the panes heartily but not doing any damage other than to leave sticky streaks on the glass and wood as the juice ran to the floor.

"D' you see the spin on that thing?" Max exclaimed.

"Ya," nodded Eberhard. "I think Coriolis."

"You guys are going to break a window," Paige said, taken aback.

"That's the purpose! Eberhard's hot. Remember?"

"I will try," Estrid said abruptly, standing up. She was thin and tall with blonde hair and a cat-like mouth. She taught math and chemistry at a private school in New Jersey and several of the high school boys had a crush on her. In fact, after she'd helped chaperone a high school dance there had been some parental concern that she was too good-looking. The parents were distrustful of an attractive foreign woman who taught male subjects.

Estrid picked out a small orange that fit her hand. "This far back I must stand?" she asked, looking worried.

"Okay, okay, you can move up a little," Dermot said loudly, coming back and taking over. The noise level had increased and everyone was on the edge of shouting. Paige had turned the stereo louder because she liked the song "Don't Stand So Close to Me". People started moving to the metronomic beat of the song.

Estrid moved forward and then forward again. She looked back once at Eberhard who nodded at her, then she threw her orange wildly. It hit the ceiling with a plop, dropped to the floor, and rolled toward them. Eberhard was laughing loud blasts of laughter. "That direction, that direction," he said pointing to home plate.

She made a face at him. "I know that direction." She took another orange from the bag. "Next time your direction," she said, shaking the orange at him.

"I have no fears," Eberhard said, standing up and taking the orange from her, still laughing, and walked to the designated pitcher's mound. Estrid sat down and delicately finished her half-eaten orange.

Eberhard threw it quickly without preamble, hitting home plate square on. The flattened orange fell to the floor and its contents raced down the wall in rivulets of faint orange, pooling where the wall met the molding, then again where the molding met

"好吧,让我来扔一个。这一下是给那个把扳手卡到分析仪上的蠢货的!"麦克斯竭力大喊。他眯起一只眼睛,用尽全身力气把橘子扔了出去。橘子重重地砸在窗户上,玻璃被振得来回颤动,发出响亮的回声。可是除了在玻璃上还有滚落到地面上时留下的一缕一缕黏糊糊的汁液以外,其他一点损坏都没有造成。

"看见它还继续在打转了吗?"麦克斯兴奋地叫着。

"看见了,"艾伯哈德点了点头,"我觉得是因为科里奥力的缘故。"〔译者注:Coriolis,科里奥利力,来自于物体运动所具有的惯性。〕

"你们这帮家伙会把玻璃给打碎的。"佩琪退缩了。

"我们就是为了这样做!艾伯哈德觉得很热,你忘了吗?"

"我也来试一下。"爱丝翠冷不丁地站了起来。她是一个又瘦又高的金发女郎,有一张像猫一样的嘴巴。她在新泽西的一所私立学校教数学和化学,有几个高中男生一直暗恋她。事实上,在有一次高中舞会她帮忙做了毕业生女伴之后,有一些家长就开始担心,她对于老师这个身份来说长得太漂亮了。让一个有魅力的外国女人来教本该男老师教的科目,那些家长感到不放心。

爱丝翠挑了一个大小适合自己抓住的橘子,"我一定得站这么远吗?"她看上去有些担心。

"好吧,好吧,你可以往前一点。"德莫特边从门口回来,边大声地指挥这个游戏。整个房间里的噪音指数都上升了,每个人几乎都快要扯开嗓子喊了。佩琪把音响的声音调得更大了,因为她喜欢正在播放的那首《别站得离我那么近》。大家都跟着歌曲强劲的节拍摆动了起来。

爱丝翠向前走了一点,又走了一点。她回头看了一下艾伯哈德,得到了一个点头首肯之后,疯狂地把橘子扔了出去。"扑通"一声,橘子砸在了天花板上,然后掉了下来,滚落到大家脚边。艾伯哈德爆发出一阵响亮的笑声。"那个方向,那个方向。"他指着本垒说道。

爱丝翠冲着他做了个鬼脸,"我知道是那个方向,"她又从袋子里取了一个橘子,"下一次可就是冲着你的方向了。"她向艾伯哈德摇晃着手里的橘子。

"我可不怕。"艾伯哈德站起身来从她手里拿过橘子,带着止不住的笑意走向指定的投手位置。爱丝翠重新坐了下去专注地吃完剩了一半的橘子。

艾伯哈德一句废话都没有多说就迅速出手,正中本垒红心。压扁了的橘子弹回地面上,同时汁液在墙面上呈浅橘色细流状喷射开来,在墙面与地板之

the floorboards. It gave the illusion that the apartment was sweating from the heat.

"You aimed!" Dermot and Max yelled indignantly.

"Yes, I aimed for ceiling," Eberhard laughed and looked at Estrid. She said something to him in German.

"Lemme try," Dermot said reaching for an orange and getting into position. He closed his eyes in concentration, taking a few practice throws without letting his orange fly. He opened his eyes and turned toward them all. "Maybe we should invite my neighbor." Anytime Dermot had everyone's attention he was loathe to give it up.

"Yeah, he probably doesn't know you're having a party!" Max yelled over the din and grabbed an orange out of the bag. He threw it at Dermot's nose but purposefully missed, though he had gotten closer than he'd expected which pleased him. The orange rolled under a table in the corner and was forgotten until the stench of its rot permeated the room two months later.

"You know what I heard the other day?" Dermot acted is if he was talking to Max, though his conversation was intended for everyone. He put his orange between his knees, holding it there in a knock-kneed stance while he rolled up his shirt sleeves. "Jimmy Carter has a degree in nuclear engineering."

"No way," Max yelled.

"It's true," Dermot replied, straightening up.

"Maybe from one of those mini-mall colleges," Max said sarcastically.

"What is mini-mall college?" Eberhard asked.

"You know, one of those technical colleges sandwiched between a 7-11 and a liquor store. Shelby used to teach word processing at one. Actually it was behind Selina's Nails and Facials. They get a lot of workman's comp. She had one guy who fell from a sixty-foot crane."

"Yeah," agreed Dermot, not to be outdone. "It's the kind of college that advertises 'Laser technology' and then they teach you how to scan groceries." This cracked Paige up.

"Paige's trashed," Max said.

"I am not!" Paige said indignantly, taking a sip from a glass.

Max glanced at Paige's drink suspiciously. It was amber and bubbly over ice cubes. "What is that?"

间的线脚处形成了小水洼。这让人产生一种错觉,仿佛房间因为过度供暖而流汗了。

"你瞄准了!"德莫特和麦克斯愤愤不平地吼道。

"是啊,我瞄的是天花板。"艾伯哈德笑着看向爱丝翠。她用德语对他说了些什么。

"让我试一下。"德莫特挑选着橘子准备就位。他闭上眼睛以集中注意力,试扔了几次但没有让橘子脱手。然后他又睁开双眼,转向大家,"也许我们应该邀请我的邻居。"不管什么时候,只要德莫特抓住了大家的注意力,他是不会情愿轻易放手的。

"是啊,他很可能都不知道你正在举办派对呢!"麦克斯的吼声盖过了屋子里的其他嘈杂声。他随手抓了一个橘子向德莫特的鼻子扔去,但是故意砸偏了。可是却比他想象中的更接近,他感到很满意。那个橘子滚到了摆在角落的桌子底下,就此被遗忘了,直到两个月后,它腐烂的臭气弥漫了整个房间。

"你知道我前几天听说了什么吗?"德莫特就好像是在对麦克斯说话,但其实是说给每个人听的。他把橘子夹在两腿之间,用膝盖内翻的姿势把它固定在那里,然后开始卷自己的衬衫袖子。"吉米·卡特有一个核工程的学位。"〔译者注:吉米·卡特是美国第39任总统〕

"不可能。"麦克斯不敢相信。

"是真的。"德莫特直起身子回答道。

"可能是在那些迷你商厦大学获得的吧。"麦克斯讽刺道。

"什么叫迷你商厦大学?"艾伯哈德有些不解。

"就是那种夹在7-11便利店和饮料店之间的技术学校。谢尔碧以前在一个这样的学校教过办公软件操作呢。那所学校就在瑟琳娜美甲美容店的后面。那里的学生会经常收到很多工伤补偿。谢尔碧的学生里面有一个家伙曾经从六十英尺高的起重机上摔下来过。"

"我也觉得,"德莫特为了不让自己被超过,也连忙表示赞同,"就是那种广告上会宣传'激光技术',但实际上教你怎么扫描货品条形码的学校。"这让佩琪放声大笑起来。

"佩琪喝醉了。"麦克斯看了她一眼。

"我才没有呢!"佩琪愤愤地拿起玻璃杯喝了一小口。

麦克斯怀疑地瞥了一眼佩琪的饮料,琥珀色的,冰块表面不停冒着气泡。"你喝的是什么?"

Paige looked down her nose at him. "Beer."

Everyone looked at Paige.

"You're drinking beer with ice?" Dermot shouted.

"I like it this way, okay? What are you going to do? Throw it down nine floors?"

"I am still warm," Eberhard shouted meaningfully to Dermot.

"Throw the fucking orange!" Max yelled. Dermot closed his eyes and stood concentrating with his arms bent and the orange touching his forehead. "I'm visualizing the space," he said mystically. Eberhard silently reached over, grabbed an orange and stood up. Dermot reared his arm back and then, just as he let the orange rip, Eberhard hurled his as well, two oranges going the speed of light. The sound of splintering glass filled the room. The oranges were nowhere to be seen, but the left window had two perfect orange-sized holes, top and bottom, with hairline cracks spreading throughout the panes. The wooden braces had kept the entire window from shattering. The change in temperature was subtle but noticeable. Sweat stopped beading up on Eberhard's face; Dermot rolled his sleeves back down. A slight breeze of cool air wafted through the apartment, making them all feel a little less aggressive, though everyone was still yelling. New guests walking down the hallway started laughing the moment they saw the window. Dermot was shouting, "Wait a second! Okay, who threw the other orange? Max, it was you, wasn't it? I know it was you!"

Max just smiled enigmatically. "I think it was Rahda." Max watched Eberhard go to the kitchen for another beer. Subterfuge must have made him thirsty.

"Did the neighbor really write that?" Hadley asked, amused but in disbelief. He leaned against the doorjamb of the kitchen. Shelby was staring out the window, trying to figure out why she felt so empty and sad. Perhaps it was watching everyone laugh and drink, and feeling so far away. They all had on too-bright faces, were laughing a little too loud, and having just a bit better than a good time. She didn't buy it. Her frustration made her want to write, to pin down this confused moment. Words beautify life. They make it music. Life can still be sad, but now it is haunting, and singable. Brutalities become ironies as they are laid on the page.

Topping off her glass and recorking the wine bottle, she realized that she was

佩琪顺着自己的鼻子看向他,"啤酒。"

每个人都转向了佩琪。

"你喝啤酒加冰?"德莫特感到不可置信。[译者注:美国人喝啤酒从来不加冰块。]

"我就喜欢这样喝,不行吗?你想怎么样?把它从九层楼给扔下去吗?"

"我还是很热。"艾伯哈德意味深长地冲德莫特叫道。

"快点他妈地扔橘子吧!"麦克斯又扯开了嗓子。德莫特终于闭上了眼睛,集中注意力弯曲双臂,橘子轻轻碰了下前额。"我正在想象本垒的位置。"他的语气里透着神秘感。艾伯哈德悄悄地探过身去,抓了一个橘子并站起身来。德莫特将一只胳膊拉到身后,然后,就在他出手的一瞬间,艾伯哈德也猛地扔了出去,两个橘子以光速并行向前。一时间玻璃破碎的声音充满了整个房间。橘子早已不见了踪影,可是左边的窗户上留下了两个完美的橘子大小的洞,上下各一个,其间的玻璃布满了发际线般的裂痕。木质框架阻止了整片玻璃窗的破碎。室内温度的改变很细微但仍然可以感觉到:艾伯哈德脸上不再不停地往外冒汗珠;德莫特也把衬衫袖子给放了下来。一小股凉爽的微风穿过房间,尽管大家还是在高声地叫喊,但每个人的暴躁程度都减轻了一些。新来的客人沿着走廊进来,一看到窗户上的景象就放声大笑起来。德莫特仍然没有降低分贝,"等会儿!说,刚才是谁在我背后扔的橘子?麦克斯,是你,对吧?我就知道是你!"

麦克斯露出了难以捉摸的笑容。"我觉得是拉达扔的。"他看着艾伯哈德走向厨房,又取了一瓶啤酒。刚耍完小花招一定是口渴了。

"真的是你的邻居写了那封信吗?"哈德利倚在厨房的门把手上问道,他虽然觉得这很有意思,却心存怀疑。谢尔碧当时正盯着窗外出神,想搞清楚自己为什么会如此空虚伤感。也许是因为看到所有人都在欢笑畅饮,而自己却有深深的距离感。他们脸上焕发的光彩有一点过于明亮,笑声也有一点过头,比开心还要更胜一筹。可是谢尔碧不相信那些都是真的。内心的沮丧让她想要写作,想要记录下这个困惑的瞬间。语言可以美化生活,使其具有音乐的韵律感。生活仍然可以是悲伤的,但是如此一来就变得难忘,可以吟咏。现实的残酷落到纸页上,就变成了嘲讽。

她喝光高脚杯里剩余的酒,拔开酒瓶的木塞,意识到自己正在把情绪投射在

projecting. She was sad. They weren't. They didn't have to deliver singing telegrams for a living. She slowly turned around, preoccupied with sipping just enough wine for the flavor, sharp and numbing on her tongue. "That's what Dermot says," she said, looking at him and turning to open the refrigerator. She felt the need to keep busy. Embarrassed that he would see she was sad. She bent her head down and, stunned by the abundance of food inside, couldn't decide where to put the wine bottle. Baggies of produce, an infinity of condiments, mysterious-looking Tupperware containers, and an absurd amount of alcohol had filled it to capacity. It reminded her of Max's parents' refrigerator. Whenever they went to his parents' house, Max would go through their refrigerator, throwing out everything past its prime. "September 30, 1980. You still want that Mom?" he would yell teasingly, holding the green cheese gingerly between two paper towels. Shelby felt that people's refrigerators were a personal matter and shouldn't be held up to the scrutiny of their children. But perhaps Max's mom liked his diligence. It was a ritual now, a way for Max to show his affection.

Shelby precariously wedged the wine bottle back in so that it balanced between the peaks of a six-pack of bottle necks. Stepping back to see if the bottle was really safe there, Shelby ran into Hadley.

"Sorry," he said, moving backward. "I was just gonna get another beer." Shelby passed one out to him and then had to re-balance the wine, propping up the corked end with the top of a mustard container, where it settled restlessly. Hadley found an opener on the sink. "So when's your bathroom getting fixed? I heard you cried at the housing office."

"Max ... " Shelby said, shaking her head. He always had to tell everyone everything. "That's not why our bathroom's getting fixed. I think Scotia must have done something." She paused for a second. "By the way," Shelby hesitated. She felt stupid saying this, but she thought it should be said. "Thanks for saving my life." She looked at Hadley quickly and then looked away. Almost wanting to laugh. Feeling nervous.

Hadley laughed. "I think you would have lived."

They heard the doorbell ring and watched as Dermot ran past the kitchen with oranges in his hand.

"How come you're not out there throwing oranges?" Hadley asked.

别人身上。她伤心,不代表别人也这样。他们不用为了生计而送唱歌电报。谢尔碧听到哈德利的问话后慢慢地回过身来,还不忘忙着小口抿酒,辛辣味道麻木了她的舌头。"德莫特是这样说的。"她看了一眼哈德利,又转到另一边,打开了冰箱门。她觉得有必要让自己看上去很忙,一想到哈德利有可能会看见自己难过的样子,她就有些局促不安。她探头进去,惊异于冰箱里食物的种类繁多,一时不知道该把酒瓶放在哪里好。成袋成袋的农产品、瓶瓶罐罐的调味汁、特百惠牌的碗碟,还有多得离谱的各种酒类填满了整个冰箱。这情景让她想起了麦克斯父母的冰箱。无论哪一次他们去造访的时候,麦克斯都会扫荡一遍他们的冰箱,把所有过期的东西都扔掉。"1980 年 9 月 30 号的。老妈,你还想留着吗?"麦克斯会用两张纸巾小心翼翼地捏起一块绿皮生干酪,充满嘲讽地大声询问。谢尔碧觉得,每个人的冰箱都是一件私人物品,不应该被迫遭遇自己孩子的仔细审查。但也许麦克斯的母亲喜欢他的这种行为,现在这已经成为一种惯例,麦克斯借此来表达他的关怀。

　　谢尔碧随手把红酒瓶塞了进去,它摇晃了几下便稳定地嵌在半打啤酒的瓶颈处。在退后一步查看酒瓶是否安全时,谢尔碧撞到了哈德利。

　　"抱歉,"他立即向后退了几步,"我只是想再拿一瓶啤酒。"谢尔碧递了一瓶给他,又不得不重新为红酒瓶寻找平衡位置。软木塞的那一头搭在芥末瓶的顶端,左右摇晃着。哈德利在水池边找到了一个开瓶器。"那么,你们的浴室什么时候才会修好?我听说你在物业办公室大哭了一场。"

　　"麦克斯……"谢尔碧欲言又止,摇了摇头。麦克斯他总是把所有事情都告诉大家。"不是因为我哭才有人来修理我们的浴室的,我觉得司考蒂亚一定帮了一些忙。"她停顿了一秒,"对了,"她又犹豫了一下。谢尔碧觉得这样说有点蠢,但又觉得有必要,"谢谢你救了我的命。"她迅速地瞥了一眼哈德利,然后看向一边。几乎想要笑出声来。有些紧张。

　　哈德利大笑了起来。"我觉得你本来就能够活下来的。"

　　门铃响了,德莫特在他们的注目下跑过厨房门口,手里还攥着几个橘子。

　　"你怎么不去外面扔橘子?"哈德利好奇地问道。

"I suppose I should be: 'Here's your pissy telegram!'" Shelby mimed throwing an orange.

"Max mentioned you were a little bummed," Hadley said nonchalantly, playing with his beer label.

"Max says too much." She shook her head and took a sip of wine. "I don't know. I hate my job and it seems to permeate my life."

"Why do you hate it so much? I thought you liked performing."

Just then several people entered the kitchen, causing Shelby and Hadley to stop talking abruptly, almost guiltily. To cover her nervousness, Shelby started talking to a woman who often came to see the band. Other people jostled them, getting beers, pouring drinks. Shelby saw Hadley looking out the window. Avoiding conversation. She tried to think of a way to get back to him, frustrated that she'd let their conversation be interrupted. Hadley made her laugh. She could use that right now. Suddenly several yells came from the living room, and they could hear Eberhard saying something about the ceiling.

"What are they doing in there?" the woman asked, starting for the hallway.

"Ventilating the living room," Hadley joked.

The kitchen emptied quickly, leaving Hadley and Shelby at a loss for words. There was a brief silence. Shelby found herself moving to the music which was so loud she could feel it through the soles of her feet. She took the words to heart, afraid to stand close to Hadley and amazed at how much she wanted to.

"So you were—"

"I don't really—" they both started to say and then stopped and laughed awkwardly.

"You were telling me why you hate your job so much," Hadley prompted.

Shelby looked at Hadley and smiled shyly. "It might seem like fun, but it's really obnoxious. Just yesterday I had to dress up as a banana. I felt like such a ..." She found herself biting her lip and staring in his eyes. She looked down at her feet. "... turd." It was an ugly word. Not a word to use with these feelings. But that's why she said it. She was frightened. Wanting to show herself in the worst light. Doing all she could to prevent—what?

"A banana?" Hadley asked, looking like he was trying not to laugh.

第十章 老鼠角落

"我想我应该大声怒吼：去你的唱歌电报！"谢尔碧做出一个用力扔橘子的动作。

"麦克斯说你最近有点闷闷不乐。"哈德利玩着啤酒瓶上的商标纸，满不在乎地说道。

"他说得太多了。"谢尔碧无奈地摇摇头，抿了一口酒。"我也不知道，我讨厌自己的工作，它似乎已经渗透进了我的生活。"

"你为什么这么讨厌它？我还以为你喜欢表演呢。"

就在这时有几个人走进了厨房，他们突然就停止了谈话，几乎有些心虚。为了掩盖自己的紧张，谢尔碧开始和旁边一个经常来看乐队演出的女人攀谈起来。剩下的人在他们之间挤来挤去，有的在取啤酒，有的在倒红酒。谢尔碧注意到哈德利正望向窗外，似乎在回避谈话。她绞尽脑汁地想找一个方法重新和哈德利聊起来，刚才对话的被迫中断，使她感到有些沮丧。哈德利有能力让她开怀大笑，而现在她正需要这一点。突然，客厅里传来的攀谈声变大了，他们可以听见艾伯哈德言语之间提到了天花板。

"他们在那儿干吗呢？"那个女人开始向客厅走去。

"给客厅通风。"哈德利戏谑道。

厨房很快就只剩下谢尔碧和哈德利两个人了，他们俩却不知道要说什么好。房间里有一阵短暂的沉默。音乐声大到脚底板都能够感觉到，谢尔碧发现自己的身体也正随之而摆动着。她用心地聆听着歌词，害怕站得离哈德利太近，但又惊讶地发现自己有多么想靠近他。

"你刚才——"

"我其实不——"他们同时开了口，然后又同时停了下来，尴尬地笑了笑。

"你刚才正在跟我说你这么讨厌自己工作的原因。"哈德利提醒道。

谢尔碧看着哈德利，有些害羞地笑了。"我的职业可能看上去有趣，但其实很烦人的。就在昨天，我就必须得穿成一个香蕉的样子。我觉得自己就像一个……"她发现自己正一边盯着哈德利的眼睛，一边咬着嘴唇，于是立刻将目光转到脚上。"像一坨屎。"这个词有些粗俗，一般不用来形容这些内心的情感。但就因为不寻常，谢尔碧才会这样用。她心里有些发怵，想要展现自己最差的一面，尽一切可能防止——防止什么呢？

"香蕉？"哈德利一脸憋笑的样子。

Shelby felt embarrassed. "See, it was supposed to be for an old-fashioned Mexican wedding. You know, mariachi band, lots of dancing, that kind of thing."

"Why a banana?" Hadley was now leaning against the kitchen counter in front of the sink. Shelby, a couple of feet away, was standing against the wall and resting her arm on the window sill.

"You know ... " Shelby hesitated. "Chiquita Banana."

Hadley just looked at her. "You're not serious."

"Hey!" Shelby said, bristling slightly. "It's a job. People do a lot of stupid things for money."

"I would just worry about somebody getting offended."

"Why do you think I wear that big coat? I didn't blow up the banana until I got there."

"You wear an inflatable banana?" He choked on a gulp of beer. "I'm not laughing at you. Honest."

"That's it, make me feel better," Shelby said sarcastically but trying not to smile. She looked out again to the building behind. Dead plants lined several window sills, as if proving it was winter.

"I'm interested," Hadley said placatingly. "I'm amazed actually. I thought you just did Wonder Woman."

"No, I do the gamut of fruits and superheroes." She looked at him mockingly. "Yesterday was different though. See, there wasn't any mariachi band or anything. It was a set-up."

"What do you mean?"

"It was at a very expensive restaurant downtown and when I went in, everyone—about five hundred people—was dressed in black—I mean it's a wedding and everyone was in black. Except for the bride, of course, who was at the opposite end of the room. Her dress must have cost a fortune; the whole thing was covered with tiny pearls. It was like I walked into *The Godfather*. And she had long blonde hair piled on her head like dessert. So I come in singing, 'Eye am Chee-quita Banana and Eye'm here to saay, half a heppy wedding on thees very speecial day.' Oh, God, it was horrible." Shelby took a huge gulp of wine, the accent having parched her.

Hadley smiled, somewhat in awe.

谢尔碧感到局促起来,"那本来是为了一场老式的墨西哥婚礼准备的,你知道的,就是那种巡回乐队表演,大家一起载歌载舞的那种。"

"为什么要扮成香蕉呢?"哈德利这会儿侧身倚在水池前的台面上。谢尔碧在几英尺远处靠墙站着,胳膊随意搭在窗台上。

"就是……"谢尔碧犹豫了一下,"奇奎塔香蕉女郎。"〔译者注:奇奎塔为美国一家以提供优质香蕉而文明的公司,吉祥物为香蕉女郎'Chiquita banana'。〕

哈德利目不转睛地盯着她,"你是在开玩笑吧。"

"喂!"谢尔碧有些微怒。"这是我的工作。人们为了挣钱本来就会做很多傻事的。"

"我只是担心有人看到你的装扮会觉得被冒犯了。"

"不然你以为我为什么要穿一件大外套呢?到了目的地我才把香蕉服给吹起来的。"

"你穿的是充气的香蕉服?"他呛了一大口啤酒。"我并不是想笑话你,真的。"

"你再继续,听你这样说我感觉好多了。"谢尔碧嘲讽地回敬他,努力地绷着脸不笑出来。她又把目光放向窗外,看着后面的那栋楼。好几户人家窗台上的植物都枯死了,就好像在证明冬天的存在。

"我觉得很好玩儿,"哈德利试图缓和谢尔碧的怒气,"事实上,我很吃惊,我还以为你只扮演神奇女侠呢。"

"不,除了超级英雄外,我还包揽了所有的水果。"她带着嘲弄的眼神看着哈德利。"但是昨天有点不一样,其实根本就没有什么巡回乐队,什么都没有,整件事就是一个圈套。"

"这是什么意思?"

"那是市中心一家非常奢华的餐馆,当我走进去的时候,每个人——大概有五百个人——都身着黑色——我真是搞不懂,在那样一场婚礼上竟然所有人穿的都是黑色。当然了,除了房间另一头的新娘。她的婚纱肯定价值不菲,上面全部都是小珍珠。我就好像走进了电影《教父》里的场景一样。还有她那一头金色的长发盘在头顶,像是某种饭后甜点。然后我就边唱边走了进去,'俺是香蕉女郎,来这儿是为了说,值此特殊日子,祝你新婚快乐。'噢,上帝啊,那种讽刺新娘的感觉简直糟糕透顶。"努力维持的西班牙语口音让谢尔碧口干不已,于是她喝了一大口红酒。〔译者注:有人为了让新娘难堪,点了香蕉女郎的唱歌电报,提醒她的过去。〕

哈德利笑了,不知为何带着几分敬畏。

"I felt like an absolute imbecile."

"Why didn't you just leave?"

"I wanted to get paid," Shelby said emphatically. "There's no fucking way I'm going to get all dressed up as a goddamn banana and not get paid. Anyway, so I march back to the bride and groom. The bride is cutting the cake and has this big knife in her hands and this smile like Jack Nicholson. Being the idiot that I am, I hand her the balloons, and she takes them and, with big stabs of her knife, she pops them all, but slowly. Frosting everywhere. I kept thinking any moment Candid Camera would appear."

Shelby felt Hadley staring at her and it made her nervous. She started talking faster, afraid she was boring him. "As soon as she started popping the balloons, the groom steered me away from the knife and gave me a hundred dollars. I handed him the scroll—"

"What is that?" Hadley interrupted.

"It's the message, like Happy Birthday, or Congratulations. So they feel like they got something. One time someone wrote, 'Hope you get it up.'"

Hadley started laughing and this made Shelby laugh too.

"Their message was 'The biggest RF is yet to come.'" Shelby said the words slowly and raised her eyebrow spylike.

Hadley tilted his head, looking uncertain.

"It's from Watergate!" Shelby pointed her finger at him in excitement. "Didn't you read *All the President's Men*? Those guys used to pull pranks, like ordering two thousand pizzas to be delivered to a rally of some candidate they didn't like. They called it rat-fucking.'"

"You make this sound so sinister and mysterious." Hadley shook his head. "And to think, all I did yesterday was work in the lab."

"I'll bet someone gets murdered!" Shelby said. "And I was their little joke, their final clue."

"I think you're being a little melodramatic."

"Hadley, this is New York!" Shelby waved her hands at him. She was starting to get a little bit drunk. "You live with a drug addict. Dermot's neighbor comes up with a gun. Get real."

"Yeah, but no one's died yet—" Hadley said dryly, then stopped abruptly.

"我当时觉得自己就是个彻头彻尾的傻瓜。"

"那你为什么不离开呢?"

"因为我想拿到报酬,"谢尔碧刻意加强了语气,"让我装扮成一个该死的香蕉却不给钱,他妈的门都没有。反正,我就开始向新娘新郎走去。那时新娘正在切蛋糕,手里握着一把长刀,脸上挂着杰克·尼克尔森[译者注:美国著名演员,扮演过许多偏执、神经质类角色]一样的笑容。我就跟个傻瓜一样,把气球递给了她,她接过气球,用手里的刀慢慢一个个地戳破。粘在刀上的蛋糕糖霜撒得到处都是。我当时一直在想,偷拍的隐藏摄像头可能随时都会出现。"

谢尔碧感觉到了哈德利盯着她的视线,顿时又紧张起来。她开始越说越快,害怕自己的话会让他感到无聊。"新娘刚开始戳气球的时候,新郎就把我领到离刀远一点的地方,给了我一张一百美元。然后我把卷轴递给他——"

"那是什么?"哈德利打断了谢尔碧的话。

"就是上面写了一句话,比如生日快乐,或是祝贺你。这样一来他们就会觉得至少得到了一些东西。有一次有人在上面写了,'希望你早日勃起'。"

哈德利忍不住开怀大笑,谢尔碧也跟着笑了起来。

"给他们的贺语是,'最大的恶作剧[译者注:rat-fucking,起源于水门事件]还在后面呢'。"谢尔碧像个密探似的挑起眉毛,一字一顿地说道。

哈德利把脑袋歪向一边,满脸的困惑。

"这句话是水门事件里的!"谢尔碧兴奋地指着他说。"你难道没看过《总统班底》这本书吗?那些家伙经常会搞恶作剧,比如说订购两千个比萨,直接派送到他们不喜欢的候选人的群众集会上,货到付款。他们把这个叫作'政客伎俩(rat-fucking)'。"

"你说得好像这件事有多么阴险神秘似的。"哈德利摇了摇头,"这样一想,昨天我做的唯一一件事就是在实验室里工作。"

"我敢打赌当时有人被谋杀了!"谢尔碧推理道,"而我的出现就是他们玩的小把戏,是最后的线索。"

"你有点太夸张了。"

"哈德利,这里可是纽约!"谢尔碧冲着他挥了挥手。她开始渐渐有了醉意。"你和一个瘾君子住在一起;德莫特的邻居带着枪找上门来。你快看清现实吧。"

"你说的对,可是至少还没有人死——"哈德利尴尬地反驳,但突然停顿了下来。

Chapter Ten Rat Corner

"What?" Shelby asked.

"I just remembered that someone did die. A friend of Ethan's."

"See?" She paused for a second, passively concerned. "Why'd he die?"

Hadley shrugged. "Some kind of drug murder. Ethan said it was because he had drugs in him."

Shelby's eyes bugged out. "Like in a little baggy or something? Somewhere reachable or somewhere sewn in?"

"I don't know!" he answered, irritated. "I didn't ask him the particulars."

"Wow, a lot of shit is happening lately. Maybe we're approaching a glacial age." Hadley looked at her and she gave him a goofy smile. "Maybe violence is propagated by a virus." She looked at him seriously. "Max says it's been tense lately. I guess Scotia pretty much jumped down Bineet's throat during group meeting?"

"He was mad," Hadley agreed. "He kept calling Bineet 'Mr. Ramanchandra'. You know it's bad when he calls you by your last name."

"Max said Rahda's been really weird too. She keeps complaining of dizziness and thinks there's some kind of gas leak."

"I didn't hear this. There were workmen supposed to look at her argon line, but I didn't know that was the reason." Hadley looked skeptical. "Rahda's always been weird, but I don't think she's nuts."

"Maybe New York has driven her psycho like it's driving me."

"I thought you liked it when you first came here."

"I did, but so many little things make me crazy. The pettiness of people. The other day I just wanted to go home. A million people got off the subway. Usually the ticket person opens that gate so everybody doesn't have to go through the little turnstile like sheep. Several people yelled, 'Open the gate', and the asshole wouldn't, wouldn't even acknowledge that we were there. It was such a silly display of power, making a million people go through a turnstile. I just lost it. I wanted to be home. So I jumped over the fence yelling, 'Fuck you!' After I did that, a bunch of people started laughing and clapping and jumping over the gate themselves. And then I got home and looked around and realized I had nothing to do. The funnest part of my day was jumping over the fence and yelling 'Fuck you.' That's what New York has reduced me to ... What are you laughing at?"

"怎么了?"谢尔碧追问道。

"我只是想起来,确实有人死了。伊桑的一个朋友。"

"看到没有?"她停了一秒,被迫关切起来。"他为什么会死?"

哈德利耸了下肩头,"可能是跟毒品有关的谋杀。伊桑说是因为他的体内藏着毒品。"

谢尔碧的眼珠子都要蹦了出来。"比如装在一个小袋子里还是什么?藏在体内够得着的地方还是缝进了身体里?"

"我不知道!"哈德利有些气恼,"我又没有问他这些细节。"

"哇哦,最近世道真是不好。也许我们离下一个冰川世纪不远了。"哈德利看了她一眼,她则报之以一个滑稽的笑容。"也许暴力倾向是通过病毒来繁殖传播的。"她认真地看着哈德利。"麦克斯说最近实验室的气氛很紧张。我猜在组会上斯考蒂亚是不是差点儿就气得跳到贝内特的脖子上了?"

"他确实很生气,"哈德利表示同意,"他一直叫贝内特'拉曼钱德勒先生'。每次他用姓氏来称呼你的时候,你就知道大事不妙了。"

"麦克斯还说最近拉达也表现得怪怪的。她一直抱怨头晕,说怀疑有什么气体泄漏。"

"我没有听说这件事。有工人来过要查看她的氩气线路,但是我不知道具体原因。"哈德利脸上露出了一丝怀疑的神色。"拉达一直以来都很古怪,但我觉得她并不傻。"

"也许纽约城已经把她给逼疯了,就跟我一样。"

"我还以为你刚到纽约的时候很喜欢这里呢。"

"刚开始是的,但是这么多琐碎的小事,还有这里人的斤斤计较,都快要让我崩溃了。有一天,我只想快点回家,当时人群却一窝蜂从地铁里往外涌。通常售票员会把大门打开,这样就不用每个人都得像绵羊那样从窄窄的旋转栅门通过了。有几个人吼了一声,'把门打开',但是那个混球就是不肯,甚至还对我们的存在视而不见。这种展示自己权力的行为真是愚蠢至极,成百上千的人都因此被迫从栅门通过。当时我火气就上来了,我想要回家。于是我就跳到栅栏上对他大喊了一声,'去死吧!'之后,许多人都开始大笑、鼓掌,还有人跳到了栅栏上来。最后当我回到家里,环顾四周,才意识到自己没什么事情可做。我的一天当中最有意思的部分竟然是跳到栅栏上大喊'去死'。就是纽约让我沦落到这样一个地步……你在笑什么?"

"Just that you're depressed and your days are so much more exciting than mine and I'm wondering why I'm not more depressed." Hadley downed his beer and threw the bottle in the trash under the sink. He looked at Shelby, who understood that he wanted another beer, and she moved from her spot at the window so that he could open the refrigerator door. Her arm brushed against his hand as she walked to the sink and she realized that she was conscious of touching him. Before she could think about it, she found herself saying, "You have a purpose. You have your Ph.D. and know where you're going. I don't have a clue."

"I thought you wanted to write."

Shelby looked at the floor and sighed. "I like writing, but the thought of it ever being something seems insurmountable. It just weighs on me. I've been writing a book about college." Shelby looked up quickly. "You wanna read it?"

"Why do you want me to read it?" Hadley frowned.

"I want someone to," Shelby implored.

"What about Max?"

"He doesn't read—except chemistry. It took him two weeks to read *Dress for Success*." They looked at each other and grinned.

"Why's he reading that?"

"Because he's starting to think about interviews and he's neurotic. Have you seen the pictures in that book? Lots of plaid."

"Where's he going to interview?"

"Well, we went to the library and looked at all the places where I was willing to move. Max admitted that when he went into chemistry, he didn't realize that most of the jobs were in New Jersey. I don't think I can live in New Jersey—at least not where we could afford," Shelby said, shaking her head. "And New York would be hell."

Hadley put down his beer suddenly. "I want to show you something."

"Where?"

"Outside. Come on."

Puzzled, Shelby set down her wine glass and followed Hadley to the front door. They could hear everyone laughing and throwing oranges in the other room.

Hadley opened the front door. "It'll just take ten minutes. They'll never miss us."

"你的一天过得比我精彩那么多,却还闷闷不乐,我在想为什么我没有比你更沮丧呢。"哈德利一口喝掉了剩下的啤酒,随手把瓶子扔进水池下面的垃圾箱里。他转过头来看着谢尔碧,她立刻就明白哈德利想再来一瓶啤酒,于是就从窗户前面挪开,好让他开冰箱门。谢尔碧走向水池的时候胳膊轻轻擦过哈德利的手,她突然意识到自己对与他的肢体接触很敏感。还没来得及细想,谢尔碧就听见自己的声音在说,"你有目标,还有博士学位,知道自己的方向是什么。而我却一点头绪也没有。"

"你不是想写作吗?"

谢尔碧盯着地板叹了一口气。"我喜欢写作,但是这个想法能成真的可能性几乎为零。它给我的压力太大了。我最近在写一本关于大学生活的书。"谢尔碧迅速抬起头来,"你想读吗?"

"你为什么会想要我来读?"哈德利皱了一下眉头。

"我想让别人读我写的东西。"谢尔碧恳求道。

"麦克斯呢?"

"他从不读书——除了和化学有关的。他花了两个星期才读完《成功着装》这本书。"他们互相觑了一眼,都忍不住笑了。

"他为什么会读那个?"

"因为他考虑要开始去面试工作了,再加上他本来就有点神经质。你看过那本书里的图片吗?有很多的格子图案。"

"他要去哪里面试?"

"唔,我们去了一趟图书馆,查阅了一些我愿意搬过去住的地方的信息。麦克斯也承认,当初他决定干化学这一行的时候,并没有意识到大部分的工作都在新泽西。我可不认为我能住在那儿——至少不是我们买得起的地段。"谢尔碧摇着头说,"可是纽约市又像是人间地狱。"

哈德利突然放下了手里的啤酒。"我想带你看样东西。"

"在哪?"

"在外面,跟我来。"

虽然很疑惑,谢尔碧还是放下高脚杯跟着哈德利来到了门口。他们可以听见大家在隔壁房间的大笑声和扔橘子的声音。

哈德利打开了门,"只要十分钟就可以了,他们不会想念我们的。"

In the elevator Shelby asked suspiciously, "Where are we going?" trying not to let the sloped floor shake them closer together.

"To see a slice of New York." Hadley looked at her. "I like New York. I think you hate it just because Max hates it."

"Because I do everything Max does," Shelby said sarcastically.

"I didn't mean it like that," Hadley said quietly.

Down on the street Shelby started shivering. "I forgot my jacket."

"Me, too. We'll run."

They started running, Shelby trying to keep up. "This better be good," she panted.

"It'll be a wildlife experience." Shelby started slowing down. Hadley grabbed her hand. "It's just around the corner," he yelled, pulling her along.

Shelby noticed the landscape changing from well-kept buildings to ones with subtle neglect. A door hung crookedly, a shattered window was held together with silver duct tape. A smoky aura of disintegration covered the buildings like kudzu.

They ran past an apartment building that was cordoned off with a yellow three-inch strip of plastic tape. The words CONDEMNED and PELIGROSO alternated down the length of it. Shelby could see lights on in the building's windows. People in jackets were sitting and standing out on the wide stone stairway in the front. Two little kids were rolling a truck up the cement ramp that topped the stone. They didn't seem troubled by the cold. Shelby noticed that in one of the windows on the second floor someone had taken pieces of the yellow tape and had used it to tie back the curtains.

Hadley and Shelby ran up to a vacant lot across the street from the building. They stopped at the battered chain link fence at the corner of 111th and Amsterdam. The fence was crooked and had large horizontal creases along its length, most likely the result of inexpertly driven cars ramming into it.

"Is this neighborhood safe?" Shelby whispered to Hadley.

"There's still a lot of people out," Hadley said confidently. He pulled her around to the other side of the fence.

"So?" Shelby said after standing at the fence for a few seconds and realizing that they'd arrived at their destination. Self-consciously, she loosened her hold of Hadley's hand, and their fingers fell lingeringly apart. She looked around her. Unknown dark

第十章 老鼠角落

在电梯里,谢尔碧用怀疑的语气问道:"我们要去哪?"同时尽量避免倾斜的底板进一步拉近他们之间的距离。

"去看纽约的一角,"哈德利直视着她,"我喜欢纽约。我觉得你讨厌这里只是因为麦克斯也讨厌。"

"因为麦克斯做什么,我就做什么。"谢尔碧讽刺地回敬他。

"我不是这个意思。"哈德利小声地嘀咕。

出了大楼之后,谢尔碧冷得打了几个寒战。"我忘了拿夹克了。"

"我也是,我们跑起来就可以了。"

于是他们开始在街道上奔跑,谢尔碧尽力跟在哈德利的后面。"你要让我看的东西最好值得我们这样做。"她气喘吁吁地威胁道。

"这会是一次野生动物探险。"感觉到谢尔碧的速度开始慢了下来,哈德利一把抓起她的手。"拐个弯就到了。"他兴奋地拉着谢尔碧向前,大声说道。

谢尔碧注意到周围的环境从悉心打理的楼房逐渐转变成了破败的建筑群。有的房门歪歪扭扭地半开着,有的窗户已经碎了,是用银色水管胶带给固定住的。一种迷蒙的破败气息如同葛藤一样缠绕着这里的楼房。

他们经过一栋公寓楼,看见它被三英寸宽的黄色塑胶条给封锁了,胶带上"危险"的英语和西班牙语字样交替出现。谢尔碧可以看见楼房窗户里的灯光。楼前的宽阔石阶上,一群人身着夹克衫,有的站着,有的坐着。石阶两旁的水泥斜坡上,两个小孩儿拿着玩具卡车在上面推来推去,他们看上去一点儿也不在意空气中的寒冷。谢尔碧无意中看到,二楼一扇窗户后的窗帘,是用从门口封锁线撕走的黄胶带固定住的。

哈德利和谢尔碧一直跑到楼房对面街道的一片空地上,在111号大街和阿姆斯特丹路交会的角落停了下来,眼前是一面残破的菱形格子钢丝网。网墙都已经弯曲变形了,横向有很多褶痕,很有可能是技术拙劣的司机的"杰作"。

"这附近安全吗?"谢尔碧小声地问哈德利。

"周围还是有很多人的。"哈德利自信满满地回答,接着将谢尔碧拉到网墙的另一边。

"然后呢?"站了几秒之后,谢尔碧意识到这就是他们的目的地了。好像注意到了什么,她局促不安地松开了哈德利的手,他们的手指依依不舍地分开了。她接着环顾了一下四周,未知的漆黑街道使她紧张起来。虽然有街灯,可它不时

Chapter Ten Rat Corner

streets like this made her nervous. There was a street light, but it fizzed and blinked occasionally, giving her the feeling that it was on its last legs. She looked around for the moon. It was full and still fairly low in the sky as if it was too heavy to rise very high. She could see a piece of it in between two buildings, its surface pitted and mysterious, like a moon unappreciated but still glowing for itself. "What are we going to see here?"

"Rats. Big ones."

"Hadley!" Shelby jumped back from the fence and into the gutter. She'd always thought those cartoons where women frantically jump on chairs at the sight of a cute little mouse were so stupid, and here she was doing the same thing.

"Don't worry," Hadley said, turning around and laughing at her. "They have a natural fear of humans. Wait a second!" He quickly turned toward the fence and Shelby cautiously stepped back onto the curb. They could hear rustling and mysterious scratching sounds.

"There's one!" Hadley whispered excitedly. Shelby looked through the angled grid of the fence to see where he was pointing.

"Oh, my God!" she whispered. It was the biggest rat she'd ever seen. The body alone was a foot long. The rat was about twenty feet from them and in the intermittent light it was hard to see the rodent clearly. But the size was unmistakable.

"'Fear of humans', my ass." She pushed Hadley jokingly and he inadvertently rattled the fence. The rat skittered sideways at the noise and ran for cover. "It's fucking huge!"

"Ssh!" Hadley laughed. He whispered to her, "You've gotta risk a little for excitement. See, you're laughing now."

"I'm in fear for my life," she whispered back. "It's a nervous reaction." Shelby stood next to Hadley, fighting the urge to giggle uncontrollably. She was freezing, she was nervous, but she felt nonsensically happy.

"This is why I like New York. Where else could you see this?" Hadley turned toward her, and she found herself watching the way his mustache moved as the wisps of steamy breath came out of his mouth with his words.

"You're insane. You brought me all this way. In the cold. To see gigantic rats!" She said this indignantly but laughed, her voice getting high and giggly, trying to break herself from studying his face.

地闪烁并发出"咝咝"的声音,谢尔碧觉得它撑不了多久了。然后她又试着去找月亮,很圆满,却仍挂在低空,仿佛是因为太重了而升不到高处。谢尔碧只能看见它在两栋楼之间露出的一部分,表面有些凹痕,散发着神秘的光芒,不被欣赏,却仍然极力地为自己而发光。"我们在这里能看到什么?"

"老鼠,很大的那种。"

"哈德利!"谢尔碧从网墙边跳开,一脚踩进了水沟里。她一直都觉得,卡通片里面那些一看到可爱的小老鼠就拼命往椅子上跳的女人们愚蠢至极,可是现在她却做着一模一样的事情。

"别担心,"哈德利转过身来嘲笑她,"老鼠天生是害怕人的。等一下!"他迅速向网墙转去,谢尔碧也小心翼翼地跟着他站到了路沿上。他们能听见"窸窸窣窣"的刮擦声,带着一丝神秘感。

"那儿有一只!"虽然很小声,可哈德利还是藏不住自己的兴奋之情。谢尔碧通过弯曲的网格,顺着他指的方向看去。

"哦,见鬼!"她小声地叫出来。这是她见过的最大的老鼠了,光是身体就有一英尺长。那只老鼠离他们大概有二十英尺的距离,在断断续续的灯光下很难看清它具体的样子,可是它那巨大的体型是绝对错不了的。

"你还说他们'天生害怕人类',鬼才信呢。"她开玩笑地推了哈德利一把,哈德利不由自主地碰晃了丝网。一听到动静,那只老鼠就飞快地沿着边缘逃窜到有遮蔽的地方去了。"真是太大了!"

"嘘!"哈德利一边笑一边低声说,"你得冒一点险才能得到兴奋的体验。看吧,你现在就笑得很开心。"

"我是在担心自己的生命安全,"谢尔碧回敬他,"这是紧张的反应。"她站在哈德利的旁边,遏制着自己想要尽情傻笑的欲望。寒冷,不安,但是荒谬无比地感到开心。

"这就是我喜欢纽约的原因。其他在什么地方你还能看到这个呢?"哈德利面对着谢尔碧说道。他每说一句话,嘴边都会哈出一缕缕白气,谢尔碧发现自己正盯着他,专心地观察着他的小胡子是怎么随之移动的。

"你真是疯了。这么冷的天,大老远地把我带到这里来,来看巨型老鼠!"她想假装愤愤不平,却笑了。她的声音开始变得有些高亢,并伴随着"咯咯"的傻笑,她试图将自己的注意力从哈德利的脸上移开。

Chapter Ten Rat Corner

"Ssh! There's two more." The reflection of the street light on a crumbled trash can illuminated the far edge of the dirt lot where they could see a mother and baby rat eating some garbage.

"Oh, that's so sweet," Shelby said, fighting the desire to push Hadley, to touch him aggressively.

"See, I knew you'd like it." In the yellowish tint of the street light, she could see him smiling at her. She smiled back, beguiled. I must be drunk, Shelby thought, suddenly disoriented.

"I know it's cold. I know you think this is weird, but I wanted to make a point," Hadley said, a little bit seriously.

"I never litter," Shelby said, mocking the tone of his voice.

He looked at her. "My point is, this is New York; this is life. You'll never see anything like it again. Maybe it's scary or infuriating or whatever, but even you are laughing about big rats."

"I'm laughing because you think this is going to make me like New York!" Shelby whispered, laughing, unable to turn her head away. They were both leaning on the fence, as close as they could get without touching.

"You forget, I know you. You'll be telling this story later. That Night at Rat Corner." His face grew calm. "You like weird. That's why you like Max."

Shelby started to say something, but then stopped, realizing that she could never tell this story later. It would seem strange to people, her and Hadley alone at night, looking at rats. She wondered if anyone at the party had realized they'd left.

"We should probably be getting back," Shelby said quietly. She sighed slowly, wanting to feel in control instead of so wild. Her heart flung itself against her ribs, and she wondered if it was trying to escape. She was shivering violently now and couldn't stop her teeth from chattering.

A group of people came up to the fence opposite them, laughing and pointing, here to see the rats. One of the girls was wearing a beret. They all looked happy. They were probably students who hailed from places other than New York, amazed at the fauna of an inner city. Shelby wanted to walk home with them, to find herself in another life with other people.

Suddenly a mammoth rat ran across the lot toward a clump of bushes. The fence was so bent and mutilated that it obviously wasn't keeping anything in. The rat ran so

"嘘！又有两只。"一只压扁了的垃圾桶反射着街灯的光,照亮了停车空地上远远的一角,那里有一只老鼠妈妈和老鼠宝宝在啃食一些垃圾。

"哦,真感人。"谢尔碧极力克制自己不去推或者碰哈德利。

"看吧,我就知道你会喜欢的。"在街灯昏黄的色调下,谢尔碧看见哈德利正在对自己微笑。她有些着迷了,也回了一个笑容。"我一定是醉了。"谢尔碧心里想着,突然就乱了方寸。

"我知道很冷,我也知道你觉得这很奇怪,但是我只是想说明一件事情。"哈德利的语气里有了一点严肃的意味。

"我从来不扔垃圾的。"谢尔碧模仿着他的语调。

他看着谢尔碧,"我想说的是,这就是纽约;这就是生活。你在别处再也看不见和这类似的事情了。也许这有点恐怖,或者让你感到愤怒,不管怎么样,那些大老鼠也把你给逗笑了。"

"我笑的原因是,你竟然会觉得这能让我爱上纽约!"谢尔碧边笑边嘀咕着,却没有办法把头转开。他们俩都倚在网墙上,近到不能再近,可是没有碰到对方。

"你忘了,我了解你。你以后一定会把这个故事讲给别人听的。老鼠角落之夜。"哈德利脸上的表情慢慢平静了下来。"你喜欢奇奇怪怪的事情,这也是你会喜欢麦克斯的原因。"

谢尔碧刚想开口说些什么,又立刻停住了嘴,她突然意识到自己永远也不能够把这个故事讲出去。因为在别人眼里这听起来会很不正常,她和哈德利两个人,单独在夜色里,看老鼠。她有些好奇,派对上有没有人已经意识到他们的离开。

"也许我们应该回去了。"谢尔碧安静地说。她缓慢地叹了口气,试图整理自己,不想再这样放任下去。她感觉到心脏不停地撞击着自己的肋骨,想要逃离。她整个人抖得厉害,牙齿也直打战。

网墙的对面,有一群人指着什么,谈笑着越走越近。他们也是来这里看老鼠的。其中一个女孩儿带着贝雷帽,每个人看上去都很快活。他们八成是从纽约市外来的学生,对这个城市中心地区的特有动物群感到惊异无比。谢尔碧想和他们一起回家,和不同的人过另一种生活。

突然,一只肥硕的老鼠从空地穿过,向灌木丛奔去。破损严重的铁丝网墙很显然已经挡不住任何东西了。那只老鼠飞速地向他们的方向冲过来,以至于

quickly toward them that both Shelby and Hadley involuntarily jumped backwards onto the street, knocking into one another, laughing. Shelby felt Hadley's hands clasp her arms, steadying her, and shivers went up her spine. "I'm fucked up," she thought, begging for the moment to continue, but Hadley dropped his arms to his side and moved away quickly.

The rat scrabbled toward an empty box of fried chicken that lay in some tall weeds just under the fence. They could hear the scraping of its teeth cracking the bones of the discarded chicken.

They started back without talking. Walking quickly, Shelby hugged herself and looked at her shoes, suddenly shy. As they approached the building, they see the glitter of broken glass sparkling on the sidewalk. Shelby said, "I thought Max said you were bummed about something, too."

"Oh ... no," Hadley said slowly, then amended, turning his head away. "Some days my work doesn't go like I'd like it to, especially when workmen mess with the equipment, but I get over it. I think I'm basically a happy person." He gestured back the way they'd come. "I like stuff like that. I don't need a lot to make me happy."

Walking into the building, Shelby asked quietly, "Do you ever get lonely?" There was a long pause. Shelby worried that perhaps she'd gone too far. The elevator opened and they got in.

"I try not to think about it. Sometimes I date." Hadley looked uncomfortable.

"What happened to Amanda?" Shelby knew she was prying but couldn't stop herself.

"Oh ..." Hadley laughed and shook his head. "Amanda thought I needed to commit more. She gave me this book by some psychiatrist called something like *Learning How to Love*—" Hadley waved his arms in the air, trying to remember the title, "—*Letting Yourself Fall In Love*."

"Jeeze."

"I know," Hadley laughed. "It's crazy to think you can give someone a book and that they'll then fall in love with you."

Shelby didn't have anything to say to this, so she just looked at the floor, embarrassed at the silence. The elevator doors opened and they could hear the loud drone of the party punctuated by individual voices. Shelby could hear Max yelling but

谢尔碧和哈德利都不由自主地跳回了身后的街道上，两个人东扭西歪地撞在一起，忍不住大笑起来。哈德利为了扶住谢尔碧便用双手抓住了她的胳膊，谢尔碧感觉到了，一种麻酥的感觉触电般地沿着脊柱直冲大脑。"我完了。"她心里想着，但暗暗渴求着这一刻可以延续，但是哈德利很快就放开双手站到了一边。

围网接地处长了一些高高的野草，那只老鼠正用爪子拨拉着草边的一只空炸鸡盒。老鼠的牙齿啃噬被丢弃的鸡骨头的"嘎吱嘎吱"声，他们听得一清二楚。

往回走的路上，俩人都默默无言。谢尔碧加快了步伐，抱紧自己，目光落在自己的鞋上，突然有些腼腆。靠近公寓楼的时候，他们看见了人行道上闪烁的玻璃碎片。谢尔碧突然想起了什么，"我记得麦克斯说过，你最近也被什么事情弄得很烦心。"

"噢……不是，"哈德利缓慢地开腔了，随即又纠正了自己，不自觉地把头转向一边，"有时候，我的研究不一定向着我想要的方向发展，特别是最近设备还被维修工给搞坏了，但是我也能看开。总的来说，我认为自己还是一个开心的人。"他指了指刚才看老鼠的方向，"我就爱那种东西，让我开心不需要很高的条件。"

走进楼里的时候，谢尔碧轻声问了一句："你有过孤单的感觉吗？"接着是长时间的沉默。谢尔碧感到担心，自己是不是越界太多了。电梯门开了，他们跨了进去。

"我尽力不去想那件事情。有时候我会去约会。"哈德利看上去有些不自然。

"你跟阿曼达后来怎么样了？"谢尔碧明知道自己在打探他的隐私，可就是不能自已。

"噢……"哈德利笑了起来，无奈地摇了摇头。"她认为我应该付出更多一些。她给了我一本某个精神病专家写的书，好像叫《学习如何去爱——》。"哈德利在空中挥了一下胳膊，努力回想着书名，"《——让自己坠入爱河》。"

"天哪。"

"我也是这种感觉，"哈德利笑了，"给别人一本书，他就会爱上你，这样的想法简直太不切实际了。"

谢尔碧对此没什么想评价的，所以她就一直盯着地板看，又一阵的沉默让她感到尴尬。电梯门再打开的时候，派对里的吵闹声和谈笑声迎面扑来，还不时有人突然提高嗓门。谢尔碧听见麦克斯在吼叫，但是听不清具体的内容。突然之

Chapter Ten Rat Corner

she couldn't make out the words. All at once everyone laughed. Hadley opened the front door, unleashing the full brunt of the party on their ears. Shelby suddenly realized what she needed to ask before they went inside.

"So you'll read it?"

"Read ... ?" Hadley, frowning mildly with confusion, turned sideways before he went through the door. The hall was too narrow to go down two abreast without touching.

"You know," Shelby said almost laughing, wondering why he was torturing her. If he didn't want to read the book she was working on, why didn't he just say so?

Hadley sighed. "Okay, but I don't know what you expect from me."

"Your honest opinion?"

Hadley half-shrugged and half-nodded, and then he went inside. Shelby paused outside, pulling down the corners of her mouth with her fingers in order to keep from smiling.

间所有人又都爆发出一阵笑声。哈德利打开前门,派对里的全部火力都在他们耳边释放。这时谢尔碧意识到,在进去之前她得问一个问题。

"所以你会读咯?"

"读……"哈德利微微蹙了下眉头,有些不解。进门之前他侧过身子来,因为走廊太窄了,不可能两个人并排通过而互不接触。

"你知道的。"谢尔碧几乎要笑出声来,不知道为什么他要明知故问。如果他不想读自己写的书的话,为什么不直说呢?

哈德利叹了口气。"好吧,但是我不知道你期待从我这里获得什么。"

"你真实的想法?"

哈德利半耸肩半点头,算是答应了,随后就走了进去。谢尔碧在外面停留了一会儿,用手指把上扬的嘴角扯了下来,消除掉自己的微笑。

Chapter Eleven   Hottentot Venus

According to Stephen J. Gould, the Hottentot Venus (a Khoi-San woman from Africa) was exhibited throughout England and Paris during the early 1800's and was a sensation for a variety of reasons, the official one being her steatopygia, a condition common to the Khoi-Sans which manifests itself as an accumulation of fat on and about the buttocks. Because of this, she was kept in a cage and ordered to move about like a beast for the entertainment of the masses. Less known was the fact that she had some facility with no fewer than three foreign languages (Dutch, English, and French) and had even confirmed in a court of law that not only was she not under restraint, but she'd been guaranteed half of the proceeds. The unofficial reason that made the Hottentot Venus such a wonder, and an attribute probably only seen after her death but which excited much rumor while she was alive, was that the woman had four-inch labia minora. Gould proposes no evolutionary explanation for this but does tell us that those labia are now pickled in the basement of France's Musée de l'Homme. Gould also points out that though there are several brains and skulls of famous men, the only thing preserved of women is genitalia. But of course.

Shelby Mitchell

She put down her pen, went into the bathroom, and sat back on the toilet seat. In the soap-stained magnifying mirror she looked at her own labia. They looked enormous, though really only measured about half-an-inch. She had nothing on the Hottentot Venus. But through the haze of ghostly waterspots that mottled the mirror, her labia seemed big and ugly to her, now that her pubic hair had been shaved off

第十一章　霍屯督·维纳斯

据史蒂芬·杰伊·古尔德[译者注：美国著名古生物学家，科普作家]研究发现，在19世纪早期，霍屯督·维纳斯（一个来自南非科伊桑的女人）在整个英格兰与巴黎地区被巡回展出。引起轰动的原因有很多，最官方的原因是她那尤其肥突的臀部。这种情况对科伊桑人来说非常常见，只是一种臀部及其周围所堆积的脂肪的表现。但就因为这种与众不同的臀部，那个女人就被关在笼子里，在指令下像野兽一般地来回走动，以此来娱乐大众。然而很少有人知道，她掌握着至少三种外语（荷兰语、英语和法语），甚至曾经在法庭上亲口确认，自己不仅没有受到禁锢，而且得到承诺，规定有一半的收入都归她所有。促使霍屯督·维纳斯如此受追捧的非官方原因是一个大概在她死后才被确认的特征，那就是她那足足有四英寸长的小阴唇，在她还在世时，这一特点就引起过无数的传言猜测。古尔德对此并没有从进化角度给出一个解释，但他告诉我们，现在那对阴唇被浸在福尔马林试剂里制成标本，存放在法国巴黎的人类博物馆地下室里。同时，古尔德还指出，那里保存的好几个大脑与头骨都是来自于曾经名噪一时的男性，而唯一来自女性身体的标本则是外生殖器。但是，这也无须多做解释。

——谢尔碧·米歇尔

谢尔碧放下笔，走进最近刚修好的洗手间，一屁股坐在了马桶上。具有放大效果的镜面上沾满了香皂的污点，她透过那面镜子观察着自己的阴唇。它们看上去非常大，尽管实际上只有半英寸。谢尔碧的阴唇绝对比不上霍屯督·维纳斯的大。但是在那被惨淡水雾所覆盖、斑驳陆离的镜面里，她的阴唇显得又大又

and was only just beginning to grow back, a prickly hedge of black that itched unmercifully, penance of a sort, she thought. Her pubic region didn't look anything like the woman's in Penthouse who looked so sexy sitting there on the beach under a striped umbrella. That's what gave them the idea. It was the kind of ritualistic foreplay that newly married couples go through. Or, in Shelby and Max's case, it was a precautionary step to reviving passion. Wild as a stand-in for emotion. Shelby believed that if she did all the requisite things—buy lover's paints, silken underwear, a game of sexual trivia—then she wouldn't find herself thinking so much about Hadley.

Max had lit candles for this tonsuring ceremony and glints of light reflected back and forth from tile to chrome, softly illuminating the tub in a ecclesiastical way. There was something ritualistic about being shorn in such a manner, and Shelby, unable to lose herself in feelings of sexuality, briefly considered the unusual relationship between religion and hair. She thought of the young boys she'd seen in the Jewelry District, pink-cheeked youths in wrinkled black linen suits straight out of *Yentl*, walking home from yeshiva in clumps, their pates cut to a military closeness except for the perfectly curled ringlets that hung before their ears. Why does adherence to religion dictate such strikingly garish fashion? A kind of forced humility? Or just bad taste?

Shelby had found herself staring up at the shower head, the one thing most directly in her sight. It was encrusted with the usual white calciferous material and made her think of the pock-marks of the moon. Thinking of the moon reminded her of how odd it had looked last night during the party, sandwiched between buildings, looking like a moon from a nursery tale, a mottled plate of curds and whey hanging in the sky.

Shelby could see the candles sputtering slightly from the sudden gust of the bedroom's radiator as a hot draft came under the crack of the closed door. She'd put candles on the back of the toilet and the back of the tub, striving for atmosphere. She could see the ones at the end of the tub dripping wax. Red streaks on white enamel. The tub rose around her, tiled on three sides—two long, one short—like a porcelain shrine. There was no curtain, no door. A total bathing environment. The uniqueness of their tub gave the bathroom a feeling of a bathhouse, where steamy clouds would billow out the just-opened door when the bath was over, warping and puckering everything in their bedroom.

丑。再加上她剃掉的阴毛才刚刚重新长出,就像黑色的棘手的篱刺,毫不仁慈地使你痒痛难忍。这也算是自作自受了,谢尔碧想道。她的私处完全比不上顶层豪华公寓里的女人,她们坐在沙滩上的条纹阳伞下,看上去那么性感。谢尔碧和麦克斯就是从这里得到的启发,才决定剃掉私处的毛发的。一种近乎仪式般的前戏,新婚夫妇一定会这么走一遭。噢,对谢尔碧和麦克斯来说,这只是重新点燃他们激情的必要措施。用疯狂的行为来做情感的临时替身。谢尔碧相信,如果自己把必要的事情都给做了——添置可食用性爱颜料、丝绸内衣,以及类似的性爱小游戏——这样一来她就不会那么频繁地想念哈德利了。

麦克斯当时还为这场"剃度"仪式点起了蜡烛,点点微光在瓷砖和器具的铬合金表面上前后游走,轻柔地将浴缸照亮,营造出了基督教会的氛围。在如此的环境中剃度私处的毛发,有了一种仪式的意味。然而谢尔碧却没有办法让自己完全沉浸在性欲中,于是她简单地思考了一下宗教与毛发之间的不寻常关系。她想起了在珠宝街区遇到的一群少年,他们面色桃红,穿着有些褶皱的黑色亚麻套装,和电影《杨朵》里的风格一模一样。他们正从叶史瓦大学[译者注:美国纽约一所犹太教信徒赞助的大学]走回家,脚步声有些笨重。他们的头发剪成了军人一般的短寸,只留两缕近乎完美的发鬈从耳边悬垂下来。为什么对宗教的遵守就一定意味着那种引人侧目的花哨风格呢?是一种被迫的侮辱?还是仅仅因为品味不好呢?

谢尔碧发现自己正盯着淋浴的花洒看,那是她视线最直接触及的东西。花洒的外面形成了一层白色的碳酸钙物质,使她联想起月球上坑坑洼洼的麻点子。而一想到月亮,她就不由自主地回忆起,昨晚的派对上它看起来有多么的奇怪,夹在楼房之间,看上去像童话故事里的月亮——一盘表面斑驳的凝乳,乳清悬垂在夜空中。

卧室里的暖气突然变强,一阵热风从门下方的缝隙里钻进来,谢尔碧看到蜡烛轻微地随之向前"噗噗"了两下。她在马桶的后面和浴缸的平台上都摆上了蜡烛,努力地营造着氛围。她注意到浴缸上有几根蜡烛已经慢慢开始滴蜡了,白色的珐琅质表面留下了一缕缕红痕。她坐在浴缸里面,三面白瓷环绕——两侧长,横向短——就像一个陶瓷质地的圣坛。没有帘子,没有门,整体形成了一个沐浴环境。这个独特之处使得他们的浴室有一种公共澡堂的感觉,沐浴结束之后,门稍微一开,云雾般的水汽就会升腾翻滚,将他们卧室里的一切摆设都裹挟起来。

Chapter Eleven Hottentot Venus

Whereas the tub was spacious, the rest of the bathroom made up for it by being crammed into a six-foot square area. Between the toilet and the sink (they faced each other sparingly) there was a person-and-a-half worth's of room. Max could brush his teeth while Shelby peed, but the situation couldn't be reversed. It was as if the bathroom had been built by someone who loved bathing but had forgotten the necessity of a toilet. The whole apartment displayed a feeling of afterthought.

Max often raved on and on about how things were done in New York. He called it incompetence wedded with bureaucracy, using their bathroom as an example. It was his way of dealing, blowing off steam, usually with a comedic effect. Shelby, however, took these rantings and internalized them, letting them bog her down. She now realized her mistake. Internalizing them seemed a way of being closer to Max when what it really did was drive her closer to Hadley.

After the shaving, they had had sex, and Shelby once again wondered why she still had so much trouble having an orgasm—at least an orgasm the normal way. Normal to Shelby meant almost anything except for the way she did it—by climbing something. Shelby started having orgasms at age five by shinnying up poles on the playground. As she grew older, and playgrounds grew out of fashion, she found that doors, and occasionally vacuum cleaner tubes, worked just as well.

One time when she was fifteen, while babysitting, she accidentally bent the tube of the vacuum cleaner, panicking as she heard a car drive up outside. Shelby had planted the bottom of the vacuum attachment on the carpeted floor near one end of the sofa. Leaning it against the arm of the sofa, Shelby straddled it. But the sofa was on rollers and when Shelby gave the tube her full weight too quickly, the sofa lurched backwards, causing the tubing to slip and Shelby to fall forward, her weight slightly crumpling the weak aluminum. The Playboys, which she'd found under the husband's side of the bed, dropped to the floor. Miss April got a little bit ripped in the process. Shelby stared in shock at the bent vacuum tube wondering how she could ever explain its condition. She heard a key in the door. In the instant it takes to realize the obvious plan of deception, Shelby threw the Playboys and the vacuum cleaner tube into the closet knowing that the boys she babysat for would get blamed. She figured they'd probably get spanked, the parents not really understanding how the vacuum cleaner tube got bent, but not wanting to hear any explanations either, and never associating the crookedness of the tubing with the subtle pheromonal odor it exuded.

正因为浴缸的占地面积很大，所以浴室剩下的部分就被迫挤在六英尺见方的区域里。在马桶和洗脸池之间（它们彼此面对面）有大概一人半的空间。麦克斯可以在谢尔碧小便的时候刷牙，但是谢尔碧却无法做到那样。就好像建造这个浴室的人对洗澡热爱至极，甚至都忘了马桶的必要性。整间公寓都展现出一种因为事后想起来才对各个部分进行补充的感觉。

麦克斯经常对纽约城的行事风格咆哮不已。他将其称作无能和官僚体制的结合物，他和谢尔碧的浴室就是一个很好的例子。这就是他对待事情的方式，尽情地发泄出来，通常伴随着一定的喜剧效果。但是谢尔碧则会将那些愤懑内化，从而给它们机会拖着她一点点往下沉。她现在意识到了自己的错误。内化不满的情绪看上去仿佛是想要离麦克斯更近一些，而事实上却将自己一步一步地推向了哈德利。

"剃度"结束之后，她和麦克斯做了爱，但她又一次感到疑惑，为什么性高潮对她来说那么难——至少是一个正常的高潮。对于谢尔碧来说，正常意味着除了她使用的方法之外的任何方法——她的方法是攀爬某样东西。五岁那年，谢尔碧在操场上攀爬滑竿的时候就开始感觉到高潮了。随着年龄的增长，操场渐渐变得不再时兴，她发现，门，或者有时候吸尘器的管子，也可以产生同样的效果。

十五岁时，有一次她正兼职代人照看小孩儿，却不小心把人家的吸尘器管弄折了，听到门外汽车的声音渐渐逼近，谢尔碧顿时感到惊慌失措。她原本是把吸尘器的底部放在铺着地毯的地面上，而另一头搭在近处的沙发扶手上，自己则骑了上去。但是当谢尔碧将自己的全部重量瞬间加在上面时，那个带轮子的沙发突然向后退去，吸尘器滑了下来，谢尔碧也不由自主地向前倒去。最终她的体重将脆弱的铝制管子微微地压弯了。她在男主人那边床下找到的《花花公子》杂志，也掉在了地上。过程中，4月份的封面小姐被撕坏了一点。谢尔碧仍然震惊无措地盯着弯曲的吸尘器，想着自己是永远也没办法解释清楚现在的状况了。这时她听见了钥匙插进门里的声音，就在意识到自己只能蒙混过关的那一瞬间，虽然明知道她负责照看的小男孩们会代她受责，但她还是将杂志和吸尘器一股脑儿扔进了衣橱里。她思忖着，他们八成会被打屁股，虽然家长也搞不清楚吸尘器是怎么折的，但是因为他们是不会愿意听取更多的解释的，于是也就不会把管子的弯曲和它所散发的微弱的费洛蒙气味给联系起来。

At twenty-seven, Shelby had never managed to have an orgasm without large accoutrements, and so climbing the door had become part of her and Max's sexual ritual. She knew that she should simply be satisfied that she could come, but still she felt in some ways sick. She wondered if that's why she required so many accessories to sex. Hand-cuffs. Ropes. Being tied up was her particular turn-on, but it limited access to the door.

A couple of months ago Shelby had mail-ordered a sheer, black merry widow with red ribbons that tied in the front and fifty million hook-and-eyes that went up the back. It had arrived last week, but because of the hook-and-eyes, it wasn't something she could just slip into. She had wanted to surprise Max. She knew deep down that wearing it was an offering, atonement for thinking so much about Hadley, but as soon as this idea surfaced, she put down the mirror and stopped looking at her labia. She had been thinking of him again. Thinking of him touching her. She had to stop.

Max had been talking about going to the Blue Rose Lounge tonight, a dingy, decrepit hole-in-the-wall where fledgling rock bands, most usually comprised of university students, played originals and obscure covers. It was the kind of seedy, divey bar that Max loved, where he could count on seeing rock music raw and at its roots, possibly out-of-tune, but spontaneous. Bands who might one day become famous and glib, but were now untapped veins of talent and brashness.

Shelby had told him that she'd rather stay home and write. As soon as the front door closed behind him, though, Shelby went to her dresser drawer and found her merry widow where it snuggled beneath her underwear. She took it out carefully and placed it on their waterbed, planning a strategy for how best to start. She tried putting the corset on the right way and realized that she could only reach around and fasten about three hook-and-eyes. Sighing in exasperation, she instead put it on backwards and painstakingly fastened all the little clasps. She then stood for a moment just breathing. It was incredibly tight. They expected you to have sex in this? She couldn't even move.

Shelby glanced at herself in the long mirror that hung on the back of the bathroom door. It looked like she had boobs in her back and nothing in the front. That briefly depressed her. She shook her head at her tendency to wallow and then began to carefully, painfully inch the cups of the corset 180 degrees, moving the

到了二十七岁,谢尔碧如果不使用大型的装备,已经无法达到性高潮了,因此爬门就变成了她和麦克斯性生活的一部分。她知道,能达到高潮自己就应该感到很满意了,可是她总觉得自己的方法有些变态。她不禁好奇,自己做爱时需要很多辅助性的物品是不是也是由于这个原因。手铐。绳子。被捆绑起来尤其能够唤起她的性欲,但是那样一来就限制了她与门的接触。

几个月前谢尔碧邮购了一件轻薄的黑寡妇情趣内衣,胸前系有红色的丝带,后背则是一排密密麻麻的挂扣。谢尔碧是上周收到的,但是因为背后烦琐的挂扣,她没办法一下子套进去。她本来是想给麦克斯一个惊喜的。但她内心十分清楚,如果她现在穿上这件衣服,就是一种主动的示好,为自己经常想着哈德利而赎罪。但这个想法刚一浮现,她就放下了手里的镜子,不再看自己的阴唇。她又在想哈德利了。每次想到哈德利都会使她动摇。她必须得停止了。

麦克斯一直在嚷嚷着说今晚要去蓝玫瑰酒吧,那是一个昏暗破旧的小酒吧,经常有初出茅庐的摇滚乐队在那里演奏原创歌曲,或是翻唱一些鲜为人知的歌,他们大部分都是大学生乐队。这种乌七八糟的酒吧是麦克斯的最爱,在这里他可以期待听见原始的摇滚乐,在它最初生根的地方,虽然很有可能会跑调,但是却毫无雕饰,纯朴自然。这里的乐队也许有一天会出人头地,然后他们的音乐就会变得流于肤浅的形式,可是现在,他们的血液里流淌的是未经发掘的天赋与不可一世。

谢尔碧告诉麦克斯自己宁愿待在家里写东西。但是他前脚关上门,谢尔碧就快步地走到梳妆台的抽屉前,找到了藏在内衣下面的整整齐齐叠好的"风流寡妇"服装。她小心地将其取出,放在她和麦克斯的水床上,盘算着怎么开始最好。她试着立刻就把紧身胸衣给穿上,但发现自己只能够得着背后的三个扣子。谢尔碧有些恼怒地叹了口气,紧接着把胸衣反过来套在身上,仔细辛苦地系上所有的小搭扣。然后她在原地占了好一会儿,调整着呼吸。真是紧得要命。怎么能期待人们穿上这个还可以做爱呢?谢尔碧差点儿都动不了了。

浴室门后面挂着一面长镜子,谢尔碧在里面打量着自己。看上去就好像她的胸长在了背后,而前面却平坦无比。这让她感到有些短暂的抑郁,但她立刻就甩甩头,打碎自己沉浸其中的倾向。随后,她忍受着痛苦,小心艰难地把胸衣转过 180 度,每拉扯一次,"风流寡妇"的套装就随之移动非常微小的距

merry widow minute amounts with each tug, until the underwiring for the breasts popped underneath her own. Suddenly the corset felt looser and she relaxed a little, taking gulps of air. She began to feel light-headed. No wonder women used to faint all the time. She remembered when she was a little kid she used to practice fainting onto her bed. At the time it seemed like something one should practice. Laughing at herself, she tried fainting now, falling to the waterbed with a plop. The wooden edge of the bed caught the side of her knee just slightly, but she was so used to banging herself up that she barely felt it. It was nice to just lie there and feel the roll of the bed carry her up and down while she thought about her childhood and why life had seemed so much easier then. She remembered wanting to grow up and become a U. N. interpreter, but she hadn't realize at the time that she needed to know another language. When she found that out, she settled on being a florist, that is until ninth grade when her science project was to sing to herbs and see if they grew better, and they all died. Obviously that she should now sing for a living was some sort of karma.

Depressing herself again, she finally got up and slowly pulled on the sheer black stockings with seams up the back. After she finished getting dressed, she put on black satin high heels with rhinestones that made her wobble when she walked. She'd heard on a talk show that Marilyn Monroe cut a quarter-inch off the heel of one shoe of every pair so that when she walked she'd wiggle. Shelby glowered as she did her make-up. Why are women raised to be so crazy? Even if they don't permanently cripple themselves like the Chinese did, then they do it temporarily. As if walking in high heels isn't bad enough. Cutting that quarter-inch seemed prophetic to Shelby, as if with every shoe Marilyn lost a little more of herself. It was something Shelby could understand. She felt the same about singing telegrams. They were a constant reminder that she never made it as an actress. She was a failure. She'd sold out to cheap theatrics.

But then she remembered her writing. It was the only thing that buoyed her up. That and Hadley. She replayed her excitement from after rehearsal today when Hadley asked gruffly, "Did you want to give me part of your book?" They'd been standing outside the taxi, waiting for Max to pay the driver.

Shelby had mumbled, "That's okay. I know you don't have much time."

"I have time."

离,直到胸撑的铁丝一下子归位到谢尔碧的胸下。一瞬间,整件胸衣就松了许多,谢尔碧也放松了一些,大大地吸了几口气,却开始觉得有点头晕。难怪以前穿胸衣的女人经常晕倒。她还记得小的时候,自己经常练习晕倒,倒在自己的床上。在那个时候,她觉得仿佛这是一件大家都应该练习的事情。想到这里谢尔碧笑了,想试着像当时一样晕倒,于是便"扑通"一声砸在了水床上。木质的床边轻微地刮到了她膝盖的一边,但她对磕磕碰碰早已习以为常了,几乎都没有感觉到。这种感觉挺好的:就那样躺在床上,让水波的起伏带着身体上下,而自己则回想着童年的生活,思考着为什么当时生活看起来如此的简单。她还记得小时候一直期待着长大,成为一名联合国的翻译,但是那时她并没有意识到,要达成这个目标,自己还必须得学习另一门语言。当她发现这一点之后,就决定开一家花店。直到九年级的时候,她的科学课项目是对着植物唱歌,看它们会不会生长得更好,但是谢尔碧的植物却都无一例外地枯死了。很显然,现在谢尔碧竟然要靠唱歌来谋生,是一种因果报应。

在又一次使自己陷入沮丧之后,她终于站起身来,开始慢条斯理地穿黑色丝袜,丝袜两侧各有一条紧带连接到腰。穿完之后,她蹬上了镶着莱茵石的黑色绸缎高跟鞋,她穿着这双鞋走路的时候,总是摇摇晃晃的。谢尔碧从一个脱口秀节目里听到过,玛莉莲·梦露会把每双鞋的其中一只鞋跟切下1/4英寸,这样一来,她每次走路时就会产生扭摆的姿态。谢尔碧在化妆的时候,对着镜子里的自己怒目而视。为什么女人越长大越疯狂?即使她们不会像中国人那样使自己永久致残[译者注:指中国裹足习俗],可还是会短暂地让自己处于那种状态。就好像脚蹬高跟鞋还不够糟糕似的。切掉1/4的鞋跟在谢尔碧看来有着预示的意味,仿佛伴随着每一只这样的鞋,梦露就又失去了一部分的自我。这一点谢尔碧可以理解。她对唱歌电报有同样的感觉。它们时时刻刻提醒谢尔碧,自己从来没有成功地成为一名女演员。她是失败者。她已经向廉价表演低头了。

但是她又想起了自己的写作,这是唯一能让她振作的事情。写作,还有哈德利。她在脑海里回放了一遍今天乐队排练完之后发生事情:当时她和哈德利正站在一辆出租车的旁边,等着麦克斯来付钱。哈德利用沙哑的声线问道:"你不是要把自己的部分书稿给我看吗?"

谢尔碧含糊不清地咕哝了一句:"没关系的,我知道你没什么时间。"

"我有时间。"

He had said this brusquely, turning away as he said it, but it made her breathe heavily, a feeling flowing through her chest. Without a word, she had taken a chapter of her manuscript out of the microphone bag. She tried not to laugh embarrassedly at her preparedness. He had stuck it in his cymbal case and left without looking at her.

There she was. Thinking about Hadley again. She had to stop. She'd been standing at the mirror, posed with the lipstick, adding a little more here, a little more there. Suddenly businesslike, Shelby blotted her lips and gargled, remembering that Max could come home any minute and she wanted to be ready. But after hurrying, she then sat around the house and waited, feeling pretty stupid, not really dressed for doing the dishes, which still needed to be done, or for anything that might splash her outfit or snag her delicate stockings, but feeling restless and wanting the time to pass quickly. And she was cold. She threw her terry cloth bathrobe on, planning to throw it off the moment she heard Max open the front door. Her plan was to pose behind the glass-paned living room door, the Penthouse picture of eroticism.

"Candles," she said aloud, startling herself with the contrast her voice made to the silence. She went to the kitchen and lit some, then turned the stereo on and played a Steely Dan record. In college she used to call Steely Dan "Get stoned and fuck music".

"Not a bad idea." She went back to the kitchen to roll a joint. She hated talking out loud to herself. But it was company. She heard steps across the marble floor outside and threw off her bathrobe as she ran into place. The steps halted and then she heard the rumble of the old elevator just to the right of their apartment, an elevator almost blinding in its just-polished copper, like it had been hammered out of new pennies.

Realizing that the footsteps had been a false alarm, Shelby put her bathrobe back on and went back to the kitchen. She knew that she smoked too much pot but she had to poof out somewhere: that's how she viewed dependencies, as a bulge in a weak spot. Whenever she tried to stop smoking pot, she started drinking more. And if she tried to curtail them both, she began to get fat. With a dependency, you might push it in one place, but sooner or later it will pop out somewhere else.

She felt herself ready to pop. To explode in some direction. She felt like she was waving a hand in Max's face, saying, "Pay attention to me." He always assumed

他突然蹦出这句话，同时转向了另一边。但是，谢尔碧的呼吸声顿时变重了，有一种感觉从她的胸膛涌过。她二话没说，就从话筒包里掏出了一个章节的手稿。自己的"早有预谋"让场面显得有些尴尬，谢尔碧努力不让自己笑出来。稿子被哈德利一把塞进钹盒里，然后他看都没有看谢尔碧一眼就离开了。

又来了，她又在想哈德利了。必须得停下来了。她一直站在镜子前，手里捏着口红，这里点一下，那里加一点。这时，她想起麦克斯随时都可能回来，而自己想准备好迎接他，于是她干脆利索地擦去口红的多余部分，接着漱了漱口。但在一阵匆忙结束之后，她坐下来开始等待时，突然觉得自己很愚蠢。有一堆碗碟需要刷，可是自己的穿着并不适合做这件事情，任何可能会把衣服溅脏或是把纤薄的丝袜给钩破的事情都不适合。可是谢尔碧感到焦躁不安，想让时间过得快一点。她还很冷，于是就披上了那件毛巾料的睡袍，打算着一听到麦克斯打开前门就迅速扔掉。她的计划是这样的，在客厅的玻璃门后面摆好姿势——像《顶层豪华公寓》里面那样的情色画面。

"蜡烛。"她大声地叫了出来，划破了寂静，连自己都被吓了一跳。她走进厨房，点燃了一些，然后打开了立体声音响，开始播放史迪利·丹合唱团的歌曲。在大学时期，谢尔碧把史迪利·丹的作品称作"嗑药之后再做爱"的音乐。

"这主意不赖。"她又回到厨房，给自己卷了一根大麻。她讨厌大声地自言自语，但那至少也是一种陪伴。听到外面传来走在大理石地面上的脚步声，她便飞速跑过去就位，同时甩开了身上的浴袍。脚步停了下来，谢尔碧听见了公寓门口老式电梯的"隆隆"声。那个电梯的铜制表面刚刚磨过光，就好像是用崭新的硬币铸造出来的，闪得人睁不开眼。

谢尔碧意识到刚才的脚步声只是虚惊一场，就又重新披上睡袍，回到厨房。她知道，自己大麻抽得有些太多了，可是她总得找个地方发泄：她对依赖性有同样的看法——虚弱部位的防线被攻破，向外凸起。一旦她停止抽大麻，就会喝更多的酒。假如她试图两者同时限制，那么她就开始变胖。有了依赖性，也许你可以把一个欲望推回原位，但迟早它还会从另一个地方挣脱出来。

她觉得自己快要迸发了，在某一个方向上爆炸。她觉得自己在向麦克斯招手，对他说："注意一下我。"而麦克斯总是想当然地认为一切都很好，除非有很

everything was fine unless something very large and noisy happened to the contrary. Shelby knew that the consequences of not getting his attention were just too severe. That's why she was wearing this silly outfit.

The sound of a key turning in the front door made Shelby jump, her heart pounding in nervousness. She ran from the sofa, threw off her bathrobe yet again, and then ran to her spot behind the glass-paned door, reaching out her hand at the last moment to switch off the overhead lights. The door swung open and Max entered in a panic.

"Shelby, you'll never believe what fucking happened!" he yelled as he immediately made the right turn into the bedroom, flicked on a light switch, and began tearing off his clothes without even seeing her, then headed toward the bathroom. "This fucking pervert—Jesus Christ—it gives me the goddamn creeps!" Max was hysterical. His voice now reverberated from inside the shower. "Shelby, the fucker whipped his dick out at me! Like, what the fuck?" There were miscellaneous sounds of water being turned on, something being dropped, more muttering. "What a fucking pervert ... Shelby! Where are you?"

Shelby looked at her feet. Her black, rhinestone-rimmed shoes were starting to hurt. She went over to her balled-up bathrobe where it had landed on the couch, shook it out, and put it back on. She felt really sad. Like she was trying with all her might, but he wasn't getting it.

Resigned to surprising Max another night, she took off her shoes and then slowly wandered into the bedroom. Max's jeans lay on the floor in a huddle, his shirt thrown over a low bookcase, his shoes, their laces trailing like the wake of a boat, looked about to collide. Listlessly she entered the bathroom. Max was face-first in the spray. He turned and saw Shelby standing there.

"Were you sleeping?" Max asked, not waiting for an answer. He gargled some water then started soaping his body furiously, as if trying to lose the first layer of skin. "This guy fuckin' whipped his dick right out at me and laid it on his chair! Jesus!"

Shelby felt really depressed all of a sudden, so she went into the kitchen for a glass of wine. Nothing like a depressant to spark you up. She could still hear Max's voice going on and on. She shook her head at the refrigerator.

Max turned around to look at Shelby, now back and sitting on the toilet seat and drinking a glass of wine. "Where'd you go?" he asked, slightly pouting.

大或是很吵的事情发生。谢尔碧知道,得不到他的注意力,后果太严重了。这也是她现在穿得这么愚蠢的原因。

听到钥匙插进前门的声音,谢尔碧一下子跳了起来,心脏也紧张地"咚咚"作响。她从沙发上弹起,又一次扔掉睡袍,跑向玻璃门后的定点,在最后一秒钟的时候伸手关了吊灯。门被猛得推开了,麦克斯有些慌张地走进来。

"谢尔碧,你不会相信我他妈的发生了什么!"他一边大吼一边毫不犹豫地右转进了卧室,推开灯的开关,然后粗鲁地扯下自己的衣服,又开始向浴室走去,他甚至都没有看见谢尔碧。"这个该死的变态——见鬼——都他妈让我起鸡皮疙瘩了!"麦克斯一直处于歇斯底里的状态,自言自语地咕哝抱怨着。现在他的声音从浴室里回响着传出来:"谢尔碧,那个智障对着我挥他的老二!真是,见鬼了?"各种混杂的声音断续传出来:打开花洒,什么东西掉到了地上,又是几句嘟哝。"真是少有的变态……谢尔碧!你在哪儿?"

谢尔碧盯着自己的双脚。那双黑色镶钻的高跟鞋已经有些磨脚了。她走到蜷皱成一团的睡袍前,把它从沙发上拎起来抖了抖,再次穿上。她感到无比难过。自己用尽了全部的力气,他却一点情都没有领。

她只好认命,另选一天再给麦克斯惊喜,于是她脱下鞋子,慢吞吞地挪进卧室。麦克斯的牛仔裤皱巴巴地躺在地板上,T恤被随手扔到了一个矮书架上,两只鞋子的鞋带像船尾的航迹,预示着即将到来的撞击。谢尔碧无精打采地走进了浴室,麦克斯在花洒下仰脸站着,转过身来的时候正好看见谢尔碧站在那里。

"你刚才是在睡觉吗?"麦克斯开口问道,但并没有等待什么回答。他用水漱了漱口,接着就开始用力地在全身打起香皂来,好像要把皮肤的第一层皮给搓下来似的。"那个家伙在我面前挥出了自己的老二,还把它放在自己的椅子上!天哪!"

突然之间一阵抑压感裹挟了谢尔碧,于是她走到厨房里给自己倒一杯葡萄酒。还有什么比大脑抑制剂更能让一个人兴奋起来呢[译者注:酒精对大脑及身体机能有抑制作用;此处为反讽]。麦克斯喋喋不休的声音还是不断传来,谢尔碧对着冰箱摇了摇头。

麦克斯转过身来,看着已经回到浴室坐在马桶盖上的谢尔碧,手里举着一杯红酒。"你去哪儿了?"他有些微恼地噘嘴了噘嘴。

"For refreshments."

"Lemme have a drink of that."

"It's wine!" Max hated wine.

"I want to sanitize my mouth."

"Why?" Shelby looked at him strangely.

"I drank off his goddamn drink!" He gave her a look of repugnance at the implication. Max then sat down in the tub and let the spray of the shower pour over him. "Okay, I'm sitting at the bar trying to ignore this guy and he keeps talking to me. Must be about fifty or sixty. He tells me how the bartender—big woman—was from Romania and it wasn't a coincidence that that's where vampires came from. Then he told me how the place almost burned down because Sonja always falls asleep with a lit cigarette, and then he pointed over to Sonja, and of course she was already asleep. Then the guy goes, Ya know, nearly fifty percent of all fires are caused by combustion." Max started laughing humorlessly. "Jesus Christ. So he asked me if I wanted another beer, and I said okay."

"You know this whole thing happened because you wanted the free beer." Shelby tried to say it with humor, but it came out more pointed than she intended.

Max ignored her. "So he comes back with two beers and some kind of liquor. 'You ever had Everclear?' he asked. He tosses it down, and the bartender pours him some more. 'Try some.' God knows why I did. It was horrible. Right then the band started setting up. I really wanted to hear them, so I asked him when they started. That's when he asked me what I was doing later tonight!" Max's voice rose in mortification, "And I said, 'Going home to my wife!'" Despite her mood, the corners of Shelby's mouth lifted imperceptibly.

"Then," Max sat up in the tub and started yelling, "he whipped out his fucking dick and started playing with it and saying, 'You sure you don't want to come home with me?' I mean, I drank off his goddamn drink!" Max wiped his mouth again.

There was a pause as Shelby took another sip of wine.

"Well, aren't you going to say something?!" Max asked.

"So the guy played with his dick. I've seen the Blue Rose Lounge. I wouldn't expect any different. Didn't you wonder why he was buying you drinks?" Shelby was tired from the pot and wine and felt like going to bed. The humor of the

"喝点东西恢复精力。"

"让我也来一口。"

"是红酒!"麦克斯是讨厌红酒的。

"我想冲一下嘴巴。"

"为什么?"谢尔碧怪异地看着他。

"因为我喝了他的酒!"麦克斯对其隐含的意义做了一个厌恶的表情。随后他一屁股坐进了浴缸里,任由花洒的水淋在自己身上。"是这样的,我正坐在酒吧里,尽量不理睬旁边那个一直在跟我说话的男人。他八成有五六十岁了。他告诉我那个酒保——一个壮硕的女人——来自罗马尼亚,而且吸血鬼也来自那里,这并不是巧合。然后他又跟我说,这家酒吧有一次差点被烧为灰烬,因为桑亚总是手里拿着点燃的香烟就睡着了,接着他就指向一边的桑亚,果真已经睡着了。那家伙继续说:'你知道吗,几乎50%的火灾都是由燃烧引起的。'"讲到这里,麦克斯假装笑了几声。"老天哪。所以他就问我还想不想再来一杯啤酒,我说好啊。"

"还不是因为你想要那杯免费啤酒。"谢尔碧试着加进些幽默口吻,但是一出口却比她的本意更多了几分尖锐。

麦克斯没有理会她。"然后他就拿着两瓶啤酒和某种烈酒回来了。'你尝过永不清醒吗?'他问我,顺势一口干了酒,酒保又给他倒了一杯。'试一下吧。'鬼知道我为什么听了他的话。简直太难喝了。就在这时,乐队开始调试设备了,我真的很想听他们演奏,于是我就问那个家伙表演什么时候开始。他就是那时问我今天晚上有什么打算的!"麦克斯的声线因为窘迫而提高起来,"我就说,'回家找我老婆!'"尽管心情还是很糟,谢尔碧的嘴角不引人注意地微微上扬了一下。

"然后,"麦克斯坐起身,开始更大声地抱怨,"他掏出该死的老二把玩了起来,还跟我说,'你确定你不想和我一起回家吗?'上帝啊,我真不敢相信我竟然喝了他的酒!"麦克斯又猛地擦了擦嘴巴。

谢尔碧小酌了一口酒,又是一阵静默。

"那么,你什么感慨都没有吗?!"麦克斯问道。

"只不过是有个家伙把玩了自己的老二。我见识过蓝玫瑰酒吧,这是我意料之中的事情。你就没有想过他为什么要请你喝酒吗?"在大麻和酒精的作用下,谢尔碧觉得有些累了,想要上床睡觉。前一秒的幽默氛围消失无踪了,取而

moment before evaporated as Max's naivet wore on her.

"I think I still have the right to be disgusted when some guy handles his pecker. What if someone had walked into the bar then? 'Oh, this looks like a nice place, honey. Let's go in here.' And then they see some shriveled up old penis hanging out of a guy's pants."

"Max. What do you want me to do?" Shelby set her glass of wine down on the back of the toilet. "I think your problem is that you go there for real life, and when you get it, you can't handle it." She knew she was being a little bit mean, but all Max ever thought about was himself. It didn't even dawn on him to ask why there were candles lit in the bedroom, or why she had makeup on.

"Thanks a lot. I thought I'd be coming home to someone who might care about me."

"I do care, but I think you're way overreacting."

"What if some guy whipped his dick out at you?"

"Are you kidding? It happens all the time. One time in L.A. even my neighbor exposed himself to me. I always felt safe because our unit had a locked grating that's supposed to separate you from the riff-raff, but not if the riff-raff live next door to you."

"Well, I'm sorry, but I'm not that easygoing." Max turned off the water and stood up. "Could you hand me a towel, please?"

Shelby reached beside her for a towel and passed it over. As he took the towel, Max said, "And I don't think you're that easygoing either."

"Not easygoing, just used to it. I think you're being a baby."

"Thanks."

"Look, I don't want to get in a fight. I'm sorry this upset you so much."

"I'm sorry that I couldn't tell you about something that was bothering me."

Shelby hated when he phrased things that way. She felt like she had to come out of her own neuroses and comfort him, while he stayed where he was. It reminded her of when he would make a "kissy face" at her, puckering his lips as if waiting for a kiss. Then she felt required to go over to him in order to kiss him, as if proving her love, as opposed to him simply coming over to kiss her. She knew thinking this was incredibly petty, but still it weighed her down. It was too trivial to air, so it lingered in her barely conscious mind, biding its time till it later became a rationalization for

代之的是麦克斯那使人倍感疲劳的天真。

"我觉得我还是有权利被玩自己阴茎的变态给恶心到吧。万一当时有人正好走进酒吧看见怎么办？'噢，这个地方看上去不错，亲爱的。我们去那儿坐吧。'然后冷不丁地他们就看见一个家伙掏出了自己干瘪皱缩的老二。"

"麦克斯，你到底想让我怎么做？"谢尔碧将手里的酒杯放在马桶后面的台子上，"我觉得你的问题就是，你去那儿本来就是为了见识真正的生活，但当你看见了，你又接受不了。"她知道，自己的话有些刻薄，但是麦克斯心里永远都只想着自己。他甚至都没有想到问一句，为什么卧室里面点上了蜡烛，或者是，为什么谢尔碧化了妆。

"真是多谢了。我以为我回到家里来，可能会有人是关心我的。"

"我不是不关心，只不过你反应过度了。"

"要是有人对你做这样的事呢？"

"你是在开玩笑吗？这种事情发生在我身上的次数还少吗？有一次在洛杉矶，我的邻居甚至都对我露阴了。我还一直认为我们住的单元有上锁的铁栅栏而感到安全呢，那个锁本来是可以把流氓无赖都拦在外面的，可是流氓在里面那还有什么用处呢。"

"那么，很抱歉你也经历过这种事情，但是我没那么随和。"麦克斯关掉淋浴头，站了起来。"能请你把毛巾递给我吗？"

谢尔碧向旁边伸手扯了一条毛巾，递了过去。麦克斯接过去，继续说道："我也不觉得你有那么随和。"

"不是随和，只是习惯了。我认为你的反应很幼稚。"

"多谢夸奖。"

"听着，我并不想吵架。我很抱歉这件事竟然让你这么不开心。"

"我很抱歉我竟然不能把自己的烦心事跟你说。"

他每次用这样的方式说话时，谢尔碧就很厌恶。她觉得好像必须从自己的精神压力里抽身出来，去安慰麦克斯，而他则待在原地，一点努力也不做。就好像有的时候，麦克斯会对她做出"亲亲脸"的表情，噘起嘴巴等待着。然后谢尔碧就觉得自己有义务走过去满足他，仿佛是为了证明自己的爱，可是麦克斯却从来没有主动走过来亲她。她知道，这些都是小事，可是现在这些正一点一点地把她压垮。那些微不足道的小事，在谢尔碧的意识层里徘徊不去，等

behavior yet to be committed.

"I'm tired. I'm just tired ... " Shelby started to say more, but knew it would only provoke a bigger fight. She shook her head. Why did their discussions always leave her feeling numb, like she just didn't care anymore? She reached behind her for her glass of wine.

"Hey!" Max paused. "What are you wearing?" The edge of the black corset showed through where the bathrobe gaped slightly open in the front.

"Nothing." Shelby sighed and got up, tightening the belt of her robe.

待着合适的时机,直到后来,为某些即将发生的行为提供合理的动机。

"我累了。我真的很累……"谢尔碧想再说些什么,可是心里很清楚这只会让吵架升级。她摇了摇头,为什么他们的对话到最后总是让自己感到麻木,就好像自己再也不在乎了呢?她转过身去拿起酒杯。

"嘿!"麦克斯顿了一下,"你穿的是什么?"浴袍微微敞开的地方,紧身衣的黑色边缘露了出来。

"没什么。"谢尔碧叹了口气,站起身,紧了紧浴袍的腰带。

Chapter Twelve   Chain Reaction

Chain Reaction: a self-sustaining chemical or nuclear reaction yielding energy or products that cause further reactions of the same kind.

Webster's New Collegiate Dictionary

Walking the six blocks to the lab, Max stared at the ground and rubbed his fingers deep into his scalp, massaging the thoughts to the surface. Sometimes it worked and sometimes it just messed up his hair. He'd been trying to break himself of this habit. He could see his hair line receding. What did they call them? Power alleys. Male pattern baldness terrified him, but he wasn't sure if he was aggressive or hairy enough to be its victim. Balding guys tended to be very shaggy everywhere else. Max tried to imagine himself bald and couldn't do it. He remembered Lenny Shames. Had the babiest face, couldn't grow a beard, hadn't gone through puberty by senior year. Guys would tease him in gym, saying that his balls hadn't even descended yet. At the ten-year high school reunion, Lenny looked like an old man, gray hairs poking from underneath his shirt, a scattering of silver around his head. He'd passed from childhood to antiquity in a decade. That's what testosterone can do to a man. Max remembered Lenny coming up to him at the reunion and declaring, "All I can say is, my dick's bigger than yours now." Max wondered if being bald would make you say stuff like that.

Still ruffling his hair, Max almost ran into a group of Girl Scouts in green uniforms and brown sashes who were patrolling the Upper West Side with laughter and giggles. He thought of Shelby dressed as Wonder Woman and smiled. For her it was a business. For him a fantasy. Of course, less so since she hated the job and refused to wear it during sex because it reminded her of work. He wondered why she didn't just quit. Was she masochistic, wanting to torture herself? She said she hated secretaries even more. She didn't mind the typing, just the people. He really should convince her

第十二章　连锁反应

连锁反应：能够自我维持的化学反应或核反应，产生的能量或者产物可以继续引起同样的反应。

——《韦伯斯特新学院字典》

麦克斯穿过六个街区，向实验室走去。他盯着地面，用手指头深深地揉搓着头皮，想把自己的想法都按摩到表面上来。这招有时候管用，有时候只是把头发弄得一团糟。他一直试图改掉这个习惯，因为他注意到自己的发际线在一点点地变高。这叫什么来着？权力线。男性的脱发模式让麦克斯不寒而栗，但是他也不确定自己的攻击性和毛发浓密程度有没有达到标准，使自己能够成为脱发的受害者。一般来说，秃头的男人身体所有其他部位都会毛发蓬乱。麦克斯试图想象出自己秃头的样子，但却没法做到。他想起了莱尼·夏姆斯，有着一张最典型的娃娃脸，怎么也长不出胡子来，到了高中时还没有度过青春期。男生们会在体操馆里取笑他，说他的睾丸还没有开始成形呢。高中十年同学会的时候，莱尼看上去就像个老年人，灰白的毛发从衬衫的下面露出来，头顶上还剩一圈稀疏的银发。十年之间，他就从童年过渡到了老年。这就是雄性激素可能给男性带来的后果。麦克斯还记得在同学会上，莱尼走到自己面前，向他宣称："我唯一能说的是，现在我的老二可比你大了。"麦克斯感到好奇，能说出这样的话是不是跟秃头也有关。

麦克斯只顾着挠头皮，差点儿撞上一群正在曼哈顿上城西区巡逻的女童子军。她们穿着绿色的制服，挂着棕色的绶带，时而大笑，时而咯咯地傻笑。谢尔碧身穿神奇女侠服装的样子浮现在麦克斯的脑海里，他下意识地笑了。对于谢尔碧来说，那是工作；而对他来说，则是一个充满梦幻的世界。当然了，自从谢尔碧讨厌自己的工作之后，她就拒绝在做爱的时候穿成那样了，因为那会使她想起工作。麦克斯不明白，为什么她不直接辞职呢。难道她有受虐倾向，想要折磨自己？她说过，自己更讨厌文秘的工作。她倒是不介意打字，只是受不了与各种各样的人打交道。麦克斯觉得自己应该劝她放弃，她会变得开心一些的。不过，那

Chapter Twelve Chain Reaction

to quit. She would be happier. It would mean less ordering out, though, and he knew she had to decide what price freedom. Chinese food or her soul?

It hit him: That's why she was depressed. She couldn't decide. Ambivalence could drive you crazy. Making the decision can be harder than living with it. He couldn't make her quit, but at least he could explain that she'd be happier if she did quit. It would be a decisive act, unlike what she was living with now. Happy to have sought a course of action, foolish enough to think it could be so easily enacted, he walked like a man with a mission. He tossed thoughts around in his mind, noticing that the weather was making him giddy. Today was one of those sunny, crisp fall days that make you think again about why you thought you hated New York.

It seemed so bright, much brighter than downtown. Max had gone down for a chemistry book. It was one more step toward trying to figure out what was going on. He was hoping that it would help him understand why none of his reactions were working. He was beginning to change his mind about Scotia's hypothesis, starting to question it. To a lot of people, changing one's mind was a sign of weakness, a thing women did, not a demonstration of flexibility or good sense. Max tried to keep his mind open to possibilities, to not shove unruly facts under the rug. It was tempting, especially when your research advisor wanted results. But Max had, he acknowledged, a mysterious feeling that Rahda's chemistry was flawed. Something about it was bugging him, but he didn't know what it was.

Going downtown for the chemistry book had taken an hour and a half out of his day, but he was hoping it would be worth it. It had been strange to be downtown. Out of his element. Wall Street was an avenue of mausoleums. The only sun one saw was when it was high overhead and a minute later there were long shadows once more, so pervasive were the buildings.

Max had found the cramped and musty bookstore down a sidestreet; its entryway piled high with thick volumes that made miniature city skylines out of the windowpanes. It was like some mystic's shop, not modern like chemistry was nowadays, but grimy and mysterious like those forgotten alchemists who were always trying to turn baser metals into gold. Alchemists had been seers of a future world. Far-sighted in their lunacy. For, indeed, you can turn metals into gold. You just need a lab to do it.

就意味着叫外卖吃的次数会变少了。他知道,谢尔碧必须要决定自由的价值是多少。中国菜还是自己的灵魂,哪一个更重要?

　　他瞬间意识到了一点:这就是谢尔碧郁郁不乐的原因。她做不了决定。矛盾的心理有时候能把人逼疯。做决定可能比忍受现状还要难。虽然自己没法强迫她放弃,但至少可以解释给她听,放弃会让她感到更快乐。做一个果断的决定,而不是像现在这样将就着生活。麦克斯为自己找到了行动方向而感到开心,并且天真地以为很容易就可以实施,于是走起路来都带着一种使命感。各种各样的想法在他脑海里盘旋,他这才意识到其实是天气使他感到这么飘飘然。正是今天这种明朗清新的秋日,会让你产生疑惑,为什么你曾经觉得自己讨厌纽约。

　　天空异常透亮,比市中心明亮得多。今天早些时候,麦克斯为了找一本化学书去了一趟市中心。这是他为了搞清楚现状做的进一步努力。他期待着可以从那本书里找到自己反应全部都失败的原因。他对斯考蒂亚的假设已经开始改变看法了,开始心存怀疑。对很多人来说,改变看法是一种软弱的表现,是女人才会做的事,而不是变通和灵敏的体现。麦克斯一直努力让自己对所有可能性都持开放的态度,不去把那些难以控制的事实给胡乱藏到毯子下面去。虽然后一种做法带来的好处很诱人,尤其是你的导师迫切地想要结果的时候。但是麦克斯——他自己也承认,有一种神秘的预感,觉得拉达的化学反应是有缺陷的。那个反应里有某样东西搅得他心神不安,但他却不知道是什么。

　　去市中心找那本书花了他一个半小时的时间,但他暗暗希望这个时间花得值得。来到市中心的感觉很奇怪,这里与麦克斯气场不合。华尔街上遍布着陵墓。你唯一能看到太阳的时候,就是它高高地在头顶正上方停留的那一分钟,很快狭长的阴影就又会卷土重来。那些高楼真是无处不在啊。

　　在一条辅街的尽头麦克斯找到了那家拥挤的、散发着些许霉味的书店,入口的地方大部头著作高高地摞起,在窗玻璃后面形成了一道迷你的城市摩天楼景。这家店更像是一个神秘主义者开的,全然没有现代化学的摩登感,反而因为有些邋遢而充满了神秘色彩,如同过去的炼金术士费尽心思要把贱金属变成金子的地方。炼金术士一直都是未来的预言家,疯癫之中却隐藏着远见。因为,事实上,将金属变成金子是可以实现的。你只是需要一间实验室来完成它。

Chapter Twelve Chain Reaction

Max had found the book he needed and returned home, happy to be back in his own neighborhood. He walked toward the university and noticed that there was more diversity on the street than usual, as if everyone had taken the subway up from Greenwich Village. The streetware ranged from Banana Republic to Victoria's Secret. Staring at a woman who was rollerskating in a G-string and bikini top under a clear plastic raincoat, Max almost collided with a bicycle courier who had stopped suddenly in front of a copy shop. Looking up quickly, Max was mesmerized by the interweaving of pedestrians in front of him, like participants in a linear square dance, do-si-doing until they reached the corner and then the dance became a parade going in all directions. And everyone was eating as they walked, folded-over pizza, ice cream, neon-colored Shave Ice; one big, greasy-looking guy even carried a store-bought birthday cake with pastel icing and fed himself hunks of it, mammoth clods clutched in his immense hand. Max imagined that this must have been how Henry VIII ate.

There was a friendliness here, different than downtown where everyone walked with an expression of "no comment", saving their emotions for people they knew. Max actually looked around smiling, breathing in deeply, exercising his sense of smell. The air was clean and peppered with winter, sharp and pungent to the nose. Occasionally other olfactory themes came through, fresh-baked bread, garlic, something sweet that smelled like almonds. Max immediately stopped inhaling. That's what cyanide smells like. It was a hard habit to break.

At 114th Max passed a bum in a ratty ski vest. The bum was leaning into a large dented green garbage can, throwing crumpled newspapers over the side. Every time the bum moved, feathers puffed loose from the ski vest through holes that looked as if they had been made by knife stabbings. After finding a half-full Coke, the bum offered it to a friend only he could see. He then proceeded to get in an argument with the guy which quickly came to blows. As he whirled around, punching the air, feathers flying, he caused passersby to suddenly swerve, creating a bottleneck with pedestrians walking in the other direction. Max gave him wide berth, and nearly ran into the plastic shelter of a bus stop a few feet further on. Sitting on the uncomfortable fold-down molded-plastic seats were several short, fat Italian women in black kerchiefs. Their hands firmly clasped their metal handcarts which were loaded with an assortment of leafy vegetables that poked tender shoots through the lattices of

第十二章 连锁反应

麦克斯找到了他需要的那本书,便动身回家,回到了自己的街区让他觉得很舒服。在去学校的路上,他注意到街上的行人要比往常更加多样化,就好像所有人都是从格林尼治村坐地铁来到了上城区似的。大家的穿着从共和党香蕉服到维多利亚的秘密内衣,各不相同。一个脚蹬溜冰鞋的女人,只穿着比基尼上衣和丁字裤,外面套着透明的塑料雨衣。麦克斯正盯着她看的时候,一个骑着自行车的快递员猛然在一家打印店前面停了下来,差点和麦克斯撞个满怀。他急忙抬起头看向前方,却被眼前交织流动的行人迷乱了双眼,他们仿佛形成了线形的方块舞阵,踩着杜西杜的节拍行进着,直到抵达了街角,随即舞阵就四散成往各个方向游行的队伍。每个人都在边吃边走,手握比萨、冰淇淋、霓虹色的刨冰。一个看上去油腻腻的大个子,竟然手里端着一个洒满彩色糖霜的生日蛋糕,并且用他那巨大的手大块大块地往嘴里递。麦克斯嘀咕着,亨利八世一定就是这样吃东西的吧。

这里有一种友善的氛围,而市中心则不同,那里每个人都带着一副"无可奉告"的表情在行走,他们只把自己的感情留给认识的人。而现在在这里,麦克斯微笑着环顾了四周,深深地吸着气,锻炼着自己的嗅觉能力。空气很清爽,布满了冬天的味道,对鼻子来说仍然有些尖锐刺激。偶尔会有其他的气味掺杂进来,新鲜出炉的面包、大蒜、一些甜甜的像是杏仁的气味。麦克斯突然就停下脚步,深深吸气。那是氰化物的气味。这种习惯很难改变。

在114大街,麦克斯路过一个穿着破破烂烂滑雪背心的流浪汉。他当时正佝偻着身子在一个有凹痕的巨大绿色垃圾桶里翻找,不时把皱巴巴的报纸扔到旁边去。每次他一动,就会有羽绒从滑雪背心的洞里喷出来,那些洞看上去就像是被刀子给捅出来的。他找到了一瓶半满的可乐,于是伸手递给身旁一个只有他能看见的"朋友"。接着他开始和那个"朋友"争吵起来,口角很快升级成了斗殴。当他侧着身子绕圈,并不停地向空气中挥拳时,羽绒也跟着在空气中飞舞。这导致正在行进的人们都必须得突然转向一旁,人流避开流浪汉缩小为一个瓶颈。麦克斯也与他保持了足够大的距离,差点儿就撞上了塑料的公交站台。不舒服的折叠塑料椅上坐着几个又矮又胖的意大利女人,头上裹着黑色的头巾。她们都牢牢地抓着自己面前的金属推车,里面装满了各式各样的绿叶蔬菜,嫩芽

steel and frothed verdantly over the handcart tops. They talked loudly to one another, cursing what the world had come to in a humorous, fatalistic way. They glanced up as Max veered quickly, nearly falling into them, not halting in their conversation, only rolling their eyes in agreement as if to say, "Sad to see in someone so young."

Fast-talkin', hip-hoppin' entrepreneurs, with their wares laid out on blankets covering the sidewalk, sold everything from "Adidas"-stenciled tennis shoes to dancing beer cans with sunglasses to black key chains that chirped when you whistled. Walking past one of these salesmen, Max heard him demo the key chain for a customer. The guy whistled a shrill whistle that hurt Max's ears. Several key chains chirped for a few seconds. Max spun around, an idea brewing. The customer, an older man in a brown trench coat, gave a plaintive whistle but the key chains remained silent.

"Gotta do it louder, man," the salesman insisted, whistling again to activate the key chains. Max came up to the blanket and the salesman eyed him while the other customer lost interest and walked on.

"How much for a key chain?" he asked the teenaged salesman. The guy was wearing a sweat jacket that looked too small for him; the hood stretched long over his head like the sheath of a pea pod. On top of this he wore another jacket which weighed down the neck of the jacket underneath. He kept twisting his head around as if his clothing was as uncomfortable as it looked.

Max picked up a key chain from one of the aligned rows across the bottom of the blanket. Above them were rows of leather wallets, two deep, black and brown, and above them were mini-walkmans, the size of a cassette tape with dental floss headphones.

"One for one, five for four-fifty, ten for nine—you get the picture?" The guy talked fast, like one of those hucksters who try to get you to gamble on which walnut shell has the pea. He spoke loudly over the warring rap music. There were many blankets laid out along the length of the sidewalk, and each vendor had his own large, two-speaker, portable radio playing his preferred station. The various songs competed with each other for one's ear, the beat sometimes in sync, sometimes out of phase, like nighttime crickets which pulse together and then mysteriously slip into white noise. The music was a discordant jumble of rhythms and words, and yet it

从金属网格的间隙里伸出来,推车的最上面也泛着一片新绿。她们大声地聊着天,口气诙谐,却带着听天由命的意味咒骂着,世界已经沦落到了如此地步。麦克斯差点撞上她们,虽然迅速转了向,她们还是瞥了他一眼,而嘴上的对话却丝毫没有停下,只是一致地翻了个白眼,好像在说:"这么年轻的人就酗酒喝得醉醺醺的真是可惜。"

语速飞快的嘻哈创业家们,在人行道上摊开一张毯子,并把所有的货物都摆在上面,品种从仿冒的"阿迪达斯"网球鞋到戴着墨镜的跳舞可乐瓶,再到会随着口哨声而"唧唧"叫的黑色钥匙链儿。麦克斯经过其中一个销售员的时候,听到他正在向顾客展示钥匙链。那个家伙吹了一声刺耳的口哨,让麦克斯的耳朵非常不舒服。有几个钥匙链"唧唧"地叫了几秒钟。麦克斯迅速地转过身来,脑海里酝酿着一个主意。那个顾客穿着棕色的军装式雨衣,上了些年纪,他带着悲伤的意味吹了一声口哨,但是钥匙链们都保持着沉默。

"伙计,你得吹大声点儿,"那个销售员坚持着,又吹了一个口哨来激活钥匙链。麦克斯走到毯子前面,销售员便一直留意地盯着他,因为另一边的那个顾客已经逐渐失去兴趣,走开了。

"一个钥匙链多少钱?"他问那个看上去只有十几岁的小贩。他穿着一件运动夹克,很显然对他来说太大了;连衣帽却盖过了他的头顶,就像是豌豆荚的一个鞘。外面他又套了另一个夹克衫,把里面的那件扯得直愣愣的。他总是不时地扭动脖子,好像他的衣服跟看上去一样,令他很不舒服。

麦克斯从毯子上的最后一排拿起一个钥匙链。前面一排放的是皮夹,有深黑色和深蓝色两种,再前面一排是迷你随身听,磁带大小,插着像牙线一样的耳机。

"一个一美元,五个四块五,十个九块——你懂我什么意思吗?"那家伙的语速很快,就像那些试图让你下注猜豆子在哪个核桃壳下面的小贩。他的声音甚至盖过了周围摊位上竞争般的音响声,他们放的饶舌歌曲一个比一个响。人行道上还有许多其他的摊位,每个小贩都有自己的巨大的双响便携收音机,播放着各自喜欢的电台。各种各样的歌曲互相竞争着人们的注意力,它们的节拍有时是和谐的,有时乱作一团,就像是夜晚的蟋蟀,同时停下来,然后又悄无声息地形成了一片神秘的白噪音。他们放的音乐称不上和谐,节奏和歌词含混一团,但却

Chapter Twelve Chain Reaction

wasn't unpleasant. Looking at the various radios, Max noticed that even though the stations were different, the radios looked almost identical. It dawned on him why the term ghetto blaster had ever been coined. He figured if he lived in the ghetto and didn't have much, he too would own a portable radio where, for whatever range the radio could reach, he could at least temporarily own the air. His brain made the odd leap. Perhaps that's why he enjoyed farting. A temporary monopoly on breathing. A kind of musk to scare off other predators. Could he be so prone to genetics as that? He paused for a moment. Who was he trying to scare off?

Putting the key chain back down, Max said, "Five for four-fifty and ten for nine is the same price." He liked to spar a little with these guys, these sellers of wares on street corners. It was like one-to-one stand-up.

"So?" The hooded gentleman looked at Max like this was obvious.

"I just thought that if I bought ten I would get a better deal than if I bought five."

"You do. You get one of these lovely bags to carry them in." The salesman pulled out a plastic grocery bag with the words "Red Apple" written on it.

Max laughed. "It was nice of the Red Apple to give you those."

The salesman said nothing but turned his radio louder, moving in time to the hypnotic and droning chant, still twisting and cracking his neck.

"Are they hot?"

"Hey, man, you crazy? If I'na steal somethin', wouldn't be no key chains." The salesman looked at Max indignantly.

"Okay." Max grinned. "I'll take ten."

"What are you going to do with ten key chains?" Hadley asked, looking skeptically at Max. Max had opened the bag in Hadley's lab, raising his eyebrows and acting like he was showing Hadley something of great secrecy.

"Are you kidding? We'll put them down the hallway and when Scotia comes through whistling, they'll all go off. It'll be great! You wait."

Hadley gave Max a long look, holding his face without expression, and then shook his head, turning to clamp a flask to his ringstand.

"You're gonna wish you thought of it," Max said, walking out to the hallway and starting to place key chains the length of the corridor.

也不恼人。麦克斯看着那些收音机,发现虽然它们各自播放的电台不同,但外形上却几乎是一模一样的。突然之间他就明白了为什么"大型手提收录机(ghetto blaster)"会被称作是"贫民窟噪音器"。他寻思着,如果他也是住在贫民区,拥有的东西很少的话,他也会拥有这样一个便携收音机,它能收到什么台不重要,至少无论拎到哪儿,麦克斯都可以短暂地拥有那一片空间。他的大脑做了奇怪的思维跳跃。也许这也是他喜欢放屁的原因。短暂地垄断呼吸的权利。是一种用来吓退猎食者的麝香。他会这么受自然法则的影响吗?接着他又停顿了一会儿。他到底想吓退谁呢?

麦克斯把钥匙链放回去,对小贩说道:"五个四块五和十个九块是一样的价格。"他就喜欢偶尔和这些街角的百货小贩争论一下,就像是双口相声。

"那又怎么样?"那个带连衣帽的"绅士"看着麦克斯,好像这是很明显的事一样。

"我就是以为如果我买十个的话会比五个更划算一点。"

"会的,我会从这些漂亮的袋子里选一个送给你,用来装它们。"他说着抽出了一个塑料的购物袋,上面印着"红苹果"的字样。

麦克斯大笑了起来,"红苹果超市能送这么多袋子给你真是不错。"

那个小贩什么都没有说,只是把收音机的音量又调大了,跟着使人迷醉的低沉嗓音律动着身体,仍然不时地把自己的脖子转得"咔咔"响。

"钥匙链是偷来的吗?"

"嘿,伙计,你疯了吗?如果我想偷东西的话,就不会偷什么鬼钥匙链了。"他一脸的义愤填膺。

"好吧,"麦克斯咧嘴笑了,"我要十个。"

"你要拿这十个钥匙链做什么?"哈德利一脸怀疑地盯着麦克斯。几分钟之前麦克斯在哈德利的实验室里打开自己的包,他挑眉的样子就像是要展示给哈德利什么特别神秘的东西似的。

"你是在开玩笑吗?我们把那些放在走廊两边,等到斯考蒂亚吹着口哨经过的时候,钥匙链就会全部被激活。效果肯定很好,你等着瞧吧!"

哈德利面无表情地和麦克斯对视了好长一会儿,然后摇了摇头,转身用夹子将一个细颈瓶固定在铁架台上。

"你会后悔自己没有先想到这个主意的。"麦克斯一边说一边向门外走去,准备把钥匙圈摆在走廊的两边。

"Uh-huh," Hadley said dryly.

"Come on, he'll never know who did it."

"Right." Hadley picked up one of the key chains and whistled. The key chain chirped loudly, embarrassing Hadley. He looked down the hall but no one came out of their lab.

"So'd you have a good time Friday night?" Max asked, placing another key chain.

"Oh," Hadley said, trying to sound noncommittal. He was thinking about how the key chain worked. The frequency of the whistle must make a piece of metal inside resonate and touch the battery which then sparked the chirping. He preferred figuring out things to figuring out people.

"Did you leave early? I don't remember seeing you when we were throwing oranges."

"I was hanging out in the kitchen." He paused. "Shelby was telling me about the ins and outs of singing telegrams."

"It's good she's talking to somebody about that," Max said, shaking his head. "Lately it's like she's on the rag all the time. She should just quit."

"She seemed kind of moody," Hadley agreed uncomfortably.

"Moody! She was all bent out of shape this morning because we'd talked about maybe going to a museum today, but I told her I have to get something done."

"Yeah ... me, too," Hadley said, wanting to change the subject. "Since the NMR's down, I tried something else. I started lowering the concentration of the catalyst to see how much is actually needed to make the reaction work. What's weird is that it doesn't seem to matter how much catalyst I use, the reaction continues to turn over. If I go much lower with the concentration, then that means ... "

"That it's turning over faster than is physically possible." Max looked at Hadley.

"What are we overlooking?" Hadley put his hands in his pockets. They both just stared at each other for a second, thinking the same thing. Something was fundamentally wrong.

Max shook his head. There was a long silence. He started to walk away and then turned around. "I just got a book on this class of reactions. I'll let you know if I find anything that might make this make sense. Oh, yeah. Shelby wanted to know if you wanted to come over to dinner tonight."

"阿——哈。"哈德利干巴巴地应付着他。

"来吧,他永远也不会知道是谁干的。"

"我可不这么觉得。"哈德利拿起一个钥匙圈,对着它吹了口哨。它立即就大声地"唧唧"叫起来,哈德利顿时感到窘迫难当。他把头伸到走廊上看了看,但是没有人从实验室里走出来。

"对了,你上周五在派对上玩儿得开心吗?"麦克斯又放下另一个钥匙圈。

"噢。"哈德利的回答听起来有些模棱两可。他正琢磨着钥匙圈的工作原理到底是什么。一定是口哨声的频率使得钥匙圈里的金属片产生了共振,触碰到了电池,然后就引发了"唧唧"的声音。比起猜人的心理,他更喜欢琢磨机器的工作机理。

"你是不是提前离开了?我们在扔橘子的时候我好像没有看见你。"

"我当时在厨房里面,"他顿了一下,"谢尔碧在跟我讲做唱歌电报的时候发生的各种事情。"

"她能跟人聊这些其实挺好的,"麦克斯摇着头接下去说,"最近她总是发脾气。她就应该直接辞职。"

"她看上去确实有些闷闷不乐。"哈德利有些别扭地附和道。

"何止是闷闷不乐!今天早上,就是因为我们之前商量着今天也许可以去博物馆参观一下,但是后来我告诉她我得去做别的事情,她就大发了一顿脾气。"

"是啊……我,也是。"哈德利心不在焉地应付着,打算着换个话题。"既然核磁共振分析仪坏了,我又试了点别的东西。我降低了催化剂的浓度,看看多少量才能使实验正常进行。怪异的是,好像不管我加入多大剂量的催化剂,反应都会继续运行。如果我再继续降低催化剂浓度的话,那么这就意味着……"

"意味着它反应的速度要比理论上的要快得多。"麦克斯看向哈德利。

"我们到底忽略了什么?"哈德利把双手插进口袋里。有那么一秒,他们俩就那么看着对方,心里想着一样的内容。肯定有哪里出现了致命性的错误。

麦克斯甩甩头,又是一阵长久的沉默。他向门外走去,但是又转过身来。"我刚买了一本关于这一类型反应的书,要是发现有什么合理的解释我会告诉你的。噢,对了,谢尔碧想知道你今天晚上想不想来吃晚饭。"

Hadley felt himself tense slightly. "Oh, you know. I've got plans," he lied.

"With who?" Max raised his eyebrows teasingly.

"No one you know," he said quickly.

Max looked at Hadley expectantly for a moment, then turned and walked toward his lab. "So bring her by sometime," he tossed over his shoulder.

Max went back to work, immediately dropping every other thought but chemistry. He had to get something done. In the book he'd bought, he'd found another possible route to Rahda's molecule which could work as a better source for his subsequent derivatives. He was beginning to set up a column so he could run the reaction when his ears perked to the sound of whistling. Scotia. Max started smiling, waiting for the wall of chirping that would ensue. Scotia wouldn't have a clue what all the noise was about. Max grinned, just thinking of the levity it would inspire. He would be remembered for a hallway of twittering key chains. He liked the idea of going down in grad student history. It certainly wasn't going to be for science, he thought glumly. Then he heard the whistling pass him, turn the corner and stop. There was silence. Max was stunned. The damn things had chirped on the sidewalk.

A few seconds later, Hadley popped his head in the doorway. "I think they're duds."

"Tell me about it." Max sighed and rolled his eyes.

"Didn't you try them out first?"

"Yes—I—tried—them—out—first." Max gave Hadley a nasty look. "You made one work. Maybe they're just too far away."

Hadley disappeared, then came back. "Do you mind if I take one home for Ethan? When he loses his keys he leaves a window open and climbs up the fire escape. How much were they?"

"Forget it," Max said glumly. "What else am I going to do with ten dud key chains?"

An hour later, the whistling returned and stopped outside Max's lab.

"So, how's it going?" Scotia asked, breezily walking in the door. He leaned back on Max's bench and crossed his arms. A formidable presence feigning nonchalance. Max knew he liked to appear low-key, but it was only an appearance. His manner during group meetings was generally that of a genial father figure, except

哈德利感到自己微微有些紧张。"哦,你懂的,我有安排了。"他撒了个谎。

"和谁呀?"麦克斯逗弄般地挑了挑眉毛。

"你不认识。"他迅速地回道。

麦克斯满心期待地盯着哈德利看了一会儿,然后转过身去准备回自己的实验室。"那么,下次带来见见吧。"他的肩头飘过来一句话。

麦克斯重新投入自己的工作当中,脑子里除了化学之外的想法立刻都被抛到了九霄云外。他必须做出点成果。在刚买的那本书里,他发现了另一个可行的办法,能够制成拉达的分子,并且更利于得到其他的衍生物。于是他立即开始准备反应所需的层析柱,同时他也听见了远远传来的口哨声,他的双耳顿时打起十二分精神来。斯考蒂亚。一抹笑意浮上麦克斯的嘴角,他静静地等待着即将到来的爆炸性的"唧唧"声。斯考蒂亚绝对猜不到那些噪音到底是怎么回事。一想到这会引起的搞笑场面,麦克斯得意地笑了。他将因为一走廊"唧唧"叫的钥匙链而被大家铭记。他喜欢自己即将被载入研究生史册的这个想法。当然不可能是因为自己的科学成就了,他有些闷闷不乐地想道。然后,口哨的声音经过他身边,拐了个弯,停了下来。走廊里面却一片安静。麦克斯震惊地愣在原地。那该死的钥匙圈在人行道上的时候明明响了的。

几秒钟之后,哈德利突然探头进来,"我觉得它们是次品。"

"还用你说。"麦克斯叹了口气,冲他翻了个白眼。

"你难道没有先试一下再买吗?"

"我——当——然——有——先——实——验。"麦克斯恶狠狠地看了一眼哈德利。"你不是也弄响了一个嘛。也许是因为它们离斯考蒂亚太远了。"

哈德利消失在了门后,过了不一会儿又回来了。"你介不介意我拿一个回家给伊桑?每次他丢了钥匙就会不关窗户然后顺着逃生通道爬进屋里。多少钱一个?"

"得了吧,"麦克斯有些抑郁地说,"我还能拿这十个次品钥匙圈做什么呢?"

过了一小时,那个口哨声又回来了,停在了麦克斯的实验室外面。

"实验做得怎么样了?"斯考蒂亚脚步轻快地走了进来。他交叉双臂,倚在麦克斯的工作台上。假装毫不在意的样子,实际上却很难对付。麦克斯知道,他喜欢行事低调,但那只是表象而已。通常情况下,斯考蒂亚在组会上会以和善的父亲形象出现,但是最近他经常让贝内特没有好日子过。这些日子,大家的状态

for recently when he would grill Bineet. These days, the heat was on. There was agitation. Things obviously weren't going as smoothly as Scotia would've liked. Bineet continued to have trouble making the catalyst, which didn't play well with Scotia. He implied that Bineet was not up to the task. Max wouldn't have wanted to be in Bineet's shoes for anything.

"Any new derivatives?" Scotia asked.

"Not yet," Max admitted. "I went downtown and bought that book you recommended—" Max gestured to it casually with his head and shoulder, "—and I've just started looking through it for similar reactions." He hurried on quickly, "You know, I've been talking to Hadley." Max paused. He didn't feel like beating around the bush, but he also didn't want to anger Scotia by challenging Rahda's competence. Weighing the pros and cons, Max decided that he was here to do research, and research meant asking hard questions. Toying with a flask, Max asked casually, "We were just thinking that this result of Rahda's is pretty amazing. Are you …" Max hesitated again. "I mean … are you at all concerned that there is something that's being overlooked?"

"Well, we've done all the checks. Rahda ran several controls. And then recently Hadley ran a scaled up control without the catalyst. It did turn over a minor extent, but I think it's pretty safe to say that there were residues on the glassware."

"Did Hadley tell you that he's been lowering the concentration of the catalyst, and the chain reaction seems to happen just as quickly? I guess the problem I have is that the reaction seems to be happening faster than seems reasonable. It appears to beat the rate at which molecules can come together—"

Scotia interrupted Max. "The movement of the molecules could be controlled by forces other than that of kinetics, perhaps gravitational forces between the molecules, ionic or electrostatic. If that were the case, the reaction could potentially beat the rate of diffusion."

"Hmm." Max was silenced. It wasn't unreasonable. But nobody had done it. Doing things that nobody's done was big in chemistry. Nobel-prize big. Max noticed that Scotia's eye was twitching. No doubt it was the pressure. Scotia had recently given a talk at the annual Steroid Society conference and had said that he'd like to thank the society but he couldn't because they did not fund the project. This had made the papers.

都有点紧张。有一股焦虑在不停地搅动着。很显然,事情没有像斯考蒂亚设想的那样一帆风顺。贝内特一直无法做出催化剂,这让斯考蒂亚非常不满。他甚至暗示贝内特的能力没有办法胜任那项工作。麦克斯可不想体会贝内特心里到底是什么样一种感受。

"有什么新的衍生物吗?"

"还没有,"麦克斯坦然承认。"我去市中心买了你推荐的那本书——"他随意地用脑袋和肩膀指了指,"——才刚开始在书里找一些类似的反应。"他有些焦急地继续下去,"我最近在和哈德利聊这件事情。"麦克斯又顿了一下,他并不想绕弯子,但是也不愿意质疑拉达的能力从而惹怒斯考蒂亚。在心里衡量了利弊之后,麦克斯决定,自己是来做研究的,这就意味着有义务把恼人的问题给提出来。于是他手里把玩着一个细颈瓶,假装随意地问道:"我们都觉得拉达的反应结果有些令人惊奇。你有没有……"麦克斯又一次犹豫了。"我的意思是……你有没有曾经担心过,反应里有什么环节被忽视了?"

"所有的核对我们都做过了。对照实验拉达也做过好几次。再加上最近哈德利也不加催化剂做了浓度递增的对照实验。确实反应发生了一小部分,但我觉得把它归因于器皿上的残留,并没什么不妥的地方。"

"哈德利有没有告诉你,他在不断降低催化剂浓度的时候,链反应仍然在以同样的速度进行? 我的疑虑是,这个反应进行的速度似乎已经超过了合理预期。它的反应速率似乎已经超过了化学分子聚集的速度——"

斯考蒂亚打断了麦克斯。"除了动力学以外,分子的运动还有可能被其他力所控制,比如说分子之间的引力,不论是离子力还是静电力。如果是这样的话,反应就有可能快于分子的扩散速度。"

"唔。"麦克斯无话可说了。斯考蒂亚的解释并不是毫无道理。但是从来没有人做到过这一点。而在化学界,做别人从未做过的事情是很大的举动。大到有可能获得诺贝尔奖。麦克斯注意到,斯考蒂亚的眼皮一直在跳。毫无疑问,肯定是压力大的缘故。前几天,斯考蒂亚在类固醇协会的年会上发表了演讲,他说,虽然他很想对协会表达谢意,但是却无法做到,因为他们并没有为项目提供资金。这件事情隔天就登上了报纸。

"The lawyers are working on the final draft of the patent and then Rahda's off to Italy to demonstrate the reaction to their scientists."

Scotia took Max by surprise. "Italy?"

"There's a pharmaceutical company there that's close to bankruptcy. If they can use the method that Rahda's worked out, it would save their company."

"Wow," Max said. He hadn't realized that she was going anywhere. He didn't know what to say, so he glanced over at his column again, watching the crude mixture of compounds trickle through the silica into the fraction collector, separating the reaction products into pure samples, the speed or leisureliness determining which of the little moving vials would hold what portion of the compound. He wondered if Hadley knew Rahda was leaving the country. Obviously these anomalies weren't bothering Scotia if the department was paying Rahda's way to Italy in order to bail out this company. It would be a pain to have Rahda gone because they wouldn't be able to check any of their results against hers. Certainly she would take her notebook. Although the thought occurred to Max that they could more easily have a look around her lab.

Scotia coughed. "By the way, you might have a look at Bineet's compounds. He still seems to be having some trouble. I'd appreciate it if you could help him with it."

"Sure." Max indicated acquiescence, his sympathy for Bineet increasing. After Scotia left, Max sat around doodling various ways that the molecule could be changing. It was like a game, figuring out the mechanism: multi-dimensional chess on the molecular level. Would a hydrogen move here or there? As he drew, he remembered Shelby saying that Scotia was a really nice guy who said exactly what you wanted to hear. But she had said it in a way that you knew she was being snide. He was surprised that Shelby didn't like Scotia because he was one of the few research directors that had female students and actually degreed them. In the very male world of organic synthesis, this was almost unheard of. More common were stories like the one about the male graduate student who walked in while his research director was getting head from a female graduate student. Another story was about the professor who had left his wife and actually moved into the dorm room of one of his students. Ultimately such behavior was considered trivial as long as one's publications were solid.

"律师们正在准备专利书的最后底稿,然后拉达就会前往意大利,给那里的科学家们展示这个反应。"

斯考蒂亚的话让麦克斯吃了一惊。"意大利?"

"那儿有一家制药公司快要倒闭了。如果他们可以运用拉达的方法的话,他们的公司就有救了。"

"哇噢。"麦克斯从没有意识到,拉达会离开。他不知道该说什么,于是又瞥了一眼自己的层析柱,看着未经处理混合在一起的化合物,缓慢地从二氧化硅层滤过,进入分流回收装置里。这个操作可以把反应产物分离成为更加纯净的样本,速度或者说缓慢程度决定了哪一部分的化合物会落进哪一个小瓶子里。他在想拉达要出国这件事哈德利是否知道。很显然,斯考蒂亚对这些反常现象并不放在心上,因为系里已经决定公费派遣拉达去意大利挽救那个公司了。拉达要是离开了事情就会变得更加棘手的,因为那样一来他们就没办法把自己的结果和她的进行比对了。她一定会带走自己的笔记本。尽管麦克斯突然想到,她走了之后进她的实验室考察就变得容易得多了。

斯考蒂亚咳嗽了一声。"对了,也许你应该看一下贝内特的化合物合成情况。他好像还是有困难。你要是能帮帮他的话我会很感激的。"

"没问题。"麦克斯表示同意,他对贝内特的同情又多了一分。斯考蒂亚离开之后,麦克斯在笔记本上胡乱设想着各种可能的分子变化的方法。这就像是一个原理分析游戏:在分子水平上进行的多维象棋。氢原子是会移动到这儿还是那儿呢?麦克斯就这样画着的时候想起来,谢尔碧曾经说过,斯考蒂亚是个很不错的人,总是说出别人想听到的话。但是她的语调让人一听就知道是在讽刺挖苦。谢尔碧不喜欢斯考蒂亚,其实有点出乎麦克斯的预料,因为斯考蒂亚是研究生导师里面招收女学生,并且真的颁发学位给她们的为数不多的几个。在有机合成这个男性占绝对主导地位的领域,这种现象几乎是从来没有听说过的。一些更常见的场景是当一个男性研究生走进导师办公室的时候,撞见一个女研究生正在给他口交。另一个流传的故事是一个教授如何离开自己的妻子,搬进他的女学生的宿舍里的情况。只要那个教授的论文发表过硬,这些行为都被认为是微不足道的。

Chapter Twelve Chain Reaction

Compared to many professors, Scotia was a saint. But Max understood what Shelby's reservations were; there was a surface to Scotia that you couldn't get through. Everything seemed pre-packaged. Like he already knew what you were going to ask him or talk to him about. He was so smart that while you were talking with him he would credibly answer all your questions. But sometime after he'd gone, you'd realize that there was still something not quite right. This diffusion thing bothered Max. Gravitational forces kind of struck him like cold fusion did. Lots of people have claimed it, but nobody's proved it. Scotia was basically proposing a new law of the universe. How often did those come along? Of course, Max remembered, making gold out of other metals had seemed impossible at one time.

Max walked out to the lunch table at the end of the hall and opened one of the day-old newspapers that lay there, waiting for his compound to finish coming off the column. He skimmed the paper, looking for any interesting tidbit, anything funny that he could use in conversation. He liked facts, numbers, clear-cut statements. Sentences that didn't extend past the turn in the page. It felt like one of those lazy afternoons when research suffered but random arguments flourished. Max thrived on conflict. He had a lot of opinions and liked to air them.

He remembered that he was supposed to talk to Bineet, so he took the paper into Bineet's lab. Bineet was pouring a colorless liquid through a sep funnel. Max sat on a stool near him. He started reading an article out loud to Bineet about insects that have sex once and then die. Max joked, "When I think about my first time, it wasn't really worth dying for."

"Perhaps I will be luckier." Bineet looked up at Max and smiled.

"I didn't say it wasn't good ... " Max said indignantly, scooting the stool further away from the bench so he could lean back and possibly get more comfortable. He turned the page and laughed, liking Bineet. He was a funny guy, never hiding the fact that he was a virgin, and also never hiding the fact that he was obsessed with sex.

"So, Bineet, whadja think of *Caligula*?" Several of them had watched the movie at Kyle's apartment last week. Kyle lived in an expensive security building that overlooked Central Park. He shared the apartment with an old friend of his father's, an artist whose paintings adorned every wall. The apartment was extravagant, filled with lots of white leather furniture and carpeted in a thick, royal blue berber. The walls had sconces where muted light slunk from the light bulbs, illuminating the

与许多教授相比,斯考蒂亚已经是圣人了。但是麦克斯理解谢尔碧对他的保留意见;斯考蒂亚身上有一层你无法穿透的表面。他说的一切都像是预制好的,仿佛他已经知道你要问他什么或是跟他谈些什么。他聪明到了跟你谈话时能完美地解答你所有疑问的程度。但是在他离开不久后,你就会意识到,还有什么地方不对劲。刚才他给出的扩散速度的解释一直萦绕在麦克斯脑海里。在他看来,这种引力的作用就像低温核融合一样,虽然有很多人都这样宣称,但却从没有人证明过。斯考蒂亚这么做其实是在建立一条新的宇宙法则。这种情况能成真的概率有多大呢?当然了,麦克斯记起来,曾几何时把其他金属转变成金子也被看作一件不可能的事。

麦克斯出了实验室,向走廊尽头的午餐桌走去。在等待化合物从层析柱完全层析出来的空当,他随手打开桌上的一份当天的报纸,大略地扫视了一遍,留意着其中的趣闻,或者是任何他可以用在聊天里面的有趣内容。他喜欢事实、数字,还有清晰明了的论断,那些不需要转到第二行的句子。与往常那些慵懒的下午一样:实验迟迟没有进展,而各式的论战却甚嚣尘上。冲突是麦克斯生活中的乐趣。他有很多的观点,而且喜欢表达出来。

这个时候他想起来,斯考蒂亚让他去和贝内特谈谈,于是他就带着报纸走进了贝内特的实验室。贝内特正在用分离漏斗过滤一种无色液体,麦克斯就顺势坐到了他旁边的凳子上。他开始大声地对着贝内特朗读一则新闻报道,是关于某种交配完就会立刻死掉的昆虫的。麦克斯开玩笑道:"我现在回想一下我的第一次,并不觉得值得我为它死。"

"也许我会走运一点。"贝内特看着麦克斯,笑了出来。

"我并不是说我的第一次不好……"麦克斯愤愤不平地说道,一边把凳子滑得离工作台远一点,这样他就能更舒服地向后倚着。他翻了一页报纸,忍不住笑起来。他喜欢贝内特,他是个有趣的家伙,从来都不隐藏自己是个处男的事实,对自己着迷于性爱这件事他也毫不忌讳。

"那么,贝内特,你觉得《喀利古拉》这部电影怎么样?"上周他们几个人在凯尔的公寓里一起看了这部电影。凯尔住在一栋能俯瞰中央公园的安保大厦里,地段非常昂贵。和他共住的是他父亲的一位老朋友,是个艺术家。房间里每一面墙上都挂着他的画。公寓的装修也很奢华,随处摆设着白色皮革的家具,铺着厚厚的皇室蓝贝伯地毯。墙上装饰着烛台式的灯盏,柔和的光线流泻而出,照亮

apartment in a restrained fashion. In the bedroom, a huge, rectangular swing painted with orchids and covered with pillows hung from the middle of the ceiling. "This guy doesn't get many women, I guess," Max had joked. It was the kind of lavish apartment that you always see in movies about New York where the person living there makes minimum wage.

Bineet glanced at Max as he continued to pour the liquid through the sep funnel. "I had not expected it to be so exhausting to watch."

"I know. After a while you just say, 'Okay, I think I've seen enough of people shoving their fists up other people's asses.'"

"It reminded me of another movie I have seen. There is a scene in the movie where these men eat the brains of a live monkey. It is very bloody. The similarities are in the feeling of being—" here Bineet paused as he searched for the right description, "—of being unable to look away, but equally unable to watch. And so you watch but wonder why you do."

"Because you live in New York where everything's fucked and how different is people eating monkey brains to what you see everyday?"

"New York is not that bad. I like New York. But at times I do wonder why I like it. I think perhaps it is for the reason you say." Bineet had stopped pouring and set down his flask thoughtfully. "I will miss New York when I eventually go back home. My village takes many hours to get to because you can only go by animal, but many times there are no animals to go by, so you have to walk many miles on foot."

"No way." Max squinted at Bineet. "I thought some company was sponsoring you and you were going to go back there and work."

"I will, but the company is in the city where my plane will land, so to go home, I must get there on my own."

"You can't rent a taxi?"

"There are no taxis. And they would never make it to my village. The roads, you see ..." Bineet held out his hands, palms up.

"Will you get married there?" Max asked curiously.

"Yes, my wife-to-be is there now, waiting for me."

"She's going to wait for three years?"

"Yes, she lives with my family and helps them. It is good for them to get to know her."

了整个公寓，稳重而不浮华。卧室里，一个巨大的长方形秋千从天花板的中间悬垂而下，表面绘饰着兰花，并且铺上了柔软的枕头。"我猜这个家伙从来泡不到女人。"麦克斯曾经说过这样的玩笑话。这就是在关于纽约的电影里经常出现的豪华公寓，但生活在这座城市里的人们却领着最低工资过活。

贝内特继续将液体倒入分离漏斗，顺带着瞥了麦克斯一眼。"我真没想到看那部电影会让人感觉那么累。"

"我也这么觉得。看了一会儿你就会对自己说，'好吧，我认为我已经看够把拳头伸进别人屁股里的画面了。'"

"这让我想起另一部看过的电影。其中有一个场景是一群男人在吃一只活的猴子的脑子。场面非常血腥。这两部电影的相似之处就是那种——"说到这贝内特顿了一下，思索着合适的表述方法，"——那种没法把眼睛移开的感觉，但是同样也没办法直视。所以你就继续看了下去，却搞不清楚为什么。"

"因为你住在纽约，这儿所有事情都乱糟糟的，有人吃猴脑和你每天看到的有什么区别呢？"

"纽约没你说的那么糟糕。我挺喜欢这儿的。我想就是因为你说的那些原因，有时候我也会质疑自己为什么会喜欢它。"贝内特放下手里的烧瓶，小心地放在工作台上。"但等我最后回家乡的时候，我会想念纽约的。我得花上好几个小时才能回到我住的村庄，因为只能骑动物进去，但有时候连动物都找不到，就只能徒步走好几英里。"

"不可能。"麦克斯斜眼看着贝内特。"我听说有个公司要赞助你，你可以回到家乡的分公司工作的。"

"是这样，但是那家公司在飞机降落的那座城市里，然后再从那里回家，我就得靠自己了。"

"你不能包一辆出租车吗？"

"那儿没有出租车，再说，它们一辈子也支撑不到我的那个村庄。那些道路，你知道的……"贝内特两手向外一摊。

"你会在那儿结婚吗？"麦克斯好奇地问。

"是的，我的未婚妻现在就在那儿等我呢。"

"她得等三年？"

"对，她现在和我的父母一起住，帮着照看他们。让我父母多了解一下她也很好。"

Chapter Twelve Chain Reaction

"Yeah, but what about you!"

"I have met her once before. She is very pretty and seemed to me to be a very nice person."

Max just shook his head.

Bineet said gently, "I know it is very strange for you to understand when everyone in America is able to pick their own mates, but even here people are not happy. Many people get divorced, so is an arranged marriage that much worse? I trust my parents. They know the kind of person I am and they are older and wiser in many ways than I. I think they are able to pick someone who will make me happy... She is very pretty." Bineet smiled.

"I'd never, not in a million years, let my parents pick my wife. They can't even pick out clothes I like."

Bineet concurred. "Your parents must know you very well and have your best interest at heart if an arranged marriage is to work. My parents are the people I respect most in the world. I am happy to do this."

There was silence for a few moments as Bineet continued working with his compound. Max thought about how much he liked Bineet, but how absolutely different they were. Bineet had been the one to tell him about Al Goldstein and Channel J, and yet here he was, calmly accepting a wife his parents had picked for him. Max realized that what he looked for in Shelby was obviously very different than what Bineet would look for in his wife. For example, he couldn't imagine marrying someone he hadn't had sex with. That was such a factor of compatibility. He wondered what Bineet would do if his wife didn't want to have sex. But maybe that was inconceivable to him. Especially after all those X-rated movies Bineet had watched.

Max thought for a moment about why he liked Shelby. She was sarcastic. Funny. She was always making observations. She liked to say that scientists have the same enormous egos as her entertainment friends, they're just not as good-looking. And that she used to think that Ph.D.s made up for this by being smart, but now she wasn't so sure. To her, all a Ph.D. meant was that you had perseverance, about a five-year pain threshold. He liked the fact that she would just announce this at parties, a kind of comic rudeness. Lately she was more subdued though. At Dermot and Paige's party she hadn't wanted to joke around at all. Was put out even when

"是不错,可是你呢?"麦克斯忍不住大叫起来。

"我之前只见过她一次。她很漂亮,看上去人也很好。"

麦克斯只是一直地摇头。

贝内特语气和缓地说:"我知道这对你来说很难理解,因为你住在人人都可以自由选择伴侣的美国,但是即使是在这里人们也不见得都是幸福的。很多人都离婚了,所以包办婚姻真的有那么糟糕吗?我相信我的父母。他们知道我是什么样的人,他们年纪大,在很多方面都比我更有经验。我觉得他们能为我选一个让我幸福的人……她确实非常漂亮。"贝内特笑了。

"我永远也不会,即使是世界末日那天也不会让我父母给我选老婆的。连他们选的衣服我都不喜欢。"

贝内特赞同地附和:"想要一场成功的包办婚姻,你的父母必须得非常了解你,并且把你的兴趣时刻放在心里。我的父母是我在这个世界上最尊重的人。所以做这件事情我很高兴。"

贝内特开始继续捣鼓他的化合物,房间里有一阵短暂的沉默。麦克斯意识到虽然自己很喜欢贝内特,可他们俩却是截然不同的两种人。把阿尔·古德斯坦和 J 频道介绍给麦克斯的人就是贝内特,但是他现在却这样,平静地接受了父母为他选的老婆。麦克斯意识到他在谢尔碧身上寻找的东西很显然不同于贝内特对自己老婆的期待。比如说,麦克斯无法想象和一个从来没有与自己做过爱的女人结婚。这是一个非常重要的两人是否能融合的标志。他很好奇,万一他的老婆不想和他做爱,贝内特会怎么做。但也许他连想都没有这么想过,尤其是在看了那么多 X 级的电影之后。

麦克斯花了一点时间来思考自己为什么会喜欢谢尔碧的原因。她说话总是带有讽刺意味,很有趣。她总是在观察周围的事物。她喜欢说,科学家和她娱乐界的朋友们一样自以为是,但是外表却比不上他们。她一直觉得获得了博士头衔的人可以用聪明来弥补外貌上的不足,但是现在她却不那么肯定了。对她来说,博士学位唯一的含义就是,你在一个长达五年的痛苦马拉松中表现出了毅力。麦克斯喜欢的一点就是,她会在派对上直言不讳地宣称这一论断,达到了粗鲁无礼的喜剧效果。但是最近她却有点蔫了。在德莫特和佩琪的派对上,她根本就一点开玩笑的兴致都没有。当别人笑闹的时候,她甚至有些恼怒。就好像

Chapter Twelve Chain Reaction

others did. Like everyone had to be morose with her. He was convinced she hadn't found her niche, the thing that would motivate her. He kept encouraging her to take classes, and she was taking one writing class, but it only seemed to aggravate her more. He believed in higher education. But he didn't know how to convince her that this would help. Even though what she said about Ph. D. s was somewhat true, a degree still made opportunities available to you that you would never otherwise have.

Sometimes Max would come home and it was clear that Shelby had been crying a long time, lying on the bed and hugging a pillow. He would tell her he loved her, but he knew that wasn't enough. He was beginning to wonder if she should go see someone. They had health insurance through the university. He wasn't sure how she'd take this suggestion either. He sighed. Life was getting so complicated lately. No wonder he watched so much TV.

Max glanced up at Bineet, watching him label a flask. "What if your wife doesn't like being married to you? What if she suddenly gets depressed?" He knew Bineet might think these were weird questions, but he couldn't stop himself.

"Many Indian men would not care. But I think this is a good question. She will have her sisters close, and her mother. And I think my mother and she like each other very much. Sometimes women can help where a man cannot."

Max nodded. Bineet was a smart guy. Shelby didn't seem to have a lot of women friends. She had the band. She had some actors she knew from summer stock that she would visit. She didn't really hang out with Paige. Or Eberhard's wife Estrid. Or any other women that he could think of. Maybe that was part of the problem. She had no one like her to confide in.

Bineet smiled, looking at Max. "Do you think my bad looks will disappoint her?"

"Just have sex in the dark. You'll be fine."

Bineet nodded as if this were good advice.

Max said, "You know ... " Then he paused. He'd had some questions that he'd been meaning to ask Bineet, but he wasn't sure if he was going too far. When would he have another chance though? He relished the opportunity to find out the truth about a culture that perplexed him. He looked Bineet in the eye, reading him. "Now let me get this straight. You can't have sex until you get married, right?"

"This is correct."

每个人都必须得跟她一样抑郁似的。麦克斯很确定,是因为她没有找到合适自己的职业,那是可以激励她的东西。他一直鼓励谢尔碧去上一些课程,她也正在上一门写作课,但是却好像使她的情况更加恶化了。麦克斯相信接受高等教育可以带来改变,可他不知道如何才能让谢尔碧明白这一点。尽管她对博士学位的见解有一部分是正确的,但是有了学位之后,那些在之前完全没可能接触的机会都会随之呈现在你的面前。

有时麦克斯回到家里,看到谢尔碧躺在床上抱着枕头,很显然是哭了很久的样子。他就会告诉谢尔碧自己很爱她,但他知道仅仅这样做是不够的。他开始思忖着,是不是应该让谢尔碧去看看心理医生。他们大学期间都是有医疗保险的。可是他并不确定谢尔碧会听从这个建议。想到这里他又叹了口气。最近生活变得越来越艰难了,怪不得自己会花那么多时间看电视。

麦克斯抬起头看向贝内特,他正在给烧瓶贴标签。"如果你的老婆不想要嫁给你怎么办?要是她突然变得很抑郁怎么办?"他知道,贝内特也许会认为这些问题很诡异,但他实在忍不住。

"很多印度男人都不会在乎的。可我认为这是一个很好的问题。她身边会有亲近的姐妹,还有自己的母亲。再加上我觉得她和我的母亲都非常喜欢对方。有时候女人的帮助是男人所无法代替的。"

麦克斯赞同地点了点头。贝内特是个聪明的家伙。谢尔碧好像女性朋友并不多。她有乐队,也会不时去拜访一些她在夏季演出剧团里认识的演员,但他们都是男性。她很少和佩琪一起逛街,也不和艾伯哈德的老婆爱丝翠经常见面,或者是任何麦克斯可以想起来的女性朋友。也许这也是导致问题的一部分原因,她没有跟自己相似的人来倾吐心声。

贝内特笑着看着麦克斯,"你觉得她会对我的外貌感到失望吗?"

"关了灯和她做爱就可以了。你没问题的。"

贝内特点了点头,似乎觉得这是一条好建议。

麦克斯继续说道:"其实……"然后他停住了。他一直有一些问题想问贝内特,但不确定自己是不是有些越界了。可什么时候才能再有机会问呢?他一直期待着有个机会可以了解这样一个使自己感到困惑的文化。他直视着贝内特的眼睛,解读着他的表情。"就让我直说了吧。你直到结婚之前都不能和别人发生性关系,对吧?"

"完全正确。"

"Can you masturbate?"

"Oh, yes, this is okay."

"What about ... oral sex?" Even Max felt he was passing the boundaries of propriety. But he really wanted to know. Everything was legitimate to him in the pursuit of knowledge.

"This is—" Bineet drew the word "is" out, thinking, "—okay, too." He nodded slowly.

Max laughed in disbelief, "Nah! You can have oral sex but no 'sex' sex? That's fucked up."

"Not everyone says this, but for me, it is okay."

"Why?"

"Because I am not having the kind of sex I will have with my wife."

"You'll never have oral sex with your wife!"

Bineet shook his head.

"Why?"

"It is not done."

"Jeeze," said Max, stunned. "That's a bummer." He wanted to ask Bineet if this was all just theoretical, or if someone had actually given Bineet head. He was thinking how he could acceptably phrase this when he noticed Bineet was looking at his sep funnel and frowning. The mixture was still the same colorless solution.

Bineet shook his head in frustration. "You know, I just cannot reproduce Rahda's results. I am unable to make her catalyst. Dr. Scotia is convinced that I am making an error, but if I am, I do not know what it is."

"Why don't you simply ask Rahda for a mass spec?"

"I did."

"And?"

"It got lost."

"What do you mean?" Max looked puzzled.

"She says she left it on my desk last Friday. I came in late Saturday and it was gone."

"I can't see the janitor throwing something like that away." Max knew that the janitors had been warned extensively about touching data. It was questionable now that they did anything. The trash was always overflowing.

"可以自慰吗?"

"噢,当然,这个是允许的。"

"那么……口交呢?"甚至连麦克斯都觉得自己的问题已经超越了得体的界限了。可他真的很想知道。在他眼里,为了追求知识而做的一切都是合理的。

"这个是——"贝内特拉长了最后一个字,一边思索着,"也是可以的。"他犹疑地点了点头。

麦克斯不相信地放声大笑起来,"才不可能!你可以口交,却不可以性交?这是什么鬼逻辑。"

"不是所有人都会这样说,但是对我来说这是可以的。"

"为什么?"

"因为这并不是我要和老婆做的那种爱。"

"你永远不会和老婆口交吗!"

贝内特摇了摇头。

"为什么?"

"没有人会这样做。"

"天哪,"麦克斯感到无比的震惊,"这可真是扫兴。"他想问贝内特这些是不是都是理论上的,还是有人真的给他做过口交。他正想着该如何表达才能更容易接受一些,却看见贝内特盯着分离漏斗在皱眉头。里面的混合物还是一样的无色溶液。

贝内特沮丧地摇着头。"你知道吗,我就是没有办法重新做出拉达的实验结果。我做不出她的催化剂。斯考蒂亚博士坚持认为我犯了什么错误,但是如果真的是这样,我不明白到底错在哪里。"

"你为什么不直接向拉达要一份质谱图呢?"

"我要了。"

"然后呢?"

"丢了。"

"什么意思?"麦克斯看上去很困惑。

"她说上周五把它放在我的桌子上了。我周六晚些时候过来的时候图谱就不见了。"

"我不觉得清洁工会把那种东西给扔掉。"麦克斯知道,清洁工们曾经多次被警告过,不允许碰实验数据相关的东西。甚至他们平时到底有没有做清洁工作都让人质疑,因为垃圾总是到处散乱着。

"Nor can I."

"Does she have a copy?"

"No."

"Hmm ..." Max said, thinking and tapping his fingers on his leg. "Have her run another one."

"She is out of catalyst and is too busy to make more before she goes to Italy."

"She doesn't even have a sample?" Max asked, eyes wide. They both knew that you never use up all your compound just in case you have to do one more reaction. It was one of those unwritten chemist doctrines.

Bineet shook his head.

"You think she's lying, don't you?" Max asked.

"Yes."

"About everything?"

"That I do not know."

"我也觉得不是清洁工。"
"她难道没有备份吗?"
"没有。"
"唔……"麦克斯思索着,手指头在腿上敲打着。"那就让她再做一遍。"
"她说她的催化剂用完了,去意大利之前她没时间再做了。"
"她连样本都没有?"麦克斯瞪大了眼睛问道。他们俩都知道,你是不应该把化合物都用完的,以防需要再多做一次实验。这是化学家么心知肚明的规定之一。

贝内特摇了摇头。

"你觉得她是在撒谎,对不对?"麦克斯问道。
"是的。"
"所有事情都是个谎言?"
"这我就不知道了。"

Chapter Thirteen Addiction

> There is very little difference between addiction and dependence. In both cases, the person's existence ... becomes centered around obtaining and using the drug. All other considerations—personal appearance, family, job, studies—become secondary.
>
> *Abnormal Psychology*, Current Perspectives

Shelby accidentally dropped her singing telegram bag as she searched deeper in her purse for her keys. A surge of anger ran through her body, and she distractedly marveled that such trivial acts could cause her so much animosity toward the world. She'd come home early because the snow had been coming down in a blizzard, and her only telegram had rescheduled. She realized that this should have made her happy, but somehow it didn't. There was too much responsibility in trying to figure out what to do with the rest of the afternoon.

Finally finding her keys in the pocket of her coat, she relaxed, her mind already taking an upswing. She knew what she could do on this dark moody day: get stoned and write. The freedom of walking around in her brain while its guard was down was intoxicating. She thought of Hadley, the confines of her mind already weakened. She would remember old conversations, playing them backwards and forwards, trying to deduce now if there were any signs of his interest in the past. One she hadn't thought of came to her. She remembered standing in his lab as he was doing chemistry. This had been a few months ago. He was waiting for something to come off the rotovap, a large machine that looked like the body of a giant glass syringe with a glass coil suspended inside, both tilted at a 45 angle. She'd told him that it reminded her of the ride at Disneyland where people shrink to the size of molecules. Not turning around, Hadley had said, "It's impossible to shrink to the size of a molecule." She'd given him a look and then said dryly, "You're gonna be great with kids." He had turned to her and smiled. "Do you think?"

第十三章　上瘾

> 上瘾与依赖之间的区别很小。在两种情况下，个体的存在……都演变为围绕着获取和食用毒品而展开。所有其他的因素——外貌、家庭、工作、学业——都变得次要。
>
> ——《异常心理学研究现状》

　　谢尔碧在钱包的更深处搜索着钥匙，却不小心碰掉了肩头唱歌电报的包。一阵怒气顿时涌遍全身，同时她又感到无比的惊讶——如此琐碎的事情也会引起她对这个世界巨大的敌意。她今天回家比较早，因为突然下起的大雪导致她唯一的一场唱歌电报也改天了。这本来应该让她开心的，但是不知为何却并没有。要好好计划把剩下的整个下午拿来做什么，责任实在太大了。

　　好不容易在上衣的口袋里翻出了钥匙，谢尔碧终于放松下来，心情也转晴了。她知道在这样一个阴暗沉闷的日子里应该做什么了：嗑药，然后写作。当大脑里的警卫放下戒备时，那种可以在其中漫游的自由使谢尔碧感到深深的陶醉。思维的边界已经被削弱了，她又开始想念哈德利。以前的对话被她一遍又一遍地回放，她试着推理，过去是否曾有任何迹象表明他对自己感兴趣。一个以前没有太注意的场景浮现在她脑海里：哈德利在做实验，而谢尔碧就站在他的身旁。这已经是几个月之前的事了，他当时正站在旋转蒸发仪旁边等待着什么结果。旋转蒸发仪是一个体型硕大的机器，看上去像是一支巨大注射器的主体部分，里面悬浮着一个玻璃线圈，两者都倾斜 45 度角。谢尔碧对他说，这让她想起迪士尼乐园里的一个体验馆，在那里面所有的人都缩成了分子的大小。哈德利没有转过身来，但一本正经地评论道："缩小到分子大小是不可能的事。"谢尔碧冲他翻了一个白眼，干巴巴地说："你肯定能和小孩子相处得很好。"哈德利转向她，笑了。"你这么觉得吗？"

Something about that moment seared Shelby's heart. He'd known she was being sarcastic but chose to take her sincerely, even though it would make him look simple. She'd been snotty, and still he'd been nice. It was a kind of decency one-ups-manship. Making her more down-to-earth by his kindness. How could she explain that sarcasm was her defense, her emotional protection?

As she started to fit the key to the lock, she realized the door was open; merely in contact with the doorjamb but not engaged. Stepping backward in surprise, she turned around for support, but noticed that the doorman was asleep in his chair and unlikely to know the recent goings on in her apartment. "Max?" she yelled, pushing the door wider. He would never leave the door like this. "Goddamn workmen," she muttered, peering down the hallway, wondering what more they'd destroyed. "Hello?" Her voice, low and dull from the constant abuse of singing rock 'n' roll, echoed hollowly in the front hall. After a particularly raucous night, her voice would rasp like an old accordion, wheezing out a memory of notes, a sad breathless melody reminiscent of locusts, or of dry air in leafless trees.

It occurred to her that she shouldn't just walk in without knowing who was in her apartment. She listened intently, wondering if someone had broken in. She was trying to decide what to do, not completely in or out of the apartment, torn between Wonder-Womaning forward, or retreating for the doorman. She couldn't decide. The spandex of her costume was pulling at her shoulders, but still she felt hypnotized. As stunned as a computer factoring the square root of two.

A deep boom boom rolled out toward her, shaking the panes of glass on their living room door, the reverberation flashing in Shelby's eyes. "Hadley." She said it as a statement. She had thought about him and there he was. Scary. She'd forgotten that he had a key, that sometimes he came over and practiced his drums. Did that mean something? That he chose now to practice? He couldn't have known she would have the afternoon off. She decided it was only coincidence and walked into the entry hall, nervous, trembling, but craving the moment. The sound stopped.

Without pausing, or she would lose her nerve, she pushed the glass-paned door to the living room open. "You scared me," Shelby said, trying not to smile at him, slightly remorseful as she said it because it was stretching the truth somewhat. Why did she always start down a conversational path she had no interest in traveling? She acted crabby because she was afraid of what acting nice would get her.

第十三章 上瘾

那一瞬间,谢尔碧的心像是被什么东西击打了一下。他明知道自己是在讽刺他,却选择把她的话当真,尽管这样会让他看起来很蠢。她一直以来都带着自以为是的态度,但哈德利却和颜悦色。这是一种很有风度的胜人一筹的作风。他的友善使得谢尔碧对他也更加坦率真诚。她要怎么向他解释,讽刺是她的自我防卫,用来保护自己的感情呢?

当她开始把钥匙插进孔里的时候,她发现门其实是开着的;只是与门边框虚掩着,并没有完全贴合。她吃惊地退后一步,转向四周寻求帮助,却看到门房躺在椅子里已经睡着了,他不可能知道谢尔碧的公寓里刚刚发生了什么。"麦克斯?"她大声叫道,同时将门推开一点。麦克斯是绝不可能让门这样大开着的。"肯定是该死的工人。"她嘟囔着,仔细审视着走廊,想知道他们这回又拆毁了什么。"有人吗?"她的声音因为长期唱摇滚乐的过度使用而变得很低沉,空荡荡地回响在前厅里。在某个狂欢的夜晚之后,她的嗓音就会变得像老旧的手风琴一样刺耳,"呼哧呼哧"地奏出记忆中的音符,使人想起成群的蚱蜢奏出的令人窒息的旋律,或是干燥空气在光秃树杈间的热切的摩挲声。

谢尔碧突然想起,自己不应该在不知道公寓里是谁的情况下,就这么走进来。她专心地听着动静,心想着是不是有人破门而入了。她就那么在门口踌躇着,不知该怎么决定,是像神奇女侠一样地向前冲,还是退后寻求门房的帮助。她没办法决定。演出服装的紧身衣勒得谢尔碧肩膀隐隐作痛,但她却感觉整个人像被催眠了一般。就像一台电脑在接收到给2的平方根分解因素的任务时一样手足无措。

一阵低沉的"嘭嘭"声翻滚到谢尔碧的耳边,把起居室的窗玻璃震得厉害,谢尔碧还能看得见它的余震。"哈德利。"她几乎是肯定地判断道。她一直在想哈德利,现在他竟然就出现在这里。真是恐怖。谢尔碧都忘了他是有钥匙的,为了偶尔来这里练鼓用。这是不是意味着什么? 他偏选择现在这个时间来练习?他不可能知道谢尔碧下午正好有空的。谢尔碧最终确定,这只是巧合,然后带着紧张走进了前厅,她甚至有些微微颤抖,但是心里却渴望着看到哈德利的那一刻。鼓声停止了。

谢尔碧却没有停顿,否则她就会失去勇气了。她一把将起居室的玻璃门推开,"你吓死我了。"谢尔碧努力不露出笑容来,但有些后悔自己夸大了事实。为什么她总是言不由衷地开始一段对话呢? 总是采取习惯性的恶劣态度,是因为她对友善行为会带来的未知结果感到害怕。

Hadley sat up and looked at her, two sticks in his left hand, an expectant expression on his face, like he was waiting for the end of a joke. He had a nerdy self-confidence, a way of being so comfortable with oddity that he made it seem cool.

"Nice boots." He pushed his bass drum pedal hard, a surprising thwop-thwop-thwop that filled the room and stopped all conversation.

Shelby waited until there was a pause in his drumming, then leaned on the living room door and pulled off her gloves. She wanted to take her coat off, but she was too embarrassed for him to see her in her Wonder Woman costume. "I thought someone had broken in."

He answered with a clatter of drums, a drummer's response. Practicing cool rhythms to pull out later in the heat of the night, in the thick of the song. "You live on the ground floor. No one's going to go past the doorman and break in your front door," Hadley said shaking his head, giving the drums a few concordant whapps. "They're going to crawl through a window."

"Great." She paused. "You want a beer?" She wondered if the suggestion of inebriants would mean something to him. A tacit acknowledgment that she was prepared to lose control.

Hadley shrugged. "Sure."

She turned around and grinned, incited by his mere acceptance. She was in over her head. Too many of her cells had switched allegiance. They wanted thrill. The majority was voting now.

Walking into the kitchen and getting two beers out of the refrigerator, she spied one lone cockroach hanging out behind the stove. For some reason it fit the Wild West of New York, the renegade mentality that had taken over her body. She closed her eyes and tried to slow herself down. She felt Hadley's presence so strongly, like some opportunity laid out for her, but what to do with it? She was married, for God's sake. It felt so unfair that she should be married when she felt so much breathlessness for someone else. When had she gone gaga for Hadley? What had done it? It was before the rats, even. She went to that party knowing something was going to make her happy. The bathroom! He'd grabbed her. Saved her. She relived his arms around her, the memory of being pulled backwards, rescued, cared about. She had felt wrestled to the floor, roughness in the pursuit of kindness. Necessary roughness. It made her want to laugh at the craziness of it. What would sex be like

哈德利坐起身,看着她,把两只鼓槌都放在左手,脸上露出期待着什么的表情,就好像在等待着一个笑话的结尾。他身上有一种书呆子式的自信,一种坦然接受自己与常人不同的态度,使得一些怪异的行为看上去都变得酷酷的了。

"靴子不赖。"他猛地踩下大鼓的踏板,一阵惊人的"斯沃扑,斯沃扑,斯沃扑"声顿时充满了房间,打断了所有的对话。

谢尔碧等待着他鼓声的间隙,然后侧身倚在起居室门框上,脱下了手套。她本来还想把外套也给脱了,可是却羞于让哈德利看到自己穿神奇女侠服装的样子。"我还以为有人入室抢劫呢。"

他用一连串的鼓声回答了谢尔碧,一个鼓手的回答。他在练习的是晚上要表演的旋律,在夜晚的热浪中,歌曲进行到最高潮时,来上这么酷酷的一段。"你住的是底楼,没人会在门房的眼皮子底下撞开你的前门的。"哈德利摇着头,在几个鼓上均匀地敲了几下。"他们会从窗户爬进来的。"

"你这么说我真是放心多了。"谢尔碧用讽刺的语气回敬他,顿了一下,她又问道:"要啤酒吗?"她不知道这个一起喝酒的建议对于哈德利来说会不会意味着什么。这是一种心照不宣的默认:她已经准备好失去控制了。

哈德利耸了耸肩。"当然了。"

谢尔碧转过身去,偷笑了一下,他答应得这么轻易让她有些激动。情况已经超出她的控制能力了,因为她体内已经有太多的细胞已经投奔了另一个阵营。它们想要刺激。大部分的细胞正在投票通过。

谢尔碧走进厨房,从冰箱里拿出两瓶啤酒,无意间瞥到炉子的后面有一只蟑螂形影单只。不知什么原因,它正应了纽约的狂野西部特质——此时她整个人都已经被反叛的思想占领了。谢尔碧闭上眼睛,试着放慢自己的节奏。她如此强烈地感觉到哈德利的存在,就像某种机会摆在了她的面前,但是拿它怎么办呢? 看在上帝的份上,她可是已经结了婚的人! 当她为另一个人感到如此窒息,无法自拔的时候,却意识到自己已婚的事实,这是多么不公平啊! 她是什么时候开始为哈德利着迷的? 又是什么引起的呢? 甚至是在他们一起去看老鼠之前。她之所以参加那场派对就是因为她知道,会发生什么事情让她开心起来的。是在浴室! 他抓住了她。救了她。她回忆了一下被哈德利胳膊环绕的感觉,被拉回来,被营救,被关心。她当时觉得自己就像是被一把摔在了地上,善意中夹杂着粗暴。必要的粗暴。这件事疯狂得让她想放声大笑。和哈德利做爱会是怎样

with Hadley? She blushed, envisioning them naked, standing abnormally like the figures sent into the outer space time capsule. Exposed. Her cheeks tingled, the nerves flaring at the thought, a biochemical reaction created by mental stimulation. How bizarre, that one's mind can cause chemicals to release, can drug the body, and make embarrassment such an aphrodisiac. She wanted to be naked with Hadley.

Hearing a noise next to her ear, Shelby instinctively jerked sideways, the beer and opener still in her hand.

"Boy. You are jumpy," Hadley said, walking into the kitchen.

Shelby said nothing, just concentrating on slowing her breath. She opened the beer and let it fizz into the sink.

He looked at the beer. "I like it like that."

Shelby looked down at the sink, trying not to smile. "You're an idiot then."

He took the beer from her now that it had stopped foaming. "Perhaps." He took a long drink. "I thought you wouldn't be home yet. I can go if my practicing is going to bother you."

"It doesn't bother me," Shelby said, cleaning up the wet counter. "My telegram was canceled because of the blizzard."

"Umm." Hadley nodded, taking another drink. She sensed he was looking at her, so she continued to wipe the counter long after it was clean.

He leaned against the kitchen doorway. "Why do you look like that?"

She turned sharply and stared at him in a kind of shock, unnerved by the intimacy of the question. "What do I look like?" she asked, trying to make her face storyless.

"Haunted."

Shelby averted her eyes. "Haun-ted?" she asked with the implication that he was mistaken. The diphthong was her defense, an affectation that hid the emotion that possessed her.

"You look like you're carrying the weight of the world on your shoulders." Hadley smiled at her.

"I'm jealous of you." It just popped out. She hadn't meant to say it, but she had to say something before the truth spilled out in a big humiliating mess. It was somewhat honest. "You and Max." She looked at him straight-on. "You have these

一种感觉？她脸红了，因为她的脑海中出现了自己和哈德利裸露着，奇怪地站在一起的画面，就像两个被送进太空时间胶囊里的人。完全暴露出来。她的脸颊有些刺痛，每根神经都被自己的想法给点燃，这是由内心的刺激引起的生化反应。多么古怪啊，一个人的大脑竟然可以释放化学物质，可以让身体迷醉，可以让尴尬都变成情欲激发剂。她想要和哈德利"坦诚相见"。

听到耳边有动静，谢尔碧本能地猛然侧过身去，手里仍然握着啤酒和开瓶器。

"天哪，你真是神经敏感。"哈德利说着走进了厨房。

谢尔碧一声不吭，只是专注地放慢着自己的呼吸。她打开了一瓶啤酒，移到水池上方，任由它"嗞嗞"地往外涌。

哈德利盯着啤酒。"我喜欢让啤酒这样。"

谢尔碧向下看着水池，努力不笑出来。"那就说明你是个白痴。"

啤酒的泡沫不再往外涌了，哈德利把它从谢尔碧的手里接过来。"也许吧。"他仰头喝了一大口。"我以为还没到你回家的时候呢。要是我练鼓打扰到你的话我可以离开。"

"并没有打扰到我，"谢尔碧一边擦拭着台面，一边回答道，"我的电报表演因为暴风雪而取消了。"

"哦。"哈德利点了点头，又喝了一口。谢尔碧感觉到他正在看着自己，所以就继续擦着台面，尽管早就没有什么可擦的了。

他向后倚在厨房的门上。"你为什么像现在这样？"

谢尔碧猛地转过身去，震惊地盯着他，被这个问题背后的亲密弄得不知所措。"我现在是什么样子？"她尽力让自己的脸看上去平静没有表情。

"不安。"

谢尔碧移开自己的目光。"不——安？"她的语气就好像在说，一定是哈德利搞错了。被过分拉长的音节就是她的自我防卫，一种可以把支配她的情感隐藏起来的伪装。

"你看上去就像整个世界的重量都被你扛在肩头了。"哈德利冲她笑了一下。

"我嫉妒你。"就那么脱口而出了。她并没有打算说这句话，但是在真相暴露出来，让她陷入无地自容的混乱之前，她必须得说些什么。而且这句话有诚实的成分。"你，还有麦克斯。"她迎着哈德利的目光看过去。"你们拥有光鲜的未

glamorous futures, and I don't even have goals." She looked at him earnestly, freed by some part of the truth.

"I read what you wrote."

There was a long silence.

"I liked it. I liked it a lot. I remember meeting your father. It's just interesting because—well, I'm sure that helps me better visualize him, but you really captured subtleties I wouldn't have known about his personality. I made a bunch of comments. I hope that's okay." He smiled again.

Shelby looked at him with shyly, a demure look that still had sex woven through it. "Yeah. Thank you."

"You should send this out. I'd also like to read more."

"You're only saying that to be nice."

"Come on. You know I'm not that nice."

Shelby laughed without meaning to, scared to death that she was going to reach over and brush the hair out of his eyes. She saw her hand moving on its own volition, rising above the kitchen counter. Petrified, she pulled it toward her beer, trying to keep it occupied. She wondered if he wanted to be naked with her as much as she wanted to with him. And if he did, what would stop them? She swallowed hard. She had thought him a better person than her, more moral. She counted on him to be the voice of reason, the brake, thinking that if she threw herself at him, he would kindly, avuncularly hold her back. But would he? She needed some space to think. She needed to not see him for a second, not feel his vibrations wafting into her own. She felt the arrow bouncing on red, warning signs going off.

"I'm going to go change my clothes," she said, stiffly moving past him in the small kitchen, almost running to the bedroom. The bedroom was stifling because the radiator was now working itself up to soft crack. Shelby found herself thinking in cooking analogies because she felt as sticky as sugar candy, sweat making her hair curly and wild. The just-laid look, she thought. Then chastised herself. Her mental conversation went back and forth in that manner: something sexual, something reprimanding. Because she was so hot, she changed into shorts and a tank top and lay down to read. It wasn't until she found herself rereading the same sentence five or six times with no comprehension that she realized she had to do something else. She wanted to go back out, but she was so restless and nervous around Hadley,

来,我却连目标都没有。"她真诚地看着哈德利,能将一部分的事实一吐为快让她感到轻松。

"我读了你写的东西。"

一阵长长的沉默。

"我喜欢。非常喜欢。我还记得与你父亲见面的场景。我觉得非常有趣,因为——好吧,见到他本人肯定也让他的形象更加丰满了,但是你的描写真的抓住了很多细节,否则我是不会了解到他的性格的。我在稿子上写了很多的评价。希望你不介意。"他又笑了。

谢尔碧有些害羞地看着他,脸上的矜持表情里还混杂着性的想法。"不会,谢谢你。"

"你应该找些地方发表。我想再多读一些。"

"你这么说只是为了表示友好罢了。"

"得了吧。你知道我这个人没那么好的。"

谢尔碧毫无征兆地笑了出来,内心却无比害怕,怕自己会靠近过去,拂过哈德利垂在眼角的头发。她看到自己的手不由自主地移动着,已经举到了台面上。她被吓呆了,用力地把它拉回啤酒的方向,不敢让它闲下来。她想知道,哈德利是否也像她一样,这么强烈地希望和她光着身子待在一起。如果他真的也那样想的话,那还有什么能阻止他们呢?谢尔碧重重地吞咽了一下。她一直觉得哈德利是一个比自己好的人,更加有道德观念。所以她一心想着让他来承担理性的刹车角色,万一自己要是控制不住"投怀送抱",他会友善地,带着慈爱之情地克制住她。但是他真的会那样做吗?谢尔碧需要一些空间来思考。需要哈德利在自己的眼前消失一小段时间,不能再让他的脉搏渐渐侵袭到自己的脉搏中来。谢尔碧感受到内心的箭头跳到了红色,警告的标志开始闪烁。

"我要去换衣服了。"她肢体僵硬地从哈德利身边移出狭小的厨房,几乎是跑进了卧室。卧室里的空气让人窒息,因为暖气自动调节到了糖膏的熔融阶段〔译者注:糖果制作的环节之一〕。谢尔碧发现自己脑子里盘绕的都是有关食物的比喻,因为她现在觉得自己就像糖果一样黏腻,汗水使她的头发卷曲蓬乱。就像刚做过爱的样子,她暗自想道。下一秒她又责备了自己的这个想法。她脑海里的对话就以这种方式反复地进行着:先是关于性爱,然后是一顿训斥。因为热得实在难以忍受,她就换上了短裤和背心,然后躺到床上开始读书。直到她意识到自己已经把同一个句子读了五六遍却一点也没有理解的时候,她才觉得自己应该做点别的事了。她想回到起居室里,但是在哈德利的身边待着让她感到不

afraid she was going to reveal her feelings that she would end up almost avoiding him, not looking at him when he spoke to her. Why did too much feeling always ruin things? You could no longer act natural. It was the bite of knowledge, just past the golden moment when you begin to realize that you are excited by someone. That being around them makes you happy. And then it becomes a drug, an addiction. Then you need to be around them to make you happy. When you aren't with them you think about them constantly. Other affections get in your way.

Shelby rolled over and over in their waterbed, trying to figure out why her life was so complicated. Finding a pen and a notebook under the bed, she tried writing, thinking maybe that she could exorcise these traitorous thoughts from her mind, and then they would leave her alone.

I have thoughts, but if I don't completely think them, I can pretend that I never really thought any particular one. It's just a glimmer of an idea hanging out in my brain. I let it stay there and soon I become used to it. I start realizing exactly how many times I've thought that thought. Daydreamed about it. Let it lead me through my day. And I know that the more I think about it, the more reality it comes to be. I'm a doer. I think something and the next thing you know, it's done. I can't stand the pain of wanting something.

I know he is tortured too. He just doesn't show it. Instead he arranges things, spends all his energy on organization. I want to mess with him. Get him dirty. I equate friendship with sex. And how not to? It seems a natural extension to translate camaraderie into carnality. If you really like someone, you'd always wonder what they are like in bed. I go to sleep thinking about Hadley touching me. And I burn. Why does this angst feel so good? Because I simply feel something? Because I can imagine passion so well in my mind that even a ghost of the experience, even a poor second to the real thing is still tangible enough to make me shiver?

Shelby lay back in a kind of stupor, absentmindedly biting her pen, only realizing it when the sharp tang of ink hit her taste buds. Getting up to wash her mouth, she realized that this kind of writing only incited her. It brought things which should remain hidden to the forefront of her mind. She wanted to write something new, something that wouldn't lead her further into this mess. She believed in rotating the crops. She'd heard somewhere that farmers must rotate the crops in order to

安和紧张。因为害怕泄露自己的感情而几乎故意躲避着他,在他跟自己说话时也不敢看他的眼睛。为什么太多的感情总是会把事情给搞砸呢?再也不能表现得像往常一样自然了。这就是知情的一个弊端[译者注:同时暗指伊娃偷食知识禁果],当你开始意识到自己因为某个人而感到兴奋,在他们身边让你觉得幸福时,黄金瞬间就已经逝去了。紧接着,它就变成了一种毒品,让你上瘾。然后,你就被迫需要待在他们身边,保持自己的幸福感。当你们不在一起的时候,会时常想念。其他的感情都成了障碍。

谢尔碧在水床上来来回回地翻着身,努力想搞清楚为什么自己的人生这么复杂。她在枕头下面找到了一支钢笔和笔记本,开始试着写点东西,思忖着写作可以帮助她驱除掉脑子里的这些背叛的想法,自己就不会这么困扰了。

我有很多想法,但是如果我不正面地思考它们,我就可以假装自己从来没有过什么特定的想法。有时候只是一点微光,在大脑边缘闪烁。我就让它在那里待着,不久之后就习惯了。渐渐地我就开始在意起这个想法出现的次数。在白日梦里出现的次数。任由它引领着我度过每一天。而且我深知,想的次数越多,它就越接近现实。我是一个执行者。在我想到一件事情的下一秒,它就已经完成了。我无法忍受渴望某样东西的那种痛苦。

我知道他也备受折磨,他只是没有表现出来而已。相反的,他开始安排事情,把所有的精力都投入一件事情的组织上去。我却想把他搞乱,不让他总是那么一副坐怀不乱的样子。我把友谊和性爱混淆了。要怎么才能不这么做呢?从同志情谊到肉欲的过渡看上去很自然。如果你真的很喜欢一个人,你就会好奇他在床上是什么样子的。入睡的时候我心里想象的是哈德利触碰我的感觉,然后我就觉得自己在燃烧。为什么这种不安让我觉得如此美好呢?仅仅是因为我对他的感觉?还是因为我可以在脑海里把激情都形象化,即使是捕捉不到的经历,即使只是一秒钟的真实体验也能够具体到使我战栗呢?

谢尔碧有些恍惚地半倚在床上,心不在焉地啃着笔,直到墨水的强烈味道刺激到她的味蕾她才反应过来。于是她站起身来去洗嘴巴,同时发现,这样的写作只会更加煽动自己的感情。它把本应深藏的想法都带到了大脑的最前端。她想写点新的东西,一些不会让她在这一团糟中越陷越深的东西。她相信翻转农作物理论。她在哪儿听说过,农夫必须要把农作物给翻转过来,才能补充泥土里的

replenish the nitrogen in the soil. That's how she saw her abilities, like so many crops. She just got worn out in one area and needed to do something completely different, something non-verbal to regain her mind's strength. Something like drinking, she chided herself, realizing that she'd finished her beer. She thought about getting up and getting another one. Then she remembered there was no more beer. Wine then.

She could hear Hadley practicing the drum solo from "Born to Be Wild." Clutching her empty beer bottle in an impassioned grip, Shelby furtively opened her bedroom door and looked through the glass-panes that separated them. Hadley had his eyes closed and so Shelby ventured further, now leaning on the living room door and looking through. Originally she had shaken the tambourine on this song but they made her stop. It wasn't in the best interest of the music, Hadley had joked. She knew she had lousy rhythm. She wondered if it was because he had such a sense of rhythm that she ached for him. She was fascinated by talents she didn't possess. Sometimes his drumming made her heart well up because it was so novel. "What an odd reaction," she thought. "I want him for his drumming. That can't be right."

Finishing the solo, Hadley opened his eyes and put down his drumsticks. Catching sight of Shelby, he tilted his head slightly, obviously wondering why she was watching him.

She opened the door and said, "There's no more beer, but there's wine and tea," marveling at her ability to play cool.

"I'm okay. I've still got half of this one left. You know, I wrote out the solo for 'Green-Eyed Lady'. Did you want to try it?"

"Oh, Hadley." He always thought her a better piano player than she was.

"I kept it simple."

"For this I'll definitely need wine." She disappeared into the kitchen for a moment, then walked into the living room with her glass. Hadley was rummaging through his drum bag. He pulled out a piece of music paper.

"Here it is."

Shelby looked at it and snorted.

"What?" Hadley asked defensively.

氮元素。谢尔碧觉得自己的能力就像那些作物一样。当她在一方面感到疲惫不堪时，就需要去做一件完全不同的事，不需要动嘴皮子，但可以帮她的大脑恢复精力。比如说喝酒，但她立刻责备了自己，并且意识到自己的啤酒已经喝完了。她想起身去再拿一瓶，却想起家里的啤酒都喝完了。那就红酒吧。

　　她能够听见哈德利在排练歌曲《天生疯狂》里的架子鼓独奏，于是偷偷地打开卧室的门，透过隔在他们之间的玻璃门看出去，空啤酒瓶被她紧紧地攥在手里。哈德利排练的时候眼睛是闭着的，于是谢尔碧又大胆地探身出去，倚在了门框上。原本她是准备在这首歌里摇铃鼓的，但是被其他成员给制止了。这对歌曲本身并不是最好的打算，哈德利这样开过玩笑。谢尔碧知道自己的节奏感不好，但她有些好奇，自己是不是因为哈德利的节奏感特别好才那么渴望他。凡是她自己没有的才能，她都为之着迷。有时，哈德利与众不同的演奏会让她的整颗心都为之振奋起来。"多么奇怪的反应啊，"她想，"我是因为他鼓打得好才喜欢他。这不可能。"

　　独奏结束后，哈德利睁开眼睛，把鼓槌放到一边的时候他瞥到了一旁的谢尔碧。于是微微地把头偏向一侧，很显然在好奇为什么谢尔碧在盯着自己看。

　　谢尔碧打开门，镇定地说道："啤酒喝完了，不过还有红酒和茶包。"连她都佩服自己装作若无其事的能力。

　　"我无所谓，我的啤酒还剩一半呢。对了，我把《绿眸女郎》的独奏部分给写出来了，你想试一下吗？"

　　"噢，哈德利。"他总是高估她的钢琴水平。

　　"我没有写很复杂的谱子。"

　　"真得练的话我必须要倒杯红酒。"谢尔碧走进厨房里，消失了一会儿，随即又握着酒杯走了出来。哈德利正在鼓包里面翻找谱子，最终抽出了一张乐谱。

　　"找到了。"

　　谢尔碧看了一眼，气愤地喷了一下鼻息。

　　"怎么了？"哈德利有些警觉地问道。

Chapter Thirteen Addiction

"You like to humiliate me," Shelby said low-voiced, sitting on the back of the sofa and facing him defiantly.

"If I only knew it was that easy." He hit a rim shot.

"These are thirty-second notes! Are you crazy?"

"Those are only sixteenth notes. Three bars would be thirty seconds."

Shelby sighed, dropping the sheet of music and falling backward into the cushions of the sofa so that her feet hung over the back edge, the rest hidden to Hadley. "I just want something to be fun." In her mind she was chanting, now, touch me, pin me down. Her eyes were closed and she imagined him rubbing his hands on her body. A frotteur with only his fingers. Knowing that he couldn't see her, she rubbed her hand slowly down the length of her torso, palm and fingers flat and outstretched so as to enlarge their surface area. Shelby felt so seductive as she fondled herself, a spectrum of sexual cues sent, none received. Pheromones gone undetected.

In the old days she would have just spilled out her feelings from the opposite side of the room, with Emily Dickinson propriety, a business proposition, explaining how much she liked the love interest at hand. She always made it clear of course that the gentleman shouldn't feel any responsibility for liking her back. She would unburden herself, praying that the feeling would be reciprocated, but generally she would make some impassioned confession only to find out that the male in question not only had no idea of her feelings but was quite perturbed by them, and especially that she would be so forward as to tell him. It was hard to know which was worse, knowing the truth and being mortified, or forever believing that there was some unrequited spark between her and another, something that kept her constantly looking for signs. Like she was doing now. Road signs of affection. Smiles, favors, unnecessary touchings. Was it only her imagination? Why did he touch her hand when he took the beer? He could have grabbed the bottle higher up. Why did he come practice today? Even if he did feel something, even if in his mind they made love, would he be so ungentlemanly as to seduce his best friend's wife?

She could only hope.

Sighing, she swung her legs around and scooted up to sit on the arm of the sofa. She listened to him practicing, the snap, crackly, pop sound of the drums making her want to be a drummer.

"What's that cymbal?" she asked, pointing.

"你就喜欢羞辱我。"谢尔碧不满地低声咕哝道,接着她半坐在沙发的背面,一脸不服地对着哈德利。

"我要是早知道羞辱你这么简单就好了。"他打了个擦边球。

"这些是三十二音符的!你疯了吗?"

"只有十六音符而已。三条杠才是三十二音符。"

谢尔碧叹了口气,松开手里的乐谱,身体向后倒向了沙发垫子,只有双脚悬空在沙发背上,其余部分都隐藏在哈德利视线之外。"我只是想让事情变得有趣一点而已。"她的脑海里却一直回荡着"就是现在,抚摸我,按倒我"的声音。她闭上了眼睛,想象着哈德利双手正在抚摸自己的身体。只用手指进行的抚摸。谢尔碧知道哈德利看不见自己,于是就用一只手缓慢地顺着自己的身体抚摸下去,手掌和手指都用力地张开,以加大接触的面积。谢尔碧抚弄着自己的时候觉得自己无比的性感撩人,但在已经发送了这么多的性暗示之后,却一个都没有被哈德利接收。费洛蒙[译者注:雌性激素]弥漫游走,却没有被察觉。

如果是在过去的时代,她早就站在屋子的另一边,以艾米莉·狄金森的风格,一吐自己的心声了,就像提出一项商务提议一样,解释清自己对目前这份感情利息的喜爱程度。当然,艾米莉总是非常清楚地表明,对面的绅士不用对返还这份爱而感到有任何压力。她倾心地诉说,祈祷着这份感情能够得到回应。但是通常情况下,她热切地吐露心声,却发现对面的当事人不但从来没有觉察到这份感情的存在,甚至进而感到困扰,尤其是她竟然主动到了告白的地步。究竟哪一种情况更好,很难判断,是知道真相之后的窘迫无比,还是永远相信自己曾和那一位之间有过互相难以启齿的相思;但后面一种情况会让自己一直不停地寻找暗示。就像谢尔碧现在在做的这样。暗含爱意的征兆:微笑,帮忙,不必要的触碰。这难道仅仅是她的想象吗?哈德利接过啤酒的时候为什么要碰她的手?本可以握住瓶子更高的地方的。为什么今天他会来这里排练?即使他真的有一些感觉,即使他真的幻想过与谢尔碧做爱的情景,他会如此没有绅士风度,引诱自己最好的朋友的妻子吗?

谢尔碧只能在心里暗暗期盼。

她叹了口气,把双腿晃到侧面,起身坐在了沙发的扶手上。听着哈德利的演奏,架子鼓那干脆、爆裂般的击打声,让谢尔碧也有了想成为鼓手的愿望。

"那个镲叫什么名字?"她指着其中一个问道。

He looked to his left. "Crash." His drumstick snapped the cymbal repeatedly. "It sounds like its name. Gets louder every time it's hit. The ride—" he switched to the cymbal on his right "—has a more pinging sound. And it doesn't build." He struck it for a moment, showing her the difference, then broke into his usual catalogue of beats, a drummer's lick library. Shelby listened, feeling the beats on her body. She watched him play, so impressed by his physical skill, the strength needed to drum, the energy he generated with sound. The whipcrack of the rhythm engulfed her, changing the conversation.

She waited until he finished his soliloquy. Then she asked, "Can I bang on your drums for a second?"

"You can play them," Hadley offered, raising one eyebrow.

"I won't break them," Shelby said snidely as Hadley stood up from the drums and moved to the side. "Pussy," she whispered dangerously as she walked past him, feeling his arm graze her own.

"What!" he asked, mock-seriously, turning to her.

The corners of her mouth wouldn't behave. She bit her lip so she wouldn't smirk. Sitting down on the stool and picking up the drumsticks, she said, "Okay, what do I do now?"

Hadley shook his head. "You're holding the sticks all wrong." He took the drumstick out of her left hand. His fingers curved around it knowingly. "Like this. See how the first two fingers go over and the second two under? Here."

He gave her back the stick and she held it the way he had showed her, but it felt really unnatural. She wondered why anyone would hold it in such a convoluted way. It seemed like drumming was hard enough as it was.

He took the right stick out of her hand. It was wet. "You're sweating all over my stick!"

"My hands always sweat." She smiled, embarrassed. It was because he had touched her. Why did the barest glance of his hands send shivers through her body?

"No, hold it farther back," he said. He enclosed her hand with his own, a dry, firm grip, completely unromantic. With his other hand, he slowly tugged the right stick until the notched end of it hung out more over the drum. Grabbing her other hand, he said, "Now, hit the drums in this pattern: right left right right, left right left left." He was leaning over her from behind and guiding the sticks. "Keep

哈德利看向左手边,鼓槌重复地击打着谢尔碧指的那个,"吊镲。它的声音就跟名字一样。每敲一下它的声音就更大一些。至于节奏镲——"他转向右手边的另一个镲,"——声音就更清脆一些。而且它的声音不会叠加。"他又敲了几下,让谢尔碧体会之间的区别,随后便爆发出一系列他擅长的鼓花节奏,这是一个鼓手的入门大全,包含了大部分的鼓花小节。谢尔碧认真地听着,用自己的身体感受着节拍。看着哈德利演奏的样子,她感到钦佩不已,不论是他的技巧、力量,还是鼓声所传达出来的能量。每一个鼓点的鞭音都将谢尔碧吞没,改变了他们俩交流的方式。

一直等到哈德利的独奏结束,她才开口问道:"我能撞几下你的鼓吗?"

"你可以敲一下。"哈德利挑起一边的眉毛,纠正道。

"我不会把它弄坏的。"谢尔碧用挖苦的口气回敬他。这时哈德利已经从凳子上起来,站到了一边。"婆婆妈妈。"谢尔碧经过他身边的时候小声嘀咕道,这样做有些危险,因为她感觉到哈德利的胳膊轻轻擦了一下她自己的。

"你说什么!"他假装严肃地转向谢尔碧。

谢尔碧的嘴角有些不听话,她必须得咬住自己的嘴唇才能不偷笑出来。她坐到鼓凳上,拿起鼓槌,说道:"好的,现在我该怎么做呢?"

哈德利摇着头,"你拿鼓槌的姿势完全错了。"他从谢尔碧的左手里一把抽走鼓槌,俨然专家一样地将手指握在特定的位置。"像这样。看到我的前两根手指是怎么绕过去,后两根手指是怎么在下面的吗?你来试一下。"

谢尔碧接回鼓槌,照着他刚才示范的样子握好,但是却感觉非常不自然。她好奇为什么会有人用这么错综复杂的方式握鼓槌。敲架子鼓本身就已经够难了。

哈德利又把另一根鼓槌从谢尔碧的右手抽出。上面汗水盈盈的。"你的汗把我的鼓槌都弄湿了!"

"我的手本来就总是流汗。"谢尔碧尴尬地笑了。是因为哈德利刚才碰到了她。为什么只是他手的轻轻触碰就让战栗流遍她的全身呢?

"不是的,再往后握一点,"他握住了谢尔碧的一只手,干燥而有力,完全没有浪漫可言。他的另一只手将右鼓槌一点一点地往外拉,直到鼓槌末端的凹口超出鼓面的边缘。他将谢尔碧的左手抓在手里,说道:"现在,按照这样的节奏敲:右左右右,左右左左。"哈德利从谢尔碧的身后向前倾着,指引着她手里的鼓

them loose."

She had no idea that he would decide to teach her, touching her professionally, embracing her in a non-embrace. She had thought that by the time they ever got this close, it would be known, the mystery solved, and she could unleash the wildness in her. Now, with him holding her hands, his back hovering near hers, his heart close, the wildness was straining to escape in an impassioned declaration of love. The word raced through her head like a flash flood, a subliminal message that refused to be sublimated. What could she be thinking? How could she love Hadley? What a mess her life would be. She reined her desire in tighter, thinking that Max could come home any moment, use sense. She wondered if such conflicts of the soul could give a person a heart attack, and she gave renewed energy to the drumming in order to direct her churning emotions.

Hadley laughed as he let go of her hands. "That's called paradiddle."

"No way!" Shelby said nervously. She played the rhythm for a little while, trying to calm herself with the beat, and then said, "Okay, now what?" wanting to see if he would touch her again.

"Now try a flam." He leaned toward her and she tried to steady her breath.

"Why are they such weird names?" she exhaled as his hands slid over hers. This time his shirt hung against her back and she could feel its gauziness slightly tickling her bare shoulder. He had to know. How could he not know? Tell me, damn it. She was softly hyperventilating.

"They seem kinda onomatopoetic to me," he said, pausing a moment in thought. He seemed completely unaware. She wondered if he could feel her pulse surging. Was he oblivious or a great actor? "Try this," he said, guiding the sticks in order to show her another rhythm. One stick he held right next to the drum head without touching the drum's surface and the other stick he held about ten inches higher. "The goal is to have the lower stick hit the drum a split-second before the upper stick does." Hadley demonstrated a couple of times, pulling her right hand down forcefully and hitting the drum with authority.

"That's a flam?" she asked, turning slightly to him, unable to think of anything more intelligent to say, but needing to say something to ground her, afraid of the alternating current running through her body.

"Doesn't it sound like one?" He made her play the thick sound again, a satisfying

槌。"手放松。"

谢尔碧一点也没有预料到,哈德利会决定教自己打鼓,像现在这样带着专业态度的肢体接触,给予她最不像拥抱的拥抱。谢尔碧本来以为,当他们俩已经到了这么接近的程度时,大家就都已经心知肚明了,窗户纸也被捅破了,她也终于可以将自己内心的野性释放出来。而此时此刻,哈德利的手就在她的手上,他的身体笼盖着她的身体,他的心跳如此靠近,谢尔碧心中的狂野正挣扎着想要以热切的爱的名义逃脱束缚。想说的那句话像山洪一样涌向她的脑际,这样一条潜意识里的信息却再也不愿意被隐藏了。她到底在想什么?怎么可以爱上哈德利呢?她的生活会变成一团糟的。于是她又收紧了自己的欲望,想着麦克斯随时都有可能到家,劝自己理智一点。谢尔碧想知道,这种灵魂上的冲突会不会让一个人心脏病发。重振精神之后谢尔碧全身心投入敲鼓中,来理清翻腾不安的思绪。

哈德利大笑着松开了手。"这就是复合跳节奏。"

"你肯定是在安慰我!"谢尔碧紧张地说道。接着她又练了一会儿,试着让节拍使自己镇定下来,然后开口说:"好吧,那么现在呢?"她想知道哈德利会不会再次触碰她。

"现在试一下装饰音节奏。"哈德利又一次俯身过来,谢尔碧努力地平稳着自己的呼吸。

"为什么鼓花的名字都这么奇怪?"哈德利的手滑过她的手时,谢尔碧吐了一口气。这一次哈德利的衬衫垂坠在她的后背,轻薄的面料摩擦在她光滑的肩头,弄得她痒痒的。他一定是知道的。怎么可能不知道呢?告诉我呀,混蛋。谢尔碧有些轻微地换气过度了。

"我觉得它们是拟声词。"哈德利停下来思考了几秒。他看上去完全不知情。谢尔碧好奇地想知道,哈德利能不能感觉到她脉搏的强烈跳动。他是真的没有察觉还是演技超群?"试一下这个。"他握住鼓槌给谢尔碧展示另一种节拍。一支鼓槌放在鼓边,却不接触鼓面,另一支则举在高出鼓面十英寸的位置。"你要做的就是让低一点的鼓槌比高的那根早几分之一秒敲击在鼓面上。"哈德利示范了几次,握着她的右手有力地向下,带着一种权威击打在鼓面上。

"这就是装饰音?"谢尔碧稍微转向哈德利一些,无法想出任何更有意义的话来,却觉得需要说一些什么来使自己镇定下来,因为她害怕那股极不稳定的电流又在她体内奔突。

"难道听上去不像吗?"他又带着谢尔碧奏了一下那个浑厚的声音,那破裂

crunching resonance that sounded somehow patriotic, like the beginning of a march. "And then of course there's flamadiddles," he said playing several, moving her arms faster. Shelby started laughing as her hands suddenly flew over the drums, seemingly on their own accord, the tempo increasing. He had stepped in closer to the stool, his face next to hers, his fists hugging her fingers. "You could do a couple paradiddles, then three flams," he said, doing it, moving her arms like a puppet's. "Or you could do some flamadiddles, some rimshots and then some paradiddles." He began linking the examples together, creating a drum fill that was an index of rhythms and beats: popping and crashing, cymbals rocking, the snare sizzling with repeated strikings. Occasionally he would call out the name of a particular rhythm, knowing how much she liked words. "That's a ruff, like a flam, but with a double beat," he shouted to her, reaching around the stool with his right foot in order to get the bass drum going. His thigh touched hers, and, not being able to stop herself, she imperceptibly moved her leg so that she could feel more of him. They were lap dancing, moving to the beat, unified in motion. She thought she was going to combust like the drummers in *Spinal Tap*, or have a seizure, or simply go for his throat, his lips, his body.

The drumming got wilder, a release for pent-up emotion, a convulsive repercussion that forced their breath in unison, gasps and exhales that made them dizzy. Shelby felt her hands on a roller coaster of movement, sailing over the drums by remote control, playing beats with a mind of their own. Hadley moved even closer during this orgy of noise, and she could now feel his chest touch her back with its own beat, swift and insistent. She felt enfolded by him, protected and exposed at the same time. The rapid-fire snap of the snare cracked back into their faces, exertion reddening their cheeks. No longer thinking, she leaned against him, still laughing uncontrollably, her arms a frenzy of syncopated activity. She tilted her head slightly to look at him and found his face next to hers and suddenly they were kissing and her head was in an awkward position but she didn't notice and his hair was in her eyes and they kissed like they were dying, like they were dreaming, like they were buddy breathing and there was no air left and it was the most heaven she could ever remember, there without oxygen, going down. His mouth tasted like beer, like milk, warm from the mouth of a baby, sour and sweet and tender. His tongue was soft and prickly both, reminding her of the sticky tentacles of a sea anemone or the fleshy part of a plum, or even the sting of honey. They were of one mind and that was to succumb to gravity, to be the

般的回音让人感到满意,与行军乐的开头很像,因此带有了爱国旋律的意味。"接下来当然就是装饰音复合跳了。"哈德利引着谢尔碧的胳膊更加快速地移动起来,又打出了几个节拍。谢尔碧看见自己的双手突然在架子鼓间飞舞,就像达成了某个协议一般,速度也越来越快,她不由自主地大笑起来。哈德利这时已经向凳子走近了一些,脸与谢尔碧的脸齐平,双手则呈握拳状将谢尔碧的手指攥在掌心。"你可以先敲几次复合跳,然后再加三个装饰音。"说着他又做起了示范,像对待木偶那样移动着谢尔碧的胳膊。"或者你可以敲一些装饰音复合跳,再加一些鼓边敲击,最后再来点复合跳。"他开始把这些例子给结合起来,编成一个鼓花组合,起到韵律和节奏的索引作用:咚咚,锵锵,伴随着重复的击打,镲剧烈地抖动着,小军鼓也间断地发出"砰砰"声。他知道谢尔碧有多么喜欢研究单词,所以偶尔也会把某个特殊节奏的名字拿出来说。"这是一个双拍装饰音,和装饰音很像,但是是双拍。"他大声地向谢尔碧解释着,为了让低音鼓继续发声,他将右脚从凳子的一侧向前伸去。哈德利的大腿触碰到了谢尔碧的大腿,谢尔碧也变得无法控制自己,将自己的大腿难以察觉地向外移动了一些,这样她就可以感受到哈德利更多的触碰。他们的双腿在进行一场缠绵的舞蹈,跟随着节奏,动作统一。谢尔碧满心觉得自己就要像电影《摇滚万万岁》里的鼓手一样燃烧起来了,或者是突发心脏病,抑或索性奔向哈德利的喉咙、嘴唇,还有身体。

鼓声越来越疯狂,这对于压抑的情感来说是一种释放,带来了痉挛一般的副作用,使得他们的呼吸都变得一致,大口地吸气、吐气令他们有些晕眩。谢尔碧感到自己的双手就像乘坐过山车一般在鼓间漂移,仿佛受遥控器指挥似的奏出有自己思想的旋律。随着这狂欢一般的噪音,哈德利靠得更近了,谢尔碧能够感觉到他的胸膛正俯在自己的后背,带着它独有的节奏,迅敏而坚定。谢尔碧觉得自己被他给环在怀里,被保护的同时也完全暴露出来。急速干脆的小军鼓声迎面扑来,他们筋疲力尽,面颊绯红。谢尔碧已经放弃了思考,倚在哈德利身上,仍然不可抑制地咯咯笑着,两只胳膊疯狂地在空中上下甩动着。谢尔碧想微微将头侧过去看一眼哈德利,却发现他的头就在旁边。突然之间,他们就在接吻了,谢尔碧的头位置很奇怪,哈德利的头发垂在她的眼睛上,但是她也不在意。他们就那样亲吻着,仿佛下一秒就会死去,仿佛陷入了梦境,仿佛在共同呼吸,没有任何的空气残留。这是谢尔碧能记起的最像天堂的状态,没有氧气,一直下沉。哈德利的嘴尝起来像啤酒,又像牛奶,如同婴儿的双唇一样温暖,酸与甜在柔软中夹杂。他的舌头既温柔又有些扎人,使谢尔碧想起海葵那黏糊糊的触角,或是成熟李子多汁的那部分,甚至是蜜蜂尾后的那根蜇针。他们当时心里都只有一个念

other. They couldn't have not kissed, even if they'd wanted to.

They broke for sanity, for air; morality suddenly pushed its ugly way between them. Shelby hated being so conscious; Hadley, so unconscious. He leaned back, breathing hard, unable to move, his hands still clenched over Shelby's. Then he got a hold of himself and let go, moving safely away. The expression on his face pinned her heart. The word "smitten" surfaced in her brain. She felt smited. Cleaved. Her head lifted on its own accord. Baring her neck. Shelby stayed this way, her breath coming in quick hiccuping gasps. Hadley walked over to the sofa.

"I'd better be going."

"I need you."

"Please. Don't say that." Hadley closed his eyes. "I lost my head. We can't let it happen again." He went over and picked up his jacket off the long window seat.

The front door opened. They both jumped. Shelby sat down and started playing flams loudly on the drums.

"What's all that racket?" Max yelled from the front door. He peered into the living room. "Jesus. I was afraid Hadley was playing and I thought, 'Oh, God, he must be sick!'"

"Thanks a lot!" yelled Shelby, still drumming. "I'm playing flams." The noise allowed her to get her breathing back to normal.

Hadley moved into Max's view.

"Oh!" Max said, turning toward Hadley, somewhat embarrassed. "I didn't even realize you were here." Max quickly turned back toward the drum set. "Shelby! Could you stop that, maybe? I think those drums are getting a headache."

Hadley grimaced slightly and Max grinned at him. Shelby put the drumsticks in the drum bag, taking her time.

"I gotta go." Hadley nodded to Max and left quickly. Max and Shelby heard the front door close.

Max said, "He really didn't seem like he was feeling too well."

"Yeah, I duh know."

Max looked at Shelby curiously. "Did you guys have a fight?"

Shelby looked up at him and said, "I don't think he was too happy about me playing his drums."

头,那就是屈服于地球的引力,与对方融为一体。即使他们都那么尽力地克制,这一切还是不可抑制地发生了。

因为理智的阻止,还有空气的稀缺,他们松开了对方;道德突然在他们中间劈开了一条丑陋的隙墟。谢尔碧讨厌自己总是这么清醒,而哈德利却是一直迷迷糊糊的样子。他向后退了一步,喘着粗气,没法再动一步,但他的手仍然紧紧地握着谢尔碧的手。过了一会儿他缓过神来,松开手,小心地站开一些。哈德利脸上的表情将谢尔碧的心钉在原地,"重击"这个词从她脑海里冒出来。她觉得自己被重重一击。被劈成两半。她的头不由自主地仰了起来,支撑着自己的脖子。她就这样一直保持着这个姿势,急促地像打嗝般地喘着气。哈德利则向沙发走去。

"我最好现在离开。"

"我需要你。"

"拜托了,别这样说。"哈德利闭上了眼睛。"我刚才失去理智了。我们不能让这样的事再发生了。"他走到靠窗的长椅旁拿起了自己的外套。

这时前门被打开了。他们两个都慌了神。谢尔碧坐下来,开始大声地敲装饰音节奏。

"这吵吵嚷嚷的是怎么回事?"麦克斯一跨进门就大叫起来。接着他把头探进起居室里来张望。"天哪。我正担心着是哈德利敲的鼓,我还想着,'哦,完了,他肯定是生病了!'"

"多谢夸奖!"谢尔碧一边吼着,一边继续挥舞着手里的鼓槌。"我正在敲装饰音呢。"巨大的鼓声让她有机会将自己的呼吸恢复到正常状态。

这时候哈德利走进了麦克斯的视线里。

"噢!"麦克斯转向他,有些尴尬。"我都没有意识到你也在这儿。"他又迅速地转过身去。"谢尔碧!或许你能停下来吗?我估摸着,那些鼓都觉得头疼了。"

哈德利微微地扯了一下嘴角,麦克斯也咧开嘴笑起来。谢尔碧便慢腾腾地把鼓槌放进鼓包里。

"我得走了。"哈德利对麦克斯点了点头就迅速地离开了。麦克斯和谢尔碧听到了前门关上的声音。

麦克斯随后说道:"看上去他真的身体不舒服。"

"可能吧,我不知道。"

麦克斯怀疑地盯着她。"你们俩是不是吵架了?"

谢尔碧抬起头看着他。"我敲他的鼓,他可能不太高兴。"

Chapter Fourteen Chirality

Chiral: Of or pertaining to the handedness or chirality of an asymmetric molecule. [Greek kheir, hand.]

The Tormont Webster's Illustrated Encyclopedic Dictionary

Syn. mirror image.

Max Carter

The only sensible reason for living in New York is if one suffers from a chronic fear of being alone. "Ermitophobia" Roget's calls it. They take the "h" off of hermit, add it to "ophobia" and try to pass it off as Greek.

Shelby was sitting in the chemistry office using the secretary's computer, trying to waste time while pretending she was writing. She could squander hours just thumbing through the thesaurus. Shelby had looked up phobias for a reason she couldn't now remember, and along with ermitophobia she found some other great alltime fears.

"Helmintophobia" is the fear of worms, "bacillophobia" the fear of microbes, "blennophobia", the fear of slime, and "albuminurophobia" is—yes, you guessed it—the fear of albumin in one's urine.

Shelby was feeling edgy, going crazy with desire and guilt. So she was trying to write a funny story about how much she hated New York, wanting to work "ermitophobia" in somewhere. Anything to get Hadley off her mind.

New York was a good topic to distract her. To put her energies toward anger and hate. Something she could live with.

New York is the kind of town where merchandise is so precious that they have to tie the garbage can lids down, yet you could equip your apartment quite fashionably with furniture found on the sidewalk. (Shelby once overheard a woman brag to another that she'd found a barber chair in perfect condition. "The hydraulics

第十四章　手征性

　　手征的：属于或关于不对称分子的偏手性或手征性。［希腊语中 kheir 意为"手"。］

——《托尔蒙特韦氏图解百科词典》

　　近义词：镜像。

——麦克斯·卡特

　　如果一个人选择住在纽约，唯一合理的原因就是他对孤独有慢性恐惧。《罗热分类词典》中收录了"Ermitophobia"（孤独恐惧症）这个词。将"隐士"（hermit）中的"h"去掉，加到"ophobia"前面，试图冒充成希腊语。

　　谢尔碧坐在化学大楼的办公室里，佯装写作的样子，其实是在用秘书的电脑打发时间。仅仅是不停地点开，浏览分类词库里的每一个词条，她就可以挥霍掉好几个小时。谢尔碧正搜索着各种以"phobia"结尾的单词，但却不记得起初自己为什么要这样做了，除了"孤独恐惧症"之外，她还发现了一些绝佳的恐惧症。

　　"Helmintophobia"是对蠕虫的恐惧，"bacillophobia"是对微生物的恐惧，"blennophobia"是对黏液的恐惧，还有"albuminurophobia"是——对，你猜对了——是对人尿液中的白蛋白的恐惧。

　　谢尔碧开始变得有些烦躁，欲望和愧疚将她推向疯狂的边缘。她打算写一个诙谐故事，讲述自己有多么讨厌纽约，把"ermitophobia"这个词也穿插其中。任何能把哈德利从她脑子里赶走的事情她都要试一下。

　　要想分散谢尔碧的注意力，纽约是一个很好的话题。把她的精力转向愤怒和厌恶。一些她还能够忍受的东西。

　　在纽约这座城市，物价高到了人们连垃圾桶盖都要锁起来的程度，可是用从人行道上捡来的家具，你照样可以把自己的公寓装扮得非常时髦。（有一次谢尔碧听到一个女人向别人炫耀说，自己捡到了一把完好无损的理发椅子。"液

even work!")

New York is a test to newcomers daring to enter the dangerous waters of unintelligible dialect and atrocious fabrication. Without blinking an eye New Yorkers can reverse everything that they have just said. Pressing them solves nothing. Digging makes them lie more outrageously. But bribing them suddenly slides the answer from their lips and finally they show you the apartment that didn't exist, or seat you at a table reserved for eighteen, all with an obsequious manner as if you were their closest friend.

In New York no one knows how to make a singlefile line. This stems not from an ignorance of basic mathematical principles, but from the fact that New York is the only true anarchy in existence. People have no conscience that tells them whoever gets to the movie theater first by rights should enter first and get the best seats. Their logic tells them that everyone is going to make a mad rush for the door, and every man for himself (including the women and children).

"In New York you can do whatever you want until someone comes along and tells you not to and then you just wait till they go away," Max always said. His plan for their last night in New York was to put all their furniture out into the street, piss on it, and leave it there. Who would stop them? Max was always so emphatic about everything, and hating New York was no different. Shelby remembered what Hadley had said, about her hating New York because Max did. He was probably right. Sometimes Shelby felt that she became whoever she hung around with, switching personality traits like clothing. It was the ultimate in empathy. Or perhaps it was just easy. You didn't have to invest time in your own beliefs.

She felt herself pulled between Max and Hadley these days, caring for them both and wondering why a person couldn't be in love with two people and that be okay. It seemed that the world was so small and petty not to allow for such complexity. Then it occurred to her that the world was not her major obstacle.

A feeling of despair settled between her shoulder blades like an ache from a strained muscle. No matter how much she changed her position, no matter how much she wrote, it stayed right with her, a kind of longing for something she couldn't have. It was a breathless feeling, as if the dissonance caused her to be without air. She felt anxious, wanting to punch something, knowing that aggression wouldn't give her relief but might exhaust her into oblivion. Shelby searched her purse, trying to

压升降装置还是管用的呢!")

对初来乍到者来说,纽约是一项测试。他们不顾这片危险水域里的晦涩方言和恶意捏造,勇敢地涉足其中。眨眼之间,纽约客们就可能把刚才说过的话反着再说一遍。给他们施压不能够解决任何问题。追问只会让他们更加肆无忌惮地撒谎。但是贿赂则会使答案脱口而出,最终他们会带你去看一座并不存在的公寓,或者把你领向一个能坐十八个人的饭桌,席上所有人都语态逢迎,就好像你是他们最亲近的朋友一般。

在纽约,没人知道怎么排成一队。之所以会这样并不是因为他们缺乏基础的数学理论,而是基于纽约是当今社会上唯一一处于无政府状态的城市这一事实。对于先到达电影院的人就应该先进入,并且选择好的座位这件事,他们的良知并不赞同。他们脑子里的逻辑是这样的:每个人都会发疯似的向门口冲去,人人为己(包括女人和孩子)。

麦克斯总是说,"在纽约你可以想做什么就做什么,直到有人来告诉你不可以这样做,而你只需要等到他们离开就行了。"他对他们在纽约待的最后一晚是这样打算的:把所有的家具都拖到街上,在上面撒尿,然后留在那里给别人。有谁会阻止他们呢?不论对待什么事,麦克斯的态度总是坚决明确,讨厌纽约这件事也不例外。谢尔碧想起了哈德利说过的话,他说她恨纽约是因为麦克斯恨纽约。他很有可能是对的。有时,谢尔碧觉得,跟谁在一起的时候,她就会变得更像那个人,变换自己的性格特点就像换衣服一样。这是同理心的最高状态。又或许只是因为这样做很容易,不用花费时间经营自己的信仰。

这阵子,谢尔碧觉得自己在麦克斯和哈德利之间挣扎。她对他们俩都很在意,可是想不通为什么一个人不可以爱上两个人,而又让大家都可以接受。如果连这种复杂性都包容不了,世界真的显得很渺小而琐碎。但她突然意识到,世界并不是她最大的障碍。

一阵绝望感攫住了她的肩胛骨,就像肌肉拉伤一般的疼痛。无论她如何改变姿势,多么投入地写作,那种感觉总是挥之不去——那种对得不到的东西的渴望。她感到窒息,仿佛这种失调让她无法呼吸。又一阵焦虑感袭来,她想对着什么挥拳,因为虽然暴力不会让她放松,但却可能使她疲惫到将这一切都抛诸脑后。谢尔碧开始在包里翻找,试图回忆自己有没有藏大麻在里面,或者是抽剩的

remember if she'd stashed any pot, any loose roaches, perhaps in a pill bottle. Finding nothing, she threw her purse on the floor beside the desk, knowing she was being childish but not caring because the place was empty. Pot was her sedative. It was the only way she knew how to cope with the realization that she loved Hadley and didn't love Max. No, that wasn't true. She really did love Max, it was just that they didn't have fun together any more. Every moment felt like an effort, constantly trying not to get on each others' nerves. Marriage was too much work. When they'd first moved to New York, life had been more magical. They used to give each other silly little presents, a rock shaped like lips, a TLC plate spotted with repeating hearts down its white chalky surface, or sometimes one of them would hide a tiny stuffed animal in odd places like the refrigerator or the bathtub so that one would think of the other and laugh. They'd been so goofy then. When had it stopped?

Shelby remembered one of those first days in New York, a year ago early fall, the weather warm and coddling. She had been lavish with her free time. Going to the Cloisters and singing in untouristed hallways or eating lunch at Grand Central, a vaulted cathedral of transit where you could sit in a restaurant above it all and watch people late for their trains, happy that you had no place to go. On a leisurely walk through her new neighborhood, she had wandered onto the university campus, sitting down near a stone fountain, feeling happy with her life. A true Californian, weather could do that to her. As twilight approached, she started seeing little flashes of green neon. She'd only ever heard about fireflies but had never seen them. They were a spectacle of nature, a seemingly modern insect fit for a stream-lined world, a world full of phosphorescence, holograms, and hallucinogens. She had wanted to catch one and take it home to Max, but it wasn't easy because their lights would illuminate in fits and starts, a kind of insect Morse code. Shelby finally managed to cup one in her hands, carefully spreading two fingers apart to see the little insect. Its tail had glowed wanly, an ugly creature made brilliant by light. She had decided she would show Max and then set it free. She only wanted to borrow its radiance for a moment.

"Look what I caught!" Shelby had yelled excitedly, finding Max in the bathtub and immediately turning out the bathroom light.

"Now how am I going to see it with the lights out?"

烟卷,也许藏在药瓶里面。一无所获的谢尔碧索性把包扔到桌旁的地板上,她知道自己在耍性子,但是四周没人,她也用不着在乎。大麻是她的镇静剂。要应对她爱着哈德利却不爱麦克斯的现实,这是她知道的唯一方法。不,不是这样的。她是爱麦克斯的,只是他们在一起时不再像从前那样充满乐趣了。每一分每一秒都需要很努力,两个人都小心翼翼地不去挑起对方的不快。婚姻需要付出的太多了。起初他们刚搬到纽约的时候,生活可比现在迷人多了。他们会互送愚蠢的小礼物。形状像嘴唇的石头,布满了心形图案的白垩质地的薄层色谱分析板;有时他们会藏一个小小的毛绒玩具在冰箱或者浴缸里,这样他们看到时就会想起对方,并且开怀大笑起来。那时他们脑子里满是这些滑稽有趣的点子。这一切是从什么时候开始停止的?

　　谢尔碧还记得刚到纽约的时候是一年以前的初秋,天气温和,似文火煨煮。她奢侈地挥霍着自己的闲余时间:去修道院博物馆参观,在游人稀少的回廊上唱歌,或是去中央车站吃午饭——那是有着拱顶设计的运输界的大教堂。选择一家高处的餐厅坐下,看着下面那些没有赶上火车的人,为自己不用赶去任何地方而感到高兴。有一次谢尔碧在新家附近散步,无意中逛进了一所大学校园,在石头喷泉的旁边坐下时,她对自己的生活感到非常满意。她成了一个真正的加州人,好天气帮了她很大的忙。暮色渐浓,谢尔碧眼前开始慢慢出现星星点点的绿色霓虹光。在那之前她只听说过萤火虫,但从来没亲眼见过。它们是大自然的奇观,这种看上去具有现代化气息的昆虫,在这个充满磷光、全息图和致幻剂的流水线世界里生存了下来。谢尔碧想要抓一只带回家给麦克斯,但却不是很容易,因为它们总是无规律地忽明忽暗,就像某种昆虫界的摩斯密码。最后谢尔碧终于成功地用双手网住了一只,十分小心地张开两根手指向里张望着。它的尾巴仍然在微弱地闪烁着,这只丑陋的生物因为发光而变得熠熠生辉。谢尔碧决定了,在给麦克斯看过之后就将它放生。她只是想把它的光辉借来用一会儿。

　　"快看我抓住了什么!"谢尔碧兴奋地大叫着进了房间,发现麦克斯正站在浴缸里,她立刻就把灯给关掉了。

　　"你把灯熄了我要怎么看呢?"

Chapter Fourteen Chirality

"Ssh!" Shelby had said, opening her sweaty hands like an offering. Nothing happened. The insect did not glow. Shelby peered closely. It didn't seem to be moving. "Shit!" she said under her breath.

"What is that?" Max had asked, moving out of the shower's spray and peering into Shelby's hands. The light from the bedroom shone somewhat into the bathroom and he could make out the insect on her palm. "Looks like some kind of beetle."

"It was a firefly," Shelby said in a sad, little-kid voice, "but I think maybe it's dead." She poked at the insect with one hand and it fell over. "I wanted to show you. It was beautiful. They were all flying around, glowing like the Pirates of the Caribbean." She felt unreasonably bad that she had killed the firefly. It seemed like a sacrilege of nature's creativity, like she had needlessly lessened one light of Mother Earth. She often thought in such grandiose terms.

Shelby gently brushed the firefly into the garbage, some of its greenish powder adhering to her hands. She turned the light back on and looked at the dusting of green. The viridescent powder reminded her of a newspaper story she'd read a long time ago about an abandoned hospital in South America where the townspeople had broken in and found some kind of X-ray machine. In the machine they found a glowing piece of Cesium, highly radioactive. But it was a beautiful blue-green color and so they took it home. To these uneducated people, this glowing ball of dust was a magical talisman. A little girl adorned herself with it, rubbing it all over her body. Many people took pieces of it for good luck. Everyone in the town was exposed. The whole area was quarantined. The next day the little girl died. Shelby felt as they must have: how could something so beautiful end so badly?

"Max," Shelby had said, kneeling on the floor beside the tub. "See this green stuff from the firefly? What is it? Is it bad for you?"

"Nyah," Max had said, in his flat nasal way. "It's luciferin."

"Is that on the Periodic Table?"

"No. It's a pretty complex organic compound. It's gotta couple of amino acids. When it oxidizes, it gives off heatless light. Fireflies and certain fish produce it."

"Luciferin," Shelby had said slowly. "Like Lucifer."

Shelby stopped daydreaming and searched her purse one more time for pot. All she could find were matches from the Lunar Room. They were in a black box with fluorescent green writing. She slid open the box, looking at the glow-in-the-dark

"嘘!"谢尔碧张开了有些汗湿的手,就像在献宝。结果什么事情都没有发生。那个小虫子没有在发光。谢尔碧仔细地盯着它观察了一会儿。似乎一动不动了。"该死的!"她低声咒骂着。

"那是什么?"麦克斯从花洒的下面走出来,往谢尔碧的手里看去。卧室里的灯光隐约洒进了浴室里,所以他可以勉强辨认出谢尔碧手掌里的虫子。"看上去像是某种甲壳虫。"

"是萤火虫,"谢尔碧的语气像个小孩子一样的悲伤,"但我想它可能死掉了。"她用另一只手拨弄了那个虫子,它被翻了过来。"我本来想给你看的。它们成群结队地飞着,发光的时候就像加勒比的幽灵海盗船一样,美极了。"谢尔碧觉得是自己杀了这只萤火虫,感到非常悲伤。这似乎是一种对大自然创造力的亵渎,就好像她做了不该做的事,捻灭了地球母亲的一盏灯。她脑子里经常有这种高尚宏大的想法。

谢尔碧轻轻地把萤火虫拂到垃圾桶里,手上还残留着一些绿色的荧光粉末。她又重新打开灯,凝视着掌心零星的绿色粉尘,想起了很久之前在报纸上读过的一个故事:在美国南部有一所废弃了的医院,当地镇上的居民们闯进去之后发现了一台 X 射线扫描仪。在仪器里面他们找到了一块发荧光的铯,具有极强的放射性。但是那块金属看上去是非常漂亮的蓝绿色,所以大家就把它给带回家了。对于那些没有受过教育的人来说,这个闪烁着光芒的粉尘球是一个神奇的护身符。有一个小女孩用它来打扮自己,浑身上下都抹了一遍。很多人都取了一小片以求好运。镇上的所有人都被辐射了。整个区域都被封锁了起来。第二天那个小女孩儿就死了。谢尔碧现在的心情他们当时肯定也经历过:如此美丽的东西怎么会有这么悲惨的结局呢?

"麦克斯,"谢尔碧屈膝半跪在浴缸的旁边,"看到萤火虫留下来的这个绿莹莹的东西了吗?这是什么物质?对人体有害吗?"

"才不会呢,"麦克斯带着扁平的鼻音回答着,"这只是虫荧光素而已。"

"在元素周期表上吗?"

"不在。它是一种比较复杂的有机化合物,包含了几种氨基酸。它在氧化的时候,就会散发出没有热量的光。萤火虫和某些鱼类都可以发出这种光。"

"虫荧光剂(luciferin),"谢尔碧慢慢地念叨了一遍,"就像撒旦(lucifer)的发音。"

谢尔碧停下自己的白日梦,又开始在包里搜索大麻。可唯一的收获就是月坊酒吧的火柴,装在写有荧光绿字体的黑色盒子里。她打开盒子,看着在黑暗中

matches, wanting to light them, to smell the smell of fresh match. She did light one, letting it burn in her hand for a moment, trying to get stoned on the fumes of what she had at hand, calmed by the creation of fire. It occurred to Shelby that, similar to fire and brimstone, misunderstood aspects of nature have always been equated with the devil. It was a good excuse for ignorance. But today there was no excuse. You can't blame your inability to understand the world on anyone but yourself. You have to face up to the fact that you're just stupid, that the modern world has zipped by you, and the evils of the past are now the money-making ventures of the future.

It just didn't seem fair. The rules had changed. Femininity had always been positively correspondent with stupidity and liberal arts, but now female civil engineers and lawyers were the sexiest. Shelby's generation at least was better off than her mother's, but she still felt useless in the world of commerce and science, slightly suspicious of female chemists who were her age. How did they get so smart? How had they known that chemistry would be a hot field for women now? To boast of a woman chemist on one's faculty made up for all the chauvinism that had gone before. And you got extra points if she had large breasts.

Shelby looked sadly at the computer screen, realizing that she always became so feminist, so reactionary when it came to viewing her life, as if shifting it to a political arena would justify past decisions. But was laying the blame on the culture really going to help her? Was it going to make her messed up life any easier to handle? She felt so sad, too numb to write anymore. Shutting down the computer, Shelby looked around the office for any smoldering matches, and left.

Walking home in the dark, she wondered if she should try harder with Max. She should, but the effort seemed monumental, and she felt so tired. They never talked these days, other than the "What do you want for dinner" variety. Maybe she should let him explain chemistry to her more. He liked to do that, but she sometimes had such a low tolerance for excess information. Especially after a grueling day of telegrams. And it was seldom reciprocal. What could she explain to him? How to hit a monkey? She couldn't even do that right.

Shelby had a rule that people could talk chemistry around her (because really, how could she stop them?), but they had to answer any questions she had, no matter how stupid. This worked okay because most of the chemists she knew were

夜光的火柴,想把它们给点着,闻一闻新烧火柴的味道。她真的就点燃了一根,捏在手里烧了一会儿,试图用飘出来的烟麻醉自己,火苗的存在让她感到安心。谢尔碧突然想起,就像火和硫黄[译者注:fire and brimstone 英语中意为"地狱之火"]一样,一直以来,人们将自然界中所有他们不能理解的事物都与邪恶等同起来。这是用来掩饰无知的一个好借口,但是在现代社会这样的理由却再也不成立了。一个人没有能力理解周围的世界,只能怪自己。你得接受自己愚蠢的事实,意识到现代社会正从你的身边飞速经过,而过去被定义为"邪恶"的种种,在未来不断的探索中,将成为获利的良器。

真是不公平。法则已经改变了:长久以来女性都被与愚蠢和文科积极地联系起来,但是如今女性土木工程师和女律师才是最性感的。至少谢尔碧这一辈比上一辈已经进步了很多,可是在这个商业和科学占主导的社会上,她仍然觉得自己毫无用处。她甚至有点怀疑与她同龄的女化学家——她们到底是怎么变得这么聪明的?又是如何预测到女性在化学界会变得像现在这么吃香的?吹嘘自己的研究组里有女化学家这件事弥补了以往的种种大男子主义现象,要是她胸部丰满的话更是有额外加分。

谢尔碧低落地盯着电脑屏幕,她发现每当自己审视生活时,最终的结论总是这么充满女权主义色彩和反动因素,仿佛把问题转移到政治立场来看就能使过去的决定变得合理似的。但是,把责任都推到文化问题上真的能帮到她吗?真的可以让她混乱的生活变得更容易控制一些?她悲伤得有些麻木了,无法再写下去。关掉电脑后,谢尔碧扫视了办公室一圈,确定没有闷燃的火柴之后,就离开了。

天色昏暗,谢尔碧走在回家的路上,思考着自己是不是应该更努力地与麦克斯相处。她应该这样做,但为此要付出的努力看上去却极其繁重,而她却感到如此疲惫。这几天,除了"你晚饭吃什么"之类的话,他们都没有聊过天。也许她应该多问他一些关于化学的问题。麦克斯喜欢给谢尔碧解释这些,可有时候过量的信息会让她无法忍受,尤其是在结束了一天令人筋疲力尽的唱歌电报之后。况且,这种信息的传递通常不是相互的。她能给他讲解什么呢?怎么敲打一只猴子玩具?连这个她甚至都做不到。

谢尔碧有个规矩,就是你可以在她身边讨论化学问题(因为想想也知道,她怎么可能阻止得了那些化学家呢?),但必须得回答她所有的疑问,无论它们有多愚蠢。这条规矩执行得还算顺利,因为她认识的大部分化学家都非常好为人

incredibly didactic. They loved to pontificate. And to explain the subtle and complex processes of chemistry to a layperson had the same kind of a thrill that a novice priest might feel at a benediction. Around here, talking chemistry was the only way to be part of the conversation. Sometimes, in the midst of conversation, she would dazzle other chemists, who would exclaim surprise when she would say, "A carbon carbon double-bond, that's an olefin, right?" Or "Would that be a Claisen rearrangement?" Of course, she only had about three of these, like you would in any foreign country, "Cerveza, por favor" "Poo ina toileta" "Voulez vous coucher avec moi ce soir?", key phrases you could spew to impress the natives.

"I'm in here," Max yelled from the bathroom as she let the front door slam. Ever since their bathroom had been "remantled" (that was how Max described it), Max spent more time in there, as if to make up for the loss. "Jesus, he lives in there," Shelby thought to herself, and then felt petty.

"Just a sec," Shelby yelled, and then immediately headed for the bong. Walking with it, she dropped her purse on the living room sofa and took a couple of long hits. It made her instantly relax, though possibly it was due more to the placebic ritual than the actual inhalation of the drug. As she felt the ooze of marijuana flow into her gray matter, making her, she believed, a nicer person, Shelby brought the bong and the baggie of pot into the bathroom and sat on the toilet seat cover. Max was laying back in a half-filled tub of water with the shower pouring on him.

Shelby asked, "So, what was the funniest thing that happened today?" and took another hit. Asking Max the funniest thing was her stock question. That and "What did you have for lunch?" It was an easy way to start conversation. She knew her only real interests were food and things that made her laugh.

Max thought for a moment as he scratched his leg and then lay back in the tub against a white bath pillow. He chuckled suddenly. "I was in the room next to the NMR, where the other computer is? There's a coffee maker in there. Rahda comes in, pours herself a fucking pint of coffee and then takes a bottle of Mylanta that's sitting up next to the sugar and pours it into her coffee!" Max started laughing at the memory.

"Like milk?" Shelby said tightly, trying to hold the smoke in her lungs. "Yuck!"

师。他们喜欢滔滔不绝。他们给一个外行人解释微妙复杂的化学过程,与一个新上任的牧师可能在祈福仪式上体会到的兴奋感一样。在这个社交圈里,谈论化学是能加入谈话的唯一方法。有时,在某段对话当中,谢尔碧的问题会让其他化学家感到出其不意,诸如,"只具有碳碳双键就是烯烃,对吧?"或者是"它们会进行克莱森重组吗?"当然了,像这么专业的问题她大概只有三个,就好像去任何国家旅游时会的那三句一样,"麻烦你,我要啤酒(西班牙语 Cerveza, por favor)","洗手间在哪儿?(希腊语 Poo ina toileta)","你愿意今晚与我共度吗?(法语 Voulez vous coucher avec moi ce soir?)",一些你可以脱口而出让当地人刮目相看的短句。

"我在里面。"谢尔碧松手让前门"砰"的一声关上时,麦克斯的叫声从浴室里传来。自从他们的浴室被"重新换了一层皮"(麦克斯的话)之后,他在里面待的时间更长了,就好像是为了弥补维修期间的损失。"上帝啊,他简直就是在浴室里定居了。"谢尔碧心里嘀咕着,但又觉得自己计较得太琐碎了。

"一会就去。"谢尔碧回吼了一声,然后径直向水烟枪走去。为了举着它边走边抽,谢尔碧把包扔在了起居室的沙发上,深深地嘬了几口。顿时谢尔碧就放松了下来,尽管也许更多的是因为这个习惯带来的心里安慰作用,而不是真正吸入大麻的效果。当她感觉到大麻开始慢慢渗透飘散进自己的脑组织时,她相信自己因此而变得更友善了一些,于是就拿着水烟枪和一小袋烟叶走进了浴室,坐在了马桶盖上。麦克斯正躺在半满的浴缸里,花洒的水淋在他的身上。

谢尔碧开口问道:"那么,今天发生的最有趣的事是什么?"接着她又抽了一口。这个问题是谢尔碧的常用储备之一,还有就是"你中午吃了什么?"这样很容易就可以开始一段对话。她真正的兴趣其实只有食物以及能使她发笑的事物。

麦克斯挠了挠大腿,向后倚在了一个白色的浴枕上,思忖着该怎么回答这个问题。突然,他自顾地笑出声来,"我当时正在核磁共振分析室旁边的房间里,就是另一台电脑所在的那个房间吧?那里有一台咖啡机。拉达走了进来,给自己倒了一杯该死的咖啡,然后拿起砂糖旁边那瓶胃能达口服液倒进了自己的咖啡里!"麦克斯被自己的回忆逗地大笑起来。

"像牛奶那样?"因为想要留住肺里的水烟,她问得很短促。"真恶心!"

"I think she thought it was Mylanta Coffeemate."

Shelby started laughing and then she started coughing and lost her hit. "Did she say anything?"

"Well, I don't think she realized I was there. But when she turned around, she mumbled something about her stomach and I said, 'Well, that coffee'll fix you right up.'"

Max and Shelby both started laughing again. Shelby felt better, at ease, happy that they were still able to enjoy one another. Why couldn't they be like this all the time? Why did it help when she smoked pot?

"Now that I think about it, she must be having some serious stomach problems." She went to the doctor the other day and he prescribed this new prostaglandin compound.

"What is it?"

"Part of the Arachidonic Acid Cascade."

"No, I mean what does it do?"

"Thickens your mucous."

"Egh." Shelby paused and took another hit. "What's it part of?"

"The Arachidonic Acid Cascade. It's a metabolic pathway in your body."

"What a strange name. 'Arachidonic Acid'."

"It's because it spreads out like a web. One chemical turns into two, they turn into four, etc."

"Hmm." Shelby was exhaling another hit. "Hmm." She said the cascade's name aloud a couple more times, stressing different syllables.

Max laughed. "You're stoned."

She looked at him pointedly. "So?" Putting the bong down and cracking her neck, Shelby asked, "Okay, so what was the most interesting thing that happened today?"

Max thought for a second. "That was it." He shrugged.

"Didn't you discover anything?"

"Oh, Bineet told me something interesting. He told me that in New York you should never answer a ringing pay phone."

Shelby started laughing.

"What? You already know about this?"

"我觉得她肯定是把那个当成咖啡伴侣了。"

谢尔碧放声大笑起来,肺里的水烟呛得她开始咳嗽,本该蓄在肺里的烟从嘴里喷射出来。"她没有说什么吗?"

"这个嘛,我想她并没有注意到我也在那里。但当她转过身来的时候,咕哝了几句自己肠胃不好的话,我就接上了话茬说,'别担心,那杯咖啡会立刻把你给治好的。'"

麦克斯和谢尔碧又一起爆发出一阵笑声。谢尔碧感觉好多了,状态也放松了下来,并且很高兴她和麦克斯还可以互相喜欢。为什么他们不能保持这样的状态呢?为什么抽大麻能帮她缓和局面?

"现在回想起来,她的肠胃肯定有什么挺严重的问题。因为有一天她去看医生,医生给她开了一种最新的前列腺素化合物。"

"那是什么?"

"花生四烯酸级联反应的一部分。"

"不,我的意思是它的作用是什么?"

"使你体内的黏液变稠。"

"呃,真恶心。"谢尔碧顿了一下,又抽了一口水烟。"你刚才说它是什么的一部分?"

"花生四烯酸级联反应。人体内新陈代谢的通道。"

"真是奇怪的名字。'花生四烯酸'。"

"因为它的结构就像花生网那样地延展。一个单元变成两个,两个变成四个,依此类推。"

"嗯。"谢尔碧又喷出一口烟,"呼",接着把那个网状物质的名字重复了几次,每次重读着不同的音节。

麦克斯突然大笑起来,"你嗑高了。"

谢尔碧挑衅地看着他,"那又怎么样?"她放下水烟管,扭转了几下脖子,"跟我说说,今天发生的最有意思的事情是什么?"

麦克斯思考了一秒。"这就是了。"他耸了耸肩。

"你的实验难道什么发现都没有吗?"

"噢,贝内特给我讲了一件有趣的事。他说在纽约永远都不要接起正在响的公用电话。"

谢尔碧忍不住笑出声来。

"什么?你已经听过这个故事了吗?"

"Hadley answered that one down on the corner the other day. The guy wanted Tom."

"Sure he did."

"So Hadley looked for him and then told the guy there wasn't anybody there and then the guy wanted to know if Hadley wanted to come over."

They both laughed.

"Well—" Max splashed some water on his chest, "Bineet said that usually the guy calling can actually see the person on the phone. He's looking down from his apartment window."

"Oh," Shelby nodded. It was so obvious.

"That's how they get the phone number. They pick the pay phone. If a cute guy walks by, they call the number. If a woman answers, they hang up."

"How does Bineet know these things?"

"He is a student of the world."

Their conversation died for a moment while Max turned on some more hot water and Shelby took a hit from the bong. After the tub filled a little deeper, Max turned off the faucet and said, "You know, I forgot to tell you, Bineet told me something odd last week."

Shelby looked at him inquisitively.

"He told me that Rahda was supposed to give him some data, but it seems to have been misplaced. She says she left it on his desk."

"And?"

"Bineet said that Rahda thought the cleaning people tossed it."

"What do you think?"

"I don't know."

"Well, considering that maintenance guys destroyed our bathroom and got a wrench stuck to the NMR, it's not much of a stretch to think that cleaning people could throw away something important."

"I guess that's true. But there are other odd things."

"Like what?"

"Well. It's a little complicated. See, Hadley and I think that her reaction happens too quickly. It doesn't seem physically possible."

Shelby frowned, wondering how he could know this.

"哈德利前几天接起了楼下拐角的那个电话,电话那头的家伙说要找汤姆。"

"很像哈德利的风格。"

"于是他就帮那个家伙找了一圈,然后告诉他电话周围并没有人。结果电话那头竟然问哈德利想不想去他家。"

他们两个同时大笑起来。

"还有,"麦克斯撩了些水在胸口,"贝内特说通常情况下打电话的那个家伙能够看见是谁接起了电话。他八成正从公寓的窗户朝下望呢。"

"噢。"谢尔碧点了点头。这是很显然的事情。

"所以他们才会知道公用电话的号码。他们选择好特定的公用电话,如果有个长相可爱的男生路过,他们就会打电话过去。要是电话被女人接了,他们就挂断。"

"贝内特是怎么知道这些事情的?"

"他可是个万事通。"

他们的对话就此陷入了沉默,麦克斯把热水开大了些,谢尔碧则又抽了一口水烟。浴缸里的水渐渐上升,麦克斯关掉水龙头,继续说道:"对了,我忘了告诉你,那天贝内特跟我说了一件奇怪的事。"

谢尔碧感兴趣地看向他。

"他告诉我拉达本来应该给他一些数据的,但是却放错了地方。她自己说是放在了贝内特的桌子上。"

"然后呢?"

"贝内特说,拉达认为是清洁工把数据给扔掉了。"

"你怎么认为?"

"我也不知道。"

"好吧,仔细想想,修理工几乎把我们的浴室都给拆了,还卡了一把扳手在核磁分析仪上,要说清洁工把一些重要东西给清理掉也不是很牵强。"

"你说的也有道理。但是还有其他奇怪的现象。"

"比如说?"

"这,有点复杂。是这样的,我和哈德利觉得她实验的反应速度太快了。在实际操作上似乎没有可能。"

谢尔碧皱起了眉头,思忖着他怎么知道不可能。

Chapter Fourteen   Chirality

"You want me to explain it to you?"

"Sure, I'm stoned." She put her feet up kitty-cornered on the edge of the tub and leaned back on the toilet seat. Shelby felt just a little bit more moral now that she'd made a plan to listen to Max talk about chemistry, and here she was, already able to put it into action. She kind of liked having Max explain things when she was fucked up. It was so much more interesting that way. And based on state-dependent learning, the theory that you remember something in the consciousness you learned it in, it was now too late to go back and learn it straight.

"Right now, in pharmaceutical companies, the starting material for steroids is made with fermentation broths. Big tubs of chemicals that have to sit around for a while. It's very expensive." Shelby knew Max was in his element. Words like "fermentation" had the ring of power to him. A modern sort of alchemy where rather than use potent words for incantations, one used them for erudition. She constantly had to explain to others what Max did. At his ten-year high school reunion, one of his old classmates, a shoe salesman, asked, "So, Max, what do you really do all day?" Max answered, "Well, my job is to synthesize—" and immediately his classmate interrupted him, waving his hands. "You know, it's just like sales. Some days you got good days, some days you got bad." Shelby later cautioned Max, "It's the word synthesize—don't use it. Use make."

"It's so expensive," Max repeated, "that everyone is trying to find another way to produce these compounds."

"Why is it expensive?" Shelby asked, already scrunching her face with frustration, wanting to understand the finer points, but feeling like she was back at school.

"Because it takes time. Because you need so many chemicals to get a small amount of starting material."

"Okay." Shelby nodded, that bit digested.

"So, what Rahda is doing is attaching a pyridine ring to a steroid then throwing in the catalyst which makes the ring capture a chlorine radical and attaches the chlorine to the nine-position of the steroid. This makes the steroid much more active as an anti-inflammatory, similar to that cortisone cream you use for your rashes. What this is is a highly functionalized starting material."

Shelby's head was thick with incomprehension. Max would always do that.

"你想让我解释给你听吗?"

"当然啦,反正我嗑药嗑高了。"她双脚交叉搭在浴缸的边缘,向后倚在马桶上。谢尔碧觉得自己的精神层次又上升了一丁点,因为不久前她刚决定要强迫自己听麦克斯讲化学方面的事,现在就已经付诸实践了。当自己状态糟糕透了的时候,她还挺喜欢听麦克斯解释东西的。在那样的情景下,连麦克斯说的话也变得更有趣了。根据情景依赖学习理论,你所记住的东西存在于学习时你的意识状态当中,现在想让谢尔碧恢复清醒状态从头开始学已经太迟了。

"现阶段,在制药公司里,制备类固醇所需要的初始原料都是在发酵培养基上生成的,成缸的化学物质就得那样一直静置着,成本非常高。"谢尔碧知道,麦克斯已经进入了自己的世界:像"发酵"这样的词在麦克斯听来有着权力的回声。这有点像现代的炼金术,只不过那些强有力的字眼不再被用来布施咒语,而是显示自己的博学。谢尔碧经常得跟别人解释麦克斯是做什么的。在他十周年高中聚会的时候,一个做鞋子生意的老同学问道:"那么,麦克斯,你整天到底都做些什么?"麦克斯老老实实地回答:"这个嘛,我的工作就是合成——"他的老同学当即就打断了他,连连摆着手。"你瞧,这就跟推销一样。有时候顺风顺水,有时候霉运连连。"在那之后,谢尔碧给麦克斯提了个醒:"是因为'合成'这个词的缘故——别再用这个词了。用'做'来代替。"

"制备成本的高昂程度,"麦克斯又重复道,"使得每个人都在试图寻求新的合成方法。"

"为什么这么昂贵?"谢尔碧早已沮丧得整张脸都皱缩在一起了,虽然她很努力地想要理解,但心里却觉得像是又回到了上学的日子。

"因为制备过程很耗时间。因为需要很多的化学试剂才能生产出少量的初始原料。"

"好吧。"谢尔碧总算消化了这一小点内容,艰难地点了点头。

"所以,拉达所做的就是把一个吡啶环附加到一个类固醇分子结构上,然后加入催化剂,使得吡啶环俘获一个氯离子基,进而使该离子基连接到类固醇结构的 9 位上。这就使得类固醇作为消炎药的效力更为明显,有点类似于用来治皮疹的可的松软膏。这种物质是一种高度官能化了的初始原料。"

谢尔碧的脑袋比灌了铅还沉。麦克斯总是这样,开始的节奏很慢,让你还能

Chapter Fourteen Chirality

He'd start slow and you'd be with him, and then he'd be off and running, so used to these terms that he'd forget Shelby's unfamiliarity. She tried to grab onto the concepts that made sense. Gathering all her working brain cells together, she said slowly, "That means it's a thing to start with to make something else, but it's further along toward what you want to make it into than it would be normally."

"Right," agreed Max, nodding quickly and forging ahead. "So what they've found is that they need very little catalyst to make this reaction work. That's a phenomenal discovery."

"Why?" Shelby took another hit so that she could better understand what Max was saying.

"Because the reaction is turning over with a minor amount of catalyst, and the catalyst is the most expensive part of the reaction. Once one molecule changes, it triggers the next. It's a chain reaction."

"Oh." Shelby's brain felt bogged down. She went to put another small bud into the bong and noticed that the bowl of the bong was clogged. She reached behind her to get the bong wire where she'd set it on the back of the toilet and plunged out the bowl.

"The only part that's really strange is that it all takes place too quickly. It beats the rate with which molecules can come together."

"Well, that doesn't make any sense!" Shelby said, indignant. How could she understand something they didn't even understand?

"Only if you assume that they are coming together in a usual way. But Scotia has an idea that they could be magnetically attracted and this could account for the speed in which the reaction is taking place ... " Max trailed off, watching Shelby mess with the bong. "Should I stop?"

"No," Shelby said, looking up in surprise. "It's just that something is stuck down in here and I can't get this thing to go through. Oh, wait. There it goes. Keep talking. I'm listening."

"So Scotia has this theory to explain why the reaction takes place so fast. There has to be some explanation for it because otherwise it violates the—"

"Wait, I know, I know! The Third Law of Thermodynamics." This was a phrase Max often used.

"Close." He grinned at her.

跟得上,接着就开始脱缰奔跑,完全忘记了这些他无比熟悉的术语在谢尔碧听来如同天书。她把所有还在工作的脑细胞集结起来,费力地抓住自己还能够理解得通的概念,语速缓慢地问道:"也就是说,这是用来制备另一种物质的初始原料,它现在体现的性能虽然离你们想要的更加接近,但却超出了正常应有的状态。"

"正确。"麦克斯迅速地点点头,又开始稳步推进。"现在他们的发现是,只需要极少量的催化剂就可以让这个反应进行。这是一个非常了不起的发现。"

"为什么?"谢尔碧顺势吸了一口水烟,以便更好地理解麦克斯说的话。

"因为所需催化剂量极少,而反应中最贵的部分恰恰是催化剂。反应中一旦一个分子改变了,就能够引发下一个分子的反应。这是个链反应。"

"噢。"谢尔碧的大脑就像陷入了泥潭之中,于是她准备再加一小坨烟丝到水烟瓶里,结果却发现烟碗被堵起来了。通水烟的铁丝被谢尔碧放在了身后的马桶盖上,她反手够到之后,用力地捅了捅烟碗。

"唯一奇怪的部分就是,反应的速率实在是太快了,超过了分子可能聚集的最快速度。"

"这根本讲不通啊!"谢尔碧愤愤不平地附和着。连化学家们都搞不懂的东西,她怎么可能懂呢?

"如果你假设分子是以最普通的方法聚集的话,这是没有可能。但是斯考蒂亚却有一个设想,认为反应分子可以互相吸引,这就解释了反应为什么会进行得如此之快……"麦克斯渐渐停了下来,看着谢尔碧与水烟"斗智斗勇"。"我是不是该停下?"

"不,不,"谢尔碧吃惊地抬起头,"只是有东西卡在了烟碗里,我没法儿疏通它。哦,等下,总算通了。继续说吧,我在听呢。"

"刚说到斯考蒂亚提出了一个理论来解释为什么反应会进行得这么快。合理的解释是必需的,不然的话这就违反了——"

"等等,我知道,我知道!热力学第三定律。"这是一个麦克斯经常用到的表达。

"非常接近了。"麦克斯对她龇了龇牙。

"The Second Law of Thermodynamics?" Max nodded. "Which says that all the molecules can't be on the same side of the room at once."

"Well," Max laughed, "not in so many words."

"That's what you said," Shelby whined.

"It's close. The actual law says that in an isolated system, spontaneous processes occur in the direction of increasing entropy."

Why did Max always have to sound like a textbook? Whenever friends of hers were around and Max talked science, Shelby felt embarrassed. People were threatened by words they didn't understand and Shelby hated to watch. Threatened people became caustic and nasty. Shelby would constantly try to soothe their provincial feelings.

"And entropy is disorder, right?" she asked, already knowing the answer but wanting to have that "good student" feeling of paying attention.

"Right."

"So if all the molecules were on the same side of the room that would be too much order?"

"It would be if no energy had been exerted to make it so. It could never happen as a random event. Except that it must have happened once."

"Why?" Shelby asked, disgruntled. Just as she was understanding something, Max always threw in more confusion.

"In order for the universe to have been formed as we know it—actually in order for life as we know it to have been created—the Second Law of Thermodynamics must have been violated."

"Why?"

"Because we're chiral." Max said this simply, like it was obvious fact. Something everyone could identify with. It was so hard hanging around with smart people. Shelby knew she was smart too, she just didn't have proof the way they did.

"Chiral." Shelby squeezed her eyes together, willing herself to remember what it meant. She had typed part of Max's thesis, noticing how often he used that word, and had asked him why. But now, for the life of her, she couldn't dredge the definition back up. It seemed to her a sign of getting old.

"Look at your hands," Max ordered. Shelby held them out in front of her. "Your hands are mirror images of each other. They are not superimposable. You can

"热力学第二定律?"麦克斯终于点头表示肯定了。她继续说道:"这个定律规定了,所有的分子不能同时存在于房间的同一边。"

"这个嘛,"麦克斯被逗笑了,"没有这么多字。"

"你自己就是这么说的。"谢尔碧抱怨地嘟囔着。

"不过已经很接近了。定律的原本内容是,在一个孤立系统中,自发反应向熵增加的方向进行。"

为什么麦克斯说话总是像教科书似的?每次谢尔碧的朋友在场,而麦克斯开始谈论科学的时候,她就觉得非常尴尬。对于自己无法理解的内容,人们总是有一种威胁感,谢尔碧讨厌看到这一幕发生。因为当一个人感到威胁的存在时,就会变得尖刻凶恶。她就得不停地试图平复大家被逼得狭隘的情绪。

"熵就是无序状态,对吧?"虽然已经知道答案,但谢尔碧还是想要获得那种注意力集中时的"好学生"的感觉。

"对。"

"因此要是所有的分子都运动到了房间的同一边就太过有序了?"

"是的,除非有外部能量使它做这样的运动。随机状态下这样的情况永远也不会发生。可是,它肯定也曾经发生过一次。"

"为什么?"谢尔碧的语气有点不满——每次当她开始慢慢理解的时候,麦克斯总是又抛出更多令她困惑的内容。

"为了使我们所认识的宇宙得以形成——事实上,也是为了生命得以被创造——热力学第二定律一定被违反过。"

"为什么?"

"因为我们人类是手征对称的。"麦克斯轻描淡写地回答,仿佛这是一个再明白不过的事实一样,每个人都能够轻易认同。和聪明人待在一块儿真是太困难了。谢尔碧知道自己天资也很好,只是她没法像麦克斯他们那样给出证据。

"手征。"谢尔碧使劲儿地努了努眼睛,回想着这个词的含义。她曾经把麦克斯的论文打印出了一部分来看,发现他经常用到"手征"这个词,她还问过麦克斯为什么。但是这一刻,无论她多么绞尽脑汁,就是没法把它的定义从记忆中给翻出来。她觉得这是自己在老去的迹象。

"看一下你的双手。"麦克斯命令道。谢尔碧听话地将双手举到眼前。"人的双手互为镜像,如果你从同一方向把一只手放在另一只上,它们没有办法重

not lay one hand on the other in the same direction and have it match. That is chiral. A lot of molecules have a left-hand version and a right-hand version. Most reactions in a biological system take place with only one of the versions. The same reaction would not take place with its mirror image."

Shelby felt very fuzzy in her head, but she wanted to understand this so much, as if understanding it would keep her from falling out of love. As if the words of chemistry were some magic spell that would stop her from being so stupid. And also, she wanted to have a grasp of something that all of Max's colleagues understood without pause. Around them she felt so ignorant. No matter that none of them could discuss literature. Money dictated importance, and there wasn't much money in literature, but in science you could recreate the world, and that was worth paying for. She asked Max slowly, "But what does chiral have to do with the Second Law of Thermodynamics?"

"Let's go way back to the beginning of the world—"

"Oh, no," Shelby muttered. The idea seemed too formidable.

"If all the chemistry and biology that went on were randomly distributed—meaning that the same reaction would take place with a molecule of either handedness—that is a less ordered system. Both the left-handed piece and the right-handed piece will work for exactly the same reaction. But that is not what happened. Somewhere along the line, a random process became ordered—Are you paying attention?"

Shelby's eyes were closed and she looked as if she were in a trance. She knew she was in trouble when they went back to the beginning of the world. Nodding that she was paying attention, Shelby kept her eyes closed. It was easier to think in the dark.

He continued. "Most reactions in chemistry and biology require a specific hand. For example, your body can metabolize only the right-handed version of sugar, which is what naturally occurs in plants. That means when you eat it, you are adding calories. The left hand doesn't have any calories because it can't be metabolized, but it still tastes sweet."

"So why don't we use that instead of, say, saccharine?"

"Can't make it cheap enough and it doesn't occur naturally. So here's the question: In the beginning of the world, why would one version of sugar, one version of anything, be chosen over the other?"

叠。这就是手征性。很多分子都有左手征和右手征两种存在形式,在生物系统中大部分的反应都只能在同种分子间进行,而无法与自己的镜面分子发生反应。"

　　谢尔碧的思绪开始迷糊,但她却执意想要去理解,似乎这样就可以阻止爱情的流逝。仿佛那些化学词汇是神奇的咒语,能够让她不再这么愚蠢。麦克斯的同事们毫不费力地就能够吸收的这些内容,她也想要了解一些。每次和他们在一起的时候她觉得自己如此无知,尽管他们没一个人可以进行有关文学的讨论。金钱决定重要性,文学领域并没有什么油水,而在科学界你甚至可以重新创造世界,这就是值得花钱的地方。谢尔碧又慢吞吞地向麦克斯发问了:"可是手征性和热力学第二定律又有什么关系呢?"

　　"现在让我们回到世界最初形成的时候看一下……"

　　"哦,不。"谢尔碧咕哝了一句。这个主意让她发怵。

　　"如果当时发生的所有化学生物反应都是随机进行的——也就是说不管手征性如何,都能互相反应——那么整个系统就不是非常的有序。左手征和右手征的分子都向着同一反应方向进行。但事实上却不是如此,在某一时刻,一个随机的过程变得有序了——你在注意听吗?"

　　谢尔碧双眼紧闭,看上去就像是被催眠了。她就知道,一回到世界之初自己肯定会有麻烦的。虽然她点头向麦克斯示意自己在听,可仍然没有把眼睛睁开。在黑暗里思考更容易一些。

　　麦克斯继续说道:"大部分的化学和生物反应都需要一种具体的手征性。比如说,人的身体只能代谢右手征的糖,而这种糖通常存在于植物当中。这就意味着当你进食那些植物时,你就在摄入卡路里。而左手征的糖就不会让你增加任何卡路里,因为它没有办法被吸收,可尝起来仍然是甜的。"

　　"那为什么我们不用那种糖来代替,比如说,糖精呢?"

　　"因为它在自然界中不存在,人工制备的成本又降不下来。那么问题就来了:在世界初始的时候,为什么偏偏那种糖,以及每一种物质的某个特定手性被选取了呢?"

Chapter Fourteen Chirality

Shelby ventured, "Gravity?"

"No, no, no. Think about it for a second. The fact that one was chosen over the other implies that the Second Law of Thermodynamics had to be violated—" Max's voice rose in excitement, even chemistry got him worked up, "—because you are ordering a system without a specific input of energy."

In the innocence of the unschooled, Shelby seized upon a tacit assumption and questioned it. "Maybe it wasn't violated, maybe there was input from somewhere."

"That's exactly the right question." Max waved his index finger at her.

Shelby smiled at him. He always told her that the concepts of chemistry were not complicated—not that she believed him—but he said everything could be understood quite easily if someone were just willing to listen.

"In fact, that's what many people think now, that there was energy from somewhere. But no one knows where."

Shelby bit her lip, perplexed. "So if Rahda's reaction seems to violate the Second Law of Thermodynamics, that's only the second time in the universe it's happened?"

Max nodded solemnly.

"Those don't seem like good odds." Shelby paused while Max folded his hands on his chest. Looking at Max, Shelby suddenly realized that he'd lead her down this path, like a storyteller reeling out the plot. Shelby had been caught like a fish, thinking she'd figured it out on her own when Max had really brought it face-to-face with his own conclusion. "You think there's input from somewhere?"

Max snorted. "That's certainly what Bineet thinks. He says she's lying, but I just can't believe that she's been lying about everything. That's a year—and—a-half of work." He paused and stood up, unplugging the tub which started draining with a loud gurgle. "Something's definitely weird though."

"Shouldn't you talk to Scotia?"

"I did already, not as bluntly as I have to you, but in his mind all the checks have been run. Basically, someone has to get ahold of her catalyst and take an NMR of it. Bineet doesn't have any, but Hadley should have some left over from his reactions. I want to be absolutely sure I'm right before I go to Scotia because you don't just ruin someone's life without knowing what you're doing."

Shelby nodded slowly, looking at her feet, feeling suddenly guilty. "No, you don't."

"重力?"谢尔碧大胆猜了一下。

"不,不,不。你再仔细思考一下,某一特征优先于其他被选择出来,意味着热力学第二定律肯定被违反了——"麦克斯激动地提高了声线,化学竟然也能让他如此兴奋,"——因为在没有外来能量的情况下,整个系统在向有序的状态发展。"

带着未经驯化的天真,谢尔碧抓住这个默认的假设追问了起来。"也许并不是定律被打破了,而是确实有外界能量的输入呢。"

"一点儿也没错!"麦克斯兴奋地上下挥舞着食指。

谢尔碧迎着他的目光笑了。麦克斯总是告诉她,化学里的概念并不复杂——倒不是她相信这一点——可是他说过,只要抱着接纳的态度去听,所有事情都很容易理解的。

"事实上,这也是现在很多人所倾向的解释,也就是曾经有来自某处的能量注入了这个系统,但是没人知道它是从哪儿来的。"

谢尔碧困惑地咬着嘴唇,"所以,要是拉达的实验真的不满足热力学第二定律的话,这就是全宇宙第二次发生这样的事情?"

麦克斯一脸严肃地点了点头。

"这听起来可不是什么好的征兆。"谢尔碧看见麦克斯将双手交叉在了胸前,便停顿了一下。她突然意识到,麦克斯就这样一步一步地将她带到了现在的阶段,像一个讲故事的人不慌不忙地展开着情节。而她自己则像一条被网兜住的鱼,以为这一切都是自己想出来的,实际上却是麦克斯带着自己的结论在一点点地向她灌输。"你认为拉达的实验里有外部能量的输入?"

麦克斯喷了一声鼻息,"反正贝内特是这么想的,他说拉达在撒谎,但我真是无法想象,她竟然从头到尾都在撒谎。这可是一年半的工作成果啊。"他停顿了一下,从浴缸里站起来,顺手拔起了缸底的塞子。登时就传来了巨大的"咕嘟咕嘟"的排水声。"但肯定有什么不对劲的地方。"

"你难道不应该去跟斯考蒂亚说这件事吗?"

"我已经跟他聊过了,没有我跟你说的这么直接,但是他却觉得所有的检查反应都做过了,不会有问题。现在要做的就是获得拉达的催化剂,然后给它做个核磁共振分析。贝内特手里一点催化剂也没有,但是哈德利应该还有一些反应剩下的。在去和斯考蒂亚说明之前,我得百分百确定自己是正确的。因为你不能在连自己在做什么都不知道的情况下,就毁了别人的人生。"

谢尔碧缓慢地点了点头,看向自己的脚,突然觉得有点内疚。"对,不应该这样。"

Chapter Fifteen Rival

> "Take three pieces of cheese from rival with most."
>
> The board game *Mousetrap*

Hadley squinted his eyes several times, but without his contacts in, he simply couldn't make out the glinting object at the bottom of the toilet. He'd been just about to take a piss when he noticed it, the light from the window reflecting off a piece of whatever it was, a kind of tinfoil radiance, shiny and cheap. Hadley could tell, even in his myopia, that it was fairly large, something that would clog their toilet for sure. He really had to pee, but he didn't, just in case he had to stick his hand in the water. He considered peeing in the sink, but it seemed like something Max would do and that decided him. Sighing, he buttoned his jeans and walked over to turn on the light, needing to be able to see his face in the mirror. After laboriously putting in his contacts, he looked back at the toilet and saw that snuggled at the bottom of the bowl, still refracting the sun's rays like some deep-sea treasure, were a set of keys.

"What the hell ..." he mumbled in annoyance, knowing exactly whose they were. Going to his closet, he found a hanger and untwisted the end of it. Dipping the hanger into the toilet water like a hook, he managed to catch a loop of the key chain on the crook of the hanger. Hadley held it above the bowl for a second, letting some of the water drip off the key chain, then he swung the hanger quickly toward the sink, but he accidentally twisted the hanger at the last moment giving the key chain a kind of angular momentum that sent it shooting over the sink where it collided with a half-full bottle of Hadley's aftershave. The aftershave skidded to the edge of the counter and Hadley, knowing he was watching the inevitability of a Saturday morning cartoon, still tried to catch the aftershave before it fell to the floor, but it was morning and his reflexes just weren't fast enough. Shattering as it made impact, the bottle's fragments flew everywhere. Hadley stared at it for a few minutes, stunned by his bad luck. It seemed like some kind of curse.

第十五章　对手

最多从对手方取三片奶酪。

——桌游《捕鼠夹》

　　哈德利眯着眼睛看了几次，但是没有隐形眼镜的帮忙，他怎么也看不清马桶底部那闪光的东西是什么。看到它的时候哈德利刚准备开始尿尿，光线透过窗玻璃照射在那片不知道是什么的东西上，折射出某种锡箔般的微茫，闪亮而又廉价。即使是近视裸眼，他也能判断出那片东西大到足以堵住马桶。尽管很急，但他还是憋住了尿，以防落得最终不得不把手伸进水里去的下场。他思忖着要不要在洗手池里解决，可这看起来像是麦克斯会做的事情，于是就放弃了这个想法。哈德利一边叹着气一边扣好裤子，走过去开灯，他需要多一些光亮才能在镜子里看清自己。十分费力地带上隐形眼镜之后，他重新回头去看马桶底的东西，它们依偎在桶底，仍然像深海宝藏一般反射着太阳的光线。是一串钥匙。

　　"这他妈是……"他恼怒地嘟囔着，心里比谁都清楚那串钥匙是谁的。他走到衣橱前面，取出一个衣架，把一头掰直。然后把它当作钩子，伸进马桶的水里，套住了钥匙链上的一个圈。拎出水面之后，哈德利提着它晾了几秒，让上面附着的水滴下来，接着迅速地将钥匙串甩向水池方向。但在最后一秒，衣架却意外地弯折了，钥匙串笨拙地改变了方向，从水池上方飞越过去，撞上了哈德利的半瓶须后水。看着瓶子紧接着滑向洗脸台的边缘，哈德利知道自己目睹的是周六早晨卡通剧里必然发生的混乱场景，可他还是尽力想要在须后水落地之前抓住它。但是，在这样的大清早，他的反应速度还不够快。接触地面的瞬间，玻璃碎片就散落了满地。哈德利盯着地面看了几分钟，不敢相信自己的霉运。就像受了诅咒一般。

Chapter Fifteen   Rival

Barefoot, he tried to figure out how he could get to his bedroom to put on some shoes before he cut himself, the next obvious catastrophe. Lowering the lid of the toilet, he started to put a foot on it when Ethan sauntered to the door of the bathroom and mumbled, "Boy, you sure make a lot of noise in the morning."

"What were your keys doing in the toilet?"

"Where were they?" Ethan made a wry face. His eyes not quite open yet, he felt for the light switch, not realizing that it was already on.

Hadley just sighed. "Can you grab the tennis shoes that are at the foot of my bed? Don't come in here, there's glass all over the floor."

Ethan moseyed into Hadley's bedroom and grabbed a left and right shoe of differing pairs out of the closet. He handed them to Hadley, who put them on without a word and walked unevenly into the kitchen to get a broom and dust pan. Trying to resolve one problem before creating more, Hadley left the keys in the sink and swept up the glass. He could feel his bladder as he moved, and regretted not pissing. Wasn't it the astronomer Tycho Brahe who died because his bladder burst? Hadley swept faster. Imagine living in the 1500's when it was ungentlemanly to leave the table and relieve oneself. Instead, you died. It was a strange passing for a man known as much for his flamboyance as for his science. He had a silver nose to replace the one he'd lost during a sword fight. Perhaps Tycho died trying to live down his reputation, getting in good with the ladies. Hadley felt this was a good argument against propriety.

Tycho's character reminded him of Max. The unrestrained part at least. Max would consider it imprudent to hold a piss. Hadley dumped the glass into the trash, realizing that his feelings for Max had changed. He felt uncomfortable thinking about Max, but in thinking about him, Hadley realized that he was angry at him. For what? For him being married to Shelby? For misunderstanding her? Hadley knew he was being nonsensical now, wanting to find reasons to justify his behavior. Wanting reasons to kiss Shelby again. His mind swept down a path of thought, all sexual in nature, and he was lost for a moment. Realizing that he was just standing there, staring into the bowl, Hadley finally relieved himself, feeling, if not happiness, than at least a fleeting moment of ease. He rinsed Ethan's keys in hot water and laid them on a double layer of toilet paper, separating each key as best he could, and dried off the chirping key chain. He'd have to remember to get another one from the lab.

此时的他光着脚,所以还得费尽心思地考虑如何回到卧室穿鞋子而不被玻璃割到脚,后者很明显容易发展为下一个灾难。哈德利把马桶盖子放下,正准备抬脚爬上去,这时候伊桑悠闲地出现在浴室门口,嚷嚷着:"见鬼,一大早的你动静真大。"

"你的钥匙在马桶里做什么?"

"在哪儿?"伊桑露出一副怪表情。他的眼睛还没有完全睁开,都不知道灯已经开了,还用手瞎摸着开关。

哈德利无奈地叹了口气。"你能把我床脚边的网球鞋给我拿来吗?别进来,地板上都是玻璃碴子。"

伊桑溜达进哈德利的卧室,从橱子里拿出一只一样的两只鞋,递给了哈德利。哈德利什么都没说就穿上了,一瘸一拐地走进厨房里,找到了扫帚和簸箕。他把钥匙留在水池里,又清扫掉玻璃,尽力在更多问题发生之前解决掉一些。每移动一下哈德利就能感觉到膀胱的憋胀感,后悔自己没有先尿尿。不是有一个天文学家第谷·布拉赫因为膀胱爆炸死掉了吗?想到这哈德利又加快了清扫的动作。想象一下,在16世纪,离开饭桌去如厕都被认为是不绅士的行为。忍耐的结果就是,死亡。这样的死法对于一个以花哨的行事风格与科学成就而闻名的人来说,未免太奇怪了。在一次决斗中他失去了鼻子,于是他就给自己安上了一个银质的鼻子。也许第谷·布拉赫之所以选择憋尿是想让别人忘记他不好的名声,给淑女们留下一个好的印象。哈德利觉得这是一个可以用来反驳得体举止的很好的例子。

第谷的性格让他想起了麦克斯,至少是不受拘束的那一面;但是,麦克斯会认为憋尿这种行为是极为不明智的。把玻璃碎片倒进垃圾箱之后,哈德利意识到自己对麦克斯的感觉变得不一样了。一想到麦克斯他就觉得不舒服,可是想着想着他就发现,其实自己是在生麦克斯的气。可是为什么呢?因为他娶了谢尔碧?因为他不理解她?哈德利知道,自己现在的想法是荒谬的,他只不过是想找理由让自己的行为看起来不那么无理取闹,想找到借口再吻谢尔碧一次而已。哈德利的脑海里卷过无数的想法,都与性有关,然后又出了一会儿神。当他发现自己只是站在那里,盯着马桶出神时,终于觉得如释重负,就算还称不上幸福,至少也是一瞬间的放松。在用热水冲洗过伊桑的钥匙之后,哈德利把它们放在双层的厕纸上,尽量让每把钥匙之间都隔开一点距离,并且擦干了会"唧唧"叫的钥匙圈。他得记着从实验室里再拿一个回来。

Chapter Fifteen   Rival

Ethan was eating a bowl of what looked like alfalfa sprouts in milk when Hadley walked into the kitchen again, but Hadley just couldn't believe someone could eat that on an empty stomach. *Time* magazine was propped up in front of him, wedged between a sugar shaker and the milk carton, and every now and then Ethan would turn the page, mumbling to himself.

"You know, why don't bag people buy tents? They must know they're going down before they get there. It's not like—boom—they're on the street without any warning."

Hadley looked at Ethan, wondering if he was an idiot savant, in his ignorance foretelling his own future. Hadley knew Ethan was trying to stall for time before the lecture.

"Okay, maybe their tents were stolen."

"You're sure in a good mood," Hadley said, pouring himself a bowl of Cap'n Crunch. Cap'n Crunch was his weakness, even though it scraped the roof of his mouth.

"I finally popped that protecting group off yesterday." Ethan waited, picking his teeth. "And I got paid for my paper on Chlorothricolide." He leaned back in his seat and grinned at Hadley.

"That's good news. Don't forget the rent." Hadley looked evenly at Ethan, knowing the only hope of getting a message across was to stare him down. Then he stopped himself. He didn't want to be forced to be a nagging person. He wanted not to be in this situation. He really had to move. Hadley sat down across from Ethan, trying not to look at Ethan's bowl of macrobiotic whatever.

"I won't forget the rent," Ethan said in a Yogi-the-Bear voice. He took his bowl and tipped it into his mouth, leaning his head back. Slurping loudly, he dropped the bowl on the table and said, "Hey, hey. Boo boo." Hadley watched in amazement, rubbing the roof of his mouth with his tongue to soothe it. It was already raw and he'd only taken two bites. Ethan then did a Pekinese coughing up a fur ball. It was a bit he liked to do, usually while Hadley was eating. Ethan's tongue somehow transforming into a dog tongue, as he cacked and humphed caninely. Cartoon sound effects were another specialty. It was hard to predict Ethan's moods. Sometimes he was so terse, like the world was coming to the end, and then other days he wanted to outfit the bag people with camping supplies.

哈德利又走进了厨房里，看见伊桑正吃着一碗看上去像是牛奶泡苜蓿芽的东西，他实在无法理解有人会在空腹的时候吃这样的食物。伊桑的面前摊开着一本《时代》杂志，夹在糖罐子和牛奶盒中间。伊桑时不时地翻上一页，再自言自语地嘟囔几句。

"你说，为什么那些流浪汉不提前买好帐篷呢？在落到最后那个境地之前他们肯定是有预感的。不可能——"砰"的一下子——他们就毫无征兆地露宿街头了。"

哈德利看着伊桑，心里想着他到底是不是一个半癫的智者，在无知的乱语中预测了自己的命运。哈德利知道，伊桑在拖延时间，好让自己迟点训斥他。

"好吧，也许他们的帐篷被偷了。"

"你心情还真是不错啊。"哈德利边说边给自己倒了一碗嘎嘣脆船长牌早餐五谷片。这种麦片是哈德利的最爱，尽管它经常会把他上颚的黏膜给刮破。

"昨天我终于把那个保护基给去掉了，"伊桑停下来剔了剔牙，"并且我还拿到了那篇关于大环内酯类抗生素论文的报酬。"说完便向后靠在了椅背上，冲着哈德利龇了龇牙。

"这可是好消息。别忘了交房租。"哈德利心平气和地看着伊桑，他知道能让伊桑听得进去任何话的方法就只有盯到他心虚为止。可是他很快就制止了自己，即使是迫不得已，他也不想变得唠叨恼人。他不想让自己置身于现在的状况，因此必须得搬离这里了。他在伊桑的对面坐下来，尽力不去看他那碗乱七八糟的养生食品。

"我不会忘了房租的。"伊桑模仿着瑜伽熊的腔调说道，然后仰头把碗里剩下的东西一股脑儿倒进嘴里。他响亮地咂着嘴，随手把碗扔回桌上，大声地叫着："嗨，嗨，砰，砰。"哈德利一脸震惊地看着他，一边用舌头舔着上颚的黏膜来减轻一点疼痛。本来表面就粗糙不平，哈德利才只吃了两口。紧接着伊桑又学起京巴犬咳嗽吐毛球时的样子，这是他爱做的一个把戏，尤其是在哈德利吃饭的时候。当他像小狗一样发出"咔咳"和"嗯哼"的喷气声时，伊桑的舌头不知怎么地就真的转变成了狗舌头。模仿卡通片里的音效是他的另一个特长。要想预测伊桑的心情实在是太难了。有时候他寡言得仿佛世界即将毁灭似的，过了几天他又想给无家可归的人都配备上露营的装备。

Chapter Fifteen Rival

Hadley couldn't stop himself. "Like you didn't forget dropping your keys in the toilet." Hadley sounded more sarcastic than critical. He just wanted to probe Ethan. Get him to talk. Ethan was on the cusp, ready to slip away, and Hadley thought someone at least should try to hold on.

Ethan looked at him straight. "I came home late last night. They must have slipped out of my pocket. I would have whistled for them, but I didn't want to wake you." Ethan gave Hadley his best "I was thinking of you" look.

"I'm relieved you didn't knowing now that it would have done no good." Hadley smiled slightly as he poured milk over a second bowl of cereal, knocking the magazine to the floor. "Sorry."

Ethan bent over to pick it up and then placed it to the side of the table. "You're really going to eat more of that?" he asked Hadley.

Hadley sighed. "Ethan, how does this compare to what you shoot in your veins?"

"Heroin is just addictive. It doesn't hurt you. But that is full of sugar."

"You scare me."

"Fine, don't believe me. But if I lived in Switzerland, I could buy my stuff legally, and it would be clean, from state-regulated pharmacists. Pointless to make it illegal, so they make it safe." Ethan paused, then got up and put his bowl in the sink. "Maybe I'll get a job with Ciba-Geigy."

"Just because they're a Swiss company doesn't mean they don't give piss tests."

"Hell, I could pass a piss test easy."

Hadley was sure that Ethan was right, but it didn't make him feel any better.

Ethan walked out of the kitchen and Hadley finished his Cap'n Crunch. A blatt of a sound came from the bathroom.

"Jesus Christ. Are you okay?" Hadley yelled.

"That wasn't me. It was the goddamn key chain."

Ethan whistled again, and the blatting continued, the pitch modulating between a duck call and the occasional chirp, as if an unusual courtship had begun. Ethan yelled, "Great, we can go hunting."

Hadley marveled. Last week Ethan's best friend had died and here he was making jokes about hunting. Hadley wanted to believe this was a healthy reaction—

哈德利实在是没有忍住,"别装得就好像你没有把钥匙落在马桶里似的。"他的语气里讽刺的意味多于批评。他只是想搞懂伊桑,让他开口说话。现在伊桑正处于边缘状态,随时都有可能失足,而哈德利觉得至少有人应该试着拉他一把。

伊桑直视着哈德利,"昨天晚上我回来得迟,它们肯定是从我的口袋里掉出来的。我本来想吹口哨让它们自动回来的,可又不想吵醒你。"他给了哈德利一个他最拿手的"我可是为你着想"的表情。

"我很庆幸你没有那样做,明知做了也不会有什么好结果的。"哈德利露出了一丝微笑,给自己的第二碗麦片也倒上牛奶,却不小心把杂志碰到了地上。"对不起。"

伊桑弯下腰去捡起来,放在桌角。"你真的还要再吃那么多谷片吗?"他问哈德利。

哈德利叹着气回道:"伊桑,这和你注射到血管里的东西相比怎么样?"

"海洛因只是会让人上瘾而已,对你的身体并没有害。但是你吃的,全部都是糖分。"

"你吓到我了。"

"好吧,那你就别相信我好了。但要是我住在瑞士的话,我就可以合法地购买了,而且还是干净的,在国家管理的药店里。他们知道让海洛因非法化是毫无意义的,所以只要确保它的安全性就好了。"伊桑顿了顿,起身把自己的碗放到水池里。"或许我会去西巴—盖吉公司找份工作。"

"就算那是一家瑞士公司,也不代表他们会让你跳过尿检。"

"管他呢,混过尿检对我来说小菜一碟。"

哈德利知道伊桑说的是真的,但心里还是没有好受多少。

伊桑走出了厨房,哈德利继续享受他的嘎嘣脆船长。突然一阵吵闹从浴室的方向传来。

"上帝啊,你没事吧?"哈德利冲着那里大叫。

"不是我,是那个该死的钥匙圈。"

伊桑又吹响了口哨,那尖利的叫声也继续着,音高在鸭鸣器[译者注:猎人打猎时用来模仿鸭子叫声的器具]和偶尔的"唧唧"声之间转换着,就像是一场不寻常的求偶仪式拉开了帷幕。伊桑大叫道:"太棒了,我们可以带着这个钥匙圈去打猎了。"

哈德利对这一切感到惊讶无比。上一周伊桑最好的朋友才去世,现在他就已经若无其事地开玩笑说要去打猎了。哈德利内心希望相信他的反应是健康

Chapter Fifteen Rival

what you can't change you laugh at—but he suspected Ethan's good mood had more to do with the promise of scoring drugs. Drugs were a closer friend to him than anyone. He didn't care who he hung out with, because his best friend was always there. For a quick moment, Hadley wanted to do drugs, to not need people. To be as cavalier as Ethan. Hadley needed Shelby. It felt like a physical sickness in his chest, an ache in his dick. He couldn't believe he was thinking so graphically. Hadley clenched, reliving yesterday's kiss, the incredibleness of it and the horror. That Shelby could kiss him like that, could want him that way was unimaginable. He'd almost lost his mind, and he couldn't even think what would have happened with Max walking in the door like that. What if they'd been naked, rutting there behind the bass drum. Hadley played it tawdry in his mind, shaming himself, but wanting it all the more. They couldn't do this. He was afraid to see Shelby, afraid that she would look at him like that again. All he wanted to do was hold her. To touch her body. God damn.

He had to get back to work. To get this nonsense out of his mind. Once out of his building, Hadley inhaled deeply, the fresh air giving him perspective. As he walked, he tried being pissed at Shelby. It felt like a farce, but he indulged. Testing every moment of their time together. She was pushy. Self-centered. He focused on how he sometimes felt used by Shelby. She would tell stories under the guise of revealing something about herself, the implication being that her revelation was indicative of how extremely close she felt to you. In actuality it had nothing to do with you. She only told you because she liked to be revealing. She'd tell anybody. But what really bothered him was that then she wanted everyone else to be revealing too. Demanded it of you. She told you about her troubled past and wanted you to disclose next. Hadley didn't want to think about tragedies in his life and try to laugh about them. He'd go to a therapist if that's what he wanted.

He knew he wasn't being fair. Shelby cared. She liked to give him grief because that was how she showed her affection. She always told him he was too placid. That he never seemed to have emotion. "What about when I'm in a pissy mood?" he had asked. "You don't think that's real emotion, do you?" she'd laughed, poking him in the side. Their juvenile shoves and nudges had transformed into X-rated material. He had the most salacious dreams about Shelby, but he would also lie in bed in the morning thinking about conversations they'd had, funny things Shelby had said,

的——无法改变的事情你只能玩笑着面对——但是他怀疑伊桑现在的好心情更大程度上是因为即将到手的毒品。毒品才是他最好的朋友，比任何人都亲密。伊桑一点也不在意自己和什么样的人为伍，因为他最好的朋友永远都在那儿。曾经有一阵子，哈德利也想过要吸毒，不需要任何人。也像伊桑那样对什么都满不在乎。可是哈德利需要谢尔碧。这种感觉就像胸口的不适，下体的疼痛。哈德利简直不敢相信，自己的想象竟然如此生动可感。他握紧了拳头，回味起昨天的吻，那种美好，还有伴随着那个吻的恐惧。谢尔碧竟然会那样亲他，竟然如此迫切地需要他，这完全出乎他的预料。当时他差点儿就被冲昏了头脑，万一麦克斯就在那时走进门，后果简直不可想象。要是他们当时都赤身裸体，在大鼓的后面不能自已的话该怎么办呢。哈德利在脑海里幻想着龌龊的画面，虽然也为自己的思想感到不齿，却忍不住地想要更多。他们不能这么做。哈德利害怕再看见谢尔碧，害怕她再像那样看着自己。他唯一想做的事情就是抱住她。触碰她的身体。该死的。

　　他必须得尽快投入工作了，那样才能把这些乱七八糟的思绪赶出脑海。一走出大楼，哈德利就深深地吸了一口气，新鲜的空气使他镇静下来。他一边走着一边试图让自己生谢尔碧的气。虽然有些滑稽，可他还是任由自己这么做了。他们在一起的每一个瞬间都被他拿出来重新审视。她有些强势，以自我为中心。哈德利集中在自己觉得有时候被谢尔碧利用了的经历上。她会给你讲故事，但其实却是为了表达关于自己的事情，暗示她觉得自己和你非常亲近。而事实上那些事情和你一点关系都没有。她告诉你的原因只不过是因为她喜欢把自己展示给大家。她一样也会告诉你以外的其他人的。但是让哈德利无比困扰的是，紧接着谢尔碧就希望对方也开始讲述自己的事情。甚至向你要求。在讲完她的悲惨往事之后，就希望你也敞开心扉。哈德利却并不愿意回忆过往生活中的所有悲剧，把它们作为笑料。就算他愿意这样做他也会找一个心理咨询师来进行。

　　哈德利知道，自己这么想她并不公平。谢尔碧是在乎他的。她之所以喜欢将自己的悲伤展示给哈德利，是因为这是她表现感情的方式。她总是说哈德利太过温驯了，从来都没什么情感波动。"那么在我心情糟糕无比的时候呢？"他曾经这样反问过谢尔碧。"你不会觉得那也算得上是一种真正的情感吧？"谢尔碧戳了戳他的肋骨，开怀大笑起来。他们一起时幼稚的推搡玩笑都变成了哈德利想象中限制级画面的材料。当他梦到谢尔碧的时候，场景都充满了肉欲，但是他也会在早晨醒来时躺在床上，回想着他们之间曾经的对话，谢尔碧说过的俏皮话，

or streams of dialogue that they'd jostled through. He remembered surprising times from the Co-op. The beginning. One time sitting outside on the cement wall that fronted the place, watching the bell curve of Co-op residents go in and out. It had been getting dark. Shelby had been prying for information about his dad. "Why did he ever become a mortician?" she had asked, trying not to laugh. Even though he knew she was making fun of him, there was a tone of sincerity in the way she ended the sentence, a solid simple inflection, untouched by all her bells and whistles. He had shaken his head. He was used to it. Everyone thought an undertaker was funny. "The smell of formaldehyde drove him to it" was his stock answer. Usually the person dropped it there. But Shelby kept pushing him, asking him more questions. Did he study for it? What did he study? Make-up? Was it something he chose in high school? What had Hadley's mom thought while they were dating? Shelby wouldn't let it go. For some reason, Hadley didn't mind. Something about the way Shelby scrunched up her nose while barraging him with questions made him not pay attention to his answers, not couch them in the usual vague responses.

"He was studying to be an architect, actually," he had admitted. "He was really good, too."

"Why did he quit? Money?"

Shelby amazed Hadley in the way that she could just ask personal questions like she was asking about the weather, offhand and casual. And you'd answer them for that very reason.

"He worked in a cannery during the summer to make money for college. After a while they promoted him to manager of canned tomatoes." Hadley smiled mockingly at Shelby. "One day, some guy was angry about something, a dock in pay maybe, and shoved my dad. Well my dad wasn't very good at keeping his temper, especially after someone shoved him. So he hauled his right hand back to hit him and ..." Hadley let the word drift in the silence. The thought shocked him every time. Even though it hadn't happened to him, and he hadn't seen it. A tragedy before he was even born.

"What!" Shelby had yelled impatiently.

"It got cut off."

Shelby just stared at him, biting her lip.

Hadley continued analytically, not letting his feeling color his dispassionate narrative.

或者是他们嬉笑打闹着聊过的话题。他还记得住在大学合作宿舍时那些充满惊喜的时光。在一切刚开始的时候。有一次他们俩坐在宿舍门口的水泥墙上,看着进进出出的学生们从稀稀拉拉到成群结队又到稀稀拉拉。天色越来越暗了,谢尔碧一直在从哈德利这里刺探他父亲的事情。"他到底为什么成为一个葬礼乐师?"她尽力憋住自己的笑意。尽管哈德利知道谢尔碧是在拿他父亲开玩笑,但是她那句话的结尾有一种真诚的意味,是非常简单而实在的语调抑扬,完全没有受到她浮夸风格影响。当时哈德利只是摇了摇头,他已经习惯了。每个人都觉得下葬人这个职业是非常好笑的。"甲醛的味道让他选择了这个职业。"这是哈德利准备好的惯常回答。通常别人得到这个回复就会识趣地住嘴了,可谢尔碧却步步进逼,追问他更多的问题。他有专门为这个职业学习吗?学习了什么科目?化妆?这是他在高中时选择的专业吗?哈德利的母亲和他父亲约会时是怎么想的?谢尔碧就是不愿意放手。不知为何,哈德利对此也不是非常介意。谢尔碧连珠炮般的发问和不时皱起鼻子让哈德利没法集中注意力在自己的回答上,没法像平时那样用模糊的回答糊弄过去。

"其实,他当时学习的是建筑,"他坦白地告诉谢尔碧,"而且还非常擅长。"

"那他为什么放弃了呢?因为钱?"

哈德利感到有些吃惊,谢尔碧可以就那样漫不经心地问起一些私人的问题,就像问起天气一样随意。而正是因为同样的原因,你也会愿意回答她。

"大学的暑假里,他在一个罐头食品厂里打工挣学费。过了不久他就被提拔为西红柿罐头区域的经理。"哈德利略微讽刺地对谢尔碧笑了笑。"有一天,有个工人不知什么原因非常生气,可能是由于工资的克扣,就猛推了我父亲一把。那时候我父亲不是很懂得控制自己的脾气,尤其是在被人推了之后。所以他就抡起右拳打向他……"哈德利的尾音在静默中被拉长。每次想到这里,他都会沉浸在震惊中无法自拔。尽管事情并没有发生在他的身上,他也没有亲眼看见。这是一场发生在他出生之前的悲剧。

"然后呢!"谢尔碧没有耐心地大叫起来。

"然后他的右手被切掉了。"

谢尔碧就那么盯着他,咬着嘴唇。

哈德利用分析的语气继续下去,尽量不让自己的感情色彩掺杂到他冷静

Chapter Fifteen Rival

"It got caught in the chain of a conveyor belt, where the belt wraps around a serrated gear. He tried to pull it out with his other hand and lost one joint of his middle finger on his left hand."

He could tell that she wanted to say something. It was almost funny. He'd never seen her speechless, even in the short time he'd known her. This was why he rarely told people, because the part that seemed to bother them most was the reason it happened. It was so horrible to lose your hand and know, inevitably, that it was your own fault. And yet losing your hand was so appalling, how could anything, even the fact that it was your fault, make it any worse?

He broke the silence. "They fired him. That's what they did in those days. You didn't sue. There was no workman's comp. They just fired you. So he had to quit school."

"He couldn't try drawing with his left hand."

"I think he was too bitter. Something like that can change you. He couldn't start over, after he'd been so good. My father isn't one for compromises."

"Wow." They both sat there in silence.

"But I think there was an artistic quality that he found in being a mortician."

He remembered Shelby's hand touching the back of his. Why hadn't he kissed her then? Why hadn't he gotten her first? It was just one of those things. He'd been accepted to the same grad schools as Max, but he chose MIT and Max chose Irvine, still close enough to Shelby and L.A. Why had he been so stupid? Or would she be tiring of him now instead?

He remembered telling Shelby that his father thought the loss of his hand was a comfort to the people. "It was his justification. That everyone has a cross to bear." Hadley had looked at Shelby, startled by a kind of revelation about his father. "That was his usual lecture. He acted like losing his hand was anything but an accident. It was his calling." Hadley paused. "I think I stopped believing in God at that moment and started believing in science."

Shelby said, "How old were you?"

"Twelve. I'd gotten into a fight at school, about my dad. He told me it didn't matter what it was about, that by fighting I was mocking him. Now I became the reason he lost his hand. He was a bitter man. It shows you just how much one thing can change your life. Everyone does things they regret, it's just that they don't always

的叙述当中。"他的右手卡在了传送带的链条里,被送向了传动齿轮。他试着用另一只手去把它拔出来,但是连左手中指的第一个指节也一并失去了。"

哈德利看得出来,她想说些什么。这几乎有些好笑。在他认识谢尔碧以来的短暂时间里,他从来都没有见过谢尔碧说不出话来的样子。这也是哈德利很少把这个故事告诉别人的原因,因为最让别人心里不舒服的部分就是这件事情发生的原因。失去一只手本就很令人痛苦了,还得再加上一个不可忽视的事实:这是你自己的过错。单单是失去一只手就可怕到了如此地步,怎么还会有任何事情(即使是自己就是罪魁这个事实)使整个局面变得更加糟糕呢?

哈德利打破了沉默。"他被解雇了。在过去他们都这么做,你没办法上诉,也没有劳工补偿这种东西。你唯一的下场就是被解雇。因此他只能辍学。"

"我想他没法试着用左手画图。"

"我觉得是因为他心里太苦涩了。那样的事故可以彻底改变一个人。他没有办法再从头开始了,特别是在曾经的优秀之后。我的父亲不是一个会退而求其次的人。"

"哇噢。"他们俩就那么默默无言地坐着。

"但我觉得他在葬礼乐师这一行里也找到了自己的艺术潜质。"

他记得当时谢尔碧轻轻地拍着自己的后背。那时候自己为什么没有吻她呢?为什么他没有先得到谢尔碧?生活就是这样。他和麦克斯被同一所研究生院录取,但他却选择了麻省理工而麦克斯选择了欧文分校,离谢尔碧和洛杉矶足够近。为什么自己那么傻?要是他们在一起了的话可能谢尔碧现在厌烦的就是自己了?

他还记得他告诉谢尔碧,他的父亲觉得自己残缺的手是对葬礼现场人们的一种安慰。"这是他给自己的合理化解释:每个人都有自己的'十字架'要背负。"哈德利看着谢尔碧,对自己讲了这么多关于父亲的事而感到惊讶。"他总是这么念叨。就好像失去那只手只是一场意外,是他命数如此。"哈德利顿了一下:"我想我就是那时候开始不再相信上帝,转而相信科学的。"

谢尔碧问他:"你当时多大?"

"十二岁。我在学校因为父亲的事跟别人打了一架。他却告诉我不论我打架的原因是什么,我这种行为就是在嘲讽他。这下我成了他失去右手的罪魁祸首了。他心里始终都非常苦闷。这也表明一件事情是如何能够改变人的一生的。每个人都会做让自己后悔的事,只是不是每件事都会有这么悲惨的

have such dire consequences."

He remembered saying that, not realizing his own regrets would prove so consequential. The freshness of the memory hurt his chest. Why hadn't he realized then? Why had he been so afraid of Shelby? She was just too in-your-face. But he'd continued to see her because of Max. It would be a sad irony if his friendship with Max lead to an affair with his wife. Will it? he asked himself cruelly, knowing that it violated every principle he stood for. And then he thought of Shelby. She was one person who, when she asked you a question, actually listened to your answer. Of course, that's probably so she could write it down somewhere. But maybe that was okay. Something positive had to come out of a story like his father's, otherwise what was the point? That a person lost his hand for no reason at all? And that stuff like that happened to people everyday. Things are only poignant after the fact. Or perhaps when they happen to someone else. When they happen to you, you just become embittered.

Embittered was how he felt right now. He couldn't shake it. He felt so angry with his life suddenly. That here was a woman he truly cared about and she was out-of-bounds. Where had he been when everyone was pairing up? In the lab? His sarcasm was not helping. He knew that feeling bitter would only make him lose twice, but it was so easy to succumb. He tried to shake himself out of his misery. There was nothing to be done about it. Shelby was married and that was that.

As Hadley mounted the stairs to the fourth floor of the chemistry building, he forced himself to think about chemistry, pushing thoughts of Shelby from his mind. He stopped at the door of the NMR, peering through the small glass window. The room was empty. The computer screen of the NMR was on—a good sign. Hadley opened the door, went to sign his name on the clipboard, but the pen was gone again. Even the string that it had been hanging from was gone. Hadley wondered why people couldn't leave a simple pen so that you wouldn't have to walk all the way down to your lab to find one. They could get all the pens they wanted in Scotia's office.

Spying a pen on the lunch table, he went to the end of the hall, stopping to get his NMR sample out of the refrigerator. He could finally re-run the uncontaminated control. Walking back to the NMR room, he had the eerie feeling that someone was watching him, but he chalked this up to guilt. He hoped he wouldn't run into Max.

后果。"

他还清楚地记得自己说的那番话,但却没有意识到自己的悔恨会起因于那时。历历在目的情景让他胸口隐隐作痛。为什么他当时没有意识到自己的感情呢?为什么他那么害怕谢尔碧呢?她实在是太咄咄逼人了。可是他之所以继续和谢尔碧见面的原因就是麦克斯。要是他和麦克斯的友谊导致自己和他的老婆有了外遇,这岂不是又伤人又讽刺吗?不是吗?哈德利残酷地质问自己,他知道这种行为违反了自己奉行的所有原则。可是他又想到了谢尔碧。她是唯一一个问了你问题,并且真的认真聆听你的回答的人。当然,她这么做也许是想要找机会把它写进故事里。但可能这样也没什么不可。像哈德利父亲身上发生的这种故事,必须要有一些积极的影响,不然的话还有什么意义呢?一个人平白无故地就失去了一只手?并且这样的事情每天都发生在人们的身上。只有在发生以后,或者是当它发生在别人身上时,人们才觉得倍加酸楚。可当事情降临到自己头上时,你只会不停地怨愤。

怨愤就是哈德利现在的感受,而他却无能为力。忽然之间,他对自己的生活怒从心生。对于一个他真正喜欢的女人,他却什么都不能做。大家都在一一配对的时候他在哪儿呢?在实验室吗?自我嘲讽也并没有多大的用处。尽管知道任由内心的酸涩肆虐只会让自己再次失去理智,但屈服于内心感受实在太容易了。他想要把自己从痛苦的抱怨中唤醒,因为什么都于事无补,谢尔碧已经结婚了,就这么到此为止了。

哈德利来到了化学大楼,在爬上四楼的过程中,他强迫自己专注在化学上,把关于谢尔碧的想法全部挤到脑海外面去。在核磁分析室的门口他停下了脚步,从那扇小玻璃窗口往里瞥去。房间是空的,核磁分析仪的电脑屏幕是亮的——这是个好兆头。哈德利推开门,想在门后的剪贴板上签上自己的名字,可是签字笔却又消失不见了。就连扣着它的那根线都不见踪影了。哈德利搞不明白,为什么有人连支笔都要拿走,害得他现在必须要一直走回自己的实验室才能找到一支。他们要是想要笔的话,斯考蒂亚的办公室里各式各样的笔随便挑选。

这时哈德利看见午餐桌上有支笔,于是他径直走到走廊的尽头,途中停下来从冰箱里取出了自己的核磁共振样本。他终于可以把完全不受污染的对照实验重新做一遍了。在走回核磁分析室的路上,他有一种怪异的感觉,觉得好像有人在盯着他看,但他很快就把这种感觉归因于内疚感。他暗自希望着不要碰上麦克斯。

Chapter Fifteen   Rival

The thought scared him and he moved quickly, wanting cover. Standing before the NMR, he went to put his tube in, but paused for a moment, deliberating. He gave in to paranoia and made a tiny mark on the underside of the red plastic top with pen. The pen was an indelible marker, but he rubbed at the spot anyway, making sure it wouldn't disappear easily. Looking at the tube straight on, he couldn't see the mark, which was what he wanted. He felt like Max, marking his belongings. It was the behavior of the possessive.

Hadley didn't trust anyone right now. Max. Shelby. Rahda. Especially Rahda. Yesterday, needing to know the conditions of the catalytic reaction, he'd looked at Rahda's notebook. Normally, he would have just asked her for it—but she wasn't around. Thumbing through the pages, he noticed something strange. Near the beginning of the notebook a page was covered completely in blue pen. Why would she do that? Her research started on later pages, and they were sequential, so it wasn't like she covered something up. It was just peculiar. He read quickly through her experimentals. Something caught his eye. Her pen color changed in the short paragraph about the addition of the catalyst. Just a little blacker. The ink seemed thicker almost.

Hadley wondered if he were losing it. But there was no question, when he looked between the two inks, something was different, even the angle of the writing was different. Hadley meant to talk to Max about this, to see if Max thought he was crazy, but now he couldn't bring himself to do it. To talk about deception to the deceived. It filled Hadley with revulsion.

Instead of talking to Max, he decided to get ahold of the catalyst. But where? He felt so stupid, using all of his up on his reactions, but she'd barely given him enough, and he figured he could always get more from her. Pity he hadn't saved even a milligram. Bineet had never been able to make it. And now Rahda said that she'd have to make more when she came back from Italy. This left a conspicuous dearth of catalyst. Then it occurred to him: she had to have microscopic samples on a TLC plate. You couldn't do chemistry with it, but you could analyze it. The question was, how could he get her to give it to him? He could go and ask her for it—but if she wasn't around ... he could just take it. He only needed a few minutes to scrape it. He'd wait till the weekend. Maybe come in early one day. This was the last piece of the puzzle. This would be proof.

这个想法一产生就把他自己给吓坏了,他赶忙加快动作,想要找个掩护的地方。站在核磁分析仪的前面,哈德利却犹豫了一会儿,没有立即把试管放进去,最终还是屈服给自己的多疑,用笔在红色盖子底部做了一个很小的记号。虽然那是支擦不掉的记号笔,他还是用手指擦了擦,确保那个记号不会轻易地消失。如果把试管拿在眼前看,完全看不见记号的痕迹,这正是他想要的效果。这会儿他觉得自己和麦克斯很相像,给自己的物品都做上了标记。这种行为是占有欲的表现。

此时此刻,哈德利谁也不相信。麦克斯。谢尔碧。拉达。尤其是拉达。昨天,因为需要了解催化剂实验的具体情况,哈德利翻看了拉达的笔记本。通常来说,他会直接开口问拉达要——但是她最近却不在。一页一页翻阅的时候,哈德利注意到了一个奇怪的现象。在笔记本最开始的地方,有一整页完全被蓝色的笔芯涂抹了起来。拉达为什么要这样做呢?她的实验记录从后面才开始,并且是连续的,因此她不见得是在隐藏什么。真是太怪异了。哈德利又接着迅速地浏览了她的实验记录,又有什么东西抓住了他的眼球。在关于催化剂加入的那个短小段落里,拉达用的笔芯颜色改变了。只是变得更黑了一些。墨水看上去似乎更浓厚了。

哈德利开始有些怀疑自己是不是疑心过头了。可是当他反复看着那两个句子时,他确切地感觉到了有什么不一样的地方,甚至连书写的棱角都不一样了。哈德利本来想把这件事情告诉麦克斯,看看他会不会认为自己是疯了,可事到如今,他也没办法这样做了。跟受欺骗的人谈论关于蒙骗的事情,这让哈德利感到厌恶。

没法与麦克斯交谈,哈德利决定还是抓住催化剂这个重要的东西。可是去哪儿抓呢?在做比例实验的时候,他把所有的催化剂都给用光了,这会儿他觉得自己愚蠢极了。可当初拉达给他的量本来就不太够,他还寻思着随时都可以向她再多要一些。连一毫克都没有剩下,真是太糟糕了。贝内特又一直都做不出催化剂,而拉达说她得从意大利回来之后才能再多制备一点。这就使得对催化剂的需求产生了一个巨大的缺口。但是哈德利灵光一闪,想起来拉达的薄层色谱板(色谱分析时使用的薄板)上肯定还有微量的样本,在第一次分离化合物的过程中留下来的。虽然不能用来做实验,但哈德利却可以用它分析出催化剂的成分。问题是,怎么才能让拉达把样本给交出来呢?他本可以直接去问她要——但要是拉达不在的话……他就可以直接拿了。只需几分钟哈德利就可以把样本给刮下来了,但他要耐心地等到周末。也许选一天早一点到实验室来。这是整个谜题的最后一块了,是关键性的证据。

Chapter Fifteen Rival

He sat back in his chair and noticed that his desk drawer was ajar. Immediately suspicious, he yanked open the drawer, wondering if something had been tampered with. It suddenly occurred to him that maybe he should start taking his notebook with him. He almost panicked, not seeing his notebook immediately. It was lying under a manila envelope that he didn't recognize. He pulled the envelope out slowly, nervous for so many reasons. He opened the envelope and pulled out two typewritten pages. His heart thumped in his chest. He took a deep breath, and then started reading.

There exists in chemistry a metabolic pathway known as the Arachidonic Acid Cascade. Say it without stopping: arachidonicacidcascade. Let it dangle from your tongue. Trickle off. For the world of science, it's a very poetic name. No less accurate for its poetry. The syllables fall after one another nicely, the vowels echo. It's a slant rhyme. Perhaps late at night in a dimly lit lab an impassioned chemist named it. There are more of them than you would think. Molecular artists, with all the foibles and temperament that go along with creativity.

Arachidonic Acid was well-named. It is the spider that strings itself across a two-dimensional diagram. As it cascades from molecule to molecule it forms a molecular web, a three-dimensional wave that interacts with the body, each reaction making a new connection. Doubling like a binary system. A multiplication process. A step toward life.

Imagine atomic scaffoldings, tinker toys of the body. Flexible. Constantly interacting. This causes the tumbling, the cascading down, as one generation metamorphoses into the next—all having a thumb in the body's chemistry. The process is repeated until a myriad of chemicals have been spawned: the daughter of one, the mother of another. Little rivulets of molecules turning over like an acrobat on a set of hurdles. It's an impressive operation. How can the body be so clever?

But the cascade is no more than the children's game Mousetrap, a Rube Goldberg creation, where one circumstance triggers the next. It is a freeway of coordinated movement, a chain of events. There is a circuitry of connections. And chemicals tumble down because molecular conditions make it favorable for them to do so. There is a pull, an attraction leading the way. Once it starts there is no turning back. The plot thickens, same as a pudding. Even our metaphors are tainted by chemistry.

想到这里,哈德利向椅背靠去,却注意到桌子的抽屉是微微开着的。顿时他就警觉起来,猛地把抽屉拉开,想知道有没有什么东西被动过了。他突然想到,也许他以后应该把笔记本给随身带着。没有立刻看到自己的笔记本,他几乎慌了。但其实它被压在一个哈德利没见过的马尼拉信封下面。他慢慢地抽出信封,各种原因让他的内心紧张无比。打开信封后,他取出了两张印着打印字迹的信纸。哈德利的心在胸前"怦怦"猛跳起来,深吸了一口气之后,他开始阅读那封信。

在化学中,存在一种新陈代谢的渠道,叫作酸串联。不要有停顿地读出这个词:arachidonicacidcascade。让余音在你的舌尖悬荡,缓缓流下。即使纵观科学界,这也是一个非常具有诗意的名字。即使从诗歌的角度来看也丝毫不失精准。音节和谐地交替相随,元音共鸣,缺陷押韵。也许某个深夜,在一个灯光昏暗的实验室里,一位充满激情的化学家给它起了这个名字。实际上这样的化合物比你想象中还要多。在分子艺术家身上,怪癖性情与创造力并行不悖。

花生四烯酸的名字取得很好。它的形状是蜘蛛在二维空间里在自己周围编织了一张网。当分子与分子之间开始串联,一张分子网就开始成形,这股三维的分子浪与人体相互作用,每一个反应都建立起新的联结。像个二进制系统一般复制延伸。成倍增长的过程,向构建生命更进一步。

想象一下,它们就像原子级的脚手架,是用来修补人体的积木玩具。非常灵活,不停地相互作用。这就引起了持续的重叠传递,第一代分子通由质的变化转为下一代——每个过程都与人体内的化学反应相关。这个过程不断重复,直到产生的化学物质多不胜数:代代衍生,绵延不绝。成串的分子在一排支架上翻转,像是杂技演员一般,整个流程令人惊叹。人体怎么会这么聪明呢?

但是这种传递与孩子的捕鼠器游戏性质相似,环环相扣,使用的都是杀鸡用牛刀的策略。一系列的连锁反应在高速通道上协调运转,又像电路系统一样互相连接。化学物质在分子状态的推动下开始分解,有一股拉力在引导反应的进行,一旦开始,就无法撤销。坐标逐渐变得厚重,如同布丁一样。就连隐喻都沾染了化学的色彩。

Chapter Fifteen Rival

The path of Arachidonic Acid is the path of anything drawn by force. In the lab, the attraction can be viewed on the molecular level. In humans, it's just a little bit higher, a bit more emotional. Chemicals catalyze in you, and suddenly you become a prisoner of your own biological urges. The mind incites the body which incites the mind. You fall in love against your will. You deceive. We all have our boiling point. We all have our carrot.

Hadley sat back, breathing heavily. He was impressed but confused. What did this mean? That it was only lust? Was she dashing his hopes? What hopes? What was he proposing? He was stunned that his first reaction wasn't one of thought, it was one of want. He wanted her mind. He wanted the package it came in. Hadley suddenly wondered if his father had ever had an affair. But he didn't even drink. In the order of things like drinking and affairs, drinking would seem to come first. Perhaps not. Some grieving widow. Some bereaved daughter. Revolted by his thoughts, Hadley shook his head violently. He noticed a cigarette paper on the ground. He picked it up and a faint smell of marijuana emanated. It must have fallen out of the envelope. He turned it over and written on it in tiny letters it said, "We don't have to do anything if you don't want."

His voice, barely a whisper, filled the room.

"That's not what I want."

花生四烯酸的合成道路与任何有牵引力的过程相同。在实验室里,可以从分子层面来分析牵引力。在人体内,牵引力的层级更高一些,牵涉了更多的情感变化。化学物质在你体内催化反应,转眼之间你就成为自己生物冲动的囚犯。大脑激起了身体的反应,身体又反向地作用于大脑。你不由自主地坠入爱河。你开始欺骗。我们都有自己的沸点。我们都有自己所爱的胡萝卜。

哈德利向后倚去,粗重地喘着气。信里的内容让他动容但也有些困惑。这到底意味着什么?她是想说他们之间发生的事情只是一时情迷?还是在试图激起他的希望?他的希望到底是什么?这真的是他想要的吗?哈德利感到有些震惊,自己的第一反应竟然是占有而不是反思。他想要知道谢尔碧的脑子里在想什么。还有她的肉体。他突然好奇地想知道,自己的父亲是否曾经有过外遇。可他连喝酒都不会。大约像是酒后情迷这种事情,先得喝酒才行。也许不一定。要是对象是某个悲伤过度的寡妇,或者是丧父的女儿的话。连哈德利自己都对自己的低劣想法感到厌恶了,他用力地甩了甩头。这时他看到地上有一片卷烟纸,于是捡了起来,一阵淡淡的大麻气味散发出来。肯定是从信封里面掉出来的。他把纸片翻过来,上面用很小的字写着:"如果你不愿意,我们可以什么都不做。"

哈德利的声音小得像是在窃窃私语,萦绕在房间里。
"这不是我想要的。"

Chapter Sixteen   Karma

> Karma: Hinduism, Buddhism, action, seen as bringing upon oneself inevitable results, good or bad, either in this life or in a reincarnation.
>
> The Random House College Dictionary

Hadley turned the page of his *C & E News* and bent back the cover so that he could hold it with one hand and take a bite of his grilled cheese. The Greek owners of the American Way made grilled cheese sandwiches with olive oil instead of butter. As a result, it was a very wet sandwich. It reminded Hadley of the way the English made their French fries, with grease that was mildly tepid, like their beer. A grease that stayed with you, bonded with your skin for a moment until it oozed onto whatever you touched, a trail of your interactions. You always had to keep one hand free if you didn't want to get whatever you were reading saturated, the grease making your magazine translucent beneath your fingertips. Hadley took another bite and wiped his hand on the two-ply napkin. It wasn't the best grilled cheese sandwich Hadley had ever eaten, but it was easily the cheapest.

Dinner at the American Way was standard for Hadley. It was close to the lab. The food was so terrible that you could often count on eating alone, no one else in the restaurant except for the cooks talking Greek in the back. In New York that was impressive. Being alone. In a weird way, the place reminded him of his elementary school's multipurpose room. The pattern of the flooring, a kind of amoebic splatter that repeated geometrically, took him back in time. He remembered how he used to stare at the splotches, making faces out of them, a kind of Rorschach linoleum, trying to think of anything at all while drying ladles and lasagna pans. (His father had forced him to volunteer for food service, thinking it life-enriching.) He always remembered how the women in charge of the cafeteria had made him wear one of those black hair nets to hold down his hair, and how kids had laughed, calling him "toilet brush" because his hair made the comparison obvious. He vowed never to

第十六章　因果报应

因果报应：印度教、佛教中的行为，给自己带来或善或恶的结果，无论是在此生或是来世，都无法避免。

——《兰登书屋大学词典》

哈德利翻开《化学与工程新闻》，一只手压住弓起的封面，以便用另一只手享用他的香煎芝士三明治。"美国风味"餐馆的希腊店主在做烤芝士三明治的时候会用橄榄油代替黄油，因此三明治就会"湿答答"的。这让哈德利想起了英国人制作薯条的方法——使用微微温热的动物油脂，就像他们的啤酒一样。这种油脂会一直跟你黏在一起，与你的皮肤形成短暂的联结，直到你触碰到某样东西，它就会慢慢地渗透到那样东西上，留下你与之互动的痕迹。要是你不想让你正在阅读的东西——不论是什么——被浸透的话，你就必须保证有一只手是闲下来的。否则，碰上那种油脂的手指再接触杂志，就会让纸张变成半透明状态。哈德利又咬了一口三明治，随即在双层纸巾上擦了擦手。这并不是哈德利吃过的最好吃的烤芝士三明治，但很可能是最便宜的。

在"美国风味"吃晚餐是哈德利的标准习惯。那里离实验室很近。那儿的食物糟糕到很多时候你可能是那里唯一的顾客，除了在餐厅后面用希腊语聊天的厨师之外，就没别人了。在纽约这可是件了不起的事。能够独自待着。虽然有些奇怪，但这家餐厅使他回忆起了小学里的多功能教室。地板的纹路将泼贱出的阿米巴虫图案以几何模式重复，他的思绪也随之回溯到那时的日子。哈德利还记得，那时他经常会盯着地板上的斑点污渍看，把它们想象成脸的形状，这算是一种罗夏油地毡[译者注：Rorschach Test 是心理学中非常著名的罗夏墨迹测验，通过被测者由墨迹联想到的内容对其进行人格测验]。他一边擦拭长柄勺和做千层面的平底锅，一边尽可能地思考一些事情。（哈德利的父亲认为在食品服务行业做志愿者有助于丰富人生阅历，于是就强迫哈德利这样做了。）他永远也不会忘记，管理咖啡厅的那个女人是如何迫使他带上那种黑色的发套来兜住自己的头发，而其他孩子又是怎么嘲笑他的。他们叫哈德利"马桶刷子"，因为他的头发支棱的样子使对比更加明显了。他曾经发誓，永

allow this to happen to his own children. There were better ways to achieve humility.

Of course, he thought suddenly, there were worse ways too.

He sighed and took another bite of sandwich, then looked down at his magazine. He was finally reading the article about the chemist blowing up at Irvine. Max had been ranting about it earlier today, mostly because he'd gone there. "The guy was a total piece of shit," Max kept repeating as they sat at the lunch table. He was all heated up because the article blamed Irvine for not having blast shields. "I went there!" he had yelled. "Every lab had blast shields! What the fuck are they talking about?" Max took his journalism seriously.

Although the chemistry student hadn't died, the doctors thought he only had a chance of returning to about a first grade level. Hadley shook his head, thinking what that would be like. Smart enough to know you'd made a mistake. Absentmindedly turning the page with his greasy hand, Hadley grimaced and then rubbed his napkin along the edge of the page, blotting the oil. Reading through the grease, he got to the part where it described the guy as liking a set of tennis in the afternoon, a line that hadn't particularly endeared him to any of the chemists on Scotia's floor. "A dilettante," Hadley had called him. "A sissified pile of shit," Max had said. "He'd be lucky to get to first grade."

Hadley did think that the article was a little one-sided, but it didn't bother him the way it bothered Max. For Max, it was as if all of chemistry had been defamed. He took his science seriously too. Hadley felt the same, but with less pomp. Max wanted to convert people to logic. Hadley hoped they'd find their way there. Why waste the effort? He didn't want to engage the way that Max did; he didn't like the masses, he'd rather spend his time with chemistry or books or … He thought of Shelby. His thoughts these days always ended with her. She brought out the best in him, made him feel like his nerdiness was a virtue. They discussed things that interested both of them. Harmonics. Bridges in resonance with the wind. Whether or not languages that read from right to left developed in areas where there was a higher number of left-handed people. Chinese foot-binding (she read him poetry from foot-bound women). Impressionism. Van Gogh, especially about how he was crazier when he wasn't painting. The bifurcation of kangaroo penises. The emerald flash. Gyotaku, the Japanese art of printing with a dead fish, something Shelby had

远也不会让这种事发生在自己的孩子身上。要是想学会谦逊的话,更好的方法多得是。

当然了,他突然想到,比这更差的方式也存在。

哈德利叹了口气,又咬了一口三明治,接着低下头看杂志。他终于读到那篇讲某个化学家在欧文分校引起爆炸的报道了。今天早些时候麦克斯拿着这条新闻嚷嚷了半天,主要是因为他去过那里。"那个家伙简直就是垃圾。"他们俩一起坐在午餐桌边时,麦克斯不停地重复这句话。他感到怒火中烧,因为那篇报道文章把事件归因于欧文分校没有配备爆炸防护屏。"我去过!"麦克斯愤愤不平地叫道,"每间实验室里都有防护屏!他们简直就是胡说八道!"麦克斯显然非常拿这篇文章当回事。

尽管那个化学学生还活着,但医生估计他最多只能恢复到一年级的智力水平。哈德利摇了摇头,想象不出那该是怎样的光景。应该足以认识到自己犯了一个错误。翻页的时候哈德利一不小心用了沾了油脂的手,他皱了皱眉头,用餐巾在杂志的边缘擦拭起来,试图把油脂给擦掉。他在残留着油迹的纸页上继续读了下去,文章讲到那个学生总喜欢在下午打一场网球,这个细节可没给斯考蒂亚实验室的化学家们留下什么好印象[译者注:该细节意味着他并没有像其他化学家一样全身心地投入化学研究]。"半吊子",哈德利这样叫他。"真是烂泥扶不上墙,"麦克斯也这样说,"能恢复到一年级的水平已经算他走运了。"

哈德利也认为这篇报道确实有失偏颇,但是他没有像麦克斯一样那么愤愤不平。对麦克斯来说,这好像是对整个化学界的诽谤。他对自己的学术研究也一样毫不含糊。哈德利虽然可以在感觉上与之共鸣,但不会表现得那么夸张。麦克斯想要亲自把所有人都转变为以逻辑为信仰;哈德利则希望人们能够自己想办法做到那一点。为什么要浪费自己的精力呢?他不愿意像麦克斯那样与人相交;也不喜欢人头攒动的场合,而宁愿把时间花费在化学上,或者是书本上,抑或是……他想到了谢尔碧。这些日子以来,他的思绪总是以谢尔碧结尾。她将哈德利身上最好的部分激发了出来,让他觉得自己的书呆子气也是一种美德。他们一起讨论的事情都是建立在共同的兴趣上的,和谐共鸣,连清风都随之附和。从右向左阅读的语言是否是在左撇子人数居多的地区发展起来的;中国的裹脚陋习(谢尔碧会给哈德利念裹脚女人写的诗歌);印象派;凡·高,尤其是当他停下画笔之后变得更加疯狂的景况。雄性袋鼠生殖器官的分叉。翡翠当中的绿光;鱼拓(Gyotaku),一种用死鱼来印刷的日本艺术形式。最近谢尔碧就尝试

recently done, a hanging of which was now on Hadley's bedroom wall, a blue and sparkly picture that shimmered at him, the scales and fins so realistic, the picture hovered at eye level when he would lie on his bed reading.

Shelby was always interested in the oddities of science. He remembered telling her about Notre Dame, about how the windows are thicker at the bottom than the top because glass is a liquid and therefore pulled by gravity. He remembered her being both charmed and suspicious at this revelation.

"Glass is a liquid? No way." She'd frowned comically at him. "Why do they call it crystal?"

"Sorry," Hadley apologized, smiling at her, wanting to be in her debt.

"If it's a liquid, then why can you drink out of it?"

"It's a very slow-moving liquid."

"You're making this up."

She had grinned at him, like she wanted to fight. He felt invigorated by her. No one had ever accosted him so completely, forcing him to produce answers.

"What makes something a liquid?" she'd asked.

"Disorganization, not having a well-defined lattice. Glass doesn't have a repeating unit cell like, for example, ice does, or salt, or sugar. That's why it breaks so randomly."

"How do you know so much?"

He had laughed. "I read."

"Literature or just science?"

"Both," he answered, a smile twisting his lips, knowing what she meant by "just science."

"You ever read *Grapes of Wrath*?" Shelby had asked.

"A long time ago."

"You remember how it ends?"

He'd thought for a second, eyes closed, the story coming back to him. "They're in a barn and someone's pregnant and the water's rising—" He'd paused and then looked at Shelby pointedly. "I remember." He felt his cheeks get hot and wondered if he was blushing. "She saves the old guy's life."

Shelby had looked at him defiantly. "I think that is one of the best endings of all time. I ask that question all the time, and nobody can remember." She had suddenly

了这种方法,成果就挂在哈德利卧室的墙上:一幅蓝色的充满生机的图画闪烁着光芒。鱼鳞与鱼鳍都极其逼真,以至于每次哈德利躺在床上读书的时候,那幅画都会在他眼前飘忽不定。

谢尔碧总是对科学领域的各种怪异事物感兴趣。哈德利还记得,他告诉过谢尔碧,圣母玛利亚大教堂里的玻璃窗底部要比上面更厚,因为玻璃是液体,会被地心引力向下拉。他的印象当中,当谢尔碧听到这个真相的时候表现得既惊奇,又心存怀疑。

"玻璃是液体?不可能。"她有些搞笑地对着哈德利皱起了眉头。"那为什么人们又叫它晶体呢?"

"对不起。"哈德利抱歉地对她笑了笑,有意地想欠她些什么。

"要是玻璃是液体的话,怎么会可以用来盛液体呢?"

"它是一种流动得非常缓慢的液体。"

"你肯定是在瞎编。"

她对哈德利龇了龇牙,像是要打架的样子。而他则因此而感到精神焕发。没有人像谢尔碧一样对他这么打破砂锅问到底,强迫他给出答案。

"什么样才能被称为液体?"谢尔碧又问道。

"结构不规则,不具有齐整的格子结构。玻璃不是由重复的单元构成的,不像冰块儿或者盐和糖那样。这就是它在随机的状态下都能破碎的原因。"

"你怎么知道这么多?"

哈德利笑了,"因为我读书。"

"读文学还是只读科学相关的东西?"

"都读。"哈德利的嘴角闪过一丝微笑,他知道谢尔碧说的"只读科学"是什么意思。

"你读过《愤怒的葡萄》吗?"她接着问道。

"很久之前读过。"

"你还记得它是怎么结尾的吗?"

哈德利闭上眼睛,想了一会儿,故事情节开始回到他的脑海里。"他们在一座农具仓棚里,当中有人怀孕了,四周的水开始漫上来——"他停顿了一下,刻意地看了一眼谢尔碧。"我记得。"他觉得双颊发烫,并不确定自己是不是在脸红。"那个孕妇救了那老头儿一命。"

谢尔碧挑衅般地看着他。"我认为这是历史上最好的小说结尾之一了。我总是问别人这个问题,可却没人回忆得起来。"她突然对着哈德利展开了笑靥,

Chapter Sixteen Karma

smiled at him, like it was them against the Philistines. "I think they block it. Someone in class told me that the critics said John Steinbeck didn't know how to end his book and I think it's because they were disturbed by it. It's too horrible to consider, and yet it's the greatest act of charity." She paused and looked off into space, as if receiving spiritual literary guidance. "What bothers people is that they can't handle ambivalence. It's too painful."

Hadley didn't tell her that one of the few times that he'd cried in his life was when he finished that book. At fourteen he had more feelings than he did now. Or perhaps now he had feelings he didn't dare recognize. Like what it was to want something. For the nth time, he remembered their kiss. He put his head in his hands, rubbing his face, trying to wrest the thought from his mind, so tired of reprising the one moment of happiness that made the rest of his life seem so unlivable.

Hadley lifted his head and sighed. It was just Shelby. Jesus. When had she become this sex goddess to him? Could she ever live up to that? There was no way. He had to stop this now. He'd felt something for her before, but after reading her writing, somehow he'd crossed a boundary. The way she wrote had moved him. Her talent was an aphrodisiac. He'd read her writing and lost his head. He remembered saying to her at Dermot's that it was crazy to think that a person can give you a book and that you'll then fall in love with that person, but it hadn't occurred to him that he would fall in love with the author.

Hadley laid the magazine on the table and turned back another page, this time with his unsoiled hand. The dim light got a little dimmer, a bad electrical connection somewhere, and a chill rippled through him, puckering his skin. The hairs on his arm stood to attention. He felt his heart bump inside his chest. He looked up at the long fluorescent tubes shining violet light over yellow Formica tables. The place had the presence of a morgue. He thought of home. How could he ever tell his parents? His common sense came back to him. He had to simply ignore her. He could not do this. He could not.

As Hadley picked the magazine back up, forcing himself to the article, he suffered another prickling chill like a thousand daddy longlegs had taken up lodgings on his back. Involuntarily he shuddered, ducked his head and looked over his shoulder. Rahda was standing diagonally behind him, six inches at most. Almost lifting out of his seat, Hadley said loudly, "What are you doing?"

就好像是他们在并肩对抗着文化艺术素养低的群体。"我觉得他们是故意忘记的。当时班里有个人告诉我,批评家们都说约翰·斯坦贝克不知道该如何给自己的书结尾,但我却坚持认为那是因为这个结尾使他们感到不安。虽然骇人到无法细想,但那却体现了最伟大的仁慈之心。"谢尔碧顿了一下,双眼出神地看向空气中,仿佛在接收精神上的文学指引。"让人们不安的,其实是他们不能直面那个情节中的矛盾心态。因为那太痛苦了。"

哈德利并没有告诉谢尔碧,在他人生当中寥寥无几的几次落泪就包括了他看完那本书的时候。那年他十四岁,感情可比现在要更丰富。但有可能,现在他只是不敢承认自己的某些感情。比如说对某样东西的渴望。不知道是第几次了,他又想起了和谢尔碧的那一吻。他把头埋进掌心,揉搓着脸颊,想把那个想法从脑海里赶走,那一瞬间的快乐在脑海里一遍又一遍地重演,使他疲累,也让他以后的生活看上去不堪忍受。

哈德利抬起头叹了口气。还不是因为谢尔碧。天哪。从什么时候开始她在自己眼里变得这么富有性魅力了?她真的有可能达到这个标准吗?根本不可能。现在就得停止了。曾经他也对谢尔碧有过一些感觉,但在读完了她写的东西之后,不知不觉中他就越过了界线。谢尔碧写作的方式让他动容,她的才华对哈德利来说如同一剂催情的药。自从读完之后,哈德利就彻底失去了理智。他还记得在德莫特的派对上,他曾经对谢尔碧说过,一个人给你一本书,然后你就会爱上她,这种想法简直就是太疯狂了。但他当时怎么也不会想到,自己会不可收拾地爱上书的作者。

哈德利把杂志摊放在桌上,又掀过一页,这次用的是未沾油脂的手。昏暗的灯光又弱下去了一些,一定是某处的电线又接触不良了,一阵寒意传遍哈德利全身,激起了许多鸡皮疙瘩,胳膊上的汗毛也一根根地竖了起来。他感到自己的心脏在胸腔里猛烈地撞击着。抬起头,哈德利看见了黄色福米加塑料桌上方的那个长长的灯管,闪烁着紫罗兰色的荧光。这个地方与太平间的氛围有些相似。他想到了自己的家。要怎么开口跟自己的父母说起他跟谢尔碧的事情呢?他的理智终于重新回来了:必须要忽视谢尔碧的存在。他不能继续这样做,不能。

当哈德利再次拿起杂志,强迫自己专注到文章上时,又一阵寒意袭来,使他感到皮肤的刺痛,仿佛有一千只长腿小怪[译者注:daddy longlegs,美国同名电子小游戏里的角色]在他的后背上安营扎寨了。哈德利不由自主地打了个冷战,将脖子往回缩了缩,像肩后望去。拉达正站在自己的斜后面,最多有六英尺的地方。哈德利几乎是从椅子上弹了起来,他大声地问道:"你在做什么?"

Rahda looked at him intently, or so it seemed. It was hard to tell because she was wearing sunglasses. "May I join you?" she asked.

He motioned to his sandwich. "Well, I'm nearly done ... " Rahda didn't move. So Hadley nodded, uncomfortable at the silence.

"Thank you." Rahda put her coke and double order of French fries on the table.

"Dinner?" Hadley asked, unable to stop himself. In his mind he could hear Max going off on Rahda's eating habits.

"I have to get back to the lab," she said nonsensically. She sat down and pulled several napkins out of the napkin holder and then placed them in front of her. "Are you going back to the lab?"

Hadley watched Rahda pour about a quarter cup of ketchup in the center of the napkins and then methodically dip one French fry at a time, rolling each until it was uniformly covered with ketchup.

"Why?" he asked pointedly, thinking his question could apply to so many things.

She stopped mid-dip and looked at him primly. "I wanted to give you the NMR data on the catalyst for Bineet. Bineet refuses to speak to me. I do not know why. But I do not want to just leave it in his lab. You heard what happened with the mass spec data?"

"And you have to give it to me? Why not Max? or Eberhard or—"

"I trust you. I think someone is ... I don't know ... "

"What?" Hadley asked sharply, wondering if Rahda was trying to get caught, or if she was just plain crazy.

"I think someone tampered with my argon line to make me sick."

"Now who would do that?" he asked.

Rahda looked over the edge of her sunglasses. "There's money involved."

"Money?"

She nodded. "Dr. Scotia said my compound is worth two to three million. I think, corporate espionage."

Hadley stayed stone-faced.

"I believe it's someone in the lab. I had a gram of catalyst sitting in a flask, and now it has been tampered with. Fortunately I took the NMR before it happened."

拉达专注地盯着他,至少看上去是挺专注的。因为她戴着墨镜所以很难辨别。"我可以坐下和你一起吃吗?"她问道。

哈德利指了指自己的三明治,"你瞧,我都快吃完了……"拉达没有动。哈德利对这种沉默感到不舒服,于是就点了点头。

"谢谢。"拉达把自己的可乐和双份薯条放在桌上。

"这是晚饭?"哈德利忍不住问了一句。在他的脑海里已经响起了麦克斯对拉达饮食习惯的滔滔不绝的评论。

"我一会儿得回实验室去。"拉达莫名其妙地说了这么一句。接着她坐了下来,从餐巾盒里抽出几张纸巾,放在自己的前面。"你要回实验室吗?"

哈德利看着拉达倒了将近四分之一的番茄酱在餐巾纸的中央,然后有条不紊地每次只蘸一根薯条,不停地旋转直到那根薯条被番茄酱均匀地覆盖。

"为什么?"哈德利刻意反问道,寻思着他的这个问题可以用来指代很多事情。

拉达停下手上的动作,一本正经地看着哈德利。"我是想把催化剂的核磁共振分析数据给你。本来是要给贝内特的,可他最近拒绝跟我说话,我也不知道为什么。可是我又不想就那么把数据放在他的实验室里。你听说了质谱图数据丢了的事儿吧?"

"你就一定得交给我吗?为什么不给麦克斯呢?或者是艾伯哈德,又或者是——"

"我信任你。我觉得有人……我也不好说……"

"怎么了?"哈德利紧追不舍,心里好奇到底拉达是快要露馅了,还是真的疯了。

"我觉得有人刻意对我的氩气线路动了手脚,好让我生病。"

"谁会那么做呢?"哈德利紧接着问道。

拉达透过墨镜的上沿看向哈德利,"肯定跟钱有关。"

"钱?"

她点了点头。"斯考蒂亚博士说我的化合物价值两到三百万美元。我认为,这是一场其他公司谋划的间谍活动。"

哈德利面无表情。

"我相信内鬼就是实验室里的人。我放了一克的催化剂在烧瓶里,结果就被人动过了。幸好我在那之前就给它做过核磁共振分析了。"她停顿的间当微

Chapter Sixteen   Karma

She nodded and paused. "I tell this only to you." She moved in, holding a French fry close to her lips, at the ready. "I suspect Bineet."

This really irritated Hadley. She had Scotia convinced that Bineet was no good as a chemist, and now this. It made Hadley angry. He stood up to throw the rest of his sandwich away. She was acting stranger than ever. Did she know he suspected her? Maybe she accused Bineet to throw him off. Did she know he was close? What would she do when it all came out? Would she disappear? Go back to India? Kill herself? The thought of her suicide crossed Hadley's mind. Still, he couldn't let that keep him from telling Scotia, but it wasn't something undertaken lightly. Telling Scotia that Rahda was falsifying data would be essentially telling him that his last year-and-a-half were a waste, that his idea was wrong, that a second-year graduate student had tricked him. Hadley needed the last piece of the puzzle before he could say anything. He had to find out what she was using as a catalyst. What had she actually made? It was the most conclusive proof—proof that she had lied.

He found that he was staring at his fingers and he looked up in time to see Rahda stuff about ten French fries in her mouth and then take the sugar dispenser and shake it all over her remaining fries.

"What are you doing?" Hadley asked.

"I do not want to eat anymore. If I put sugar on them, I will stop."

"Ohhhh," Hadley said almost under his breath.

"So I will meet you at the lab." Rahda immediately stood up. "I will give you the data." She then hit her head with the heel of her hand almost comically. "I forgot my backpack at home. It has the data. I will be up there in some minutes."

Hadley nodded in a daze and bussed his plate, wondering why he attracted all the loonies.

As Hadley walked to the lab, he got an idea. He'd been planning to search for Rahda's TLC sample of the catalyst while she was in Italy, but he could do it now if he was quick. At some point she would have had to take a TLC, spotting the compound on a small glass slide and then looking at it under ultraviolet light. The size of the TLC was the problem. No bigger than half-an-inch by three inches, but most people—he found himself rolling his eyes, likening her to most people—just laid them on the back of their bench. Finding it could be difficult, but perhaps she'd forgotten its significance and it was still there. This was his chance. It would take her

微点了下头。"这件事我只对你说,"她凑近了一些,一只手拿着一根薯条在嘴边随时准备着,"我怀疑是贝内特。"

这让哈德利非常生气。她已经让斯考蒂亚相信贝内特不是一名称职的化学家了,现在又来这一套。哈德利站起身来扔掉了自己剩下的三明治。拉达的行为真是越来越古怪了。她知道自己怀疑过她吗?也许她说贝内特的坏话是想借机摆脱掉他。她知道自己已经快要查出真相了吗?当一切真相大白的时候她打算怎么办?她会就此消失吗?回到印度?自杀?她会自杀的想法掠过哈德利的脑海。这虽然不足以改变他告诉斯考蒂亚的想法,但这件事情牵涉众多,不能轻举妄动。告诉斯考蒂亚拉达在篡改数据,实际上就是在跟他说他这过去的一年半完全就是浪费,他的想法是错误的,一个二年级的研究生把他给耍了。哈德利需要最后的一片拼图才能开口指证。他得找到真正被拉达用作催化剂的东西。她合成的到底是什么?那才是最确凿有力的证据——证明她说谎了。

当哈德利发现自己正在盯着手指头看时,便匆忙抬起头来,正好看见拉达把将近十根薯条全部塞进嘴里,然后拿起糖罐儿在剩下的薯条上撒了个遍。

"你在做什么?"哈德利惊奇地问。

"我不想再吃了,如果我撒糖在上面的话,我就能够停下来了。"

"噢——"哈德利的声音小到几乎听不见。

"那么实验室见了。"拉达随即站起身来。"我会把数据交给你。"紧接着她用手掌的根部夸张地打了一下自己的头,"我把背包落在家里了,数据放在里面。我过几分钟再上去找你。"

哈德利茫然地点点头,收掉自己的盘子,心里嘀咕着为什么所有的怪人都会被自己给吸引过来。

走在去实验室的路上,一个想法出现在哈德利的脑海里。之前拉达在意大利的时候,他就打算过去查看一下拉达对催化剂的薄层色谱分析样本,但如果他动作利索一些的话也许现在就能做到。曾经的某个时间里,她肯定做过薄层色谱分析,把那个化合物点在一片很小的载玻片上,然后放在紫外线光下观察。最大的问题就是薄层分析样本的大小,不超过半英寸乘三英寸,但是大多数人——他意识到自己不自主地翻了个白眼,因为他把拉达与大多数人分成了一类——就会把它放在自己工作台的靠后位置。找到样本可能有点难度,但是拉达有可能忘记了它的重要性,而把它留在了原地。哈德利的机会来了。拉达回家再重

Chapter Sixteen Karma

at least twenty minutes to go home and then come back to the lab. He started running.

Throwing open the door to the Scotia's floor, he decided to quickly check his NMR sample first. He tore the sheet of data from the machine. It looked good. Then he pulled the probe out and checked the cap. Where was his mark? He couldn't believe it. It was gone. Glancing at the data, he realized the information was useless.

He decided to worry about that later. He didn't have much time. He walked quickly to Rahda's lab. He'd give himself ten minutes. The first place he looked was her bench. There weren't any TLC plates anywhere. Now where would she keep them? He checked her hood, nothing. Some people taped them to there notebook pages, not a great idea, but it was done. She, however, did not. He closed her notebook and tried to think like her. She was weird. Secretive. Perhaps she'd keep them in a drawer. He opened the top drawer of her desk. It was a mess. He felt overwhelmed by the task ahead of him. How would he ever find something that small in ten minutes? But her next drawer was virtually empty. In her third drawer he found a home pregnancy test. He closed the drawer immediately, feeling guilty at invading her space so. Still, he couldn't now unsee it. Could she be pregnant? Was that why she was so strange? He didn't know that much about pregnancy, but that seemed not enough of an explanation to justify her oddity. Still, if she was, it certainly wouldn't make her more normal.

In the bottom drawer he found them, a stack of TLC plates, perhaps twenty. He shuffled through them rapidly. They had numbers written on them which he figured corresponded to her notebook pages. He realized this was a leap of faith, because, again, she wasn't like most chemists. He took the first four early numbers and, quickly checking his watch, moved to her bench to find the page in her notebook where she recorded her work on the catalyst. He thumbed hastily, remembering where he'd found it before, the page with the two inks. There it was. Page twenty. He slipped the TLC plate with "20" written on it into his jacket pocket and zipped it up, then carefully put the rest back in her desk drawer.

He was starting to get nervous. He was a few minutes over his ten minutes and he didn't feel like a confrontation. He took a deep breath and scrutinized the lab once more to make sure everything was as he'd found it. It was then that he noticed a rack

新来到实验室至少需要二十分钟。哈德利想着的时候脚下已经开始奔跑起来了。

　　猛地推开斯考蒂亚办公室所在楼层的大门，哈德利决定先迅速地检查一下自己的薄层色谱分析样本。他将数据单从机器里扯出来，看上去一切正常。接着他又把探针给取了出来，查看试管的盖子。他做的标记去哪儿了？哈德利简直不敢相信，标记不见了。有人偷换了他的样本。他又瞥了一眼数据，意识到那些信息已经丝毫用处都没有了。

　　哈德利决定过后再考虑这件事，剩下的时间不多了。他快步走向拉达的实验室，在心里给了自己十分钟的时间。他搜寻的第一个地方是拉达的工作台，完全没有样本的影子。那么她能放在哪儿呢？接下来是通风橱，可还是一无所获。有的人会把样本粘在笔记本里，虽然这不是什么好主意，但至少也安置好了。然而拉达，却没有这么做。合上她的笔记本，哈德利开始尝试像她一样思考。诡异的，遮遮掩掩的。她也许会把样本放进抽屉里。最上面的抽屉打开之后，呈现在眼前的一团乱糟糟的景象。哈德利感觉到眼前的任务艰巨。怎么可能在十分钟之内找到那么小的一个东西呢？但是第二个抽屉抽开后却是空空如也。在第三个抽屉里面哈德利发现了一个家用的验孕棒。他像是触电般地把它推回去，为自己入侵了她的私人空间而感到内疚。可是，他没法装作从来没有看见过。难道她怀孕了吗？是不是因此她才行为这么奇怪？哈德利对孕期的症状也不是非常了解，但还是觉得就算怀孕也不能完全解释拉达的古怪表现。即使她真的有了身孕，她也不会因此变得正常多少的。

　　在最下面的抽屉里，哈德利终于找到了那一沓薄层色谱分析板，大概有二十个。他赶忙挨个地翻看，猜测着每一个板上的数字与拉达的笔记本页码是相对应的。他意识到自己又在放手一搏了，因为拉达和大部分的化学家都不一样。他取了前四个号码，迅速瞟了一眼手表，然后走到拉达的工作台前，翻到笔记本上记录催化剂的相应页码。他匆忙地用拇指翻着，试图回忆之前翻到的那一页，上面有两种墨水的颜色。找到了。第二十页。哈德利将标记着"20"的色谱分析板滑进夹克的口袋里，顺势拉上了拉链，接着小心地把剩下的样品放回她的抽屉里。

　　这时已经比他给自己分配的时间超出了好几分钟，哈德利开始有些紧张了，他并不想与拉达正面冲突。深吸一口气之后，他又扫视了一遍实验室，确保一切与自己刚进来时没有差别。就在这时，哈德利注意到拉达的通风橱下排列着一

of NMR tubes with a variety of colored tops sitting in the back of her hood. His marked one had had a red cap. She had two red ones sitting there and, wondering if he was pushing his luck, he decided to check them. Hadley prided himself on his ability to maintain composure. He fancied himself somewhat adept at biofeedback, and attempted it now. Breathing slowly as he walked toward her hood, calming himself. There was no sound of doors closing or footsteps in the hallway. He was doing okay. He had good presence of mind. He'd had practice. When he was younger, he would have to help out in the funeral home, ushering hearses, holding supplies while his father attended to a body. He was used to things most people would find unsettling. Consequently, he could make good money.

He remembered working at the Gross Anatomy Lab during spring break his junior year. You'd walk in and there'd be naked bodies hanging from meat hooks, like so much dry cleaning. After the initial shock, it didn't seem sinister anymore, just vile. At least at a funeral home there was some dignity. Hadley's job was to cut the bodies up for medical students to practice on. He remembered seeing one woman's body, stunningly beautiful, ready for detachment. His boss, a creepy, wizened old guy with a wall-eye and bad dandruff who'd worked there for years and seemed to like his job, took a chainsaw and without flinching once, separated her chest from her torso, right under her breasts. You couldn't help wondering how someone that beautiful ever ended up that dead.

It was his and another guy's job to take the pieces and package them up in green zippered bags for delivery to the medical school. One day someone unfortunately found a body that had been forgotten in the back of the cold storage and had never been embalmed. Things like this always happened on his shift. Without actually looking at the disintegrating body, four of them lifted it (you couldn't even tell what sex it was) onto a kind of gurney and then wheeled that to an elevator. Outside the elevator, they all took a big breath hoping that they'd get to the fifth floor before they'd have to breathe again. The elevator had only made it to the second floor before Hadley was forced to inhale through the filter of his teeth, a horrifying stench that came a circuitous route to the olfactory sensors, the teeth being a poor sieve for the likes of putrefaction. A lifetime later, the elevator doors opened onto the fifth floor, and they wheeled the rotting body to the incinerator. As they lifted it, a sickening mucous-colored fluid ran from the carcass, almost as if the body were

排彩色盖子的核磁分析试管。自己做了标记的那个试管盖子是红色的,而拉达那一排里安坐着两个红盖试管。哈德利决定检查一下,自忖自己的运气是不是快到极限了。他简直快要为自己保持镇定的能力感到自豪了,想象着自己能够熟练地控制自己身体里的生物反馈机制,并准备放手尝试一把。他一边放缓呼吸,一边走近拉达的通风橱,使自己镇静下来。走廊里并没有关门声或是脚步声传来。目前一切正常。哈德利沉着的功力是曾有过类似练习的结果。早些年,当他的父亲忙于与尸体打交道时,他就必须得在殡仪馆里帮忙,做些引导灵车、端贡品之类的活儿。对于令大部分人感到不安的事情,他已经习以为常了。因此,他的收入也相当可观。

他还记得大三那年的春假,在系统解剖实验室工作时的经历。走进去,第一眼你就能看见裸露的尸体用挂肉钩成排地吊在那里,像极了干洗店里的情景。起初的震惊褪去之后,那个场面不再有不祥的意味了,而只是让人觉得简陋。至少在殡仪馆里,还给尸体留存些许尊严。哈德利的职责就是肢解尸体,供医学学生练习。他还记得曾经见过一个女人的尸体,异常美丽,静静地等待切割。他的上司是一个怪异干瘪的老头儿,双眼向外斜视,头皮屑旺盛,他在那儿工作已经有些年头了,似乎挺享受这份工作。只见他拿起电锯,从那具女尸的胸部以下将其切割开,连眼都没有眨一下。人们会不由自主地好奇,那么漂亮的人怎么会落得个死挺挺的下场。

哈德利和另一个家伙的工作就是把肢解后的尸体部分打包进带拉链的绿色大包里,以便运送到医学院去。有一次,一个倒霉的家伙在冷冻室的最里面发现了一具被遗忘的尸体,从来都没有进行过防腐处理。像这样的事情总是发生在哈德利当班的时候。他们四个人连看都没有看一眼那具已经腐烂分解的尸体,就把它给抬了起来(性别几乎都无法分辨了),放在轮床上,向电梯推去。在电梯外面,他们每个人都深吸了一口气,暗自期盼着在吸下一口气之前就能到达五楼。事实上刚到二楼的时候,哈德利就不得不透过牙缝吸了另一口气,一股骇人的臭气迂回地到达了嗅觉神经,牙齿则可怜地成了那腐烂气息的筛子。似乎过了漫长的一辈子之后,电梯的门终于在五楼打开了,他们一刻不停地将溃烂的尸体推到焚化炉前。当他们再次抬起那具尸体的时候,一股令人恶心的黏液从那躯体上流出来,仿佛是融化了的样子。哈德利当时心里想:"我们最终变成的

melting. Hadley had thought at the time, "It isn't dust that we turn to but pus," a distinction that mattered only to the living.

Hadley wanted to tell Shelby this story. Maybe he would try to write it down for her. He liked the idea of their written communication. It was a way to connect without others knowing. A very intimate interaction. He'd learned in the Gross Anatomy lab that humans, without life, are undemanding. It's too late for them. You needn't waste your tears. And perhaps people who are not quite dead are the same way. He wanted to tell Shelby how much Ethan bothered him. In some ways the weirdness of Rahda reminded him of Ethan. They were both turmoiled for reasons unknown. Both on their way down. But he didn't live with Rahda. Ethan he got to see daily, got to witness his decline. One had to get pretty callous in order to watch someone's life deteriorate day by day. He'd done it once already. He hated to do it again.

"Come in. Door'zopen," Ethan slurred.

Rahda pushed the front door tentatively. It swung slowly, panning the room as it extended the view. She stood there, afraid to walk in. Ethan was sitting in a beanbag chair inches from the television watching "Dr. Who". She'd thought that he might be here, hoped, in fact, so that she would be able to get into the apartment. She wanted to search Hadley's room. It occurred to her that she might find his notebook. Steal it if necessary. She knew he wasn't keeping anything in the lab anymore. No data, no spectra, nothing. He was even locking his lab drawer. She had jammed a ruler hard against the thin piece of metal that held it closed. The lock had sprung, but the notebook wasn't there. Where else could it be but in his apartment? It was a long shot, but she was running out of options. Anyway, no one would suspect her. She didn't look like a criminal.

It had occurred to her that Ethan might not be here. It was late and he often worked nights. And so, she would have left and tried tomorrow. She had meant to come earlier, but her father had called and ranted on the phone about how she was not making the wedding plans any easier. She was supposed to meet with her aunt and get new clothes, but she kept putting it off. She had told him that her science was important and she didn't have time to shop, and he had yelled that her family was more important and that they were all flying to New York to see her get married and that she'd better remember this so that the family was not shamed by her.

不是尘土,而是脓水。"而这个区别也只有活着的人才在乎。

哈德利一直想给谢尔碧讲这个故事。也许他会试着为她写下来。他喜欢这个通过写作来交流的想法。这是一种可以不让其他人察觉的建立联结的方法。一种非常亲近的互动。在系统解剖实验室,他领悟到了一个道理:人,没有了生命,就不再苛求了。对他们来说任何事情都太迟了。也无须为他们浪费你的泪水。也许,有些还没有死亡的人却也处于这样的状态中。他想告诉谢尔碧伊桑的事有多么让他烦心,而拉达的鬼祟怪异在某种程度上又让他想起伊桑。他们两个都因为某些不可名状的原因而处于混乱之中。都在往下沉。但是他不用和拉达住在一起,却要每天都见到伊桑,不得不见证他一点点地堕落。一个人得有冷酷无情的心肠,才能眼睁睁看着另一个生命日复一日地退化。他已经做过一次了,不想再来一次。

"请进,门是开着的。"伊桑咕哝着。

拉达犹疑地推开了前门。门缓慢地滑开弧线,视角逐渐增大,直到整间屋子都呈现在眼前。她站在那里,不敢走进来。伊桑正窝在懒人沙发里看《神秘博士》,电视离他只有几英寸远的距离。事实上,拉达已经估摸到他可能会在家,并且这样期望着,因为如此一来就能够进到公寓里面来了。她想要搜查哈德利的房间。没准儿能找到他的笔记本,就算要偷也在所不惜。她知道哈德利早就不把任何东西存放在实验室里了。不管是数据,还是图谱,什么都没有。他甚至都把自己实验室里的抽屉给上了锁。拉达曾把尺子抵在薄薄的锁片后面,用力撬起。锁登时弹了开去,可是笔记本却不在里面。除了公寓以外还有可能在哪儿呢?虽然这样的猜测很大胆,但拉达别无选择了。无论如何,没有人会怀疑她的。她看上去并不像一个罪犯。

之前她也想过,伊桑也许不在家。因为天色已经晚了,他又经常晚上工作。当真是那样,她就打算先离开,第二天再来。本想早一点出发,结果她父亲却打来电话,在那头大声地嚷嚷着,责骂拉达阻碍了婚礼计划的顺利实施。她本应该与婶婶见面,并且一同去置办新衣裳的,但却一直借口拖延着。拉达在电话里告诉父亲自己的科学事业很重要,没有时间去购物,但他仍然大吼着驳斥说她的家人更加重要,而且他们即将一起飞往纽约来见证她的婚礼;并警告拉达最好牢记这一点,不要让家族蒙羞。

Chapter Sixteen Karma

It had taken her some time to calm down. And her time was running out. Her wedding had been moved up to the end of next week. She had to go to Italy for a couple of days and confer with a pharmaceutical company—of all the ill-timed meetings—and then come back to New York and get married. Neither filled her with much excitement. Her fiance requested that the wedding be here, not home in India. He used his studies as an excuse, but it was an insult to her. With the first bit of trepidation that she'd felt in a long time, she realized that there was a plan that had backfired. She'd thought for sure that the pregnancy test would have released her. She'd mailed him the damaging result, a small plastic square with a simple " + " in the center. Wrapped around it had been a short note saying that she thought it was only right that he know first. It had been ten days now since she'd sent it, and she'd heard nothing from him. Nothing from her mother, no crying or remonstrating, just a request last week from her father to move the wedding up because he had an important meeting to go to that conflicted with the original date. Rahda knew this was a lie, but what could she say? It was not acceptable to disagree with one's father.

She hadn't realized how much of a dowry her family was giving her husband-to-be. It must be enormous. The thought of giving money to her fiance gave her a very American irritation. The ease with which the irresponsible get money. Her head ached from the knowledge that she would never see any of it. He had not struck her as a generous man. More than ever, she needed money. It would buy her freedom from this detestable union.

As she stood at the threshold of Ethan and Hadley's apartment, she realized that she had never meant to let things get this far. It was Scotia's fault. He didn't pay attention. He didn't hear her mumbled explanations. He always told her what the result should be, and she didn't want to disappoint him. She'd seen his disappointment with others. It was a kind of biting sarcasm he had that made you feel about a foot tall. Her father was the same. He could smile and scorn you at once, the ultimate of insults.

She knew she would never marry. She would find a way out of her predicament. She had good karma. She believed in karma, but it was too often the explanation for bad things. A bridge in India fell down on a pilgrimage going to Holy Land. Thousands were killed. The king declared it karma. That was stupid. The bridge was obviously of poor quality. Karma took the blame off the king. But when

她花了一些时间才平静下来。时间却快不够了。她的婚礼被提前到了下周末。她得去意大利待几天，与一家制药公司协商事宜——正如所有不合时宜的会议一样——然后回到纽约结婚。没有一件值得她兴奋的事。她的未婚夫要求婚礼在美国举行，而不是印度的家乡。虽然他以自己的学业为借口，但其实却是对拉达的侮辱。这么久以来，拉达第一次产生了不安的心绪，随即她就意识到自己的计划并没有如愿实行。她满心以为孕检的结果能够解救自己的。一个方形的塑料小片，中间有一个清晰的"＋"号——拉达把这个具有毁灭性的结果寄给了未婚夫。在包裹着这个结果的纸条上，拉达写着，觉得应该让他提前知道。自从寄出之后已经过去十天了，拉达却没有收到任何回音。母亲那边也动静全无，没有哭闹，也没有抗议，只是上周他父亲要求把婚礼提前，因为他有一个重要的会议与原定日期冲突。拉达明知这是个谎言，可她又能如何反驳呢？不服从父亲的意见，这是不能被社会接受的。

目前，她还不知道家里到底给她的未婚夫准备了多少嫁妆，但肯定庞大得惊人。拉达一想到这件事情，一股美国式的气恼情绪就油然而生。完全不负责任的人却轻易地得到金钱。想到自己连这些钱的一分都看不见，拉达的头开始痛起来。他在拉达心中没有留下很大方的印象。她现在比以往任何时候都更需要钱，因为钱可以在这场令人憎恶的联姻中买回她的自由。

站在伊桑和哈德利公寓的门口，拉达意识到自己从来就没有打算让事情发展到如今这个地步。是斯考蒂亚的错，他没有注意，没有听见她当时小声嘀咕的解释。他总是把应该产生的结果告知拉达，而拉达并不想让他失望。她见识过其他人让斯考蒂亚失望时的情景。那种酸涩的讽刺语气让人觉得顿时矮了半截儿。她的父亲也是这样，可以在微笑的同时予以嘲笑，这是侮辱的终极形式。

拉达知道，自己是不会结婚的。她要找到一个摆脱目前困境的办法。她的命相很好，因为她相信印度教中的因果报应，可那却通常是用来解释不好的事情的。印度有一座桥坍塌在了朝觐圣地的路上，上千人因此丧命，国王将其定性为因果报应。愚蠢无比。很显然是因为那座桥的质量原因。而因果报应却将罪责从国王身上揽了下来。但是当你将事情掌控在自己的手里，让事情

you took things into your own hands, when you made things happen, that was karma. Karma favored those in control.

Rahda noticed Ethan staring at her.

"Do I know you?" Ethan asked. "You're one of those little people." He had a perplexed look on his face.

"I work in Scotia's lab." She pushed her sunglasses so that they perched on her head. "Is Hadley here?" She knew he wasn't, because she'd just left him at the diner, but the question seemed like a logical one.

"Nah. He's out. Out and about. Come on in, though."

Rahda closed the door behind her so that she could hear it open if anyone entered, and walked over beside Ethan. "You are watching 'Dr. Who'. I like that program."

"I like the dog. K-Nine. What a great name." Ethan shifted slightly in the chair and it made a noise like sand filtering through a hourglass, amplified molecules shuffling past one another with the dryness of ping-pong balls. "You know that there is an 'ine' word for every animal? Feline, bovine, ursine, caprine, porcine, aquiline."

Rahda looked around her while listening to Ethan talk on about nothing. He seemed odd. Perhaps very drunk. "Hadley has an article about folate inhibitors he said I could borrow. He told me I could pick it up." Mixing truth and lie was her specialty. An alloy of the most unsuspecting kind.

"Room'zat way." Ethan nodded in the direction of Hadley's bedroom. He continued chanting. "Serpentine, equine, asinine, elephantine, hircine ..."

Rahda walked slowly past the kitchen, no detail of the apartment lost on her. The bedrooms were next to each other and out of Ethan's eyesight. She glanced at him from the hallway and he continued talking nonsense to the TV, laying very sideways in the bean bag like he might fall over. She could hear bits and pieces of bizarre jabbering.

"John Glenn, like the daughters of Fatima, went into outer space to see if his magnetism falls off ... New York is not indivisible from all the other stars on the flag. We're not just suing New York, we're suing all the stars."

Rahda shook her head in wonder. It was possible he wouldn't even remember her being here. She stepped into one of the rooms. A black stereo system centered

发生时,那才是因果。因果青睐于具有掌控权的人。

拉达注意到伊桑正盯着她看。

"我认识你吗?"伊桑开口问道,"你就是那些小侏儒里面的一个吧。"他脸上呈现出一种困惑的表情。

"我在斯考蒂亚的实验室工作。"她把墨镜向上推去,架在了头上。"哈德利在吗?"虽然她刚在饭馆里跟哈德利告了别,明知他这会儿不在家,但这个问题的提出显得很符合逻辑。

"没有,他出门了,出门去逛逛了。不过你还是进来吧。"

拉达关上了身后的门,这样如果有人进来的话她就会听见开门声了。接着她走到了伊桑的身旁,"你在看《神秘博士》啊,我挺喜欢这个节目的。"

"我超爱那条狗。K9,多棒的名字啊。"伊桑在椅子上微微挪动了一下位置,发出了沙子缓缓滤过沙漏般的声音。放大了的分子带着乒乓球般的干燥质地互相之间摩擦着。"你知道吗,在每一个指代动物的词语里面都有'ine'这个成分。Feline(猫科的),bovine(牛科的),ursine(胸科的),caprine(绵羊科的),porcine(猪科的),aquiline(鹰科的)。"

一边听着伊桑滔滔不绝地说些废话,拉达趁机环顾了四周。他看上去有些奇怪,也许是醉得厉害了。"哈德利有一篇关于叶酸抑制剂的文章,他说可以借给我,让我自己来取。"将真相和谎言混合起来是拉达的专长,形成了最不容易让人怀疑的合金产物。

"房间在那边。"伊桑向哈德利卧室的方向点了点头,又继续喋喋不休地继续下去,"serpentine(蛇科的),equine(马科的),asinine(驴科的),elephantine(象科的),hircine(山羊科的)……"

拉达缓步经过厨房,不放过公寓里的任何一个细节。两个卧室是连在一起的,都在伊桑的视线之外。她从过道瞟了伊桑一眼,他还在继续对着电视喃喃自语,侧躺在懒人沙发上,仿佛随时都有可能摔下来似的。一阵怪异的窸窸窣窣声不时传到拉达耳朵里。

"约翰格伦,就像法蒂玛的女儿们一样,前往外太空来检测重力是否会消失……纽约完全可以从国旗上的星星中分割出来。我们起诉的不仅是纽约,而是所有的星星。"

拉达惊奇地摇了摇头,伊桑很有可能已经不记得她还在这儿了。她一步踏进其中一个房间,那小小的空间中一个白色的书架占据了主导位置,书架中间放

on a white bookcase dominated the small space. She stared at it for a moment, it's blackness drawing her eye. Whose room was it? It had the feeling of Hadley's. Neat, generic. She opened a drawer and ouijaed her way around the clothes she found there, her hands receptive, feeling for vibrations, sensitive to the nuances of the owner. She felt something hard and pulled out a framed picture of a boy who looked like Hadley but with much darker hair. Probably a brother. He had long hair and bell-bottoms and a peculiar expression on his face. There was a wonderful feeling that went with snooping, that you might find out something you shouldn't know. You could get close to someone without ever getting close to them. That had an odd appeal for Rahda.

But she put the picture back and moved on. Where would his notebook be? Quickly she felt through every drawer, looked under the bed, under the mattress, behind pictures, in his closet, all through his desk, beneath the stereo. The notebook was nowhere to be found. He must have it with him. In his backpack? Was he suspicious? Had he talked to Bineet? She knew that Bineet was close to figuring things out, but Scotia would never believe him. He would believe Hadley though. Had he figured out there was no catalyst? Did Hadley have proof? That's what she needed to know. When would Hadley tell Scotia? Probably when she was in Italy and couldn't defend herself. She would have to do something.

She left Hadley's room, finding nothing of worth, and then snuck into Ethan's, a dark cavern of black light posters hanging at rakish angles. Rahda had decided to search it as well. Why not? Ethan was close to unconscious. Unhurried, she looked around, pivoting slowly, amazed by the profusion of pictures and objects that filled every available space. It was a dizzying array of articles so foreign to her, tall water pipes and ornate lighters, and some very familiar. She recognized a lab balance, a bottle of solvent. She frowned, wondering why he would have taken those from the lab. Still turning in awe, Rahda had a sensation of the room tilting. She saw little moving holes on the periphery of sight, circling, her own personal shooting stars. Heavily she sat down on the bed and shook her head, trying to get rid of the fog that had suddenly enwrapped her mind. Lately she had been beset with dizziness. The doctor who had told her it was from drinking coffee had also advised her to see a therapist. As if she would take his advice. Sitting there a second and breathing, she noticed that she was sitting on something hard, a lump she could feel through the

置着一个黑色的音响系统。拉达被那黑色给吸引了,盯着它看了一会。这是谁的房间?感觉像是哈德利的。整洁,毫无特色。她打开一个抽屉,双手如同占卜一般迂回地在衣服之间摸索,格外的敏感,努力感受着突出的物体,从细微差别当中判别它的主人。她突然摸到一个硬硬的东西,拉出来之后是一个相框,照片上的男孩儿与哈德利很像,发色却更深一些。大概是他的弟弟吧。蓄着长发,穿着喇叭裤,脸上的表情别扭着。拉达感受到了一阵窥探别人隐私带来的特殊快感,因为你可能会发现一些你不应该知道的东西。不用真正的接近本人,就可以了解他们。这对拉达有一种特殊的吸引力。

但她放下照片又开始继续自己的搜寻。他的笔记本会放在哪儿呢?拉达十分迅速地把每一个抽屉、床底、床垫下面、画框后面、橱子里面、桌子还有音响的下面全部摸索了一遍。笔记本却仍不见踪影。他肯定是随身带着了。在他的背包里?难道他起疑了?是不是和贝内特通过气了?她知道贝内特已离探清真相不远了,但是斯考蒂亚是不会相信他的。但斯考蒂亚一定会相信哈德利的话。难道他已经发现根本就没有催化剂的事实了?哈德利有证据吗?她只需要知道这个就够了。哈德利会什么时候告诉斯考蒂亚呢?八成会在她去意大利期间,那样她就不能给自己辩白了。她必须得做些什么了。

在哈德利的房间毫无收获之后,拉达转身溜进了伊桑的卧室。里面像一个昏暗的洞穴,荧光海报以放浪不羁的角度悬挂在墙面上。拉达决定把这里也搜查一遍。为什么不呢?伊桑现在已经几乎没什么意识了。她不紧不慢地四下扫视着,缓慢地转动着身躯,对充满每一个角落的物品和照片数量感到惊奇。这一系列令人目眩的物品对拉达来说都十分陌生,长长的玻璃管、华丽的打火机,还有一些非常熟悉的东西。她瞟到了一个实验室天平,还有一瓶溶剂。拉达皱了皱眉头,不禁想知道为什么伊桑会把这些从实验室给带回家。在她仍然沉浸在震惊中时,拉达突然感觉到房间开始倾斜。在她眼睑的边缘出现了不停旋转的小洞,形成了她的专属流星。她重重地坐在了床上,甩了甩头,试图摆脱那突然裹挟住大脑的混沌感。最近她一直被晕眩困扰,医生告诉她这是喝咖啡引起的,同时还建议她去看心理医生。好像拉达会把他的话当回事儿似的。她大口地喘着气,短暂地坐了一会儿之后,意识到屁股下面有一个硬硬的突起的东西,隔着

mattress. She looked under the bed. Tucked underneath the thrashed boxsprings she spied an old green suitcase. Rahda tugged it toward her until it partially cleared the mattress. Slowly she let each springlock pop open onto the fleshly part of her thumb. She lifted the lid, the middle of it hitting the bottom of the mattress but still giving her a good four inches to peruse the contents. It was filled with baggies. Baggies of white powder. She exhaled slowly, putting the pieces together. The balance. The solvent. The water pipes. She lifted one baggy out of the suitcase, fingering the whitish powder between the slick coolness of smooth plastic. Sliding her finger down the tread of the ziplock and unsealing the bag, she wet the tip of her nail and then lightly touched the powder, first sniffing it then touching it to her tongue. Bitter but mostly tasteless. It made her tongue numb. Perhaps she'd take one with her. Or two. It was too risky to take more. She was sure she could arrange that later.

Quickly stashing the suitcase back under the bed and smoothing the covers, Rahda listened at the door before she went out. She could hear heavy breathing and the voice of Dr. Who. She didn't hear any more mumbled rhymes. Would he remember her being here? Rahda walked back toward the living room, passing the kitchen. She stopped abruptly. There were keys laying on the kitchen counter. Five on a square black key chain.

"May I get a drink of water?" Her voice sounded loud, but there was no answer. She put the water glass into the sink underneath the nozzle, then turned the tap on, the merest stream leisurely making its way into the glass, tinkling loudly, obscuring any other sound. She fingered the keys, and then stuck them in her pocket, cushioned by the baggies. She was sure, for a price, she could find someone who was interested in what she had.

床垫她也感觉到了。她弯腰向床底看去,在破旧的弹簧床垫下面塞着一个绿色的手提箱。拉达将箱子向外拉,直到它的部分露出床垫以外。接着她慢条斯理地让弹簧锁一个一个地弹开到自己的拇指上。箱盖被打开的时候,中间部位被床垫底部给抵住无法完全打开,但是仍然留有四英寸左右的缝隙供拉达一探究竟。里面塞满了小袋子,盛着白色粉末的小袋子。拉达缓慢地吐着气,把线索一点一点地拼凑起来。天平。溶剂。玻璃管。她从箱里提起一个小袋子,隔着油滑阴凉的塑料用手指摩挲着那白色的粉末。她用手指沿着密封袋的滑索将拉链打开,然后用口水将指尖弄湿,轻轻地蘸了一下那粉末,先是闻了闻,然后点在了舌头上。有些苦,但总体来说没什么味道。她的舌头却因此而麻木了。也许她该拿一袋走,或者是两袋。再多拿就太冒险了。她自信满满,认为日后可以再安排回来拿。

拉达迅速把手提箱塞回床底,掸了掸表面,出门之前侧耳在门上听了一会儿。只有沉重的呼吸声和神秘博士的声音传来。除此之外她再没有听见那喋喋不休的蹩脚韵律。他会记得拉达曾经来过吗?拉达向起居室走回去,中途经过了厨房。突然,她停下了脚步。厨房的桌面上躺着一串钥匙,五把钥匙串在一个黑色的方形钥匙链上。

"我可以喝点水吗?"她的声音听起来很大,可是却没有得到回复。于是她便径自将玻璃杯放在喷嘴下的水池里,拧开水龙头,一股涓细的水流不紧不慢地落到杯子里,发出"丁铃铛"的声音,淹没了其他的一切声响。拉达用手指捏起钥匙串儿,顺手放进了自己的口袋里,被装白粉的小袋子给包围着。她可以确定的是,只要价位合适,她肯定能找到对她手里的东西感兴趣的人。

Chapter Seventeen   Piltdown Man

> Piltdown Man: A species of early man, Eoanthropus dawsoni, postulated from bones found in an early Pleistocene gravel bed in 1912, and proved in 1953 to have been a forgery based on the artificial modification and juxtaposition of the cranium of a modern man and the mandible of an orangutan.
>
> *The Tormont Webster's Illustrated Encyclopedic Dictionary*

"You never heard of the Piltdown man?" Hadley asked, breaking his resolve of not conversing with Shelby. How could he not? He felt so aware of her, like he must interact. She loomed large in his brain.

They were sitting next to Eberhard in the back of a taxi streaking toward midtown. "I majored in theater. Leave me alone," Shelby answered loudly, purposely confrontational. It was her enjoyed method of interacting, parrying, thrusting.

Max sat in the front because he had lost the race for the back seat—not that it was a completely conscious race. More like nonchalant competition, as everything was for the group. It wasn't that sitting next to the cab driver was so awful, it was that you might be expected to talk to him.

Max leaned over from the front seat and looked at them through the open plastic window that separated the two seats. "You do too know," he insisted. "Where a human skull was discovered next to an ape's jaw and for years everyone thought it was the missing link."

Shelby narrowed her eyes and smiled mockingly. "Sure," she agreed, obviously unconvinced.

The cab driver took his right hand off the steering wheel, yawned, and stretched his arm out, resting it on the length of the front seat like he owned the place, which he probably did. "Oh yeah. I heard a that." He nodded. "So you guys scientists?"

第十七章　皮尔当人

> 皮尔当人：早期人类的一种，拉丁学名为 Eoanthropus dawsoni，据1912年发现于更新世（地质时代第四纪）早期沙砾层中的遗骨推测而来，1953年被证实为一场骗局，实为现代人的颅骨和猿猴的下颌骨拼凑而成的赝品。
>
> ——《托尔蒙特韦伯斯特图解百科词典》

"你从来都没听说过皮尔当人？"哈德利问道，就此打破了自己不和谢尔碧说话的决心。他怎么可能做得到呢？谢尔碧的存在感在他心中如此强烈，渐趋赫然，使他不得不与之交涉。

他们正坐在艾伯哈德的旁边，一辆疾速向市中心驶去的出租车后座。"我大学专业是戏剧，我怎么会听说过。"谢尔碧大声地回答着，语气故意咄咄逼人起来。她就喜欢用这种方法交涉，回避，或是攻击。

麦克斯正坐在副驾驶位置上，因为在奔向后座的赛跑中他失利了——倒也不是有心的竞争。更像是无心的攀比，如同这个小团体里所有其他事情一样。坐在司机旁边倒没那么糟糕，只不过你可能得跟他攀谈。

麦克斯从前排倾过身来，隔着开口的塑料挡板看着他们。"你不可能不知道那件事吧，"他坚持道，"一个人类的头骨和猿猴的下颚骨一起被发现，而人们长久以来都以为那是考古史上缺失的关键一环。"

谢尔碧眯缝起了眼睛，露出讽刺的笑容。"当然了。"她同意道，但很显然一脸的不相信。

出租车司机从方向盘上拿下右手，打了个哈欠，舒展了几下胳膊，顺势搭在了前座的靠背上，好像他拥有这个地方——不过很有可能也没错。"噢，可不是嘛。我听说过。"他点了点头，"所以你们都是科学家？"麦克斯看了看哈德利，他

Chapter Seventeen Piltdown Man

Max looked at Hadley. Hadley made a face of worry. Max raised his right eyebrow. Shelby mugged at them, risking that the cab driver would see her in his rearview mirror. It was a shared moment.

"How did you know?" Eberhard asked the driver, filling the silence. Max was making his "spool down" face at Shelby.

"That area, you get a lot of scientists." The cab driver nodded, as if it was something he'd studied.

"Do they pay usually?" Hadley asked, cracking Shelby up. He wanted her attention. He felt jealous as he watched Shelby and Max out-spoof each other. They seemed made out of the same mold. So then why had she kissed him? Why did he feel under her observation? It was hard not to succumb.

"So what kind of scientists are you?" the cab driver asked.

"Chemists."

There was a long pause.

"That's like a pharmacist right?" The cab driver asked, coughing phlegmatically into his hand.

"Yeah. We prescribe a lot of Valium," Max said, bugging his eyes out at Shelby and then dropping the look instantly as the cab driver turned to him. "It's a great job."

Hadley couldn't see Shelby's reaction as she was sitting next to him, but he sensed her playing along. It was clear that she and Max were so alike, so irreverent. So why had she written him that letter? What could he give her that Max couldn't? But he knew. Occasionally Hadley made the mistake in thinking that he and Max were alike—they had similar interests, similar talents, and had known each other for almost nine years now—but then Max would say or do something that reminded Hadley how far apart their sensibilities were. It was clear that Max had never read anything Shelby had written. Max didn't seem to realize that Shelby needed more encouragement than he was giving her. Hadley would watch them telling stories at parties, each trying to get out the funniest lines, top one another. Hadley was willing to stand back and let Shelby effervesce. He didn't want to compete with her. He didn't need to. Just watching her was enough.

She'd given him something else to read, something she'd written about life at the Co-op. It had made it all come back to him so clearly. He had been almost afraid of

做了个担心的表情,麦克斯紧接着挑了挑右眉。谢尔碧对他们做了个鬼脸,也不顾司机可能会在后视镜里看见她。那个瞬间是他们所共享的。

"你怎么知道的?"艾伯哈德的发问填补上了那阵静默。麦克斯做了个夸张的表情,让谢尔碧镇定下来。

"那片区域,本来就有很多科学家。"那个司机点着头,仿佛曾经做过研究似的。

"那么那些科学家们平时打车付钱吗?"哈德利开口问了句,谢尔碧被逗得大笑起来。他想要谢尔碧的注意力转移到自己身上。当他看着谢尔碧和麦克斯互相戏弄的时候,心里就妒火难耐。他们俩就像是一个模子刻出来的。那么谢尔碧为什么还要吻他呢?为什么他总是觉得谢尔碧在观察自己?要想不投降,实在太难了。

"所以,你们是哪种科学家?"司机问道。

"化学家。"

一阵长久的沉默。

"就像药剂师一样,对吗?"司机用手捂着嘴巴平静地咳嗽着。

"对,我们经常开很多安定剂。"麦克斯对着谢尔碧鼓突着眼珠子,可是就在司机转向他的一瞬间立刻又恢复了正常。"这可是份不错的工作。"

因为谢尔碧就坐在他的旁边,哈德利看不见她的反应,可是却能感觉到她也在和麦克斯一唱一和。她和麦克斯非常相似,都一副玩世不恭的样子。那么为什么她要给自己写那封信呢?他能给她什么,是麦克斯所给不了的?可哈德利立刻意识到,自己其实知道答案。有些时候哈德利会误以为自己和麦克斯是相像的人——他们有相似的兴趣、天赋,并且已经相识差不多九年了——可是麦克斯有时说的话或做的事,会提醒哈德利其实他们俩的感性差距到底有多大。很显然,麦克斯从来没有读过谢尔碧写的任何东西。他并没有意识到,他给予谢尔碧的鼓励远远不够。哈德利曾经看着他们俩在派对上一起讲故事,双方都想讲出最搞笑的那句话,试图胜过对方。而哈德利则愿意后退一步,让谢尔碧能够兴高采烈地得偿所愿。他不想和谢尔碧竞争。也不需要。只要看着她就够了。

谢尔碧又给了他一些自己写的东西,是关于在大学合作宿舍的那段日子的。这使得一切记忆都清晰地向哈德利涌来。那些日子里,他对谢尔碧几乎是

her in those days. She'd looked like the girlfriend of a Hell's Angel then, mascara under the eyes, bed hair hung crookedly, sexy and messy at the same time. Her writing brought forth so many previously submerged thoughts, now frothing in his conscious mind, jostling for actualization. How could he stop himself?

He remembered, shortly after meeting her, telling her a story about his being locked in a U-haul with a girl who had come to see their band play. He wasn't sure why he was telling her, but Shelby inspired confidences. He'd been explaining to Shelby why he and the girl were even in the U-Haul, explaining that he'd been sharing a hotel room with the three other band members and he'd been locked out of the room. It was clear why. He could hear all sorts of moaning coming from inside. So he'd gone back to the bar to hear another band play and he'd met this girl. She had liked their band, and so they both got some beers and ended up just hanging out in the U-Haul talking.

"So we're there, just sitting inside, when suddenly my friend Brendan shows up, laughing uproariously, and closes the back of the U-Haul on us. He thought it was the greatest joke. We're thinking that he's going to come back in a few minutes and let us out. But an hour goes by and we realize that he's probably not coming back. I knew he was really drunk and figured that he'd forgotten about us. As it turns out, he passed out in the hallway next to the hotel room. So we pound on the walls for a while and yell, but no one comes."

"What did you do?"

"What could we do? We were locked in a U-Haul. I reassured her that, you know, I was a gentleman, and so we sat and talked. She was a waitress. I just remembered that she told me a funny story about how she'd hit a woman in the head with an omelet and little pieces of egg had gotten in the woman's hair and how she, Kelly, had laughed at the time, not meaning to of course, and the table still gave her a big tip. She asked me if I thought she got a big tip because she had laughed, or because they didn't really like the woman. Of course, how could I know, not being there, but she seemed to think that I should be able to figure it out." Hadley's gaze had strayed to his hands, but now he turned to Shelby. "People think all sorts of weird things when they hear you play music. They look up to you as if have more answers than the next guy."

There was a pause.

抱着害怕的态度的。她当时看上去就像是"地狱使徒"的女朋友,下睫毛涂得浓黑,头发就像刚起床时那样糟乱地散着,既邋遢又性感。谢尔碧写的故事引出了他脑海里许多曾被压抑的想法,现在它们在哈德利的意识中争挤,想要被实现。

他还记得,在刚认识谢尔碧不久之后,他就给她讲述了自己如何与一个来看自己乐队演出的女生一起被关在 U-Haul 搬家车里的故事。他当时在给谢尔碧解释,为什么他和那个女生会在搬运车里,是因为他当时是和另外三个乐队成员共住一个宾馆房间,但他却被锁在了门外。原因很清楚。他都能够听见门里传来的各种呻吟声。于是他就回到了酒吧里,看另一个乐队的演出,然后就认识了这个女生。她喜欢哈德利的乐队,自然而然地,他们俩就一起喝了些啤酒,最终站在了 U-Haul 的搬家车里闲聊。

"就那样儿,我们当时就坐在车里,我的朋友布兰登突然出现,发狂似的大笑了几声,猛地关上了车后门。他可能觉得这是最棒的恶作剧了。我们本以为几分钟之后他就会回来放我们出去的。可是一个小时就那么过去了,我们才开始意识到他已经把我们给忘了。其实事实是,他在酒店房间旁边的走廊里醉得不省人事。所以不论我们当时多么用力地捶打墙壁,扯着嗓子叫喊,都没有人来帮我们。"

"那你们是怎么做的?"

"还能怎么做?我们被锁在车里了。我就向她保证了,你懂的,我是一个绅士,所以我们就一直坐在那里聊天。她是个服务生。我还记得她给我讲了一个很好笑的故事,她有一次把煎蛋卷打翻在了一位女顾客的头上,以致她的头发里都嵌满了蛋渣。虽然当时并不想,可是她,凯莉,还是忍不住大声笑了出来。但那桌的人仍然给了她很大一笔小费。她问我,她得到那笔小费是因为她笑了,还是因为他们都不喜欢那个女人。可是,我当时又没在场,怎么会知道呢。她似乎就认定了我应该能弄明白。"哈德利的目光游离到了自己的双手上,这会儿又转向了谢尔碧。"人们一听说你是玩音乐的,就会联想到各种奇怪的事情。他们期待地看着你,就好像你的答案比其他人的都多似的。"

接着有一阵短暂的沉默。

"And do you?"

He had laughed. "Only when I'm playing."

"What about when you're locked in a U-Haul?"

"Certainly not."

"Women around here are much choosier you know."

"I don't doubt it," Hadley had said, looking levelly at Shelby. "The next morning Brendan came back, apologizing like crazy and then nudging me when she couldn't see."

"Why?"

Hadley had given Shelby a twisted smile. "Because I was a virgin."

At the time Hadley wondered why he even told her that. Now, years later, he knew. Something about Shelby made you disclose. You had no fears.

"And?" she'd asked, meaningfully.

"Give me a break. That was two years ago."

"So you're a consummate lover now?"

"No one's complained yet."

"That could be because you date women in U-Haul's."

Hadley smiled at the recollection, turning his head and looking out the window of the cab. He felt Shelby's presence so completely, his leg pressed against hers, the memory of her impertinence when he'd not yet appreciated it. Why had he let Max get her first? Why was he always so slow?

Broadway slithered past as the cab quickly twined in and out of slower cars. A light rain drizzled, misting the cab windows. The inside of the cab was so hot and muggy, though, that Hadley had his window rolled down slightly and every so often little pinpricks of rain would hit his face or hand. Shelby watched as raindrops landed on Hadley's mustache and got lost in it. He looked at her watching him, and smiled slightly. Acknowledgingly. Her heart clenched in her chest. It was a sign. He'd read her letter. He was encouraging. She closed her eyes, imagining them alone.

The cab driver suddenly gunned the engine before an intersection, not making the yellow, but going for it anyway. The acceleration flung a large drop of water into Shelby's face. She flinched at the icy wetness, forcing herself not to ask the cab driver to slow down. It only made them drive faster.

"你真的有吗?"

哈德利笑了,"只有在我打鼓的时候。"

"那么当你被关在搬家车里的时候呢?"

"当然没有。"

"你知道吗,这里的女人选男人可挑剔了。"

"我毫不怀疑。"哈德利给了谢尔碧一个认真的眼神。"第二天早上布兰登回来了,像疯了似的跟我们道歉,却在凯莉看不见的时候一直用肘部拱我。"

"为什么?"

哈德利给了谢尔碧一个扭曲的微笑,"因为我那时还是一个处男。"

那个时候哈德利还莫名其妙,不知道自己为什么会把那件事告诉她。多年之后的现在,他知道了。谢尔碧身上有一种魔力,能让人坦诚相见,没有恐惧。

"所以呢?"她意味深长地接下去。

"饶了我吧。那可是两年前的事了。"

"所以你现在是一个技艺精湛的情人咯?"

"目前为止还没人抱怨过。"

"这也许是因为你都是在搬家车里和女人约会的缘故。"

哈德利回忆到这里的时候嘴角不觉浮起一丝微笑,他转头向计程车窗外看去。他彻底地感受着谢尔碧的存在,他们俩的大腿互相碰触着。哈德利回忆着她的粗鲁无理,那时他对此还不感到欣赏。为什么他让麦克斯捷足先登了?为什么自己总是这么慢?

出租车左右穿梭,超过了其他缓行的车辆,百老汇的景色在两边的车窗外闪过。雨势很小,飘洒在车窗上,蒙了一层薄雾。车里则又热又闷,哈德利于是把窗户稍微摇开了一些,不时会有小雨滴打在他的脸上或手上。谢尔碧看着雨点着陆在哈德利的胡子上,又消失在里面。哈德利在车窗里看见她盯着自己的样子,微微地笑了。秘而不宣地。谢尔碧的心脏在胸膛里猛地收紧了。这是一个迹象。他已经读过她写的信了。而他现在正鼓励着她。谢尔碧闭上了双眼,想象着他们俩正单独待在一起。

司机突然在岔路口猛踩了油门,虽然没赶上黄灯,但还是直接闯了过去。瞬间的加速使一大滴的水珠砸在谢尔碧的脸上。那湿漉漉的冰凉让她下意识往后缩了一下,她勉强忍住,没有开口让司机开慢一点。因为那只会刺激他们开得更快。

Eberhard chuckled and said, "I belief we mate Mach 1."

"You know, on the Concorde they have an LED read out so you can know exactly when you break the sound barrier," Shelby said. She heard her voice talking away without completely realizing that she'd said anything. She felt so nervous. In some ways, she wanted to go back in time, before they had this perverse awareness of each other. "You feel yourself pushed back in your seat by the force." She heard her voice going on without her, saying nothing. It sounded tight and snotty when all she meant to do was sound in need.

"How do you know that?" Hadley asked challengingly.

Feeling the presence of Max, she turned her head away. "I was an air courier. I had to take someone's heart valve to England—"

"They served partridge. Isn't that like eating someone's pet?" Max threw this out for discussion, but Shelby was irritated that Max had interrupted her, her anger an excuse, a reason to want Hadley. She felt cheap using it, but used it all the same. She hid her annoyance by going along with the redirected topic, driving into the skid to regain control of the conversation. "I have Concorde coasters," she added.

"But could you feel how fast you were going?" asked Hadley, his voice deep and husky, like the question had great import.

"Yah," Eberhard agreed. "Were you stuck in your seat?"

"How was the partridge?" the cab driver wanted to know, looking over his shoulder for a second.

Max, seeing trouble ahead, yelled, "Watch out!" With a quick look forward, the cab driver cranked the wheel hard to the left. The cab jolted sideways, narrowly missing a double-parked truck. Horns honked all around. The truck's hazard lights were on and the segmented back door, like the cover to a roll-top desk, was at half-mast. Two men sitting on the truck's floor and eating big sandwiches in waxed paper laughed and pointed at the cars and cabs as the vehicles nearly sideswiped them.

Shelby fell against Hadley, her hands catching his ribs. Eberhard fell on top of her, and she found her face pressed into Hadley's chest. It was warm. A man's chest. He was a man and she was touching him. She felt twinges between her legs. The weave of his madras shirt softly scratched her face, warning her of the risk. She had slipped into his gravity zone. There was danger here. A button dug at her temple, but it went unnoticed because her face was now in resonance with his heartbeat, a

艾伯哈德咯咯笑着说:"我觉得我们刚才超越了音速[译者注:航空用语 Mach I]。"

"你们知道吗,在协和飞机上安装有一个 LED 读数器,这样你就可以知道达到音速的确切时间了。"谢尔碧听着自己的声音就那样说开去,可她却对此毫无意识。她感觉到无比紧张。某种程度上来说,她想要回到过去,他们还不会因为对方的在场而感到尴尬的时候。"你在座位上会感觉到自己被那股力量向后推了一下。"谢尔碧听着自己的声音抽离了自己,内容空洞。她的声线紧绷,带着自以为是的口吻,而其实她只是想让别人听出自己亟须帮助。

"你怎么知道的?"哈德利挑衅地问道。

谢尔碧感觉到了麦克斯的存在,于是把头转向一边。"我曾经做过航空快递员,有一次我必须得把某个人的心脏瓣膜给护送到英国——"

"英国有道菜是山鹬。那不就像是吃了某个人的宠物似的吗?"麦克斯突然抛出这个问题来让大家讨论,但是谢尔碧却因为他打断了自己而恼怒起来。这给了她一个生气的借口,一个想要哈德利的理由。虽然她觉得利用这一点有些卑鄙,可还是这么做了。藏起愠色,她继续着新话题讲下去,接着长驱直入,又夺回了话语权。"我现在还收藏着协和式飞机上的杯垫。"她补充道。

"但是你感觉得到飞机的速度有多快吗?"他深沉的嗓音有些沙哑,仿佛这个问题有多重要似的。

"就是,"艾伯哈德附和道,"你当时是卡在座位上不能动了吗?"

"那个山鹬尝起来怎么样?"司机好奇地想知道,便把头转到肩膀这头来。

麦克斯看到了前方的危险,大声叫起来:"当心!"司机迅速向前瞥了一眼,猛地将方向盘打到左边。出租车扭转到了一边,与一辆双排停车的卡车擦肩而过。四周响起一阵鸣笛声。卡车上的危险警告灯是亮着的,残缺的后门就像拉盖书桌的掀盖,现在已经"降了半旗"。两个男人坐在卡车的地板上,一边啃着油皮纸包着的巨型三明治,一边指着那些险些撞到他们的轿车和出租车大声叫笑着。

谢尔碧被一下子甩到了哈德利的身上,双手不自主地扶住了他的肋骨位置。艾伯哈德也压在了谢尔碧的身上,把她的脸挤到了哈德利的胸膛上。很温暖。一个男人的胸膛。他是一个男人,而她正触碰着他。她的两腿之间感觉到了一阵微微的刺痛。哈德利身上马德拉斯布料的衬衫轻柔地刮擦着谢尔碧的脸庞,警告着她风险的存在。她已经滑入了他的禁区,那里潜伏着危险。有颗纽扣顶到了谢尔碧的太阳穴,可是她却丝毫没有察觉,因为她的脸蛋儿现在和哈德利的心跳处于一个频率上,感受到的猛烈的撞击让谢尔碧自己的心跳也随之加速起

furious pounding sensation making her own beat faster. She could feel her cheeks grow warm and was glad it was a dark day. She couldn't move because Eberhard was crammed against her, but then Eberhard reached quickly for the door handle and righted himself. Embarrassed, she placed her hands against Hadley's chest, feeling his body solid under his shirt, the heat of it, the flesh, imagining it unclothed. In the space of an instant, she grasped him as hers, her fingers holding him to her chest, the barest rub of her breasts, unknowable to the rest, a message, a pulse of energy. Then she quickly pushed herself back to sitting position, feeling her body shooting sparks, electrons flying. She glanced at him. He wouldn't look at her. Time expanded. She tried taking inaudible deep breaths to regain her composure. Her only concrete thought was: Don't. Don't even.

"They must be most hungry," Eberhard laughed, referring to the men eating in the double-parked truck. He dealt with New York by assuming that everything stupid was funny instead, which meant he laughed more than most people.

"Nah. They do it for sport," the cab driver said. "I seen guys like that everyday a the week."

"I thought it was a fifty-dollar fine if you honk," Max said, still wincing from the noise.

"Only if they hear ya," the cabby laughed. "It's like that tree." He slowed down at a stoplight. A man with a rag and a squirt bottle walked up and started cleaning the front window. The cab driver turned on the wipers and the man left and went to the car behind them. "Damn bums."

"I wonder if they make any money doing that," Max said congenially.

"Oh, sure," the guy answered, like he really knew. He reached down to turn on the radio, dialing in Paul Harvey. "So what kind of music do you guys play?" He'd helped them pile their instruments into the trunk.

"We play—the Sixties. Do you remember them?" Eberhard asked.

"Ya know," the cab driver shifted to a more comfortable position and belched lightly, "not a lot a people know this, but the Sixties was my idea, and somebody else got all the credit."

There was a silence. Shelby remembered again why she tried never to get into conversations with cab drivers.

来。她很庆幸当时的天色昏暗,因为她能感觉到自己的两颊开始逐渐变暖。有艾伯哈德压在身上,谢尔碧动弹不得,可他迅速地伸手抓住了门把手,坐正了身体。谢尔碧这时才感到尴尬,因为她的双手正撑在哈德利的胸膛上,感受着衬衫下面结实的身体、温度、肌肉,想象着他赤裸身体时的样子。在千分之一秒的时间里,谢尔碧紧紧地拥住了哈德利,手指将他拉近自己胸前,让他感受柔软胸脯的摩擦,其他人却毫无察觉,这是一条讯号,一次能量的脉冲。接着她迅速地将自己推回原位坐好,体内却火花四射,电子飞蹿。她瞟了一眼哈德利。他却不愿意回看一眼。时间开始横向地扩张。谢尔碧试着在不引人注意的前提下深呼吸了几次,以此来重新镇定下来。她脑海里唯一坚定的想法就是:不要。想都不要。

"他们一定是饿疯了。"艾伯哈德放声大笑起来,他指的是那卡车里吃东西的两个男人。他与纽约周旋的方法就是把任何愚蠢的事情都看作是有趣的,也就是说他笑得频率比大部分人都高。

"才不是呢,他们这样做是为了逗乐的,"司机回应道,"这样的家伙我每天都看到。"

"我还以为按喇叭是要罚款五十美金的呢。"麦克斯仍然因为刚才那阵噪音而蹙着眉头。

"除非被他们听到了,"出租车司机笑了,"就像树林里倒下的树一样。"他在一个红绿灯前面放慢了速度,一个拿着破布和喷水瓶的男人走上前来,开始擦洗车前窗。一看到司机打开雨刮器,那个人就离开了,走向了后面的一辆车。"该死的流浪汉。"

"我有点好奇他们这样能挣到钱吗?"麦克斯同情地说道。

"哦,当然了。"那个家伙回答道,就好像他真的了解似的。他又伸手去打开车载收音机,调到保罗哈维的频道。"你们演奏的是哪种音乐呢?"之前是他帮着把乐器给抬进后备厢的。

"我们表演的是六十年代乐队[译者注:美国著名摇滚乐队 the Sixties]的歌。你还记得他们吗?"艾伯哈德问道。

"你们知道吗,"司机换了一个更舒服的姿势,惬意地打了个嗝,"虽然懂的人不多,组建六十年代这个乐队可是我的主意,却被别人给抢了功劳。"

取而代之的是一阵沉默。谢尔碧这时想起了自己为什么从来都不愿意和出租车司机攀谈的原因。

"Ah! We are here!" Eberhard said to the cab driver, leaning into the front and pointing to the curb.

"You know, I just hate people who take credit for things they didn't do," the cabby said, pulling quickly to the curb. "Get a lot of that in this business. That's why I keep a gun."

Shelby reached over and opened Eberhard's door for him, pushing him out, then climbing out quickly herself. She couldn't take it any more. The idiocy of the driver, the proximity of Hadley. Her head was going to explode.

The sidewalk glistened with water and occasional rainbows of grease. Soggy Kleenex lay next to a battered garbage can as if someone with a bad cold had been shooting baskets and missed. Several men wearing blankets and cardboard hats huddled around the entrance to the building. An overhang reduced the amount of rain there, and the men stood under it, holding paper bags in hand and occasionally taking swigs of whatever was inside.

The band walked into the low entryway, carrying cases, the steel doors crashing behind them. The place was an eyesore of clashing colors and scrawled graffiti. Along the walls someone had haphazardly thrown buckets of paint. Perhaps the moment had been art, but the walls were far from it. Staples, thumbtacks, and long black skid marks from unwieldy instrument cases added to the hieroglyphics of band culture. Many of the walls were covered with flyers from bands with names like Mondo Boffo, Power Tool Theology, Spam Shaft, and La La La Fuck You. Shelby often read the flyers in order to discover potential places to play, though many of the clubs, she suspected, were a higher class of dive bar than they were ready for.

As they walked toward the elevator, the low roof of the entryway opened up to a high ceiling where one lone fire sprinkler incautiously dripped a salty tasting fluid on the unsuspecting. Skirting the precipitate, Eberhard pushed the button for the elevator and they waited as the banging machine descended toward them.

"God, and he seemed so normal," Shelby said. Max laughed and put his arm around her. She tried not to pull away.

A woman who looked like a member of the East German swim team walked through the front door and stood next to them as they waited for the elevator. When the woman turned her head, Shelby realized that half of it was shaved. She tried not to stare, but kept finding reasons to look in her direction, which was mostly up. Shelby

"啊！我们到了！"艾伯哈德将身体倾向前去，指着马路边对司机说道。

"说真的，我最恨明明没有做过，却抢别人功劳的人了，"司机一边迅速停向路边，一边继续说着，"在这一行经常发生，所以我随身带枪。"

谢尔碧伸手开了艾伯哈德那边的门，一把将他推了出去，接着自己也忙不迭地钻了出来。她实在是忍受不了了。不论是那个司机的愚昧，还是哈德利一直在身边的即时感。她的脑袋就快要爆炸了。

人行道的地面反射着水光，还有偶尔的油光折射的彩虹。湿软的纸巾散乱在有凹陷的垃圾桶旁边，仿佛有个重感冒的人一直在用纸团儿投篮可是总是不中。几个身披毯子，头戴硬纸壳帽子的人蜷缩在大楼的入口边上。突出的屋檐挡住了一部分的雨，于是有一些男人就站在下面，手里拎着纸袋子，不时从中拿出藏在袋里的瓶子来喝上几大口。

乐队一行人提着乐器走进了低矮的入口，铁门在他们身后"哐当"一声关上了。

这个地方充满了互相冲突的色彩，潦草的涂鸦，丑陋得异常显眼。一路走来的墙上都被人胡乱地撒上了彩漆。也许泼洒的那个瞬间可以算作是艺术，但现在的这堵墙却离艺术差了十万八千里。笨重乐器盒上的订书钉、图钉，以及长长的黑色划痕，构成了乐队文化的象形文字。相当面积的墙体都被乐队的宣传单给覆盖了，那些乐队的名字千奇百怪：蒙多波甫（Mondo Boffo：非常成功，最佳结果）、电力工具神学（power tool theology）、肉质长矛（spam shaft），还有啦啦啦操你（La La La Fuck You）。谢尔碧经常会为了找到下一个演出场所而把这些海报都读一遍，虽然她怀疑里面有许多俱乐部都比他们乐队的档次要高很多。

在走向电梯的途中，低矮入口的后面天花板豁然变高了，一个孤零零的消防喷头冷不丁地掉下几滴咸味的液体，砸在毫无防备的人头上。艾伯哈德绕开"突袭"，按下了电梯的按钮，在那个机器"哐当哐当"的声音中等着它降到面前。

"天哪，他明明看上去挺正常的。"谢尔碧回忆道。麦克斯大笑着搂住了她，谢尔碧强迫自己不把他推开。

一个长得像东德游泳队队员似的女人穿过前门，停在了他们的旁边。当她转头的时候，谢尔碧意识到她有半边头发是剃光的。虽然她尽力不去盯着那个女人看，可是总是找理由向那个方向看过去，她几乎是要仰着头的。谢尔碧仔细

Chapter Seventeen Piltdown Man

studied the woman's face, her nose ring, her chiseled jawbone. Shelby felt her own jaw. A double-chin wasn't far away. How did people handle getting old? Shelby felt along her jaw where it matched up to her skull, feeling the hinge as she opened and closed her mouth, the action well-oiled from use. She recalled their conversation in the cab. "How long did people think this ape-man thing was the missing link?" Shelby asked. "Wouldn't the jaws have had to fit together incredibly well?"

"Someone planted it there," Hadley said, walking into the open elevator. He waited for them all to get in and for the woman to push the button for her floor, then he pressed the button for floor five with the end of a drumstick because someone had stuck a wad of gum on the button. "It fit together well because it was a hoax," he added quietly, not looking at her.

"Oooh!" Shelby exhaled. "I thought it was just bad archeology."

"Well, it was that, too. People were suckered for about forty years," Max added. "The scientists wanted to believe it because they'd all made their careers on the Piltdown man. It proved all their theories. One guy was even knighted for it."

"Did they unknight him later?"

"No. He died," Eberhard laughed as the elevator doors opened. Everyone just stood there. "I think this is four," Max said to the woman. The numbers didn't light up over the door, so it was hard to tell what floor you were on. You had to listen. Two was reggae and the doors would open to the intoxicating smell of reefer. Three was heavy metal. Four and five were straight rock. But the people on four wore darker clothes and had planned accidents with razors.

The elevator started to rise to the next floor as the doors lethargically closed after the woman. They could see graffiti on the elevator shaft.

"Every time I ride this I think we should start taking the stairs," Hadley said, shaking his head.

"That's what I thought until I took them," Shelby said wryly. "You have to step over bodies on the landings and everything smells of urine mixed with puke."

"Ah, well then, this is bet-ter," Eberhard agreed.

Shelby had actually only once opened the door to the stairs and that was enough. A man was sprawled in the corner of the stairwell. He'd been living there, a human soul between ascent and descent. It was like finding a troll under a bridge. And knowing he might have been an accountant at one time.

研究了她的脸、她的鼻环，以及轮廓分明的颌骨。然后她又感受了一下自己的颌骨，离双下巴不远了。人们都是怎么对待老去这件事的？谢尔碧沿着自己的下巴寻觅着，一直到它和头骨连接的地方，借着嘴巴张合感受两者的衔接部分。那个部位因为经常使用而运行良好。她突然想起了计程车里的对话。"有多长一段时间人们认为那个猿人颌骨是考古学上缺失的一环？"谢尔碧又提起了这个问题。"难道那颌骨和颅骨不应该完美地衔接才对吗？"

"是有人事先埋在那里的。"哈德利走进了打开的电梯。等所有人都进去，那个女人也按过自己的楼层后，他才用鼓槌的末端按下五楼，因为有人在那个按钮上粘了一块口香糖。"衔接之所以那么完美是因为这整件事就是一个骗局。"哈德利没有看谢尔碧，静静地补充道。

"天哪——"谢尔碧深吸了一口气，"我还以为只是考古学家出错了呢。"

"好吧，那也是一部分原因。大家被耍了四十多年。"麦克斯也插了进来，"科学家们愿意那样相信，是因为他们的职业生涯就指望着皮尔当人的发掘了。那次考古证实了他们的理论。有个家伙甚至因此而被授予了骑士头衔。"

"那后来他们把头衔给撤销了吗？"

"没有，他死了。"艾伯哈德在电梯门打开的时候大笑起来。每个人都站在原地没有动。"我觉得这是四楼。"麦克斯对那个女人说。电梯门上的数字并没有亮起来，所以很难辨别到底处在哪一层楼。得仔细听着。二楼放的是雷盖音乐［译者注：一种节奏强劲的西印度流行音乐］，门一开醉人的大麻烟味就扑面而来。三楼是重金属音乐。四楼和五楼则是纯摇滚。但是四楼上的人习惯穿深色的衣服，会用剃须刀在身上割划。

那个女人出去了，电梯门没精打采地慢慢合上，继续向下一层攀升。就连电梯的通风井上都画着涂鸦。

"每次我一坐这个电梯，我就开始觉得我们应该走楼梯的。"哈德利边说边摇着头。

"在我没走过楼梯之前我也是这么想的。"谢尔碧语气挖苦地回应道。"每走一步你都得小心地绕开地上的人，那里的所有东西闻上去都像是尿液和呕吐物的混合气味。"

"啊，好吧，那还是电梯更好。"艾伯哈德做了个总结。

其实谢尔碧只打开过一次通向楼梯的门，但那也就足够了。在楼梯井的角落里，有个男人四仰八叉地躺着。他一直住在那里，灵魂在上升和堕落之间徘徊。谢尔碧的感觉就像是在桥下发现了一个怪物，而心里却知道他也许曾经是个会计师。

Chapter Seventeen Piltdown Man

The elevator doors opened and a cacophony of bands could be heard coming at them in all directions, the music competing for air space. The screeching wail of an out-of-tune guitarist pierced the din. Shelby could feel the vibrations sonicating her organs. It made her want to throw up. The wail stopped for a moment, and Shelby felt her spine unclench. Then it started again, harsh and jarring as if the sound had been fried on hot pavement and scraped up with a rake, caught in the guitar's larynx and making its bloody way, claw by claw, up the trachea.

They rounded the corner and the sound cut by a meager ten percent, but enough to make them think that they still had their hearing. Their rehearsal space was on the other side of the building, a quieter area, but the repulsiveness of the owner offset the momentary serenity they'd gained by discovering they weren't yet deaf. They called him "the Pirate" because he wore a black patch over his left eye. One time early on, without their requesting it, he even took off his patch to show them the vacancy, a stitched concavity that absolutely grossed Shelby out and didn't do a hell of a lot for the others. "It was some kind of test," Max had said, "to see if we were man enough to play at Rogue Studios."

They stood at the solid metal door, waiting for the Pirate to answer the buzzer. Sometimes it took him a while. Shelby dropped the mike bag she'd been carrying and sat on it, taunted by an idea that had been dangling in front of her. What was it? There were too many ideas fighting for space in her brain. It related somehow to their previous discussion. Some way to impress Hadley, to get him embroiled in conversation. Something about the Piltdown man. She got a corner of the thought, tugging it through a hole in her consciousness. The idea slowly coalesced. She formed it in her mind for a moment before she spoke, wanting them to take her seriously. Slowly she asked, "What good is science if a major discovery could be that wrong, and for forty years? Then a theory is as good as faith."

Hadley looked at her straight-on. "But the truth will out. Science is something that can be repeated, that can stand face to face with time. Is that true with faith?"

"Well ..." she paused, wondering if she should go on. "Isn't it faith if molecules can come together faster than is possible?" She now spoke quickly, unsure that Max would want her to bring this up. She wanted to show them all that she was smart, too. That she knew what was going on.

"Ah!" Eberhard smiled. "You are talking about Scotia's theory. I too have

电梯门又打开了，各式乐队演奏的刺耳声音从四面八方向他们袭来，在空气中互相竞争着领地。其中一个吉他手跑调了，尖厉的声音穿透了整片嘈杂。谢尔碧能够感觉到自己的器官在跟随声波一起振动。这让她想吐。那刺耳的声音停了一会儿，谢尔碧就觉得自己的整个脊柱都放松了下来。可是转瞬间它又重新开始了，粗糙又尖刻，仿佛是在滚烫的路面上煎过，被耙子刮下来之后，卡在了吉他的下弦位，然后一点一点地抓挠着沿着琴颈向上。

一转过拐角，音量就轻微减弱了百分之十，但却足够让他们确定自己的听力仍然健在。他们的排练地点在大楼的另一边，相对安静些，可是这里主人的可憎程度却能够抵消刚刚发现自己没有聋掉而获得的那点安宁。他们把那个楼主叫作"海盗"，因为他的左眼上蒙了一块黑色的眼罩。早前些的时候，没有人要求他，他就取下了那个眼罩，露出空荡的眼窝，凹陷的表面处有着针线缝合的痕迹。谢尔碧被恶心得够呛，可是其他人却没什么大反应。"这是一种测试，"麦克斯说，"看我们够不够男人，能够获得在'流氓'工作室排练的资质。"

他们站在厚重的金属大门前，等待"海盗"来应门铃。有时候他会过上好一会儿才来。谢尔碧把一直背在身上的麦克风包往地上一扔，坐在了上面，脑子里一直挥之不去的一个想法此时正嘲笑着她。是什么想法呢？她脑袋里实在有太多的想法在争抢地盘了，但那个想法与先前的对话有关。某种可以让哈德利印象深刻，投入到交谈中的方法。某件关于皮尔当人的事。她抓住了那个想法的一个小角，想要从一个洞口将它从自己的意识里扯出来，然后开始逐渐拼凑成形了。在开口之前谢尔碧在脑海里斟酌了一会儿，因为她想让其他人重视她说的话。她终于慢慢地开口了："要是一个重大发现都能够错得如此离谱，并且还持续了四十年，那么科学还有什么用处呢？可以说科学理论与宗教信仰没什么差别。"

哈德利直接迎上她的目光。"但是真相最终会浮现的。科学是可以经受重复验证的东西，也可以经受时间的考验。信仰也是这样吗？"

"这个嘛……"谢尔碧犹疑了，不知道自己是不是该继续。"如果分子能够以超出常理的速度聚拢，那么这不是一种信仰吗？"这会儿她的语速加快了，因为她并不确定麦克斯希望自己提起这件事。她想要证明，自己也很聪明，她了解正在发生的事情。

"啊哈！"艾伯哈德笑了，"你指的是斯考蒂亚的理论。我也正纳闷呢，难道

wondered. A new law of the universe?" Eberhard gestured in a way that made it clear he thought it unlikely.

"But Scotia's explanation of energy sinks, where one reaction could speed the next is not really a violation of the second law. Our model just isn't good enough." Hadley looked at Max when he said this and shrugged. "And perhaps the science isn't either."

"It's an interesting theory, but it's beginning to look like there is no science to back it up. And that a second-year graduate student should stumble upon an example of it ..." Max looked at the others, opening his hands.

"Serendipity," Shelby said sarcastically.

Hadley looked at Shelby curiously. "You think she's lying, too?"

Shelby nodded.

"You don't know her chemistry. How can you be so sure?"

"I like to think that I am fairly intuitive. Why else be a woman?"

"She's certainly on the edge of a wig," Max agreed. He sat down on the floor. Hadley crouched down next to him.

"A wig?" Eberhard asked.

"Max has expressions no one's heard of. Not even us Americans," Shelby said wryly.

"Yes you have. She's wigged out."

"I got a sample of her catalyst," Hadley said off-handedly.

"How'd you get that?" Max turned to Hadley. "Bineet's been bugging her for weeks for the stuff, and I thought you didn't have anymore."

"I took her TLC plate and scraped it."

Max looked at Hadley admiringly. "Well, what is it?"

"I can't tell from the NMR ... I know how she's faking it though." Hadley paused for a dramatic moment.

"So tell us jism!" Max yelled, pushing Hadley.

"She's switching NMR tubes."

"Now how do you know that?" Max asked.

"I marked a tube," Hadley said, eyeing Max.

"You put a marked tube in the NMR and got a different one back?" Max was astounded. "When?" They heard the studio door's padlocks unlatching, causing a

产生了一条新的宇宙法则?"他做了个手势,明显地表明自己并不相信。

"但是斯考蒂亚给出的势能阱的解释,关于一个反应可以引发下一个的假设,也并不完全违反热力学第二定律。只是我们的模型不够好罢了。"哈德利说这句话的时候看着麦克斯,然后耸了耸肩。"也许科学本身就不完美。"

"这个理论挺有趣的,"麦克斯接口道,"但是就现状看来,这背后根本就缺乏科学依据。更何况竟然还是一个二年级的研究生乱打乱撞地发现了这个特例……"他扫视了一眼大家,两手向外一摊。

"多巧啊。"谢尔碧讽刺地评价道。

哈德利好奇地看着她,"你也觉得拉达在撒谎吗?"

谢尔碧点了点头。

"你又不了解她做的化学研究,你怎么能够确定呢?"

"我认为我是一个直觉很准的人。不然的话,做女人还有什么好处呢?"

"不消说,她已经离假发不远了。"麦克斯表示同意,接着一屁股坐在了地上,哈德利也随即在他身旁蹲了下来。

"假发?"艾伯哈德有些不解。

"麦克斯总是说一些没人听过的谚语。甚至本土美国人都不知道。"谢尔碧挖苦道。

"你听过的,用来说一个人精神不正常[译者注:英文短语 wig out 有精神不正常的意思;wig 假发]。"

"我搞到了她催化剂的一点样本。"哈德利漫不经心地抛出这么一句。

"你是怎么办到的?"麦克斯转向他,"贝内特跟她磨了好几个星期,都没能要到催化剂,我还以为你也一点都不剩了呢。"

"我拿了她的层析色谱板,从上面刮下来的。"

麦克斯一脸崇拜地看着哈德利,"那么,那个催化剂究竟是什么?"

"从核磁共振结果来看,我看不出是什么……但我知道她是在作假。"为了达到戏剧效果,哈德利故意停顿了一下。

"快告诉我们,你这家伙!"麦克斯推了哈德利一把,冲着他叫道。

"她偷偷调换了核磁共振的试管。"

"这你又是怎么知道的?"麦克斯又发问了。

"我在一个试管上做了标记。"哈德利给了他一个眼色。

"你放了一个有标记的试管到核磁分析仪里,但是取回了一个不一样的?"麦克斯感到无比的震惊,"什么时候的事?"他们听到了工作室大门的挂锁打开的声音,

ripple of standing from the group, a percolation of heads as they each grabbed their instrument and prepared to head in.

"Yesterday."

"It did not, for example, rub off?" Eberhard asked.

Hadley shook his head. "I snooped. It was in her lab. Empty."

Max blew out through his lips. "When do we tell Scotia?"

"When we figure out what the catalyst really is," Hadley said. "She was supposed to give me the NMR data. Not surprisingly, that never happened."

"After we rehearse," Eberhard said. "We will solve this problem."

Shelby groaned, feeling ignorant in not foreseeing the eventual outcome of her question. Usually they went out to lunch afterward. She had wanted more time with Hadley.

The heavy iron door swung toward them and the Pirate leered at them for a brief moment, then picked up his carton of Beef Lo Mein and resumed tossing the contents into his ever-chewing mouth. They walked into the studio, a medium-sized room with blue egg-carton foam covering every surface except for the deeply carpeted floor. The foam transformed the room into a special haven of softness and convolution. It was an odd feeling for one not used to it, to talk loudly and hear your voice end abruptly, no resonance, as peremptory as a period, the sound making a full stop when it encountered the wall. The foam was a magnet for noise, sucking up the vibrations into its network of cavities. Lots of surface area would be the chemist explanation. Shelby could hear Hadley's soft voice in her head, explaining about convolutions and crevasses, his voice tranquil and rough at the same time. She touched the keyboard, thinking of touching him, and shocked herself, literally. The electricity flew off the keyboard into her third finger. Everything was punishment. No one had warned her that there was so much static in New York City. It made her feel oddly deceived. Even when she kissed Max she could sometimes see sparks. Now they tentatively touched hands before they kissed, checking the atmosphere, their lips too sensitive to subject themselves to jolts of personal lightning.

As they began to play, Shelby lost herself in the music. The harmony of their voices felt so thick and satisfying that she felt she could almost lie down on it, let it buoy her like the blue cushioned walls. Clean harmonies, where the notes were so physically present in space, like fifth position in ballet, or the coherent beam of a laser

便顺次站了起来,像渗滤式咖啡壶里渐次突突的水泡,拿起自己的乐器,准备进去。

"昨天。"

"有没有可能,比方说,记号被蹭掉了?"艾伯哈德问道。

哈德利摇了摇头,"我后来四处打探了一下,在拉达的实验室里发现了,是空的。"

麦克斯迫切地脱口而出:"我们什么时候告诉斯考蒂亚?"

"等我们搞清楚那个催化剂到底是什么之后,"哈德利回应说,"她本来是应该把核磁分析的数据交给我的,可从来没有发生过,我想也没什么可意外的。"

"在排练之后,"艾伯哈德接着说,"我们就把这个问题给解决掉。"

谢尔碧暗自"哼哼"了一声,竟然没能预见到自己提出这个问题带来的最终结果,她觉得自己有些被捉弄了。大部分时候排练完他们会直接去吃午饭的——她想要更多和哈德利相处的时间。

沉重的金属门向外转开,站在门里的"海盗"色迷迷地斜睨了他们一会儿,接着又捧起他的那盒牛肉捞面,继续往那张没停过的嘴巴里扔吃的。他们一行人走进了工作室,那是一间中等大小的房子,所有表面都用蓝色的鸡蛋盒泡沫给覆盖了起来,地板上则铺了厚厚的地毯。整个房间被泡沫改装成了一个特殊的避风港,柔软,起伏不平。对于不熟悉这种环境的人来说,可能会觉得很奇怪:当你大声说话时,声音会戛然而止,没有回响,如同句号一样干脆,声音一旦接触墙面就迅速销匿无踪。泡沫对于噪音来说就像一块吸铁石,把所有的声波振动都吸进了自己的孔腔网络结构里。专业的化学术语是"接触表面积大"。谢尔碧的脑海里萦绕着哈德利沉静又有些沙哑的嗓音,温柔地给她解释着褶合和裂隙的含义。她抚摸着电子键盘,想象着抚摸哈德利的感觉,却真的被电到了。电流从键盘上传进了她的手指。每一件事都是惩罚。从来没有人警告过她,纽约市乐器里的静电会这么频繁。这让她有种莫名被欺骗了的感觉。甚至在和麦克斯接吻的时候她都看见过电火花。所以现在他们都会先试探性地碰一下手,以此来检测空气,嘴唇这个部位实在是太敏感了,承受不了人际闪电的电击。

开始排练之后,谢尔碧就完全沉浸在了音乐之中。她和哈德利的和音如此胶着,令人舒心,她觉得自己几乎可以浸身其中,就像被那些蓝色泡沫托着一样,身体随之沉浮。在那干净的和声中,音符的空间存在感非常强烈,像是芭蕾的五

light. She thought of the book *Flatland* where in the one-dimensional world inhabitants had to sing in harmony when they fell in love because they had no other way to demonstrate unity. (One dimension had no plane of movement. If you didn't fall in love with the beings next to you, singing was your only communion.) Harmonizing with someone was like falling in love for the moment, being sensitive to that person's every nuance, mirroring the voice in every way but pitch. Or occasionally mirroring the pitch, but at some distance, to give the sound thickness, a claiming of harmonics, creating more sound because the notes encouraged each other. The more Shelby sang with Hadley, the closer she felt to him, their voices paired snugly together, rising and falling precognitively. It was the closest she could ever get to sex. The thought saddened her. No, that wasn't true. He was willing. She was sure of it. Now she was afraid. Where would it lead? She closed her eyes, listening to her voice ride Hadley's, then punctuate his guttural melody with sixths and octaves, contrapuntal offbeats that hung in the air and twanged in resonance. Hadley glanced at her and smiled. She lived for those sideways steals, a moment too cool for words but thrilling to the pulse all the same.

The band made the rest of Shelby's life bearable. She wasn't sure she could live without it. Max always told her that she was an emotional person. That she didn't hold herself back. That whenever she liked someone, she couldn't just like them just a little bit. If Hadley knew the depth of her feelings he might be scared to death. He might think that he had some feeling for her, probably some sexual feelings, but she doubted that he would ever consider that she had such diabolically well-developed feelings for him that they'd caused her to write page upon passionate page in an effort to alleviate their torturous effects upon her mind. If she had sex with Hadley and if Max found out, what would happen to the band? What would happen to Max? She realized that the band was significant to her because all three of them were in it. But it would have to end sometime. Eventually she and Max would move. It wasn't likely that the three of them would end up together again. How could she bear that? She was forced to choose. She questioned the concept of marriage if such feelings, such desires for someone other than one's spouse, could arise unbidden. Her constant reflection compelled her to admit that if, in some different universe, she were married to Hadley right now, she could very easily be wanting an affair with Max. It wasn't the individual but the institution that was the source of ennui. If marriage,

位,或是镭射光锐利的光柱。谢尔碧想起了《二维世界》那本书里这样形容过,在一维的世界里,当人们陷入爱情时,他们唱出和谐的曲调,因为没有其他方法可以用以展现结合。(一维空间里不存在可供移动的平台。假使你爱上的不是你旁边的人,那你唯一交流的方法就是歌唱。)与一个人合唱就像是暂时地与之坠入爱河,对方的一切细节你都格外敏感,除了音高以外,你声音的所有方面都与之相呼应。有些情况下音高也需要呼应,但还是要有一定间隔,给予和声以厚度,产生谐波,同时音符之间互相激发,也会衍生出更多的声效。和哈德利一起唱歌,让谢尔碧觉得他们的距离更近了,他们俩的声音紧密地贴合在一起,了若指掌般地升降自如。这是她能达到的与性爱最接近的程度了。她因为这个想法而有些伤心。不,不是这样的。哈德利也是愿意的。谢尔碧可以肯定这一点。而现在她却害怕了。最终会发展成什么样子呢?她索性闭上了眼睛,听着自己的声音穿梭于哈德利的声线之间,不时地用六度和八度音阶点缀他粗嘎的韵律,形成与之平行对位的弱拍,悬垂在空气中,发出弹拨般的回响。哈德利给了谢尔碧一瞥,然后笑了。这样一些微妙的瞬间就是谢尔碧生活的动力,不需要语言做任何装饰,就已经足够点燃你的脉搏。

　　谢尔碧的后半生因为有了这个乐队而变得可以忍受了,否则的话,她并不确定自己能够继续生活下去。麦克斯总是告诉她,她是一个感情用事的人,没有办法掩藏自己的情绪,无论她爱上谁,都没有办法只爱一点点。如果哈德利知道她内心的感觉有如此强烈的话,八成会被吓掉了魂儿。也许哈德利对自己只有些许的感觉,很有可能是和性爱相关的,但她觉得哈德利永远也不会料想到,她的情感已经发展到了如此地步,以致她必须得将自己的激情倾注在纸页上,以求削减精神上承受的折磨。要是她和哈德利做爱并且被麦克斯发现了,乐队的最终结局会怎样?麦克斯会怎么办呢?谢尔碧意识到了乐队对她的重要性,因为他们三个都身处其中。但是总归有一天会解散的。她和麦克斯会搬走的。他们三个再次聚到一起的可能性小之又小。这让她如何承受呢?她要被迫做出选择。要是这种对于除了配偶之外的人的感情和渴求自然而然地会产生,这让谢尔碧不得不对婚姻的概念产生怀疑。经过翻来覆去的思考,她终于被迫承认,假如在另一个时空里她嫁的是哈德利,这会儿她很有可能是渴望和麦克斯有一段韵事了。厌倦的情绪与个人无关,而来源于制度本身。婚姻,就意味着单调乏味。这

Chapter Seventeen Piltdown Man

then monotony. Was that true? It was such a sad thought.

But as a band, they weren't monotonous. They created something, something that couldn't exist without cooperation. As a band, they were an altered state without the drugs. Even their bad nights could be fun. And after dealing with slimy bar owners who tried to date her, and empty rooms where they performed for themselves, Shelby still felt the band was the high point of her life. She remembered the Doo-Wop club, a drug store of a bar, where white limos pulled up out front, and body guards lounged massively against tinted windows while skinny pockmarked guys would slither through the front door for frequent negotiations with the one-eared owner (the other ear looked as if it had been shot off, a bullet crease searing the flesh where the tragus would have been). The night of their gig, the owner ultimately paid them a hundred dollars not to play. So they returned to their hundred-dollar rented station wagon and wryly joked about scum-sucking bar owners while smoking a joint Shelby had had tucked into the case of her keyboard. It was depressing, but a shared depression. They could laugh about misery and feel happy that they were among friends, happy that in their forays into New York night life, at least they broke even.

But how much longer could it last?

是真的吗？这真是一个令人悲伤的想法。

但是作为一个乐队，他们却不再单调了。他们有所创造，而创造离不开合作。当他们聚到一起时，如果不嗑药，便是完全不同的状态。即使是观众反响不好的夜晚也可以充满乐趣。即使要应对那个想约她出去的油腻的酒吧主，即使观众席空无一人他们只能为自己演奏，谢尔碧仍然觉得乐队是她人生的最高点。她还记得那个"嘟·喔普"俱乐部［译者注：Doo-wop 是流行于 20 世纪 40 年代至 60 年代的重唱形式］，担当酒吧药店双重身份的地方，会有白色的豪华轿车停在门口，成群的保镖清一色列队在茶色的车窗前，瘦得皮包骨的伙计顶着麻斑点点的脸在车和酒吧前门之间频繁穿梭，与那个只有一只耳朵的酒吧主（他的另一只耳朵看上去像是被枪给射掉的，原来耳屏所在的位置留有清晰的子弹灼痕）传话协商。那天晚上他们本来是要表演的，可最终酒吧主给了他们一百美金让他们休息。于是他们就回到了每月一百美金租来的旅行车里，拿那些混蛋酒吧主开玩笑。谢尔碧取出早前塞在琴盒里的大麻烟卷，大家轮流抽了起来。那种情景虽然令人沮丧，可那是一个分享的瞬间。他们可以尽情地嘲笑生活的悲苦，仍然为自己有身边的朋友而感到欣喜。至少在对纽约夜生活的初步尝试中，他们扯平了。

但是这样的时光可以持续多久呢？

Chapter Eighteen Mannitol

Mannitol: a slightly sweet crystalline alcohol $C_6H_{14}O_6$ found in many plants and used esp. in testing kidney function.

Webster's New Collegiate Dictionary

Baby laxative.

Street Drugs: A Reference Guide to Controlled Substances

It seemed like night and it was only three o'clock. The rain cast a pall on the day, giving it the Edgar Allan Poe treatment. A premonition hung over Shelby, but she wasn't psychic enough to latch onto it. There were unabating sheets of water now. The guys ran from the cab into Max and Shelby's apartment to drop off the instruments. Shelby, unhappily holding the cab so it wouldn't leave, watched them run, Max with a guitar, Eberhard his bass, Hadley, a microphone bag and a cymbal case. It looked like a band video, rain obscuring the image. A man stood at the side of the street with a sign, "Need work. Will do anything, beats nothing." It made her cry. She searched her wallet, but all she had was a ten. She knew that her life was so busy that she'd probably forget him as soon as they drove on. Crying was cheating. It gets out the emotion with no resolution. Crying was negative pleasure. Like pushing a bruise. There was something so reassuring about pain, at least you know you're having a rotten time.

She wiped her eyes before they made their way back to the cab, noisy and flinging water in their hurry to take cover. Shelby was continuing on to the lab with them, even though she felt an appendage. Superfluous. No. Worse than that. Like she would get in the way. They talked on a level above her. She wasn't used to not making conversation, to not knowing things. There was no way she could compete. Except for sex. Was it that low? That basic her need for them both? She was stoned, having smoked some in the bathroom outside the studio. The cramped lavatory smelled of strongly of urine and cigarettes. Who'd notice? It could only improve the odor.

第十八章　甘露醇

甘露醇：存在于许多植物中的一种微甜结晶醇（化学式为 $C_6H_{14}O_6$），尤其使用于肾功能测试中。

——《韦氏新大学词典》

婴幼儿通便剂。

——《街售药物：管制类药物的参考指南》

　　看上去如同夜色已经降临，可其实才下午三点钟。因为下雨，天气显得阴郁乏味，有了爱伦·坡笔下的氛围。谢尔碧的心头盘旋着不祥的预感，但她并不怎么相信灵异这一套，所以便没有抓住不放。雨势丝毫没有减弱，甚而达到倾盆的地步了。男生们从出租车里鱼贯钻出，跑进谢尔碧和麦克斯的公寓里把乐器放下。谢尔碧则蛮不高兴地坐在车里好让出租车等着，只能看着他们狂奔：麦克斯拎着吉他，艾伯哈德提着他的贝斯，哈德利则一手麦克风包，一手钹盒。那场景就像是乐队的专辑视频，画面因雨水而变得有些模糊了。马路边站着一个手里拿标语的男人："需要工作。什么都做，好过没有。"谢尔碧顿时伤感得眼睛有些迷蒙，可她搜遍了钱包却只有一张十美金。可她心里十分清楚，等到他们的车一开动，自己就会忙到把这件事给抛诸脑后了。流泪就像是作弊，释放了情感，却没有解决的办法。哭泣给你带来负面的快乐，就像按压青肿的部位时的感觉。关于疼痛，有一点特别让人安心，至少你明确地知道它的来源是腐烂。

　　在他们回来之前，谢尔碧擦了擦自己的眼睛，他们急着躲雨，嘈嘈杂杂地带进了"扑刺刺"的雨水。谢尔碧打算继续和他们一起去实验室，尽管她觉得自己就像一个附属品，是多余的。不，比那还要糟糕。就好像自己会碍事儿似的。他们聊天的层面总是高于谢尔碧，而她却不习惯被排除在聊天内容之外，不习惯一无所知。她根本就没有办法和他们竞争，除非是在性爱方面。真的有这么低级吗？她对他们两个的需求真的就这么基础？谢尔碧刚才在录音室外面的洗手间里吸了一些大麻，这会儿有些亢奋。那个狭小的卫生间本来就充满了强烈的尿味和烟味，有谁会注意到呢？这只会让那里的气味有所改善的。

Chapter Eighteen Mannitol

Hadley ran back first. He sat in the front seat. Shelby looked at him pointedly. "Do I make you nervous?" she asked, knowing that for a moment she could say anything.

"You're stoned, aren't you?"

She didn't answer as Max slid into the car, followed by Eberhard. As the taxi drove on toward the campus, Shelby steered the conversation around to Ethan, knowing it was a discussion they could all participate in, and so she could have a reason for addressing Hadley. Earlier that day, Hadley had been complaining about how friends of Ethan's continued to sleep over, sprawled on the living room couch till noon. She now asked him why he didn't start a bed-and-breakfast. Max and Eberhard laughed loudly. Hadley smiled but ignored her. He told Max and Eberhard that he'd been to the housing office twice, and they'd said there was nothing available. Shelby felt him not look at her. He was only talking to the men now. His sleeping arrangements were his own business.

Max marveled out loud that the son of a chiropractor would be so dependent on drugs. He likened it to the wild oscillations of fad. Capricious father breeds capricious son.

"I've been to one." Hadley tossed this casually into the conversation.

Shelby was startled. "To a chiropractor? Are you nuts?"

"He fixed my back. There are legitimate ones out there."

Shelby made a face of skepticism, then started shaking her head.

Hadley said seriously, "Don't shake your head at me. I don't hit people."

"I only hit in self-defense," she said. "I don't let people run all over me—"

"Ethan doesn't run all over me—"

"No, you just front him money all the time."

Hadley looked at the window and said nothing. Shelby bit her lip, trying to stop herself from talking. Why was she acting this way?

Max coughed. "Hadley, what if police raid your place—"

"Do you think he's making drugs?" Shelby interrupted, wanting somehow to backtrack, to let him know that she confronted him because she cared about him.

"No."

"Not yet," Max said.

"What else can a Ph. D. chemist do with no Ph. D. ?" Eberhard asked.

哈德利首先跑回来了。他坐进了副驾驶的位置。谢尔碧尖锐地盯着他，"我是不是让你紧张了？"她知道这会儿没人，她什么都可以说。

"你是不是嗑高了？"

这时麦克斯也钻进了车里，艾伯哈德紧随其后，谢尔碧便没有回答。当计程车向校园方向开去的时候，谢尔碧把话题转向了伊桑，这样大家就都可以加入讨论，而她也有理由直接和哈德利说话了。那天早些时候，哈德利抱怨说伊桑的朋友们总是过来借宿，他们横七竖八地躺在在客厅沙发上，直到中午才起。谢尔碧这会儿问哈德利为什么他不就此开一家民宿旅馆。麦克斯和艾伯哈德放声大笑起来。哈德利也跟着笑了，但是却没有搭理谢尔碧。他告诉麦克斯和艾伯哈德，自己已经去过住房办公室两次了，可总是被告知没有合适的房子。谢尔碧觉察到了，他故意不看自己。他现在只在和其他两个男人说话了，表明他要睡哪儿是他自己的事儿。

麦克斯突然大声感叹，作为一个脊骨按摩治疗师的儿子，伊桑对药物的依赖性竟然这么大。他把这比作怪癖的突变。变化无常的父亲养育了阴晴不定的儿子。

"我曾经去看过。"哈德利漫不经心地抛出一句话。

谢尔碧被震惊到了，"看过脊骨按摩治疗师？你疯了吗？"

"他把我的背给矫正好了。正规经营的治疗师还是大有人在的。"

谢尔碧一脸的怀疑，不住地摇着头。

哈德利严肃地说："别冲我摇头。至少我不打人。"

"我只在自卫的时候打人，"谢尔碧回应道，"我不会让别人欺负到我头上来——"

"伊桑并没有欺负我——"

"是没有，你只是总给他钱。"

哈德利看向窗外，什么都没有说。谢尔碧咬着自己的嘴唇，试图不让自己再说话了。她为什么总是这样做呢？

麦克斯咳嗽了一声，"哈德利，要是警察突然来搜查你们的公寓怎么办——"

"你觉得伊桑在合成毒品吗？"谢尔碧打断了他的话，想要回到原来的话题上，好让哈德利知道，自己之所以与他交锋是因为关心他。

"没有。"

"只是还没有而已。"麦克斯补充道。

"一个没有获得博士学位的博士生还能做什么别的事呢？"艾伯哈德问道。

Chapter Eighteen Mannitol

"He's going to get his Ph. D. " Hadley turned his gaze to Max, even though the angle was more acute than simply looking at Shelby. She felt the impact of this and opened her door the moment their cab stopped at the curb. She wanted not to care about him, not to have him within cab proximity. Shelby felt angry, a two-year old's petulance. Misunderstood. She had bugged Hadley, in her mind for his own good. There she was. Trying to change him. It was something she vowed she would never do. What's the point? Men always spring back.

She was drifting, letting them talk chemistry while she thought her own thoughts. The rain had lessened and so she followed them at a distance, up the stone stairway of the chemistry building. But Max slowed down momentarily. "What kind of pizza do you want?" he asked her.

"Goat cheese," she said loudly, knowing he would make a face at this. Still yelling "goat cheese", she started to run into him as they walked down the lab hallway, trying to trip him, suddenly feeling renewed affection for Max as he tried to trip her back.

She was showing off. Holding him under Hadley's nose. Her absence of decency made her stop. In the cease of frenetic activity, she heard the odd chirping sound, like the backtrack to a farm movie. She looked around. It was as if a band of crickets had tuned in on a frequency of pheromones and were resonating their mating song back to the source.

"What is that sound?" Shelby asked, somewhat baffled, worrying that some machine was out of whack. A wild sonicator. A Büchi kuglerohr. She couldn't remember what a kuglerohr was exactly, but she loved the sound of the name. Bew-key koo-gull-roar. Whatever it was obviously needed attention. She turned to Max and saw he had a stunned look on his face.

"They work!"

"What work?" The hall was alive with the noise of twittering, chattering chirping.

"Shit," Max said, starting to laugh.

A couple of people came out of their labs to find out what the racket was. Bineet, walking to his door, asked, "What is going on?"

"Shelby's voice set off the key chains," Hadley said, stunned as well. "Your voice must hit their perfect frequency."

第十八章 甘露醇

"他会拿到博士学位的。"哈德利转过身坚定地看着麦克斯,尽管直接看向谢尔碧的话转身的角度要更小一些。谢尔碧感受到了那种刻意的回避,于是车停在路边的瞬间她就打开门钻了出去。她不想再关心他了,不想再和他像同坐一辆出租车一样这么靠近了。因为被误解,谢尔碧心底一阵愤怒,像是两岁孩子耍性子般的情绪。她追着哈德利问个不停是为了他好的。她又这样了,试图改变哈德利。她发过誓永远不会这样做的。有什么意义呢?男人总是本性难改的。

谢尔碧的思绪飘荡着,任由他们谈论化学,她则盘算着自己的心思。雨势已经小了很多,于是谢尔碧保持着一定的距离跟在他们后面,沿着化学大楼的石阶一直向上。但是麦克斯突然慢下脚步来,"你想要什么口味的比萨?"他问谢尔碧。

"羊奶干酪味的。"她大声地回应道,明知道麦克斯会对这个答案做鬼脸表示不屑的。这会儿他们正走在实验室的走廊上,可是她仍然大喊着"羊奶干酪",然后开始向麦克斯冲过去,试图绊倒他。当麦克斯也反过来想绊倒她时,谢尔碧顿时觉得自己对麦克斯的感情又重新点燃了。

她是在炫耀。在哈德利的眼皮子底下和麦克斯打闹。最终她觉得有失体统,便也就停下了。在那疯狂的玩闹结束之后,谢尔碧听见了一阵奇怪的"唧唧"声,就像是农场电影里的背景音乐。她环顾了四周。那声音仿佛是一群蟋蟀在某种费洛蒙的吸引下,开始合力向信息源唱响求偶之歌。

"那是什么声音?"谢尔碧有些困惑地问道,她担心是有什么仪器出故障了。也许是一台疯癫了的声波定位器,或是瑞士布奇公司产的滚珠循环导管(Büchi kuglerohr)〔译者注:Büchi 瑞士布奇公司;德语 kuglerohr,短程蒸馏中使用的滚珠循环导管〕。她不记得那个导管到底长什么样子了,可她就是喜欢这个短语的发音。英语的音标就是 Bew-key koo-gull-roar。不论是什么,它很显然非常需要别人的注意。她转向了麦克斯,看见他一脸震惊的表情。

"它们是管用的!"

"什么是管用的?"整个走廊都因为那"唧啾唧唧"的声音变得生动了起来。

"该死。"麦克斯忍不住大笑起来。

有几个人从实验室里走出来,查看那喧闹声究竟是什么。贝内特一边走向自己的实验室,一边问道:"到底发生了什么?"

"谢尔碧的声音触发了那些钥匙链儿。"哈德利也吃了一惊。"你的声音肯定完美地匹配上了它们的频率。"

Not believing him, Shelby followed the sound of the diminished chirping to a key chain that was laying on the floor next to a bookcase. She picked it up and whistled. Nothing happened.

"I thought these worked when you whistled," she said.

Immediately the noise started up again. Max and Hadley laughed, both of them slapping their legs. Shelby giggled, not knowing who to look at. Wishing suddenly that they were both bi. Oh, what a female fantasy. And probably not something that would really make you happy. But who knew?

"Why are these here?" she asked, whispering, trying not to think of watching the two of them naked—wasn't there a famous scene of men wrestling in *Women in Love*? Shelby thought of Max and Hadley naked, wrestling for her. She was losing her mind. She walked down the hall and picked up the key chains, one by one, trying a differently pitched whistle with each new recruit, and getting nothing in return. "There's a lot of them!" Her hands suddenly radiated sound, a muffled cackling that continued to crack the rest of them up. Laughter comes easy in the wake of stress.

"Your husband had some fool idea about playing a joke on Scotia," Hadley said.

In Shelby's mind she repeated the words, "Your husband." It was a taunt.

Eberhard said, "We must use them in the band."

"No fucking way," Shelby said, in a deep, husky voice that made Eberhard laugh, her pedal tone, where the reverberations were slower and not as apt to jostle anything in her hands.

"Perhaps 'Sympathy for the Devil'. When Shelby woo-woos, she'll have accompaniment," Max said, laughing.

"I'm going to order pizza now," Shelby said in a low, dignified voice. She gave the wad of key chains to Max and then walked down the hall.

Shelby was going to order pizza and then write. She didn't know what else to do with this emotion that expanded inside of her, making her crazy, making her say things she didn't want to say. She felt so close to the edge, and started writing quickly with her eyes closed so that she couldn't see how close she really was.

I have no little tollbooth that stops me midway between affection and lust. That charges me with my behavior. Reroutes my progress.

谢尔碧不相信他，跟随着渐渐小下去的声音，在书架旁边的地板上找到了一个钥匙链。她将其捡起来，对着它吹了声口哨。什么都没有发生。

"我还以为你吹口哨的时候它们会叫呢。"谢尔碧说道。

顷刻间，又"啷啷"声四起。麦克斯和哈德利都放声大笑起来，使劲儿地拍打着自己的大腿。谢尔碧也不由得咯咯笑起来，不知道该看谁。她突然希望他们两个都是双性恋。噢，多么典型的女性幻想啊！就算那样八成也不会让她真正地开心。可是谁又知道呢？

"这些为什么会在这里？"她小声地问了一句，努力让自己不去想象他们两个赤身裸体在一起的样子——《恋爱中的女人》那本书里不是有个很有名的两个男人摔跤的场景吗？谢尔碧的脑海中又浮现出了麦克斯和哈德利赤裸着身体，为她摔跤的场面。她已经开始渐渐失去理智了。她沿着走廊一个一个地将钥匙链捡起，每一次都用不同的音调吹口哨，却没有得到任何回应。"这么多！"她的双手突然发射出一阵闷闷的"咯咯"声，又连带着把剩下的钥匙链也给唤醒了。压力之后欢笑往往更容易紧随而至。

"你的老公想出了这个愚蠢的主意，想要捉弄一下斯考蒂亚。"哈德利开口了。

谢尔碧的脑子里重复着那几个字，"你的老公"。这是对她的奚落。

艾伯哈德这时插了进来，"我们一定要在乐队表演的时候用上。"

"门都没有。"谢尔碧压低声音，用沙哑的嗓音反驳道。艾伯哈德笑了起来，因为谢尔碧启用了自己的踏板音，这样声带震动就会减慢，不至于触发她手里的那些玩意儿了。

"也许可以在表演《同情魔鬼》这首歌的时候用，这样在谢尔碧唱和声部分的时候，就会有伴奏了。"麦克斯边笑边建议道。

"我去订比萨了。"谢尔碧用低低的，略显庄严的嗓音搪塞过去。她把那一把钥匙链递给麦克斯之后就沿着走廊向外走去。

谢尔碧打算订完比萨就开始写作。在她体内蔓延的这股感情，让她发狂，让她说一些言不由衷的话，除了写下来之外她也想不出该拿它怎么办了。她觉得自己与陷落的边缘如此靠近，只能闭上眼睛开始飞快地写作，这样就不会看见到底离边缘多近了。

在喜爱和性欲之间，没有可以中途将我拦截的收费亭，对我的行为进行收费，强制我改道。

Chapter Eighteen Mannitol

She tried to convince herself it was lust, to bad-mouth the emotion she felt for Hadley. She turned her thoughts to Max, wanting to shame herself into caring for him again, hoping it would help her figure things out. She had woken up yesterday feeling very weird. She remembered that she had had a strange dream about being pregnant. She'd delivered her own baby because no one else was around to help. It only took a minute. "So this is why they make such a big deal about home births," she'd said in her dream.

Shelby would often lie in bed analyzing her dreams, but this one seemed pretty obvious. What good is sleeping if you can't even get away from your troubles? Her most recent trouble was that Max wanted to have a baby. As if she didn't have enough on her mind. It had started simply enough on the subway. Max had said under his breath, "I just figured out what a bandanna does."

Shelby glanced to where he was looking. "What?"

"Hides a receding hairline."

Shelby had given a half smile. It was a funny observation but it felt like a distraction to her. It didn't dawn on her till later that Max was thinking of his own hairline. She realized that Max was starting to feel old. So wrapped up in her own unhappiness, it didn't always occur to her that Max might have his own fears. There was a connection between them that was missing, a void that sucked their conversation dry of inference, of innuendo, leaving only brittle declarations that were usually misinterpreted.

Wishing she could go back to a dreamless sleep, Shelby unconsciously flicked a fingerfold of sheet under her nose, back and forth, whish-whish-whish-whish, the tactility of the fabric hypnotizing her, relaxing her to a more thoughtful mood. She often got mad at Max because he didn't read her mind, but she was sometimes as obtuse. How had they gotten so far away from one another?

Maybe Max knew something was different. Shelby stopped flicking for a moment as she contemplated what he could know. After the bandanna comment, he'd started again, hedgingly working an angle that wasn't yet clear to Shelby. "You know, I'm going to be interviewing during the next few months and I'll probably start a new job by May if not sooner," Max had said.

Startled, Shelby had looked at him. He sounded as if he was making a business proposal. "So?"

她想说服自己那只是性欲，想把自己对哈德利的感情抹黑。她又把思绪转向麦克斯，想要用羞耻心让自己再度爱上麦克斯，并希望这能够帮助解决目前的困境。昨天醒来的时候，谢尔碧心里有一种怪异的感觉。她还记得自己做了一个奇怪的梦，梦见自己怀孕了。她给自己接了生，因为周围一个人都没有。只花了一分钟。"我还以为在家里生产是什么大不了的事情呢。"在梦里她这样说道。

谢尔碧经常会躺在床上分析自己的梦境，但是这个梦的含义挺显而易见的。假若入睡了都没有办法摆脱生活中的烦心事，那睡觉还有什么用处呢？最近让她烦心的事情，就是麦克斯想要个孩子。好像嫌谢尔碧脑子里考虑的事情还不够多似的。这件事只是从地铁上一次简单的对话开始的。麦克斯低声地对她说："我刚发现了班丹娜头巾的用处是什么。"

谢尔碧朝麦克斯视线落下的地方看去。"是什么？"

"隐藏变高的发际线。"

谢尔碧给了他一个勉强的微笑。虽然是个有意思的观察，但对她来说却更像是无关紧要的分神打岔。直到后来她才意识到，麦克斯其实是在担心自己的发际线——他开始感觉到自己的衰老了。而谢尔碧却一直沉浸在自己的烦恼中，从没想过麦克斯可能也有自己的担忧。他们之间缺失了一种联结，那个虚隙抽干了他们的对话，没有推理，没有影射，只剩下脆弱的宣言，还经常被对方误解。

指望着能够再睡一个无梦的回笼觉，谢尔碧下意识地把床单的一角扯到鼻子下面，来回摩擦着，"窸窸窣窣，窸窸窣窣"，织料的触感催她入眠，使她放松到更深的思绪中去。她经常会因为麦克斯不能读懂自己的心思而生气，可有时候她实在是太艰涩难懂了。他们是怎么走到像现在这么生疏的地步的？

也许麦克斯已经知道有什么不对劲的地方了。谢尔碧暂时停下手里床单的摩挲，沉思着他可能知道的事情。在那个头巾的对话结束后，他又旁敲侧击地从另一个角度开始对话，当时谢尔碧还不甚了了。"你瞧，我接下来几个月会开始进行面试，最迟五月份我可能就会开始一份新工作了。"麦克斯这样说道。

谢尔碧有些惊讶，抬头看着他。他的语气听上去就像是在提出一份商业提议。"所以呢？"

"Well," Max had looked at her gently, "I was just thinking that we might want to consider having a baby."

Shelby said nothing.

"Don't you think it would be nice to have a little baby?" Max had put his arm around her.

"Maybe," Shelby had said tentatively, feeling claustrophobic. "I just don't know if I'm ready right now." Shelby tried to squelch the immediate feeling of panic that overcame her. A child seemed like such a ridiculous idea when one was planning an affair.

Shelby had sighed at the thought, forcing herself out of bed, not wanting to contemplate babies, or new jobs or moving. She, who couldn't stand New York, now didn't want to leave it. She heard Max in the other room practicing the guitar. He seemed to be playing it more as job interviews loomed. He was going on one in a few days. Shelby tried not to consider what that could mean for her and Hadley. Instead she listened. He wasn't a bad guitar player. He always said that it was a good thing he wasn't a great guitar player because he'd probably be dead by now. Max was not the kind of guitar player who played a blizzard of notes in a show of technical virtuosity. He played on a more visceral level, with unexpected choices, notes that surprised you when you heard them because they fit even though you might never have thought to choose them yourself.

Shelby went to the bedroom door to look out at Max. He was sitting on the sofa playing the guitar in his underwear. It made her smile. She knew that he probably hadn't even had breakfast yet. A surge of emotion went through her. What was she thinking? She loved Max. But then she thought of what Hadley would look like playing the drums in his underwear. The physical strength drumming required impressed the hell out of Shelby. Drumming was power and violence, but with a purpose. It had all the elements of seduction.

Shelby shook her head and went to brush her teeth. She couldn't have a thought but that it would lead her back to Hadley. As she got dressed, she replayed her courtship with Max, remembering when they had first started seeing each other, how exciting it had been. She had once felt about Max what she now felt about Hadley. What did that mean? Would she always need to move on? It was a sad thought, that what she took for love was really just the opposite of boredom.

"所以,"麦克斯温柔地看着她,"我只是在想,也许我们该考虑要一个孩子。"

谢尔碧什么都没有说。

"你难道不认为生个宝宝是件很美好的事吗?"麦克斯用胳膊环住了她。

"也许吧,"谢尔碧感到了被幽闭的恐惧,略带犹疑给出了这个回答,"我只是不知道自己现在有没有准备好。"她试图镇压住那阵突然袭来的惊慌。在一个人还在计划一场外遇的时候,生孩子这个想法听上去简直就是荒谬至极。

谢尔碧想到这里叹了口气,硬逼着自己起了床,她不想停留在考虑孩子、新工作或是搬家这些事情上了。作为一个一度无法忍受纽约的人,她现在竟然不想离开了。麦克斯在另外一个房间里弹吉他的声音传来——随着面试的临近,他好像练习吉他更频繁了。再过几天就有一个面试。谢尔碧试着不去想那对她和哈德利来说意味着什么,而是专心听了起来。麦克斯是个不赖的吉他手。他总是说自己没有成为一个伟大的吉他手也许是件好事,不然他现在可能已经不在人世了。他不是那种会突然迸发出一阵激烈的旋律来炫耀精湛技艺的人,而是更加偏向自然地流露,再加上一些出人意料的发挥。当你听到其中一些音符组合时,会感到意外,因为它们结合得很完美,尽管你自己从来都没有想过要这样搭配选择。

谢尔碧向卧室门口走去,想看一眼麦克斯。他坐在沙发上弹着吉他,下半身只穿着内裤。谢尔碧笑了。她知道他八成还没有吃早饭呢。一阵爱怜之情涌遍谢尔碧全身。她到底在想什么?她是爱着麦克斯的。可是紧接着她又开始想象哈德利只穿着内裤打架子鼓会是什么样子。打鼓所需要的力度让谢尔碧赞叹不已,这是一种带着目的的力量和暴力。诱惑需要的所有元素它都具备了。

谢尔碧甩了甩头,去刷牙了。她产生的任何思绪,最终都会停留在哈德利身上。在穿衣服的时候,她开始回忆自己和麦克斯的恋爱过程,还记得当初他们刚开始约会的时候,是多么令人兴奋。曾经她对麦克斯的感觉和现在对哈德利的是一样的。那意味着什么?她总是需要重新开始吗?原来她投奔爱情的原因只是想摆脱无聊,这个想法真是令人伤感。

Chapter Eighteen Mannitol

She opened the door to the living room and watched Max as he finished a solo, playing over a pre-recorded tape he'd made of a blues progression. He was standing now, bending over in a primal way as he played a particularly difficult riff. He often got dirty when he performed, some sexual quality came out in the way he bent the strings, the twanginess of the strumming, the lowering of his knees. At one time it used to make her crazy.

Max stopped playing and turned off the tape recorder. She watched him put his guitar away, and she sighed, wondering for the millionth time why she was so stupid.

They'd gone to lunch in the Village, Max taking the morning off as a favor to her. Shelby had found a little café on a side street that had a wine bar and the ubiquitous baked brie that she liked so much. It wasn't Max's favorite kind of place, but he went there for Shelby. The interior of the café was of whitewashed stone with fresh flowers on the table. Unframed pictures done by local artists hung on the walls. The aroma of French roast was discernible, as was the scent of basil and oregano. Gabrieli played in the background. Shelby loved antiphonal music. She felt like such a snob sometimes, but she really liked places like this, good wine, clean, stylish decor. Very yuppie.

While they ate, Max pointed out that a large furniture van had pulled up outside the restaurant and workmen were carrying floral cushions into the building next to the restaurant.

Shelby was thinking about what it would be like to have a baby. The hardest part would be to give up pot. Alcohol too, but pot was the thing she craved. And it wasn't just giving up the drugs, it was giving up a way of life, freedom. Suddenly, once you had a kid, you were a grown-up.

"Max." Shelby said this sadly. She looked at him over her brie. "Do you really think we get along well enough to have a child?" Shelby noticed there was something white just above Max's lip. She pointed to her own face, tapping it several times.

Max was watching the workman who were now moving a large sofa out of the truck and onto the street. They disappeared with the sofa next door. He looked back at Shelby. "What, I gotta booger?" With a napkin, he wiped at his face.

"Do you?"

Max said, still wiping, "Did I get it?" Shelby nodded, rolling her eyes.

第十八章 甘露醇

谢尔碧打开通向客厅的门,看着麦克斯跟着一盘事先录好的蓝调和弦曲,以独奏收尾。他现在站起来了,用一种原始的姿势弓着身子,弹奏着一段难度极大的即兴演奏重复段。在乐队演出的时候,他经常会展现出不羁的一面,他竭力拨弦的方式带有些性爱的特质,包括扫弦的缭绕鼻音以及膝盖的弯曲弧度。这些一度都让谢尔碧为之癫狂。

麦克斯停下来,关上了磁带录音机。看着他收起吉他,谢尔碧叹了口气,第一百万次地质问自己为什么这么傻。

他们一起去格林威治村[译者注:纽约曼哈顿著名街区]吃午饭,麦克斯专门为了她空出了早上的时间。谢尔碧在辅街上发现了一家小巧的咖啡馆,里面有个葡萄酒吧台,到处摆放着谢尔碧最爱的酥烤布里芝士。虽然这不是麦克斯喜爱的风格,可他还是为了谢尔碧来了。咖啡馆的内部是粉刷成白色的石头墙,桌子上摆放着鲜花。墙上挂着当地艺术家的画作,没有加任何画框。空气中萦绕着明朗的法式烘焙咖啡的香气,还有罗勒和牛至的气味。背景音乐放的是加布里埃利指挥的古典乐。谢尔碧喜欢铜管重奏的表演形式。有的时候,她觉得自己很小资虚荣,可是她真的很喜欢这样的地方:上好的葡萄酒,整洁、雅致的布景,非常有雅皮士的风格。

用餐的时候,麦克斯看见一辆运送家具的大卡车停在了餐馆的外面,工人正往隔壁的大楼里搬运有鲜花图案的垫子。

而谢尔碧当时正思考着有了孩子会是什么样的情景。难度最大的一条应该是要戒掉大麻,还有酒精,但她对大麻的欲望更强一些。这不仅是放弃嗑药,更是放弃一种生活方式,放弃自由。一旦有了孩子,突然之间,你就是一个成年人了。

"麦克斯,"谢尔碧略带悲伤地叫了一声,目光越过布里干酪看向他,"你真的觉得我们的关系融洽到了可以要孩子的程度吗?"谢尔碧注意到麦克斯的嘴唇上沾了什么白色的东西,于是指着自己的脸,轻轻弹了几下。

麦克斯正聚精会神地看工人将一个相当大的沙发从卡车里卸到街道上,接着消失在隔壁的门口。他回过头来看着谢尔碧,"怎么了,我脸上沾了鼻屎吗?"接着他用餐巾擦了擦脸。

"你觉得呢?"

麦克斯反问道,手里的动作并没有停下来。"擦掉了吗?"谢尔碧点了点头,

Maybe she had lost her sense of humor. She used to find Max funny, his obliviousness to social norms. Now it just depressed and irritated her. But it wasn't his fault. She had changed. She wished that knowing it was her fault could help in some way, but it only made her feel more guilty.

"Shelby, I would love to have a family with you. Everybody disagrees sometimes." Max reached out and held her hand as it lay on the white linen.

Shelby sighed. Max just didn't get it. He didn't even hear her, and she couldn't just come out and say it. What? That she didn't love him? Did she really not love him? Could it happen that fast? She was afraid if he weren't around she would miss him desperately, but when he was around he drove her nuts. What was wrong with her? A tear ran down her face.

Max leaned forward suddenly, and wiped her cheek gently with his napkin. "Why are you crying?"

Shelby shook her head. She knew without question that she was going to hurt him and it made her sad. She'd switched her loyalties. She couldn't tell him the truth anymore. Unable to answer, she glanced outside at the sudden action on the moving van. "The guys in the street are having an argument," was all she said, not able to put words to anything she felt, but feeling like the whole world was unhappy.

Max turned to see the workmen standing on the ramp of the van in postures of anger: lots of arm gestures and grimaces. One big burly guy shook his finger in the face of another. A skinnier guy just sat down on the curb. Max and Shelby watched as the men disappeared next door and then reappeared carrying the sofa back into the van. Shortly after, the cushions followed.

"Sometimes I feel like there's no future for us." Shelby flinched inwardly, wondering if she'd revealed too much.

"Why do you say that? I think it's New York. We won't always live here. I know it's hard now, but it's just a few more months."

Shelby tried to imagine living somewhere else, somewhere where Hadley wasn't. Maybe Max was right. Maybe that was the answer. But the thought was almost more than she could bear.

Max suddenly said, "Look at that." He nodded toward the window where they could see the big burly workman pull out a saw and proceed to saw the brand-new sofa in half. The sofa was hanging out over the edge of the van floor, forming an

翻了个白眼。也许她已经失去幽默感了,因为在以前,麦克斯对社会准则的不屑一顾在她眼里是一种风趣。而现在,他的行为只会让她感到恼怒抑郁。这并不是麦克斯的错,是她自己变了。她希望承认这一点能够在某种程度上帮助自己,可内疚感却越发浓重了。

"谢尔碧,我非常愿意和你组建一个家庭。争吵不和对谁来说都是难免的。"麦克斯握住了谢尔碧放在白色亚麻桌布上的手。

她叹了口气:麦克斯还是不明白。他甚至都没有听懂她问的是什么,她又不能直脱脱地说出口来。难道要说,说自己不再爱他了?这是真的吗?有可能发生得这么快吗?要是麦克斯不在身边,她担心自己又会疯狂地想念他,可当他在的时候,却又快把她给逼疯了。她到底是出什么毛病了?一滴泪水顺着她的脸颊滑落下来。

麦克斯突然倾过身来,温柔地用他的餐巾擦拭着谢尔碧的脸庞。"你怎么哭了?"

谢尔碧摇着头,她清楚地知道自己会伤害到麦克斯,而这使她感到十分难过。她改变了忠诚的对象,不再能够和麦克斯讲真话了。她感到自己无法回答,于是将目光瞟向了窗外突然移动起来的卡车。"马路上的那些家伙在吵架。"她只能说出这句话,却无法用话语表达出自己内心的任何感受。她觉得整个世界都是忧郁的。

麦克斯转头看向那些工人,他们站在卡车的斜板上,形容愤怒:挥舞着臂膀,面部表情也十分扭曲。一个身材魁梧的家伙对着另一个人不停地摇着食指,另一个瘦些的家伙索性就坐在了马路牙子上。麦克斯和谢尔碧看着那些人消失在餐厅的隔壁门里,然后又再出现,将沙发重新搬回了卡车里。没过多久,沙发垫也被请了出来。

"有的时候我觉得我们两个没有未来。"谢尔碧内心有些退缩,不确定自己是不是袒露得有些太多了。

"你为什么这么说?我觉得是因为纽约的原因。我们不会一直住在这儿的。我知道现在很艰难,但是再过几个月就好了。"

谢尔碧试着想象生活在别处的样子,一个没有哈德利的地方。也许麦克斯是对的。也许这就是答案。但是光是这样一想她就已经无法承受了。

麦克斯突然说道:"快看。"他朝窗户的方向点了点头,只见那个强壮的工人抽出一把锯子,开始切割那个崭新的沙发。沙发的一半悬在卡车底部的外面,

Chapter Eighteen Mannitol

acute angle with the ramp of the van. The skinny guy was standing on the ramp and holding onto the end of the sofa that hung out into space. The other workmen stood by watching. Shelby turned her head as the two halves of the sofa slowly fell apart. The sofa pieces were then returned to the apartment next door.

"Why would they do that?" Shelby squinted in confusion.

"Because this is New York," Max said, laughing.

The sawn sofa seemed like a metaphor to Shelby, so susceptible was she to any outward phenomena that fit her mood. Everything was so ludicrous that rules were unnecessary. The world seemed to be ending, or at least the world that she knew, and it freed her to behave in any way possible.

They both watched as the cushions went back into the apartment. "You ready to go?" Max asked as he watched Shelby mop up every last bit of brie on her plate with a piece of bread. She nodded and downed her wine, so he signaled for the bill. As they left the restaurant, they paused on the sidewalk for a second and watched as the workmen carried the two pieces of the sofa out of the building, the sawn edges raw like a wound and spurting polyester. Without ceremony, they dumped them into the back of the van and then drove away. Obviously the severed sofa had not suited the owner. Shelby tried to grasp at some kind of moral there, but it taxed her brain. She still took it for a sign of something even though she didn't know what the sign was. These days everything had portent.

Hadley, Max and Eberhard walked into Max's lab, prepared for a long afternoon. Hadley went to the chalkboard and quickly drew line segments connected by "C"s. "From the NMR data, the catalyst seems to have a backbone of carbons."

"Jesus. A million things have a carbon backbone," Max said, shaking his head.

"It also appears that there are no nitrogen, and that several hydrogens are attached to oxygen-bearing carbons."

"We need a mass spec," Eberhard said. "That will solve it." The mass spec wouldn't tell them what the compound was, but it would tell them the molecular weight and how many of what kind of molecules made up the compound. Between that and the NMR data, they could puzzle out the structure.

"Those guys take a week." Max looked glum.

"Ah!" Eberhard smiled. "But one is German, and my parents are coming

与斜坡形成了一个锐角。瘦削的那个工人站在斜坡上,手扶着露在外面的那半沙发。其余的工人都在一旁观看着。当那个沙发缓缓地断成两半的时候,谢尔碧把头转了回来。被分尸后的沙发又被还回了隔壁的公寓里。

"他们为什么要那么做?"谢尔碧困惑地眯缝起了眼睛。

"因为这里是纽约。"麦克斯笑着回答。

那个被锯开的沙发对于谢尔碧来说像是有着什么隐含的意义,现在任何与她心情相衬的外界现象都使她分外善感。一切都荒唐可笑,以至于规则都没有存在的必要了。似乎世界——至少是她所知晓的这个世界,即将进入末日,这一想法让她能够自由地在无限的可能性中做自己。

他们一起看着沙发垫也被抬回了公寓。"走吗?"麦克斯看着谢尔碧用一片面包抹光了碟子里残余的布里奶酪屑,然后问道。她点了点头,一口气喝光了杯子里的葡萄酒。于是麦克斯就打了个买单的手势。离开餐馆的时候,他们在人行道上停留了一小会儿,看着那个断成两节儿的沙发又被搬了出来,新鲜的锯痕就像一个伤口,里面的聚酯纤维露了出来。这次什么后续反应都没有,他们把沙发扔进卡车里,然后开走了。很显然,公寓主人对那个断成两节儿的沙发并不满意。谢尔碧试图理解这整件事情的寓意,但是这样的思索让她头疼。尽管不知道是什么,她仍然将其看作是某件事情的征兆。最近这段时间里,所有事情都有先兆。

哈德利、麦克斯和艾伯哈德一同走进了麦克斯的实验室,他们都准备好了要迎接又一个漫长的下午。哈德利走到白板面前,迅速地画了一条碳原子连接的碳链。"从核磁共振分析数据来看,催化剂应该是由碳链支撑的。"

"天哪,有碳链结构的物质数都数不清。"麦克斯摇着头说道。

"同时,里面不存在氮原子,并且有几个氢原子连接在了携氧碳原子上。"

"我们需要测个质谱图,"艾伯哈德说,"这就能把问题给解决了。"质谱图虽然不能告诉他们化合物是什么,但可以测出分子质量,以及构成化合物的分子类型及数量。再加上核磁共振的分析数据,他们就能够把整个结构拼凑出来了。

"那些家伙做个质谱要花上一个星期呢。"麦克斯看上去有些忧心忡忡。

"啊哈!"艾伯哈德笑了。"但他们中有个是德国人,我的父母就快从德国来

to visit soon. We will deal." Eberhard smiled again, as if mocking himself, the perpetual happy camper. "Where is this catalyst?"

Hadley went to get a small vial from the back of his hood. Taking it, Eberhard said, "I will be back."

Hadley, feeling restless and jumpy around Max, stood up and walked out of the lab after Eberhard, like he had something to do. He went toward the end of the hallway, but not as far as Scotia's office where Shelby was, guided by the afternoon light coming through the window, an icy light, late-breaking in the clouds, the last morsel of the day. The hall was empty but looked lived in. Newspapers were spread on the round lunch table that cantilevered uneasily near the lead-paned window. A skateboard was in the corner. That hadn't been here before. Paige's? You never knew. Paige was always trying new schemes to lose weight. Hadley thought for a minute about Paige. How he'd never asked her out. He didn't think that they could find a place to be real to one another, a truth that united them. Their interests were so opposite. She seemed to take too much energy. But so did Shelby. And what united him with her? He stopped for a moment, trying to figure out why he felt such an amazing need of her. Was it music? Was it doom? Their melancholy aspects were a seduction to each other. He wasn't an unhappy person, he just had this aspect of sedateness that people took for more serious than it was. And now it was true.

He noticed that he was standing in front of Bineet's door. Bineet was looking at him. "Were you coming to see me?" Hadley could tell that Bineet thought him strange just standing there, but Bineet was too nice to ask questions.

"I have a puzzle," Bineet said, drawing him in. Bineet could put anyone at ease.

"And?" Hadley sat down on a stool.

"I take product from one flask, put it in one tube and on Tuesday the electrons spin differently than on Wednesday. I ask why?"

Hadley scanned Bineet's face, realizing that Bineet was being rhetorical.

"Because she's switching NMR tubes."

Bineet exhaled slowly. "This is as I thought."

"I marked a tube and I found it in her lab. But I don't think we should go to Scotia until we know what her catalyst is. He'll realize there's never been a catalyst. It's just something she pulled off the shelf. We're pretty sure it has a carbon backbone ..."

看我了，我会让他们带些特产来的。"他又笑了一下，仿佛是在嘲笑自己，永远都是这么乐天派。"催化剂在哪儿呢？"

哈德利走到自己的通风橱前取出一个小药剂瓶。艾伯哈德接过去，转身向外走去，"我一会儿就回来。"

有麦克斯在身边，哈德利总是感觉焦躁不安，于是他站起身跟在艾伯哈德后面走出了实验室，好像打算要做什么似的。他向着走廊的尽头走去，但是还没有到斯考蒂亚的办公室——谢尔碧正在里面。午后的阳光从窗玻璃直射进来，冰冷的，刺透云层，透出白昼的最后一抹微光。走廊空荡荡的，但是却充满着有人居住的气息。圆形的午餐桌由悬臂固定在铅窗框边上，看上去不是很稳定，上面平摊着一些报纸。角落里倚着一个滑板，之前没有的。是佩琪的吗？说不准呢。她总是为了减肥尝试各种新的花招儿。哈德利的思绪在佩琪身上停留了一小会儿。他从来都没有约佩琪出去过，因为他觉得找不到任何一个能让他们俩坦诚相待的地方，互相倾吐真相，从而产生联结。他们的兴趣实在相差太大了。佩琪看上去需要太多的精力投入了。可谢尔碧也是一样的。那又是什么铸就了他和谢尔碧之间的关系呢？哈德利顿了一下，想搞清楚自己对谢尔碧的需求感为什么会这么强烈。是音乐吗？还是曾经的苦难？他们性格当中忧郁的成分正是对方眼中的魅力所在。其实哈德利不是一个郁郁寡欢的人，只是人们往往将他个性中沉静的因素视作过于严肃。而如今却成真了。

这时他才注意到自己一直站在贝内特实验室的门口，而贝内特正盯着他看。"你是来看我的吗？"哈德利看得出来，贝内特觉得自己一直站在那里的行为很诡异，可是他人太好了，不好意思追根究底地询问。

"我有个未解的谜团。"贝内特说着示意哈德利进来。他有为别人解除尴尬的能力。

"是什么？"哈德利坐在了凳子上。

"周二我从烧瓶里取了产物，放进试管，可是电子旋转的情况却和周三时不一样了。所以我想问，为什么会这样？"

哈德利扫视了一下贝内特的脸，意识到他是在影射什么。

"因为她调换了核磁共振的试管。"

贝内特缓缓地呼出一口气，"我也是这么猜测的。"

"我在一个试管上做了标记，结果却在她的实验室里找到了。但是我认为，我们要在搞清楚她所谓的催化剂到底是什么之后才能向斯考蒂亚告发。那样他就会意识到从来就没有这么一个催化剂的存在。那只不过是拉达从架子上随手拿下来的东西罢了。我们现在非常确定那东西有碳链基础结构……"哈德利注

Chapter Eighteen   Mannitol

Hadley paused, noticing the change on Bineet's face.

Bineet coughed politely and said, "It is mannitol."

Hadley looked at him blankly.

"I know that what she calls the catalyst is actually mannitol."

Hadley noticed their evasion of Rahda's name. "You mean baby laxative?"

"Yes."

Hadley tried to remember what the structure of mannitol was. He turned to the blackboard. "This?" He drew a map of the molecules, lines connected to other lines with letters at the junctures naming the atoms: carbons, oxygens, hydrogens.

Bineet took the chalk. "An alcohol at both ends." He corrected the structure.

Hadley nodded. "Does she know you know?"

Bineet paused. "No. When the mass spec data disappeared, I was suspicious. Did it ever exist? I have a friend who runs the mass spec. I found the code for the catalyst in her notebook and yesterday had him search through his discarded sample vials. She was very smart. Mannitol has the same molecular weight as her purported catalyst. But its fragmentation pattern is not the same. That is why she hid the data. I took the discarded vial and had another friend at Rockefeller run an NMR. I did not trust to do it here. I plan to go to Scotia on Tuesday, when he comes back from Cincinnati. I will leave it up to him to tell her."

"If you want, we'll go with you."

"I would like that." Bineet smiled wryly. "Dr. Scotia is not so fond of me."

意到内内特的神情发生了变化,于是停了下来。

贝内特礼节性地咳嗽了几声,然后说道:"是甘露醇。"

哈德利茫然地看着他。

"我知道,被她称作催化剂的那个东西实际上是甘露醇。"

哈德利发现,大家都刻意避开了拉达的名字。"你是说,是婴幼儿通便剂的成分?"

"是的。"

哈德利试着回想了一下甘露醇的结构是怎样的,然后转向了黑板。"这个?"他画出了一个分子结构图,线与线之间的连接处用字母标识出原子:碳原子、氧原子、氢原子。

贝内特接过粉笔,"在两边的结尾处加上羟基。"他修改了哈德利画的结构式。

哈德利点了点头。"她知道你已经发现了吗?"

贝内特犹豫了一秒。"还不知道。当质谱图数据消失不见的时候,我就开始怀疑了。那东西到底有没有存在过呢?我在质谱实验室有个朋友,在她的笔记本里找到她记录的催化剂代码之后,昨天我让那个朋友在废弃的样本药瓶堆里找了一圈。她很聪明,利用甘露醇和她所宣称的催化剂分子量相同这一点。但是它们的质谱裂解模式却不一样。这就是她要把数据藏起来的原因。我拿了那个废弃的样品药瓶,去找了洛克菲勒公司的另一个朋友又做了一遍质谱。在这儿做,我不放心。我打算周二等斯考蒂亚从辛辛那提市回来的时候去找他,并由他来最终和她挑明。"

"如果你想要的话,我们可以跟你一起去。"

"那最好不过了,"贝内特面部不自然地笑了一下,"斯考蒂亚博士对我不是很有好感。"

Chapter Nineteen   Rate-limiting Reaction

> Return for the moment to the Embden-Meyerhof pathway of glycolysis. Of the ten reactions involved in this pathway, the slowest is usually at step 3. Thus Reaction 3 ... is said to be the rate-limiting reaction.
>
> Biology Today

Hadley was dreaming that he went to a psychiatrist who gave him a bill like a dinner check. All of his various problems were itemized separately. He was even charged for office decorations. The bill metamorphosed into a chemistry book that he was reading in the lab. It had a chapter entitled, "What to do when the police arrive," and then there the police were, walking down the hallway of the chemistry labs, guns drawn. He could hear them knocking over things. The sound got louder until Hadley suddenly realized that he was awake and the noise had not stopped. He froze, his eyes still shut, listening intently. There was nothing. No, there it was again. Something was being shoved across a floor. Maybe Ethan was just getting a drink of water? Sometimes he had insomnia and wandered the apartment, so moving furniture didn't seem impossible. Hadley thought about calling out "Ethan?" but for some reason stopped himself. Then he panicked. He remembered. Ethan was staying at his girlfriend's house. Hadley was alone. Or rather he wasn't alone. He felt very afraid. Goddamn Ethan. It was one of his goddamn friends. Hadley started to sit up but then heard a slight creaking. Someone was opening the door to his bedroom. He tried to breathe normally. Just stay quiet. It occurred to Hadley that Ethan's friends didn't move around this much. It must be someone looking for drugs. So why were they in his room? He just hoped they weren't so fucked up that they would kill him when they didn't find them.

If I make it through this night, he thought, I'm moving. Goddamn Ethan! he thought again. He was trying to get angry rather than scared, but it wasn't working.

第十九章　控速反应

重现糖酵解反应中埃姆登—迈耶霍夫途径发生的瞬间。这一途径所包含的十个反应当中,最慢的通常是第三步。因此,反应三……被称作控速反应。

——《今日生物》

哈德利梦见自己去看了心理医生,他收到了一张像晚餐账单似的条子,上面一一列出了他的所有问题,甚至连那个医生办公室装潢的费用都算在了他的头上。霎时间,场景又变幻到了实验室里,手里的账单幻化成了一本化学书。里面有一章节题目是"警察来的时候该怎么做",紧接着一群警察就出现在了化学大楼的走廊里,荷枪实弹。哈德利能够听见他们在不停地打翻东西,声音越来越大,直到他突然意识到自己是清醒着的,可是那噪音却并没有因此停止。他一动不动,仍然闭着双眼,专注地听着。什么动静都没有。不,又来了。什么东西在地板上挪动的声音。也许是伊桑起床喝水了?他失眠的时候会在房间里来回走动,所以给家具挪挪位置也不是没可能。哈德利本想叫一声"伊桑?"但出于某种原因他制止了自己。他慌了,因为他猛然记起伊桑今天留宿在女朋友家了。哈德利只身一人。但又不是。他感到恐惧袭来。该死的伊桑。肯定是他的那些狐朋狗友。哈德利准备坐起身来,这时却听见一阵轻微的"吱呀"声——有人在开他卧室的门。他努力地保持正常呼吸,尽量不发出任何声响。哈德利意识到伊桑的朋友不会活动范围这么大的。一定是来找毒品的人。可是为什么他们会来自己的房间呢?他现在只是默默祈盼着这帮人没有丧心病狂到没有收获就杀人的地步。

要是我活着度过今晚的话,哈德利心想着,我就搬家。该死的伊桑!他又在心里咒骂了一遍。本想着可以用愤怒来代替恐惧,但好像没起什么作用。他开

He started to shake. Was this retribution? He wanted another man's wife and now he would die for it. Jesus. At least let him do something to make it worth it. He hadn't done anything. One kiss. He thought of Shelby. He didn't want to die.

Hadley slowly reached up above the headboard for a pen, clutching it in his hand like a weapon. The phone was across the room. Useless to him. Anyway, in New York 911 was a courtesy call. Just letting the police know where to find the body. Suddenly he heard the front door open and close. He hadn't even heard the intruder leave his room. A great witness he'd be. Hadley counted to one hundred, trying not to exhale too loudly. Still afraid, he counted to one hundred again.

Not hearing any more sounds, he quickly got out of bed, threw on his clothes, grabbed his backpack, and made for the door. He ran down the two flights of stairs and out to the street. There was no one on 110th, which made him nervous, so he sprinted to Broadway, just under a block away. As he turned the corner, he saw a huddle of rough-looking individuals near a fire hydrant. "Great," thought Hadley. "People."

He ran up Broadway, past the outdoor market where tired-looking youths in red smocks were restocking vegetables. One was sweeping up some broken glass. Lights made him feel better. Activity. Here there weren't a lot of people, but enough to ease his paranoia. Bums lay in the doorways of buildings, covered up with green trash bags and ripped open cardboard boxes. The yellowish street lights gave everyone the look of jaundice.

Hadley turned left onto Max and Shelby's street. He knew he shouldn't be doing this. He thought about going to Eberhard's, but it was all the way over on Morningside and that was a risky prospect, and anyway he was here now. He tried the lobby door. Open. Hadley walked daintily past the night doorman who had slid down in his plush red armchair, legs sticking out, a human table. He hurried to Max and Shelby's door and knocked on it loudly, thinking of the two of them lying in bed. He realized that he shouldn't be doing this, but he was desperate.

Shelby woke up with a start. "Now who in the hell is that?" she asked sleepily, pushing Max to wake him.

"Mmm?" Max mumbled, pulling the covers tighter.

"It's Dermot." Shelby yawned. "Either he wants us to party or his neighbor's

始不自主地颤抖。这是因果惩戒吗？垂涎了别人的妻子，现在就要为此而丧命。上帝啊，至少让他先做些什么，让这一死也值得。他还什么都没有做呢。只有一吻。他又想到了谢尔碧。他不想死。

哈德利缓缓地伸出手去，取了床头板上的钢笔，像武器一样紧紧攥在手里。电话在房间的另一头，对他一点用处也派不上。再说纽约的911报警电话形同虚设，只是为了让警察知道要去哪里找尸体罢了。突然，公寓前门打开又关上的声音传进了哈德利的耳朵里。他甚至都没有注意到那个人是什么时候离开他房间的，不然他就可以成为绝佳的目击证人了。他尽力降低呼吸声，从一数到了一百。可仍然惊惶未定，于是他又从头数起。

在安静了好一会儿之后，哈德利迅速地从床上爬起，草草穿上衣服，一把抓起背包，夺门而去。小跑下了两层楼后，他来到了空无一人的110号大街。这空旷仍然让他感到紧张，于是他以冲刺的速度向一个街区之隔的百老汇跑去。刚转过拐角，哈德利就看见一群面相凶恶的人站在消防栓的旁边。"太棒了，"他心想，"有人了。"

他继续沿着百老汇向前奔跑着，途中经过了一个室外集市，穿着红色罩衣的年轻人正在搬运蔬菜补给，一脸的倦意。还有一个人在清扫地上的玻璃碎渣。灯光让哈德利心中放松了不少——那意味着人烟。只有寥寥几人，但已经足够打消他不必要的迫害妄想了。高楼大厦的门前歪斜倾趔着许多的流浪汉，身上覆盖着绿色的垃圾袋和撕扯开的纸盒箱子。在昏黄的街灯下，每个人的脸色都像是染上了黄疸病。

哈德利在路口左拐，来到了麦克斯和谢尔碧住的街上。他知道，自己不应该这么做的。本想去艾伯哈德的住处，可那要一直跑到晨边大道上去，再加上路上可能存在的风险，还有……无论如何，他现在已经到门口了。他试探了一下公寓前厅的大门，开着的。守夜的门卫睡着了，半个身体顺着毛茸茸的红色扶手椅滑了下来，两腿成九十度杵在地上，形成了一张人肉桌子，哈德利于是轻手轻脚地从他身边走过去了。匆忙来到麦克斯和谢尔碧的门前，他用力地捶响了门，脑子里想象的是他们俩躺在床上的样子。他再一次觉得自己不应该这样做，但实在是无计可施了。

谢尔碧先被惊醒了，"到底是谁呀？"她推了推麦克斯，睡意蒙眬地问道。

"嗯？"麦克斯模糊地应了一声，又把被单拉紧了一些。

"肯定是德莫特。"谢尔碧打了个哈欠，"不是想让我们加入他的派对就是他

Chapter Nineteen Rate-limiting Reaction

come after him."

"Whaddya talking about?" Max asked, thinking he was dreaming. The pounding on the door resumed.

"That," she said pushing him. Max rolled over and fell back asleep. "Okay, okay, I'll see who it is." She threw on her terry cloth bathrobe and made her way to the front door in the dark.

"Hadley!" she said, spying him through the peephole and then immediately opening the door. Was he here to see her? she wondered stupidly, still confused by sleep. The thought played in her head, a continuous loop, each round able to incite her heart. It was her heart because she could feel it move, lift up, press against her breasts. "What's going on?" Shelby switched on the hall light.

"Someone broke into my apartment."

"Oh, my God." She touched his shoulder as she guided him into the apartment. Twice. "You're sweating. Do you want something to drink? Beer? Rum."

"Just some water, actually."

Shelby went into the kitchen to get some water and saw Max standing at the bedroom door in his boxers. "Someone broke into Hadley's apartment," she said. Max wavered a little on his feet, trying to focus. Perplexed, he scratched his head, then went into the living room and sat down on the upholstered chair.

"Someone after drugs?" Max asked.

"I don't know." Hadley took the glass from Shelby and drank some water. "All I know is I was having this weird dream about police in the lab and then I woke up and found it was worse than that. Someone was in my room."

"Wow," Shelby exhaled.

"I just lay there and waited and finally got the nerve to get up."

"Jesus," Max said.

"I don't know how they got in."

"What are you going to do?" Max asked.

Hadley looked at Max. "I was ... I was wondering if I could stay here for a few days until I can find somewhere else to live?" Hadley asked hesitantly.

"Sure," Shelby said. She looked at Max.

Max shrugged. "If you can sleep on this couch."

被邻居追杀了。"

"你嘟囔什么呢?"麦克斯仍然半睡半醒。"砰砰"的敲门声丝毫没有停下来的意思。

"听啊。"她又推了麦克斯一下。

麦克斯翻了个身,正面朝下,彻底失去了意识。

"好吧,好吧,我来看看这到底是谁。"谢尔碧披上毛巾织料的浴袍,在黑暗中向门口走去。

"哈德利!"她透过猫眼看出去之后立刻就打开了门。他是来这儿看自己的吗?谢尔碧傻乎乎地想着,明显还没有完全从睡意中清醒过来。这个想法在她的脑海里不断盘旋着,每一次都能在她心里激起涟漪。确定是她的心脏无疑,因为她感受到了它的移动,上升,以及在胸口处的撞击。"发生了什么?"谢尔碧打开了门关处的灯。

"有人闯进了我的公寓。"

"上帝啊。"她携着哈德利的胳膊引他进屋。然后又把手搭在了他肩头,"你在流汗。想喝些什么吗?啤酒?朗姆?"

"其实,水就行了。"

谢尔碧走进厨房去倒水,这时她看见麦克斯只穿着四角裤出现在了卧室的门口。"有人闯进了哈德利的公寓。"她转述道。麦克斯脚下有点打晃儿,他试着想站稳。带着一脸困惑的表情,他挠了挠头,走到客厅在有软垫的椅子上坐了下来。

"嗑了药的人吗?"麦克斯问了一句。

"我不知道。"哈德利从谢尔碧的手里接过玻璃杯,喝了点水。"我只知道,我当时正做着奇怪的梦,梦见有警察来实验室了,接着我一醒来,发现情况比梦里还要糟糕:我的房间里有人。"

"哇哦。"谢尔碧吐了口气。

"我就一直躺在那里等着,最终才有胆量起来。"

"天哪。"麦克斯也感到无比惊讶。

"我不懂他们是怎么进来的。"

"你现在打算怎么办?"麦克斯问道。

哈德利看向他。"我想……我在想我能不能先在你们这儿待几天,等我找到住的地方就搬走?"他的口气有些犹疑不定。

"当然了。"谢尔碧看了麦克斯一眼,抢着答道。

麦克斯耸了耸肩。"要是你愿意在这张沙发上将就的话。"

"For a few days. Just to figure out what to do next."

"We got tons of room," Shelby said, motioning to the half-empty living room.

"Whatever you want," Max said, yawning and standing up. "Do you need—"

"I'll get them," Shelby said rising and going to the living room closet for a blanket and pillow.

"I really do appreciate this. I'm sorry I had to wake you guys up."

"Don't be ridiculous." Shelby turned toward Hadley. "You're our best friend."

"What she said," Max mumbled, nodding. "I'm really sorry, but I can't keep my eyes open. I'll see you in the morning." Max clapped Hadley lightly on the back and almost lost his balance. "Sorry."

Hadley turned to him and said, "Thanks." Max nodded as he walked to the bedroom door and went inside.

Shelby started covering the sofa with a sheet and then spreading a blanket on top of it.

"I can do all that," Hadley said quickly.

"I don't mind. Did you want more water?" Shelby asked, noticing that his glass was empty.

"I'll feel worse if you wait on me. It's bad enough that I woke you both up."

"We would do anything for you."

Hadley lifted his head to look at her. "Thank you," he said softly. He smiled and said, "Go back to sleep." Shelby nodded and walked out of the living room.

For hours Shelby thought of Hadley sleeping in the living room on the sofa she and Max had bought from a woman whose marriage was falling apart. There in the dark, Shelby burned. But what could she do, trapped as she was in bed, Max breathing heavily on one side of her? He moved toward her in his sleep, throwing one arm over her as if unconsciously aware of her emotional duplicity. She felt trespassed.

Feigning sleep, she turned over and moved away. Max's arm slid to the mattress and he snored softly. This was hell. She couldn't sleep and the more she thought, the more she went crazy. What if she got up for a drink of water? And what would that give her? How would that make her ache any less? "Fuck you," she chastised

"几天就好,几天我就能想清楚接下来该怎么做了。"

"我们多的是地方。"谢尔碧指着几乎是半空状态的客厅说。

"你舒服就好,"麦克斯哈欠连天地站起身来,"你需不需要——"

"我会去拿的,"谢尔碧说着也起身走向壁橱去取毯子和枕头。

"真的非常感谢。很抱歉把你们都给吵醒了。"

"别犯傻了,"谢尔碧转过身来,"你是我们最好的朋友。"

"她说得对。"麦克斯含糊地附和着,又点了点头。"真对不起,但我实在是睁不开眼睛了。明早见。"麦克斯轻轻在哈德利的背上拍了一下,差点儿又没站稳。"抱歉。"

哈德利转向他说了声:"谢谢。"麦克斯点着头走回了卧室。

谢尔碧开始动手把床单铺到沙发上,然后又在上面加了一层毯子。

"我自己来就好了。"哈德利赶忙说道。

"没事儿。你想再来点儿水吗?"谢尔碧注意到他的杯子空了。

"要是你这么服侍我的话,我只会感觉更愧疚的。把你们俩都吵醒已经够糟糕的了。"

"我们愿意为你做任何事。"

哈德利抬起头来看着她,"谢谢。"他温柔地说了一声。笑了一下,他又继续说道:"回去睡觉。"谢尔碧点着头走出了客厅。

连续好几个小时,谢尔碧的脑海里全都在想,哈德利此时正睡在客厅里那张她和麦克斯从一个婚姻即将破裂的女人那里买来的沙发上。黑暗之中,谢尔碧感到欲火焚身。可像她现在这样被困在床上,伴随着一旁麦克斯沉重的呼吸声,她能够做什么呢?睡梦中麦克斯向谢尔碧这边靠过来,一只胳膊甩在了她身上,仿佛下意识里感知到了谢尔碧情感上的表里不一。她感觉到自己的领域被入侵了。

于是她假装睡着的样子,借转身向外挪了挪。麦克斯的胳膊滑到了床垫上,并传出了轻微的呼噜声。这对谢尔碧来说如同地狱一般。她睡不着,越想,越接近发狂的边缘。要不起床去喝点水?那又能给她带来什么呢?能减轻她的痛苦吗?"去你的。"她咒骂了一句那个主张退缩的自己。"别总碍事

herself. "Stop getting in my way."

Shelby moved the covers aside slowly and eased her way out of the waterbed. She shifted her weight hesitantly to the floor so that the water level wouldn't change abruptly and wake Max. He mumbled and she froze, silently begging him to stay asleep. She walked to the door of the bedroom. The floorboards creaked loudly with the weight of her body, raspy warnings of betrayal, but Max didn't stir. Shelby peered out toward the living room. The glass-paned door hung halfway open, allowing Shelby to hear Hadley's soft breathing. She could see the mound of Hadley underneath the faded blue blanket she'd given him. The wallpaper shades in the living room hadn't been pulled down, so the soft yellow moonlight illuminated the room in bands of eerie paleness. It was a chiaroscuro of vaulted living room, transformed by the alternating shades. She could see the reflection of hairs in his mustache, but not whether his eyes were opened or closed. What excuse could she have to go in? To go stroke his cheek? What could she do? With Max in the next room. She closed the bedroom door, one step closer to adultery.

"You're a fool," she thought sadly, not knowing how to relieve the torment. How could marriage mean that she would never again kiss another man? Sex with the same person year in and year out ... it had seemed possible at one time, but it always seems possible when passion and matrimony coincide in those first months of bliss. But soon fidelity feels like a restraint. It's so arbitrary, so small-minded. A concept conceived by puritans with no strength of personality, nothing to ignite them.

She wanted economic freedom, because with that would come sexual freedom. She could love them both. She could live in her own house, and not need either of them. They could come visit her when they wanted, when she wanted. They would all be free to choose. She wouldn't be owned or claimed by either of them. Men did it. They had their concubines, their wives. Why couldn't women? You just needed power, status, money. And lacking those, she cheated. She went behind the back, in the dark of the night. In the world of men she'd be a rake, but in the world of women she was an adulteress. Not yet, but soon. She fantasized, about the next time they would meet, what they would say. It's a web that she climbed down cautiously, trying not to stick to anything. Trying not to say anything that would stick to her, denominate her, and yet saying everything in a way that exuded passion.

"Shelby."

儿了。"

谢尔碧掀开身上的被子,蹑手蹑脚地慢慢从水床上下来。为了防止水波突然涌动弄醒麦克斯,她小心不迭地转移着自己的体重。麦克斯嘟囔了一声,谢尔碧立时冻在了原地,暗自期盼着他不要醒来。她又继续向卧室门口走去。地板因为她的体重而"吱呀"响了起来,刺耳如同提醒背叛的警铃声,可是麦克斯丝毫没有被惊动。谢尔碧先是从门缝向客厅里窥探——玻璃滑门半开着,因此她能听见哈德利轻柔的呼吸声。在那条有些褪色的蓝色毯子下面,她能够看见哈德利的身形。客厅里的墙纸百叶窗没有拉下来,浅黄色的月光撒了进来,屋子里苍白得有些怪异。交替翻飞的百叶帘让客厅的穹顶产生了明暗交替的效果。谢尔碧能够在玻璃上看见哈德利胡子的倒影,但是却不能确定他的双眼是睁是闭。借什么为由进客厅呢,去抚摸他的脸呢?麦克斯就在隔壁的房间里,她还能做什么?关上身后卧室的门,谢尔碧离通奸又近了一步。

"你真是个傻瓜。"她悲伤地想着,不知道该怎么减轻这种折磨。婚姻怎么可以意味着永远都不允许再亲另一个男人呢?与同一个人做爱,年复一年……放在曾经,这看起来还有可能,因为在那最初几个月的欢愉里,激情和婚姻是相挽并行的。但很快,忠诚就变成了枷锁,独断而狭隘。这是清教徒们想出来的,他们毫无个性色彩,没有东西能够点燃他们的激情。

谢尔碧想要实现经济上的独立,因为那样性的自由才会随之而来。那时她就可以同时爱他们两个人了。住在属于自己的房子里,不需要依靠他们任何一个。愿意的时候,他们随时都可以来拜访她。大家就都能拥有选择的自由了。谁都不能声称拥有她。男人就是这么做的:既有妻,又有妾。为什么女人不行?只要有权力、地位和金钱就可以了。谢尔碧一样都没有,所以她出轨了:趁着夜色漆黑,鬼鬼祟祟。在男人的世界里她就是个浪子,但她生而为女,只能是奸妇。虽然现在还不是,但快了。她脑海里想象着他们再次见面时的情景、会说的话。谢尔碧沿着这张网小心翼翼地爬行着,尽可能不被任何东西给粘住,不说任何会束缚住自己,给自己贴上标价的话,可是她所说出的一切,都洋溢着热情。

"谢尔碧。"

His voice stopped her cold. Her heart beat dangerously close to the speed limit. She felt twittery with the attention, like a glistening fish twitching on a line. "Yes." She said it so softly that only someone listening intently could have deduced the word from the molecules of air that it collided through.

"I can't sleep either."

Shelby saw him sit up on the sofa, pulling his knees into his chest. She swallowed hard and then walked into the living room. "Are you okay?"

"I'm frightened."

His honesty took Shelby aback. She blinked and then asked, "That they'll follow you?"

"No."

The breathiness of his voice hung in the air. It made her ache. Was she in love? She didn't even care to find out. She just wanted this now. Like a child wants a pacifier. Something to ease her pain.

Shelby sat down on the far edge of the sofa, perched on the padded arm. She felt pulled, unable to stop herself from sliding down to the seat. They looked at each other, afraid to move closer, knowing there was a point at which critical mass would take over.

"I scare you." She spoke, but it could have been either of them.

"Yes."

"Me, too."

"We have to think about Max."

"I know. I love him." She looked at Hadley, reading his face. "I can't help it. I love you. I want to live with you both."

Hadley laughed. "You are."

She smiled sadly. The moment was lost, she had ruined it. Instead of being amorous, she'd been truthful.

"We would be too morbid together." He said this as he looked toward the bedroom.

"I know."

"Max is uplifting."

"Yes."

They looked at each other. Then they heard the toilet flush. Shelby smiled at

第十九章 控速反应

哈德利突然响起的声音让谢尔碧不知所措地愣在原地。她的心跳直蹿限速标准,对哈德利的注意感到既紧张又兴奋,就像被勾住的鱼在水面上扑腾出闪闪的金光。"是的。"谢尔碧的声音十分轻柔,只有凝神倾听的人才能从它摩擦而过的空气分子中推断出那个单词。

"我也睡不着。"

谢尔碧看见他从沙发上坐起,蜷起双腿抱在了胸前。她用力地吞咽一下,走进了客厅。"你还好吗?"

"我很害怕。"

他的坦诚让谢尔碧吃了一惊。她眨了眨眼追问道:"怕他们会跟踪你?"

"不是。"

哈德利伴着呼吸声的嗓音飘浮在空气中,令谢尔碧感到心痛。她陷入爱情了吗?谢尔碧甚至都没有心思去寻找答案了。只要拥有现在就好,如同婴儿对安抚奶嘴的渴求一样,她需要某样可以缓和她痛苦的东西。

谢尔碧坐在沙发另一头的扶手软垫上,却像被牵引着一样,不受控制地滑坐在了沙发上。他们看着对方,不敢再靠近丝毫,深知再向前的某个点处,他们就会被临界质量[译者注:critical mass 维持链式反应所需要的裂变材料的最小质量]给控制住了。

"是我让你害怕了。"谢尔碧开了口,但哈德利本也可能说出同样的话。

"是的。"

"你也是。"

"我们得想想麦克斯。"

"我知道。我爱他。"她直视着哈德利,试图从他的脸部读出什么。"我控制不了自己。我也爱你。我想和你们两个住在一起。"

哈德利忍不住笑了。"你现在就是了。"

谢尔碧也悲伤地笑了。最好的时机已经错过了,被她给毁了。本可以含情脉脉的,可她却选择了直抒胸臆。

"我们俩在一起的话就太消极了。"他看着卧室的方向,说了这句话。

"我懂。"

"麦克斯是让人振奋的性格。"

"是的。"

他们又把目光投向了对方。这时传来了马桶冲水的声音。谢尔碧对哈德利

Hadley, the sadness of a lifetime in the glance of a second. She jumped off the sofa and raced toward the kitchen. The bedroom door opened and Max looked out. "Shelby?" She followed him inside. The bedroom door closed. Just like that.

Hadley tried not to let disappointment set in. But it would always be like this. He would be the outsider. He knew that there was no way he could go back to sleep, so he got up and left the apartment. Might as well do some chemistry. It was 5:38 in the morning. Instead of black, the city had become dark gray, lightening slowly as the shadowy grime was washed clean by the sun. He had another moment of grief that he quickly submerged, his mind perfecting a choke hold on errant feelings, pushing them under, subduing them. Shelby was the rate-limiting step. She controlled them both. Lead them on. He had to break free. Chemistry. He'd think about that. Everything else was meaningless.

莞尔一笑，在那一秒钟的凝视中仿佛充满了一辈子的忧伤。接着她从沙发上一跃而起，冲向了厨房。卧室门被推开了，麦克斯向外张望着，"谢尔碧？"她跟着麦克斯进去了。卧室的门又关上了。就那样，关上了。

　　哈德利努力不让沮丧占据自己的内心，但往后永远都会是这样了：他永远都是外人。知道自己不可能再睡着，他起身离开了公寓。不如做做化学实验。现在是清晨5:38，这个城市已经由漆黑一片转变为深灰色了，蒙浊的污垢被渐露的阳光清洗一新，天色一点一点地明亮起来。又一阵悲伤向哈德利袭来，但被他迅速掩埋住了。他不断精进着将出轨情感掐死的能力：向下推，或者压制住。谢尔碧就像是化学实验中的控速反应步——控制住了他和麦克斯，再进一步地诱惑。他必须要挣脱出来。化学，他应该专注在这上面。其他一切都没有意义。

Chapter Twenty Moth to Flame

And all wild longings of the insatiate blood Brought me down to my knees. O who can be Both moth and flame? The weak moth blundering by ...

> Theodore Roethke, 1964

Hadley was panicking. He'd searched his whole apartment, hating every terrifying moment of being there. He knew he was prone to panic these days. Wild oscillations, from guilt to jubilation, left him bereft of common sense. He almost laughed. Common sense? That had gone long ago.

His notebook was gone. He remembered taking it home Friday and putting it on his desk in his bedroom so he could write his research report. Then what did he do? He closed his eyes, trying to replay the insignificance of his movements. He'd put it in his desk drawer. Ah, but then Sunday night he'd pulled it out again so he wouldn't forget it Monday. Wait—Rahda had called him Sunday night. He'd looked up a yield for her. Played along. Like she was normal. It was so hard for him to put himself in Rahda's shoes. What could she be thinking? He paused for a moment, wondering if she'd taken his notebook. But when? Had he taken it back Monday? Had he left it sitting out at the lab, unattended for a moment? He just couldn't believe she'd go that far. Although, he had thought someone had gone through his lab drawers, but people do that, looking for things. It pissed him off. He remembered Max needling him, whispering loudly to Shelby. "His balance was rotated by eight degrees."

"I'm tired of people going through my drawers." Hadley had said. "I don't think irritation is an unreasonable emotion."

"Look, you set a trap. You buy the John Holmes Dick Enlarger. You put it in a drawer. Then every time they pass you in the hall they'll check your pants. You got 'em easy."

第二十章 飞蛾扑火

> 贪嗜血液中的一切渴望使我屈膝。哦，谁能既是飞蛾又是火焰？虚弱的蛾子跌跌撞撞地飞过……
> ——西奥多·罗特克，1964

哈德利慌了神。待在这里的每一秒都让他不寒而栗，虽然讨厌，但他还是里里外外地把公寓给搜寻了一遍。他知道自己最近很容易陷入惊恐之中。情绪在极端之间变幻，从内疚到欣喜，连常识都完全丧失了。他差点儿就笑出声来了。常识？老早就没有了。

哈德利的笔记本不见了。明明星期五那天为了撰写研究报告带回了家，放在自己卧室的桌上了。然后他做了什么？哈德利闭上眼睛，尝试回忆当时自己一些细小不重要的动作。他把笔记本放进了桌子抽屉里。啊哈，但是为了防止周一忘记带，周日晚上他又把它给拿了出来。等等——拉达周日晚上打电话来找过他，让哈德利给她查一下产物的产量。哈德利当时也陪着她演了下去，把她当作正常人一样对待。对哈德利来说，要他从拉达的角度来看问题实在是太难了。她到底是怎么想的？哈德利想到这儿顿了一下，他开始怀疑是不是拉达拿走了他的笔记本。可在什么时候呢？星期一自己有把它带回实验室吗？是不是有一阵子就放在了实验室里无人看管？他实在无法相信拉达会做到这种程度。他确实觉得有人翻过自己实验室的抽屉，可有时候会有人这样做的，为了找些什么东西。这让他很有些恼怒。还记得麦克斯也故意大声地对谢尔碧耳语过："他的电子天平被挪转了八度。"

"我受够了别人来翻看我的抽屉，"哈德利回应道，"我也不觉得因为这件事情生气有什么不合理的。"

"听着，你该设计一个陷阱。可以买一个约翰·福尔摩斯牌的阳具放大器，放在抽屉里。然后翻你抽屉的人每次从你身边经过的时候就会盯着你的裤裆看。你很容易就可以抓个正着了。"

Chapter Twenty Moth to Flame

Hadley remembered Shelby laughing and swatting Max. They seemed to get along so well. The perfect couple. Then why? Why had she touched him? Why did she want him to touch her? And what if he did? What if he took her away from Max? It was the first time he actually thought the thought. The deed. What an act of betrayal it was. He hadn't done anything, but he felt like a sinner. He had done something. He'd kissed his best friend's wife. He'd gotten letters from her. He could no longer call theirs a platonic relationship.

Maybe it was a game with her. Was she toying with him? She wasn't like that. He knew her well. Even intimate stuff, like the fact that she'd sucked a woman's nipple once, during a ménage à trois. This was years ago. She said she'd arranged it for an old boyfriend because he was only making minimum wage. And they'd broken up a month later. He remembered now that she'd said the saddest thing about going out-of-bounds is that you may never see that person again. That thought played over in his head as he locked his apartment and headed for Max and Shelby's.

The subway doors opened and a guy on a skateboard got on. No legs but a skateboard. It reminded Shelby that her troubles were all of her own making. She was a big whiner. New York constantly thrust alternative lives in your face, making you shape up. Sometimes you were thankful for your life, and sometimes you were in awe of how much better it could be. Of course, the subway was destined to cheer you up in these matters, making you almost always more thankful.

Shelby hated Gary, her boss. She'd been looking for another job because he'd been pressuring her to do stripping telegrams. Not completely naked, but down to a corset. She'd done one, at a Lindy's restaurant of all places. She made two hundred dollars. It was a lot of money, but it was also one of the most demeaning experiences she'd ever had, singing "Makin' Whoopee" to frowzy, happy hour women while she swung a feather boa in their faces. She couldn't decide if it was more sexist to sing to the women or to ignore them completely. She pretty much avoided the men. She didn't want to hit anyone.

The subway car stopped shudderingly and glitter fell into her eyes. Another lame idea of Gary's. She had tried to tell him that Wonder Woman wouldn't be caught dead in glitter. He was unrelenting and she knew he'd find out if she didn't wear the stuff. It was like getting a sudden case of fourteen-karat dandruff.

哈德利还记得当时谢尔碧大笑不止,不住地拍打着麦克斯。他们俩看上去非常合拍,是一对完美的情侣。那为什么呢?为什么谢尔碧还故意与自己有身体接触?为什么她想要他也做同样的事?万一做了会怎么样?要是他真的把谢尔碧从麦克斯的身边夺走会如何?这是哈德利第一次产生这个想法。这种行为,是多么明目张胆的背叛啊。虽然什么都还没做过,他已经觉得自己像个罪人了。其实他有过行动了:他亲了自己最好的朋友的老婆;还收了她的信。他们之间的关系无法再被称作是柏拉图式的了。

也许这对谢尔碧来说是一场游戏。她是不是在玩弄自己?可她不是那样的人,哈德利了解她。甚至连一些私密的事都了如指掌,比如说她曾经在过去三人同居的日子里吮吸过一个女人的乳头。很多年前的事情了。她说是为了旧日的男朋友有心安排的,因为他当时的薪水微薄到了刚够上最低薪资的程度。一个月之后他们就分手了。哈德利还记得她说过,做出格的事情最令人难过的一点是,可能因此这辈子都不能再和那个人相见了。他锁上公寓门,向麦克斯和谢尔碧的住所走去,这个想法却一直在他脑海里盘旋不去。

地铁门打开了,上来一个带着滑板的家伙。没有腿,只有滑板。谢尔碧顿时觉得,所有的烦心事都是她自己一手造成的。她总是抱怨个不停。纽约时不时地将不同的生命形式猛地推到你面前,催你振作起来。人有时对生活充满感激,有时又对它可以改善的空间感到震惊。不消说,从这方面来说地铁上的所见是注定能够鼓舞人的,几乎每次经历都会让你变得更加感恩。

谢尔碧对她的老板加里憎恶至极。他不断施压,想让谢尔碧做脱衣舞电报,因此她一直想另谋出路。倒不需要完全脱光,但要到只剩一件紧身胸衣的程度。她试过一次,还偏偏选在了在林迪餐馆里[译者注:纽约一家低档餐馆]。那次的小费有两百美金之多,可却是她做过的最有损尊严的事情之一:对着一群在欢乐时光买醉的邋遢女人唱着《纵享狂欢》,边用羽毛披肩在她们眼前撩拨。她也无法确定哪一种做法更带有性别歧视的色彩,对着她们唱,还是完全忽略她们。全场下来她几乎刻意避开了所有的男性顾客,她可不想再动手打人了。

地铁停下来的时候,车身剧烈地抖动了一下,谢尔碧的眼睛里飘进了亮片——这是加里的另一个烂主意。她试着争辩说神奇女侠死的时候是不会飘下亮片来的,可加里却一意孤行。谢尔碧知道自己要是不照做的话他一定会发现的。那感觉就像是突然头顶上多了十四克拉的头皮屑。并且粘得到处都是,演

Glitter covered her wardrobe. The stuff stuck to everything, even her contacts. Once the glitter was on the lens, it was a bitch to get off. She would feel her eyelid close over it, scratched every few seconds by a tiny piece of gold mylar.

Getting off at 110th, she found herself hoping that Hadley would be there. Would he have come home for lunch? Would he be on her wavelength? She started running.

"Lose your key?"

"No." She smiled wanly at the doorman. She'd been listening at the apartment door. "I was ..." she couldn't for the life of her think of any plausible explanations. "... just getting my keys." She pulled them out of her purse and opened the door slowly, prepared for anything.

Hadley looked up from the sofa as she walked in. He was standing in front of it, tossing things out of his backpack. "I'm looking for my notebook. I can't find it anywhere. I'm supposed to do a research report at five."

"You think it was stolen?"

"Maybe."

Shelby stood nervously, vacillating between taking off her coat and leaving it on. It was hard to carry on a normal conversation dressed as Wonder Woman.

"Shit." He went over and sat on the window seat. "I don't know what I'm going to do."

"Is anything else gone?"

"Not that I know of." He sighed and looked out the window. "Why is everything going wrong?"

"What else is going wrong?" She could barely breathe after she asked this, settling for sitting down on the sofa instead of inhaling.

Hadley turned and looked at her without blinking. "Ah." He shook his head and laughed.

"Give me a hint."

"A hint is way too short."

"So take your time."

"What if Max walked in right now?"

"We're just talking." She smiled at him.

The phone rang. They both jumped. "I'll get it," Shelby said stupidly,

出服,甚至是隐形眼镜上。有一次就发生了这种情况,想取下来比登天还难。每过几秒钟她闭眼的时候,那一小片的聚酯树脂薄膜都会刚擦到眼皮。

从110号大街出站后,谢尔碧意识到,自己暗自期待着哈德利这会儿正待在家里。他有可能回来吃午饭吗?他会不会也怀揣着和自己一样的想法?谢尔碧开始跑了起来。

"钥匙丢了吗?"

"没有。"她给了门卫一个心虚的微笑,因为她已经趴在自己公寓门口听了一会儿了。"我只是……"绞尽了脑汁她也想不出任何合理的解释来。"……在找钥匙。"说话间她从包里抽出钥匙,慢吞吞地打开了门,做好了应对所有场面的准备。

站在沙发前的哈德利抬起头看着她,从背包里拿东西的动作也停了下来。"我在找我的笔记本,哪儿都找不到。下午五点我就要做实验汇报了。"

"被人偷了?"

"也许吧。"

谢尔碧紧张地站在原地,纠结到底要不要脱掉外套。穿成神奇女侠的样子要想进行一场正常的对话实在是太难了。

"该死。"哈德利走到一边坐在了窗座上。"我真不知道该怎么办了。"

"其他东西有丢吗?"

"我还没发现。"他叹了口气,向窗外看去。"为什么所有事情都不对劲?"

"还有什么事出错了?"话一出口谢尔碧几乎无法呼吸了,她决定先在沙发上坐下来,而不是站在原地大口吸气。

哈德利转过身来看着她,眼睛都没有眨一下。"啊。"他摇着头笑了。

"提示我一下。"

"一个提示根本不够长。"

"那就慢慢讲。"

"要是麦克斯现在走进来怎么办?"

"我们只不过是在聊天啊。"谢尔碧对着他笑了。

电话铃在这时响起了。他们俩都跳了起来。"我来接。"谢尔碧的心沉了

her heart sinking. Max often called about now.

She picked up the phone and then looked perplexed. "It's for you."

Hadley took the phone from her.

"Hello? What?" Hadley's voice raised. "Jesus." Shelby could hear loud talking on the other end.

"Oh, Ethan—No, I'm not starting on a lecture!" He paused impatiently. "I'm worried about you, frankly. What about your dad? —Well, you've got to ask him."

Hadley looked at Shelby and raised his eyebrows in an exasperated way. "Yeah. I'm moving. I don't know." There was more gurgling from the other side and then Hadley said slowly, "Listen to me carefully. Don't do it. If you make it in the lab and someone finds out, you will never work as a Ph.D. again. Get the money from your dad. I'm telling you, don't do it."

Shelby waited while Hadley finished his conversation. There was a faint but constant tinfoil rattle of the radiator interfering with her concentration. Shelby could only think of Hadley kissing her. The tempo changed, and now it seemed that the radiator tattled lightly on the air current that disturbed it, until the current gusted in defiance and the radiator's noise blurted out a faster story. It seemed only Shelby noticed the confession.

"A hundred thousand dollars' worth of cocaine was stolen," Hadley explained as he hung up.

"From where?" Shelby had no idea that Ethan trafficked in amounts that large.

"Under his bed. He said it was in a big green suitcase. And now it's gone."

"Where did he get that kind of money?"

"He didn't. But now he'll have to."

"Or else someone'll kill him?" Shelby bit her fingernails.

"Yeah." Hadley walked over and rested one knee on the window seat.

Shelby followed him. "I'm sorry." She didn't know what to say. "I'm sorry we don't have a better view for you to forget your troubles."

"I like the view. It's the biggest rock in Manhattan." He smiled sadly at her. "Ethan reminds me of my brother. A loser with a heart. I know he's going to fuck up. It's hard to care for someone who's going to fuck up."

Shelby searched Hadley's face. "I didn't know you had a brother."

下去,傻乎乎地说了一句。麦克斯通常会在这个时间点打电话回来。

拿起听筒,谢尔碧脸上的表情变得困惑起来。"是找你的。"

哈德利从她手里接过电话。

"你好?什么?"哈德利的声线提高了八度。"上帝啊。"谢尔碧能够听见电话那头的人在大声地讲话。

"噢,伊桑——不,我不是想给你讲道理。"他不耐烦地停顿了一下。"坦白说,我很担心你。那你父亲呢?——可是,你总得问问他。"

哈德利看了谢尔碧一眼,恼怒地挑了挑眉毛。"是的,我要搬走了。我不知道。"那头又陆续传来伊桑的声音,哈德利接下去慢慢地说:"你认真听我说,不要这么做。要是你在实验室里做被人发现了的话,你永远都不可能拿到博士学位了。钱可以向你父亲要。千万不要那么做。"

谢尔碧一直等到哈德利挂上电话。暖气片持续不断地传来锡箔摩擦的"咔嚓"声,虽然微弱,却让谢尔碧无法集中。她的脑海里只有哈德利亲吻自己的画面。那声音的节奏突然改变了,现在听上去像是暖气片在空气中絮絮地讲述着什么,直到被扰乱的气流奋起反抗,那噪音才一鼓作气地讲完了那个故事。似乎只有谢尔碧注意到了空气中的忏悔。

"十万美金的可卡因被偷了。"哈德利放下电话后解释道。

"在哪儿?"谢尔碧完全没料到伊桑走私的数量这么惊人。

"在他床底下。他说装在一个绿色的大行李箱里。现在不见了。"

"他从哪儿弄的那么多钱?"

"并没有,不过现在他必须要开始筹集了。"

"否则就会有人追杀他?"谢尔碧咬着自己的手指甲。

"对。"哈德利又走回去,单腿跪在窗座上。

谢尔碧跟在后面,"我很抱歉。"她也不知道该说些什么。"抱歉这儿的视野不太好,不能让暂时你忘记这些烦恼。"

"我喜欢这个风景。这是曼哈顿最大的岩石了。"哈德利笑了,表情有些悲伤。"伊桑让我想起了我的哥哥。虽然是失败者,心地却还是善良的。明明知道他不会有好的结局,所以要对这样的人给予关心是很难的事。"

谢尔碧扫视着他的脸,"我从来不知道你还有个哥哥。"

"I know." He sat down on the window seat. "Simon was a lot like Ethan. Everyone thought he was such a genius. He was good at math, science; he played a bunch of instruments in the junior high band. I think he had a crush on his band teacher and this way he was in the music room a lot. He kept bugging the teacher to let the band play 'JoJo'. Finally, she told him that if he wrote out all the parts he could conduct it, thinking this a way to get him to shut up. But she didn't know Simon. He spent weeks color-coding the instruments. We shared the same room and he'd be there with pages laid out before him, a sixty-four pack of felt pens scattered all over his desk."

"You mean every instrument was a different color?" Shelby smiled.

"It was a work of art ..." Hadley paused, " ... but it was all in the same key. He was so busy writing them out in all those fucking colors that he forgot to transpose."

Shelby looked at Hadley, smiling, and he gave her an odd look.

"A month later he brought it to rehearsal. He was all fluffed up, thinking he was so important. He clicked the conductor's stand about thirty times, then hit the down beat. Oh man. It was awful. I mean, way worse than normal for junior high. He realized immediately. I was at the back of the room, and I watched as my brother carefully folded the conductor's score, placed it under his arm, and walked out of the multi-purpose room."

Hadley looked levelly at Shelby. "He went home and hung himself with the rope swing."

"No!" Shelby said, stunned that Hadley had kept this a secret all this time. She could think of nothing to say.

"I remember when I was younger he stayed in a mental hospital for a while. When he came back home, he told me that they put him on lithium because that's what they use to cool down nuclear reactors." Hadley paused. "I could never tell if he was joking."

"Wow," Shelby said. She wanted to touch him, to hug him, but she felt unable to initiate intimacy. She was married. She kept chanting this in her mind. Anyway, she was the one who'd said they were just talking. "Hadley, I'm really sorry." She tried to communicate all her conflicting emotions in her that one sentence, knowing it would only get her into trouble. "He was older?"

"我从没讲起过。"他坐了下去,"西蒙和伊桑很相像。大家都觉得他是个天才,他在数学和科学方面都很出色;还在初中的校乐队里演奏很多种乐器。我想,他当时对乐队老师产生了爱慕之情,所以经常在音乐教室里待着。他一直缠着那个老师,想让乐队演奏'JoJo'[译者注:披头士乐队的一首名为 Get Back 的歌曲]。终于有一天,她对西蒙说,要是他能把所有部分的指挥谱都给写出来的话,就可以由他来指挥演出。她八成指望着这可以让西蒙断了念头。可她不了解西蒙。从那以后的几周里,他专注地用不同的颜色标注起了各种乐器的演奏部分。我们俩当时住在一个房间,他经常面前摊着好多纸页,六十四支装的油毡笔散落在桌子上。"

"你是说每种乐器都用不同的颜色标记?"谢尔碧笑了。

"那对他来说是一件艺术品……"哈德利停了一会儿,"……但全篇都在一个调上。他太倾心于用那些该死的颜色来书写不同部分,结果忘记变调了。"

谢尔碧微笑着看着他,可哈德利却回以一个古怪的表情。

"一个月之后他把指挥谱带到了排练的现场,踌躇满志的样子,觉得自己的角色无比重要。结果他用指挥棒敲了大概三十次才让所有乐手集中了注意,最后才正式开始。唉,别提有多糟糕了,比一般初中生的水平都差了一大截儿。我当时就坐在教室的后面,看着他一丝不苟地把指挥谱整理好,夹在胳膊下面,走出了多功能教室。"

哈德利直视着谢尔碧的眼睛,"他回到家之后用秋千绳上吊自杀了。"

"天哪!"谢尔碧震惊地大叫出来,哈德利竟然一直以来将这作为秘密来保守。她也想不出还能说什么了。

"我还记得,在那件事发生的前几年西蒙在精神病院待了好一阵子。回来以后,他告诉我那里的人让他服用锂,因为核反应堆就是用它来抑制的。"哈德利停了几秒,"我始终不知道他是不是在开玩笑。"

"哇哦。"谢尔碧想要触碰他,给他拥抱,可却觉得无法主动做出亲密的举动。你已经结婚了。她不住地在脑海里重复着。无论如何,刚才说他们只不过是在聊天的人可是她自己。"哈德利,我真的很抱歉。"虽然明知道这样会让情况变得不可控制,她还是试着把自己所有冲突的感情都注入那一句话里。"他比你大?"

Chapter Twenty Moth to Flame

Hadley nodded. "I didn't tell you this to feel sorry for me. I just want you to know I'm not the greatest guy in the world."

"What do you mean?"

Hadley didn't say anything right away. He stood up again and looked out the window, grasping the crosspieces in his hands, his head framed by one square of the grid. His face reflected back at Shelby, faint and ghostlike, a hologram throwing its voice.

"I knew he was doing it wrong. I guess I thought it was funny, you know, that he was so stupid. I was jealous that everybody always thought he was such a brain. He probably thought everyone could transpose as fast as he did."

"Yeah, but Hadley," Shelby said shaking her head, "this was obviously one incident in the big picture. It sounds like he did have a crush on his band teacher. He was humiliated."

"If I had changed one thing, it might not have happened." Hadley's face shimmered in the glass.

"Are you okay?"

"No." Hadley abruptly turned to face her. "I'm in love with my best friend's wife. Who toys with me. And I find myself thinking that I deserve this because I let my brother die."

Staring at Hadley, Shelby touched his shoulder and they melted to one another, body clung to body. Heat-seeking devices. Lip-syncing. Holding so tightly to each other that they started to fall, catching themselves on the windowseat and smiling, then kissing again.

"I'm not toying with you." Shelby whispered in Hadley's ear, rubbing her lips along its edge. "I am not your punishment." She kissed his eyes closed, lightly covering his face with the merest brush of her painted lips, leaving no prints. His face moved down her neck, nuzzling her breasts, his head heavy and pressing.

"Max could walk in any moment," she sighed, then she kissed his lips quickly and gestured for him to come, a follow-through from her index finger stroking underneath his chin. Not looking to see if he was coming, she walked to the front door and opened it.

"Where are we going?" Hadley asked as he followed her to the stairwell, a public room that afforded relative privacy for those who walk. Hadley's voice

哈德利点了点头，"我告诉你不是让你为我难过的。我只是想让你知道，我并不是好人。"

"什么意思？"

哈德利没有立刻回答，他又站起身来，目光投向窗外，双手紧紧握住了横杆，脑袋正好镶嵌在了窗户的一格里。谢尔碧能够在玻璃里看见他脸部的镜像，苍白得像个幽灵，声音如同从玻璃上的那张全息图里传出来一般。

"我明知道他当时做错了，但我可能只是觉得有趣，就是，他也会犯那种愚蠢的错误。大家都觉得他天赋过人，这让我产生了妒意。他八成以为每个人都像他一样可以临场变调呢。"

"虽然是这样，可哈德利，"谢尔碧摇着头，"那很明显只是一次意外。从我听的角度来看，西蒙的确爱上了乐队的老师，却被羞辱了。"

"要是我做了什么的话，可能事情就不会发生了。"哈德利的脸庞在窗户上闪烁着光芒。

"你还好吗？"

"不好。"哈德利猛地转过身来。"我爱上了最好的朋友的老婆，对方却只是在玩弄我的感情。我现在觉得自己是罪有应得，因为我曾经眼睁睁地看着自己的哥哥走上绝路。"

谢尔碧目不转睛地盯着哈德利，碰到他肩膀的瞬间他们俩就融为了一体，紧紧地依附着对方。互相取暖，嘴唇也同步地胶着在一起。拥抱得过于用力以至于他们失去了平衡，跌坐在窗座上。之后他们相视一笑，又忘我地吻起来。

"我并没有玩弄你的感情。"谢尔碧轻柔地在哈德利耳边说道，嘴唇在他耳朵边缘摩擦着。"我不是你的惩罚。"接着她吻过哈德利闭合的双眼，涂红的双唇又轻拂过他面颊的每一寸，却没有留下任何的唇印。哈德利的头顺着谢尔碧的脖子往下移动，用力拱擦着她的胸。

"麦克斯随时都有可能进来。"她叹了口气，快速地亲了一下哈德利的双唇，并示意他跟着自己走——食指轻抚下巴，并没有回头看哈德利是否紧随其后，她径直走到门口，打开了门。

"我们要去哪儿？"哈德利跟在谢尔碧后面进了楼梯井，这里给所有想谈话的人提供了相对私密的空间。哈德利的声音听起来与谢尔碧印象中的丝毫不

Chapter Twenty Moth to Flame

sounded so much like Hadley that Shelby almost felt shock. How accustomed she was to it. The familiarity and unfamiliarity of Hadley made her breathless. For years she'd thought of him like a brother. It was a strong bond that had never verged on the sexual. And now that it had, it made her crazy. Some people liked sex with strangers. But for her the aphrodisiac was knowing someone so well, and then suddenly crossing that line. In many ways it made her more dangerous.

He asked again, "Where are we going?"

She didn't answer him right away because those words might pull him back from the insanity of their plan. She wondered if he was thinking of bailing. Was that an aphrodisiac to him? The uncertainty of conflagration. She turned and said "Shh!" then started running up the steps, nine flights of them, not talking until they got to the top. Finally she turned to him. "I don't want you to think that I take this lightly."

Touching her waist almost imperceptibly, Hadley reached past her and opened the door. The light before them was muted and white, a shimmering of sheets, a heaven of bedding. "You couldn't take this lightly." He held the door open for her and she crossed the threshold. Taking his hand, she walked with him down a corridor of starched bedclothes. The sheets smelled of lemon and purity, smells anomalous with their mission.

"How did you know this was here?" Hadley asked, looking around.

Smiling and pulling a sheet off the line, Shelby motioned for him to do the same.

"Because of our bathroom." Just the word *our* brought Shelby a pang of guilt, and she closed her eyes for a second.

Ducking under several rows, they finally made their way out of the flapping maze and came to a side of the building Shelby hadn't seen. The view was to the west, and they saw the darkness of the Hudson and the industry of New Jersey. Spreading out the sheets on the ground, they sat down next to one another.

"I'm afraid."

Hadley nodded. He turned to Shelby and hugged her. They held on to each other for a long time, sitting there, not kissing, not saying anything. They held each other and watched the barges on the Hudson, the sanity of commerce next to the insanity of concupiscence.

差,她几乎被吓到了——她对这声音竟如此习惯。关于哈德利的一切,不论陌生还是熟悉,让谢尔碧连呼吸都感到困难。这些年,她都把哈德利当作兄长看待,这强壮的纽带直到最近才掺杂上了性欲望的色彩。事实既成之后,谢尔碧再也无法平静了。有些人喜欢和陌生人做爱,但在她的眼里,对一个熟识的人突然越过禁忌线的瞬间,才是一剂催情药。很大程度上来说,谢尔碧因此而成为更危险的角色。

哈德利又问了一遍:"我们要去哪儿?"

她还是没有立刻回答,怕那几个字会吓得他从他们极端疯狂而愚蠢的计划当中退缩出去。谢尔碧担心他心里是不是已经敲响了退堂鼓。内心熊熊燃起的火焰所带来的不确定性,这对他来说也是催情剂吗?"嘘!"谢尔碧转过头来,随即又回身开始小跑着上楼梯。九级,到达楼顶之前谁都没有说话。终于,谢尔碧转过身面对着哈德利,喘着粗气。"我不想让你觉得,我把这当作儿戏。"

哈德利伸出手,几乎难以察觉地触碰到了她的腰部,又越过她,打开了顶楼的门。缄默无声的白色光影迎面在他们眼前展开,床单闪烁翻飞,这里是床上用品组成的天堂。"你不能把这当儿戏。"哈德利抵住门,让谢尔碧先跨过门槛。他们俩牵着手走过一个由浆洗过的床单被罩搭起的走廊,柠檬和洁净的气味在鼻息间萦绕,甚至因为他们的秘密行动而增添了不寻常的气息。

"你是怎么知道有这么个地方的?"哈德利四处打量了一下。

谢尔碧咯咯笑着从晾衣绳上扯下一条床单,并示意哈德利也学她照做。

"因为我们的浴室。"仅仅在"我们的"这个词出口的瞬间,一阵愧疚便劈头而来,谢尔碧短暂地闭上了眼睛。

蹲身钻过好几排晾衣绳之后,他们终于逃脱出了那个在风中"啪啪"作响的迷宫,来到了谢尔碧从未见过的大楼另一边。西面的景色尽收眼底,黝黑深邃的哈德逊河,还有新泽西林立的工厂。他们将床单铺在地上,相邻而坐。

"我很害怕。"

哈德利点了点头,侧身抱住了她。他们就那样相拥着坐了很久,没有接吻,也没有任何交谈,只是静静地看着河上的驳艇船只,理智如常的商贸活动反衬着性欲勾起的狂热。

Chapter Twenty   Moth to Flame

Hadley turned his head and kissed Shelby just underneath her ear where the convolutions of the skin become complicated. He whispered, "You know. We don't have to do this if you don't want." She groaned softly, turning to him, and they found themselves suddenly on a linear path to coition. In the midst of kissing, an equation hit her. Sex plus friendship was the more dangerous, because that's when you fell in love.

Hadley undid her coat and laughed. "You're dressed as Wonder Woman."

"I know."

"I can't believe my luck."

She tried to hit him and he grabbed her arm, wrestling her down playfully. They rolled against the roof, feeling the sting of gravel through the sheets. Wordless, breathless, overlooking the slow-moving Hudson, they clung together because they were the only available warmth. They couldn't deny themselves this moment. She realized that this was an incredibly selfish reason for an incredibly tactile experience. She felt more naked than ever, though they removed no clothes, only shifted them a bit, pulled here and there, lifted, slid past, exposed briefly. They looked for various skin-to-skin combinations, sheltering the rest of their bodies, but allowing portions to have connections, interactions, conjugal visits. Hadley started to talk dirty to her, and the words, his hot breath, his doing the incredible things he was saying, drove her to the brink of her self, a place where you can only step down and become a selfless mass of trembling intensity.

What seemed like years later, Shelby said, "What time is it?"

Hadley found his watch a couple of yards away, surprised at the ground they'd covered. They might have rolled off the building. What a fitting end. "It's four-thirty."

"Jesus. I've got to go. I have a telegram at five."

He looked at Shelby and smiled as she pulled her spandex top back down. "Now what?"

"Tomorrow?"

Hadley nodded.

哈德利侧过头亲吻着谢尔碧耳下的肌肤,纹路从那里开始变得错综紊乱。他柔声耳语着,"其实,如果你不愿意,我们不一定要这样做的。"谢尔碧无限柔情地呻吟着转过身来,电光火石之间,他们仿佛搭上了性的快速列车,不顾风险忘情地提速起来。在那间当儿谢尔碧的脑中突然蹦出一个方程式:性加友谊就带上了更多危险色彩,因为这就是爱情悄然来临的时候。

哈德利脱去谢尔碧的外衣,忍不住笑出声来。"你穿的是神奇女侠的服装。"

"我知道。"

"我简直不敢相信自己有多幸运。"

谢尔碧本想打他一下,哈德利却一下子抓住了她的胳膊,嘻嘻哈哈着带着她一起倒下身去。他们在屋顶上打着滚,任由床单下面的沙砾硌得生疼。没有言语,只有呼呼的喘气声,远处的哈德逊河缓缓流淌着,他们紧紧缠绕在一起,这是四下里唯一的温暖。此刻他们谁都无法否定内心的感情。但谢尔碧觉得,对这场充溢着肉欲的经历来说,这个理由是非常自私的。尽管并没有褪去衣服,她却觉得比以往任何时候都要赤裸——他们仅仅是将衣服左右地拉扯,掀起,滑下,有短暂的暴露。他们寻找着不同方式的肌肤接触,其余的身体仍然遮蔽着,但却允许部分的亲昵,互动,做爱。哈德利开始在她耳边挑逗地说些下流话,那些话,他温热的喘息,还有与此同时与话相符的动作,都将谢尔碧推向自己的极限,接着就只能向下,成为一个热切的不停战栗的无我质体。

似乎过了很久很久之后,谢尔碧开口了:"几点了?"

哈德利发现自己的手表在几码之外的距离,不禁对他们所占用的面积感到吃惊。没准儿都有可能滚摔下楼呢。多么合时宜的收场,"四点半。"

"天哪,我得走了。我在五点有个唱歌电报的活儿。"

他带着笑意看谢尔碧把涤纶上衣重新拉扯着穿上。"现在怎么办?"

"明天再见?"

哈德利点了点头。

Chapter Twenty-One Proof

> Proof: evidence sufficient to establish a thing as true and believable.
>
> *The Random House College Dictionary*

The bartender who ran the Blue Rose Lounge had a bad case of steatopygia. This was further compounded by the black polyester pants that clung so tightly to her thighs, the dimples of her cellulite were mapped mogul for mogul. Max watched in mesmerized revulsion as she moved along the bar, making drinks, taking money, and talking in her thick Romanian accent. Occasionally she would pause, using both hands to give some torque to her black wig. It sported a large rhinestone brooch pinned just north of her forehead which weighted the widow's peak. Toward the end of the evening, she tended to look like Cousin It.

The Blue Rose was dimly lit; it had taken Max's eyes a long time to adjust, and now he was sorry they had. He'd been there before, but never completely sober. The place looked like it had been throttled. Stuff was everywhere. Sheets once tacked to the ceiling had pulled loose and now hung like performance art set pieces, perhaps a university production. Something Brechtian. More sheets covered grimy windows, but they obviously hadn't done the trick because large pieces of plywood had been carelessly nailed to both. Too much sunshine can befuddle the profoundly drunk.

The Blue Rose actually consisted of two rooms with the adjoining wall knocked out, certainly from one of the trashings. A support had been left in the center of the room, an unpainted steel brace partially covered with plaster and chicken wire. It was a stumbling block to many a lush. The entrance (and exit) to the Blue Rose was at the west end of the narrower room. A fractal path for the tanked. But if they could find the upholstered bar, they were home free. It ran the length of the smaller room and terminated at the bathrooms, no doubt so the very inebriated would have a handhold the whole way to the pisser.

第二十一章　证据

证据：足够证明一件事情是真实或者可信的材料。
　　　　　　　　　　　　　　　——《兰登书屋大学词典》

蓝玫瑰酒吧的女主人有严重的臀部肥突症。紧绷住大腿的涤纶裤子使情况加剧了，皮下脂肪团的旋涡像地图般地凸起。麦克斯带着迷惑和厌恶，注视着她在吧台后游移，调酒，收钱，用浓重的罗马尼亚口音与人交谈。偶尔停下来，两只手合力扭一扭头顶的黑色假发套。前额正上方别着巨大的假钻石饰针，让这个寡妇的头显得更加沉重了。夜晚将尽的时候，她看上去就像《亚当斯一家》里的表亲伊特[译者注：伊特是电视剧中最早出现的变性人；伊特为英语中性代词 it 的音译]。

蓝玫瑰里光线暗淡；麦克斯费了好久功夫才让双眼适应，这会儿他又后悔了。他来过这儿许多次，但没有一次是在完全清醒的状态下。室内整体看上去像是垂死挣扎过般的凌乱。杂物散落得到处都是。原本用钉子固定在天花板上的布单脱落了，松散地挂在那儿，像是行为艺术表演的场景设置，带着些许大学剧社的味道，以及布莱希特[译者注：德国戏剧家，诗人]的风格。更多的布单被用来遮盖住了污垢层生的窗户，但很显然没有收到预期的效果，因为后续又有人随意地在外面钉了大块的胶合板——过多的阳光可能会让本已醉醺醺酒客们更加迷糊。

蓝玫瑰其实是由两间毗邻的房子打通而成的，肯定是某个醉汉耍酒疯的"杰作"。一个未上漆的金属支架被遗忘在房子正中，上面附着斑驳的水泥，还缠绕着铁丝线。许多酒鬼在这附近都不免绊个趔趄。出入口位于狭窄一些的房间最西边，是专门留给醉酒的人的曲折小道。但若是他们摸索到了垫着软垫的吧椅，就能一路到西。吧椅顺着较小的那间房一字排开，终止在卫生间的门口，为神智混沌的泡吧客们提供了前往小便器的扶手。

Chapter Twenty-One Proof

Eventually the Blue Rose Lounge would be turned into the trendy and upscaled Bugsy's Surfeteria. Surf boards affixed to the walls, and beachy colors everywhere, Bugsy's would be a much bigger hit than the Blue Rose had ever been. The passing of the Blue Rose would be another casualty in the gentrification of the Upper West Side. As Shelby liked to point out, these days, everywhere you look the decor is cute and pastel. Or at least things started with pastoral winsomeness but now the colors remind one more of pastels gone bad. Hard chartreuses and vulgar purples. The kind of maturity that happens to Easter colors when they've spent some time in the big city.

The Blue Rose couldn't pay its fire insurance. That was the rumor. And of course, with patrons like the old floozy who would ask to draw your picture for money and then later fall asleep with a lit cigarette hanging from her lips as her head sagged closer and closer to the cheap flammable material that draped her body, it was a problem. Shelby had let the woman draw her. The finished portrait looked nothing like Shelby, but she had paid the woman two dollars all the same. Max knew that quality wasn't something Shelby expected from a woman littered with ashes.

As he waited for the bartender, Max thought of that drawing. Shelby'd stuck it to the refrigerator with a fortune cookie magnet. The face was more sullen than Shelby's, the kind of pout seen on anorexic models dying for a hamburger. It didn't look like Shelby's face, but the woman had captured something. Anger? Frustration? Shelby was different these days. He didn't know what to do to help her. Everything he suggested was met by a kind of underlying hostility. And he knew sometimes the way he acted wasn't much help. The other day she threw away some canker sore medicine that was two years past the expiration date. He'd been a little irritated, even though she pointed out he was always throwing away moldy food in the refrigerator. "This is different. I know what's in this stuff. It's just hydrogen peroxide. Okay, so it's only ninety-five percent effective." He thought he had the right to keep his own drugs. But when he tried to make amends, jokingly accusing her of making sweeps of the house, that anything not labeled or bolted down was history, she wouldn't talk to him. They both took everything too seriously. Why? Max frowned at the pain of analysis. He hated problems he couldn't solve.

The bartender finally made her way down to Max's end of the bar, and Max, glancing in her direction, forgot what he'd been thinking because in the gloom he

不久的将来,蓝玫瑰就会被改造成一家时髦高端的巴格西冲浪俱乐部。墙上挂着各式的冲浪板,到处都是海滩的颜色,它受欢迎的程度会远远超越蓝玫瑰曾经的辉煌。蓝玫瑰的逝去是上西区中产阶级化热潮的又一个连带损失。就像谢尔碧感慨的那样,过去不管是哪儿,装潢风格都有着蜡笔画的可人触感,或者至少会从恬静的田园风入手;但如今,店铺的色调让人觉得是一幅被搞砸了的蜡笔画。浅黄浅绿和庸俗的深紫生硬地搭配在一起。复活节的色彩在大城市停留太久,就会发酵变成这个样子。

蓝玫瑰付不起火灾保险了。谣言是这么传的。当然了,再加上有个收费替人画肖像,却中途睡着的轻佻老妪做老板,随着她的脑袋不停地下坠,嘴角垂着的香烟也越来越接近她身上裹的廉价易燃布料,问题就变得不可忽视了。谢尔碧曾经让那个女人画过自己,虽然作品没有抓住丝毫相似之处,可她还是付了两美元。麦克斯知道,谢尔碧从一个身上落满烟灰的女人那里,本就不会期待很高的质量。

等待那个女酒保的间当儿,麦克斯又想起了那幅画,它被谢尔碧用一块幸运饼干磁石固定在了冰箱上。画中人的脸比谢尔碧更阴沉一些,带着患有神经性厌食症的模特极度渴望一个汉堡时的那种不满神情。虽然毫无形似可言,可那个女人捕捉到了谢尔碧身上的某样东西。愤怒?沮丧?这阵子谢尔碧的性情变得不一样了。他不知道该做什么才能帮到她。无论是什么建议,谢尔碧都会以一种本能的敌意来回应。他明白,有时候自己的行为方式只会火上浇油。前几天,谢尔碧把一瓶过期了两年的溃疡药给扔了,麦克斯因此有些愠怒。尽管谢尔碧争辩说,他也总是把冰箱里生霉的食物给扔掉。"那不一样。我知道这药里的成分是什么,只不过是过氧化氢而已。懂吗,所以过期只是少了百分之五的药效而已。"他觉得留下自己的药是他的权利。但当他试图弥补,开玩笑般地控诉她清扫房间时会把所有没标签或没有一股脑儿全吃完的东西都变成历史时,谢尔碧便不再愿意和他说话了。他们俩都把一切看得太认真了,为什么呢?深度分析带来的痛苦让麦克斯不自觉地皱起了眉头。自知无力解决的问题令人厌烦。

酒保终于沿着吧台向麦克斯这头走来,他也把目光投过去。但转瞬间他竟

Chapter Twenty-One Proof

noticed the pervert who had pulled his dick out of his pants last week. The old geezer was sitting halfway down the bar talking to himself. Max bristled at the thought of the guy recognizing him. But the guy seemed too preoccupied with his own conversation. And Max probably wasn't the first person he'd exposed himself to, anyway.

"Yes." The bartender said this abruptly, her strong accent making it sound like a command, as perhaps it was.

"'The Dingoes Ate My Baby'. We're still set for the twenty-seventh, right?" Max asked the bartender, watching her wig slide forward as she slowly lowered her heft onto a barstool and pulled out an extremely worn calendar. With a sigh of exhaustion, she plopped it down in front of her and opened it to the month of November. Tracing down one of the weeks with her index finger, a finger thick and corpulent and weighted down with cheap flashy rings, she examined the day and said, "Yess, I haf you for the twenty-seventh. 'Dingoes eat Baby'."

Max glanced sideways at the calendar. The twenty-seventh fell on a Monday. But they'd booked a Friday.

"Hold on," he said. "I thought we were playing Friday. What day is the twenty-seventh?"

"Oh, not to mind, it is the olt year," she said reassuringly. Suddenly someone at the other end of the bar started coughing and hacking, a horribly human sound of diseased phlegm making its sticky way up a convulsed esophagus. The bartender didn't seem to notice the gagging. With two of her long tusklike nails, she flipped the calendar closed and slid it to the edge of the bar.

Turning his head to read the year, Max saw that it was a 1965 calendar. Jesus Christ! This place was the Twilight Zone. The bartender put the calendar back underneath the bar and then, conversation over, waddled down to the other end to pour drinks. Her tight pants allowed little movement and so every time she walked, there was a ratchety sound of thigh scraping thigh.

Max wandered into the other room, imagining how they would set up, checking for electrical outlets. He was struck by something odd. At first he thought that the room had been widened. What was different? It took Max a second to realize—There was no P. A. The huge public address system that had been stacked on both sides of the room was no longer there. "Shit." He felt anger beginning to erupt,

然忘了刚才的思绪,因为在那幽暗的光线下他瞄见了上周的那个露阴癖。那老家伙正坐在吧台约莫中间的位置上自言自语。麦克斯一想到他可能认出自己来就不自觉地汗毛直竖,可他看上去正忙于和自己对话,暂时无法抽身。再说,麦克斯八成也不是他的第一个受害者。

"没错。"酒保突然开口了,她浓重的口音听上去如同命令,也许确实如此。

"《野狗吃了我的孩子》。原定 27 号的演唱仍然照常,对吧?"麦克斯话音刚落,只见她吃力地放低下半身,把所有重量压在了一把吧椅上,假发随之荡到了额前,接着又伸手掏出了本磨损不堪的日历。一声疲乏的叹息之后,她把日历"扑通"一声扔在面前的桌子上,翻到了 11 月。她翘起食指,划拉着寻找某一周的标记。那根粗肿的手指被几个廉价艳俗的戒指压得似乎快要抬不起来了。检查之后她回复了麦克斯,"没差儿,我定了你们 27 号的表演。《野狗吃孩子》。"

麦克斯斜眼瞥了一下日历,上面 27 号对应的是星期一,可是他们定好的明明是周五。

"等会儿,"他急忙澄清,"我还以为我们是周五表演呢。27 号到底是周几?"

"噢,别在意,这是本旧日历。"她宽慰麦克斯道。这时,吧台另一边的尽头有个人开始猛烈地咳嗽,发出令人恐惧的声音,仿佛裹挟着病菌的痰液黏着在震颤的食管上一点点地向上蠕动。那个女吧主似乎一点儿也不在意,她用两个长如獠牙似的指甲盖儿合上日历,顺势推向一边。

当麦克斯转过头仔细瞧那日历时,突然发现上面赫然写着 1965 年。见鬼!这个地方简直就是年月不分的结界地区。女酒保把日历塞回吧台下面,对话既已结束,她便扭摆着身躯回到吧台另一头调酒。紧绷的牛仔裤不允许有任何大幅度的动作,所以她每走一步,都会发出大腿根之间相互摩擦的"咔嚓咔嚓"声。

麦克斯漫不经心地踱进了另一个房间,检查着电插板,并在脑子里盘算着乐队位置的编排。突然,他觉得有什么地方不对劲。起初他还以为是因为房子被拓宽了。到底什么变得不一样了呢?不消多久麦克斯就意识到了——扩音装置不见了。过去被安置在房间两边的整个巨大组合音响都不翼而飞了。"混蛋。"他感到怒气开始向上喷涌,太多的压力和无法解决的问题终于累积到了爆发点。

the culmination of too many stresses, too many unresolved questions. Where were they going to find a goddamn P. A. ?

Quickly Max made his way through the gloom, past the man who was still in the throes of asphyxiation, skirting the old pervert, down almost to the bathroom. The bartender hung out back here, a black widow in her web, only reeling herself down the bar only when she had to. A smell claimed this area, of human excrement and warm beer. A smell that staked out territory. It made you feel on unfamiliar ground, knowing that someone could prefer this stench.

"The P. A. that was here—?" Max started to ask, following the bartender as she ignored him and moved toward the cash register.

"The P. A. that was here, used to be stacked against—" Max gestured with his hand, like of course there was some confusion. Maybe someone had only borrowed the P. A.

The cash register chinged and shot its drawer.

"Vat P. A. ?"

"You know, the one that used to sit right there." Max pointed to the emptiness.

"No."

"Come on, you know. The one that's been here every time I've come to the Blue Rose Lounge!" Max yelled. He realized he was over-reacting. It was an unpleasant situation, what would yelling solve? Nothing. Except that yelling made him want to yell even more.

The man's cough had changed into a kind of grotesque hiccup, a constant staccato, worsened from the uproar. Crouched low, like an angel of misery, he listed toward the floor, every racking inhalation ready to knock him to the ground.

Max decided to try another approach. "Did someone come and take the P. A. ?" he asked in gentle, measured tones.

"You must to bring your own."

"We had an agreement!" Max yelled, realizing that he was risking the band gig, but he didn't care. The woman was a harpy. It didn't even matter that the gasping man suddenly lifted his head and puked his guts out all over the bar, drowning out the bartender's response. It was cascade of foul-smelling regurgitation, his stubbled cheeks sucking inward after each retching heave.

第二十一章 证据

哪儿能找到一套该死的音响设备呢?

很快,麦克斯就在幽暗之中往回走去,经过了那个仍然在剧烈咳嗽几经窒息边缘的男人,绕过那个老变态,几乎快到了洗手间的门口。那里是女酒保通常待的地方,就像黑寡妇匍匐在网上,只在迫不得已的时候才沿着吧台走动。这片区域的空气被一种气味充盈着,是人的排泄物和温热啤酒的混合气味。这是为了标明自己的领地,让外来者感到不自在,因为你知道有人有可能对这臭气情有独钟。

"原来在这里的音响——?"麦克斯张嘴问道,可却遭到了她的忽略,她径直向收款机走去,麦克斯只能紧紧跟上。

"过去这儿的那个音响,紧贴着安装在——"麦克斯打着手势,仿佛在说一定是存在什么误会,也许只是被人借走了。

收银机"磬"的一声吐出了抽屉。

"啥么音响?"

"你瞧,就是原来蹲那儿的。"麦克斯指着现在空荡荡的地方。

"不知道。"

"得了,你知道的,就是我每次来蓝玫瑰都看见的那个。"麦克斯激动地大叫起来。可他立刻就意识到自己有些反应过度了。现在的情景确实令人恼火,可大声嚷嚷能有什么帮助呢?什么都解决不了。反而激起了他继续喊叫的欲望。

那个男人的咳嗽已经演变成了诡异的打嗝声,时断时续,看来周围的吵闹喧嚣加重了他的不适。他蹲在那里,身体痛苦地弓着,每一声沉重的吸气都可能会把他撂倒在地。

麦克斯决定换一个方式,"有人来把音箱搬走了吗?"他尽量让自己的语气听上去柔和克制一些。

"你们须得自己带来。"

"我们之前说好了的!"麦克斯禁不住吼出声来,尽管这样做相当于是拿乐队的演出机会冒险,可他也顾不上了。这个女人形容无异泼妇。那个一直费力喘息着的男人突然间抬起头,连肠子都吐得满地,盖过了女吧主的声音。小瀑布般的呕吐物散发出酸臭的气味,那张满是胡茬的脸颊在每次干呕带来的剧烈抖动下深深地凹陷了下去。

Chapter Twenty-One Proof

She scuttled toward the man with surprising agility yelling, "Out! You out of here!" When the sick man didn't move, she came through the break in the bar, lifting the bartop up so fast it slammed down on the other side. She grabbed the man by his arm, pulling him off his stool like a leg of mutton. Muttering Romanian vulgarities, she lugged the stumbling man through the entryway and outside into the freezing weather. The swinging door let in a gasp of cold air that caused everyone at the bar to huddle closer to their alcohol. Of course, the place now reeked of throw up. Max felt like he was going to be sick himself if he didn't leave. Trying to catch the bartender outside, he nearly collided with her, a monolith of black polyester. Sliding to safety by smacking into a small table, Max wondered if they had touched, what bacteria might have been transmitted. A bruise was well worth it. She looked weathered. Traveled. From the old country.

"Okay. Look. Where can we rent a P. A. ?" He had no choice but to admit defeat.

Without a word, she wrote something and then ripped off the corner of the napkin. "Fifty dollars." Her heavy hand came at him like in a John Waters movie, a hand magnified by his sudden fish-eyed view as the darkened bar receded. It must be the puke, he thought, holding onto the bar, waiting for his dizziness to subside. He took the offering and she instantly retreated, lumbering back to refill drinks, her wig riding sidesaddle. (In the men's bathroom, someone had aptly written, "I thought she was a stegosaurus.") The old pervert was cleaning up, circling the mess with a string mop, changing the landscape minimally. The bartender yelled loudly at him, coming out of the bar and pushing at his buttocks with her slippered foot. Afraid to see more, Max left.

The band was to make exactly fifty dollars for the night. Max was so angry he kicked a bottle on the sidewalk and it hit a newspaper vendor's stand, breaking in a scatter of glass, forcing him to walk in the street to avoid the shards. The hardest part about New York was knowing that people are taking advantage of you and realizing that you can't do anything about it.

Max decided to go home and take a bath. Just thinking about hot water made him happy. He planned the quickest route. Shoes off first, socks, then pants and shirt simultaneously, glasses on the back of the toilet. Two minutes tops. That's what good planning was all about. Then he remembered that Hadley was staying with them.

第二十一章 证据

她迈着迅疾的碎步走过去,敏捷得出奇,还一边大喊着:"出去!你给我出去!"当看到那个可怜的男人丝毫未动时,她穿过吧台的间隔处,被猛然掀起的隔板重重地摔在了另一边。一把抓住他的胳膊后,她像拎一只羊腿般将他从凳子上提了下来。她用罗马尼亚语咕哝咒骂着,拖得那个男人步履趔趄,最终扔进了门外刺骨的寒冷中。门板反复摆动了几下,一阵冷风顺势钻了进来,屋里的每个人都往自己的酒杯蜷缩得更紧了。毫无疑问,这个地方现在充溢着呕吐物的气味。麦克斯觉得要是再不离开的话,自己会真的犯恶心的。为了在门外截住女吧主,他险些与她撞个满怀——一个裹在黑色涤纶衣料里的巨大物体。在滑步趔倒在一旁的小桌子上之后,麦克斯揣测着,假如他们刚才真的接触到了,可能会有什么细菌传播到自己身上。所以就算撞出了瘀青也值得。她皮肤黝黑,仿佛经过长途的跋涉,从曾经的故乡来到这里。

"得了,告诉我,我们在哪儿能租到音响设备?"麦克斯别无选择,只能认栽。

她一声不吭地开始在餐巾纸上写些什么,随后将那一角撕下。"五十美金。"她那粗重的手向麦克斯袭来,如同约翰·沃特斯电影中的情景,突然之间麦克斯眼中的酒吧变得愈加昏暗朦胧起来,那只手也被无限放大了。一定是刚才的呕吐物在作祟,他一边寻思着,一边牢牢抓住吧台,等着眩晕消退。麦克斯一接过那张纸,她立刻就吃力地退回原位去给客人补酒,假发如同马鞍侧座一样甩在一边。(有人在在男卫生间里写下的那句话显得恰如其分,"我还以为她是剑龙呢。")这会儿,那个老变态正用拖把圈罗着呕吐物,清扫效果甚微。女酒保气势汹汹地吼叫着走出来,提起穿着拖鞋的脚,踹向他的屁股。麦克斯连一眼都不想再多看,直奔门外。

乐队一个晚上演出的收入正好是五十美金。麦克斯气不打一处来,飞起一脚向人行道上的玻璃瓶踢去,瓶子在击中了报刊亭之后炸裂了满地的碴子,他不得不走到车行道上去。在纽约生存,最艰难的部分就是明知道别人在占你的便宜,你却无能为力。

麦克斯决定回家,洗个澡。仅仅是一想到热水他的心情就好了不少。他在心里盘算着最快捷的流程:先甩掉鞋子,接着是袜子,然后裤子和T恤双管齐下,眼镜搁在马桶的后座上。最多花费两分钟。好的计划就是应该这样高效。可他突然想起,哈德利正在家里借住,便产生了一阵不可抑制的恼火。麦克斯是喜欢

Chapter Twenty-One   Proof

He felt a sense of irritation. Max liked Hadley. But he liked it better when he lived at his own apartment.

Max decided that he'd give him a couple more days, then he'd ask him to leave. He didn't want Hadley living with them when Max went on job interviews next week. "Call me neurotic," Max said to himself, but he also felt uncomfortable at the thought of Shelby and Hadley alone. He shook his head, realizing that the smell of throw up had confused him, unbalanced his good sense. He trusted Shelby. What was he thinking?

Instead, Max thought about his future, seeing as how it was looming before him. There were two routes a chemist could go: academics or industry. Academics were considered the more prestigious. The stellar scientists generally went toward the tenure track. But you ended up goofier. And divorced. Look at C. K. Crenshaw. Had a huge name for himself. Thought he was God. Outside his office he had a red light and a green light. If you bothered him when the red light was on, there went your degree. Academics seemed to insure assholeness. But the problem with industry was the risk that you might end up being nothing more than a number, one chemist in a long white hallway of other chemists, working on other people's ideas. The thought of working at a large company didn't thrill Max, but long ago he had decided not to go into academics because he wanted to stay married. In academics you had to give yourself up to research if you hoped to be tenured; eighteen-hour days, seven days a week were quite common. With a company, you didn't work as long hours, but you also usually didn't get the fame and glory either. However, Max thought it was worth it to stay married. He loved being married. He loved Shelby. The thought that maybe she didn't love him could make him crazy. So he willed it out of his mind.

"We're in here," Shelby yelled as Max walked in the front door. Shelby was sitting on the sofa and Hadley was sitting at his drums. Max rubbed his hand through his hair, unable to break himself of the habit. The roots prickled his fingers as he lightly pressed the tips against the bent hair shafts, the most buoyant part of the hair, newly synthesized, untamed by rinsing and repeating. Imagining that he could feel the hairs loosen from his scalp, Max abruptly pulled his hand forward into a half-hearted wave. He was feeling the strain of confinement, being subjected to small spaces with more than the appropriate number of people. He noticed Shelby and Hadley looking at him expectantly.

哈德利的，可还是更希望他住在自己的公寓里。

他决定再宽限哈德利几天，不然就得开口送客了。他不希望下周自己去工作面试的时候哈德利还是跟他们住在一起。"我就是疑神疑鬼。"麦克斯对自己说了这么一句，但他一想到谢尔碧和哈德利单独待在一起就感到很不舒服。甩了甩头，他开始认为是刚才恶心的呕吐气味让自己神智有些混沌了，失去了基本的判断。他是信任谢尔碧的。刚才都在想些什么哪？

麦克斯转而开始考虑自己的将来，其实就在不远处隐隐浮现。对于一个化学家来说有两条路可以选择：学术或者工业应用。学术通常能够带来名望，大部分杰出的科学家都会奔着终身教职的方向去。可最终人会变得怪里怪气，婚姻惨淡离散。看看 C. K. 克兰肖就知道了：曾经名噪一时，自视甚高。在他办公室的外面设有红灯和绿灯各一盏，要是谁胆敢在红灯亮的时候打扰他，就可以跟学位说拜拜了。学术似乎注定会沾染上混蛋气息。可投身工业界的问题又在于，或许最终你只能沦为一个数字标号，白色走廊进驻的众多化学家中的一员，每天实践着别人的想法。麦克斯对于在大公司工作的场景毫无憧憬，但很久之前他就已经决定不会投身学术了，因为他不想毁掉自己的婚姻。要是怀有获得终身教职的希冀，就得为了研究完全放弃自我；每天十八个小时，一周七天是家常便饭。在公司里，工作时长虽然短不少，但名气和荣耀也跟你丝毫沾不上边儿。综合下来，麦克斯仍然认为只要能维持好婚姻，都是值得的。他热爱自己的婚姻，更爱谢尔碧，一想到谢尔碧有可能不爱自己，他就几近奔溃。因此他总是随着自己的意愿将这个想法驱逐出脑海。

"我们在里面。"麦克斯刚走进前门，谢尔碧的声音就传了过来。她正坐在沙发上，而哈德利则坐在鼓架的后面。麦克斯下意识地又将手指插入头发，往后揉搓着，这个习惯一时还是无法改掉。他轻轻地按压着弯曲的发根，手指感到微微有些刺痛。这是他头发最蓬松的地方，刚长出不久，经历了冲洗和反复揉压，仍然桀骜地挺立着。麦克斯感到头发从头皮上隐约松动了一些，立即迅速地放下手来，漫不经心地在空中划过。同时一股幽闭的紧张感袭来，他感到自己受困在这多于应有人数的狭小空间里。这时他注意到谢尔碧和哈德利都用期待的眼神盯着自己。

Chapter Twenty-One Proof

Shelby pointed to Hadley and said, "Talk to him." Hadley played a drum fill. It occurred to Max that there was an inherent need for drummers to participate in conversations by way of drumbeats. Consequently, talking to a drummer can take more time.

"What?" It had the ring of impatience.

Hadley stood up. "I think we should go talk to Rahda."

Max looked at him like he was crazy. "Why?"

"I think it's the fair thing to do."

Max rubbed his forehead, wincing in obvious disagreement. "So we're going to go over there and say, 'Rahda, we know you're a liar, so if you need more time to cover up ... '?"

"I'll do the talking."

"We could call." Shelby smiled, wanting to be part of the conversation.

Hadley shook his head.

"I don't know," Max hedged, truly irritated. "What's it going to get us?"

"I think Rahda has a right to be there when we go to Scotia."

"As far as I'm concerned, that's something Scotia can handle later." Max slumped down in the easy chair, flicking on the TV.

"Okay, I'll go by myself." It was phrased like an offer, but Max took it as a taunt. He ran his hand through his hair again, wanting the intensity of his life to be turned down to dim.

"I'll go," Shelby said.

Max shook his head and sighed, letting them know that he thought it a mistake. The TV droned on for a few minutes, no one speaking. Max picked up the remote and turned the TV off. "Let's get it over with."

Out on the street the cold made them aggressive, chatty for strength, the air so numbing that Max felt sorry for the homeless because it was only going to get worse. And it did. It started to snow. As far as Max could tell, there was only one real use for snow in the city, and that was to write swear words with his boots.

Max skipped a step and farted loudly as he walked into Rahda's building. Shelby said, "Max!" He knew it was childish, but it was his version of a rim shot. He didn't have instrument stand-ins like Hadley. He had to make do. Besides, he had to fart.

谢尔碧指着哈德利说道："你说吧。"哈德利却顺势敲了一段鼓花。麦克斯突然意识到：用鼓点说话，是鼓手与生俱来的天性。因此和鼓手聊天可能花费更多的时间。

"到底什么事？"麦克斯语气中透露出了一丝不耐烦。

哈德利站起身来。"我觉得我们应该去和拉达聊一下。"

麦克斯看着他，仿佛觉得他疯了。"为什么？"

"我觉得这样做才公平。"

麦克斯揉了揉额头，明显不赞成地蹙着眉。"所以我们要去她公寓，然后对她说：'拉达，我们已经知道你是个骗子了，要是你需要更多时间来掩盖事实的话……'？"

"由我来开口好了。"

"我们可以打电话。"谢尔碧笑了，她也想加入对话当中来。

哈德利摇了摇头。

"我不懂，"麦克斯真的有些恼怒了，但尽量回避着正面的冲突，"这么做能给我们带来什么？"

"我觉得我们去找斯考蒂亚的时候拉达有权利在场。"

"在我看来，斯考蒂亚可以稍后再和她对质。"麦克斯一屁股坐在安乐椅上，"咯哒"一声打开了电视。

"好吧，我自己去。"虽然是提议的语气，可在麦克斯听来却是一种奚落。他又伸手撸了一下头发，暗自希冀着自己生活的激烈程度可以减小为零。

"我也去。"谢尔碧应道。

麦克斯摇着头叹了口气，表明自己觉得这是个错误。有几分钟，没人开口说话，只有电视机低沉单调的声音喋喋不休。麦克斯拿起遥控关掉了电视，"那就赶紧把这件事给解决了吧。"

街道上的寒冷让人变得暴躁，要不停地说话才能有动力继续走下去。刺骨的寒气麻木了肌肤，麦克斯开始同情起那些无家可归的人来，因为天气只会越来越糟糕。下一秒就立刻应验了，雪花开始慢腾腾地飘落下来。在麦克斯看来，城市里的雪只有一个真正的用途，就是用脚在上面写脏话。

走进拉达的公寓楼时，麦克斯跳下一级台阶，响亮地放着屁。谢尔碧恼怒地叫道："麦克斯！"他知道这种行为很幼稚，但这是他自己版本的"鼓边击"[译者注：一种架子鼓击打技巧 rim shot]，他不像哈德利那样有一套自己的乐器装备，

Chapter Twenty-One Proof

"I want you to know that my labmate Kyle wrote a friend back in England that no one here farts in public. His friend wrote back, 'Come home immediately.'"

"And?" Shelby looked at him pointedly.

"It's a cultural thing. I emulate the British."

"You take far too many baths," Shelby said, stepping into the elevator, one foot over the line, then immediately backing up, trying to knock into Max. He was glad to see her so happy. Her rim shots took a physical form. His and Hadley's were both aural. Shelby enjoyed a kind of primitive slapstick, consisting solely of running into you. Max liked Shelby's anti-social quality. Lately this part of her had been dormant. It made him feel good to watch the old Shelby.

As the elevator doors started closing, a man carrying a rolled-up carpet stuck his hand between the narrowing doors and shoved roughly. The doors reopened and he got in, making them huddle closer to the walls because the rug was a body-and-a-half wide.

"I know someone who broke their hand that way," Max said conversationally. The man said nothing. Max nudged Shelby, pinching her bottom. She laughed softly and Max turned to Hadley. "So. You gonna do the talking, right?"

"I'm just going to tell her how I know she switched my NMR tube—"

"And that her catalyst is baby laxative?"

"—and that we are going tomorrow to tell Scotia that we know her catalyst is mannitol. She should be there. I have to admit, I want to see her reaction. I want to find out if she realizes that the reaction working without the catalyst is still a significant discovery. Why would she lie?" He tapped his fingers on the walls of the elevator. "You know, I'm trying to think of when anything else this big has happened."

"Piltdown?" Max asked.

Shelby laughed loudly.

Hadley said dryly, "Eighteen months is not Piltdown."

"It's the length of our marriage," Max said, "but I prefer to measure it in lifetimes."

An unpleasant sound punctuated his comment. Shelby pushed him and then made a tcching sound of revulsion, a non-verbal profanity.

"That wasn't me," Max said indignantly, turning to her. "It was more the drumbeat type."

只能凑合着来。再说，放屁是人的正常生理需求。"你知道吗，我实验室里的同事凯尔有一次写信回英国说，这里没人会在公共场合放屁，结果他的朋友回信劝他立刻回国去。"

"所以呢？"谢尔碧故意瞪着他看。

"这跟文化有关，我只是倾向于英国人而已。"

"他们可不像你洗澡的次数那么频繁。"谢尔碧边说边将一只脚踏进了电梯里，可立马又收了回来，想要出其不意地撞麦克斯一下。麦克斯看到她心情这么好，心里也不觉亮起来。她的"鼓边击"采取的是肢体接触的形式。麦克斯和哈德利的方式则与听觉相关。谢尔碧享受那种原始的打闹剧的感觉，仅仅包含身体的碰撞。麦克斯喜欢谢尔碧身上反社会的气质，可近来她的这一面总是处于休眠状态。再次看到从前的她让麦克斯心情大好。

正当电梯门缓缓合上的时候，一个扛着地毯的男人突然将手伸进渐窄的门缝里，粗鲁地一把推开。门又开了，那个男人走了进来，他们几个只能向电梯壁再凑得紧些，因为他肩上的地毯有一人半宽。

"我知道有人因为那样做而折了手。"麦克斯试图开启一段对话。可那个人什么反应都没有。于是他用胳膊肘轻轻拱了拱谢尔碧，捏了一下她的屁股。谢尔碧轻声笑了出来，麦克斯同时转向了哈德利，"所以，由你来开口，对吧？"

"我只是打算告诉她，我是怎么知道她调包了我的核磁试管的——"

"还有她所谓的催化剂只是婴幼儿通便剂？"

"——还有我们打算明天去向斯考蒂亚表明一切，告诉他催化剂是甘露醇。她也应该在那儿。我得承认，我想看看她会有什么反应，她到底有没有意识到即使反应没有催化剂就能够进行，这仍然是一个重大发现。为什么要撒谎呢？"他的手指在电梯的墙壁上敲着，"我在想，上一次这么轰动的事情发生是在什么时候。"

"皮尔当人事件？"麦克斯接嘴道。

谢尔碧放声大笑起来。

哈德利冷冰冰地回了一句："皮尔当人事件可没有持续十八个月。"

"这正好是我们婚姻的长度，"麦克斯忽视了他的话，"不过我更愿意用一辈子来衡量。"

他的深情告白被一声令人不快的声音打断了，谢尔碧推搡了他一下，发出厌恶的"啧啧"声，省略了言语的咒骂。

"不是我发出的，"麦克斯一脸愤愤地转向她，"更像是鼓点的类型。"

Chapter Twenty-One Proof

Shelby continued to give him the evil eye.

"It wasn't."

She looked at Hadley.

"It wasn't me."

She started laughing again, obviously embarrassed. Gas had been passed and there was only one other person in the elevator, the man with the rug. The sound happened again, louder. But it wasn't farting. It sounded more like a slow door buzzer. The elevator opened on the eighth floor and the man got off, the peculiar sound moving with him. The doors closed as they saw him hoist the rug over his left shoulder.

"That man was making that sound," Max said, baffled. New York was stranger than fiction. Weird guys carrying large objects around, suspiciously body-size. And then the guy's got a buzzer that sounds like you're choppin' one.

"This is going to sound incredible." Hadley looked at both of them. "But I swear to God, that sounded exactly like Ethan's key chain."

Max eyed Hadley warily. "Now why would that man have Ethan's keys?"

"I have no idea." The elevator doors opened onto the ninth floor and they got off, Hadley walking ahead but glancing back. "Ethan dropped his keys in the toilet, and they sounded exactly like that. They've been missing for almost a week." He turned around quickly, stopping their progress. "And we know Shelby's voice sets them off." Hadley got excited and waved his finger at Max. The inference was that Hadley was practiced at listening. At placing pitches. That he could certainly recognize identical sounds.

"But I didn't say anything."

"You laughed."

Max watched Shelby look at Hadley in a way that made his stomach drop. He couldn't define it. But he felt goose bumps charge up his arms.

"I think it's more likely the guy dropped his in the toilet too ..." Max said, his voice laden with exasperation. He walked past Hadley. They were silent for a moment as they came to Rahda's door. Hadley glanced at them, then raised his hand to knock.

"Wait a second ..." Shelby's voice drifted off.

谢尔碧继续用凌厉的眼神盯着他。

"真的不是。"

她转而看向哈德利。

"也不是我。"

她又忍不住咧嘴大笑起来，很显然有些害臊。臭气的声音在狭小的空间里回荡着，电梯里只剩下另一个人了——扛着地毯带着遮秃假发的男人。那声音又来了，这次更响一些。但不是放屁，听上去更像是缓慢的门铃声。电梯门在八层开了，那个男人头也不回地踏出去，那阵奇怪的声音也一直尾随而去。门缓缓地开始闭合，麦克斯他们从渐小的门缝中看着他将地毯举到了左肩上。

"是那个男人发出来的。"麦克斯的声音里充满了困惑。纽约发生的事情甚至比小说里的还要离奇。那古怪的家伙肩上扛着可疑的一人多宽的巨大物体，还随身携带着蜂鸣器，发出像剁肉时的声音。

"这听上去可能不可置信，"哈德利把目光投向他们两个，"但我敢发誓，那声音和伊桑的钥匙链声一模一样。"

麦克斯警惕地注视着哈德利，"那个家伙和伊桑的钥匙链怎么会扯上关系呢？"

"我一点儿头绪也没有。"九楼到了，哈德利走在最前面，但是不时地回头看看。"伊桑有一次把钥匙掉进了马桶里，发出的就是这种声音。这回他的钥匙已经丢了一个多星期了。"他突然猛地转身，大家的脚步也被迫停下。"而且我们知道谢尔碧的声音能够激发那些钥匙链。"哈德利激动了起来，不住对麦克斯挥舞着手指。言下之意，他的音感很好，能够熟练地定音。因而一定能将完全一样的声音辨识出来。

"可我什么话都没有说呀。"

"你笑了。"

看到谢尔碧凝视哈德利的眼神，麦克斯的心重重地沉了下去。他不知道该怎么形容，可双臂不自觉地蹦起了鸡皮疙瘩。

"我看八成是那个家伙也曾经把钥匙链掉进过马桶里……"麦克斯的恼怒溢于言表。他从哈德利身边擦过，一直到走到拉达的门前，没有人说话。哈德利瞥了他们一眼，接着抬起手要去敲门。

"等一下……"谢尔碧的声音轻飘飘地传了出来。

Chapter Twenty-One   Proof

Max read her mind. The last time they were here, throwing oranges and insulting Dermot about his crazy neighbor. His mind did that track again.

"The neighbor." They said it at once, in a kind of mind meld of suspicion.

"What did Dermot say his downstairs neighbor sold?" Max asked.

Shelby looked worried. "Indian rugs."

Max saw Shelby look at Hadley and then quickly glance at him. He knocked on the door forcefully. "Well, Indian rugs are certainly one way to distribute drugs. If it can be delivered in pizza boxes, why not rugs? But if the neighbor stole Ethan's cocaine and stashed it in the rugs, how'd he get the keys?"

"He could have followed him," Shelby said.

"Ethan loses his keys all the time," Hadley said. "Someone could have easily taken them from him."

"Shit." Max started to swear excitedly, jumping up and down. "Shit, shit, shit. Baby laxative! You use—"

"You know, I can't figure that one out," Hadley said pensively. "She grabbed whatever was on the shelf, but you've got to ask, why was mannitol on her shelf? Was she doing sugar chemistry?"

"Because, shit-for-brains, that's what you use to cut cocaine!"

Dermot answered the door. "Sure a lot of yelling out here."

"Is Rahda here?" Max asked this quietly. Catching Hadley's glance. Maybe this really wasn't such a good idea.

Dermot looked at them with surprise. "She's gone. Went to Italy," he whispered. "Why are we whispering?"

"She's gone already?"

"She left the beer, though. Want some?" Dermot asked, walking toward the kitchen.

"No, we were just leaving." Shelby started pulling at Max.

Hadley explained. "We think it's likely that Rahda's been lying. She's been obstructing experiments. And her catalyst appears to be nothing more than mannitol."

"Mannitol?" Dermot turned around, looking shocked. He walked back toward them. "Does Scotia know this?"

麦克斯读到了她内心的想法。上一次他们在这间公寓房里扔橘子的时候，还拿他的疯狂邻居这件事儿讽刺过德莫特。他顺着记忆的藤追溯了一下。

"那个邻居。"他们同时脱口而出，仿佛两人的大脑合二为一似的。

"德莫特说他楼下的邻居是卖什么的来着？"麦克斯问道。

谢尔碧的表情开始凝重起来。"印度地毯。"

麦克斯看到谢尔碧先是看向哈德利，又迅速瞥了他一眼。他用力地砸着门，"不过，印度地毯确实能用来偷运毒品。如果比萨盒可以的话，地毯有什么不行呢？可要是伊桑的可卡因是那个邻居偷的，又藏在了地毯里，那钥匙是怎么会在他那儿的？"

"他可能一直在跟踪伊桑。"谢尔碧推测道。

"伊桑总是搞丢钥匙，"哈德利接过话茬来，"谁都能很轻易地拿到。"

"该死，"麦克斯开始兴奋地上蹿下跳起来，不停地咒骂着，"该死，该死，该死的。婴儿通便剂！用来——"

"是的，我一直搞不懂这点。"哈德利仿佛在沉思。"她随手抓了一个药品架上的东西，但问题是，她的架子上怎么会有甘露醇呢？难道她在做制糖的实验？"

"因为，我们真是脑子短路了，那是用来稀释可卡因的东西。"

德莫特打开了门。"你们在外面大喊大叫什么。"

"拉达在吗？"麦克斯低声耳语道，顺便和哈德利交换了一下眼神。也许这真的不是一个好主意。

德莫特吃惊地看着他们。"她不在，去了意大利。"他也跟着放低了音量。"为什么我们要这么小声？"

"她已经离开了？"

"可她没有把啤酒带走，要喝吗？"德莫特说着转身向厨房走去。

"不用了，我们得走了。"谢尔碧拉扯着麦克斯的胳膊。

哈德利则解释开了："我们觉得拉达很有可能一直在撒谎，在阻碍反应的进行。而她的催化剂只不过是甘露醇而已。"

"甘露醇？"德莫特一脸震惊地回过头，重新向他们走来。"斯考蒂亚知道吗？"

"No." Hadley shook his head. "Bineet's the one who figured it out. We're going with him to tell Scotia tomorrow."

Dermot stood there for moment, a stunned look on his face. "I mean I know she's weird, but this is serious. Are you sure?"

"It may be worse."

Max wished Shelby hadn't said that.

Shelby whispered, "How well do you know your neighbor?" She pointed down.

Dermot rolled his eyes. "We don't hang out or anything."

"Did Rahda know him?"

"Actually, I think she hooked him up with some relative of hers. He imports Indian rugs you know."

"Shelby, forget it." Max didn't want to explain all the complexities to Dermot. He just wanted to go back home.

Shelby ignored him. "Someone broke into Hadley's apartment and stole a hundred thousand dollar's worth of cocaine."

Dermot looked inquiringly at Hadley.

Hadley looked aggrieved. "It was Ethan's."

"And you think it was my neighbor?" Dermot panned the bunch of them. "You guys watch way too much TV."

Walking out of Dermot's building, Max felt the cold cutting through his jeans, climbing up his legs. The weather had changed recently. The chill dropped down on you, pinning your joints, making it harder to move. You skittered from one enclosure to the next, clutching yourself, instinctively burning fuel. You noticed the change in the bag people. They became more aggressive. Confronted you. Moved in close. Sometimes it felt medieval. Max remembered a guy who lived in the instant teller alcove of his bank. The door was broken and the guy was in there every night; you could see him through the glass, nice guy, told the weather, did bag person stand-up. Reassured you that he wasn't going to steal anything, he was just cold. He talked constantly, a news commentary, predicting the next day's weather, maybe mentioned sports. It was unnerving, on the edge of street theater. A creative solution, at least until they fixed the lock. Max felt better afterward, though he kind

"还不知道。"哈德利摇着头,"是贝内特第一个发现的,我们明天就和他一起去见斯考蒂亚。"

德莫特在原地站了一会儿,脸上像是被打了一记闷棍儿。"我只觉得她性格有些古怪,但这件事实在是太严重了,你们确定吗?"

"情况还有可能更糟呢。"

麦克斯希望谢尔碧没有把那句话说出口。

谢尔碧毫不在意地继续小声询问着:"你对你的邻居了解多少?"她指了指楼下。

德莫特翻了个白眼。"反正我们从来没有一起出去玩过。"

"拉达和他相熟吗?"

"这么说起来,她确实通过亲戚的关系结识了他。他是进口印度地毯的。"

"谢尔碧,算了吧。"麦克斯不愿意把那些错综复杂的事都解释给德莫特听。他只想回家。

谢尔碧却丝毫不理会。"有人闯进哈德利的公寓,偷走了价值十万美金的可卡因。"

德莫特向哈德利投去探询的目光。

后者则是满腔的怨怼:"是伊桑的。"

"所以你们觉得是我的邻居干的?"德莫特严词推翻了他们的猜测。"你们电视剧看得太多了。"

走出德莫特的公寓楼,麦克斯感到寒风像刀子一样割穿了自己的牛仔裤,顺着双腿向上拱着。近来的天气变化很大,寒气会扑头盖脸落在你身上,刺进关节处,动弹都十分艰难。人们飞快地从一处暖巢奔向另一处,裹得紧紧的,本能地燃烧着体内的能量。流浪汉身上发生的变化也显而易见。他们变得更加暴躁强硬了,迎面向你走来,越凑越近。有时这场景感觉就像中世纪。麦克斯还记得,有一段时间,他所用的银行自动取款机门坏了,便有个家伙每天晚上住在里面;透过玻璃一切都看得一清二楚。他人不错,有时播报天气,有时来段流浪人的单口相声。这就让人放心不少,至少他不会趁机偷东西,只不过是觉得冷而已。他总是滔滔不绝地在讲,新闻评论,天气预报,甚至有时会提到体育赛事。几乎都能够称得上是街头戏剧了,多少让人有些不知所措。这个办法很新颖,至少直到他们把门给修好为止。在那之后,麦克斯感觉上好了

of missed the guy.

There were fewer homeless in the area by the university. One walked more easily on the street. But a change of a block could mark the difference in climate. Go over to Amsterdam, it was lonelier. Go up seven blocks and you were in Harlem. This was one of the first things white people warned other white people about when coming to Manhattan. Never take the Express train past 96th Street. Max would constantly impress the point on Shelby. "Yeah, yeah, yeah," she'd say. "And don't talk to strangers."

Max laughed to himself. She liked to play tough. But lately she was so vulnerable. He could tell that she was irritated with him now, because he hadn't wanted her to go on and on about the neighbor. He knew Dermot would think they were nuts. And they were. They had no proof. But she got so indignant if she perceived that you were trying to control her. Why didn't she just come out and tell him to stop instead of sulking? Max liked it when someone disagreed with him, met him head on. So many people thought you had to get nasty in debates and either they did, fighting dirty and malicious, or they avoided disagreement altogether. This was what frustrated him about Shelby lately. She had no interest in spirited conversation. He missed a sparring partner, someone who didn't give him lip service. He felt intimidated by her quickness to accuse him of being mean. She got mad if he interrupted her, even if he was in agreement. She'd just stop talking if he started to say something. Pouting even. He'd say, "But I was agreeing with you!" And she'd say, "Nod then!"

He always had so many ideas and they welled out of him boisterously. He didn't want her to think that he wasn't interested in what she said; it wasn't like that. She used to interrupt him sometimes, and he recognized it as her excitement. They often told stories together, one finishing the sentence the other had started. When had that stopped? He realized that he'd been so busy with work, things had shifted between them, but he hadn't noticed when or how. He could see it from Shelby's side, too. He was probably pretty annoying sometimes, always having to have his say. But if she really wanted him to change, she'd be nicer about it. She didn't understand that his schooling, hell, his whole life had trained him to be outspoken. Just when you were being rewarded by your peers for your force of character, suddenly at home you're condemned for the same behavior. What do you do?

不少,可他竟然有些想念那个家伙了。

大学附近流浪汉要少一些,因此一个人走在路上宽心不少。可一旦换个街区,气氛就有可能发生翻天覆地的变化。上到阿姆斯特丹区,人烟更加寂寥。再上七个街区,就到了声名在外的哈林区。初到曼哈顿,这是白人之间会互相警告的首要几件事情之一。永远不要搭电车去96街区或者更远的地方。麦克斯总是给谢尔碧强调这一点。而她则会不耐烦地敷衍:"对,对,对,还有不要和陌生人讲话。"

麦克斯想到这儿忍不住笑了。她总是爱逞强,可是最近却变得很脆弱。麦克斯能够感受到,她现在就在和自己怄气,因为自己不愿意让她一直在那个邻居的事情上说个不停。他知道德莫特会把他们都当作傻瓜看待的,事实也确实如此。他们一点证据都没有。可如果谢尔碧认定了你是在试图掌控她,就会立刻义愤填膺起来。为什么她不能直截了当地阻止自己,而非要生闷气呢?对于反对的意见和迎面争辩,麦克斯一点儿都不觉得排斥。许多人都偏执地认为在辩论中就一定要凶狠恶毒,一部分人确实那么做了,手段下作,口出恶言,而其余的人干脆就完全回避了意见的分歧。谢尔碧近来就完全采取了后一种态度,对开诚布公的谈话兴味索然,这让麦克斯觉得非常沮丧。他想念过去的那个能与他唇枪舌剑的伙伴,不会只在口头上敷衍了事。谢尔碧最近总是不分青红皂白地就判定他刻薄,令他担惊受怕的。要是说话被打断了,即使是附和的话,她也会立刻翻脸。当麦克斯开口时,她索性就一声不吭了,甚至会赌气般地撅着嘴。麦克斯有时愤愤不平地回一句:"可我是在同意你的观点啊!"她也毫不示弱:"那点头不就好了!"

麦克斯的脑子里总是想法无数,热热闹闹,争先恐后地向外涌着。他不想让谢尔碧认为自己对她的观点不感兴趣,因为事实并非如此。她有时候也会打断麦克斯,可他总是将其看作是她兴奋的表现。他们俩以前经常一起讲故事,你一言我一语地争相赶向结尾。那样的时光是何时消匿无踪的?最近忙于工作,以至于他们之间的微妙变化发生于何时,又是如何发生的,他都不曾留心。从谢尔碧的表现上也能够看得出来,也许有时他着实讨人厌,总是要有自己的发言权。可如果谢尔碧当真希望他做些改变的话,就应该更加委婉柔和点。她一点儿也意识不到,麦克斯的学业,见鬼,还有他全部的生活,都养成了他现在这样直言不讳的性格。正当同龄人对你的人格力量称赞有加时,在家庭生活里同样的行为突然就招来了谴责。这该如何是好呢?

Chapter Twenty-One Proof

He watched her now as she talked to Hadley. She was flipping him off for some reason. Max hadn't been paying attention.

"The girl way. And the boy way," Shelby was saying, giving Hadley two views of her middle finger. They had both told her that she gave the finger backwards. Max watched Shelby laugh and then run toward the building, stopping for a moment on the sidewalk to yell at them that she was freezing.

Max jumped up on the curb and walked quickly, cold, but not willing to run. Hadley behind him, Max slowed his pace to walk with him. He looked quizzically at Hadley. "So?"

"She called me an enabler."

"Shouldn't you be flipping her off?"

"I must have said something she didn't like."

Hadley laughed for a moment. His laugh had a quality, a leit-motif running through it that made Max look at him differently. It was the sound of knowing someone well, like Hadley was laughing about his kid sister.

A twinge, a light convulsion of nerves on Max's neck pulsed for a moment, giving him the chills. The cold was making his head ache, and it disoriented him. He felt like he was having an intense head rush. Second time that day. "I need something to drink," he said to Hadley as he started walking faster toward the building. He figured he must be dehydrated. He hurried to their apartment, pushing the solid door open, hearing the music to "Jeopardy" infect the air. Max paused. Shelby never turned on the TV. He looked into the living room and saw her sitting on the floor, holding the remote. Max went to get a beer in the kitchen.

Opening the refrigerator, Max froze for a moment, his thoughts confused and unavoidable. He tilted his head sideways with one hand, like pushing a needle out of a record groove, hoping to stop the constant repetition surfacing in his mind. It was a question he couldn't get rid of. A yammering uncertainty that started quietly and then crescendoed to schizophrenic voices volleying between his temples. Why was there glitter on Hadley's mustache? He had noticed it when Hadley laughed, reflecting the street light. Max breathed deeply. Drank some cold water. There could be many reasons. What were they? Should he ask Shelby, or would it be too accusatory? What if she told him? What could she tell him? It wasn't a lot of glitter.

第二十一章 证据

他望着正在和哈德利说话的谢尔碧,突然她就对哈德利竖起了中指,麦克斯之前没有留心听,有些不明所以。

"女性的版本,和男性的版本。"谢尔碧边说边将中指翻转过来对着哈德利。他和哈德利都曾经告诉过她,她竖中指的方向是反的。麦克斯看着谢尔碧跑向公寓楼,留下一串爽朗的笑声,又突然在人行道上站住,对着他们大喊冷死了。

麦克斯也跳上路沿,步速不自觉地加快了,虽然冷,却不愿意跑动起来。哈德利就在身后不远处,于是他又放慢脚步与他并排走着。"所以刚才发生了什么?"麦克斯满心好奇地问起。

"她说我是背后唆使者。"

"那不是应该你对她竖中指才对吗?"

"一定是我说了什么不称她心的话。"

哈德利忍不住笑了起来。他的笑声里交织着一种不一样的东西,让麦克斯不由得向他看去。那笑声里透露出无比的亲密,仿佛他是在笑话自己的妹妹一样。

突如其来的一阵神经痉挛在麦克斯的脖颈处停留了一会儿,使他身上的寒意更深了,头也不可抑制地阵痛起来。瞬间又有一股强烈的眩晕袭来,今天已经第二次了。"我需要喝点儿东西。"他加速前进,把这句话丢给了身后的哈德利。他觉得自己肯定是有些脱水了,于是匆忙地一把推开门,电视节目《险境》的音乐声便穿透了空气袭来。麦克斯立在了原地——谢尔碧从来不看电视的,可现在客厅里,谢尔碧正手握着遥控器坐在地板上。他又继续走进厨房去拿啤酒。

打开冰箱门的瞬间,麦克斯怔怔地停下了手里的动作,因为总有一些疑惑在脑海里挥之不去。他将头慢慢地倒向一侧,就像将唱片机的针头推离轨道一般,希望借此止住那个阴魂不散的猜测。起初的悄然开始的"窸窸窣窣"声由不确定变得渐强,直到最后,演变成精神分裂般的撕扯,在麦克斯的太阳穴之间凌空冲撞。为什么哈德利的胡子上会有闪光的亮片?他在笑的时候,麦克斯注意到那里反射着路灯的光亮。他深吸了一口气,喝了几口冷水。也许有很多解释,到底是什么呢?应该直接向谢尔碧发问吗?会不会太像是责问了?要是她直接告诉自己一切怎么办?她能说些什么呢?亮片并不多,仅仅有几小片粘在哈德利

Chapter Twenty-One   Proof

A couple of sparkles embedded above Hadley's upper lip. Max kept thinking how the stuff was like a radioactive compound, a tracer, a record of Shelby's day. There was no doubt they had touched.

No. He stopped himself. He was making something out of nothing. Maybe it was totally innocent. Maybe they'd accidentally bumped heads. Maybe it was from the other day when he'd used her microphone. Max could think of a hundred plausible excuses, but none of them made him feel any better. The problem was Shelby. She was different. It was that damn job. He kept telling her to quit. They didn't need the money. But she punished herself with it. Felt it was all she deserved. He couldn't even bring it up anymore because she would get mad at him. And then she would cry. He felt really bad when she cried. Helpless. He thought of earlier today when he and Shelby were downtown. Shelby had nearly run into a man pushing a baby buggy filled with newspapers and magazines. Hanging off the handlebars was a huge bag of bottle caps.

Shelby waited until the man trundled on. "And you wonder, what is he going to do with all those bottle caps?"

Max had smiled at her. Liking her good mood. They'd just had lunch and she was drunk. It made her philosophical. Max answered her with the same degree of humored seriousness. "Maybe bag people collect all of society's leftovers, all the things that no one else could possibly want."

Shelby began to walk along the edge of a cement wall, then jumped off when it met a building. "What do the bag people want with them?"

"Could be an intrinsic human need for possessions," Max had said, waiting for her as she now looked in the window of an antique store. She'd turned to him, almost surprised.

"What?" he'd asked.

She'd smiled at him. "So they collect things there's no demand for, to insure they can keep them."

Max shrugged. "Newspaper might not be of any use to you, but to someone on the street, it's shelter, camouflage—lots of things."

"But bottle caps?"

Max grinned. "Maybe he brews his own beer."

嘴唇上面一些的位置。麦克斯一直觉得,这亮片像是种具有放射性的化合物,被用作追踪剂,可以记录下谢尔碧一天的行程。这就是证据,他们一定有过亲密接触。

不,麦克斯制止了自己。他是在无中生有,也许那亮片只是意外。也许他们不小心撞到了头,又或许是前几天他用谢尔碧的麦克风时蹭上的。麦克斯能想出上百个貌似合理的解释,可没有一个能让他心里好受些。问题其实在谢尔碧身上——她变得不一样了。就是因为那份该死的工作,他一直劝她辞职来着,他们并不需要她的那份工资来维持生活。可谢尔碧一意孤行,用那份工作惩罚自己,并觉得这就是自己应得的。麦克斯现在甚至都不能够提起这件事,否则她准会发飙,紧接着又哭起来。看到她哭泣无助的样子,麦克斯觉得很心疼。他想起了今天早些时候,他们俩在市中心,谢尔碧差点儿撞上一个推着婴儿车的男人,车里堆满了旧报纸和杂志,把手上挂的大袋子里全部都是塑料瓶盖儿。

谢尔碧等待着,直到他慢吞吞地推着车离开。"真是奇怪,他要那么多瓶盖儿干吗呢?"

麦克斯看着她,脸上带着微笑。他喜欢谢尔碧心情好的时候。这会儿他们刚吃完午饭,她处于微醺状态。每当这种时候,谢尔碧就会带上哲学的色彩。麦克斯也用同样故作严肃的幽默语气回答道:"也许流浪汉就爱收集社会上所有的残留物,那些别人不太想要的东西。"

谢尔碧开始沿着水泥墙的墙根走起来,到了大楼的跟前便轻轻跳了下来。"那流浪汉能用它们来做什么呢?"

"可能只是为了满足人性天生的占有欲。"谢尔碧停下来向一家古董店的橱窗里望去,麦克斯则站在一旁等着,慢条斯理地说道。她回过头来,表情几乎是讶异的。

"怎么了?"

谢尔碧报以微笑。"所以他们收集那些没人要的物品,这样就可以保证自己能够占有它们了。"

麦克斯耸了耸肩。"报纸在你眼里可能没什么用处,可对露宿街头的人来说,既是庇护,也是伪装——可能还有其他作用。"

"可瓶盖儿呢?"

麦克斯龇着牙笑了。"也许他留着自己酿啤酒的时候用呢。"

Chapter Twenty-One Proof

Shelby had started pushing him down the street, sticking her tennis-shooed foot into the immediate vicinity of his calves. "Hey, spunky," he had yelled at her, happy to be in love in New York. One's happiness had an audience. Why couldn't they always be like this? Max grabbed her shoulders to steady himself and she used it to her advantage, trying to pull him off balance, laughing at her almost victory. It was a campy vaudeville they did, physical comedy. A style they'd all learned during college, when the way to be affectionate was to slug each other. A guy thing. Max knew that Shelby liked to hang with the guys.

They'd ended up breathless, walking down the street cuddled together, a wind break against the world. The day was getting bleaker, and the cold started looking for places to inhabit. Max had hugged Shelby tightly and turned to her. The sunlight hit her profile, and Max noticed the glistening of her cheek.

"You're crying."

Shelby didn't say anything.

"Why?" Max asked as one would ask a faun, fearing to frighten it off.

"I don't know," Shelby managed to exhale, unable to stop a fresh surge of tears. He had hugged her as she'd continued to weep, having no idea what was troubling her.

He thought of that now, and even in the hot apartment, a feeling of chilliness came over Max. That was twice now that she'd started just started crying for no reason. What could it mean? He knew she wasn't pregnant. He closed the refrigerator without getting a beer. He walked into their bedroom and shut the door, glancing first to see them both watching TV in the living room. When had they ever watched TV together? In the bedroom he found himself standing in front of her dresser, so he opened the top drawer. He just wanted to see if it was there. To see if it looked recently used. At first he thought it was missing. He had to feel around in the drawer to find it, sliding his hands through her underwear and nylons. He felt like such a sneak, but he was too committed to go back now. His fingers jammed against it. Pulling it out between the silky folds of a negligee, he tried to memorize its position so he could put it back exactly as it had been. This was his basest moment, but he had to know.

It was in a molded blue plastic case, like a special Tupperware accessory, bulging on top, yet to be burped. Max felt like he was opening an oyster. Would the pearl

谢尔碧把他往街道上一推,穿网球鞋的脚伸到麦克斯小腿肚儿之间的空隙里。"嘿,调皮鬼。"麦克斯冲着她嗔怒般地叫了一声,能在纽约拥有一份爱情让他感到幸福,而这份幸福也有了观众。为什么他们不能永远都像这样呢?麦克斯握住她的肩膀来稳住自己,却反被谢尔碧利用,顺势又被扯得失去了平衡。她大声地笑着,庆祝自己只差一点儿的胜利。夸张的杂耍动作,这是一种运用肢体语言的戏剧。这一招儿是他们在大学的时候学到的,从那时起他们表示亲昵的方式就是互相偷袭。男生之间比较流行,可麦克斯知道谢尔碧爱和男孩子混在一块儿。

他们气喘吁吁,紧紧相拥着继续沿街道向前走,形成了对抗这个世界的防风屏障。天气愈发的凛冽起来,寒风削尖了脑袋想要找地方躲藏。麦克斯将谢尔碧搂得更紧了一些,又转过头看着她。阳光洒在她的侧脸上,却有点点金光闪烁。

"你在哭。"

谢尔碧默默无言。

"为什么?"麦克斯的语气轻柔得如同对待弗恩神兽一般[译者注:faun 希腊神话中半人半鹿的自然和丰收之神],担心会把它给吓跑。

"我也不知道。"虽然仍然无法阻止新一波的泪水涌出,却总算能够吐出一口气来。麦克斯无措地抱住仍在小声啜泣的谢尔碧,完全不知道是什么在困扰她。

麦克斯现在想起当时的场景,即使房间里热浪袭袭,也没能阻挡一阵寒意钻入他的脊髓。像这样没头没脑的哭泣,已经是第二次了。这能意味着什么呢?况且他知道谢尔碧并没有怀孕。想到这儿麦克斯关上冰箱门,再也提不起对啤酒的兴趣了。他径直走进卧室,关门之前瞥了一眼客厅——他们俩都在看电视。他们什么时候一起看过电视?卧室里,麦克斯站在谢尔碧的梳妆台前,打开了第一层抽屉。他只是想看一下那个东西是不是还在那儿,最近有没有使用过。起初他还以为不见了,在谢尔碧的内裤和尼龙丝袜间摸索了好一会儿。虽然感觉到了自己的鬼鬼祟祟,可他一心想要弄清楚,不愿放手。他用手指夹住,从折叠整齐的女式晨衣里抽出来。同时记下了它的位置,以便丝毫不差地放回原位。尽管这个瞬间无比可耻,他还是必须要知道。

它被装在一个蓝色的塑料盒子里,像特百惠的特制单品,盖子有些鼓起,等待着消气。麦克斯觉得自己就像在打开一个河蚌,里面的珍珠还在吗?会不会

be there? Would it look used? He closed his eyes as he opened it, afraid to know, afraid to not. He sighed. It was there, powdered with cornstarch, which he accidentally sprinkled everywhere, almost panicking. It was anticlimactic. What had he expected to find? Having not really examined a diaphragm before, he didn't know what might be out of place about it if it had been recently used. It didn't have pieces of paper towel stuck to it like it might if she'd dried it off quickly, but surely she'd be too clever for that. Standing there looking at it suddenly disgusted him. Was his life reduced to this? To suspecting his wife of God-knows-what? He couldn't live like that. He'd never been a jealous person and it was too late to start. He loved Shelby. What could he do? Another wave of helplessness came over him. Putting the diaphragm back, Max sat down on the waterbed and let the swells rock him, trying to lose this feeling. His cheek itched, and he scratched it, feeling his fingers come away wet.

被用过了?打开的瞬间他闭上了双眼,害怕知道,又害怕未知。他叹了口气——还在那儿。麦克斯不小心把包裹在上面的干燥剂玉米粉抖落了满地,几乎慌了神。这样的结局真是扫兴。他本来期待能发现什么呢?因为他从来都不知道怎么检查子宫帽[译者注:避孕用具],就算最近真的被使用过了他也看不出有什么不对劲的地方。上面没有粘着匆忙擦干时可能留下的纸巾屑,但谢尔碧肯定比那精明多了。麦克斯站在原地,就那么盯着,心底突然升起一股对自己的厌恶之情。他的生活真的堕落到了这种程度吗?因为莫须有的事情而怀疑自己的妻子?不能够这样继续下去了。他从来都不是一个嫉妒心强的人,现在要开始也太迟了。他对谢尔碧的爱是真心的。那到底该怎么做呢?又一股无助感笼罩住了麦克斯。把子宫帽放回原处后,他一屁股坐在水床上,任由水波晃来晃去,试图赶走那份思绪。他觉得脸颊痒痒的,便伸手挠了挠,手指移开的时候,便是潮湿的了。

Chapter Twenty-Two   Adulterate

Adulterate: 1. to debase by adding inferior materials or elements.
2. to make impure by admixture.

The Random House College Dictionary

Max always said that in chemistry, people only remember the first and the best. He usually said this loudly at parties, punctuating the sentence with jabs of his finger. It was common knowledge, but Max had a proprietary air, claiming ideas by the sheer robustness with which he presented them. Hadley knew what he meant in this case: people remember the first and best routes to a molecule. How a person makes something like dynamite, for example, or laetrile. A procedure similar to a recipe, but with many more dictates of temperatures and quantities, requiring constant checking and rechecking by complex methods, like noting the direction of the spin of atoms at certain frequencies, and the breakdown of a wave into component waves, methods that seem shaman-like to the layperson. That's why the more elegant the solution, the more it is remembered because that is the one everyone will use. The first guy is considered lucky. But one would rather be considered smart.

Sitting at his desk and thumbing through *TetLet* (which Max liked to call it the journal of trendy chemistry), Hadley hoped that this would be true, that people would remember the stuff that worked, and not the liars and the braggarts who skimmed the horizon brightly and then fell from the sky. Look at cold fusion and perpetual motion machines. Every few years these would resurface with someone claiming that they'd found the key. The media would whip the public into a mindless frenzy, and then, finally, the hoopla would die down and everyone would be very skeptical until the next uprising of ignorance. It was a sad sate of affairs for mankind, but Hadley was relieved to think that it might preserve the reputation of someone in Scotia's group.

Knowing that active participation would also save the reputation of someone in

第二十二章　掺假

掺假:1. 通过加入劣质材料或元素降低成色；2. 混合添加使之不纯净。

——《兰登书屋大学词典》

麦克斯总是说,在化学领域,只有先驱和最优秀的人会被铭记。他会在派对上大声地宣称这一定律,并不时激动地挥舞几下手指。其实大家对这点都了然于心,可麦克斯在表达想法时总有一股架势,斩钉截铁,不容置疑。哈德利知道他的话在此情此景下的具体含义:人们只会记住合成某种分子的第一条和最优途径。比如,炸药是如何合成出来的;又例如苦杏仁苷。这个过程如同遵循菜谱一般,但是却需要更加严格的温度以及分量控制,运用复杂的方法不断地检测,例如记录以某一频率旋转的原子的转向,或是光波分解为成分波的过程。对外行人来说,这些方法听起来如同萨满法师的巫术。这就是为什么合成方法越简洁优雅,被载入史册的可能性就越大,因为人人都会选择使用它。通常第一个发现者会被冠以幸运之名,可本人八成宁愿将其归功于自己的才智。

哈德利此时正坐在自己的桌前翻看着 *TetLet* 杂志(麦克斯喜欢把它称作"时髦化学杂志"),暗自希望着这是真的——人们只会记住奏效的方法,而不是抓住骗子和说大话的人不放。他们在绚丽地滑过天际之后,无法避免悲惨的坠落。冷核聚变以及永动机的妄想就是很好的例子。每隔几年,就会有人跳出来,宣称自己找到了解决的关键点。媒体便鼓起劲头造势,使整个公众陷入盲目的疯狂之中。最终,势头渐熄,人人又重操怀疑态度,直到新一轮的无知再度涌起。这种现象是人类的悲哀,但哈德利竟为此感到轻松不少,因为这种普遍的健忘性能够让斯考蒂亚组里的某个人名声得以保存。

哈德利觉得通过积极表现还可以挽救一下自己被拖下水的名声,便借着这

Chapter Twenty-Two Adulterate

Scotia's group, the momentum of thought propelled Hadley into action. He tapped one last drum cadence on the edge of his desk, then went over to his bench to find the oleic acid. He had the slows, probably all that sex, he scoffed, his mind drifting for a moment. Disbelieving his luck ... Remembering ... No. He had to force himself to do something. Run a reaction. Even with all this mess, he might actually have something worth publishing. He'd run controls to prove that you didn't even need the catalyst to get the product. That was interesting research. Why had Rahda been so stupid as to lie? He kept asking himself this question because it didn't make any sense. She had good research and she lied to make it great. He simply couldn't understand that.

Hadley started to do a diglyceride. It was a way of making an artificial membrane which he could then test Rahda's product against. With all the focus on her nonexistent catalyst, they'd almost forgotten that the product was still useful. He unstoppered a brown-tinted bottle and poured the remains, a gram-and-a-half, into a graduated cylinder. Damn. It was empty and he needed two grams. He'd meant to order more but had forgotten. This early into it, and he was at a halt. He almost sat down and read *C & E News* again, wanting to daydream. Thinking of Shelby made him buck up. Happy. Wanting to accomplish something. To deserve his good luck.

He was pretty sure Bineet had some oleic acid, so he went to see if Bineet was around. It was still an hour before their meeting with Scotia. Hadley looked in Bineet's lab, seeing what he needed there behind the stirrer. Bineet wasn't there, and Hadley deliberated. He knew Bineet wouldn't mind if he took the chemical, but he knew he sure would if someone did it to him. People were always taking things. He rocked back and forth at the door, suddenly seized by a kind of indecision. He couldn't make up his mind. It shocked him. He had to concentrate. He kept flashing on how Max would feel if he knew. If he knew that Hadley had fucked his wife. The crude word sickened him. He shook himself out of his trance. Take the bottle, he decided, anything but standing here paralyzed. Feeling like so much more than a hypocrite, he grabbed it, and went back to his lab. Unstoppering the acid, he noticed a puff of brownish smoke drift out. Puzzled, he watched the plume lazily spin over the bottle like a playful genie. The stuff must be old. Odd. The thought flitted away when Hadley noticed a piece of glitter on his shoe. He thought of Shelby, her hair like Glinda the Good's. Shimmering and bobbing when she danced

股动力行动起来。在桌子边缘敲击完了最后一个鼓韵之后,他便站起身,走向工作台去找油酸试剂。此时的哈德利有些疲乏——八成是因为他和谢尔碧的那场"翻云覆雨",他走了一会儿神,自我嘲弄着。他有些不相信自己的运气……回想起……不能这样。得强迫自己做些正事了,比如开始一项反应。即使在现在这样一团糟的情况下,兴许还能有什么值得发表的成果呢。对照实验值得一做,这可以证明催化剂并不是获得产物的必需条件。拉达为什么会这么愚蠢,撒没有必要的谎呢?这个问题总是纠缠着哈德利,他怎么都想不通。拉达的实验本来就够好了,可她偏要通过谎言来使它更好。哈德利实在无法理解。

他开始着手准备甘油二酯了,用来制作测试拉达产物的人造薄膜。经过她假催化剂这么一闹腾,大家几乎都忘记了产物本身也是有作用的。哈德利取下一个浅棕色玻璃瓶的瓶塞,将剩下的试剂——一共 1.5 克,都倒进了量筒里。该死,瓶子已经空了,可他一共需要 2 克。之前本来想着再多订购一些,可却忘得干干净净。实验才刚刚开始准备阶段,就不得不停手了。哈德利几乎都想重新坐下来读《化学和工程新闻》了,顺便做做白日梦。一想到谢尔碧他就感到精神抖擞,幸福感油然而生,并且想要有所成就,这样才能对得起自己的这份幸运。

他很确定贝内特还有些油酸试剂剩下,便抬腿去贝内特的实验室看看他来了没有。离他们约好与斯考蒂亚见面的时间还有一个小时,哈德利在贝内特的实验室里张望了几眼,发现了摆在搅拌器后面的油酸试剂瓶。可贝内特本人并不在,哈德利于是犹豫了。虽然明知贝内特不会介意,可要是有人随意动自己的试剂,哈德利肯定会愠怒不已。总是有人未经允许乱拿别人的试剂。在门口踌躇了一会儿之后,他突然发现自己正被一股优柔寡断的气氛笼罩着,无法抉择。他感到惊讶无比,虽然努力想要集中注意力,脑海里却不断浮现麦克斯发现事情真相后的情景,如果他知道自己睡了他的老婆,会作何反应。那个粗鲁的字眼让哈德利一阵恶心,他用力甩了甩头,从出神状态中挣脱出来。他终于决定了,拿上试剂瓶——做任何事都比僵站在这里好。一把抓过瓶子后,尽管内心不断鄙视着自己的伪君子行径,他还是头也不回地走回了实验室。瓶盖儿打开的瞬间,一小缕略带棕色的烟雾"噗"地一下子冒了出来。哈德利困惑地盯着那缕轻烟在瓶口上方闲适地漂移着,如同爱开玩笑的精灵。肯定是因为试剂保存时间太久了,真是奇怪。当哈德利瞥见自己鞋面上的亮片时,刚才的疑惑瞬间就被取代了。顿时谢尔碧的形象就浮现在了他的脑海里,她的头发就像《绿野仙踪》里的善良女巫葛琳达,跳舞的时候便整个人都散发着蒸腾的光芒,灵巧地弯曲着身

Chapter Twenty-Two   Adulterate

around, she was her own confetti dispenser. He started to smile, when he noticed a tiny piece of glitter on his arm. He scratched at it, and it took a moment to fall to the floor, seemingly magnetized to his skin. He looked in the window, seeing a dark reflection of himself. There was a piece of glitter stuck to the side of his nose. And he hadn't even seen Shelby since yesterday. What must he have looked like yesterday? He felt a tightness in his throat. Had Max noticed? He looked closer at his face, scratching off the particle of glitter. It was infinitesimal, but it reflected light amazingly well. It was something he hadn't even considered.

Maybe he was just being neurotic. This Rahda thing was making everyone a little psycho. He unconsciously shook his head, trying to rid his mind of thoughts he had no answers for. Swirling Bineet's bottle of oleic acid and releasing more smoke, Hadley tried to make a circle with the trailing vapor, thinking of things he'd like to show Shelby. Phosphorescence and things that go boom. He took a deep breath, and forced himself to stop thinking about Shelby. Pouring half a gram of Bineet's acid into the graduated cylinder, Hadley looked at the mixture and frowned. It looked a little murky. He thought about finding more oleic acid, but he didn't think it being old would hurt the reaction. He took the cylinder to his hood where the flask of glycerin and solvent was suspended over an oil bath. Slowly pouring the acid into the flask and cranking the gear on the lab jack so that the oil bath would heat up, he watched the mixture swirl around inside, hypnotizing him, relaxing him, bringing him back to his theme. Every thought led to Shelby. And what good did that do? He had no right to even think about her. Hadley wondered again how much Max would hate him if he found out. He tried to imagine himself in Max's shoes and wondered what his own reaction would be. Without meaning it to, the word adultery came to mind. He was an adulterer. He'd had sex with another man's wife. Some places that was still illegal, though probably not in Manhattan. He almost laughed, the idea of anything to do with sex being illegal in Manhattan.

He'd read recently, in *Natural History* maybe, about adultery among animals; it was a kind of scam, a way to protect the offspring. Male animals will often kill offspring that isn't their own, but if the female has had sex with several males, then all the males seem to think that the offspring is theirs and will let them live. Pretty clever. But when it came to people, you couldn't really see that line of reasoning holding up in court. Hadley's mind went so far as to imagine Shelby pleading to a

体,五彩的亮片也随之从她身上抖落。哈德利情不自禁地翘起了嘴角,就在这时,他发现自己的胳膊上也粘着一个小亮片。挠了几下之后还是像吸铁石一般粘在皮肤上,又过了一会儿才弄下来。他抬起头看着窗户里自己的身影,鼻翼的一侧也在闪光。可从他昨天起就再也没有见过谢尔碧了,那昨天他身上该粘有多少亮片啊?想到这儿哈德利的喉咙顿时紧了起来。麦克斯注意到了吗?他又凑近玻璃一些,试图把脸上的亮片刮下来。虽然小得不能再小,可反光的效果却惊人。他从来都没有料想到这一点。

也许只是自己过度紧张了,毕竟拉达的这次事件让每个人都变得有点神经质。哈德利下意识地甩着头,想脱离这些无解问题的纠缠。他捏住油酸试剂瓶的瓶颈,前后抖动着,更多的烟雾随之飘散出来。哈德利用手引领着烟雾在空中画了个圈,脑子里同时思索着想做给谢尔碧看的其他事情。磷光现象,还有会产生轻微爆炸效果的反应。他深吸了一口气,强迫自己的思绪从谢尔碧身上移开。继续向量筒里倒了半克的油酸之后,哈德利对着有些浑浊的混合物皱起了眉头。本想再去其他地方找找油酸,但他又觉得试剂存放的时间不会影响反应的正常进行。最终他还是拿着量筒来到了通风橱前,混合在烧瓶里的甘油和溶剂正处在油浴当中。哈德利先是缓慢地将油酸加进烧瓶中,接着转动升降台上的齿轮,使之浸没。混合物在烧瓶里旋转的画面如同在给他催眠,使得大脑渐渐放松了警惕,于是旧把戏又开始卷土重来——不论想什么,最终都会落在谢尔碧身上。这样做到底有什么好处呢?他甚至连想她的权利都没有。麦克斯发现之后,一定会对自己恨之入骨。他又试着换位思考,想着如果自己是麦克斯他会怎么做。"通奸"这个词毫无预兆地从哈德利脑子里跳出来——他是"奸夫"。与他人之妻有染,尽管这在某些地区仍然被视作违法,但曼哈顿八成不在其中。一想到任何与性相关的事情会在曼哈顿被列为违法,哈德利几乎笑了出来。

最近他读到一篇关于动物之间通奸的文章,也许是在《自然历史》杂志上;文中说这对动物来说是一种欺骗的手段,用来保护后代的方法。雄性动物通常会残忍杀害非自己血亲的年轻一代,但假若雌性与多个雄性发生性行为,所有雄性便都会认为孩子是自己的,不会惨下狠手。这一招很聪明。可当同样的情况发生在人类的身上时,这条理由在法庭上就站不住脚了。哈德利的思绪越飘越远,脑海竟然浮现了谢尔碧向法官求情的场景,"我这么做是为了救我还没出生

Chapter Twenty-Two Adulterate

judge, "I did it to save my unborn children."

Hadley shook his head, untwisting the clamp that held the flask and lowering it closer to the oil bath. The thoughts he had lately were goofier than he could ever remember. That had to be Shelby's influence. He went from absurd to perverted, tortured to resigned. Why was life so fucked? He said the word again loud in his head, defiant, challenging his religious upbringing which had prepared him for none of this. Religion only had stock answers. It didn't have any advice for when you got in this deep.

Hadley went to turn the temperature of the bath down when a sudden heat seared his face. He was knocked backward, a catastrophic roar clouding his ears, a pounding whoosh of force that sonic boomed around him in a fraction of perceived time. The sash on his hood dropped quickly, a large piece of safety glass intended to contain any explosions. It protected his body but the solid weight of the metal frame caught his hands underneath, wedged at the forearm. He screamed from the pain of the exploding reaction. In a flash of chilling fear, he wondered if he would lose his hands. He tried to lift the window with the strength of his forearms, working his shoulders hard, but it was a good 200 pounds. The cable must have broken. He leaned his body against the fiery glass, trying to lift it with the pressure of his chest and his arms, but it seemed stuck. Intense pain blazed up his arm and clenched at his chest and he tried not to panic.

Suddenly he was somewhere else and someone was licking his face. He smiled. Where was he? His eyelids fluttered. He thought he saw sheets. No, it was water. He felt wetness. Icy cold wetness. Pouring on him. Covering him. Now he was shivering uncontrollably. Someone was holding him, lifting his arms. He was in a shower.

"They don't seem to have hot water. Sorry."

"Max," Hadley whispered.

"Yes."

"What happened?"

"I'm not sure."

"My hands."

"They're still there. I'm hoping your dick's gone though."

The cable connecting the counterweight to the sash had broken because of the

的孩子。"

哈德利清了清脑袋,稍稍松开用来固定的铁夹,将烧瓶向下移动至更接近油浴的位置。这阵子他总是会有奇奇怪怪的想法,连自己都感到吃惊。肯定是受谢尔碧的影响没跑儿。他的想法从怪诞转为扭曲,倍感折磨之后便渐趋听天由命了。为什么生活总是充满了窘境?他又在脑海里咒骂了一遍,带着反抗的意味,仿佛是在挑战自己一直以来接受的宗教教育。因为它对哈德利现在面临的困境没有丝毫启示或是帮助。宗教只会提供格式化的答案,假如你太深入生活,那它便束手无策了。

哈德利正准备调低油浴的温度,却有一阵突然的热浪滑过他的脸颊,留下灼烧般的刺痛感。他不禁连退几步,在难以察觉的短短时间里,炸裂在他耳边的声波"嗖"地一下形成一股力量,可怖的轰鸣声冲撞着他的耳膜。通风橱上的防护玻璃迅速落了下来,这块巨大的玻璃是用来隔离爆炸反应的。虽然哈德利的身体因此幸免,可他的双手却被沉重的金属窗框牢牢地压在了下面,正好卡在小臂的前方。爆炸所带来的痛苦让哈德利失声尖叫起来,在恐惧袭来的最初几秒,他觉得自己可能会因此而失去双手。整块玻璃足足有两百磅重,哈德利无论是试图用小臂的力量,还是再加上肩膀,都徒劳无功。控制的缆绳肯定断了。哈德利又将整个身体都抵在灼热的通风橱上,想借助胸部的压力把它抬起一点,可它似乎卡住了。尽管剧烈的疼痛沿着哈德利的胳膊向上蔓延,啃噬着他的胸膛,哈德利还是努力地保持着镇静。

突然,他发现自己身处另一个地方,有人在舔他的脸。他笑了。这是在哪儿?哈德利的眼皮震颤了几下,他以为自己看见了大片大片的床单。但不是,其实是水。湿漉漉的触感,冰凉冰凉的。不断浇淋到他的身上,覆盖了每一寸皮肤。这会儿他已经不受控制地浑身发起抖来。有个人一直架着他的胳膊,他在淋浴室。

"好像没有热水,真是抱歉。"

"麦克斯。"哈德利虚弱地叫了一声。

"是我。"

"发生了什么?"

"我也不确定。"

"我的手。"

"它们还在。可我希望你的老二已经被烧掉了。"

在爆炸的威力下,连接能够拉起防护玻璃平衡物的绳索断了。要把它给硬

Chapter Twenty-Two Adulterate

explosion's force. Pushing the sash back up was harder than Max had expected and he couldn't do that and drag Hadley out of the hood. He yelled for someone to come help him. Bineet ran across the hall and yelled something as he lifted the sash so Max could drag Hadley backwards to the emergency shower in the hallway. Hadley's hands were on fire. Max pulled the shower chain and then stood in the cold water, turning Hadley into his own chest to smother the flames. They stood there in a moment of embrace. Hadley mumbled, "Thank you."

"Don't thank me. I want nothing from you." Max said it very gently, factually. He didn't want to threaten Hadley. He wanted him to know he knew. He would save his life, but he would never talk to him again.

Bineet ran out of Hadley's lab. "Is he awake?"

"Yeah. He's not in a coma. Here, help me get his clothes off."

"What was he running?" Bineet yelled over the roar of the shower, helping Max off with Hadley's shirt.

"I don't know," Max grunted, struggling with Hadley's pants. He motioned for Bineet to hold Hadley against the wall while Max lifted his feet and then yanked on the bottoms of Hadley's jeans. The wet clothes moved uneasily. Max tugged harder, wanting this part of his life to be over, wanting not to be this close to someone he hated so much. Max couldn't even think about the proximity of Hadley's flesh, how he wanted violence. Graphic pictures flashed inside his head, making him feel like throwing up. Making him want to do damage. He felt so wronged. Hurt to the point of despondency. His heart really did feel the added weight of sadness. And then this cycled back into savage anger. He wanted retribution, but he could only achieve it in his mind, over and over again. Civilization means civilized behavior. But our thoughts are still as barbaric as they ever were.

He glanced at the door to Hadley's lab. There was a Far Side comic taped to it. Ed's Dingo Farm next to Doreen's Nursery. All the dingoes were lined up along the fence looking into the next yard at two babies sitting in a play pen. The caption read, "Trouble brewing." It was the comic that gave Max the idea for the band's name. But now he thought about the caption. He kept unconsciously repeating the words, trouble brewing, trouble brewing, as a kind of mantra, a thing that he should have known, that he should have seen a mile away, no less obvious than the meeting of dingoes and babies.

第二十二章 掺假

推回去比麦克斯想象中还要难,仅凭他一人之力根本做不到,更别提把哈德利给拖出来了。他只能大声呼叫其他人,贝内特闻声从大厅里跑过来,一边鬼喊一边奋力抬起玻璃罩,麦克斯赶忙把哈德利拖进大厅里的紧急淋浴室中。看见哈德利的双手上仍然跳动着火苗,麦克斯拉开喷头后便与哈德利一同站在冷水中,将他搂向自己的胸膛,以此来熄灭火焰。他们俩就这样以相拥的姿势站了一会儿,哈德利含糊地咕哝了一句:"谢谢。"

"别谢我,我不想接受你的任何东西。"麦克斯平静地轻声答道。他无意威胁哈德利,但希望他知道自己已经知晓一切。他会向哈德利伸出援手,可却永远都不会再和他说话了。

这时,贝内特也跑出了哈德利的实验室。"他醒了吗?"

"醒了,没有昏迷。来,帮我一起把他的衣服给脱了。"

"他到底在做什么实验?"贝内特一边帮麦克斯一起脱去哈德利的衬衫,一边大声询问着,试图盖过淋浴的声音。

"我不知道。"麦克斯低声咕哝了一句,继续忙活着给哈德利脱掉裤子。他示意贝内特扶住哈德利倚着墙,自己则抬起他的脚,猛地拉扯牛仔裤的裤脚。衣料因为沾了水特别不容易脱,麦克斯又加大了力度,暗自期盼着这部分的人生能够尽快结束,可以不用离自己恨到骨子里的人这么近。他甚至不能细想,否则便忍不住冒出暴力的念头来。脑海里不断闪现的画面激起他一阵想要呕吐的感觉,加剧了麦克斯破坏的欲望。这整件事让他感到无比的委屈、沮丧,连悲伤的重量也实实在在地压在他的心上。这些感情又不可避免地循环成了原始的愤怒,麦克斯想要报复,可却只能在脑子里实现,一次又一次。文明在行为上得以体现,但是我们的思想却一如过往,粗野蛮荒。

麦克斯瞥了一眼哈德利实验室的门,上面贴了一张"远侧"(美国著名漫画家盖瑞·拉尔森的系列漫画 Far Side)的漫画,爱德华澳洲野狗农场与朵茵托儿所相毗邻,所有的野狗在栅栏后面一字排开,垂涎三尺地盯着隔壁坐在游戏护栏里的两个宝宝。旁边写着,"风雨欲来"。正是这幅漫画给了麦克斯灵感,才有了他们乐队的名字。可现在他再读那上面的配字,下意识地不停重复着,风雨欲来,风雨欲来,仿佛是一句咒语。在最初出现苗头的时候,他早就该预见的,因为那暗示与野狗和宝宝的相遇同样显而易见。

Chapter Twenty-Two   Adulterate

Max heard the paramedics running up the long stairway as he and Bineet wrapped Hadley in a blanket and laid him down. Bineet ran to the door at the end of the hall and yelled so they would know where they were. Gurney in hands, they burst through the swinging door and quickly ran to where Hadley lay on the floor. They stuck an IV in him, checked his pulse, loaded him up, and started to roll him down the hall. "What's he got on him?" a remaining medic with a clipboard asked Max.

"I don't know. Possibly an acid. I'll find out. Give me a number to call."

"Anyone going with him?" the paramedic asked, starting down the hallway. Max hesitated and Bineet looked at him, surprised.

"No." Max said. "I need to find out what happened." It dawned on Max that Hadley might have been trying to kill himself. Maybe he actually felt terrible. Max found himself wishing that Hadley had been trying to kill himself, wishing that he thought it would bother Hadley that much. No. He didn't want that. It wasn't in him. He really couldn't take his revenge that far. He was much too sad for that.

"I will go," Bineet said, running with long strides down the hallway, his lab coat flaring behind him as he tried to catch up.

Max went back into Hadley's lab. The hood had an automatic extinguisher which had put the explosion out, but inside there was glass everywhere. The sash to the hood had pretty much contained the destruction, but the stench in the air was unbearable, the smell of burning rubber, probably the seals to the sash. Max went to open the windows at the end of the hall. Propping the sash and looking around the hood didn't tell him much. He'd put on gloves, but now he went to get a lab coat, something he rarely wore. There were chemicals everywhere and he had no idea what they were. As a last thought, he added a face mask. Who knew what kind of toxic substances might have been released?

Max finally found Hadley's notebook. It had fallen behind his desk. But it had no mention of his most recent reaction. In fact, it hadn't been written in for a couple of days. That wasn't much help. He went to Hadley's bench and started checking what bottles were out: glycerin, oleic acid, a couple of solvents. Fortunately Hadley was so meticulous, it was easy to tell what he'd used recently. Max realized that if his own hood had exploded, someone would be there for days, reconstructing. Of course, there was a reason his hood hadn't exploded. He wasn't a hack. He felt a

麦克斯听到急救人员在楼梯上匆忙的脚步声,便和贝内特一起将哈德利用毛毯包起来,使其平躺在地上。贝内特紧接着向走廊尽头的大门处跑去,并大声喊叫着以便让他们确定方位。转门"砰"的一声被撞开,医护人员推着轮床急速向哈德利躺着的方向赶来。他们立即给哈德利打上点滴,检查了脉搏之后便将他抬上轮床,分秒不停地向外推去。"他身上的化学物是什么?"一名手里拿着病例板的医生留了下来,他开始询问麦克斯一些信息。

"我不知道,很有可能是酸。我会查出来的,留一个号码给我。"

"有人跟他一起去医院吗?"轮车仍然快速沿着走廊前进着。贝内特看到麦克斯脸上犹豫的神情,感到有些惊讶。

"我不行,"麦克斯开口道,"我得留下来查清发生了什么。"突然有个想法闯进麦克斯的脑子里:哈德利也许是在自杀。因为太内疚的缘故。麦克斯发现,内心深处他希望这是真的,希望这件事真的有让哈德利良心不安到这种程度。不,这不是他所期望的,他的性格不是如此。就算是复仇也不能到如此地步,否则他就太可悲了。

"我跟着去。"贝内特沿着走廊大步向前跑去,试图追上他们,他的实验服在身后被风鼓起。

麦克斯起身回到了哈德利的实验室里。虽然通风橱自带的自动灭火装置已经将爆炸产生的火焰熄灭,可是里面四处散布着玻璃碎渣。通风橱将毁坏性降到了最低,空气中却弥漫着令人难以忍受的橡胶燃烧的臭气,八成是玻璃罩的塑封边缘。麦克斯走到房间尽头打开了窗户,继续在通风橱周围检视,可是收获寥寥。虽然已经戴上了手套,可他又去取来了实验服,平时他根本不屑一穿。因为现在四处散落着化学品,他完全不知道都有些什么。最后细细一想,他又给自己带上了防毒面罩。谁知道有哪些有毒物质都被释放到了空气中呢?

麦克斯终于在哈德利的桌子后面发现了他的笔记本,可是上面却只字未提他正在做的这个反应。事实上,上面已经有好几天没做任何记录了。没什么实质性的帮助。于是他走到哈德利的工作台前,查看哪些试剂瓶被取出来用了:甘油、油酸,还有几种溶剂。幸运的是,哈德利做事一向有条不紊,因此很容易判断哪些试剂是刚刚使用过的。麦克斯心想着如果事情发生在自己身上,肯定需要有人花上好几天来做现场重现工作。当然,爆炸没有发生在自己的实验室是有原因的——他的能力可没那么弱。这么想让麦克斯觉得有些愧疚,因为哈德利

Chapter Twenty-Two Adulterate

little guilty thinking this, because Hadley wasn't a hack either. So why did his reaction explode? Max opened the bottle of oleic acid and a puff of smoke came out. He watched it, confused for a moment. Could be old, he thought. He looked at the bottle and noticed Bineet's handwriting. Hadley had borrowed this. Bineet had a writing style that wasn't easy for Max to read. A kind of Sanskrit-looking alphabet, more curvaceous than one normally saw. Turning the bottle, Max noticed that on the upper left corner of the label was a date. This was only a month old. Something pinged in Max's brain. The sound of a correct answer. Nitric acid emitted smoke, too. Always. Of course, how would nitric acid get in the oleic acid bottle? He froze, the brunt of the truth hitting him. Nitric acid and glycerin. Nitroglycerine. Dynamite. Max took the bottle and went to measure its acidity. Nitric acid has a greater acidity than oleic acid. It only took him a moment to do the test, and he was right. Either the bottle had been mislabeled, or someone had switched the compounds.

Was Hadley trying to kill himself? Why would he bother switching the bottles? No. This had to be accidental. Maybe even criminal. But if Rahda really had done this, she'd meant to blow up Bineet. Both stories seemed too unbelievable. Max went to call the hospital. Scotia would have to call the police.

也非常优秀。那么,到底为什么他的反应会突然爆炸呢?麦克斯打开油酸的瓶盖,一缕轻烟随之冒了出来。他就那么呆看着,一时有些困惑。也许是放得时间久了,他对自己解释道。这时他注意到了瓶身上贝内特的字迹——哈德利借了他的试剂。贝内特的书写风格很难辨认,看上去近乎梵语字母,比常见字迹带有更多的弯曲。麦克斯将瓶子反转过来,同时注意到了标签左上角标的日期——才一个月。有什么东西在麦克斯的脑子里"叮当"作响——真正的谜底。硝酸在打开时也会飘出烟雾,每次都会。但是,硝酸怎么会装在油酸的试剂瓶里呢?麦克斯霎时怔在了原地,真相不断有力地撞击着他。硝酸和甘油在一起,硝酸甘油,炸药。麦克斯迅速拿起试剂瓶,去进行酸性检测,因为硝酸的酸性比油酸要大。不消一会儿就完成了,结果也证实了麦克斯的猜测。如果不是标签被贴错了,那么一定有人刻意把试剂给调包了。

是哈德利意图自杀吗?那他为什么要大费周折地调换试剂瓶呢?不,这肯定在他的意料之外,甚至有可能是一场有预谋的犯罪。拉达的名字不可抑制地在麦克斯的脑海里浮现。可如果拉达真的是始作俑者,那么她本来想加害的其实是贝内特。不论是哪一种可能性,都太令人难以置信了。麦克斯给医院打了电话,报警的工作应该要留给斯考蒂亚来做了。

Chapter Twenty-Three

Unresolved: to Stay Together

Resolve: to separate into constituent or elementary parts; break up.
The Random House College Dictionary

Unresolved: to stay together.
Common sense

Shelby was in the throes of cleaning. When in doubt, she threw things away. And she was in doubt. She'd found Max in the shower, crying, his eyes blood-shot. He knew. He'd seen them kiss in the reflection of the living room windows that morning. Innumerable window panes reflecting their indiscretion. But he hadn't told her until after Hadley's accident, life having scared him by its fragility. He wanted his wife back. So she had confessed, having told herself that if he ever asked her point-blank, she would tell the truth. That was her one moral. If things weren't so dire, she might have laughed. Could you get into heaven with one moral?

She was beset by indecision. She didn't know what to do. If she stayed, she knew her danger. She'd had one affair. How long would be it before she had another? Having two affairs is like having two abortions: One is an honest mistake, two suggests indiscretion. That you're a slow learner. Stupid, possibly. She knew having an affair was the chickenshit way to affect change. But leaving one's husband was simply too conscious. She felt like Anaïs Nin. Screwing Henry Miller, screwing the psychiatrist she was seeing because she was screwing Henry Miller, and then making her husband meet her at the train afterward and never showing up. Three times. Her sins felt no less than that. Her awareness was a curse. Just because you know something doesn't mean that you are able to change it. She still wanted Hadley. Even as much love and gratitude as she felt for Max, it didn't rid her of her desire.

She found that thinking made her crazy. So she threw things away. Anything to

第二十三章　未溶解：保持一体性

溶解：分解成为相应成分或者基础部分；瓦解。

——《兰登书屋大学词典》

未溶解的：保持一体性。

——常识

谢尔碧正无比煎熬地清扫着房间。每次犹疑不决的时候，她就会开始扔东西。现在便是这种情景。她看见麦克斯一个人在浴室里流泪，眼睛布满了血丝。他早就知道了一切。那天早晨，她和哈德利亲吻的场景映在客厅的窗玻璃上，麦克斯看得一清二楚。无数的倒影让他们的不检点无处躲藏。但直到哈德利的意外发生之后，麦克斯才说出一切，生命的不堪一击让他心生后怕。他想要老婆回到自己身边。谢尔碧也毫无隐瞒地坦白了一切，她跟自己说假如麦克斯曾经直言质问，她肯定会如实相告的。这是她唯一的一条道德标准。要不是现在的境况近乎悲惨的话，她没准会因此而大笑出来。只有一条道德标准，足以进天堂吗？

谢尔碧深陷踌躇，不知该如何是好。如果选择留下，她清楚自己的处境很危险：已经有过一次外遇了，隔多久会有另一次呢？两次外遇与两次堕胎的暗含意义是一样的：初次是无心之失，再犯则是生活不检。这证明你学得慢，甚至有些愚蠢。谢尔碧知道，用外遇来达到影响别人的目的未免卑劣，可是如果真的选择离开麦克斯，这最终的决定必然是在十分清醒的状态下做出的。她觉得自己就像阿娜伊斯·宁[译者注：世界著名的女性日记小说家]一样。与亨利·米勒有染，又与因此而认识的心理医生发生关系，事后约了自己的老公在火车站见面，却放了他三次鸽子。谢尔碧觉得自己的罪行与之也没差多少。她贯穿始终的清醒意识就像一种诅咒，讽刺着无力改变的事实。她仍然对哈德利存有欲望，对麦克斯的爱意与感激也没能将这种欲望消除。

谢尔碧发现思考正逐渐将她逼向疯狂的境地，因此她转而开始收拾要扔的

keep busy. It was a purging. A ceremony. Shelby felt like the world was ending and that protocols were the only thing that kept one balanced. Even when she was little she would have rites, anointing sacred rocks and hiding them under her pillow or in particular fairylike places in the yard. She made pentagrams and burned incense, all to give life some kind of significance. She didn't believe in religion, but still she needed ritual to satisfy something in her. For her, ceremony was a way to sanctify things that make one feel uncomfortable. Weddings consecrate sex, bar mitzvahs puberty, funerals death—primal urges and things out of our control. Ceremonies acknowledge change. Shelby realized that she felt change but had no way to acknowledge it. Throwing things away was the best she could come up with.

Shelby stopped walking for a moment and sighed, balancing the box she was carrying against a fire hydrant. She wished her life could end now, so much did she hate this pain. She didn't care enough to kill herself, she just wanted to be dead. She thought sadly about the band. It was over. The one thing in her life she had truly enjoyed.

Hitting herself hard on the forehead with her fist, she looked up and saw a woman sitting on the sidewalk next to the subway, rocking herself. It was late, after two in the morning. As Shelby approached the woman on the street, she started having doubts. Was she asking for trouble? Would she get mugged? If she died, she didn't want that to be painful either. Death didn't scare her. Just pain.

The carbony smell of car fumes made her wrinkle her nose, forgetting her worries for all of a second. Even this late at night, the air had a hint of traffic in it, a kind of diesel vapor that smelled like the waftings of an empty bus terminal. The occasional fumes skimmed through one's nostrils, never habituating themselves, so one was constantly hit anew by the acrid smell of exhaust. It made you breathe more shallowly. Inspired light-headedness. Wispy thoughts. It made Shelby want to crawl in bed and hang on the edges of sleep, that moment of unreality that is still malleable to one's wishes.

As she got closer to the woman, she stared at the pavement again to give them both some privacy. But the frequency of the cracks in the ground hypnotized her. She popped her ears because they felt plugged up, like she was underwater. She wanted to be underwater, the almost-silence lulling her mind, the movement of the waves calming her. She imagined the chug of slow turbines, like blades of a paddle

东西。不论什么事，只要不让她闲下来就可以。这是一种净化，一种仪式。她觉得整个世界都在沦陷，礼仪是唯一仍然规范着人类行为的东西。即便是在小的时候，谢尔碧就已经创造出了自己特有的仪式：给石块施以涂油礼，然后藏在枕头下面，或是院子里某个带有童话色彩的角落里。她还会折叠五角星，焚香，一切都是为了赋予生命更多的重要性。虽然不相信宗教，谢尔碧仍然需要仪式来满足自己内心的某种需求。对她来说，仪式可以把让人不自在的事情变得神圣化。婚礼将性加以合法化，酒吧是青年人的成年礼，葬礼则祭奠死亡——这些都是原始的欲望，无法抑制。仪式是对变化的一种承认。谢尔碧感觉到了变化，却做不到承认。清理物品是她能想出的最佳策略了。

谢尔碧停下脚步，叹了口气，借着路边的消防栓平衡了一下怀里抱着的纸盒。她看着路面，愤恨着此时此刻的痛苦，希望生命可以就此结束。她下不了手自杀，但只想一了百了。一想起他们的乐队，悲伤便一股脑儿地涌来——都结束了，唯一真正给她的生命带来享受的东西。

谢尔碧不停用拳头懊恼地捶着自己的额头，再抬头时，她看见一个女人坐在地铁站旁边的人行道上，抱着双臂左右晃着像是在哄自己睡觉。现在已经很晚了，至少有凌晨两点。谢尔碧在走近那个女人的时候，不断有退缩的念头冒出来。这是不是在自找麻烦？会被抢劫吗？如果真的要死，最好没有痛苦。死亡并吓不住她，只有痛苦能够。

汽车尾气中的碳化物气味让谢尔碧不由得皱起了鼻头，一时间忘记了所有的烦忧。尽管已是深夜，空气里仍然残余着车来车往留下的痕迹，如同空荡荡的汽车终点站飘忽着的柴油蒸汽的气息。那气味不时撩拨着你的鼻孔，也不停留，总是有新的刺鼻气味再次袭来。于是你只敢浅浅地呼吸，因而产生了一些晕眩，思绪也随之飘忽起来。此时的谢尔碧只想要爬到床上，进入似睡非睡的境地，停留在那个能够被主观意志影响的梦幻瞬间。

随着她和那个女人的距离越来越近，谢尔碧再一次将目光调转向人行道的方向，为双方都保留一些私密的空间。可地面上密密麻麻的细小裂缝却产生了催眠的效果。她觉得耳朵堵，仿佛浸在水底的感觉一般，便打了个哈欠来平衡气压。她喜欢待在水底，任由思绪被那近乎绝对的寂静麻痹，柔动的水波使她趋于平静。她在脑海中想象着"突突突"慢吞吞前进的涡轮机，双脚如同桨轮上不停

Chapter Twenty-Three Unresolved: to Stay Together

wheel, as her feet broke the surface of the water. She had once asked Max if the sound was from the surface tension being disturbed, all those molecules having to readjust. She remembered him saying that water liked to interact with itself. "Imagine a flexible lattice of H's and O's, little springy X formations. Like molecular netting. That's why it crystallizes so easily. Water molecules tile a three-dimensional plane well. There's a place for everyone." Shelby had said that maybe those water molecules just enjoyed hanging out together and it was hard to break up the party. Max had smiled at her. They were a team: he supplied the facts, she made them into stories. How could she have been so blind?

He had told her he didn't want her to leave. They could see someone. He loved her. Shelby had had her hackles raised, ready for him to be angry. She felt defiant. But then he told her that even if she left, she could always come back to him. That he would hope she wouldn't be too proud to do that. It made her cry. How could he be this nice to her? After what she'd done. The thought of what it would be like to leave him hit her for the first time. A kind of emptiness. A piece of her gone. She felt scared. Like she needed him to help her make this decision.

He'd been taking a bath when she came back from her telegrams, the shower pouring over him. Seeing Max there, his little rabbit eyes red and blurry, she'd started crying too, having to sit down on the toilet seat suddenly, her knees buckling. She was actually glad he knew because she hated the duplicity. The actingness of it. It occurred to her that some women might revel in this, having two men in love with them, but it simply drove her nuts. She wasn't that kind of person. She told him that if he wanted, she could leave. He could keep the apartment. It was the least she could do.

"The last thing I want you to do is leave," he'd said. Shelby had started crying uncontrollably, using yards of toilet paper to blow her nose. She couldn't help it. She'd never seen him vulnerable before. He always was in control, sarcastic, unflappable. She was moved to see a side of himself he had never before revealed. And yet it made her feel horrid that she had brought him to this. She had this knack for hurting people. She sucked them in. She had more men wanting her than ever before. Or so it seemed, because one plus one's husband is an infinite amount.

Max lying there, naked and crying, had broken her heart because she had broken his. How could she have hurt her best friend? After wiping her dripping

旋转的叶片一般,撩碎水面。谢尔碧曾经问过麦克斯,水底的声音是否因为水面的张力被搅扰了,所有的分子都必须要重新调整位置的缘故。麦克斯则回复说水确实喜欢进行自我互动。"想象一下,一群自由的氢原子和氧原子晶格弹性排列成了小小的 X 结构,如同在织一张分子网。所以水分子结晶化才会这么容易。水分子在三维平面上排列得非常服帖,每个分子各占其位。"谢尔碧又补充说,没准儿那些水分子享受一起度过的时光,不想结束那场派对呢。麦克斯则报以一笑。他们俩是绝佳搭档:麦克斯提供事实,谢尔碧以此编出故事。她怎么能够忽略这一点呢?

麦克斯跟她表明过,不希望她离开,他们可以一起去见婚姻咨询师。他是爱着谢尔碧的。谢尔碧本已竖起浑身的刺,准备好迎接麦克斯的怒气了。可面对她挑衅的态度,麦克斯却说,即便她真的离开了,随时都可以再回到他身边来。他不希望谢尔碧因为放不下面子而选择不回头。谢尔碧哭了。在她做了这一切之后,麦克斯怎么还能够对她这么好呢?谢尔碧第一次开始认真地考虑,离开麦克斯会是怎样的一种光景。一种空洞感,缺失了一部分的自我。她心生恐惧,仿佛需要麦克斯来帮助她一起做这个决定。

从谢尔碧做完唱歌电报回来,麦克斯就一直在洗澡,站在淋浴头下任由水流冲刷着。麦克斯的眼睛朦朦胧胧的,红得像兔子眼睛一样,谢尔碧看到这样的情景,膝盖一软,瘫坐在马桶盖上,眼泪也止不住地掉下来。麦克斯知道实情反而让她轻松了一些,因为她厌恶自己表里不一的欺骗行为。每次都要刻意伪装。虽然同时拥有两个男人的爱会让有些女人陶醉不已,谢尔碧却只觉得抓狂。她不是那种人。她告诉麦克斯,如果他愿意,自己可以随时离开,公寓则归他所有。这是她能做到的最起码的事了。

"你离开是我最不想看见的事情。"麦克斯的回答让谢尔碧又一次失声痛哭起来,轱辘轱辘地拉扯了老长的卫生纸来擤鼻涕。她无法自控,因为她从来都没有见过麦克斯如此脆弱受伤的样子。他总是对一切胸有成竹,擅长挖苦搞笑,却又处变不惊。看到他从没展现过的这一面,谢尔碧内心受到了触动,可同时心情也无比糟糕,因为这是她一手造成的。她总是这样伤害别人,使他们陷入其中无法自拔。现在对她感兴趣的男人比以往都要多,至少看起来是这样,因为有了老公,再加上另一个男人就已经是相当大的数量了。

麦克斯躺在浴缸里,赤裸着身体哭泣,谢尔碧看了觉得心痛无比,但毕竟是自己先伤了他的心。她怎么能够伤害自己最好的朋友呢?想到这儿,谢尔碧擦

nose, she had climbed into the shower with him, kneeling down in her clothes and hugging him. They both cried and laughed as the water poured on them. Even in the midst of this they could be so nice to each other. She'd always said you don't really know someone until you break up with them. And here they were doing it.

She was a cacophony of loose ends. How could she live without Hadley? How could she leave Max? The idea of leaving them both occurred to her for a moment as perhaps the fairest thing to do. She could enter a nunnery. Like Guinevere. She remembered Hadley telling her about two people he knew who were in love but both decided to dedicate their lives to God. The woman had already entered a nunnery. And the guy was planning on entering a monastery as soon as he finished law school. Hadley and Shelby had marveled. At the time celibacy had seemed like such an odd response to love.

She'd tried to call Hadley that same night, needing to talk to him, but no one was answering. He was living at Eberhard's, having been bandaged up and released from the hospital. They didn't keep him long. Too many knife fights, too much domestic violence took precedence. He'd had Eberhard come over and move his things. She'd been home when Eberhard had dropped by, hearing the whole story from him, that Max had saved Hadley, that Hadley was okay. She watched Eberhard tell her. He'd looked directly in her eyes, kindly. Eberhard knew. She could tell. She wondered if he thought her a slut. She said the word vulgarly in her mind. But he gave her a note from Hadley, and she realized that Eberhard was not one to judge. He was her friend. She read the note while he was there, wondering if she would have to respond. No. It was only three sentences:

"Max knows. He saved my life. I feel like the worst person in the world."

Shelby had to turn her head so Eberhard wouldn't see her cry.

She had thought Hadley would have been too good to fall. That's probably why she'd picked him, an unconscious defense. She'd thought he was more moral than her, but then lately it seemed that everyone was more moral than her. Or maybe that was only when it came to scrutinizing others. But then, it's always easier to be moral with other people's lives.

The tuneless humming brought Shelby back to earth as she approached the bag woman slowly, carrying a box of things she no longer wanted. She felt shy about giving them to this woman, like who was she to give her rejects to someone else.

了擦鼻子，穿着衣服就爬进了浴缸里，蹲下来，抱住了麦克斯。在不断喷洒的水流下，他们俩一会儿哭一会儿笑。即使是在这种时候，他们仍然能够温柔相对。谢尔碧总是说，直到分手的时候你才能看清一个人的真正面目。现在就是那个时刻了。

一切未知的结局都在她的耳边嘈杂不休。离开了哈德利她能够活下去吗？她又真的舍得下麦克斯吗？突然一下子，她觉得同时离开他们两个才是最公平的做法。进修道院似乎是个选择，就像格温娜维尔［译者注：传说中亚瑟王之妻，兰斯洛特爵士的情妇］一样。她还记得哈德利跟她讲过一个他认识的人的故事，两个人明明相爱，却双双决定将自己的一生献给上帝。那个女人现在就在一座女修道院里，而男方则打算一完成法学院的学业也投身一所男修道院。那时谢尔碧和哈德利都对此感到不可置信，因为用禁欲主义来回应爱情简直是太奇怪了。

出事那天晚上，谢尔碧迫切地需要和哈德利聊一聊，就给他打了电话，却一直没人接听。哈德利包扎完之后就出院了，暂住在艾伯哈德那里。医院并没有收留他太久，因为有太多的持刀斗殴和家庭暴力受害者占据了优先权。他拜托艾伯哈德来帮他取自己的东西，正好谢尔碧也在家，便从他那里听到了故事的始末——哈德利的命是麦克斯救的，现在已经没什么大碍了。艾伯哈德讲述的时候，谢尔碧目不转睛地盯着他，而他也带着善意直视回去。他知道他们之间的事情，谢尔碧看得出来。不知道他会不会认为自己是一个放荡的女人，谢尔碧愤恨地默念了一遍荡妇这个词。但是艾伯哈德递过一张哈德利写的纸条，让她意识到他并不是来这儿评头论足的。他们是朋友。没等艾伯哈德离开，谢尔碧就打开了字条，寻思着自己是不是得回复。但她其实多虑了，上面只有三句话：

"麦克斯知道了。他救了我。我觉得自己是世界上最烂的人。"

谢尔碧转过头去，不让艾伯哈德看见自己的泪水。

起初，谢尔碧以为像哈德利这么正直的人是不会与自己同流的。这很有可能也是她选择哈德利的原因——出于下意识的自我防卫。她一直认为哈德利比自己具有更强烈的道德观，可最近看来，所有人的品行都比她端正。或许人们只是在审视别人时才用上道德这个标杆，这样毕竟更容易些。

恼人的嗡鸣声将谢尔碧拉回现实，她继续端着一盒自己不想要的东西，慢慢向那个流浪女人靠近。这么做她心里有点过意不去，她有什么资格把自己淘汰的残次品施舍给别人呢？谢尔碧想起了小时候的情景：她们一家会带着所有的

Chapter Twenty-Three   Unresolved: to Stay Together

It reminded Shelby of when she was a kid: her family used to take all their cast-off clothes and toys to this black family of nine children. The eldest daughter had one half-white child who was the offspring of Shelby's uncle Sid. Sid refused to acknowledge the child, so the rest of the family felt it was their Christian duty to visit them twice a year, spreading around their white guilt and feeling mostly uneasy until they left.

As Shelby walked up to the woman, she thought of that household, the pictures of white Jesus on the wall, all the little girls with asymmetrical pigtails, the bareness of the floor. Nothing was ever out-of-place, the children all scrubbed clean. How could that be the constant state of someone with nine kids? Their deference had bothered Shelby. Ma'am this and sir that. Thanking them for giving them things that Shelby's family couldn't bring themselves to throw away. And, as she looked down at the box in her arms, she wondered, was she any different? She almost turned around, but the woman had stopped humming and was looking up at her suspiciously.

"Uh. I just wondered if you'd be interested in any of this stuff," Shelby said, lowering the box so that the woman could see inside. Without saying a word, the woman started picking through things, lifting up a moth-eaten wool scarf and wrapping it around her neck, taking out a yo-yo and putting it behind her.

"You can have the box," Shelby said, placing it in front of the woman.

The woman grunted something which Shelby took for thanks. Walking slowly backwards, Shelby watched the woman sort through the box's contents. As she pulled things out, she laid them around her in some master plan. The eight-track tapes she found quickly, holding one up to her ear, then rooted around in the box, looking for something. The woman pulled out an old walkman, turning it over and over as if marveling at the invention, pulling the attached cord slowly, until the headphones got caught on the edge of the box and struggled like a fish on a line. She slowly disentangled them, then placed them over her ears and pushed the buttons. Taking an eight-track tape out of a box, the woman tried to force it into the walkman. Shelby felt a little guilty, knowing that not only were there no cassette tapes in the box, the walkman also needed batteries.

"You know, that's the wrong kind of tape," Shelby said watching her. "You need a cassette."

旧衣服和玩具,送到一户有九个孩子的黑人家庭去。那家最年长的女儿生下了一个有一半白人血缘的孩子,而孩子的父亲是谢尔碧的叔叔西德。西德拒绝承认那个孩子,于是家里其他人都觉得作为基督教徒,他们有义务每年去看望那家人两次,流露出白人式的内疚之情,心神不宁到离开为止。

随着谢尔碧离那个女人越来越近,她脑海里开始浮现那一家人的景象:墙上挂着皮肤白皙的耶稣像,家里年幼的女孩子们扎着两边不对齐的小辫子,地板光秃秃的。所有的物品都摆放得井井有条,孩子们也都打理得整洁利索。他们表现出的尊敬着实让谢尔碧有些困扰:一口一个"女士""先生"。对于谢尔碧一家人带来的舍不得扔掉的东西,他们不住地表达着感谢。此时谢尔碧低下头看着臂弯里的盒子,开始怀疑自己的做法跟那时有什么不一样。就在她几乎要转身离开时,那个女人止住了低声哼唱,满脸警惕地盯着她。

"呃,我只是想看看你对这些东西感不感兴趣。"谢尔碧边说边把盒子放低一些,好让她看见里面。而那女人则一言不发,径直开始挑拣了起来:她先是提溜出一条被飞蛾蛀食的羊毛围巾,裹在自己的脖子上,又搜罗出一个溜溜球放在了身后。

"你可以整个盒子都拿走。"谢尔碧说着把盒子放在了她的面前。

她咕哝了些什么字句,谢尔碧权当是感谢的话了。谢尔碧慢慢向后退着,看着那女人饶有兴致地整理盒子里的物件。每拿出一样东西,她都按照某种大师的章法排列在自己周围。她找到了几盘八轨道磁带,迅速抽出后把其中一个举到耳边,转而接着在盒子深处继续摸索着。一个老式随身听被拉了出来,她翻来覆去地把玩着,仿佛在感叹这一神奇的发明。她顺着插在上面的连接线继续向外拉扯,直到耳机纠缠在盒子的边缘,像被勾住的鱼一般挣扎着。那个女人动作迟缓地解开耳机线之后,分别将其塞进两耳,按下了按键。从盒子里取出的八音轨磁带,任凭她怎么费力都没法塞进去。一阵内疚感涌上谢尔碧心头,因为她带来的箱子里并没有盒式磁带,随身听里也没有电池。

"其实,这种磁带不是放在随身听里的,"谢尔碧看着她开口了,"你需要的是盒式磁带。"

Chapter Twenty-Three Unresolved: to Stay Together

"You got one of them in here?" the woman asked abruptly, rummaging around. Shelby almost laughed. It would be foolish to expect good manners from a woman who lived on the street.

"Wait a second," Shelby said. "I'll go get you one." It seemed a shame not to make someone happy when it was so within her power. She ran back the three blocks to the apartment.

"What are you doing?" Max asked, looking up. He was sitting on the floor, working out the solo to "Hotel California". He smiled at her sadly. Studying her face. She knew he was looking for a sign. Would she stay or would she go? Their band used to do that song. Who would have ever guessed it would be prophetic?

"Nothin'," she answered, biting her lip. Max watched her take the batteries out of her walkman, and waited patiently.

Shelby looked at him, then back at the batteries lying in her hand. "I gave this woman all that stuff and she was trying to put the eight-tracks into the Walkman, and I felt bad that here she probably had her best find in days and couldn't get it to work." Shelby paused for a moment, feeling as if she was going to cry again. "So I was going to give her this Willie Nelson tape and some batteries," she said quickly.

Max looked at Shelby affectionately. "I know I don't tell you this enough," he said, setting his guitar on the floor and standing up and hugging her, "but I love you." She hugged him back, holding him like a rock. They were both sad, for different reasons. But their sadness united them. Shelby wondered if she could leave Max. She was a pair-bonder, a deuce, part of a matched set. If she left Max, she wasn't sure Hadley would want her, and she couldn't imagine going it alone. How would she support herself? It was a terrible reason to stay married. But her uncertainty was a terrible reason to leave too.

The fact that she'd deceived Max humbled her. Deceit was such a vicious activity. And lately it was so prevalent. She wondered suddenly whether Rahda felt as badly as she. Could you lie and not feel the repercussions? Max was convinced that Rahda had caused the explosion in the lab. Could a person like that feel remorse? Shelby, who tried to understand the motives of everyone, still couldn't figure Rahda out. If marriage had made Shelby feel so entrapped, just think what an arranged marriage could do. Perhaps Rahda was tired of living a life she hadn't chosen for herself. But why hadn't she just said no? She came from a wealthy family.

"你在箱子里放了吗?"那个女人一边唐突地质问,一边又开始了翻找。谢尔碧差点儿就忍不住大笑起来。期待从一个流落街头的女人身上看到彬彬有礼的举止,简直就近乎愚蠢。

"你等一会儿,"谢尔碧回答道,"我去给你拿一个。"如果让一个人开心只是举手之劳,而你却没有这么做,这几乎使人羞愧。谢尔碧跑过三个街区,回到了公寓。

"你在做什么?"麦克斯抬起头看着她。他这时正坐在地板上,研究着《加州旅馆》的独奏部分。他带着悲伤的微笑,细细地解读着谢尔碧的脸庞。谢尔碧知道,他是在寻找自己是去是留的征兆。这首歌他们的乐队曾经表演过,可谁能猜想到它的歌词竟然如此精准地预测了他们的未来呢?

"没什么。"谢尔碧咬着嘴唇。麦克斯看着她把随身听里的电池取了出来,耐心地等待着。

谢尔碧看了他一眼,然后又把目光收回手里的电池上。"我把一箱旧东西给了路边的一个女人,看见她试着把八音轨磁带塞进随身听的样子,我觉得很内疚,因为这八成是她这几天最大的收获了,可却没法让它出声儿。"她顿了一下,仿佛眼泪又要夺眶而出了。"所以我打算把这盒威利·尼尔森的磁带和电池一起送给她。"她加快了语速。

麦克斯看着谢尔碧的眼神里满是深情。"我知道我不经常说这样的话,"他把吉他放到一边的地板上,站起身,将谢尔碧拥在怀里,"但是我爱你。"谢尔碧也紧紧抱住了他,像抱住一块岩石一样。他们俩的悲伤,各有所因,可是这共同的悲伤却将他们紧紧相连。谢尔碧不知道自己是否能够离开麦克斯,她是双飞鸟的一只,持平局的一方,更是组合的一部分。即使她真的离开了麦克斯,哈德利也不一定会张开双臂迎接她,单枪匹马她是决计做不来的。她要怎么养活自己呢?虽然这是个用来保存婚姻完整性的烂理由,可是她飘忽不定的情感也无法支撑起断然离开的这个决定。

欺骗麦克斯这件事让谢尔碧变得卑微不堪。欺骗堪比暴行,近来更是随处可见。突然,她好奇拉达的内心会不会也和自己一样糟糕。有人能够做到撒谎之后完全不被它造成的影响所折磨吗?麦克斯已经无比笃定地认为,拉达就是实验室爆炸事件的元凶。像那样的一个人会感到懊悔自责吗?就连试着去理解每个人的动机的谢尔碧,都看不透拉达的心理。假如一场两情相悦的婚姻甚至让谢尔碧如陷囹圄,包办婚姻带来的打击便更无法言说了。也许拉达是厌倦了自己不能做主的生活,可她为什么不直接拒绝呢?她来自一个富有的家庭,

Chapter Twenty-Three Unresolved: to Stay Together

Her father was a high level chemist in India. She had a ready-made career. She didn't need to lie; she didn't even need to marry. It made no sense.

Shelby sighed, thinking of Rahda plotting in her lab. The elaborate ends she went to in order to perpetuate her fraud. Shelby tried to imagine this haunting kind of compulsion, a compulsion that is so prehistoric in your makeup, all ties to the original cause are lost. Doing something that you know is so wrong but still cannot stop yourself from doing. She tried to imagine herself in that situation, and then shook her head at her stupidity. She was in that situation. She was as compulsive, perhaps more even than Rahda. Rahda wanted success. Shelby wanted meaning. Neither of them unreasonable pursuits, except for the ruthlessness with which they'd sought them.

Did Rahda, thinking little details insignificant, conveniently forget them because they wouldn't further her goal? Crumbs of science trod into the floor. And did she, Shelby, thinking that having an affair would make her life more meaningful, suddenly realize her mistake when all it did was make it more complicated? For all their effort, neither of them got what they wanted.

Shelby now recognized that she had been carried by the passion of the moment, imagining intrigue, conspiracies to unite herself and Hadley. It turned out that Rahda had stolen the cocaine. Not the neighbor. The psycho neighbor had nothing to do with it—Rahda had simply given him Ethan's key chain as a present. Dermot found this out, taunting them with their theories, making Shelby question her tendency to overreact, to immediately jump to the farthest conclusion. It was simple really. Rahda had done everything except steal Hadley's notebook. He'd lost that on his own. She was a one-woman mystery, falsifying data, obstructing research, hiring someone to steal the drugs (who later got caught). She'd learned how to cut the cocaine with mannitol, coincidentally having a ready supply of the laxative, and then selling it cheap. The money was gone and so was Rahda. Ethan's dad had finally fronted Ethan the cash so he wouldn't be murdered, and as a result, Ethan was now in an upstate rehab facility where apparently he was dating the heiress to the ziplock fortune. Shelby marveled. How did someone so obnoxious always end up on his feet? She was jealous that Ethan could come out unscathed, and that her life would never be the same.

父亲是印度的高级化学家。而她的职业生涯也一帆风顺,完全没有撒谎的必要;婚姻对她来说甚至都不是必需品。她这么做根本就解释不通。

拉达在实验室里密谋的情景在谢尔碧脑海里浮现,她不由得叹了口气。为了延续她的欺诈行为,精心设计着结尾。谢尔碧试图去理解这种近乎阴魂不散的强迫症行为:明知不对,却无法停手。这种强迫感在你的伪装中潜藏已久,以至于最初的动机已经无处可寻。她试着想象自己深陷其中的情形,随后又因为自己的愚蠢摇了摇头。她已经身处其中了。至于强迫症的强度,至少与拉达齐平,或许更甚。拉达想要的是成功,而谢尔碧则是在追寻意义。两者都合情合理,但她们使用的手段却过于残忍无情。

拉达是否认为琐碎的细节无足轻重,也不利于她实现目标,便轻巧地回避了它们?科学的残渣被践踏在地板上。谢尔碧本以为一场外遇能够为她的生活带来更多的意义,却发现它只平添了更多的错综复杂,她又是否意识到了自己的错误呢?费尽心力之后,她们却都没有得到自己想要的东西。

谢尔碧现在才看清,自己一路都任由瞬间的激情引领,想象着密谋事件给生活添油加醋,以此拉近她和哈德利之间的联结。结果拉达才是真正偷走可卡因的人,那个变态邻居是清白的——伊桑的钥匙链只不过是拉达给他的礼物。德莫特知道之后,借此把他们的推理嘲笑了一番,这使得谢尔碧开始怀疑起自己反应过度的倾向来,因为她总是迅速地跳到最疯狂的结论上去。其实整件事并不复杂:除了哈德利的笔记本是他自己搞丢了的之外,所有事情都是拉达做的。一个单枪匹马的神秘女人——造假数据,阻碍研究,雇人偷窃毒品(后来被缉拿归案)。她自己学会了用甘露醇稀释可卡因,再加上碰巧实验室里有现成的婴幼儿通便剂[译者注:成分为甘露醇],完工之后再以低价售出。钱已经挥霍一空,拉达也不见了踪影。伊桑终于收到了父亲给他寄来的钱,免于被追杀的下场,他也因此住进了一家边远地区的康复中心,现在正和密保诺财团的女继承人约会当中。这让谢尔碧感叹不已,为什么像他这样如此可恶的人总是能够东山再起呢?其实,她是嫉妒伊桑在经历了这一切之后可以毫发无损,而她的生活却再也回不到过去了。

There was a rumor that Rahda had gone back to India, but when Scotia contacted her father, her father maintained that Rahda still lived in New York. Rahda's traits obviously had a familial component. Shelby imagined that Rahda was in India now. She tried to picture her there, maybe even working in her father's lab. Did she dwell on the past? Did she know that Hadley had blown up, that her lab had been dismantled? Shelby wanted to know what Rahda thought because for some reason—she didn't know why she thought so—she sensed she could get a clue about herself. She could see Rahda's compulsion from a different angle, whereas hers only had this one tangential view. Rahda's was a different obsession with different needs, but the rhythm, the beat was the same. Rahda lied, Shelby took off her clothes. The similarity was in the unconscionableness of it. In the monomania. Shelby realized that she herself simply couldn't let her unexamined behavior dictate her life.

Walking back down the street, Shelby noticed that the homeless woman had laid out her new possessions on the dirty blanket: a deck of cards, a yo-yo, a broken frame, several plastic cups. They were arranged with precision, the cards square with the frame and eight-track tapes, the yo-yo and cups opposite them. Behind her she had stashed the more valuable stuff, an old iron and a cracked flashlight still hidden inside the box.

Handing the woman the cassette tape, Shelby said, "I brought some batteries too," and held her hand out, gesturing for the Walkman. The woman pursed her lips suspiciously, then picked up her Walkman and held it close, not wanting to give it back.

"Don't worry, I'm just going to put the batteries in for you."

With a deep scowl on her face, the woman slowly let go of the Walkman, her thin scabby fingers sliding over the plastic as Shelby took it from her. Shelby inserted the batteries, showing the woman how they fit, then slid the plastic cover back on.

"Other way," Shelby said as the woman tried to insert the Willie Nelson tape backward. Then she watched as the woman heard the music come through the headphones, adjusting the volume control like a pro.

"You got any other tapes?" the woman asked, lowering the headphones. Shelby laughed. Willie Nelson wasn't Shelby's favorite singer either.

"They sell them along here. You might be able to trade for something in the morning," Shelby said diplomatically.

有传言说拉达回了印度,当斯考蒂亚联系上她的父亲时,他却坚持说拉达还生活在纽约。很显然,拉达撒谎的特性是家族遗传的。谢尔碧觉得拉达现在一定已经在印度了,她在脑海中拼凑着拉达现在的生活,也许进了她父亲的实验室。她对过去发生的事能够释怀吗?对哈德利在爆炸中受伤,她自己的实验室被拆除的事情,她又是否知晓?谢尔碧希望了解拉达的想法,因为冥冥之中——她也不知道这种想法从何而来——她能够从中获得一些自我透视的线索。谢尔碧能够从不同角度来看拉达的强迫行为,可对待自己,她却只有这一个切肤的看法。她和拉达被不同的东西迷住心窍,可是她们的规律和节拍,是一样的。拉达扯着谎言,谢尔碧脱下了衣衫。两者相似之处是行为的极端性,以及偏执。此时的谢尔碧意识到,她不能够让这种不加检视的行为主宰自己的生活了。

重新回到那条街上之后,谢尔碧注意到那个女人把新近财产都摆在了一条脏毯子上:一副扑克牌、一个溜溜球、一个残缺的相框,还有几个塑料杯子。摆放的顺序经过了精心的设计——纸牌与相框和八音轨磁带相互垂直,对面放着溜溜球和塑料杯。价值更高一点的物品诸如老旧的电熨斗和变形了的手电筒,仍然留在箱子里,被她藏在了身后。

谢尔碧把磁带递过去,"我还给你带了几节电池,"又伸出手,示意她把随身听拿过来。那个女人带着怀疑的神色噘了噘嘴,拿起随身听往怀里塞了塞,不想还回来。

"别担心,我只是想帮你把电池放进去。"

她的脸上仍旧满是怒容,但慢慢将随身听递了出来,谢尔碧接过来的时候她结满疮痂的瘦削手指依依不舍地划过塑料外壳。谢尔碧将正确的安装方向展示给她,然后合上了塑料盖子。

"换个方向。"当看见她反着将威利·尼尔森的磁带塞进去时,谢尔碧忍不住提醒道。音乐声通过耳机传进那个女人的耳朵里,她像个专家似的调节着音量,谢尔碧则在一旁看着。

"你还有别的磁带吗?"她放下耳机,开口问道。谢尔碧笑了,威利·尼尔森也不是她的最爱。

"这条街上有人卖磁带,明天早上兴许你可以用东西交换到一盘其他的磁带。"谢尔碧圆滑地回应道。

Chapter Twenty-Three   Unresolved: to Stay Together

The woman grunted and put the earphones back on.

Shelby heard her name being called. She looked up. Max was running toward her. "Here," he yelled. "Give her this thing. You don't need it anymore."

Shelby smiled wryly at him, shaking her head. He was carrying Chuckles, that ratty monkey that represented so much of what she hated about her life. "Assuming I quit, I need to give that back to Gary—" she started to say, but before she could say more, he'd already handed it to the women who looked at it appraisingly, then hugged it to her chest and rocked.

"I don't think you should go back there. I want you to do something that will make you happy. You should go back to school. It'll give you a goal." He paused. "I know you feel for Hadley. I don't like it, but I accept it because I don't want you to leave. But I want you to remember that not getting what you want can sometimes contribute to one's happiness." He smiled. "I think you said that. Don't judge our marriage because you're sad about your life. You like to write. That's what you should do." He held her shoulders gently. "I should have said this before, but I want to read what you write. Slowly maybe." She looked at him and he kissed her face. "And see, she loves the monkey." The woman had found the battery compartment and batteries were rolling across the sidewalk.

Shelby smiled sadly and took his hand. They walked toward home, leaving the woman to her sudden prosperity. Deep down Shelby felt beholden to Max; it occurred to her that it was a feeling that might have been love, but she wasn't yet skilled enough to recognize it, or happy enough to believe it. Shelby had no doubts that she had once loved Max with the same intensity that she now loved Hadley. An eerie habit? Could it happen again? What if she and Hadley ended up hating each other? Who could believe in everlasting romance now that Carly Simon and James Taylor had gotten a divorce? What did that bode for the rest of them? No wonder so many stories have such dire resolution: someone perishes or enters a convent. The cataclysm is too great. Nothing remains to patch back together. The romantic ideal. Shakespearean. Better to die than remain unresolved. Ambiguity is inherently stressful. And irresolution was a lot more work. It required extensive therapy.

Shelby looked over her shoulder one last time, watching the woman cuddle the monkey and arrange her wares for an unseen public who would probably trample her during morning rush hour, so close was she to the subway steps. The bag woman

虽然咕哝了几声，那女人最终还是把耳机重新戴上了。

谢尔碧听见有人叫她的名字，回过头，她看见麦克斯正朝自己的方向跑过来。"还有这个，"他大声地叫着，"把这个玩意儿也送给她。你不再需要它了。"

谢尔碧苦笑着看向麦克斯，摇了摇头。他手里拿的是"咯咯笑"，那只脾气暴躁的猴子，见证了她所厌恶的自己生活中的绝大部分。"就算我不干了，我也得把它给还给加里——"她话音还没落，麦克斯就已经把"咯咯笑"塞进了那女人的手里。她先是用打量的目光上下看着，接着一把搂进怀里，左右摇晃了起来。

"我觉得你不应该再回去了。我希望你能够做一些让自己开心的事情。比如重回学校，这样你就有奋斗目标了。"麦克斯顿了一下，"我知道你对哈德利还有感情，虽然我不喜欢，可我能够容忍，因为我不愿意让你离开。我还想让你知道，有时候得不到想要的东西也能够提升一个人的幸福感。"他笑了，"这是你曾经说过的话。不要仅仅因为对自己的人生不满，就把我们的婚姻也一并否定掉。你喜欢写作，应该坚持下去。"麦克斯轻柔地握住谢尔碧的肩膀，"我早就应该跟你说的，我想要读你写的东西。也许可以慢慢来。"谢尔碧抬起头时，麦克斯亲吻了她的脸。"啊，看哪，她对那猴子爱不释手。"那个女人随手掀开电池盖儿，电池便"骨碌碌"地滚落到了人行道上。

谢尔碧悲伤地笑了，她牵起了麦克斯的手，与他肩并肩地往回走，留下身后的女人和她从天而降的财富。内心深处，谢尔碧非常依赖麦克斯；她觉得这种感情有可能是爱情，可却没有足够的经验能够确认，也无法天真地欣然接受。虽然她从来没有怀疑自己曾经爱过麦克斯，如同现在对哈德利的感情一样强烈。难道这是一种怪癖吗？会不会再次发生呢？假如她和哈德利最终反目相向了怎么办？就连卡利·西蒙和詹姆斯·泰勒都离婚了，谁还会再相信爱情能够持久呢？这对其他人来说预示着什么呢？难怪很多故事都有着悲惨的结局：死亡，或者出家。这样的悲剧性太强烈了。剩下的残片无法再拼凑复原。这是一种浪漫的理想主义状态，带着浓重的莎士比亚风格。比起悬而不决，死亡似乎是更好的选择。模棱两可本身便预示着压力。踌躇不决的状态则需要更大的投入，还有全面的心理治疗。

谢尔碧最后一次向身后看去，那个女人怀里搂着"咯咯笑"，对着不存在的过客将所有物品摆放一齐。早高峰来临时，拥挤的人群八成会踩着她经过，因为她离地铁入口的楼梯实在是太近了。她还是不停地摆放着那些廉价的小玩意

Chapter Twenty-Three Unresolved: to Stay Together

continued to lay out her trinkets, not even caring whether it was night or day, the presence of merchandise enough to sustain her. A woman on the street but more self-sufficient than Shelby. It was something Shelby would have to work on.

The End

儿,丝毫不在乎是白天还是黑夜,拥有这些就足够让她心满意足了。一个露宿街头的女人,却比谢尔碧还要自给自足。在这方面她还需要继续努力。

结束